PENGUIN BOOKS

TRINITY

'Frank Close is one of Britain's most distinguished physicists. He studied under Peierls and eventually occupied the post held by Fuchs as head of theoretical physics at Harwell's Rutherford laboratory. Close's narrative weaves the tale of treason into that of the development of the atomic bomb . . . a fluent writer who retells the bomb story very well' Max Hastings, *Sunday Times*

'Close has produced a work that could go toe-to-toe with any historian specializing in events surrounding the beginnings of the nuclear age. He has delved into the archives to produce a remarkable story . . . meticulous but highly readable' Manjit Kumar, *The Times*

'*Trinity* reads like a spy novel: Close writes the human stories well . . . by framing Fuchs's career with the story of his humane mentor Peierls, *Trinity* reveals a man familiar with betrayal, with motives he thought were pure' Ann Finkbeiner, *Nature*

'With the benefit of declassified intelligence files in Britain, America and Russia, *Trinity* is by far the most comprehensive account so far, and Close's diligence in the archives is deeply impressive' Andrew Glazzard, *New Statesman*

'Professor Close's thorough and sometimes exciting book is a great window into how the first nuclear weapons were developed, how the Soviets were able to recruit so many agents at the heart of the British state, and how Britain worked in the late 1940s' Clovis Meath Baker, *Standpoint*

'Meticulously researched . . . thought-provoking' Martin Uli Mauthner, *AJR Journal*

D1465150

Frank Close is Professor Emeritus of Theoretical Physics at Oxford University and Fellow Emeritus in Physics at Exeter College, Oxford. He was formerly Head of the Theoretical Physics Division at the Rutherford Appleton Laboratory at Harwell, vice president of the British Association for Advancement of Science and Head of Communications and Public Education at CERN. He was awarded the Kelvin Medal of the Institute of Physics for his 'outstanding contributions to the public understanding of physics' in 1996, an OBE for 'services to research and the public understanding of science' in 2000, and the Royal Society Michael Faraday Prize for communicating science in 2013. As a young man he worked with Rudolf Peierls, in circumstances he describes in this book.

FRANK CLOSE

Trinity

*The Treachery and Pursuit of the Most
Dangerous Spy in History*

PENGUIN BOOKS

PENGUIN BOOKS

UK | USA | Canada | Ireland | Australia
India | New Zealand | South Africa

Penguin Books is part of the Penguin Random House group of companies
whose addresses can be found at global.penguinrandomhouse.com

First published by Allen Lane 2019
Published in Penguin Books 2020
001

Copyright © Frank Close, 2019

The moral right of the author has been asserted

Typeset by Jouve (UK), Milton Keynes
Printed and bound in Great Britain by Clays Ltd, Elcograf S.p.A.

A CIP catalogue record for this book is available from the British Library

ISBN: 978-0-141-98644-9

'It seemed . . . that you treated him as if he were your son.'
Nobel Laureate Max Perutz
to Rudolf Peierls, 19 May 1987

Contents

PART FIVE
The Haunting: 1949–50

PART SIX
Endgame: 1950

PART SEVEN
Fallout: 1950–59

Acknowledgements

Six years ago, Lorna Arnold – the spritely ninety-seven-year-old historian of the British atomic and hydrogen bombs – shared with me her first-hand memories of the atomic spy, Klaus Fuchs. She insisted that Fuchs' importance as a scientist, as well as his personal morals, had yet to be assessed in light of the (then) newly released security files. She described him as an honourable person – a portrayal utterly opposite to the received wisdom about the man once dubbed 'the most dangerous spy in the history of nations'.

Lorna's assessment reminded me of an occasion decades earlier, when I was a graduate student in theoretical physics at Oxford University and Rudolf Peierls was the departmental head. State secrecy meant that none of us knew any details of his singular role in 1940 as father of the atomic bomb, but we did know that his assistant had been Klaus Fuchs, and that Fuchs – like Peierls a refugee from the Nazis – had lodged in the home of 'Prof' and his wife Genia. The Peierlses had treated Fuchs almost 'like a son', only to see him betray his adopted country, his professional colleagues and the Peierls family with his duplicity. I had asked the Peierlses about Fuchs and was astonished when Genia described him as one of the most honourable men she had known.

Lorna Arnold's endorsement of Genia Peierls' testament inspired the investigation that led to this book. I am indebted to Graham Farmelo for having directed me to Lorna, to both Lorna and Graham for many conversations about the history and politics of the early British work on the atomic bomb, and to Graham for reading some early drafts on that part of *Trinity*. Lorna sadly died before this book was completed.

Two dedicated biographies of Fuchs had been published before his British Security files were available, and during my own researches three further books appeared that dealt at least in part with Klaus Fuchs. I am indebted to the authors Norman Moss, Richard Chadwell Williams, Tony Percy, Mike Rossiter and Peter Watson for discussions about their own research into Klaus Fuchs. I am also grateful to Gaby Gross (Peierls) for a personal memory of Fuchs, and to Jo Hookway (Peierls) for presenting me with her father's annotated copy of Norman Moss' biography, as well as for sharing and recalling many memories of her parents and allowing me to see some family documents. Sabine Lee, who has edited and collated

Peierls' works, graciously shared her knowledge with me, and read parts of a preliminary manuscript.

Christopher Andrew made available the academic thesis of his former student Timothy Gibbs, which includes the case of Klaus Fuchs. This is the most complete fully referenced study of Fuchs' espionage and its political implications, and I am indebted to Professor Andrew for access to this.

I am grateful to Jeremy Bernstein for having read a first draft of the manuscript, and for numerous discussions about the history and dynamics of the atomic bombs and of the early work on thermonuclear weapons; Alex Wellerstein for his use of Freedom of Information in the United States, which brought the content of Fermi's 1945 lectures on this topic into the public domain, and through this helped reveal a previously unknown aspect of Fuchs' duplicity; Jack Connors, Steven Cowley and Bryan Taylor for educating me about the history of fusion, in all its forms; Jonathan Smith at the Wren Library, Trinity College, Cambridge, for access to G. P. Thomson's papers; David Schwartz, for his help in pursuing Fuchs' history in New York; Brian Pollard and the archives of Bristol University where Fuchs was once a student; Tony Comer, historian at GCHQ; Malcolm Crook for access to Harwell memorabilia and with Ben Greenstreet for locating the sites of Fuchs and Skinner residences and offices at Harwell; Abingdon School and Abingdon Historical Society for help identifying Fuchs' presence in the town; Chris Fletcher, Colin Harris, Stuart Ackland and the staff of the Bodleian Library, Oxford, for unravelling the various files of papers of Rudolf Peierls and for allowing me access to the previously unseen photographic file of Tony Skyrme; Allen Packwood and the staff at the Churchill College archives, Cambridge; Herbi Dreiner and Emmanuel Drees at the University of Bonn for help with Fuchs' German articles; and Alexander Vassiliev for clarifying some of his annotations of KGB archives.

I am also grateful to my daughter Katie whose house near the National Archives enabled me to spend many hours in the Archives' Reading Room before large swathes of documents were suddenly and inexplicably removed from public view at the end of 2018.

Many others have helped me along the way, including Jim Baggott, Philip Ball, Gill Bennett, Brian Cathcart, Catherine Colglazier, Tony Comer, Norman Dombey, Freeman Dyson, Roger Elliott, Graham Farmelo, Margaret Farrell, Michael Goodman, Bryson Gore, John Grieve, Michael Hart, David Holloway, James Jinks, Peter Knight, Sabine Lee, Robin Marshall, Michael Marten, Andy Paterson, Rudolf and Genia Peierls, Gaby Gross (Peierls), Jo Hookway (Peierls), Harry Chapman Pincher, Kate Pyne, Mikhail Shifman, Andrei Starinets, Carey Sublette, Simone Turchetti and

Alexander Vassiliev, Philip and James Waller, Alex Wellerstein, Kati Whitaker and Nishi Yamamoto for contact with Klaus Fuchs-Kittowski. In addition, I am grateful to two individuals who wish to remain anonymous.

Finally, I give special thanks to my wife, Gillian, for having lived with this project for so long and for having read some early drafts; to Ben Sinyor at Allen Lane, and Amanda Russell, for their help with diagrams and image research; Richard Mason for his perceptive questions and copy-editing; and my agent Patrick Walsh, and editor, Stuart Proffitt, for having helped to bring these ideas to fruition.

List of Illustrations

Illustrations in the Text

Plates

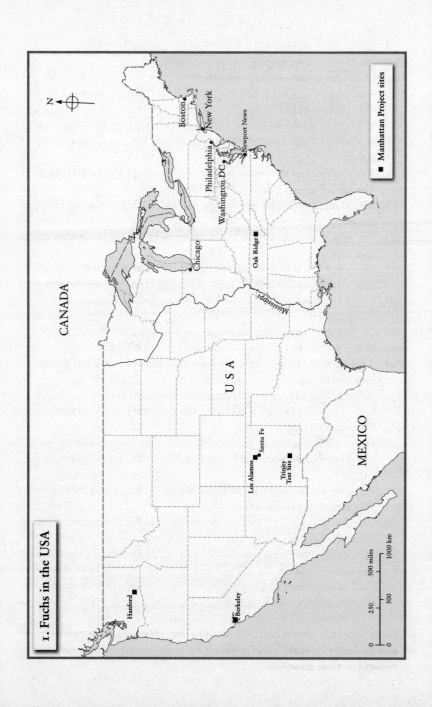

1. Fuchs in the USA

Manhattan Project sites

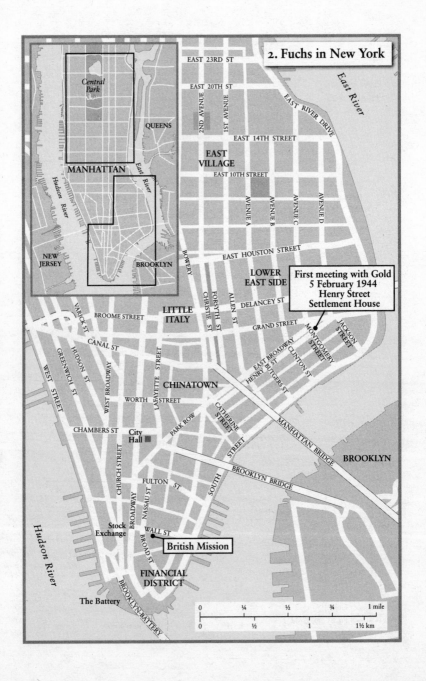

2. Fuchs in New York

Central Park

MANHATTAN

QUEENS

Hudson River

East River

NEW JERSEY

BROOKLYN

EAST 23RD ST

EAST 20TH ST

2ND AVENUE

1ST AVENUE

EAST RIVER DRIVE

EAST 14TH STREET

EAST VILLAGE

EAST 10TH STREET

AVENUE A

AVENUE B

AVENUE C

AVENUE D

EAST HOUSTON STREET

BOWERY

LOWER EAST SIDE

DELANCEY ST

FORSYTH ST

CHRISTIE ST

ALLEN ST

GRAND STREET

First meeting with Gold
5 February 1944
Henry Street
Settlement House

JACKSON STREET

MONTGOMERY STREET

BROOME STREET

LITTLE ITALY

VARICK ST

GREENWICH ST

HUDSON ST

CANAL ST

WEST BROADWAY

LAFAYETTE STREET

WEST STREET

CHINATOWN

WORTH STREET

EAST BROADWAY

HENRY ST

CLINTON ST

RUTGERS ST

CATHERINE STREET

PARK ROW

MANHATTAN BRIDGE

CHAMBERS ST

City Hall

STREET

BROOKLYN

CHURCH STREET

FULTON ST

BROOKLYN BRIDGE

SOUTH STREET

BROADWAY

NASSAU ST

Stock Exchange

WALL ST

BROAD ST

British Mission

Hudson River

FINANCIAL DISTRICT

The Battery

BROOKLYN-BATTERY

| 0 | | ¼ | | ½ | | ¾ | | 1 mile |
| 0 | | | ½ | | 1 | | | 1½ km |

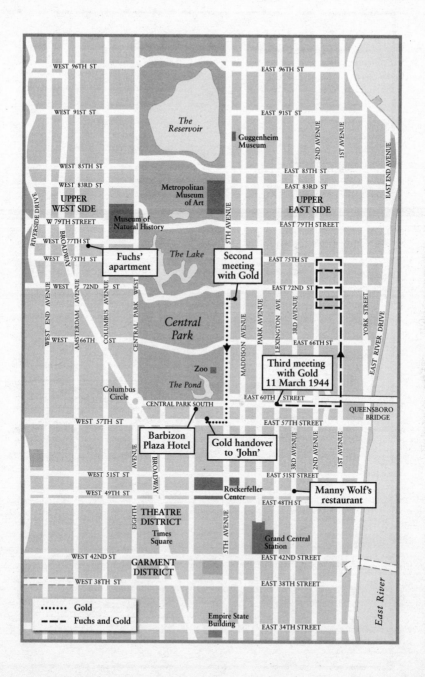

WEST 96TH ST   EAST 96TH ST

WEST 91ST ST   EAST 91ST ST

The Reservoir

Guggenheim Museum

2ND AVENUE

1ST AVENUE

EAST END AVENUE

WEST 85TH ST   EAST 85TH ST

WEST 83RD ST   EAST 83RD ST

RIVERSIDE DRIVE

UPPER WEST SIDE

Metropolitan Museum of Art

UPPER EAST SIDE

W 79TH STREET   EAST 79TH STREET

Museum of Natural History

BROADWAY

WEST 77TH ST

WEST 75TH ST

5TH AVENUE

Fuchs' apartment

The Lake

Second meeting with Gold

EAST 75TH ST

WEST 72ND ST

EAST 72ND ST

WEST END AVENUE

AMSTERDAM AVENUE

COLUMBUS AVENUE

CENTRAL PARK WEST

PARK AVENUE

LEXINGTON AVE

3RD AVENUE

YORK STREET

EAST RIVER DRIVE

WEST 66TH ST

Central Park

MADDISON AVENUE

EAST 66TH ST

Third meeting with Gold 11 March 1944

Zoo

Columbus Circle

The Pond

CENTRAL PARK SOUTH

EAST 60TH STREET

QUEENSBORO BRIDGE

WEST 57TH ST   EAST 57TH STREET

Barbizon Plaza Hotel

Gold handover to 'John'

BROADWAY

AVENUE

3RD AVENUE

2ND AVENUE

1ST AVENUE

WEST 51ST ST   EAST 51ST STREET

WEST 49TH ST   EAST 49TH STREET

Rockerfeller Center

Manny Wolf's restaurant

EAST 48TH ST

EIGHTH

THEATRE DISTRICT

Times Square

5TH AVENUE

Grand Central Station

WEST 42ND ST   EAST 42ND STREET

GARMENT DISTRICT

WEST 38TH ST   EAST 38TH STREET

•••••• Gold

- - - Fuchs and Gold

Empire State Building

EAST 34TH STREET

East River

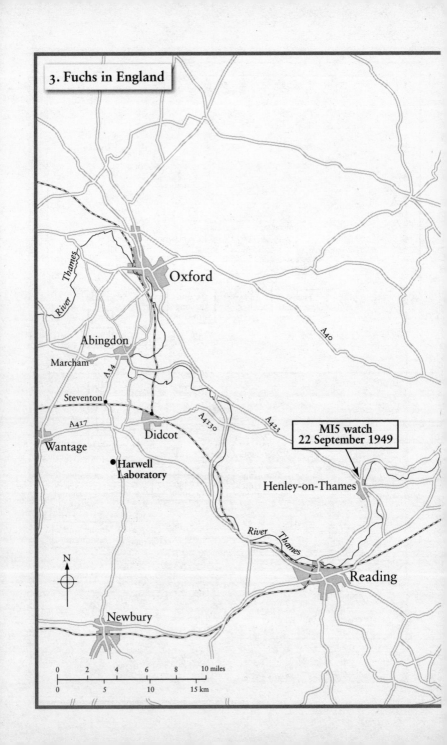

3. Fuchs in England

Oxford

River Thames

Abingdon

Marcham

A34

Steventon

A417

Wantage

Didcot

A4130

A423

MI5 watch
22 September 1949

Harwell
Laboratory

Henley-on-Thames

A40

River Thames

Reading

N

Newbury

| 0 | 2 | 4 | 6 | 8 | 10 miles |

| 0 | 5 | 10 | 15 km |

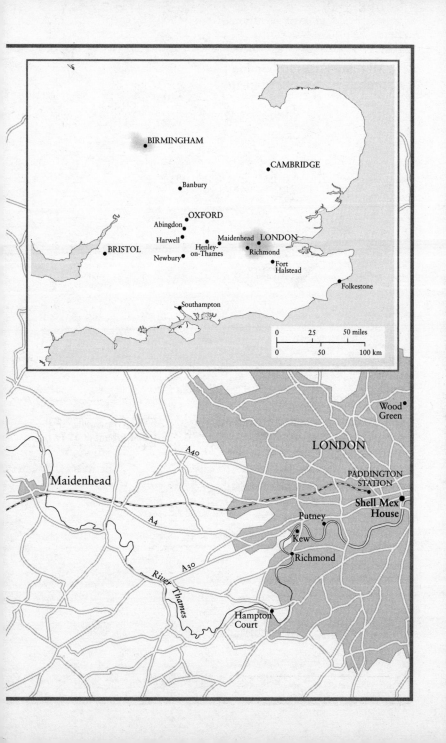

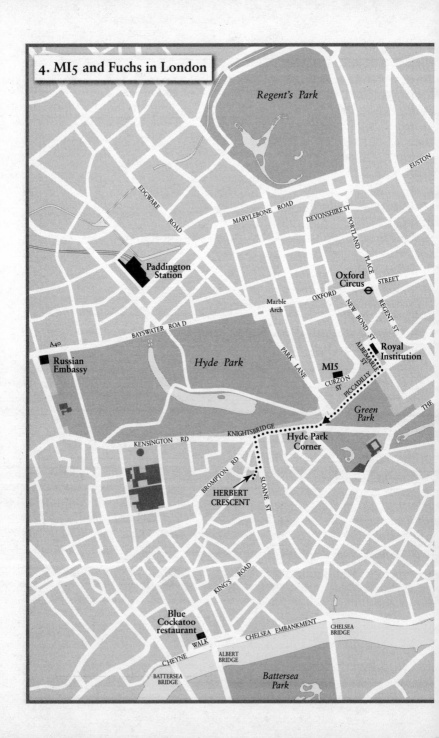

4. MI5 and Fuchs in London

Regent's Park

EDGWARE ROAD

MARYLEBONE ROAD

DEVONSHIRE ST

PORTLAND PLACE

EUSTON

Paddington Station

Oxford Circus

OXFORD STREET

Marble Arch

NEW BOND ST

REGENT ST

BAYSWATER ROAD

A40

Russian Embassy

Hyde Park

PARK LANE

ALBEMARLE ST

Royal Institution

MI5

CURZON ST

PICCADILLY

Green Park

THE

KNIGHTSBRIDGE

KENSINGTON RD

Hyde Park Corner

BROMPTON RD

SLOANE ST

HERBERT CRESCENT

KING'S ROAD

Blue Cockatoo restaurant

WALK

CHELSEA EMBANKMENT

CHELSEA BRIDGE

CHEYNE

ALBERT BRIDGE

BATTERSEA BRIDGE

Battersea Park

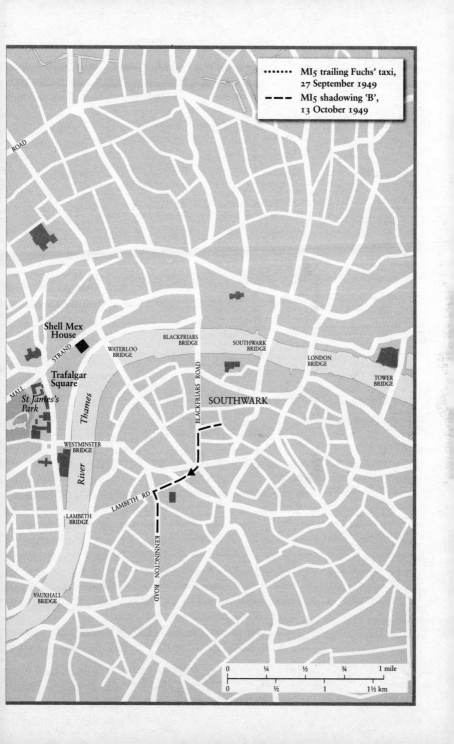

MI5 trailing Fuchs' taxi,
27 September 1949

MI5 shadowing 'B',
13 October 1949

Shell Mex
House

BLACKFRIARS
BRIDGE

SOUTHWARK
BRIDGE

WATERLOO
BRIDGE

LONDON
BRIDGE

STRAND

Trafalgar
Square

TOWER
BRIDGE

MALL

St James's
Park

SOUTHWARK

BLACKFRIARS ROAD

Thames

WESTMINSTER
BRIDGE

River

LAMBETH RD

LAMBETH
BRIDGE

KENNINGTON ROAD

VAUXHALL
BRIDGE

ROAD

| 0 | ¼ | ½ | ¾ | 1 mile |

| 0 | ½ | 1 | 1½ km |

Prologue: Oxford 1967

'I am Piles!'

The source of this enigmatic statement was a bespectacled, white-haired man in his sixties, wearing a drab grey sports jacket with a pouch of tobacco protruding from one pocket. His right hand fiddled with the pouch's contents, while the left played with a pipe that refused to light. He was five feet seven and a half inches tall, as I would later learn from MI5 files.

It was a September morning in 1967. The encounter took place in the hallway of 12 Parks Road, a Victorian house in north Oxford, an ample and slightly down-at-heel building that could easily have doubled for a vicarage in an Agatha Christie novel. In those days 12 Parks Road was home to the university's Department of Theoretical Physics. I was a nervous new graduate student on my first day in Oxford. I had walked up the gravel drive opposite the University Parks, and entered: as the front door swung closed behind me, the thud echoed back from the rafters two flights of stairs above. I found myself in a silent, gloomy hallway.

Linoleum covered the floor; a stairway of dark wood led to upper landings; imposing oak doors were all shut. A musty smell hinted at decades of decay. The walls were painted ochre, their only decoration a large board that listed the scientists who had offices there. Against each name was a tag, which indicated whether the individual was 'IN' or 'OUT'. It appeared that everyone was 'OUT'.

Alone in this apparently empty mansion, I was wondering what to do, when from the subterranean depths of the basement a man appeared like a mole from its burrow. He greeted me in a strong central European accent, with stress on every word: 'Can I Help Yo?' Taken aback by this strange encounter with (I assumed) the janitor, I replied 'I don't think so', to which the apparition made the bizarre reply that he was 'Piles'.

Flustered, I then realized that he had actually said 'I am Peierls':

Pi-Urls – Rudolf Peierls, the father of the atomic bomb, and one-time mentor to Klaus Fuchs, the most damaging spy of modern times. More than three decades after he had fled Nazi persecution, Peierls' Germanic cadences remained. Breathless at failing to recognize the head of Theoretical Physics, I stuttered, 'I am Frank Close.' I was about to explain why I was there when Peierls proffered his hand as if my arrival was the highlight of his day. 'Plizzed to Mit Yo,' he said firmly, nodding his head in welcome as he led me into his office.

At my high school in Peterborough, entering the inner sanctum of the head's study had been a journey of dread. But in Oxford, Peierls ushered me kindly into a new world. Here I was welcomed as a new member of an international family of scientists. I was twenty-two years old, the same age as many of the physicists who had designed and built the atomic bomb – and the same age as Klaus Fuchs when he first settled at university in England, like Peierls a refugee from Hitler.

PART ONE

Escaping Hitler

I

From Berlin to Birmingham

The Father: Peierls' Story to 1941

Rudolf Peierls was born in Berlin in 1907, the youngest of three children of Elizabeth and Heinrich. His mother died when he was fourteen years old, leaving his widowed father – director of the AEG Cable Factory – to inspire Rudolf's early fascination with machinery, railways and radio. At first he wanted to become an engineer, but when his father said that his eyesight wasn't good enough, Peierls became a physicist, and partly by accident of history and geography midwife to the atomic age.

In 1925 he enrolled as a student at Humboldt University, Berlin, and attended lectures by Walther Nernst, who impressed Peierls as a 'great physicist of rather small stature and even smaller sense of humility'.[1] For the young student his home city of Berlin was an 'exciting place, full of intellectual life, theatres, cabarets, lectures on any topic imaginable', but after two terms he felt ready to leave. The greatest teacher in theoretical physics at that time was Arnold Sommerfeld, in Munich, so Peierls transferred there. Not only had Peierls moved to the right place, fortuitously his timing couldn't have been better. He arrived in the midst of a scientific revolution.

For 250 years, Isaac Newton's laws of motion and of gravity had successfully described the dynamics of objects such as planets, the moon and falling apples, and had never failed; but when applied to very small things, such as atoms, they were nonsensical. An atom consists of electrons encircling a compact central nucleus, the whole held together by electrical forces. According to the laws of Newtonian physics, these forces accelerate the orbiting electrons. Acceleration of an electric charge leads to electromagnetic radiation, and loss of energy, so these electrons should spiral into the nucleus and destroy the atom in a flash of light within a fraction of a second. In other words, neither we nor anything else should be here. That Newton's laws are inadequate in the atomic domain was thus obvious, but the way forward was only discovered with the advent of quantum mechanics in 1926. Quantum mechanics, in effect, extends Newton's laws of motion into the atomic realm. When Peierls arrived in Munich that year, 'everyone was studying' the new theory.[2]

So Peierls began his career as a theoretical physicist at a most opportune moment, and Arnold Sommerfeld was the ideal guide. Sommerfeld's technique for educating students is today standard practice: set the novice a challenge, ideally a problem that has not previously been solved. To this end, he encouraged Peierls to investigate what quantum mechanics implied for the conduction of electricity in metals. Peierls started work on this, but in the spring of 1928 Sommerfeld left to spend a year in the United States, and on his advice Peierls moved to Leipzig. Sommerfeld had shown Peierls the way into the quantum world, now in Leipzig the young theorist could work with one of the founders of the new physics and a giant of German science: Werner Heisenberg.

The previous year Heisenberg had produced his eponymous 'uncertainty principle', which is today recognized as the core of quantum mechanics. Heisenberg's rule governs the behaviour of atoms, atomic nuclei and the particles – electrons, protons and neutrons – that constitute the seeds of all earthly matter. In a nutshell, it states that there is a fundamental limit to the precision with which you can measure both the position and motion of an object. The more accurately you measure its position, for example, the more uncertain is your knowledge of its motion. The same holds true in reverse: precision measurement of an object's motion comes at the expense of accuracy about its location. This indeterminacy is an intrinsic property of nature, not simply a failure in the measuring apparatus. The effect of this restriction is so small that it can be ignored in everyday affairs, but it is dramatic for atoms and their constituent particles. The motion of particles subjected to these constraints is known as quantum mechanics.

With Heisenberg, Peierls deepened his understanding of quantum physics. Yet for all Heisenberg's brilliance in having founded the subject, by 1929 his greatest contribution was in the past. In the spring of that year Peierls moved again, this time to Zurich, ever nearer to the core of activity in the still novel field. The star in Zurich was Austrian Wolfgang Pauli, father of the 'exclusion principle', which posits that electrons are like cuckoos, and no more than one can occupy the same quantum nest. Today Pauli's principle is recognized as key to the structure of atoms, the basis to the periodic table of the elements, and the quantum mechanical capstone to all structure and form in the material world. For that insight, Pauli would win the Nobel Prize for physics in 1945. In 1929, however, his principle was still a radical hypothesis.

Pauli was renowned for his brilliance both as a physicist and for his acerbic wit, with its cutting criticisms of anything that in his judgement was less than perfect. His opinion of one theorist's idea was so poor that Pauli witheringly dismissed it as 'not even wrong'.[3] Another starlet's reputation was destroyed with Pauli's assessment that he was 'so young, and already so unknown'.[4] That Pauli soon came to regard the young Peierls as on a par with himself was praise indeed, and perhaps the sharpest illustration of the international reputation that the twenty-three-year-old Peierls was already building.

By 1930, Peierls had worked as an assistant variously for Heisenberg, Sommerfeld and Pauli, respectively the co-founder and leading practitioners of the new quantum mechanics, for three years. He himself was applying this profound theory, and with it successfully explained many physical properties of solids, metals and crystals. His groundbreaking papers in this dawn of his career addressed the conduction of heat in a crystal, and how electric currents arise when electrons flow freely through a metal, or instead jump from one atom to another.

The first of these articles, which dealt with thermal conduction in crystals, built on work by Erwin Schrödinger, inventor of the equation that describes the quantum mechanics of atoms and electrons. Peierls' improvement of Schrödinger's theory of thermal conductivity filled forty-six pages of the leading journal *Annalen der Physik* in 1929 with formulae, interwoven with carefully phrased logical arguments. Within a year, Peierls developed his ideas further with a twenty-seven-page paper on both electrical and thermal conductivity.[5] Peierls' successful description of the phenomena incorporated Pauli's exclusion principle into its argument, thus both confirming quantum mechanics as the viable description of the atomic level of reality and demonstrating the centrality of Pauli's principle.

TWO FATEFUL ENCOUNTERS

The course of Peierls' life was determined in the 1930s by the rise of fascism, the discovery of the neutron – the key to the explosive release of nuclear energy – and by two fateful encounters. The first came in the summer of 1930, when he went to the Soviet Union to attend a physics conference in Odessa. Still a student, he was used to paying his way to attend conferences and to sitting up all night in third-class carriages on long-distance trains, so he was pleased to be invited to the Soviet Union where all expenses would be paid. He went to Odessa for the adventure, as well as the physics, because so little was then known in Germany about life in the Soviet Union. Those who had visited tended to have their existing prejudices confirmed, and would return home saying either that the Soviet Union was a paradise, or that it was hell. Peierls went to Odessa to find out for himself.

He could not have anticipated the outcome. Amidst what he later described as a 'pervasive impression of things being run down', of economic hardships and shortages, and intolerable political pressure, he found something wonderful, which would last a lifetime in the person of Eugenia Kannegiser, recently graduated in physics. It was a *coup de foudre*. As Peierls recorded in his memoir: 'She seemed to know everybody, was known to everybody, and was more cheerful than everybody.'[6] Her family was famous, her cousin Leonid Kannegiser having assassinated Moisei Uritsky, head of the Leningrad Cheka – the Secret Police – after the onset of the Red Terror in 1918. For her part, Genia fell in love with Rudolf 'partly because of his "easy-goingness". Compared to others he was a treat to look after. He ate everything, slept under any conditions. Insects did not sting him; germs did not attack him. He was game to try anything, organize anything, take part in anything.'[7] As Rudolf spoke no Russian, and Genia knew no German, they conversed in English.

At the end of that conference, Genia and Rudolf decided to visit Kislovodsk, a spa in the North Caucasus region of Russia. This involved a train journey, overnight, in 'hard' class, with unreserved seats. The young couple entered a crowded carriage full of what Rudolf described as 'wild-looking local types'.[8] Genia squeezed into a space between them, but there was no seat for Rudolf. His love of challenges was second only to his enthusiasm for finding creative solutions: he noticed a gap in the wooden luggage racks, climbed up, and tied himself in place with the belt of his trousers so that he would not fall off while asleep. Genia later said, in her idiosyncratic English, 'That moment I knew; this man I marry.'[9]

Rudolf Peierls was intellectually brilliant, a scientist with an exceptionally broad understanding of the physical world. Like many successful mathematicians and theoretical physicists, however, he was shy, more at home with algebraic symbols than people. For Genia, who complemented him with a remarkable intuitive intelligence, Rudolf's shyness was an attraction. She had a singular ability to see through the facades that people create, and her insights into human behaviour were as if she had inherited the wisdom of several lifetimes. There was no point in putting on a front with Genia: she knew you better than you knew yourself.

Peierls' manner was to gather evidence, assess it, and not take a decision until he was certain he had all the available facts. Once his mind was made up, however, he trusted his judgement absolutely. That applied not only to his physics and, later, to moral and political problems, but also to his personal life, not least to the phenomenon of Eugenia. Within a year they married and planned to settle in Germany.

If Genia fell in love with Rudolf's vulnerability and 'easy-goingness', then Rudolf fell for her vivacity. Theirs was a German-Russian parallel to the short story by Maupassant, 'The Englishman of Etretat', in which a Frenchman has fallen for an English girl.[10] Pretty and adorable, the most enchanting thing about the girl was the idiosyncratic way she spoke French. In the story, years later a colleague meets the hero, who looks gloomy and dejected: 'What happened? Did she die?' 'No, she learned French.' Genia told Rudolf this cautionary tale and must have taken it to heart as, through the years to their Golden Wedding anniversary and beyond, Rudolf recalled: 'She managed to retain her Russian accent and her special way of using any language.'[11]

Genia's spoken English when I knew her was fluent, but like most for whom English is not their first language, the music and tempo of its delivery revealed her history. There are no definite or indefinite articles in the Russian language, and Genia omitted them in her English too. Her 'special way' was like a linguistic metaphor for quantum physics, where the smooth legato waves of an eloquent native were replaced by the staccato burst of individual quanta – verbs, nouns and occasional adjectives produced a form of auditory shorthand. The cadences of normal English would become the plainsong monotone of a native Russian speaker, which made every phrase sound like an indisputable assertion of fact, yet uttered with such charm that it was impossible to disagree.

By 1932 Rudolf Peierls was already acknowledged as one of the world's leading experts in quantum mechanics. He had won a Rockefeller Fellowship, which enabled him to visit the University of Cambridge for a year, and while he was there the University of Hamburg offered him a tenured teaching and research position. This would be ideal. It would enable Rudolf and Genia to end their peripatetic lifestyle and achieve their ambition of settling in Germany. He duly accepted Hamburg's offer and prepared to return from England to Germany and start work there at Easter 1933.

This was also the year in which Hitler and the Nazis came to power in Germany. The Reichstag was set on fire just weeks before Peierls was due to settle in Hamburg. The Nazi dictator instigated a reign of terror, which overwhelmed Germany. The young couple, both Jews, watched these events with horror. Rudolf decided not to leave England, and withdrew from the Hamburg post.[12] Instead, they took refuge in Cambridge thanks to a temporary extension of his fellowship at the university.

Although his personal life was in turmoil, with his parents and extended family in Nazi Germany, Rudolf was in paradise in his professional life. Cambridge was then the world's foremost experimental laboratory in a new field of research – nuclear physics – and attracting the attention of the world's leading theorists.

In 1932 James Chadwick in Cambridge discovered the neutron, one of the two fundamental constituents of atomic nuclei and, as it would soon transpire, the means to liberate energy from within the nucleus. An atom is mostly empty space, with negatively charged particles – electrons – encircling a massive dense kernel at its centre: the nucleus. The nucleus carries positive charge whereby the electrical attraction of opposite charges – negative electrons and positive nucleus – provides the force that holds an atom together. The nucleus of a hydrogen atom is the simplest of all, consisting of a single positively charged particle, which its discoverer Ernest Rutherford in 1920 called a proton. By 1932 Rutherford was head of the Cambridge research team, and had deduced that the proton was fundamental to the nuclei of all atomic elements.

The chemical elements are distinguished by the complexity of their atoms. Hydrogen, the simplest, consists of a single electron encircling a single proton, while helium has two protons in its nucleus, carbon has six, onwards to uranium with ninety-two. The chemical identity of an element is a result of its electrons, and chemical reactions occur when electrons move from one atom to another. Up to this juncture, Peierls had studied the behaviour of those electrons as they moved around solid materials under the influence of electric and magnetic forces. This was about to change, as attention focused on the nucleus following Chadwick's discovery of the neutron.

Neutrons are similar to protons but carry no electric charge; they cluster in atomic nuclei and add to the nuclear mass without changing the total charge. The resulting massive nuclei are known as 'isotopes' from the Greek for 'same place' – the same place in the periodic table of the atomic elements. We now know that neutrons are an essential component of all atomic nuclei except for that of hydrogen, which normally consists of just a single proton. The stability of an atomic nucleus can change radically if the number of neutrons varies by just one or two. Within a decade this delicate balance between stability and explosive fragility would be exploited in the case of the heaviest naturally occurring element – uranium.

Peierls arrived in Cambridge soon after James Chadwick's discovery of the neutron. Nuclear physics was still in its infancy; in due course it would become Peierls' forte, but not yet. In Cambridge he continued to build his reputation by applying quantum mechanics to the behaviour of electrons in metals and the phenomenon of diamagnetism, where some materials are repelled by a magnetic field. His appointment expired in 1933, but return to Germany was out of the question. Fortunately, Peierls received a two-year Fellowship at Manchester University from the Academic Assistance Council – a privately funded organization that helped displaced scholars. At Manchester he was reunited with Hans Bethe, whom he had known as a fellow student in Munich. Bethe too had a Jewish background and had left Germany. So began a lifelong friendship, Bethe now helping to defray the Peierlses' expenses by living in a spare room at their small house.

The pair began to work together on nuclear physics. In 1930 Wolfgang Pauli had hypothesized that a particle called the neutrino can be produced when an unstable isotope spontaneously stabilizes in the phenomenon known as radioactivity; in 1934 Bethe and Peierls wrote the first papers that quantified the circumstances under which the neutrino would interact with matter and be detectable. Two decades elapsed before their work bore fruit with the neutrino's discovery.[13] In 1935 they wrote one of the first papers applying quantum theory to the structure of atomic nuclei. They explained how the simplest nucleus – the isotope of hydrogen consisting of a proton and a single neutron – is formed when a proton captures a neutron, and how it disintegrates when bombarded by electrons.[14] Later that year, Peierls returned to Cambridge, where he wrote further papers on magnetism and on nuclear physics.

Peierls' depth was becoming joined to remarkable breadth. Two years later, in the summer of 1937 and aged thirty, Rudolf Peierls became the youngest professor in the country, at Birmingham University.*

Meeting Genia in 1930 had been the first fateful encounter for Rudolf; the second came in 1936. Still only twenty-nine years old, he was at the fulcrum of British physics, much in demand, his opinion valued. Neville Mott, a future Nobel laureate who had befriended Peierls in Cambridge, discussed the implications of quantum mechanics with him on a regular basis. In 1936 Mott, now at Bristol University, invited Peierls to give a talk to the physics department. It is likely that this was the occasion when Rudolf Peierls – the maestro – was first introduced to Klaus Fuchs, an outstanding student and fellow refugee from the Nazis.†

Fuchs and Mott had been working on a theory of electrical conduction

---

* This was an era when 'Professor' equated with 'Head of Department' – in Peierls' case, Applied Mathematics – and not its modern ubiquitous use to describe a university teacher of almost any rank.

† Peierls was a delegate at an international physics conference in Bristol from 2 to 5 July 1935, and Fuchs – in his first weeks as a research student – attended the sessions. It is unlikely that the pair met more than passingly, however. See chapter 2.

in thin metals, inspired by some enigmatic results that no one could understand. Peierls discussed this with them, and was impressed some weeks later when Fuchs presented the complete mathematical explanation of the phenomenon.*

The following year, Peierls was invited to a nuclear physics conference in Moscow. He planned to take Genia with him, but went alone because he was 'worried that her presence might prove an embarrassment to her relatives'.[15] Those are Peierls' understated words, which hide a starker reality of the terror that was engulfing the Soviet Union.

Back in the summer of 1934, Rudolf and Genia had taken their newborn daughter, Gaby, to visit Genia's family in Leningrad. This had been a happy time, though no one anticipated that it would be the last occasion on which Genia would see her parents. The first hint of looming disaster came on 1 December with the assassination of Sergey Kirov, who was head of the Communist Party in Leningrad. Stalin immediately instigated mass repressions in the city, which many regard as a rehearsal of the subsequent Great Terror. Genia's mother, sister Nina and stepfather Isai Mandelshtam (her biological father had died in 1909) were caught up in this purge and in 1935 were exiled for five years to Ufa in the Urals, 2,000 kilometres east of Leningrad. Nina was allowed to return to Leningrad after two years, but their mother and stepfather were sent from one exile to another, with Isai spending three years in a Gulag camp. By all accounts their life was miserable. An aunt and uncle also spent years in the Gulag.†

The Peierlses were sensitive to the reality of life in Stalin's autocracy and the dilemma that Genia's return would create for members of her family: should they welcome her like some prodigal, and draw the attention of the secret police, or take the politically safer course of shunning a Russian-born citizen who chose to live away from the homeland? Xenophobia was rampant in Russia then; all foreigners were suspected of being spies, and Soviet citizens who chose to marry a foreigner and leave Russia were also distrusted.

Peierls wryly noted a book that was popular in Russia at the time, which remarked: 'The best time for spies to work is just before or during the outbreak of a war, when there is a general spy hysteria, and everybody suspects everybody else of being a spy [making it] virtually impossible to detect the real spies.'[16] This observation would be triply ironic. First, Isai Mandelshtam was interrogated and accused of espionage en route to the

---

* Fuchs' paper is described in chapter 2.

† Genia's aunt and uncle and their children eventually managed to migrate to Paris before the Great Terror only to be captured by the Nazis and perish in Auschwitz. Her cousin joined the French Resistance, was caught by the Gestapo and shot on the spot.

Gulag, because of his connection to Rudolf Peierls. Soviet suspicion of the ex-patriot Genia would be an uncanny mirror image, later, of British unease at her Russian origin. Furthermore, Rudolf's theory of spies is an ironic preview of his own future, as his visit to Russia led to MI5 creating a file on him in 1938. In April that year he visited Niels Bohr in Copenhagen and upon his return the immigration officer at Harwich noted 'during examination of [Peierls'] passport it was noticed that it contained a Soviet visa and Russian control stamps for 1937, but the alien, when questioned, beyond confirming that he had in fact visited the Soviet Union last year, did not appear to be willing to give any reason for his visit to that country'. The immigration officer did not question Peierls further 'in view of his substantial position as a professor'. Nonetheless this was recorded as 'of possible interest to Special Branch'. On 25 April 1938 this became the first entry in Peierls' MI5 file.[17]

In May 1938 Peierls applied for naturalization as a British citizen. By mid-1939 nothing had happened. With war looming, on 31 August Peierls wrote to the Under-Secretary of State at the Aliens department. He pointed out that he was an alien, a German, who had lived in the United Kingdom for six years and had applied for naturalization in May 1938. He was very anxious to become an air-raid warden, but could not be enrolled before his naturalization was completed. He asked: 'Is my application being considered?' Peierls said he wanted to be able to help when there was a need for volunteers, 'even in capacities that involve no responsibility and confidential information'.[18]

On 4 September 1939 Britain declared war on Germany. Peierls was now seriously worried: still formally a German subject, his application for British naturalization became bogged down in bureaucracy.

The restrictions imposed on Germans in the United Kingdom were for Peierls a minor matter, however, but that he was also refused permission to help in emergency work in any capacity made him feel impotent. He pointed out to the naturalization authorities that he had not lived in Germany since 1929. In addition he explained that in March 1933, even before the anti-Jewish laws, he had declined the offer of a job in Germany because the Nazi regime had just been established and 'I did not want to submit to it.' He had only returned to Germany once, in 1934 to visit his parents, and after that, 'I suppose I would not have been allowed to return even if I wanted to.' His parents and near family had, like him, now left Germany.

Peierls wrote to influential scientists in the hope of being assigned to useful war work. To Edward Appleton, the chair of the Department of Scientific and Industrial Research and as such the most senior British government post associated with physical science, Peierls wrote on 13 September 1939, 'I have more personal experience of, and hence more animosity towards, the present regime in Germany than most other people in this country.' He had even 'tried to get rid of my German nationality but . . . this was technically impossible while my papers were at the Home Office with my naturalisation papers'. Peierls' German passport had expired in May and he had 'taken no steps to renew it'. He was in limbo. Despite his brilliance, as Peierls was technically German the United Kingdom was unready to use his talents in the war effort.[19]

Peierls was based at Birmingham University, where the head of the physics department, Mark Oliphant, was working on radar. It was the most secret scientific enterprise of the war, from which the alien Peierls was excluded. Even after he finally managed to become a British citizen, in March 1940, he was excluded from the top-secret research into radar on grounds of his origins. He had, however, been welcomed in the City of Birmingham Auxiliary Fire Service, and received a certificate that he had 'completed in a satisfactory manner a course in anti-gas precautionary measures'.[20] He summarized his feelings pithily in a letter to Sir William Bragg, the President of the Royal Society: 'I shall get a very beautiful uniform but I still think I might help the country in more efficient ways than sleeping in a fire station.'[21] He was indeed given a uniform with a helmet and an axe, and as he foresaw in his letter to Bragg he spent 'long hours at the station just sitting around'.[22] Peierls was frustrated, but fate was about to cast him into a leading role. With radar a secret and off limits, Peierls decided to devote his intellectual energy to a field that in 1940 had no obvious relevance for the war: nuclear physics and fission. Without knowing it, in March of that year he was about to redefine the war effort.

NUCLEAR FISSION

The key to nuclear fission was a rare form of the element uranium, known as 'U235'. The nuclei of these atypical uranium atoms are so fragile that a mere touch by a slow neutron can be enough to split the pack – in an analogy made at the time, this was like disturbing a large drop of water whereupon it breaks into two smaller drops. This phenomenon, named 'fission', had been discovered in Germany by Otto Hahn, Lisa Meitner and Fritz Strassmann in 1938, and might have remained a mere curiosity, except for two features. First, when the nucleus of a uranium atom splits, the total energy released is over a hundred times greater than in radioactivity. The comparison to chemical reactions is stark, fission freeing nearly a billion times the energy, atom for atom. Here was the first hint of how to liberate nuclear energy on a larger scale than had hitherto appeared possible. The second discovery, early in 1939, was that the fission of a uranium nucleus also liberates neutrons – by analogy, these extra neutrons are like tiny droplets in the space between the two big drops. If these 'secondary' neutrons hit other atoms within the lump of uranium, causing them to divide with the release both of energy and further neutrons, a self-sustaining nuclear 'chain reaction' is possible. This creates the potential for an immense release of energy and, in extremis, a nuclear explosion.*

When news of fission broke in 1938, scientists immediately wondered: Why are the rocks around us, which contain uranium and are being hit continuously by neutrons from cosmic rays, not liable to detonate spontaneously? The great Danish theoretical physicist, Niels Bohr, gave the answer. Uranium nuclei come in different forms – isotopes – such as 'U238' and 'U235' (the U signifies uranium and the number denotes the total number of constituent protons and neutrons within the nucleus). Bohr made the key insight: fission is more likely in an isotope with an odd number of constituents, such as U235, than an even number, such as U238.[23] The fission of natural rocks is rare because they contain so little U235 – less than one per cent.

A flurry of experiments soon established that whenever a neutron hits uranium, the outcome depends on what isotope is hit, and at what speed. If a neutron impacts a nucleus of U235, for example, the latter almost invariably breaks up whatever the speed of the neutron. If a nucleus of U238 is hit, however, it usually remains intact but the result depends on the neutron's speed. If the neutron is moving fast, which is likely to be the case if it was spawned by fission of U235, it will be captured by the U238. This converts the uranium into another isotope, U239, removes the

* Ernest Rutherford's assistants John Cockcroft and Ernest Walton first observed fission – the splitting of an atomic nucleus into smaller parts – in April 1932. They fired protons at the third lightest element, lithium, and split it into two alpha particles – nuclei of helium. The following year Rutherford remarked that this liberated much more energy than the proton supplied, but he realized that it was so inefficient that 'anyone who looks for a source of power in the transformation of atoms is talking moonshine'. When the Hungarian Leo Szilard read what Rutherford had said, he had a brilliant thought: if instead of a proton, a neutron struck lithium, the fission would also return a neutron (Appendix, p. 427, fig. 1(b)). The breakthrough insight was that this neutron could initiate another fission, and so on in a chain reaction. Unfortunately, in the case of lithium, this liberated neutron is too feeble to make further fissions. Nobody seems to have applied Szilard's reasoning to the heaviest elements in the periodic table, such as uranium. Indeed, when fission of uranium was discovered in 1938 (Appendix, p. 428, fig. 1(c)), Szilard's idea had existed for five years, but no one seems to have been aware of the fact.

neutron from activity and prevents it contributing further to a chain reaction. If the neutron is moving slowly, however, with kinetic energy similar to the molecules in the room, it will bounce off the U238 and live on. If its next collision is with U235, fission will occur; if it hits a U238 it will bounce off once more; if it exits the target, however, it is lost to the chain reaction.

In natural uranium, the dominant U238 acts as a blanket that covers any nearby U235, making a succession of fissions rare, and the chance of a chain reaction negligible. Only if the neutrons encounter some of the rare isotope U235 before exiting the uranium target can a chain reaction occur. The scarcity of U235 stabilizes the natural world, which is a good thing, but makes it difficult to extract nuclear energy from raw uranium.

Difficult isn't the same as impossible, however. By the summer of 1939 experiments in France, England and the United States had shown that a chain reaction might be possible if the neutrons are slowed – in the jargon 'moderated' to 'thermal energies' – by bouncing off atoms of carbon in graphite or of deuterium in 'heavy water'.

When atoms of hydrogen in water are replaced by those of deuterium, where the single proton of the hydrogen nucleus is accompanied by a neutron, the result is heavy water. The neutron leaves the chemistry unaltered – hence the resulting molecule is still one of water – but adds to the mass. Heavy water is more efficient than ordinary water in slowing neutrons.

So slow neutrons are the spark that can light the nuclear fire, but the flame is fickle. Uranium fission provides the kindling but the neutrons released in fission are fast, so the problem returns. To liberate nuclear energy effectively requires both 'enrichment' – an increase of the relative amount of U235 in the target – and lots of uranium.[24]

Niels Bohr published his insight about U235 in *Physical Review* in September 1939,* in the same week that the Second World War began.[25] At this critical moment in history, there was at best only a hope that with several tons of uranium, and some means to slow neutrons to make them effective, scientists could construct a nuclear reactor. This could liberate energy and produce power for industry, but an atomic bomb small enough to be delivered by a plane or gun seemed out of the question.

---

* The paper was received by the editor on 26 June 1939 and published on 1 September. Germany invaded Poland that day; Britain and France declared war on Germany two days later.

EINSTEIN'S LETTER

Europe was at war. Meanwhile in the United States, President Roosevelt was constrained by the 1937 Neutrality Act, which forbade America from becoming embroiled in foreign conflicts. Roosevelt, who was near the end of his second term, felt that the United States had a duty to stop the spread of fascism and he wanted the Act repealed. For many Americans, however, the priority was to escape from the aftermath of the Great Depression, not to commit troops to fight Hitler thousands of miles away.

Many Jews had fled from central Europe, like Peierls, and escaped to North America. Among these was a trio of Hungarians: Edward Teller, Eugene Wigner and Leo Szilard. In August 1939 this group of émigré physicists visited Albert Einstein, who was spending the summer on Long Island, told him that it might be possible to build atomic weapons, and urged him to alert Roosevelt. This was the first that Einstein had heard of the chain reaction and he understood its implications immediately. Without hesitation he signed the letter, which mentioned 'the almost in-finite power' of atomic energy and warned of its potential for 'bombs of hitherto unenvisaged potency and scope'.[26]

When Roosevelt received this news, his reaction was immediate. To ensure that 'the Nazis don't blow us up', he charged Lyman Briggs, head of the National Bureau of Standards, to form an 'Advisory Committee on Uranium'.[27] Briggs was a worthy bureaucrat but unfortunately no vision-ary. The committee's first report to the President in November 1939 had the uninspiring recommendation that the government should put more funds into the study of nuclear chain reactions.

The United States project came alive the following year with the arrival of Vannevar Bush, the energetic vice-president of MIT. In June 1940 he gained Roosevelt's ear with an idea to revitalize the American economy – still in the doldrums after the Depression – by coordinating scientific research and the development of military equipment and weapons. Roosevelt liked what he heard, and appointed Bush head of a National Defence Research Committee.

Prominent in the early American work was Nobel laureate and Italian émigré Enrico Fermi, who made rapid progress at Columbia University investigating chain reactions and establishing that the bombardment of uranium with neutrons might be a route to the controlled release of nuclear energy. At this stage, however, nuclear weapons weren't in this new vision. While Einstein's letter is often cited as the start of a nuclear weapons development programme in the United States, this is only true in hindsight.

In 1939 and into 1940 physicists anticipated nuclear weapons being too heavy for delivery by aircraft, and hence having to be 'carried by boat'. So although a terrifying super-weapon could be imagined in principle, a practical one seemed out of the question. The British scientist A. V. Hill, who visited the USA and Canada in March and April 1940, was so unimpressed that he reported back to his colleagues in the United Kingdom it would be a waste of time to do this work here at home. He argued that it was scientifically very interesting 'but for present practical needs probably a wild-goose chase', and 'if anything likely to be of war value emerges, the [US scientists] will certainly give us a hint of it in good time'.[28]

What neither Hill nor anyone in the United States knew was that back in March, in the United Kingdom, Peierls and Otto Frisch, another refugee from Nazism and like Peierls prevented from working on radar, had made a discovery that would utterly change the nature of warfare. The pair had calculated that the energy liberated by a 0.5kg bomb of U235 would be equivalent to that of several thousand tons of dynamite. With this insight, Peierls and Frisch had made a key breakthrough: an atomic bomb could be light enough to be dropped from an aircraft.

THE CONCEPTION OF THE ATOMIC BOMB

This is what had happened. Peierls and Frisch, working together at Birmingham University, had read Bohr's paper, checked its conclusions, and agreed that if fission were to be a practical energy source, uranium must first be enriched in U235. So Frisch began some experiments to see how feasible enrichment might be. To do this, he used the phenomenon of 'thermal diffusion'. When a mixture of two gases is in a container, one end of which is hot and the other cold, a gentle breeze develops in which the lighter gas molecules drift towards the hot end while the heavier ones accumulate at the cold end. Frisch used uranium hexafluoride – in chemical shorthand 'UF_6', and colloquially known as 'hex' – which is the only practical gaseous compound of uranium. Most of the uranium in UF_6 consists of the heavy isotope U238, while about seven molecules in every thousand is in the lighter form, U235. In principle Frisch hoped to enrich the U235 by extracting gas from the hot end, where the relatively light U235 would gather, then he would repeat the exercise, over and over, progressively increasing the concentration of U235.

Frisch established that, even if he could enrich uranium this way, it would be slow. Adding to his problems was that his goal was unclear, as he had no idea how much U235 would be needed to make a practical fission engine. A ton was out of the question, and the task looked impractical even if 100kg were sufficient. Then in March 1940 Frisch asked Peierls the seminal question: If neutrons were to hit a lump of pure U235, how much would be required to make a significant explosion? Peierls worked out a formula to compute the critical mass – the minimum lump of uranium capable of sustaining a chain reaction before too many neutrons escaped through its surface. What he didn't then know was the probability that a neutron would hit an individual nucleus of U235 and cause it to fission, for in March 1940 no one had isolated enough U235 to be able to measure this critical quantity.[29]

Peierls had read Bohr's paper and understood it sufficiently to realize that if a neutron hit a nucleus of U235, at any speed, fission was almost certain to occur, at least in theory. So he assumed this to be true, and worked out the implications in his formula. The two young physicists were astonished by the answer: where previously they thought that a weapon would require at least the mass of a champion weightlifter, they had now established that a lump the size of a pineapple would be enough. A question remained, however: Would this actually explode or merely fizzle?

The chain reaction would spread through the uranium, the first fission liberating typically two neutrons, this pair inducing two further fissions, which would spawn four neutrons, each successive generation doubling up the number of neutrons and increasing the amount of subsequent fission reactions exponentially. Peierls estimated that the time between successive generations would be about five-millionths of a second, the number of active neutrons doubling each time.[30] After about eighty generations, the lump of uranium would be vaporized into fragments smaller than the critical size, and fission would stop, but by then the damage would have been done. The implication was staggering: in less than one-thousandth of a second, the uranium would be hotter than the centre of the sun and the explosive effects of this small piece of metal would be greater than several thousand tons of dynamite. Frisch recalled the moment: 'We stared at one another and realised that a bomb might after all be possible.'

Had they stumbled on such an apocalyptic vision in peacetime, they would probably have abandoned the project at once, and told nobody. But, as Frisch explained later, 'we were at war, and the idea was reasonably obvious. Very probably some German scientists had had the same idea and were working on it.'[31]

The implications were so sensitive that Peierls typed the report himself, on his typewriter, while Frisch dictated from their notes. They were in Peierls' office on the ground floor of the physics department and, as it was a warm day, the window was open. At one moment, while they were debating a particularly sensitive point, a face suddenly appeared in the open window. Their momentary panic passed when it turned out to be no more than a colleague 'digging for victory', who was planting tomatoes by the south-facing wall. The secret was safe – for now.[32]

If there was a 'secret' to the atomic bomb it was this: fast neutrons will induce nuclear fission reactions fast enough to be potentially explosive, and pure U235 avoids neutrons being lost through capture by U238. Frisch and Peierls immediately informed Oliphant, the departmental head, who had security clearance in Whitehall. In a secret memorandum, written in the middle of March 1940 for the attention of the British government, the pair pointed out that no material could resist the blast of this 'atomic bomb'. Their report is today known as the 'Frisch-Peierls Memorandum'.* It is a remarkable document in the breadth of its vision and foresight.

The implications of Peierls and Frisch's discovery were so awful that the two scientists believed the weapon would prove impossible for a civilized society to employ, as both the initial blast and lingering radiation would kill thousands of civilians. In just 1,428 words, not only did they announce the key to making this fearsome weapon, but they also laid the foundations for a new science – the biological effect of radiation – and foresaw a strategy of defence through mutually assured destruction.[33] While this might not seem remarkable to modern eyes, reflect for a moment that before 1940 all conventional weapons had been *chemical* in nature. A single *nuclear* weapon, such as Peierls and Frisch were describing, when dropped by a lone aircraft, would create a blast whose strength would compare to a conventional air raid by hundreds of bombers. But it would do far more, as the pair realized with horror. There would be a qualitative change in the nature of war. They pointed out that as there was no material that could resist its blast, the military and governments would need to develop new strategies. Radiation would spread with the wind, and its threat would linger long after the dust had settled, literally. This meant that even those who exploded such a bomb would have to take care when advancing later into the devastated area. Where conventional weapons could liberate an area for occupation, the atomic bomb would create a 'danger-zone' where no one could enter for days or more.

Their status as refugees from Nazism must have influenced the opinion of both Peierls and Frisch that such an awful invention might be 'unsuitable as a weapon for use by this country', while at the same time fearing that Germany might be developing an atomic bomb itself, and be prepared

---

* The memorandum is shown in full at the end of this chapter.

to use it. Eight decades later, their foresight about atomic weapons being a form of mutual defence continues to be correct. With hindsight, their only significant error was their estimate that production could take months in a relatively compact plant: the scale and effort of the Manhattan Project, which would involve up to 100,000 workers for three years, were as yet unimagined.

The British took action: Peierls and Frisch's work was classified so secret that the government committee which evaluated their discovery even barred attendance at its meetings by the two émigrés themselves.

MAUD*

The result of Peierls and Frisch's discovery was that the government set up a research and development programme for an atomic weapon. Initially run by the enigmatically named MAUD committee of scientists, it later matured (end of 1941) into an industrial project under the bland code name of 'Tube Alloys', both names chosen in order to hide their purpose.

The origin of MAUD reads like an Ealing comedy. In April 1940 the Nazi army occupied Denmark, the home of Niels Bohr. Soon afterwards news of Bohr arrived in London in a telegram. It stated that he was safe and included the enigmatic instruction to 'inform Cockcroft and Maud Ray Kent'. John Cockcroft, one of the duo who had first artificially split the atom, thought 'Maud Ray Kent' was an anagram for 'Radium taken' and that Bohr was covertly telling them that the Germans had availed themselves of radioactive materials and were actively pursuing atomic research. Only later did Cockcroft learn that in fact the message referred innocently to the Bohr family's governess, Maud Ray, who lived in Kent. In any event, Maud Ray has become immortalized by the morphing of her name into the code name of Britain's atomic committee.[34]

Peierls was a mild-tempered man who had initially been merely frustrated at having his war effort limited to duties as a fireman. When as an 'enemy alien' he had been unable to work on radar, he had contributed through the intermediary of his departmental head at the university, Mark Oliphant. Their manoeuvres had elements of farce. Peierls would share ideas with Oliphant, who would transmit them to Whitehall. Upon returning to Birmingham, Oliphant would then discuss the resulting

* The original members of MAUD in April 1940 were George Thomson, James Chadwick, John Cockcroft, Mark Oliphant and Philip Moon. For details of MAUD's work see Margaret Gowing, *Britain and Atomic Energy, 1939–1945* (Macmillan, 1964).

physics questions with Peierls, who would hand down replies. This creative solution to a problem was characteristic of Peierls, and sweeter still as it represented victory over the jobsworths who, in his opinion, obstructed progress through a myopic application of regulations. By this means some headway was made without formally breaching the Official Secrets Act. On 22 April, however, restricted from working on his own invention, Peierls was incandescent, haranguing the head of the MAUD committee, Professor G. P. Thomson of Imperial College, London, until this lunatic bureaucracy was broken.

In one of its first actions the MAUD committee noted in May 1940: 'Two enemy aliens . . . PEIERLS and FRISCH have put forward certain suggestions in this connection which seem worthy of consideration. It seems desirable that we should use their knowledge and advice.'[35] Winston Churchill's science advisor, Frederick Lindemann, wrote to Peierls asking why the bomb should now be taken seriously, to which Peierls replied that the probability of the bomb working 'is sufficiently high to make it important to investigate the matter as rapidly as possible'. He continued: 'While there is no evidence that the Germans realise the potentialities of a U235 bomb . . . it is quite possible that they do, and for all we know they may have almost completed its production.'[36]

Peierls met Lindemann and presented his ideas face to face. The two men never felt comfortable together. Lindemann was ill at ease in the presence of a scientist whose understanding significantly exceeded his own, while Peierls, in common with several colleagues, regarded Lindemann as a scientific lightweight. Afterwards, Peierls was asked about Lindemann's reactions and said: 'I do not know him sufficiently well to translate his grunts correctly.'[37]

So it was that in June 1940, in the same week that France surrendered to the Nazis, leaving the United Kingdom isolated, Peierls was included in the atomic team. Having initially been an outsider, he soon became one of the lead theorists, if not formally, then in practice: of the first seventy scientific reports issued with code-numbers fronted by the Tube Alloys acronym 'TA' during 1941 and 1942, all but a handful carried Peierls' name, and a substantial majority of these were written by him alone.[38]

Peierls initially set out the strategic questions. For an explosion to happen, what are the critical mass and optimal design of the uranium? How will the shock wave develop? In order to produce the fuel for the weapon, what is the best way to enrich U235? Initially there were several ideas on enrichment – electromagnetic separation, thermal methods, or diffusion of the gaseous compound, uranium hexafluoride. By August 1940 Peierls' analyses led the British to pursue gaseous diffusion as the means.

The key feature, as Peierls realized, was that U235 is about one per cent lighter than U238. As a force will shift a tennis ball more easily than a lump of rock, so in gaseous uranium will a relatively light atom of U235 respond to pressure more readily than its slightly heavier sibling U238. If the gas is in a cylinder, with a piston applying pressure at one end while the other end consists of a porous membrane, the U235 will be forced through the membrane faster than the U238. So the gas on the far side of the membrane will be richer in U235. The enrichment will be very small, but the process can be repeated, starting with the already enriched gas; after sufficient repetitions the proportion of U235 could become considerable. The idea is simple, but the practical questions were hard to answer. How many stages would be needed to enrich U235 to the level needed for a bomb? For how long should the pressure be applied in each stage?

At first sight the answer to the second question might seem to be: 'The longer the better.' This is flawed, however. It is true that the amount of U235 on the far side of the barrier increases early on, but it does so at the expense of its depletion in the original sample. Eventually there is no longer enough U235 in the source to compete with the excess of U235 seeping back through the membrane from the enriched side. The implication is that after some amount of time the gases on either side of the membrane will reach equilibrium. So a crucial question for the theorists to answer was: How long is the equilibrium time and how does it vary with the pressure?

Peierls' initial estimates were that for realistic pressures the equilibrium time would be days, and to enrich the uranium adequately would take up to three hundred individual stages. This is so impractical that it would never have been contemplated, but for the imperatives of the war.

Nonetheless, this method of gaseous diffusion appeared to be more efficient than other ideas such as thermal separation, which Frisch had tried. At Oxford University, Franz Simon, also an émigré from the Nazis, fabricated fine wire with which he could bore holes less than one-hundredth of a millimetre in diameter. The resulting porous membranes were then used to make test measurements of diffusion. By the autumn of 1940 Simon's team was confident that the concept would work.

Meanwhile in Cambridge experiments were being conducted to see whether a divergent chain reaction really happens and if so how rapidly it can develop. The Cambridge team irradiated uranium oxide with neutrons that had first been slowed by bouncing off atoms of heavy water. Slow neutrons are more effective at causing fission, and the experiments demonstrated that a divergent chain reaction happens. This opened a possibility – albeit still theoretical – of a self-sustaining engine, producing power by fission: a nuclear reactor. Whereas $U235$ would be needed to make an explosion, the irradiation of the dominant $U238$ in a reactor would produce a new element: plutonium. Cambridge theorists Egon Bretscher and Norman Feather predicted that plutonium could be a super-explosive material, more so even than $U235$.

For fission to happen, a neutron first has to bump into uranium. The likelihood of this happening is measured by a quantity called the 'cross section', figuratively, how big the uranium appears to the neutron. The bigger the cross section, the greater the likelihood of an encounter and of fission. The magnitude of this cross section was poorly understood; Peierls and Frisch's estimate that a pineapple-sized lump of $U235$ would be sufficient for an explosion relied on theoretical estimates for this quantity. Liverpool University had the necessary apparatus – a cyclotron – with which Frisch, who had moved there from Birmingham, now measured the cross section. This turned out to be less than Frisch and Peierls had assumed, which implied that the amount of $U235$ needed for a bomb would be some 50 kilograms, nearly a hundred times larger than Peierls' original estimate. Had this been known from the start it is possible that the MAUD project would never have begun, but although the challenge was now more difficult at least the goals for Simon's enrichment experiments were now clear. Peierls, Frisch and Simon – three émigrés who for security reasons had been excluded from other war work – had now been entrusted with the greatest wartime secret of all.[39]

Back in Birmingham, in addition to Peierls' work on diffusion, scientists were investigating how to prepare uranium metal. The reason for metal is that it is dense, which increases the chance of neutrons bumping into uranium atoms and inducing fission. First, however, the overriding task was to prepare enough $U235$ by diffusion.

Diffusion requires a gas, and uranium hexafluoride UF_6 was the only compound of uranium that was practical. It had the advantage that fluorine has only one stable isotope, so the diffusion would be determined by the uranium and not by the fluorine. That was the extent of the good news, however. To keep 'hex' gaseous, the laboratory had to be hotter than the Sahara Desert in high summer or the pressure lower than at the summit of Mount Everest; otherwise, hex solidifies. It is also highly corrosive and interacts with many substances, including water, to form solid compounds. The ease with which hex could solidify threatened to kill the diffusion plant with an exotic arteriosclerosis. But unless some other substance was found, hex would have to be used. And if a less lethal fuel were available, it would be unlikely to have the advantage that uranium alone determined its diffusion. Would that be a problem? This was but one of the many questions that Peierls had to deal with.*

Questions were in fact growing exponentially. By November 1940 Peierls was overwhelmed with work for MAUD and in desperate need of an assistant. He said later: 'I found many theoretical problems piling up and I could not deal with them fast enough.'[40] He found help in unexpected ways. For example, the Nobel laureate theorist Paul Dirac had done an experiment on isotope separation and developed a mathematical theory of how to separate isotopic mixtures most effectively.[41] Meanwhile, Frisch had joined a team at Liverpool University where one of his colleagues, the theoretician Maurice Pryce, worked out how to estimate the efficiency of an explosive chain reaction. These contributions were gems, admittedly, but Peierls was still in desperate need of a full-time assistant: 'I needed some regular help – someone with whom I would be able to discuss the theoretical technicalities.'[42]

Most competent theoreticians were already doing something important, and when Peierls heard that Klaus Fuchs, whom he knew and respected as a physicist from his work at Bristol, was available, it seemed a good idea to get him to come to Birmingham.

Fuchs had the kind of ability Peierls was looking for. Furthermore, like Peierls, Fuchs detested what Hitler had done to his country and, now, much of mainland Europe. Peierls recalled: 'I knew he had left Germany because of his opposition to the Nazis and I respected him for this. I knew of his association with left-wing student organizations in Germany since at that time the communist-controlled organizations were the only ones putting up any active opposition.'[43]

The United Kingdom itself feared invasion, and Peierls thought Fuchs 'might welcome an opportunity to participate in a project that was intended to forestall Hitler'. On 10 May 1941 Peierls wrote to Fuchs and invited him to join in 'theoretical work involving mathematical problems of considerable complexity', adding that he 'cannot describe the nature or the purpose of the work'.[44] By inviting Fuchs into the team, Peierls had unwittingly started a chain reaction that would have vast and unforeseen consequences.

---

* For uranium hexafluoride to remain gas at normal atmospheric pressure requires the temperature to exceed 130° F (55° C). If the pressure is reduced to that at the top of Mount Everest, the temperature still has to exceed 100° F (38° C). At normal room temperature, the pressure must be less than one-tenth of atmospheric pressure, which is like the atmosphere 10 miles above sea level.

THE FRISCH-PEIERLS MEMORANDUM*

Strictly Confidential
Memorandum on the properties of a radioactive 'super-bomb'

The attached detailed report concerns the possibility of constructing a 'super-bomb' which utilises the energy stored in atomic nuclei as a source of energy. The energy liberated in the explosion of such a super-bomb is about the same as that produced by the explosion of 1000 tons of dynamite. The energy is liberated in a small volume, in which it will, for an instant, produce a temperature comparable to that in the interior of the sun. The blast from such an explosion would destroy life in a wide area. The size of this area is difficult to estimate, but it will probably cover the entire centre of a big city.

In addition, some part of the energy set free by the bomb goes to produce radioactive substances, and these will emit very powerful and dangerous radiations. The effect of these radiations is greatest immediately after the explosion, but it decays only gradually and even for days after the explosion any person entering the affected area will be killed.

Some of this radioactivity will be carried along with the wind and will spread the contamination; several miles downwind this may kill people.

In order to produce such a bomb it is necessary to treat a few cwt. [few hundreds of kg] of uranium by a process which will separate from the uranium its light isotope (U235) of which it contains about 0.7%. Methods for the separation of isotopes have recently been developed. They are slow and they have not until now been applied to uranium, whose chemical properties give rise to technical difficulties. But these difficulties are by no means insuperable. We have not sufficient experience with large-scale chemical plant to give a reliable estimate of the cost, but it is certainly not prohibitive.

It is a property of these super-bombs that there exists a 'critical size' of about one pound [about half a kg]. A quantity of the separated uranium isotope that exceeds the critical amount is explosive, yet a quantity less than the critical amount is absolutely safe. [The phrase after 'yet' was initially

---

* Frisch and Peierls produced two versions of their memorandum; one contained some technical details and the other, 'pedagogic' version was written specifically for decision-makers who were not primarily physicists. The technical version is discussed in detail in Jeremy Bernstein, 'A Memorandum that Changed the World', *American Journal of Physics*, vol. 79 (2011), pp. 440–46. Here I display the pedagogic version. TNA AB 1/210.

omitted and added as an insert.] The bomb would therefore be manufactured in two (or more) parts, each being less than the critical size, and in transport all danger of a premature explosion would be avoided if these parts were kept at a distance of a few inches from each other. The bomb would be provided with a mechanism that brings the two parts together when the bomb is intended to go off. Once the parts are joined to form a block which exceeds the critical amount, the effect of the penetrating radiation always present in the atmosphere will initiate the explosion within a second or so.

The mechanism which brings the parts of the bomb together must be arranged to work fairly rapidly because of the possibility of the bomb exploding when the critical conditions have just only [sic] been reached. In this case the explosion will be far less powerful. It is never possible to exclude this altogether, but one can easily ensure that only, say, one bomb out of 100 will fail in this way, and since in any case the explosion is strong enough to destroy the bomb itself, this point is not serious.

We do not feel competent to discuss the strategic value of such a bomb, but the following conclusions seem certain:

1. As a weapon, the super-bomb would be practically irresistible. There is no material or structure that could expect to resist the force of the explosion. If one thinks of using the bomb for breaking through a line of fortifications, it should be kept in mind that the radioactive radiations will prevent anyone from approaching the affected territory for several days; they will equally prevent defenders from reoccupying the affected positions. The advantage would lie with the side which can determine most accurately just when it is safe to re-enter the area; this is likely to be the aggressor, who knows the location of the bomb in advance.

2. Owing to the spreading of radioactive substances with the wind, the bomb could probably not be used without killing large numbers of civilians, and this may make it unsuitable as a weapon for use by this country. (Use as a depth charge near a naval base suggests itself, but even there it is likely that it would cause great loss of civilian life by flooding and by the radioactive radiations.)

3. We have no information that the same idea has also occurred to other scientists, but since all the theoretical data bearing on this problem are published, it is conceivable that Germany is, in fact, developing this weapon. Whether this is the case is difficult to find out, since the plant for the separation of isotopes need not be of such a size as to attract attention. Information that could be helpful in this respect

would be data about the exploitation of the uranium mines under German control (mainly in Czechoslovakia) and about any recent German purchases of uranium abroad. It is likely that the plant would be controlled by Dr. K. Clusius (Professor of Physical Chemistry in Munich University), the inventor of the best method for separating isotopes, and therefore information as to his whereabouts and status might also give an important clue.

At the same time it is quite possible that nobody in Germany has yet realized that the separation of the uranium isotopes would make the construction of a super-bomb possible. Hence it is of extreme importance to keep this report secret since any rumour about the connection between uranium separation and a super-bomb may set a German scientist thinking along the same lines.

4. If one works on the assumption that Germany is, or will be, in the possession of this weapon, it must be realized that no shelters are available that would be effective and could be used on a large scale. The most effective reply would be a counter-threat with a similar bomb. Therefore it seems to us important to start production as soon and as rapidly as possible, even if it is not intended to use the bomb as a means of attack. Since the separation of the necessary amount of uranium is, in the most favourable circumstances, a matter of several months, it would obviously be too late to start production when such a bomb is known to be in the hands of Germany, and the matter seems, therefore, very urgent.

5. As a matter of precaution, it is important to have detection squads available in order to deal with the radioactive effects of such a bomb. Their task would be to approach the danger zone with measuring instruments, to determine the extent and probable duration of the danger and to prevent people from entering the danger zone. This is vital since the radiations kill instantly only in very strong doses, whereas weaker doses produce delayed effects, and hence near the edges of the danger zone people would have no warning until too late.

For their own protection, the detection squads would enter the danger zone in motor-cars or aeroplanes which are armoured with lead plates, which absorb most of the dangerous radiation. The cabin would have to be hermetically sealed and oxygen carried in cylinders because of the danger from contaminated air.

The detection staff would have to know exactly the greatest dose of radiation to which a human being can be exposed safely for a short time. This safety limit is not at present known with sufficient accuracy and further biological research for this purpose is urgently required.

As regards the reliability of the conclusions outlined above, it may be said that they are not based on direct experiments, since nobody has ever yet built a super-bomb, but they are mostly based on facts which, by recent research in nuclear physics, have been very safely established. The only uncertainty concerns the critical size for the bomb. We are fairly confident that the critical size is roughly a pound or so, but for this estimate we have to rely on certain theoretical ideas which have not been positively confirmed. If the critical size were appreciably larger than we believe it to be, the technical difficulties in the way of constructing the bomb would be enhanced. The point can be definitely settled as soon as a small amount of uranium has been separated, and we think that in view of the importance of the matter immediate steps should be taken to carry out certain experiments which, while they cannot settle the question with absolute finality, could, if their result were positive, give strong support to our conclusions.

[Signed] O. R. Frisch [and] R. Peierls.
The University, Birmingham.
[Date March 1940]

2

The Red Fox

The Son: Fuchs' Story to 1941

Emil Julius Klaus Fuchs was born in Rüsselsheim, near Frankfurt in Germany, on 29 December 1911. Named after his authoritarian father, Emil, the boy created his own identity by choosing to be known by his third name: Klaus. His mother committed suicide by drinking hydrochloric acid; his grandmother and one of his two sisters also killed themselves. Even so, when on trial at the Old Bailey in London for espionage in 1950 he claimed that his childhood had been 'very happy'.[1] Socially withdrawn, Klaus Fuchs was later described to me by Genia Peierls as 'penny in the slot': he would say nothing unless spoken to and then the floodgates would open. He himself described his mental state, finely tuned through years of duplicity, as 'controlled schizophrenia'.[2]

Slim and boyish looking, even into his forties, Fuchs wore round spectacles, which gave him a quizzical look and the air of a bookworm. His quiet, reserved outward appearance hid a deep inner toughness, however, whose core was a strong belief that one should always do 'what is right, whatever the cost'.[3] This dictum of their martinet father was drilled into the children.[4] In a letter to his surviving sister, Kristel, Klaus remarked perceptively on the 'family weakness where we feel so strongly about our convictions that we take a good deal on ourselves [and] we have to pay for it'. He added it was 'characteristic that we do not complain [about] the price'.[5] Even when the cost of his beliefs included betrayal of the trust of Rudolf and Genia Peierls, Klaus would nevertheless remain for them one of 'the most decent men we knew'. In the judgement of Genia, for whom Klaus Fuchs would become like one of the family, he was fundamentally an 'honest man' destroyed by the intensity of his ideology.[6]

Unlike the Peierls family, who as Jews were a prime target of Hitler's persecution and watched the rise of Nazism with fear, the Fuchses were Aryan liberal socialists, who detested the fascist creed politically and bravely 'did what was right' by opposing it openly. Klaus' father, Emil, was the first parson to join the German Socialist Party and defy Hitler.

He inspired the political consciences of his four children: Elizabeth born in 1908, Gerhard in 1909, followed by Klaus in 1911, and his younger sister, Kristel, born in 1913.

Emil, himself the son of a Lutheran minister, had married their mother Else Wagner in 1906. Else too came from a liberal background, her parents enthused by the national liberalism inspired by the March Revolution of 1848 across Germany.[7] Emil was a deeply religious person of immense courage and integrity, who saw left-wing politics as the only way to lead a Christian life. By the start of the First World War he was known throughout Germany for his ministry with the working classes. These were the very people who would soon be slaughtered in the trenches of the Western Front, an experience that converted Emil into a militant pacifist by the time of the armistice.

In 1925 Emil became active with the Quakers.[8] Klaus was at this stage thirteen years old, and a top student at high school. Lonely and friendless, he was fascinated by mathematics and showed little interest in public affairs, but now Emil aroused Klaus' political awareness.[9] When Klaus was very young the family had moved to Eisenach, midway between Frankfurt and Leipzig and most famous as the birthplace of Johann Sebastian Bach. One day at the high school in Eisenach there was a celebration of the Weimar Constitution, the founding text of the democratic republic that had replaced the imperial monarchy following the German Revolution of 1918. Outside the school, the flags of the Weimar Republic were on public display. Inside, however, 'large numbers of pupils' appeared with the imperial badge'. Here in microcosm was the tension beneath the surface in Germany. Klaus recalled 'all the other pupils knew who my father was', a fact that 'forced' the young Fuchs to become politically mature. Klaus Fuchs now made his first statement of allegiance when in response to this imperial display he 'took out the badge showing the colours of the republic' and put it on, only for other students to rip it off immediately.[10]

Emil's socialist connections interfered with Klaus' education directly in 1928 when Klaus was declared to be the best student in the school. This carried a prize, which was normally awarded in a public ceremony, but that year Klaus received the award in private because officials disapproved of his father's socialism.

Four years younger than Peierls, in 1928 Klaus Fuchs enrolled at the University of Leipzig to study mathematics and science. This was exactly when Peierls too was studying there, but four years is a significant amount of time when you are sixteen years old and Peierls was by this time already making his entrée into research. He had just left Leipzig for Zurich, as we have seen, never to return to his homeland. There is no record that he and

Fuchs ever met in Leipzig, or even that they knew of one another, and it is almost certain that as yet they occupied utterly different spheres.

Fuchs, the undergraduate, now joined the German Socialist Party, the SPD, and took part in the organization of student activities. He also had some discussion with communists but 'despised' them because 'they accepted the official policy of their party even if they did not agree with it'.[11] On the one hand the communists proclaimed support for a united front against fascism, and yet at the same time they would attack the leaders of the SPD. Such political tensions paled, however, beside Fuchs' hatred of the fascists. In Leipzig, Klaus made his first break with his father's pacifism: he joined the Reichsbanner, a paramilitary group that fought street battles against the Nazis.

In May 1931 the family moved to Kiel on the Baltic coast following Emil's appointment there as professor of religion at a teacher-training college. This was a period of great personal tragedy. On 9 October Emil returned home to find his deeply depressed wife, Else, Klaus' mother, lying on the floor, having drunk hydrochloric acid. It seems that she suffered from 'dementia praecox', a form of schizophrenia that begins in early adulthood.[12] Her dying words, apparently, were 'Mother I am coming'[13] – a testament to Else's own mother, who had also committed suicide. Only now did Klaus and his siblings learn that their grandmother as well as their mother had killed themselves. Later, in 1939, his sister Elizabeth would end her life by jumping onto railway tracks, and a decade after that his other sister, Kristel, would enter a mental hospital. Whether or not Klaus Fuchs also shared these tendencies, he would certainly have been scarred by such events, which may explain his actions during his own dark night of the soul in 1950.

That was the year in which he described his childhood as 'very happy'.[14] Closer examination of his account, however, reveals that the stage on which Klaus Fuchs played out this childhood memory seems cold, with moral and political concepts as its only scenery. Love was present by implication, in the support of Emil for his children, but there was no sense of warmth, or joy, or of the naïve fun of a childhood that is 'happy' other than as a cliché. There is no mention of Klaus Fuchs' mother.

POLITICAL AWAKENING

Following his mother's suicide, Klaus made the family home his base by transferring from Leipzig to Kiel University in 1932.[15] This was a time of political awakening for both Klaus and his siblings. In 1931 Elizabeth had joined the cell of the Communist Party (KPD) in Kiel and become involved in passive resistance to the Nazis. Emil's fair hair and politics, both of which were inherited by his children, inspired a German newspaper to dub them the 'red foxes [Fuchs] of Kiel'.[16]

Klaus Fuchs' political epiphany, which led him to join the Communist Party and become a target for the Brownshirts, can be traced to the SPD's support of General Paul von Hindenburg as Reich President. Fuchs believed that the only way to stop the Nazis was through a united working-class movement of socialists and communists against both Hindenburg and Hitler. In his view, to support Hindenburg was to cooperate with bourgeois parties. Like so many in the 1930s, Fuchs now saw communism as the only bulwark against fascism. He openly opposed the SPD policy, and even offered to speak in support of the Communist Party presidential candidate, Ernst Thaelmann, in 1932.

By the latter half of 1932 political polarization in Germany was growing. Supporters of the Nazis instigated violence against opponents on a daily basis. Fuchs, by now chairman of the Socialist Students' Union, became a target for the local Nazi students. Their attacks on him were at first verbal, but soon turned physical when Fuchs stood up to the bullying during a demonstration at the university. The Nazi students, supported by Brownshirts, tried to enforce a strike on the university campus. Fuchs urged the Socialist Students' Union to stand up to them, and as their leader he went to the university 'every day' to show he was not afraid.[17]

This action illustrates Fuchs' strength of character and moral fortitude. Thin, bespectacled, a typical 'boffin' (in a modern idiom a 'nerd'), he had no physical presence with which to confront a bully. A contemporary described him as a 'weed', like someone 'who has never breathed any fresh air'.[18] Fuchs was clearly no pushover, however, as he stood up to the Brownshirts, who were already infamous for killing their opponents. And indeed, they duly tried to kill Fuchs too after he was sentenced to death in a 'lynching trial'.[19] He was thrown into the Forde River. He managed to clamber to safety, but lost three front teeth and wore a dental plate for the rest of his life.[20]

In January 1933 Adolf Hitler became Reich Chancellor, appointed by Hindenburg under the mistaken impression that the Nazis would behave responsibly once given office. Emil and his entire family now became a target for Nazi persecution. For Klaus this was proof that he had been right to oppose the policies of the SPD, which had led to the debacle. On the evening of 27 February the seat of government, the Reichstag, was set on fire. The Nazis declared this to be the result of a communist plot, and Joseph Goebbels immediately initiated waves of arrests of communists and socialists.

The twenty-one-year-old Klaus Fuchs escaped arrest by chance. Unaware of what had taken place the previous night, he left home early the following morning to take a train to Berlin for a meeting of student communists. He bought a newspaper at Kiel station. When he opened it on the journey and read about the arson attack on the seat of German democracy, he 'immediately realised the significance'. Fuchs took this as the signal that 'the underground struggle [against Nazism] had started'.[21] Klaus Fuchs had habitually worn the badge of the hammer and sickle in his lapel; now, to avoid drawing further attention to himself, he immediately removed it. Fuchs could not risk a return to Kiel, where he would face arrest, so he remained in Berlin. And just in time: on 1 March, the day after he left Kiel, the Security Police had searched his house and found communist literature.[22]

The red foxes had run. Gerhard, who was himself active and had learned from a tip-off that Klaus had been condemned to death, fled Kiel for anonymity in the hurly-burly of Berlin. Elizabeth hid with friends in Kiel. Kristel by this time was working away from Kiel, but she too fled to Berlin later that year.

In the spring of 1933 Emil was dismissed by the University of Kiel and almost immediately arrested by the Gestapo. He was interrogated in prison for five weeks before he was released, following a campaign by Quakers throughout Germany. Elizabeth too was arrested, along with her husband, Gustav Kittowski, but she was released at Christmas, once again following Quaker pressure. Gerhard was arrested, together with his pregnant wife, Karin. Their child was born in prison, where they remained incarcerated for two years.[23]

Throughout the spring of 1933 Klaus stayed in the apartment of a female Communist Party member, and on 1 June he enrolled at the Friedrichs Wilhelm University in Berlin for the summer.[24] That month, however, all political parties other than the Nazi Party were made illegal, and the thugs who had tried to kill him earlier were now in control. Fuchs' communist links became known to the university and, following a tip-off that the Gestapo were closing in, Fuchs fled to France in July, with the excuse that he was to attend a Congress in Paris. Barely adult, poor and with few personal belongings, Klaus Fuchs had left his homeland. His departure was organized by the Communist Party, who said that he must finish his studies because 'after the revolution in Germany, people [will] be required with technical knowledge to take part in the building up of the Communist Germany'.[25]

In Paris, Fuchs found cheap lodgings at 70 bis Blvd-Ornano, in Montmartre.[26] The Congress, which had provided the excuse for him to leave

Germany, was run by the Comintern – the organization that promoted world communism. At the Congress, Fuchs met a married woman, six years his senior, named Margarete Keilson. 'Grete', a stenographer and member of the German Communist Party, was also a courier for the Comintern who travelled between Paris and Prague, and later would become a counter-intelligence officer for the Communist Party in East Germany. She was attracted to Klaus whom she found good company – a quality that her husband failed to recognize as, in his recollection, Fuchs had 'little to say' when he came regularly for meals in their flat.[27] He registered with the Quaker Bureau, through which he came to the notice of a well-to-do family, the Gunns, who lived in England. A relative of the Gunns told them that Klaus had fled to Paris, and the Gunns, who knew of his father, Emil, by reputation, agreed to sponsor Klaus as a political refugee.[28] The Gunns were leftist sympathizers, possibly themselves communists, who had been identified through Grete's contacts. Years later, Klaus Fuchs described them as Quakers; MI5 files, however, reveal that the Gunns had a chequered history, Ronald Gunn having visited the Soviet Union in 1932 and again in 1936, while a document in 1941 affirms 'Gunn is mixed up with Communism.'[29] Fuchs' Quaker story seems likely to have been a means to protect both the Gunns and him. In any event, thanks to the lifeline provided by them, Fuchs escaped to England, beyond the reach of the Gestapo and with a long-term goal.[30]

REFUGE IN BRISTOL

On 24 September 1933 Klaus Fuchs crossed the English Channel by ferry, and landed at Folkestone with the intention of studying at Bristol University. He was allowed to enter the United Kingdom on condition that he immediately registered with the police, and he 'proceeded to the residence of Mr Gunn', near Bristol, 'a friend of his father'. The immigration officer's report commented: '[Bristol University] had no facilities for the particular branch of applied mathematics which Fuchs wishes to study, but offered alternatives. Fuchs said that he proposed taking one of these alternatives: Physics.' He was allowed to immigrate as he 'was of good class'.[31]

Somehow Fuchs made his way from Folkestone, on the east coast, 150 miles to Clapton-in-Gordano, near Bristol in the west of England, where he settled as the guest of Ronald and Jessie Gunn. Ronald Gunn was about ten years older than Fuchs, 'very tall' and 'angular' in appearance. An accountant, he was also a director of the Imperial Tobacco Company in Bristol and a cousin of fellow director Henry Hubert Wills, whose largesse

funded the H. H. Wills Physics Laboratory at Bristol University. The
Gunns too were well off, and lived in a large house with a 'staff of
servants'.[32]

Fuchs then enrolled as a student of physics at the University of Bristol.
He had studied at Leipzig and Kiel, of course, but never formally graduated; with this background already in place, in Bristol he registered for
'B.Sc. by research'.[33] He felt no need to hide his political beliefs, and
almost immediately it became apparent that he was well connected to
socialists on the continent.[34] At a meeting of the university's Socialist
Society in February 1934, for example, Fuchs produced a message that
had come from a contact. The name of his informant was not revealed
but on the basis of what he had received Fuchs told the gathering that
Georgi Dimitrov, who had been charged with arson for setting the Reichstag on fire, would be released or executed within days. Fuchs' prediction
was dramatically confirmed when, about three days later, Dimitrov was
indeed released. The meeting was reported in the *News Chronicle* but
seems to have attracted no special attention at the time. Dimitrov, we now
know, was head of the Comintern in Western Europe.

Ronald Gunn became Klaus Fuchs' rock in an alien land. Gunn's liberal
socialist beliefs matched those of the young scientist. Gunn had visited
the Soviet Union in 1932, and would do so again during Fuchs' tenure; he
was founder and first chair of the Bristol branch of the Society for Cultural
Relations between the Peoples of the British Commonwealth and the
Union of the Soviet Socialist Republics.* Its members included 'several of
the [university] physics staff', and one Erna Skinner, wife of the Bristol
physicist Herbert Skinner, of whom more later. The group met regularly,
often at Miss Brownlee's in Charlotte Street or at Gunn's substantial
house.[35] This brought Gunn to the attention of the Security Services when
the Chief Constable of Bristol alerted MI5's head of investigations, Brigadier Harker, 'foreigners regularly call at his house and they are made much
of there'. What's more, the police chief added, the local postman had
noticed unusual items in the mail, including a package from Moscow and
postcards referring to a 'Left Book Club'. Investigations revealed that this
book club – in reality the Cultural Society just mentioned – held meetings
at the Gunns' house, and at one of its gatherings there was a talk on *Mein
Kampf*. This left the security authorities confused as to Gunn's allegiances, which they described as 'leaning towards either Communism or
Nazism'.[36]

---

* Now known as the Society for Co-operation in Russian and Soviet Studies: http://www.
scrss.org.uk/aboutus.htm

All went well for Fuchs in England until 3 August 1934, when he asked for an extension of his passport. The German Embassy in London rejected the request because of Fuchs' well-known political allegiance in Kiel, and said that he would have to apply in person at his home town in Germany.[37]

Two months elapsed before Fuchs took action. On 6 October he sent a registered letter to the Municipal Offices in Kiel asking for a certificate from the Kiel police for issue of a new passport.[38] Ten days later the police chief of Kiel told the German Consulate in Bristol that there were 'political doubts against the issue of a passport to Fuchs'. On 23 October the consulate informed Fuchs that the issue of a new passport had been declined. Their London Embassy was prepared to issue a short-term certificate, however, which would 'only enabl[e] the voyage back to Germany'.

Fuchs knew that the moment he stepped on to German soil he would be arrested. With no passport, and effectively stateless, his future lay in the hands of the British authorities. He received temporary respite when in July 1935 they allowed him to remain in the United Kingdom to complete his degree and to undertake research in Bristol under the guidance of Neville Mott. Mott, who as we have seen was a former colleague of Peierls at Cambridge, suggested that Fuchs apply the new quantum theory to understand the dynamics of metals and electrical conductors.

The university declared him 'fitted to pursue research for Ph.D. or M.Sc.' on 4 June 1935.[39] The timing was fortunate because at the start of July the physics department hosted a major conference on the nature of metals. Fuchs is visible in the conference photo (see Plate 3), partly hidden in the back row. Luminaries at the conference include several destined to play roles in Fuchs' career. Edward Teller, father of the American hydrogen bomb, sits cross-legged at the right (as we view the image) of the front row; seated on a chair at the right is Herbert Skinner, whose wife, Erna, would a decade later have an affair with Klaus Fuchs; four places to the left of Skinner sits the bespectacled Rudolf Peierls.

This would have been the first time that Fuchs came across Peierls, though as Fuchs was a novice it is unlikely that they had close contact. It was in the following year, 1936, that Fuchs wrote the physics paper which established him as an outstanding new talent and brought him to Peierls' attention. A group at Bristol University had measured how easily an electric current can pass through conductors only a few atoms wide. The results disagreed utterly with the standard theory, which had been formulated by the discoverer of the electron itself, J. J. Thomson, three decades earlier. Fuchs investigated the reasons for the large discrepancy and found the culprit: in deriving his celebrated formula, Thomson had made a conceptual error.

We can visualize the phenomenon and get a sense of the error if we compare the current of electrons through a wire to the flow of water in a river or stream. Not all pieces of flotsam travel at the same speed: some go slightly faster or slower than the average. When the stream is very narrow, surface debris frequently hits the banks. Individual pieces of slow flotsam return to the main stream in a different pattern to faster elements. Fuchs realized that Thomson had taken the average of the range of speeds in a way that, while correct for a wide river, did not adequately allow for the different responses of fast or slow flotsam in a thin stream, where collisions with the banks play a more important role. Fuchs had found the flaw; now he had to correct it.

It was at this juncture that Rudolf Peierls visited Bristol at the invitation of Neville Mott for the seminar alluded to in chapter 1. While there, he learned of the anomalous experiment on electrical conduction in thin films, of Mott and Fuchs' interest in it, and of Fuchs' insight as to why Thomson's theory was inadequate. Peierls listened to Fuchs' explanation of Thomson's error, understood the idea, and suggested how Fuchs might derive a mathematical formula to encapsulate it.

In the middle of the 1930s Mott and Peierls were among the founding fathers of quantum mechanics, in at the start with the first generation of theorists who had explored its mysterious promise. So fast had progress been that Fuchs, less than five years younger, was already of the next generation. He and his contemporaries were presented with the viable quantum theory, and applied it to an ever-increasing range of phenomena. It was Mott who had introduced the tools of the trade to Fuchs, pointed him to potential applications, and guided him through his first exploration. By 1936 Mott and Peierls were already maestros; Fuchs was an outstanding pupil.

Peierls analysed the puzzle after their discussion and informed Mott on 20 November that he had found a theoretical description of the conductivity problem.[40] He was impressed two weeks later when he heard back from Mott that Fuchs 'can get your answer by a more elementary method'.[41] Mott suggested that Fuchs, Mott and Peierls 'in alphabetical order' should write a paper, but Peierls judged that Fuchs' method was neater than his own, and that Fuchs should take the full credit: 'I see no reason why my name should be added to Fuchs' paper: all I did was to obtain the same result by a more complicated method.'[42]

Fuchs duly wrote a paper, published in January 1938 under his name as sole author, in which he fulsomely acknowledged Peierls.[43] Fuchs' formula both explained the Bristol data and also showed how the 'bounce' of electrons from the surface (the 'banks' of the stream) varies if the surface is smooth or lumpy. Today this breakthrough is still used in microelectronics. First you measure the electrical resistance of a thin film when different amounts of current flow. Then, using Fuchs' mathematical analysis, the results are translated to deduce the roughness – at the atomic scale – of the surface of a thin film. His paper has been acknowledged as seminal in over one thousand subsequent scientific papers; in other words, it has been referenced, on average, every month for more than eighty years. It is now cited more often than the basic work of Otto Hahn and Fritz Strassmann on nuclear fission.[44]

Fuchs did more than physics in Bristol, however. He also kept up his political interests by making contact with Jürgen Kuczynski, the leader of the German Communist Party (KPD) in Britain. Kuczynski, based in London, was active in the Society for Cultural Relations between the Peoples of the British Commonwealth and the Union of the Soviet Socialist Republics, and it was probably during his visit to the Bristol caucus in 1937 or 1938, hosted by Ronald Gunn, that he met Klaus Fuchs for the first time.

Fuchs' Bristol University colleague Herbert Skinner remembered him at this time as 'an uncouth and callow youth', who 'never made friends with anyone in the laboratory and quite obviously lived in left-wing circles'.[45] It is not clear, however, to what extent Skinner's description has been coloured by his wife's membership of those very circles, and her subsequent relationship with Fuchs. If reliable, this picture of him as withdrawn and closeted hints at the beginning of a change in Klaus Fuchs' persona. His success as a political activist in Kiel suggests he had been a charismatic speaker, able to excite his fellow students. The English Klaus Fuchs was different. With as yet limited command of English, he protected himself carefully by keeping quiet. Only when in company with those with whom he felt confident would he open up. So was born the Klaus Fuchs whom Genia Peierls would later refer to as 'penny in the slot'.

In 1936 the Spanish Civil War broke out, and it soon became an issue for intellectuals. At Bristol University this was true no less than on campuses throughout Europe and the United States. Fascist Italy and Nazi Germany supported General Franco's Nationalists, whereas the Communist Party aided the Spanish Republicans. Many saw the war as the frontier in a fight for the survival of culture in the face of fascist tyranny. In this climate the Soviet Union became the champion of decency; Stalin's genocidal purges and mass deportations to the Gulag were yet to be widely known. In the fight against fascism many intellectuals chose to follow the red banner of the Communist Party, as camp followers if not full members. Klaus Fuchs, while deeply sympathetic to the cause, as manifested in his membership of the Society for Cultural Relations between the Peoples of the British Commonwealth and the Union of the Soviet Socialist Republics, kept his communist beliefs largely to himself, however. His ties with Nazi Germany were certainly cut, as he ignored a letter from the German Consulate in Bristol reminding him that – as a German national – he was required to register for military service.[46]

That same year Kristel managed to leave Germany to enter Swarthmore College, Pennsylvania, in the United States. She travelled via England and was reunited with Klaus. Any joy at this meeting, the first time that brother and sister had been together in three years, was soured by her news that the Gestapo had got wind that Emil, together with Gerhard, Elizabeth and their spouses, were smuggling Jews and socialists out of Germany. Klaus learned that Gerhard and his wife had spent two years in prison, but were now released. Kristel told Klaus that Elizabeth and Gustav had also been arrested. Elizabeth, who had subsequently been released, was now living with their father, Emil, in Kiel, but Gustav was in a concentration camp.

At this juncture, Fuchs' life-story looked similar to those of many others in his situation: a chronic fear for family trapped in Hitler's dictatorship while maintaining anonymity for oneself in the shadowy world of German refugees and communist sympathizers in Britain. Lost in the canvas of a looming war, his tale would never have merited special attention. The course of Klaus Fuchs' life, however, would be determined by his meeting with Rudolf Peierls. Their lives would become entwined, like father and son in a Greek tragedy.

1939–41: INTERNMENT AND RELEASE

In 1937 Klaus Fuchs obtained his doctorate from Bristol University.[47] The Home Office allowed him to stay in the United Kingdom for one more year in order to move to Edinburgh University to do research with Max Born, another of the great founders of quantum theory and, subsequently, a Nobel laureate. Born and Fuchs wrote some physics papers together, but nothing as significant as Fuchs' earlier opus on conductivity.*

---

* When Fuchs joined Peierls in 1941 he submitted a CV listing his scientific publications (Peierls papers, Bodleian Library, File C111). His first seven papers, written between 1935 and 1938, applied quantum mechanics to the theory of solids and electrical conduction. During 1940 and 1941 he wrote a series of papers on a quantum mechanical idea of Max Born's – 'reciprocity' – which made no impact. He wrote only two papers on nuclear physics, one on beta radioactivity and one discussing the application of statistical physics to nuclear stability. Neither of these papers was central to the mainstream questions of nuclear physics, and fission seems to have made no impact on Fuchs at this time.

Nonetheless, his talent was recognized sufficiently for the Home Office to grant Fuchs permanent residency in Britain in 1938.[48]

He was funded by a Carnegie Fellowship at Edinburgh, and received a D.Sc. from the university in 1939.[49] On 17 July of that year he applied for British citizenship, but the outbreak of war intervened and in September he was listed as an alien.[50] Fuchs appeared before the Aliens Tribunal in Edinburgh on 2 November. He was given exactly one week to obtain and bring letters of support.

Max Born provided one, which testified that Fuchs was 'devoted to liberal and social ideas' and that he had been a member of the Social Democratic Party in Germany between 1930 and 1932; there was no mention of Fuchs' association with the Communist Party.* Nonetheless, Born was certainly aware of and sympathetic to Fuchs' pro-Soviet views, which seem to have been discussed openly in their circle. At the end of 1941, for example, a few months after Fuchs had left Edinburgh to work with Peierls, Born wrote that the news from Russia seemed quite hopeful, and: 'You must be gratified that your belief in the Russians is so much justified now.'[51]

In his letter to the Aliens Tribunal, Born merely testified that Fuchs had 'avoided the persecutions of the Hitler government by coming to this country', where he had joined Born's department and become 'my best an most efficient collaborator'. Born established Fuchs' stature at this

---

* After Fuchs' conviction for espionage in 1950, MI5 was widely criticized for having over-looked evidence of his communist affiliation, which had supposedly been presented at the Aliens Tribunal. MI5 pursued this and confirmed there was 'no documentary evidence' to support such a claim (minutes of meeting at the Foreign Office, 3 May 1951, TNA KV 2/1257, s. 836b). One R. J. Mann contacted Edinburgh City Police to examine the original files of the Aliens Tribunal of 2 November 1939. This confirmed that Born's statement that from 1930 to 1932 Fuchs had been a member of the Social Democrat Party in Germany was 'the only reference to politics on the files'. Shorthand notes of the hearing had long since been destroyed, but Mann spoke to the detective officer who was Clerk to the Proceedings and he assured Mann that 'so far as he can remember there was no mention of the Communist Party when Fuchs was before the Tribunal' (TNA KV 2/1257, s. 837a, R. J. Mann to J. Robertson, 7 May 1951).

On 5 June 1951 the MI5 Director General Sir Percy Sillitoe sent a note to the Prime Minister (KV 2/1257, s. 849a), which summarized the evidence from Edinburgh, and added the cogent remark: 'it hardly seems believable that Fuchs would gratuitously have drawn attention to his communist past at a time when the position of Russia in the war was by no means clear – in November 1939 she had recently signed a non-aggression pact with Germany.'

The myth that Fuchs announced his communism at the Aliens Tribunal in 1939 appears to have been a creation of the writer Rebecca West in 1950 with no basis in fact. Contrary to a widely held misconception, there is no evidence that Fuchs ever admitted to membership or support of the Communist Party, at least in any publicly available document.

juncture by rating him to be 'the best theoretical physicist of the younger generation in Scotland'. In Born's estimation Fuchs was 'a man of excellent character, deeply devoted not only to his science but to all human ideals and humanitarian activities', who was 'passionately opposed to the present German Government'. He concluded: Fuchs 'hopes for the victory of the Allies'.[52]

The application succeeded. Fuchs was 'exempted until further notice from internment and from the special restrictions applicable to enemy aliens', as he was a 'Refugee from Nazi oppression'.[53]

Oppression indeed. As we have seen, in 1936 Klaus learned that the Gestapo had arrested his siblings and their spouses. Following their release, Gerhard and Karin fled to Prague. Elizabeth's husband, Gustav, who was in a prison in Germany, somehow managed to escape, and he too made his way to Prague. Elizabeth, meanwhile, lived with their son, Klaus Kittowski, and her father in Germany.

The tragedy escalated rapidly once the Nazis annexed Czechoslovakia in March 1939. Gerhard, who had contracted tuberculosis, had entered a sanatorium in Switzerland, but Karin was thrown into a concentration camp and her fate is lost in the vastness of the Holocaust.[54] Gustav, after his escape, was a marked man. For Elizabeth, the worry about her husband's fate was too much and she killed herself on 7 August 1939.[55]

The details of this history vary in the telling, however. In one version Elizabeth had learned that the German concentration camp where Gustav languished was near the Elbe River. The communist underground hatched a plan for his escape, and Elizabeth swam the Elbe to alert him. The pair successfully fled to Prague. It was in Prague that she 'ended her life by jumping off a bridge into the path of a moving train'.[56]

Gustav actually survived the war, so it is not clear in this story why Elizabeth should feel so desperate for him while she herself was also living in Prague. The derring-do of swimming across the Elbe might appeal to an action adventure, but an alternative version seems to me more plausible.

As in the previous tale, Gustav had been sentenced to six years in a prison in the Berlin suburb of Brandenburg, but escaped. In this account, however, he 'made an arrangement to meet Elizabeth in secret, but did not keep the rendezvous'. Elizabeth then received a postcard from Gustav, which had been sent from Prague. In August 1939, five months after the Nazis took control of Czechoslovakia, Emil went to a Quaker conference in Bad Pyrmont, and Elizabeth went with him. The train journey took several hours. Elizabeth had not heard from Gustav again, and feared that he was now dead. Emil sensed her depression, and decided to take her to see a doctor when they returned to Berlin, but during the journey back, while he was briefly away from their compartment, 'she threw herself out' of the train. Other passengers 'pulled the emergency cord, but she was found dead beside the track'.[57]

In any event, whether Elizabeth's life ended on the railway tracks in Prague or in Berlin, the sad conclusion is that her death made three generations of suicides in the maternal line of Klaus' family. Emil was left to look after his grandson, 'little Klaus', Klaus Fuchs' nephew.

Klaus Fuchs, now granted permanent residency in the United Kingdom, was at last relatively settled, but he still dreamed of Hitler's overthrow and of some future return to his homeland. The dream seemed unlikely to come true, however, as Germany continued its invasion of European countries from the autumn of 1939. Then in 1940, as fear of a German invasion and a fifth column overtook the United Kingdom, Fuchs found himself classed as an 'enemy alien'. As a result, he was interned, briefly on the Isle of Man, and then in July transferred to an internment camp in Canada.

Fuchs and over two thousand internees were sent to Canada in two ships. The first of these to depart – the *Arandora Star* with 1,500 people on board – was torpedoed and sunk on 2 July 1940. Among the 700 who drowned were active anti-fascists, well-known opponents of Hitler who had fled Europe, and many others – not least Italians based in Scotland – who had lived in the United Kingdom for years but by accident of birth had been caught in the net. A report claimed 'there was hardly an Italian family in Scotland unaffected by this tragedy'.[58] The tragic waste of lives of people who were Hitler's enemies highlighted the cruel and inefficient nature of the internment policy.

Fuchs departed on 3 July in the other vessel, the SS *Ettrick*, in appalling, overcrowded conditions. A fellow passenger, Max Perutz, a biologist and future Nobel laureate, recalled 1,200 men herded in airless holds, who were suspended in hammocks 'like bats from the mess deck's ceilings'. News of the *Arandora Star*'s fate arrived on the second day of the voyage, and 'after that we were issued lifebelts'. In heavy seas the prisoners' 'eruptions turned the floors into quagmires emitting a sickening stench'.[59] After two weeks of this hell, they reached the port of Quebec.[60]

The lost *Arandora Star* contained all the records for both ships, however, and when the *Ettrick* arrived, there was no information about the internees. The narrative gaining traction within MI5 was that almost the sole knowledge the Canadians had of Fuchs was that he was not Jewish, so they placed him in a camp intended for 'active Nazis only'.[61] MI5's mistaken belief that the internees were predominantly Nazis would frame its judgement of Fuchs throughout the subsequent decade.* Given this false premise, MI5 deduced that Fuchs would have enormously resented this treatment, and so he was pleased to meet a kindred spirit in the person of Hans Kahle, who had also been sent to the camp 'by mistake'.[62] Far from Kahle and Fuchs being two misfits drawn together by this chance, as MI5's narrative would insist, in reality Kahle recognized an opportunity in Fuchs, the communist dreamer, at a time when Fuchs must have been very disillusioned about the British. Kahle was a 'well-known [German] communist' who after the war became a senior member of the Soviet Security Police. Fuchs' baptism into the communist ideal, which his hatred of the Nazis had inspired, was now confirmed and his subsequent career in espionage conceived.

Internee's No: 417.

NAME: FUCHS

Given Names: KLAUS EMIL JULIUS. Hut 16

DESCRIPTION

Age: 28 Years

Height: 5 Ft. 10 inches

Complexion: dark

Colour of eyes: brown dark

Colour of hair: brown dark

Weight (approximate): 9 stone

Clean shaven or not: clean shaven

Chin: pointed Nose: straight

General build: tall

Scars: etc.: none

Remarks: wears glasses

3 false teeth in front.

Fuchs' internment card, 1940

* See the Epilogue for the denouement of this factoid.

Years later, after Fuchs had been jailed for espionage, MI5 attempted to control its reputation. In 1951, when the author Alan Moorehead requested information for a book, MI5 initially dismissed Fuchs' friendship with Kahle as 'of relatively little significance and a natural result of the presence of two anti-Nazis in a crowd of active sympathisers'.[63] In 'supplementary' notes given to Moorehead this cosy description was qualified, however. 'Hans Kahle is not thought to have been a spy. He may have been a talent spotter [who] reported on Fuchs' suitability to the Russian Intelligence Services.'[64] It is then ironic that part of the breakthrough that would eventually expose Fuchs came from another, innocent, liaison. In the camp, Fuchs was supplied scientific journals by Israel Halperin, a Canadian communist mathematician. As part of this exercise, he added Fuchs' name to his address book. Six years later, when Halperin was arrested and accused of espionage in Canada, this innocent address-book entry would have repercussions.

In the meantime, scientists in Britain were actively trying to get Fuchs released. Max Born wrote: 'Fuchs was the soul of my research group; he is responsible for about half of the dissertations partly finished, partly in progress, which he suggested and supervised. He is in the small top group of theoretical physicists in this country.'[65] The Royal Society included Fuchs in a list of mathematicians and physicists that they wanted freed urgently. On 17 October 1940 the Home Office communicated Fuchs' case to the High Commissioner for Canada as 'a man to be repatriated to this country if he were willing to come'.[66]

After five months in the camp, Fuchs was released on 17 December 1940, twelve days before his twenty-ninth birthday. Upon arrival at Liverpool on 11 January 1941 he was given a travel warrant and went directly to a post as a research physicist at Edinburgh University. He also contacted his communist friends in London, whom he made arrangements to visit. Among those friends were Hans Kahle and Jürgen Kuczynski.[67]

In those days trips from Edinburgh to London were a major venture as the train took up to ten hours and the round trip would occupy two or three days. As an alien, Fuchs needed permission from the police to travel, and his alien record reveals that he made but a single extended visit to London. This unique occasion was from 3 to 15 April 1941, which was approved subject to him being 'indoors there between 10.30 pm and 6 am'.[68] At some point during those twelve days Kuczynski hosted a party at his London home in Lawn Road, south of Hampstead Heath, to celebrate Fuchs' return to the United Kingdom. As this was Fuchs' only recorded trip to London, it is likely that it was during this visit that

Fuchs met Colonel Simon Kremer, intelligence officer at the Soviet Embassy.*

Fuchs claimed later he told Kuczynski that he wanted only to make the Russians aware there was atomic research going on in the United Kingdom, and he had no plans to become involved in espionage.[69] This is plausible: in April, Fuchs had yet to join Rudolf Peierls, and was only aware of atomic research in broad terms.† At that stage he had no reason to anticipate that he would have access to useful information.

Kuczynski introduced Fuchs to the Russian (Kremer), a courteous, intelligent man, with perfect English, who could masquerade as an Englishman in the presence of an alien such as Fuchs. Kuczynski completed the deception by telling Fuchs that his friend's name was 'Johnson'.[70] Johnson expressed interest in science and the pair talked about the potential use of atomic energy. Fuchs was about to return to Edinburgh, and promised to 'prepare for Johnson a short account about the possibilities of atomic energy'.[71]

We can probably conclude that at this stage Fuchs believed Johnson to be English, or at least not Russian. The Soviet Union had signed a non-aggression pact with Hitler in August 1939, and as such was no ally of the United Kingdom. Fuchs would have been on dangerous ground as any aid to the enemy in wartime could be classed as treason, for which the penalty was death.

That said, in April 1941 Fuchs would have nothing to tell the Russians that they did not already know or could discover for themselves in the open literature. The initial scientific breakthrough from which atomic weapons and reactor technology would subsequently emerge had been the discovery of the fission of uranium by Otto Hahn, Lisa Meitner and Fritz

---

* Chapman Pincher, *Treachery: Betrayals, Blunders and Cover-Ups: Six Decades of Espionage against America and Great Britain* (Random House, 2009), chapter 15. Pincher gives no source for the claim that Fuchs was introduced to Kremer at the party in April 1941. In 1950 Fuchs confirmed that his first Russian courier was Kremer, 'to whom he had originally been introduced in the house on the south side of Hyde Park' (Fuchs to MI5, 8 February 1950, TNA KV 6/134, s. 147a). Fuchs also admitted having visited Kremer on one subsequent occasion at the Russian Embassy (TNA KV 2/1252, s. 519). It is possible here that Fuchs' memory has conflated and confused two locations. Lawn Road in the gentrified gardens of Hampstead is south of vast parkland – Hampstead Heath; a visit to the Russian Embassy, meanwhile, would have taken him to the west end of Hyde Park and the grandeur of Kensington. If we assume that after nine years Fuchs' memory has jumbled these two, mixing the greenery of Hampstead Heath with Hyde Park, a coherent account of various events emerges, which is consistent with Pincher's unsourced claim. In any event, it is clear that Fuchs met Kremer during April 1941, as this was the only occasion he had permission for extended travel to London.

† The extent of this foreknowledge is discussed in the following pages.

Strassmann in Germany. That had been in 1938 and was well known. That fission of a uranium nucleus liberates both energy and neutrons, enabling these neutrons to cause further fissions and potentially a chain reaction, had been demonstrated in several experiments during 1939, and this too was widely known throughout the physics community. Fuchs would have reminded Johnson/Kremer of all this and perhaps told him of Niels Bohr's insight that fission occurs in the rare isotope, U235.

As we saw earlier, Bohr published his findings in the same week that the Second World War started. It is ironic that the means that would help bring the conflict to a close made its debut in the same week the war in Europe began. Fuchs could not have foreseen this, of course, still less that he would be instrumental in the history of the atomic bomb. In April 1941 he was unaware of Peierls and Frisch's breakthrough and at the most could have alerted Kremer to uranium fission's potential to be an energy machine – a nuclear reactor – but not as a weapon.*

Fuchs enjoyed drinking, although he was able to hold alcohol and remain sober. Whether or not that was the case at Kuczynski's party, his visit seems to have been a great success because Fuchs stayed too long: due to return to Scotland on the evening of 15 April, he missed the train from King's Cross to Edinburgh. He reported to the King's Cross Road police station at 11.45 p.m. The police told him to get the train at 04.30 the next morning.[72]

It was shortly after that party that Fuchs received the letter from Peierls which invited him to join in work whose purpose Peierls 'cannot now disclose'.[73] The result was that before the end of May 1941 Fuchs had moved to Birmingham, to begin working out with Peierls the feasibility of an atomic bomb.

---

* In the autumn of 1940 in the Soviet Union, Yulii Khariton and Yakhov Zeldovitch independently discovered the same phenomenon as Peierls and Frisch. The USSR also kept this secret. So by the autumn of 1940 the USSR already knew everything about U235 through its own efforts. Fuchs would have had nothing new to tell them about this anyway. In any event, he did not know any of this when he met Kremer in April 1941. It is probable that Fuchs was already aware of Peierls' interest in him – see chapter 4 – though perhaps not the reason why. If so, he might have passed this news on to Kremer, which would explain the reason for Kremer's continued interest in Fuchs. Fuchs later claimed that at the time of his meeting with Kremer he regarded the atomic energy project as 'at best, a long term possibility for the production of power' (Fuchs to Perrin, 30 January 1950, TNA KV 2/1253, s.558).

3

Defending the Realm

The Ghosts: Defenders of the Realm, 1909–41

'C', the code name for the chief of the British Secret Intelligence Service, or MI6, originates with Mansfield Cumming, its first head. On 4 October 1909 Cumming, then a fifty-year-old naval commander, met army Captain Vernon Kell, fourteen years his junior, at the office of a private detective near London's Victoria Station. Over drinks, they discussed the state of the nation.

The Prime Minister, Herbert Asquith, had charged the Committee of Imperial Defence to consider the question of foreign espionage in the United Kingdom. Its report stated that the British government was worried that 'an extensive system of German espionage exists in this country' and there was 'no organisation for keeping in touch with that espionage' for determining its objectives.[1] This was the agenda for Cumming and Kell as they discussed how 'to deal both with espionage in this country and with our foreign agents abroad'.[2] Their concern was timely: five years later the First World War began.

The conversation led directly to the creation of the British Secret Service, initially a modest organization whose sole officers, Cumming and Kell, worked on a shoestring budget from a single office across the road from the Army and Navy Store at 64 Victoria Street, London SW1. The reality was thus utterly unlike the myths propagated by some spy novels set in the Edwardian era, which have advertised a modern version of the Elizabethan secret service, made infamous by Sir Francis Walsingham.

Cumming focused on matters abroad, which subsequently became the realm of the Secret Intelligence Service, MI6, while Kell took on internal security, the remit today of the Security Service, MI5. Even at the start of the First World War, Kell, by now 'Director' of counter-espionage, had only nine officers and detectives, together with 'six clerical staff and a caretaker'.[3]

Kell's good fortune was that in 1910 Winston Churchill became Home Secretary. During the Boer War, Churchill had gone behind enemy lines and had espionage in his blood. He supported Kell in gaining the assistance of chief constables around the country in his counter-espionage strategy. By the start of the war in 1914 this network of senior policemen had provided Kell with a register of aliens and potential German agents, and there had been 'a wholesale round-up of [German] secret service agents in England'.[4]

By 1934, sixteen years after the defeat of Germany, the rise of Adolf Hitler encouraged the growth of fascism within the United Kingdom too. Sir Vernon Kell, as he had become, now reactivated his network of chief constables to draw together information on membership of the British Union of Fascists, or 'black shirts'. Kell and his senior police were watching just as keenly for activities by communists, although membership of the Communist Party was never illegal in the United Kingdom. So on 5 November 1934, when C. G. Maby, OBE, the Chief Constable of Bristol, received a damning letter from the German consul in the town, he contacted Kell at once.

Klaus Fuchs' covert political agenda might have remained hidden but for the expiry of his passport in August 1934, which (as we have seen) brought him to the attention of the German authorities. When they realized that Fuchs could not be bullied into returning to Germany, at the start of November the German Consul in Bristol alerted the police: 'Klaus Fuchs is a notorious communist.' Maby informed Sir Vernon Kell of this but added: 'During his stay in this City, Fuchs is not known to have engaged in any Communist activities.'[5] The British gave Fuchs the benefit of the doubt, and leave to remain.

Thus began one of the most infamous files in MI5's history. Over the next seventeen years it would grow to more than two dozen volumes containing thousands of documents.

KLAUS FUCHS AND GUY LIDDELL

That the British Security Service didn't immediately identify Fuchs as a danger was partly the result of an experience that a member of MI5 had had just one year earlier. This was Captain Guy Liddell, at the time a junior officer but destined to rise later to become Deputy Director General of the organization.

Guy Liddell was a second cousin of Alice Liddell, the inspiration for *Alice in Wonderland*. A pudgy man with a high forehead, a round face, and a square moustache on his upper lip, he had the appearance of a bank manager. He was a first-rate cellist and had a calm and kindly manner that endeared him to his staff. His family life was a disaster, however, for he was unhappily married to the Hon. Calypso Baring, the daughter of an Irish peer. According to colleagues, Liddell endured life with her 'through a haze of cigarette smoke' and 'would surely have strangled Calypso' had he been a 'less patient man'.[6] In 1943 she would desert him for her American half-brother, taking their four children to California. From then on Liddell would effectively be married to the defence of the realm.

The saga of Klaus Fuchs would be a recurring professional nightmare in Liddell's life of private pain. Liddell's obsession with communists and, inadvertently, his perceptions of Klaus Fuchs, began quite innocently in 1933. The Nazi government, which had persuaded itself that Germany was under siege by a conspiracy of communists, Jews and leftist pacifists, had called upon MI5 to cooperate. At the end of March, Liddell began a ten-day visit to Berlin. He was hosted by Hitler's foreign-press bureau chief, the charismatic Ernst Hanfstaengel, met the head of the Prussian Secret Police, Rudolf Diels, and upon return to London, wrote a report that the *Authorized History of MI5* describes as 'the lowest point in a distinguished career'.[7] In it he wrongly assessed Nazi brutality to be a passing phase and the Comintern to be a greater threat. Years later, when the Cold War was at its height, and following further misjudgements by Liddell, some conspiracy theorists would claim that he himself was a communist mole at the heart of British security. This was completely untrue.

In one respect that fateful visit to Berlin in 1933, when Diehls informed him of their intention to 'exterminate communism', had a lasting impact on Liddell's thinking. Many thousands had already been arrested, and disposing of them was becoming a serious problem. 'Perhaps,' the police chief said, 'the British Government could set aside an island somewhere which could be jointly used as a penal settlement.' At first Liddell thought he was joking, but he later discovered that the suggestion had been made 'in all seriousness'.

Liddell reported back to London: 'The Germans have dealt the third international a serious blow by liquidating its European centre. In addition the German communist party has been completely broken up. Some of the arrested leaders ... will be interned indefinitely.' Although Liddell seems to have been impressed with the result, he was horrified by the methods. 'A good deal of "third degree" work is going on,' he wrote, adding: 'Communists and even Social Democrats have been submitted to every kind of outrage' – a statement with which Klaus Fuchs would certainly have agreed.

For Liddell and MI5, realpolitik seems at that point to have won over morality. Liddell noted that the German police, who believed they had 'saved Europe from the menace of communism', were 'proud of what they have done and are anxious to convince the world that their action was fully justified'. Liddell recommended that personal contact be maintained with specific officers, who seemed more sensible, for a day 'when the present rather hysterical atmosphere of sentiment and brutality dies down'.

Liddell had seen enough to form his own opinions of the amateur methods of the German secret police, which had raided houses, 'thrown documents in lorries, and then dumped them in disorder in some large room'.[8] Nothing had been packed or labelled. There was no means to connect any claim with a reliable source, nor was any of their 'evidence' worth more than passing attention.

The Nazi agenda during Liddell's visit was to get MI5 on board for an anti-communist purge. Unwittingly, however, they created an impression that any information about 'communists' that originated with the Gestapo was almost certainly worthless.* Indeed, Liddell was so unimpressed by their record-keeping and corruption of evidence that later, when there was a message from the German Embassy in London with genuine information about a communist – Fuchs – his chief, Sir Vernon Kell, ignored it.

On 8 November 1934 Kell responded to the chief constable's alert about Fuchs, noting simply that the Aliens Branch had been informed and that the Home Office file revealed nothing untoward about him. In sum: MI5 was sceptical about the information, which had originated with the Gestapo, and on 21 November the Fuchs file was closed.[9]

MI5's interest in Fuchs reawakened temporarily in January 1938 when he required a new travel certificate. The Home Office phoned MI5, who replied that they had no evidence that Fuchs was a communist except for the Gestapo's assertion, which they continued to discount.[10] These were the first in a litany of oversights.

VERNON KELL'S LEGACY

MI5's failures with Fuchs, and other errors in that era, have been variously cited as bad luck, incompetence, or evidence of a well-placed Soviet mole in the organization. While one or all of these may have played a role, it is certainly true that between the two world wars MI5 was significantly

* The Gestapo was formally established by combining various security police agencies on 26 April, a fortnight after Liddell's departure.

under-resourced. By the time of the armistice in 1918, Vernon Kell's
bureau had a total staff of over 800 individuals, of whom eighty-four
(almost all men) were officers. By 1919, however, the role of the Intelligence Services in peacetime was being questioned. Kell, who suffered from
asthma, was on sick leave and, outmanoeuvred in Whitehall, lost control
of UK Intelligence. Soon he was fighting for MI5's very survival. By 1920
his staff had been cut by 80 per cent.[11]

Meanwhile, communist revolutions on the continent and the Russian
Civil War (1918–21) led to concern in the United Kingdom about Soviet
subversion. Soviet espionage, however, was not yet perceived as a threat. In
1920 the Secretary of State for War and Air was Winston Churchill, not
only a great advocate of espionage but also deeply concerned about communist disruption. The threat of Bolshevik insurrection in the army and
navy trumped any opposition, and MI5's future was agreed.[12] Even so, in
1923 Rear-Admiral Hugh Sinclair, chief of the Secret Intelligence Service
(MI6), doubted the need for MI5 to exist 'as a separate entity'. In his opinion MI5 needed no more than five people and all its duties could be subsumed within MI6.[13] MI5 survived, though with a minuscule staff. In 1929,
MI5's officer contingent consisted of Kell and just a dozen others.[14]

During his thirty years as head of the bureau, Vernon Kell gradually
built up MI5's strength. Even so, by 1937, when he rightly judged war
with Germany to be unavoidable, MI5 still only had twenty-six officers.
By July 1939, just weeks before the start of the Second World War, it still
had just thirty-six officers.[15] Kell retired just before Fuchs' run of espionage began, so he was not directly involved in the saga, but people who
were senior in the organization after the war, when the Fuchs affair would
reach its climax, were hired on Kell's watch.

Among the recruits during Kell's tenure, Guy Liddell and three others
would play leading parts in the Fuchs affair: two future Director Generals,
Roger Hollis and Dick White, and a remarkable woman, Jane Sissmore.*
Sissmore married an MI5 officer, Wing-Commander John Archer, 'in the
lunch hour the day before war was declared'.[16]

Kell had recruited Sissmore in 1916, when she was eighteen, as MI5's
first female intelligence officer. Her face in profile had the elegance of
Marianne, the figurehead of France. Proud and determined like the symbolic Marianne, Jane Sissmore brimmed with fun, so much so that 'one
never knew what she would do next'. Guy Liddell, who was her divisional
chief, described her as the 'court jester', and on one occasion a colleague

---

* MI5 files refer to her variously by her maiden or married name; for consistency I shall
refer to her as Sissmore or Sissmore/Archer throughout.

recalls her 'dropping to her knees and shuffling into [Liddell's office] with hands pressed together in prayer' that Liddell would grant whatever request she put to him.[17] But Sissmore's frivolity concealed a deep and penetrating mind. She was exceptionally clever and trained as a barrister in her spare time. This honed her skills as an interrogator and as a judge of evidence. By 1929 she was responsible for Soviet counter-espionage in MI5.

MI5's limited revitalization began in 1931. Intelligence in the United Kingdom was now rationalized into two separate organizations with clear boundaries of responsibility: MI6 (SIS), which was to 'confine itself to operations at least three miles from British territory', and MI5, responsible for 'the Empire'.[18] As part of this reorganization, MI5 acquired the section of Scotland Yard's Special Branch that dealt with communist subversion. This brought MI5 an influx of able officers, notably the avuncular Liddell, who became deputy head of B Branch – Counter-Subversion and Counter-Espionage. His boss in B Branch was the irascible Oswald 'Jasper' Harker, who had spent fourteen years in the Indian Police. The person whose quality Liddell most quickly recognized and relied on was Jane Sissmore. She was involved in the hiring and then the training of the two recruits who would later become Director Generals of MI5 and would be central players in the Fuchs affair.

The first of the pair, Dick White, joined MI5 in 1936. In contrast to most officers in MI5 at that time, White had neither gone to one of the top public schools nor had a military background. He had, however, studied history at Christ Church, Oxford, and won a blue for athletics. In those days MI5 hired from the old-boy network, or by recommendations from within or from trusted outsiders. White had taken up teaching, and through this became known to another Security Services officer, Malcolm Cumming, who was the more traditional establishment type – Eton and Sandhurst. Cumming was impressed by White's ability and judgement, and so tipped off Harker, who in turn informed Kell. In January 1936 White began work at MI5. First, however, he spent time in Berlin and Munich, where he quickly became fluent in German and an expert in the realities of Hitler's regime.

Although at first sight White appeared shy and diffident, he had a friendly, outgoing personality that worked nicely in Whitehall. He got on well with the mandarins in the Foreign Office; for the inhibited Kell, by contrast, relations in Whitehall were difficult. White impressed Kell, and in 1937 he convinced him that Germany was dangerous and set on war. Kell was able to expand his small organization a little further. Most notable among the new intake was Roger Hollis, who seventeen years later would succeed White as Director General of MI5.

As in White's case, Hollis came to MI5's attention via a trusted outsider, a Major Meldrum, one of Hollis' relations. Meldrum also knew Jane Sissmore through their mutual membership of Ealing Tennis Club.[19] Hollis had the right family background – both his father and elder brother were bishops, and he had gone to Oxford University to read English, although he left without completing a degree. He then worked in the Far East, but returned to England because he was suffering from tuberculosis. Hollis was therefore not an immediately obvious recruit and so MI5 decided that he should be informally interviewed at a social occasion to see whether he was worth more formal treatment. Jane Sissmore duly had Hollis invited to play tennis at the Ealing club, on Sunday 28 August 1937, and White was asked to take part and to give his opinion.[20]

At the tennis game Hollis impressed them as 'gritty and hard-headed' and so Sissmore and White recommended that he be given a formal interview. The MI5 panel initially rejected him and suggested that he try MI6, in view of his experience abroad. When MI6 assessed Hollis, they too turned him down, due to his poor health. Sissmore, however, was convinced that Hollis had the right qualities to succeed in Intelligence. She persuaded Kell that Hollis should indeed join MI5, and he gave her the responsibility for training him.

Hollis and Sissmore concentrated on Soviet affairs; White meanwhile focused on the fascist powers. On 11 March 1939 Kell alerted the Foreign Office of Nazi plans to invade Czechoslovakia, and in early April White warned of Italy's impending excursion into Albania. The Foreign Office and the Prime Minister Neville Chamberlain were sceptical, but on each occasion the Intelligence Services were proved to have been correct.[21] Although Kell was correct about Germany, his grasp of Soviet espionage was much less impressive and in January 1939 he declared Soviet activity in the United Kingdom to be 'non-existent'.[22] Far from being non-existent, however, there was a concentration of communists in Hampstead, north London. Jane Sissmore especially had been aware of this for some time.[23] What no one foresaw, of course, was that in 1941 this left-wing cluster of individuals would be the scene of Klaus Fuchs' entrée into Soviet espionage.

THE KUCZYNSKI CLAN

Back in 1934 a four-storey apartment block was built in Lawn Road, Hampstead. Designed in the style of the German Bauhaus – literally 'construction house' – the minimalist design from the side looked like an ocean liner with four decks, whose cabins were recessed behind extravagantly cantilevered white stone balconies that ran along the length of each floor. The occupants of the Lawn Road Flats constitute a *Who's Who* of the famous – such as crime writer Agatha Christie and the first celebrity chef, Philip Harben – and the infamous, for the Lawn Road Flats became the hub of Soviet espionage in Britain at a time when the Soviet Union was still allied to Nazi Germany.*

It is, of course, all too easy to be wise after the event, but MI5's files at the time are pregnant with clues. In November 1936 thirteen communists had arrived at the House of Commons and requested interviews with 'various members [of Parliament] for various purposes'. Among these was a Bridget Lewis, who gave her address as '4 Lawn Road Flats'.[24] Bridget Lewis, sister of Jürgen Kuczynski, was a secretary at the London School of Economics (LSE), where she was a member of the Communist Party and worked as a volunteer at the party's St Pancras branch. By 1938 she had created enough interest that her file was passed to 'Miss Sissmore B.4a', who immediately arranged for the Post Office to intercept Lewis' correspondence.[25] This seems to have enabled MI5 to identify the members of a web of communists, which was duly recorded but unearthed nothing of real significance, certainly no evidence of espionage.

Arnold Deutsch was another of the early residents in the flats, based at number 7.[26] An academic at the University of London, he recruited for Soviet Intelligence, his notable protégés including Kim Philby and Anthony Blunt. During the Spanish Civil War, Deutsch used his Lawn Road flat as a base to run Philby as a Soviet agent.

Deutsch also attracted artists and intellectuals to meetings in a café on the premises. Speakers at the café included Hans Kahle, who met Klaus Fuchs during internment in Canada in 1940. In October 1939, MI5 had become suspicious of Kahle, allegedly a 'direct agent of Moscow'. According to MI5's informant, Kahle was running an espionage network – assisted by Kuczynski.[27] The British Security Services in fact already had a file on Kuczynski, who had come to their attention back in 1931 while he was still living in Germany. He had fled from the Nazis and arrived in England in 1936 to join his parents, who had already escaped and were living in the next street to the Lawn Road Flats.

Jürgen and his wife, Marguerite, would themselves set up home at 6 Lawn Road Flats in March 1940. Before this, however, as we have seen,

---

* Some of the infamous will appear in the following pages. For a long list of Lawn Road residents see 'Dramatis Personae' in David Burke, *The Lawn Road Flats: Spies, Writers and Artists* (Boydell Press, 2014).

Jürgen had set about coordinating the German Communist Party (KPD) in Great Britain and was well enough connected within the communist movement in August 1936 to become known to Klaus Fuchs, still a student in Bristol.[28] On 25 March 1937, MI5 had a report that Kuczynski was 'in touch with the Soviet Embassy', though for what purpose they had no idea. He moved into sharp focus for MI5 by November 1939* when they learned that Kuczynski is 'assisting Hans Kahle in espionage work among refugees'.[29]

By November 1939 Jane Sissmore, MI5's main Soviet expert, was increasingly worried by these 'scraps of information'. The seriousness of the threat became clear when she interrogated a Soviet defector, Walter Krivitsky.[30] Krivitsky had defected to the United States and in articles written with the American journalist, Isaac Levine, hinted that there were two Soviet agents in London, one in the Foreign Office and one in the Cabinet Office.[31] Sissmore decided on 10 November 1939 that 'to get to the bottom of Soviet military espionage activities in this country, we must contact Krivitsky'.[32]

Krivitsky duly came to Britain, voluntarily, in January 1940. Initially he feared that he might be walking into a trap, but 'with Jane Sissmore taking the lead role in the questioning, Krivitsky began to open up.'[33] Sissmore's debrief of Krivitsky unearthed the name of Simon Kremer as the intelligence officer at the Soviet Embassy – the same Kremer who as 'Johnson' would befriend Klaus Fuchs in 1941. Sissmore also learned that there were agents, who with hindsight could have been Donald Maclean and Kim Philby, two British traitors at the heart of government and the Intelligence Service, whose treachery would not be established until after 1950. In 1940, however, Krivitsky's information was too muddled to make identification possible, even though he did muse that one agent's name 'began with P'.[34]

---

* TNA KV 2/1871, s. 73h, written on 4 April 1940, states that Jürgen Kuczynski 'has been known to us as a communist since June 1931 when he was employed by Communist Central Organisations in Berlin. He is believed to have been in touch with the Soviet Embassy in London in 1937 but for reasons unknown.' In serial 77a, written on 9 April, Hollis asserted that he 'didn't believe for a moment that Kuczynski is an OGPU agent', and Dick White endorsed his junior colleague's judgement because Hollis 'knows Kuczynski personally'. Fuchs later implied that he had two meetings with Kuczynski before becoming a Soviet agent himself in August 1941. KV 2/1879 s. 546a records an interview with Fuchs by MI5 officer William ('Jim') Skardon on 30 November 1950 in which Skardon noted: 'At that time [when Fuchs first made contact with the Russian Intelligence Service] he had casually met Jurgen Kuczynski on a couple of occasions and did in fact recognise him as head of the German Communist Party here.' One of these was the April 1941 meeting referred to in chapter 2. The date of the other is unknown but probably before Fuchs' internment, as the visit to London to celebrate his release suggests that he was already known to the Hampstead set.

Although it was not possible to identify Philby, the pieces were there in Sissmore's memory, and would have consequences later, as we shall see. Indeed, when Philby saw a report of Sissmore's debriefing of Krivitsky with its 'tantalizing scrap of information about a young English journalist whom Soviet Intelligence had sent to Spain during the Civil War', Philby 'recognised himself'.[35] Krivitsky could not have fingered Philby or Maclean at that time, yet his testimony should have alerted MI5 that Soviet espionage was certainly not 'non-existent' and, indeed, was potentially active. Meanwhile the circumstances that would bring Klaus Fuchs alive as a spy were converging on Lawn Road. Not only did Jürgen Kuczynski move into 6 Lawn Road Flats in March 1940, but within a week his other sister, Ursula Beurton – a Soviet spy resident in Switzerland – was ordered by Moscow to move to the United Kingdom to be the head of the GRU military intelligence network. Bigamously married to Len Beurton, a British citizen, as well as to the German architect Rudolf Hamburger, she obtained a British passport. This manoeuvre was noted by MI5.[36]

With the Lawn Road Flats at the centre of this vortex of communists and spies, one would have expected MI5 to mount saturated surveillance in Hampstead. That it failed to be more proactive was partly the result of a hiatus within the organization, which led to Sissmore transferring to MI6 and the Soviet desk devolving to the relatively raw Roger Hollis.

The debacle arose following the sudden ending of Kell's leadership. By the start of the war Kell was sixty-six years old and had been director for thirty years. He had exploited his experience and the secrecy of his office to build a strong organization. He had a chauffeur who drove him in a magnificent Invicta car, a blue pennant at its vanguard, as if the occupant were a head of state. The pennant's decoration was a tortoise with the motto 'Safe but Sure'.[37]

No thought seems to have been given to Kell's successor, but poor health overtook him as the war led to an exponential increase in MI5's responsibilities. Whereas before the war MI5 had dealt with a mere handful of extremists and subversives, it was now suddenly charged with a host of new tasks, including the vetting of thousands of recruits for government jobs, managing the new security constraints that grew out of the Emergency Regulations, and also having to monitor some 50,000 aliens. Perhaps overwhelmed by the scale of the task, Kell simply urged the wholesale internment of aliens.

In an uncanny parallel to the United States in the 1950s, when communist witch-hunts began with the start of the Cold War, in 1940 aliens in the United Kingdom were seen as potential saboteurs and spies. Kell had no evidence for this, however. Home Office officials were unimpressed and 'within Whitehall, respect for MI5 sank'.[38] Churchill's fascination with secret intelligence had been Kell's good fortune when he built up the Security Service back in 1910; now, however, it would be his downfall. Churchill monitored secret intelligence avidly and decided that Kell was no longer up to the job. Having lost the confidence of both the Prime Minister and Whitehall, on 10 June 1940 Kell was dismissed.

For MI5, the transition to his successor, Jasper Harker, was like the proverbial leap from the frying pan into the fire. Harker – 'good looking but not clever', whose recreations were 'fishing, riding and big-game hunting' – was quickly found to be inept.[39] It was unfortunate that his tenure had hardly begun when the loss of the 700 'enemy aliens' on board the *Arandora Star* happened. In Whitehall, when it was realized that many of those drowned were not really 'enemy' at all, one Foreign Office official blamed the Security Service for 'incompetence' in its 'cruel and foolish treatment' of aliens.[40] Churchill castigated MI5 for 'witch-finding activities'. Harker was too closely linked with Kell as one of the *ancien régime* and was perceived as an architect of the disaster. Harker too was now replaced, early in 1941, but not before he had sacked the brilliant Jane Sissmore in November 1940 for 'insubordination'.[41] Sissmore had publicly articulated what other officers seem to have felt about Harker, and was punished. Liddell, who shared her opinion of him, failed to change Harker's mind: Sissmore had openly denounced his leadership and had to go. She was not lost to the British Intelligence Services, however, because she soon joined MI6.

With dramatic irony, though no one at the time could realize this, Sissmore's new boss in MI6 was Kim Philby. Guy Liddell described her move from MI5 as 'a very serious blow to us all', not least because MI5 itself was 'on the verge of collapse'.[42] Over the following years Liddell's assessment would be confirmed, as we shall see, but even he didn't perceive that Jane Sissmore's absence would have serious repercussions within a month.

With Sissmore now gone, the Soviet desk became Hollis' responsibility. One of his first actions, on 9 December 1940, was to write to Colonel Valentine Vivian of MI6 about a 'Walter [*sic*] FUCHS' whom a source had identified as a Gestapo agent from Prague and claimed to have seen in London. This was a red herring, but Hollis' letter noted that the description 'corresponds in a remarkable way to that of a man called Gerhard FUCHS, son of a Kiel clergyman, who belonged to the Communist Party in Prague and had corresponded regularly from there with the Society of Friends'.[43] Vivian's reply showed that the link between Walter and Gerhard was spurious, and Hollis then seems to have forgotten all about this for nine more years. Although there was no direct link between Gerhard and his brother, the communist scientist, Klaus' first name – Emil – was identical to that of the aforementioned Kiel clergyman, and the Society of Friends was mentioned in the file of his sponsor, the suspected communist Ronald Gunn. When questions about Klaus Fuchs came into Hollis' view later, such clues might have linked Klaus with his communist brother Gerhard – had Hollis' vision been as keen as that of his predecessor, Jane Sissmore.[44]

That was but the first slip on Hollis' watch. In that same month the American Embassy asked MI5 for a list of foreign communists in the United Kingdom.[45] According to the journalist Chapman Pincher, the reply to the US Embassy failed to include any mention of Jürgen Kuczynski or his entourage of associates. Pincher gives no source for his astonishing claim, so one explanation could be that he was simply incorrect. MI5 was certainly aware of Kuczynski at this time, there being at least two notes on file that show their concerns. One, written in December 1940, referred to him as 'a GPU agent', and this was copied into his personal file.[46] Then in February 1941, MI5 recorded, 'from various sources it is claimed that he [JK] is an illegal contact with the Soviet Secret Service'.[47] This is a remarkable insight just two months before Kuczynski became matchmaker for Klaus Fuchs and the Soviet Embassy. Even if Pincher was wrong, however, and these suspicions were passed to the Americans, neither of MI5's observations appears to have led to any meaningful action.

MI5's failure could be an oversight that occurred during the fractured transition from Sissmore to Hollis. Pincher regards it as but one of several failings that conspiracy theorists have associated with Roger Hollis, arguing that he was himself a mole working within MI5 on behalf of the Soviet Union. While this has never been proved, and on the evidence available seems unlikely, it is not easy to dispel questions about the state of their organization around the time that Klaus Fuchs was being courted by the Soviet Union.

Harker's successor as leader in March 1941 was Sir David Petrie.* Petrie had the unenviable task of revitalizing MI5 in the midst of the Second World War, at a time when German agents were the perceived enemy. Meanwhile, as these changes took place in the corridors of power, behind the scenes Klaus Fuchs was preparing for espionage.

---

* In a bureaucratic manoeuvre, Director Harker was rebranded as Deputy Director General, while Petrie became MI5's first Director General. See Andrew, *Defence of the Realm*, p. 236.

PART TWO

Tube Alloys: 1941–3

4

Klaus Fuchs in Birmingham

Much confusion and misinformation abounds as to exactly when Klaus Fuchs started his espionage. Throughout his life Fuchs remained coy about precisely when the Soviets first realized that he would be useful to them as a spy. When questioned, he always claimed it to have been in 1942 or, at the earliest, 'late 1941', in any event long after he joined Peierls.[1] This is, however, an example of Fuchs' crafty setting of false trails, as he was in fact spying by the summer of 1941, and possibly even earlier. The date is of more than scholastic concern, for if he began to spy soon after he joined Peierls that would have been in the period when the Soviet Union still had a non-aggression pact with Germany, and was by implication an enemy of the United Kingdom.

There has been considerable doubt too about the circumstances that brought Fuchs to the heart of the atomic bomb project, and which enabled him later to become one of the key figures in the post-war development of the hydrogen bomb.* For example, how was Fuchs cleared by the Security Services in the first place? Were they asleep on the job, or duped, or was the government right to claim later that it was impossible to have foreseen that Fuchs was a threat?[2]

Peierls' memoir of his fateful recruitment of Fuchs, written three decades later, is a good place to start:

As regards the question of how Klaus Fuchs was recruited, the answer is that I recruited him. In 1940, when it was clear that an atomic weapon was a serious possibility, and that it was urgent to do experimental and theoretical work about this, I wanted someone to help me with the theoretical side. Most competent theoreticians were already doing something important, and when I heard that Fuchs, whom I knew and respected as a physicist from his work at Bristol, was back in the UK, temporarily in Edinburgh,

---

* Fuchs' involvement with the H-bomb is described in chapters 10, 12 and 22.

it seemed a good idea to get him to come to Birmingham. There was at first
some difficulty about security clearance, and I was told I could not tell him
what it was all about. (I presume, but do not know, that this was because
as a student in Nazi Germany he had joined a left-wing organisation of
students to oppose the Nazis, and had eventually to flee for his life.)[3]

Peierls explained to the Security Services the reasons why Fuchs was
ideal for the task, and this seems to have clinched matters. Much later, the
government described Fuchs' singular appeal thus: 'The very finest brains
available were needed to assist in that research and such brains as Dr Fuchs
possesses are very rare indeed. He was known as and has proved himself
to be one of the finest theoretical physicists living.'[4] This description,
designed to excuse the mistaken decision to hire an embryonic spy, over-
states his quality. Fuchs was never in the class of nuclear physicists such
as Niels Bohr, Enrico Fermi, or indeed Rudolf Peierls; within the needs of
the United Kingdom in 1941, however, Fuchs had the skills required, and
Peierls was fortunate to be able to call on them. Approval was granted but
on the condition that Peierls told Fuchs only 'what was absolutely necessary
for his work'. Peierls replied that if he could not take Fuchs into his confidence, Fuchs would be of no use to him. This must have been agreed as 'In
due course he got full clearance and he started work in May 1941.'[5]

This narrative in which Fuchs was given security clearance 'in due
course' and 'started work in May' is both vague on chronology and ambiguous. For example, did the difficulty with Fuchs' clearance delay the
start of their collaboration, or did Peierls stress to Fuchs that it was imperative to press ahead, and the security clearance only arrive later? The
available record also raises questions of how much Fuchs already knew of
Peierls' programme when he visited the Lawn Road Flats in London on
15 April 1941.

INTERLUDE

This phase in the saga had begun in the summer of 1940 when Fuchs was
interned as an enemy alien. Max Born, his colleague and professor at
Edinburgh University, had written to the authorities on 29 May urging
that Fuchs be released, and had solicited Peierls' support.[6] Peierls replied
in July and apologized for not having answered earlier. He was at that
time, of course, fully engaged with the implications of his work with
Frisch, which had raised the spectre of the atomic bomb.

In this correspondence Born had also expressed his frustration at being unable to contribute to the war effort due to his German background. This is evident in Peierls' enigmatic response:

> I know exactly how you feel, and could very well understand what you wrote, in fact I was thinking just along the same lines. I am afraid I cannot make any suggestions as to any pieces of research that are likely to be of practical importance.[7]

Here, 'practical' means applicable to the war effort. Born had shared Peierls' disappointment at being sidelined as an enemy alien and was looking for ideas to develop that would make him indispensable in the fight against the Nazis.

Like many of his contemporaries, Born was aware of the fission of uranium and of Bohr's insight that using $U235$ rather than $U238$ was key. Indeed, in 1939, when he and Fuchs were in Edinburgh, the pair had 'discussed the possibility of exploiting the gigantic energy involved'. Furthermore Born had been at Cambridge before the war and heard the Hungarian physicist Leo Szilard talking about a chain reaction and the possibility of a nuclear explosion. Already Szilard feared that Hitler might develop this 'super-weapon and thus conquer the world'. Born's memory, thirty years later, was 'I think I discussed this with Fuchs [in 1939] after my return from Cambridge. In any event Fuchs was much more expert than I was as he knew much more about nuclear physics.'[8] There may be an element of false memory here as Fuchs' main work by then was not in nuclear physics, but like many of their colleagues Born and Fuchs would have been broadly aware of the potential for releasing vast amounts of energy from the atomic nucleus. Fission and the possibility of a chain reaction were sensational ideas, but not secret.

At most their interest was that of physics kibitzers who followed developments with interest: they did no meaningful research into the phenomenon. Born's discussion with Fuchs in 1939 was probably no different from those between many other theoretical physicists in the aftermath of the discovery of fission: first, to marvel at the prodigious energies involved, and then wonder how they might be realized in practice by experiment and technology. That nuclear power could be of service to humanity was an obvious possibility; that a deliverable bomb was feasible, however, was far from clear – the surprise of Werner Heisenberg and his German colleagues in 1945 when they learned that the Allies had succeeded at what they had thought to be impossible is testament to the received wisdom absent Peierls and Frisch. Heisenberg and his team were, like Born and Fuchs, unaware that only a few kilograms of $U235$ would be needed. In July 1940 Peierls' reply to Born's enquiry meticulously protected this terrible secret.

Within the constraints of that secrecy, Peierls elaborated on his current work:

> The problems I am interested in just now do not really offer much scope for theoretical work, it is mainly a question of getting somebody to do the experiments.* In a general way, if anybody can think of a new and efficient way of separating the isotopes of heavy elements, that would no doubt be of importance for many purposes. But I really think that all possible methods have already been explored, for example in Urey's article ['*Separation of Isotopes*'] in the Physical Society reports.[9]

Peierls interest in separating isotopes of 'heavy' elements and the importance of fission in the heaviest known element, uranium, would have made his strategic goal rather obvious. But it gave no indication of any progress – if anything, quite the opposite.

Although Peierls' war work would turn out to be the most far-reaching long-term consequence of that letter, the main content concerned one of Born's students, a Polish graduate named Wolfgang Hepner. Peierls' interest in Hepner is relevant to understanding the context of the hiring of Fuchs. Hepner had studied quantum mechanics with its founder, Erwin Schrödinger, as well as with Born, and so was a strong prospect. Peierls was keen for Hepner to study for a Ph.D. in Birmingham and had been negotiating with the university for him to begin in October 1940. Unfortunately – as Peierls explained to Born – the authorities at the University of Birmingham 'are just now very reluctant to accept any new foreign students'. In this period when fear of a fifth column was rife, xenophobia within the university was no different from that in the population at large. Peierls stopped going to faculty meetings after he heard negative remarks that 'former enemy aliens' were attending them.[10]

Despite this, Peierls must have received approval, for by October Hepner was at Birmingham – but without any funds to support him. Faced now with a potentially destitute student on his hands, Peierls wrote to Born at the start of November and asked whether there was any possibility of Hepner moving back to Edinburgh! To sugar the pill, Peierls added that he had heard from Neville Mott that Fuchs was about to be released from internment and would soon be returning to the United Kingdom but was without a job. Peierls explained: 'I am doing some consulting work for a

---

* Born was a theoretician, not an experimentalist.

Government Department at present and am trying to get some relief from teaching.'[11] Peierls asked Born whether Fuchs – already with a Ph.D. and some post-doctoral experience – would like to come to Birmingham as a temporary lecturer.

Born did not know when Fuchs would return to the United Kingdom, however. As a result of this uncertainty Peierls decided not to proceed with Fuchs and instead continued to pursue the case of Hepner with the university. He told the authorities that he proposed to employ Hepner as a 'private part-time assistant in order to enable me to devote more time to consulting work of National importance'.[12] He explained that Hepner would spend most of his time as a research student in the university, and that the teaching would be a private matter between the pair of them – Peierls paying Hepner 'One pound, eight shillings and ten pence per week' for this work. Peierls stressed to the university that he had made 'exhaustive enquiries to get a suitable assistant of British nationality but was unsuccessful'.

The university approved Hepner's appointment. This satisfied Peierls' needs in the short term, but once Hepner graduated and took a full-time job Peierls would be back at square one. So with an eye to the future, and aware that Born had no funds in Edinburgh to maintain Fuchs, Peierls asked Born to keep him informed if Fuchs returned.

By 12 March 1941 Peierls must have learned that Fuchs was back in Edinburgh and that Born had not yet found a job for him because he wrote again to Born about Fuchs' prospects. Born responded immediately. In a letter of 16 March Born confirmed that Fuchs was back from internment in Canada and added that he would be 'very grateful if [you] could help [me] find a suitable post for [him]'. On 22 March Peierls replied that there was no chance of a regular staff position for Fuchs at Birmingham, but there might be an opening for a temporary lecturer, or alternatively a hybrid position, part-time as a lecturer and the rest as Peierls' research assistant.

Peierls gave Born the background. Hepner was about to complete his Ph.D. and seemed likely to take a job in industry; his departure would create room for Fuchs in one of those positions. Peierls' question to Born was whether he would judge that to be 'sufficient advance on Fuch's [sic] present situation to justify his leaving Edinburgh?'

Born was very positive and wrote of Fuchs in glowing terms. He regarded Fuchs as one of the most outstanding young theorists at that time, describing him as 'extremely gifted, on quite a different level from all my other pupils at Edinburgh'. His pen portrait of Fuchs was 'a very nice quiet fellow with sad eyes', who was both 'shy' and 'penniless'.[13]

Nearly two months then elapsed before Peierls sent a written offer to be passed to Fuchs in May. The autobiographies of Peierls and of Born hint at conversations that took place off the record during this period. Peierls' autobiography is not specific about dates but the implicit chronology is tantalizing. First, on 22 March, Peierls asked Born whether Fuchs was 'willing to join us'.[14] Peierls' narrative explains that he has asked for official clearance, and was 'at first' instructed to say as little as possible, to which he had replied that this would be impractical. Peierls continues: 'In due course he got a full clearance and he started work in May 1941.'

Recall that Born had probably deduced that Peierls was interested in nuclear physics – possibly even U235 – when Peierls mentioned 'separating the isotopes of heavy elements' back in July 1940. This conclusion is supported by Born's own memoir, which reveals that, when Peierls' cryptic letter with its offer of employment arrived on 10 May, Born and Fuchs 'both knew what it meant'.[15]

Peierls had raised the prospect of Fuchs working at Birmingham back on 22 March. Although no formal offer was made until 10 May, it seems possible that Fuchs could have been aware of Peierls' interest in uranium isotopes, if only implicitly, when he visited Jürgen Kuczynski in the middle of April.

MORE EFFICIENT THAN THE SECURITY SERVICES

Thus on Saturday 10 May 1941 Peierls sent his letter to Fuchs setting out the terms and inviting him to join in work 'for the Ministry of Aircraft Production'. Peierls added that he 'cannot now disclose the nature or the purpose' other than to say that it involved 'mathematical problems of considerable difficulty'. The job would be 'temporary, probably for six months at a time', though 'I do not see an end to the work at present'.[16] Peierls' letter of 10 May was probably the formality required to complete rather than initiate the move. Fuchs would have received Peierls' letter on Monday 12 May at the earliest; by 13 May the Edinburgh City Police had already given him permission to travel by night train to Birmingham so that he could talk the offer over with Peierls.[17] Whatever the truth, Peierls, Born and Fuchs certainly moved faster than the Security Services.

Fuchs carried with him a handwritten letter of introduction from Born to Peierls. The letter refers to 'war work', which is 'important as you yourself say'.[18] This strongly suggests that Born and Peierls had had some unrecorded conversation because there is no mention of the 'importance' of 'war work' in the available written correspondence, which had focused on Fuchs as a teacher and part-time assistant to Peierls. The correspondence between 10 and 16 May also suggests that Born and Peierls were tying up loose ends such as in a cunning scheme to get round some bureaucratic restrictions. The money for Peierls' war work came from the Ministry of Aircraft Production.* This would be a serious problem in the case of Fuchs, who was still classed as an enemy alien. Peierls suggested a clever solution: if Fuchs were to remain technically in the employment of Edinburgh University, he could then be 'lent' to the Ministry, who would 'refund the salary' to the university. Peierls added that this ruse 'might facilitate [Fuchs'] return to Edinburgh when the temporary job expires'.

Born agreed that Fuchs' later career would be helped 'if he had a war job and a good record', but then raised a problem with Peierls' suggestion: Fuchs, unfortunately, was not in the employ of the university. Born immediately proposed a way around this too, however: he would declare Fuchs to be his 'personal assistant' and receive the money for Fuchs. He also looked forward to getting Fuchs back to Edinburgh 'when the work with you is finished'.

With no clear evidence against him, Fuchs' scientific transfer moved on rapidly. On 27 May he relocated to Birmingham, and lodged in the home of Rudolf and Genia Peierls.[19] Their two children, aged five and seven, had recently moved to live with family and friends in Canada, away from the threat of bombing. Fuchs filled their empty nest and Genia's personality provided motherly care as Fuchs was treated 'like a son'.[20] She found him to be 'exceptionally companionable and nice with children, very kind, and extremely reliable', and recalled that Klaus liked animals: 'He was good with dogs and cats. Dogs liked him!' She theorized this was due to his shyness: 'He never pushed with his personality. Some people like [a] more outgoing personality but children and animals like reserve.'[21] For the first time in many years, and perhaps in his entire life, Fuchs experienced the genuine happiness of being part of a loving family. Later, at Los Alamos, Fuchs found the Peierls' children amusing, and in turn they liked him.

In Rudolf Peierls' home, he and Fuchs discussed physics, but the secret project was off limits. This was the beginning of a deep friendship that developed over the next decade. Of course they shared Germanic roots, but also a common style of behaviour, even down to small details at mealtimes. The Peierls' home was like a hostel for transient scientists – 'every British physicist of note has spent an evening at our home', Genia would

* His letter of 10 May makes clear that the holder would be 'on the payroll of the Ministry'.

later claim. In this warm-hearted environment Klaus Fuchs absorbed the Peierls' sense of honour, and became part of a 'physics family' that shared its members' lives beyond just equations. All this would come out later.[22]

Conversation often focused on their common heritage. That Fuchs openly espoused anti-fascist and socialist views was of no particular surprise to Rudolf and Genia Peierls. His views about the Nazis mirrored theirs; that he had adopted such a stance, when as an Aryan he could have taken the safe option and stayed silent, only added to his attraction. So by the end of May 1941, Rudolf Peierls seemed to have achieved an ideal situation. He had found a talented assistant for his physics research, a fellow refugee from Nazi Germany who shared many of his ideals, and who had become a welcome and congenial addition to his family home. What could go wrong?

BIRMINGHAM AND MAUD

The timing of Fuchs' recruitment by Peierls could not have been more dramatic, as it coincided with three momentous developments in the course of the war. First, this was a key moment for science. The invention of radar had helped win the Battle of Britain in 1940; now the race to develop an atomic bomb could decide not just a battle but also the outcome of the war, and determine subsequent global hegemony. Second, the timing was hugely significant for global politics, as the Soviet Union, formerly an ally of Nazi Germany, was invaded by Germany in June and the following month became allied with the United Kingdom. For Fuchs, this confluence would be seminal. Third, political pressures within the United Kingdom put development of an atomic weapon in the balance. In Whitehall, radar was still perceived as the leading research field for the war effort. Attitudes to an atomic bomb were mixed. If the project was believed in at all, it was as a long-term hedge. The fear that Hitler might get there first spurred the scientists, many of whom were émigrés and saw the race against the Nazis as a personal cause.

Fuchs also arrived when the project was moving forwards rapidly. In March 1941 Peierls had had a brainwave: the idea of wrapping a layer of iron around the lump of U235 in order to reflect some of the escaping neutrons back into the uranium and thereby increase the number of fissions. This promised to reduce the amount of U235 required for a weapon, but the design of such a device would first need careful evaluation by theorists.

The immediate goal of MAUD scientists was to enrich uranium and eventually isolate U235. Peierls and another émigré, Franz Simon of Oxford University, had sketched a first outline design of a practical diffusion plant, while Simon's team had built a half-scale model of a single stage. Peierls had made estimates of the plant's manpower and costs, and the contract with Metropolitan Vickers for the twenty-stage plant had been agreed.

Fuchs' arrival as Peierls' assistant helped to release the master's creativity. Peierls' vision was clear: the first task must be the production of the raw material – U235 – for the weapon and in sufficient quantity to make at least one bomb. The immediate goal was therefore to separate U235 from natural uranium. This would require the uranium to be in a gas, for which the only practical substance was uranium hexafluoride, a compound of uranium and fluorine. The first assignment that Peierls set Fuchs when he joined in May 1941 was: How can one ensure that when a gas passes through a diffusion plant, uranium isotopes are filtered out rather than those of other elements?*

Fuchs solved this problem. His report that summer kept the variety of gas secret, as it referred only to elements 'A' and 'X', with no mention of uranium or fluorine. He examined the hypothetical case of 'an element X in a compound with element A, where A has two isotopes, A1 and A2'. The question that he now had to solve was 'How far [does] the existence of two A isotopes affect the efficiency of separation of the X isotopes?'[23] As Fuchs had not yet signed the Official Secrets Act, Peierls seems to have given him this abstract problem without revealing the identities of the elements A and X. Fuchs had almost certainly deduced their identities, however. To see why, recall what was already in the public domain at that time.

Fission had been discovered in 1938, and the idea of a chain reaction had attracted wide attention among scientists. In 1939 the 'Great Dane' – the atomic theorist Niels Bohr – had published his insight that the rare isotope U235 is key to the phenomenon, but from that moment research in nuclear physics became secret. Even so, the implication of Bohr's observation would have been clear to any competent physicist presented with

---

* In the case of uranium hexafluoride, six lightweight atoms of fluorine weigh about half as much as a single atom of uranium. So in the molecule, fluorine carries about one-third of the whole mass. Although fluorine has only one stable isotope, F19, the isotope F18 is radioactive, with a half-life of about two hours. This leaves only trace amounts of F18 in normal fluorine, however, so it should not have presented a problem in practice. As discussed in chapter 1, there was a hope that an alternative might be found to hex, and it is possible that Peierls wanted Fuchs to assess this general problem in order to be sure that a huge and expensive diffusion plant would not produce large amounts of isotopes of some other element while leaving the precious uranium undifferentiated.

a problem about separating isotopes, especially within a top-secret war programme. That the element 'X' was uranium would have been obvious to Fuchs; perhaps the only unknown for him would have been the nature of the compound, but as uranium hexafluoride is the only practical gaseous compound of uranium, he might, with a little more effort, have been able to deduce this also.

Peierls was impatient to press ahead even before Fuchs was formally approved.* On Wednesday 11 June 1941 he wrote to a colleague who was working on the secret project at Cambridge: 'I propose to be in Cambridge next Sunday afternoon and Monday . . . I shall bring Fuchs with me, who has now started work here, and I would like him to meet [theorists in your team] as their problems are similar in some ways from the mathematical point of view.'[24]

It is unrealistic to suppose that Fuchs could have discussed mathematics with any of the Cambridge team without both parties knowing the context of the physical problems that the mathematics was intended to solve. Mathematics can provide a set of tools that enable analysis of a physical problem, but there is little point in forging ahead without first ensuring that the tools are the right ones, and that first requires a deep understanding of the physical processes themselves.

In the circumstances Peierls' decision to take Fuchs with him to Cambridge was natural. To defeat Hitler was the urgent task; Fuchs was fully committed to that end and his abilities were critical to Peierls' capacity to move forward. Peierls was a scientist, totally focused on that goal. There was every reason for him to believe that Fuchs' motivation was the same. Signing documents was important for the mandarins, but in the meantime there was work to be done. One of Peierls' fundamental beliefs was that research was most effective when 'guided by the necessity to get the best answer in the shortest possible time rather than by questions of formal organisation and prestige'.[25] As if to reinforce his sense of urgency, five days later the German army invaded Russia, which now became allied with the United Kingdom in the war against the Nazis.

---

* Documents found in Fuchs' home, in February 1950, revealed that he received notification about the Official Secrets Act only on 11 October 1941 (TNA KV 2/1252, s. 505a.). In his trial it was claimed he signed the OSA on 18 June 1942 (sic). In any event, he had not been cleared until the late summer of 1941; see chapter 5.

5

The Amateur Spy

On 22 June 1941, less than a month after Klaus Fuchs began working with Peierls, Germany invaded Russia. That evening, Prime Minister Winston Churchill spoke to the nation on the radio and said, 'We shall give whatever help we can to Russia and the Russian people.'[1] A few weeks later a formal military alliance was signed between the United Kingdom and the Soviet Union. If Fuchs had needed permission to take action, that alliance and Churchill's rhetoric would have been it. In any event, Soviet archives record that Fuchs remembered his 'former [sic] acquaintance' with Kremer – the Soviet intelligence officer – and decided to transmit what he knew about the atom bomb project to that 'representative of Russia as part of the war against fascism'.[2] At some point over the summer Fuchs contacted Jürgen Kuczynski and told him about his new role in nuclear research.[3] Kuczynski passed on Fuchs' message.[4] The London chief of GRU (Soviet Military Intelligence), Ivan Sklyarov (code name BRION), was alerted. He in turn consulted the GRU Centre in Moscow, which instructed him to recruit Fuchs.[5]

Fuchs and Kremer met in London on 8 August 1941, a date established by the GRU and KGB records and which belies Fuchs' later claims that he began espionage only in 1942.[6] A deciphered GRU message from London to Moscow Centre on 10 August (see note 2), which referred to Fuchs as a 'former acquaintance' of Kremer, confirms that they had met earlier, most probably at Kuczynski's party in April. Before the GRU decided to recruit Fuchs as a source they would have had to satisfy themselves that he was legitimate and not MI5 bait. This would have taken some time, which suggests that Fuchs approached Kuczynski at the latest in July, and possibly even earlier – in which case the timing is pushed tantalizingly close to the time that the Soviet Union's role in the war changed. Such a timetable fits naturally with the thesis that Fuchs took his initiative upon hearing Churchill's broadcast, although he never advanced this defence later. In any event, it would appear that 8 August 1941 was the date when

Fuchs was formally 'signed on' by the GRU with the code name OTTO, and that his decision to spy for the Soviet Union had preceded that.

Fuchs had become privy to official secrets in the spring, was passing them to the Soviet Union by the summer, yet he did not receive warning about the Official Secrets Act until 11 October.[7] That summer he joined the exclusive club of insomniacs haunted by knowledge that an atomic bomb was both possible and indeed likely. There was a practical method to concentrate U235, the amount needed for a single bomb was small, and the contract had just been placed with Metropolitan Vickers to design a twenty-stage diffusion plant that was expected to be ready by the end of the year.[8] Fuchs knew the data on which these conclusions relied.

By the time of Fuchs' arrival in Birmingham, Peierls had elucidated the problems in nine papers.[9] Fuchs would have learned from the start that when a neutron hits a lump of uranium, the results depend not just on whether the target is U238 or U235 but also on the neutron's speed. You can liberate energy from natural uranium when the neutrons are slow because 1 in every 140 atoms contains U235. This can be the basis for a heat engine – in modern language a 'reactor' – but does not create an explosion. If the neutrons have high energy they can induce fission in U238, but the secondary neutrons liberated in these reactions do not have enough energy to induce further fissions in U238. They can, however, cause fission in U235 if by chance they happen upon one of these atypical isotopes. Unfortunately, these 'fast' secondary neutrons tend to be captured by U238 atoms and are lost to the fission engine, so even if the amount of U235 is larger than normal, some means of slowing the neutrons is needed in order to maintain a chain of fission reactions.[10] Start with about 50 kilograms of pure U235, on the other hand, and according to Frisch and Peierls an explosion would in theory be possible, whatever the neutron's speed.

By the summer of 1941 Peierls and his new assistant were deep into the theoretical physics of gaseous diffusion and the design of a practical enrichment plant. There were so many variables that the work was both time consuming and difficult. Peierls produced a series of papers on assembly problems, and on different designs with fanciful names such as 'rabbit', 'cul-de-sac' and 'cascade of cascades', chosen, no doubt, to give no clues to their content.[11] Fuchs' study of uranium enrichment, when the uranium is in a compound molecule, formed the basis of his first papers with Peierls.[12]

This was the state of knowledge in the summer of 1941, and of Fuchs' particular contribution to it. When Fuchs met Kremer in August, he handed him six sheets of data, the first transmission of many over the next seven years. Kremer showed Fuchs' documents to Sklyarov, who had some scientific training. On 10 August Skylarov – BRION – radioed a message to the GRU Centre, which when decoded read:

Barch [Kremer] conducted a meeting with the German physicist, Klaus Fuchs, who reported he is in a special group in Birmingham University working on the theoretical aspects of creating a uranium bomb. The work is expected to take three months and then the results will be directed to Canada for production purposes. Assuming that at least one per cent of the atomic energy of uranium explosive is released, a ten kilograms bomb will be equal to 1000 tons of dynamite.[13]

The six pages of notes were sent to Moscow by diplomatic pouch that same day, but the war delayed them, and they did not reach the GRU Centre until early September. Meanwhile, the radio message had excited Moscow, as on 11 August came the response: 'To Brion: Take all measures for obtaining information about the uranium bomb. Director.'[14]

The transfer of top-secret information from Fuchs to Kremer was the classic spycraft of novels. The pair would meet at a busy bus stop, and sit side by side on the bus. Fuchs would be carrying copies of his papers in an envelope, or wrapped in packing paper, and when he was ready to alight would leave these on the seat for Kremer, who remained on board. On one occasion they met on a quiet residential street after dark and cruised around the neighbourhood in a car.[15]

Fuchs would claim later that initially his conscience allowed him only to communicate his own work on diffusion.[16] Moscow's reaction suggests this is untrue. Fuchs' own work at this early stage primarily showed that the presence of multiple isotopes in gaseous compounds of uranium would not confound the goal of diffusion enriching $U235$. While this was clearly of some importance, in the grand scheme of things it was relatively trifling. The sensational debut of Fuchs' material in Moscow must have relied on the context rather than this particular contribution. The Director of GRU, General Alexei Panfilov, was technically trained and rated Fuchs' notes 'very important'. His assessment was that they revealed the British to be researching a weapon that 'would put humanity on the road to Hell'.[17]

Such a response would have been unlikely if Fuchs' notes consisted solely of his two months' work on diffusion. Instead it suggests that Fuchs – or someone else – also transmitted the key to the entire project: the Frisch-Peierls Memorandum of May 1940 itself. Fuchs' message to Kremer that 'the work is expected to take three months' was Peierls and Frisch's original estimate. Moscow's reaction that the British were researching a weapon that 'would put humanity on the road to Hell' is also a fair paraphrase of Peierls and Frisch's conclusion.

One consequence of Fuchs' initiative was that Moscow Centre instructed Skylarov to find out about 'work on uranium in other British establishments, such as Metropolitan Vickers and Cambridge University.'[18] These institutions were mentioned in a MAUD scientific committee report, whose first draft was discussed by committee members on 2 July. During the summer, the MAUD committee reviewed the document, and although Peierls was not formally a member, he too was 'fully consulted'.[19]

Of the thirty-one university scientists actively engaged in MAUD work, five were at Birmingham University, namely Peierls and Fuchs, along with two chemists, and Mark Oliphant, who was also on the MAUD committee.[20] Peierls was fully aware of the project's status, as outlined in the draft MAUD report, and Fuchs probably knew the preliminary report's content when he met Kremer on 8 August; it might even have been his reason for doing so. When the final version arrived in Whitehall, on 27 August, the British civil servant John Cairncross passed a copy to his own Soviet handler. So by the start of September 1941, Fuchs and Cairncross had alerted the Soviet Union to this top-secret development.

Meanwhile, on 4 July 1941, G. P. Thomson, the chairman of the MAUD committee, learned that the Germans were trying to obtain heavy water.* He urged Frederick Lindemann, Churchill's science advisor and newly ennobled as Lord Cherwell, to develop a scientific intelligence programme to evaluate German progress. As this was too specialized to be an activity suitable for MI6, Thomson recommended that this needed 'someone with knowledge of physics and especially of the personalities and specialities of German physicists'.[21] The chosen intelligence gatherers were Peierls and Fuchs. What Thomson and Cherwell did not know was that while Fuchs was analysing German work on behalf of the British, he was already leaking the fruits of British work to the Russians.

In September he and Peierls visited London to 'obtain copies of German scientific periodicals from MI6 and to deduce the location, travel, and research activity of German nuclear scientists'.[22] The pair wrote a report, which concluded that German scientists were fully aware of the importance of separating isotopes to produce the fissionable U235. Peierls and Fuchs judged the centres of German basic research to be Heidelberg and Munich, in addition to Berlin. When MI6 asked 'what steps were

---

* The use of heavy water is a means to moderate neutrons. The interest in heavy water thereby points to potential interest in the development of a nuclear reactor or weapons programme – see chapter 1.

being taken to find out the movements of German scientists skilled in nuclear physics', they were informed that Peierls and Fuchs were on the case. In reality Peierls was the main player as Fuchs had never been in German academic life long enough to know the background. Peierls showed Fuchs his findings, and consulted him on specific items. Their collaboration to assess German activity seems to have been between master and assistant, as was consistent with their relative standing and experience.

Fuchs produced his first solo contribution in March 1942 with an analysis of a German paper, which worryingly dealt with separation of isotopes. Was this a clue to a German military programme, or harmless? He wrote to Perrin on 4 April 1942 and agreed with him that although 'the more harmless interpretation appears to me more plausible . . . the other one should not be neglected'.[23] This typifies the difficulty in assessing the threat from German science, for while Peierls and Fuchs' reports identified tantalizing work relevant to the development of an atomic weapon, they produced no conclusive evidence that Germany had a significant active programme to that end. As Peierls summarized for Perrin on 29 August 1942: 'We unearthed no very startling information, [but] there are some points of interest.'[24]

SHE COULD 'SMELL A RAT AT TWENTY PACES'

Fuchs moved to Birmingham in May, yet not until August, with Fuchs already at work on secret material, was his sparse MI5 file reopened.[25] In early 1941 Klaus Fuchs' file contained no more than four entries: the remarks from the Gestapo about communist activities in 1934, the repetition of the same in 1938, together with MI5's dismissal on both occasions.

For anyone seeking to answer the question 'Who cleared Klaus Fuchs?' and in particular whether it was Roger Hollis, later accused of being a Soviet mole, the trail starts on 6 August 1941, when the Ministry of Aircraft Production applied for an Aliens War Service permit so that Fuchs could work with Peierls. Mr Cochran-Wilson in the Division of Alien Control took action. Having noticed the 1934 remark that Fuchs was 'an active member of the Communist Party in Germany', Cochran-Wilson contacted Milicent Bagot in section F.2.b – responsible for monitoring activity by the Comintern in the United Kingdom – and asked that enquiries be made about Fuchs' activities.

John Le Carré's fictional Moscow expert, Connie Sachs, was modelled on the formidable Milicent Bagot. In 1941 she was ten years into an outstanding career, where her superb memory and ability to detect patterns in reams of data became legendary. By the time of her retirement, in 1967, she had become MI5's leading expert on communists, and famous for being the first to alert the Security Services in the 1950s that Kim Philby, the notorious double agent then working in MI6, was not who he appeared to be. Utterly discreet, she never revealed her source. One of the memorials written after her death aged ninety-nine, in 2006, asserted that she could 'smell a rat at twenty paces'.[26] Her reaction to Cochran-Wilson's request suggests that she sensed all was not well with Klaus Fuchs.

Large numbers of names of potential communists came to MI5's attention and only the most important were referred to Roger Hollis, head of Division F.[27] Miss Bagot seems to have highlighted the Fuchs case at once, because by 9 August 1941 Cochran-Wilson's request to her had risen even further: the in-tray of the Director General, Sir David Petrie. This would presumably have gone via her division head, Roger Hollis, but there is no indication of this on the paperwork; if Hollis was informed, he failed to recall his exchange with Colonel Vivian eight months before about Gerhard Fuchs.* That same day Petrie contacted the Birmingham chief constable in a letter, which Bagot signed. 'As this man was reported by the German Consul in Bristol in 1934 as being an active member of the Communist Party in Germany,' Petrie asked, 'has [he] come to notice in Birmingham on account of his political activities or associates?'[28] Petrie stressed that this was urgent, and the chief constable obliged, by return reaffirming that Fuchs had 'not come adversely under notice' in Birmingham, and that he was working with 'PEIERLS – a brilliant mathematician'. The letter added that Peierls' wife was 'a Russian subject' and that Peierls' 'bona-fides have never been questioned'.[29] The same day that the Director General contacted Birmingham, the Security Services ran checks through their own records. Miss Bagot's section asked Mr Robson-Scott – another double-barrelled old-school member of Alien Control – whether he had information on Fuchs, who had been reported in 1934 to be 'an active member of the Communist Party in Germany'.[30] Robson-Scott evidently did not reply, as on 29 August there was a further request to him, this time with 'DG' appended to the anonymous sender's code-number.[31] On 18 September he was sent yet another reminder because 'MAP [the Ministry of Aircraft Production are] press[ing] for a decision'.[32]

Fuchs had worked on the top-secret project all summer, yet as autumn began the Security Services had not completed their background checks.[33] Only in October – two months after the initial enquiry to Robson-Scott – did the vetting officers in MI5 learn that one of his undercover

* See chapter 3, note 43.

agents – 'Contact KASPAR' – had reported Fuchs to be 'very well-known in communist circles'.[34] Unfortunately KASPAR would be unable to give more definitive information for some considerable time, and his report remained simply on file. Apart from KASPAR's intelligence, the only negative information on Fuchs remained the discounted Gestapo report. Clues latent in Hollis' December 1940 query about Gerhard Fuchs lay dormant.

Yet there was already information in Security Service files that could have raised alarms if it had been properly handled. For example, recall Hollis' interest in Klaus' brother, Gerhard. Back in July 1939, Gerhard had attempted to land in England to visit Klaus but was refused admittance and returned to Switzerland.[35] Gerhard was a strong anti-Nazi and British Security had already identified his communist links. The first occasion was in 1932 when in an SIS (MI6) list of German publishing houses he was recorded to be 'working under communist direction' as the editor of the journal *Mahnruf*.[36] Next, in 1933, he was described as 'directing the General Secretariat of the Workers' International Relief at The Hague'. By 1940 the files record that 'an MI5 source reported that [Gerhard Fuchs] had at one time belonged to the communist party in Prague'.[37] All of these remarks were stored in the registry of MI5 and MI6 files before 1941, yet at no point in the vetting of Klaus Fuchs, when claims of his communist association were being assessed, and dismissed, and later his suitability for the Manhattan Project evaluated, does this information about his brother appear to have surfaced. Today, computerized records make such cross-checks by search engines straightforward; back then, when information was stored in vast archives in the basement and indexed on reams of card files, correlations were harder to uncover. Nonetheless, it seems remarkable that at no stage did Roger Hollis join the dots.

Unaware of these nuggets, in October 1941 when there was 'no knowing when KASPAR's further information' would arrive, one D. Griffith – a colleague of Miss Bagot – felt that they could not 'hold the case up any longer' and advised that if anything serious should come to light about Fuchs later, 'we should consider the cancellation of his permit'.[38] Hedging against the possibility of MI5 having to carry the can someday, Griffith suggested that in the meantime it would 'be as well to warn the M[inistry of] A[ircraft] P[roduction] of this man's Communist connections'.[39]

The lack of urgency within MI5 reveals what with hindsight is obvious: they had no idea of the singular nature of Peierls and Fuchs' work. Most of all, the perceived enemy was not the Soviet Union but Germany. Ironically Fuchs' history of anti-fascism and his status as a refugee from Nazi persecution were in his favour.

Communism nevertheless remained a spectre for the British Security

Services. Following Griffith's advice to alert MAP about Fuchs' communist connections, on 10 October J. O. 'Joe' Archer of MI5 – husband of Jane Sissmore – phoned Mr W. Stephens, head of security at the Ministry. Given that Fuchs was German, and in Archer's words had 'some connection with the Communist Party', Archer asked Stephens whether it would be 'really serious if information about this work left the country'. Archer added that it was more likely 'information would go to the Russians than to the Germans'. Stephens had a delicate judgement to make and, hoping for a safe way out, he replied that he would like to consider whether 'someone other than Fuchs' could be employed on this particular work. Archer agreed this was 'the crux of the matter', and that if the work could not be done without Fuchs they should 'have to accept such risk as there might be'.[40] We don't know whom in MAP Stephens consulted, but five days later he gave Archer their answer: 'Dr Fuchs' assistance is urgently required at present, and since he will have knowledge only of a small part of the work as is necessary for the performance of his duties, we think that there will be no objection to employing him.'[41]

Here Stephens and Archer were victims of the intense secrecy surrounding MAUD. Stephens was aware that the project was active in several institutions around the United Kingdom, but didn't realize how intimately their investigations were entwined. For example, experiments at Liverpool University's nuclear cyclotron tested the theoretical assumptions made in Peierls and Frisch's original memorandum; together with work on chain reactions at Cambridge, these refined the estimates of the critical mass of $U235$ and hence the magnitude of the challenge facing the diffusion facility. Experiments on diffusion in Oxford then tested the Birmingham theorists' calculations, the results in turn setting new challenges and refinements in the design.* Finding the answers is the goal, of course, but the most difficult part of research can be in identifying the right questions. To do this effectively required an understanding of the whole programme. Recall that Peierls himself had said that if he was not allowed to take Fuchs into his confidence, Fuchs would be of no use to him.†

The mandarins at MAP were ignorant of this profound organism, as were the officers in MI5, who knew only that what they were overseeing was top secret. Stephens compounded the perception that there would be

---

* A major decision about the design, taken early on, was that gaseous rather than thermal diffusion would be more effective. This was determined before Fuchs joined. As a result he was unaware of it in 1944 when his Soviet contact in the United States – who had experience in thermal diffusion – raised the concept in conversation, with fateful results; see chapter 21.
† See chapter 4, note 3, 13 November 1978 letter to Andrew Boyle, Peierls papers, Bodleian Library, File D53, and note 5, Peierls, *Bird of Passage*, p. 163.

a firewall with the assurance, 'We will again [*sic*] bring to the attention of the Birmingham authorities the necessity for the minimum disclosure to Fuchs.' He added a gentle nudge as a handwritten afterthought, 'and we should be glad if the necessary formalities could be expedited.' Archer duly recorded that there was no objection to the issue of an Aliens Work Service permit, and this was completed on 18 October.[42]

By this stage Fuchs had been working with Peierls for nearly half a year, had visited the Tube Alloys team at Cambridge University, and already passed on information about the Frisch-Peierls Memorandum and progress with enrichment of U235 to the Soviet Union in his August meeting with Kremer.[43]

By November 1941 his freedom in the United Kingdom fully approved, Klaus Fuchs had become a settled part of the British scientific fight against Hitler.[44] One consequence was that now he could travel without prior need of permission from the police. Almost immediately Fuchs went to London, anxious to know what had become of the information that he had handed over to Kremer back in the summer and to check whether the secret of his role was secure. In a remarkably risky breach of normal procedure, he contacted Kremer by telephone more than once.[45] A GRU memoir even suggests that Fuchs went to the Soviet Embassy, unannounced, to find Kremer, and delivered forty pages of notes on the state of the atomic bomb programme in the United Kingdom.[46] Fuchs was exceptionally fortunate that MI5 did not identify him as a result of this visit, or by intercepting one of his phone calls, and end his espionage in its infancy. His behaviour shows that this exceptional theoretical physicist was still very much an amateur at espionage.

The sole clue to Fuchs' stress was that when he returned home to Birmingham after a liaison with a Soviet contact, he would develop a nasty cough. Years later, after his double life had become known, Genia Peierls would claim that she could in retrospect pinpoint his spying activities by this cough: 'He didn't usually have much temperature or practically any temperature but he would lie in bed and cough, looking very miserable and very depressed.' In her opinion it was 'psychosomatic self-punishment', which was 'probably subconscious, and because he was feeling bad that he was betraying his friend and I was looking after him'.[47]

DIFFUSING DIFFUSION

Thanks to his natural intelligence Fuchs' spycraft quickly improved. During his first six months as a spy, he passed documents to the Soviets on several occasions, though the precise number is uncertain.[48] Fuchs' normal procedure at this stage seems to have been to make contact with a courier, most likely Brigitte Kuczynski, sister of Jürgen. Fuchs later described Jürgen's flat in Lawn Road, Hampstead, as 'my secret residence'. If he were seen by MI5 in the vicinity of the house, he would have a perfect explanation: visiting a German friend. At his first meeting with Kremer in August 1941, Fuchs had handed over six pages of information. Russian GRU archives show that in December Fuchs delivered a report that ran to forty pages and that by July 1942, when Kremer was recalled to Moscow, Fuchs had given him some 200 pages of information.[49]

The MAUD report of August 1941 had defined the immediate milestones and during the next year Fuchs was able to report on progress with designs for a diffusion plant, of measurement of the fission cross section of U235, and on the estimate of the critical size for U235 to become explosive. In this case, at least, Fuchs was able to report on his own work, as it was his calculations in 1941 and 1942 that turned out to be the most accurate theoretical predictors of the critical size.[50] The chemical properties of 'hex' were being investigated in order to find the best way to work with this highly corrosive gas. There had been decisions about the nature of the membranes through which the gas diffuses, the optimal strategies for pumping hex through the plant, and how to recycle the gases as they became progressively enriched during their journey through the sequence of stages. Much of this involved mundane, repetitive work, which scientists in the Soviet Union could have replicated in due course for themselves, but Fuchs' regular updates from England saved them considerable time and expenditure, at the very least.

He was able to tell them that the United States too was interested in the opportunities with uranium, although they were far behind the United Kingdom, not least because the USA was neutral and not driven by the imperatives of war. Norman Feather and Egon Bretscher, a Swiss-born British physicist working at Cambridge, had theorized that plutonium, which could be 'bred' in a nuclear reactor, would be more fissile than U235, and thereby be a novel way to creating an atomic weapon. In California, Ernest Lawrence had managed to make microscopic traces of plutonium in the Berkeley cyclotron and confirmed Bretscher's prediction that plutonium-239 has a fission cross section larger than U235.[51] In addition, Lawrence was investigating a third way of separating U235 by the use of electromagnetic forces. When electrically charged atoms move through a magnetic field their paths curve in circles whose radii depend on the masses of the atoms. A light isotope, such as U235, will follow a smaller circle than the heavier U238, for example. Lawrence found that this 'centrifugal' effect could isolate the precious U235, at least in the laboratory. Whether it could prove viable for the amounts required for a weapon remained to be seen.

By the start of 1942 Fuchs was able to pass along news about progress in the United Kingdom, from first-hand knowledge, and in the United States, also thanks to exchanges of information between MAUD scientists and American colleagues. These contacts were the result of talks between Prime Minister Churchill and President Roosevelt. Within a year the exchange of scientific information would inspire the collaborative 'Manhattan Project' to build an atomic bomb in New Mexico (see chapter 6).

A SCHOLARLY BRITISH GENTLEMAN

The fourth occasion when Fuchs' background came under scrutiny from MI5 was in the spring of 1942, when he applied for naturalization.[52]

Fuchs' petition stated that he wished to become a British citizen because the United Kingdom had 'given him refuge, a livelihood, and personal freedom'.[53] The Home Office checked with MI5, who replied that they had 'certain records of this applicant' but before giving a considered opinion on his suitability for naturalization from a security point of view, 'would be grateful to see your papers in case there are fuller details available regarding his present activities and mode of life'.[54] MI5 was hedging its bets. It wanted more information about Fuchs, especially 'a police report showing whether he has taken any recent interest in politics'. An internal MI5 memorandum also commented: 'It would be interesting to know why his naturalization would be "in the national interest".'[55]

In an extract from the Home Office file on Fuchs, the Chief Constable of Birmingham reported much as he had the previous year: there was nothing known to Fuchs' detriment. Fuchs spoke excellent English, German and French. 'Discreet enquiries' revealed that 'if he still has any interest in politics it is not an active one and he has not been known to associate with Communists in this District.'[56] The Chief Constable added, 'he says himself as one given hospitality by this country it was his duty not to take more than a passive interest in affairs'. Based on this assurance, that Fuchs had taken no part in politics in the United Kingdom, the vetting officer deemed there was no reason 'from the Communist point of view' to object to the application.[57] On 7 August 1942 Klaus Fuchs became a British citizen and thus no longer of particular interest to MI5.[58] He was now free to be a mole within Peierls' scientific establishment.

Another missed opportunity linked to KASPAR came to light years later. In 1942 a British intelligence agent named Robert Fischer infiltrated the '70 club', a group of communists in Birmingham. In anticipation of the James Bond novels, he obtained its membership list 'after having incapacitated its female secretary to start with by alcohol'. (The significance of 'to start with' was not explained.) The said list included the name of Klaus Fuchs, which could have proved seminal had it been made known to the relevant authorities at the time. Fischer passed this to an intermediary code-named 'Victoria', who was following leads on both Klaus Fuchs and his brother Gerhard. Gerhard had lived in Prague, and the file reports that Victoria 'does not remember if the report went to the Czechs or to [KASPAR]'.[59] Presumably it was to the Czechs, as no record of this derring-do appears on released files until 1950, long after the damage had been done.

For eight years from the summer of 1941, Klaus Fuchs would slip through MI5's wide-meshed net. Later, in 1949, when he had come under suspicion, MI5 reviewed Fuchs' history. It cleared itself of oversight: 'The Birmingham Police report (in connection with his application for naturalization) adduced nothing to the detriment of Fuchs' character, describing him as a man known to his colleagues as gentlemanly, inoffensive and a typical scholar.' The police had stated that if Fuchs still had any interest in politics it was not an active interest, and 'he was so absorbed in his research work as to have little time for political matters. He had not been heard to discuss either domestic or international politics or to associate with Communists in the Birmingham district. He himself had said that having been offered hospitality by this country, he conceived it his duty not to take more than a passive interest in political affairs.'[60] Fuchs was being doubly diligent in doing his 'duty': the Soviet Union specifically required its agents to avoid overt support for the Communist Party.

6

The Atomic Industry

Back in the spring of 1940 German victory seemed possible. Few in the United Kingdom could see how Britain could emerge victorious, with defeat likely after a long drawn-out conflict. Against this background Peierls and Frisch's discovery that an atomic bomb might be possible offered hope for a 'decisive weapon' that might tip the scales.[1] A year later, after Hitler invaded Russia, the alliance with the United Kingdom gave new hope, so long as Russia could withstand the Nazi army. But as fighting on the Eastern Front became ever more bloody and over a million Soviet troops lost their lives, Russia's presence in the war seemed likely only to delay an inevitable Nazi victory. The trump card of an atomic bomb was still years away, and unlikely to be ready in time. Furthermore, British scientists worried that Germany too might be developing nuclear weapons. Churchill desperately wanted the United States to join the fray as an ally. To this end, in July 1940 he authorized a mission to give the Americans a dowry: information about some of Britain's most valuable technical secrets that might help the US military.[2]

Scientists in the United States had been studying nuclear fission themselves, of course. The discovery in 1938 that the splitting of uranium atoms potentially releases vast amounts of energy naturally led scientists to investigate how this energy could be controlled and put to use. The design of a heat engine – a nuclear reactor – is an obvious example of such use that was independent of a war. As a natural phenomenon, uranium fission demanded investigation. The United States formed a Uranium Committee, which included a National Defence Research Committee (NDRC) chaired by Dr Vannevar Bush, Vice-President of MIT and science policymaker in Washington, assisted by Dr James Conant, the President of Harvard University.

As soon as the idea of a chain reaction in uranium was mooted, Enrico Fermi, at Columbia University, investigated whether graphite could slow neutrons enough to achieve this. His first results looked promising, and in October 1939 he decided that uranium-235 should be separated from natural uranium in order to determine which of the isotopes – U235 or U238 – caused fission with slow neutrons.

As a first step to finding the answer, Fermi wrote to Alfred Nier at the University of Minnesota, who had a mass spectrometer, a device that uses electromagnetic forces to separate ions of different masses, such as U235 and U238.* Fermi asked him to separate some U235 this way, which Nier did by using uranium tetrafluoride, a green crystalline solid compound of the element. He made his first separation on 29 February – he recalled the date later because 1940 was a leap year. It was a Friday afternoon. He pasted little samples of U235 onto pieces of nickel foil and attached them to the margins of a handwritten letter, which he sealed in an envelope. He reached the Minneapolis post office at about 6 p.m., in time for the precious package to be transmitted to Fermi in New York by airmail, special delivery. Fermi received it on the Saturday and set to work, irradiating the uranium with neutrons from the Columbia University cyclotron.

Early on the Sunday morning Nier was woken by his telephone. One of Fermi's team, John Dunning, had worked through the night taking measurements. The U235 sample was excellent, and the results showed clearly that U235 is the isotope responsible for slow neutron fission – as Niels Bohr had theorized.[3]

The proof that U235 was indeed key had an unexpected consequence: American scientists doubted that a chain reaction would be possible in natural uranium, where the U235 content is so small. They felt no great urgency to pursue this question – the United States was not at war – and awaited the results of Fermi's large-scale experiments on natural uranium and graphite at Columbia University. Fermi judged that the irradiation of uranium by slow neutrons could be a possible future source of power but would have no military use – the amounts of U235 required would be huge and impractical, and its nugatory presence in natural uranium provided a natural damper of the energy release. This was the received wisdom when Archibald 'A. V.' Hill arrived in Washington from the United Kingdom, on 22 March 1940, as yet unaware of Frisch and Peierls' breakthrough.

'I HAD TO TAKE SLEEPING PILLS'

The United Kingdom, meanwhile, was fighting for its survival. The war effort gave its scientists an 'intensity and purpose' that was absent in the

* The principle is that described on page 82.

United States.[4] While Peierls was overseeing the theoretical work through-out the United Kingdom, the national experimental programme was organized by James Chadwick, the Nobel laureate who had discovered the neutron, which is the key particle in initiating a chain reaction. This dapper, hard-working scientist also showed his brilliance as an administrator of science. Like many experts, he initially thought that nothing would come of the atomic project until after the war. Then, in the spring of 1941, as a result of experiments on the separation of uranium isotopes and the theoretical analyses driven by Peierls, British scientists found that it was possible to extract the fissile U235 from naturally occurring uranium. What's more, the costs of doing so made this method of diffusion practical. In Chadwick's opinion this made the atomic bomb not just possible but 'inevitable'.

This judgement raised the stakes dramatically. Fears spread that the Germans might possess the weapon. Indeed, so profound was the anxiety experienced by those aware of what might be happening that, as Chadwick recalled: 'I had to take sleeping pills; it was the only remedy.'[5]

The quest for a bomb was of primary importance, and it occupied the bulk of the MAUD report in 1941, but the potential use of fission as a source of energy was a long-term goal also. Its undoubted commercial potential excited ICI, who were involved in the chemical engineering of the diffusion project. ICI's management doubted that the United States, still neutral, would make rapid progress and saw their company's involvement with the MAUD project as a means to commercial advantage post-war.

Following the MAUD report, in September 1941 Winston Churchill authorized a top-secret development project to go ahead under the bland code name 'Tube Alloys'. Wallace Akers, a senior executive of ICI, was appointed its manager. He was excellent at his job, but his ICI background would later hinder smooth collaboration with the Americans, who distrusted his split loyalties. Tube Alloys' technical committee consisted of a Dr Slade from ICI and four MAUD scientists, one of whom was Peierls.[6]

When the British shared the MAUD report with the United States that September, Vannevar Bush and James Conant were impressed, not least by the startling news of Peierls and Frisch's breakthrough and the British belief that a bomb was feasible. No one in the United States had forseen this conclusion, which had 'escaped some of the most distinguished scientists in the world'.[7] Bush and Conant immediately sent two leading scientists involved with uranium research, Professors Pegram and Urey, across the Atlantic to learn about research in the United Kingdom, in line with President Roosevelt's brief to encourage 'exchange of information on recent scientific developments of importance to national defence'.[8] Scientific opinion in the United Kingdom was split: several scientists were keen to cooperate, but Chadwick was cautious.[9]

On 11 October President Roosevelt proposed to Churchill that the work of MAUD and United States' scientists 'be coordinated or even jointly conducted'.[10] At this stage Britain was the leader in nuclear physics, and Lord Cherwell advised Churchill against sharing its know-how with America. The Prime Minister, who desperately wanted the USA in the war but who also believed that any bomb should be totally British, blew hot and cold on the American advances. In November, with an irony that would only become clear much later, Sir John Anderson – a member of Churchill's War Cabinet – advised that before the British collaborated with the United States, the Americans 'needed to improve their security so that it was on a par with Britain's'.[11]

On 7 December 1941 Japanese aircraft attacked the American fleet at Pearl Harbor. This finally brought the United States into the war, allied with the United Kingdom and Soviet Union, against Japan and the European fascist axis of Germany and Italy. What some in the USA had dismissed previously as a remote European conflict was now truly a world war. The news from Great Britain that an atomic bomb was viable raised fears that Germany too could be developing the weapon. If so, defeat would mean subjugation by a global hegemony greater than any before, like the Roman Empire but with atomic weapons to enslave and dominate. If Nazi scientists won the race to build an atomic bomb, Hitler's dream of a thousand-year Reich could no longer be easily dismissed.

Churchill visited Roosevelt immediately, to show solidarity with the Americans. The President's welcome couldn't have been warmer. He met Churchill at Washington's new National Airport on 22 December and hosted him at the White House. They discussed strategy late into the night, lubricated by liquor. On Christmas Eve Churchill joined the President for the ceremonial lighting of the White House Christmas tree, and two days later he addressed Congress with a bravura speech. The British Prime Minister lived in the White House like 'one of a big family', so much so that on one occasion the President entered the room to find Churchill, fresh from a bath, pacing up and down while dictating memos, completely naked. Churchill greeted his visitor: 'You see Mr President, I have nothing to conceal from you!'[12]

During those precious days and nights, the two leaders agreed their nations' joint strategy for the war. However, Churchill did not mention the atomic bomb, which left Roosevelt with the impression that the British didn't think it to be important. Within days of Churchill leaving the United States, on 19 January 1942 Roosevelt 'approved a secret proposal to build a bomb'.[13] America now proceeded with gusto to develop an atomic weapon.

In 1941 the United Kingdom had built on Peierls and Frisch's breakthrough and established a lead in the race to build an atomic bomb. They had made an experimental investigation of U235 enrichment in trials at Oxford, and were well advanced in the theoretical workings of a uranium bomb, thanks especially to Peierls and Fuchs. This is why Churchill had avoided sharing information on the atomic bomb with the Americans. During 1942, however, the initiative shifted to the United States.

FERMI'S PILE

Tube Alloys' manager, Wallace Akers, was a good listener, charismatic, and full of energy. He proved to be ideal to oversee the vast industrial project that building a bomb would entail. He quickly saw that this was unrealistic in the United Kingdom and that a merger with the American project would be necessary.

In January 1942 the leaders of the American project invited Akers, Franz Simon and Peierls to visit, together with Hans Halban, a French physicist now working in England, who had been the first in Europe to establish the possibility of a chain reaction. The quartet set off on 21 February.[14] The four scientists soon discovered that, whereas the United Kingdom led in the *theory* of nuclear weapons, the United States was far ahead *experimentally*. Britain was under siege, and had to make the best of strained resources; meanwhile America had immense productive capacity, which enabled it to pursue expensive development work. So whereas the UK was focused on gaseous diffusion, together with some small studies of centrifugal separation, the USA was actively pursuing four approaches on a much bigger scale. It was building test plants for gaseous and thermal diffusion in Columbia University, New York, electromagnetic separation at Berkeley, and a centrifugal plant in Virginia, with the goal of seeing which worked best.[15] What took the British by surprise, however, was that the United States was also enthusiastic about a fourth route to a weapon, using the newly discovered element: plutonium.

In the United Kingdom, plutonium had been relegated to the background; the theory that it could be fissile was speculative and some MAUD scientists doubted that it would be suitable for a weapon. Even if it were adequate, to produce plutonium would require a nuclear reactor, which itself seemed a major enterprise and a long-term project for peacetime, rather than a priority for the war effort.

To make plutonium from uranium required neutrons much more powerful than the United Kingdom could produce with the technology at Liverpool or Cambridge Universities. In the United States, however, the Berkeley cyclotron had the capacity, and already in March 1941 Berkeley scientists had secretly demonstrated that the plutonium isotope 'Pu239' was fissile with a larger fission cross section than U235. Plutonium would eventually prove to be the fuel for the first atomic explosion.

In Chicago the British team learned that research into plutonium was already well underway. They also met Fermi, who was by then designing a prototype nuclear reactor. Fermi's initial experiments at Columbia University had convinced him that a chain reaction could be maintained, at least in theory. Now, in Chicago, he planned to build a machine to demonstrate this in reality by creating a self-sustaining chain reaction using neutrons and uranium. A second goal would be to produce plutonium.

Fermi's reactor was built from solid uranium oxide, in lumps the size of tennis balls, encased in blocks of graphite. The role of the graphite was to slow the neutrons and thereby increase their efficiency for creating fission in the uranium. The graphite blocks were stacked in a pile, which led to the colloquial description of this type of nuclear reactor as a 'pile'. Fermi's experiment would prove to be the most significant development in nuclear physics, short of the actual explosion of the atomic bomb itself.

The message for the British scientists was clear: the Americans were making real progress developing the technology for a weapon, whereas in the United Kingdom research was driven by theoretical expertise but practical advances were at the margins. In June 1942 Akers' assistant, Michael Perrin, visited the United States and within four days of his arrival reported progress to be 'enormous'.[16] On 17 June, Vannevar Bush gave an upbeat account of progress to Roosevelt. He told the President that five basic methods for preparing a bomb were being investigated and that the construction of pilot plants could soon prepare the scientists for the design of production facilities. Under ideal conditions, Bush asserted, this might lead to a weapon 'ready in time to influence the outcome of the present war'. In reality, as the Uranium Committee members agreed the following week, centrifuge and diffusion pilots were not yet ready, and it might be some time before plants were designed. Nonetheless, there was real focus to the work and commitment to the goal: 'To provide our armed forces with a weapon that would end the war and to do it before our enemies could use it against us.' This required that the project move ahead 'with the utmost speed'.[17]

One consequence of Perrin's visit was that Akers recommended that Tube Alloys be fused with the American programme. Churchill's advisors, however, were 'in denial about American industrial and organisational capacity' and continued to insist that Britain was in the lead. Small wonder that Akers' memo to Churchill recommending that Britain merge with the American atomic programme said the UK's 'pioneer work is a dwindling asset' and 'unless we capitalise it quickly we shall be outstripped'. There was real danger that to refuse a merger 'would risk giving Germany the bomb first'.[18]

'SONYA'

During 1942 Kremer returned to Moscow. Bizarrely, with Kremer no longer in the United Kingdom, Moscow seems to have made no arrangement to maintain contact with their prolific atomic spy.

For Fuchs this was frustrating because he and Peierls had just made a big advance with the diffusion plant and produced their conclusions on the 'equilibrium time'.[19] This is an important parameter in determining how long a plant will take to produce enriched uranium of a required amount, and the answer was encouraging. Their report, which updated a preliminary version of 1941, was produced in May 1942 and, it seems, this prompted Fuchs to re-establish contact with the Russians.

In Birmingham, Fuchs had no secure links with the Communist Party, and so made use of his contacts from his time in Scotland. He knew two members of the underground German Communist Party working in Glasgow – Hugo Groff, a well-known communist and a former member of the Reichstag, and Hannah Klopstech, who was the Welfare Secretary in the Free German League of Culture and, unknown to Fuchs, a Soviet contact with the code name Marta.[20] At the end of May 1942 Fuchs had to travel to Stockton-on-Tees in the north of England on business with Tube Alloys, and took advantage of the visit to ask the Chief Constable of Edinburgh 'for permission to visit Edinburgh from May 30 to June 2nd'.[21] This was ostensibly to see Max Born, but it is clear that Fuchs made contact with his communist colleagues during the visit, as within days news of his approach had been passed to Jürgen Kuczynski, still the leader of the underground German Communist Party in the United Kingdom.*

* On 30 November 1950 Skardon interviewed Fuchs at Brixton Prison about Fuchs' initial contact with the Russian Intelligence Service in 1942 [sic]. The report says Fuchs 'instinctively

Kuczynski had been interned but released almost immediately, on 23 April 1940, following pressure from influential friends: his father was a political scientist at the London School of Economics with contacts in Parliament, who were lobbied to have Jürgen released. The Home Office consulted MI5, who 'believed [Jürgen] to be a communist' but for some reason wrongly claimed he was 'not a particularly red-hot communist'. When pressed further, MI5 hedged and said they were 'not prepared to say that if Kuczynski were released the safety of the state would be endangered'.[22] He was released. His family first heard the news from the brother of Clement Attlee, the leader of the Labour Party.

Jürgen Kuczynski was not a spy, but his sister Ursula was. She had moved from clandestine activities in Switzerland to England at about the same time as Fuchs returned from Canada. Separated from her first husband, she had married Len Beurton, a French-born naturalized British citizen. She was thus able to move to England, and settled with her father in Oxford. In May 1941 she became the GRU's head 'illegal' – a spy who operates outside the protection of the Embassy – in the United Kingdom, with the code name 'Sonya'.[23]

Ursula had young children, and smuggled part of her radio transmitter in a teddy bear. On one occasion, stopped by the local police, she informed the constable that the transmitter itself was a child's toy.[24]

In July 1942, on one of Ursula's visits to see her brother and family in London, Jürgen told her that he had been informed that 'a physicist by the name of F. had lost contact with a representative of the Soviet Embassy's military department, who called himself Johnson'.[25] Sonya sent a coded signal to Moscow, and was told to make contact with Fuchs.[26]

In October, she took the train to Birmingham, where she met Fuchs in a café opposite Snow Hill railway station. It is possible that Fuchs had met her already, at Jürgen's party in 1941, as he seems to have trusted her implicitly from the start. According to one report, at that first meeting

---

decided that the person through whom he should make contact was the head of the German Communist Party in the UK'. At that time Fuchs had 'casually met Jurgen Kuczynski on a couple of occasions and did in fact recognize him as the head of the party here'. Accordingly Hannah 'KLOPSTECH' arranged for Fuchs to see 'KUCZYNSKI', 'possibly at the Free German Club in Hampstead' (TNA KV 2/1879, s. 546a). What Fuchs described to Skardon was his renewal of contact that year following Kremer's departure and not his initial, 1941, encounter. It is possible that Fuchs has conflated events here, either because of memory lapses after the passage of nine years, or deliberately to obscure his true entrée into espionage in spring 1941 at the time of the Nazi-Soviet non-aggression pact. He met Kuczynski at the club in 1941; there appears to be no independent record that the 1942 meeting also took place there. His reference to 'a couple of occasions' is in accord with his visit to Kuczynski in April 1941, and their pre-war meeting in Bristol – see note 3 in chapter 5.

Fuchs handed over eighty-five pages of secret documents, including 'several reports by different scientists about their work on the Tube Alloys Project'.[27] All subsequent meetings were to take place 'in country roads near Banbury'.* During the final months of 1942, and throughout 1943, Fuchs and Sonya met at regular intervals near Banbury, always at weekends. She would come from Oxford by train in the morning, Fuchs arriving from Birmingham in the afternoon. One meeting was in Overthorpe Park, two miles east of Banbury, and within easy reach by bicycle or on foot.[28]

To arrange meetings they used a classic espionage technique of a 'letter-box'. Sonya found the hiding places and arranged the venues outside town in secluded places so she could use her bicycle. One hiding place was a spot in the undergrowth near the edge of a wood, where she dug a hole between the roots of a tree where messages could be exchanged. They could have completed their essential business in thirty seconds, but to avoid raising suspicion they masqueraded as a courting couple, walking arm in arm in the surrounding countryside. They never met in the same place twice, each assignation lasted less than an hour, and, Sonya later recalled, they became close, as she discussed many things – books, films, current affairs – with the 'sensitive and intelligent comrade' who was 'calm, tactful and cultured'. Klaus told her that he was pleased to be out of the city. Sonya recalled: 'No one who did not live in such isolation can guess how precious these meetings with a fellow German comrade were. Our common involvement in trading in danger also added to our feeling of closeness.' For Fuchs, a bachelor who was totally immersed in his work and who lodged with his boss's family, the meetings with Sonya were rare chances to be unguarded. At these meetings Sonya, a highly experienced spy who had worked for the GRU in China and Switzerland, was able to reassure Fuchs and hone his skills in espionage. Neither knew the other's address and, she remained sure, Klaus never knew that she was Jürgen's sister.[29]

Of course Fuchs had to cover his tracks with Peierls, and we can reconstruct one such occasion. On Thursday 8 July 1943 Peierls received a letter

* Fuchs to Skardon, TNA KV 2/1252, s. 518. Fuchs told Skardon that 'on one occasion she came to Birmingham and met in a café', but he does not specify it as their first meeting. Mike Rossiter, The Spy who Changed the World (Headline, 2014), p. 100, and Pincher, Treachery, chapter 19, both cite this as the first meeting, but give no source. Sonya refers to their first meeting in the countryside, and makes no mention of Birmingham. I have assumed that Birmingham was their first meeting, in line with Rossiter and Pincher, as a first contact with a stranger has, at the least, to have a clear location, a means of identification and of aborting the rendezvous if necessary, for which merging into a crowd has the advantage over exposure in open countryside.

from a Dr Hune-Rothery, who had written a book on atomic theory and asked Peierls whether Fuchs might like the job of checking its equations 'for a fee of about £10'. Peierls promised to ask Fuchs but explained: 'Fuchs is on holiday this week.' By the following Monday, 12 July, Fuchs must have returned because Peierls replied, 'I have now put the proposition to Fuchs, and as I feared, he does not feel he would be able to tackle the job.' That same day, Moscow was sent a shipment of information that came from Sonya's most recent meeting with Klaus Fuchs. Fuchs' 'holiday' would seem to have included a visit to Banbury.[30]

Fuchs successfully kept his duplicity hidden from the Peierlses, though there was one occasion when his mask may have slipped. At the end of 1942 there was a party on New Year's Eve at the Peierls' home. Genia, her natural extroversion oiled by the occasion, took the floor and sang Russian folk songs. Klaus Fuchs was overcome and Genia noticed him staring at her. There was only a four-year difference in their ages and his trancelike state disturbed her. Thinking that Klaus might be falling in love with her, she made a mental note to ensure this did not develop further. Years later, when it emerged that Fuchs' real love affair was with communist Russia, Genia recalled his look that evening and for the first time understood its significance.*

Between 1941 and the end of 1943 Peierls wrote nearly a hundred secret reports for Tube Alloys. He produced the majority alone; eleven were co-authored with Fuchs. One of these, produced at the end of 1942, would have been included in Fuchs' gifts to Sonya. It provided the basic formulae and data for determining the destructive power of an atomic bomb.[31]

By then the Tube Alloys team members were certain that neutrons create an explosive chain reaction in enriched uranium. The mantra was that a single atomic bomb would be equivalent to many thousands of tons of high explosive, but this conclusion came from a naïve scaling up the ratio of the energy released in the two types of explosion. In reality, there would be large differences in their natures, rendering the simple estimate inadequate. For example, in a chemical explosion the blast arises from the sudden expansion associated with the release of heat. This might be typically a few thousand degrees, whereas in a nuclear explosion the temperatures exceed a million degrees, which rips apart atoms in the air and alters the nature of the shock wave. In addition, the explosion would be much more rapid than in a conventional weapon. How might these differences affect the estimates of the bomb's destructive power?

---

* This event is recalled in Norman Moss, *Klaus Fuchs: The Man who Stole the Atom Bomb* (Grafton Books, 1987), p. 45. It appears to be a true record because Peierls' personal copy of Moss' book, which I now have, contains several pencilled critiques or corrections, but the account of this episode has drawn no comment.

The damage from an explosion is caused by the blast wave, a sudden change of pressure in the air akin to a gigantic sonic boom, which mechanically disrupts objects in its path. In a conventional explosion the wave propagates thanks to molecules in the air banging into one another like billiard balls. The individual atoms, however, tend to survive. By contrast, a nuclear blast occurs at temperatures of millions of degrees, akin to the heart of the sun where atoms are stripped of their orbital electrons – they are ionized. In order to calculate how a blast wave propagates through such a plasma – electrically charged gases of ionized atoms – you first need to know what percentage of atoms are ionized, and whether all their electrons are ripped away or just one or two. That is what Peierls and Fuchs were examining in 1942.

They studied the physics of nitrogen and oxygen – the main atomic elements in air – at temperatures up to 2 million degrees. In a tour de force of over sixty equations, with eight tables of numerical results, they computed how the amounts of ionization grew with temperature in the shock wave. This described the nature of the air – or what is left of it – on the high-pressure side of the wave, and computed various quantities needed for calculation of the wave's propagation. They already knew from work in March 1941 that a good amount of the energy in an explosion would be released before the bomb's material dispersed, the uranium shards became sub-critical and the nuclear reactions died. Put all of this together and the conclusion was that the bomb would indeed be as destructive as thousands of tons of TNT, on top of which there would also be a lethal release of radiation.

The collection of Tube Alloys papers established that an atomic bomb was a realistic goal. It was via Fuchs and Sonya that Moscow received news of effectively all the scientific data produced by the Tube Alloys project for over a year. Sonya later recalled that on one occasion alone Fuchs gave her 'a thick book of blueprints' – most probably drawings and formulae – more than a hundred pages long.[32] Thus Stalin, who Churchill and Roosevelt thought knew nothing, was aware throughout the last four years of the war of the atomic bomb project, and its enormity. The Russians duly gave the Allies' project the code name 'ENORMOS', and began work of their own.

AMERICA TAKES THE LEAD

A key technological development, which would move atomic power from theory towards reality, was already well advanced in Chicago where

Enrico Fermi had spent much of 1942 building and refining his prototype nuclear reactor. Fermi and a handful of colleagues manhandled 6 tons of uranium metal, 50 tons of uranium oxide and 400 tons of graphite into a pile 6 metres high. At 3.20 in the afternoon of 2 December 1942 Fermi achieved his goal when this 'pile' liberated energy at a steady rate of about one-half a watt, which was increased to 200 watts ten days later.[33] This demonstrated not only the validity of the theory of fission and chain reactions, but also implied that if his pile had contained $U235$ instead of the less reactive, naturally occurring uranium, much of Chicago would have been destroyed by an atomic explosion. Pursuit of an atomic bomb, based on $U235$, had moved out of the realm of the hypothetical.

Fermi's success also opened another route to an atomic weapon. In the process of liberating energy by, in effect, 'burning' uranium, the residue of atomic 'ash' contained the element plutonium. Recall that Egon Bretscher and Norman Feather, working at Cambridge in 1941, had identified plutonium as potentially an even better explosive fuel than $U235$. Experiments at Berkeley had confirmed their predictions and now Fermi had constructed a machine capable of producing the element. So nuclear reactors could breed plutonium as an alternative and potentially more effective fuel for an atomic bomb. With Fermi's breakthrough, the Manhattan Project was born.

Several American officials meanwhile suspected the 'wily British' and feared that after the war Tube Alloys' ICI managers would 'exploit the secrets and knowhow of the innocent American inventors'.[34] Suspicions of ICI were not helped by visitors' first sight on arriving in Tube Alloys outer office: a large map of the United Kingdom divided up into ICI sales divisions.[35] The British, on the other hand, felt no such power over the Americans; indeed, by the end of 1942 they were aware that without US help they could not build a full-scale separation plant to enrich $U235$. The United States held the initiative and in January 1943 proposed collaboration once more. In contrast to 1941, where the British lead gave Churchill leverage, the memorandum presented to the British in 1943 was a one-way street: knowledge would flow to the United States, but no information would return to the United Kingdom about atomic weapons, or the production of plutonium, which later turned out to be key to their operation. Furthermore, Britain would have to give up all rights to commercial and industrial development after the war.

The British response was somewhat puerile. Seemingly blind to the reality that the Americans were now key to the endeavour, Whitehall retaliated by forbidding its scientists to attend meetings in the United States. The Tube Alloys' team members had no idea of this political infighting; all they saw was that information from America had dried up. The United Kingdom had been shut out except in areas where British knowledge might be useful to the USA.[36] Meanwhile, Peierls was elected a Fellow of the Royal Society in the spring of 1943 and with this visible recognition of his scientific authority he warned that government indecision was causing him and his fellow scientists in Tube Alloys to lose momentum.[37] The British team, unable to build a full-scale separation plant on its own, was impotent.

THE HIGHEST DEGREE OF SECRECY

In May 1943 Major G. D. Garrett – MI5's security liaison officer within the Department of Scientific and Industrial Research – visited Birmingham University. He was impressed with the security measures taken by the various teams working on Tube Alloys and wrote a favourable report. Garrett included in the brief commentary that he spent two hours with Peierls, who had 'a staff of about eight' and ran the operation so efficiently that 'an outsider could gain no information as regards the project as a whole'.[38] Garrett, aware now of the singular importance of Tube Alloys, made a note in Fuchs' personal file that he was involved in work of the 'very highest degree of secrecy'.[39] This news was also passed to section F.2.a, responsible for monitoring the Communist Party in Great Britain, and then on to Milicent Bagot's team in section F.2.b.[40]

In February that year Bagot's colleague Daphne Bosanquet had filed the report from agent KASPAR that said that Klaus Fuchs had 'belonged to the German Communist Party' but had 'never achieved any prominence'. She had written a memo in March about Fuchs in which she concluded, 'He is believed to be still a Communist and to engage in the normal propaganda activities although he is not prominent politically and has a good personal reputation.'[41] Garrett's news that the importance of Fuchs' secret work was now deemed to be 'of the highest degree' caught her attention. So on 7 July she contacted Captain Dykes, MI5 field officer responsible for Birmingham.

Bosanquet told Dykes that since taking out an AWS (Aliens War Service) permit, MI5 had known Fuchs was engaged on secret research work but now had learned this to be 'work of the highest degree of secrecy and importance'. She included a copy of her March memo and added that, while this was not a police matter, could Dykes give an opinion on Fuchs, knowledge of his university contacts, and his address.[42]

Dykes' reply of 12 July has been removed from the files, but it seems to have quoted an opinion of the police that Fuchs was 'clever and dangerous'.[43] Bosanquet wrote back that 'there is no more we can do about Fuchs at present and as he has been in his present job for some years without apparently causing any trouble, I think we can safely let him continue in it'.[44]

Dykes, in the field, avoided the groupthink that seems to have pervaded head office in London. On 15 July 1943 he responded with a cogent observation. He was not impressed by reports that Fuchs had 'apparently caused no trouble' during the years in his present job: 'Surely the point is whether a man of this nature who has been described as being clever and dangerous should be in a position where he has access to information of the highest degree of secrecy and importance?' Then Dykes made his key point: 'He would not be likely to cause trouble but might well be expected to be passing information to undesirable quarters.' This clearly impressed someone, because an unknown hand has added a pencilled graffito of an exclamation mark in the margin of the file against this comment. Dykes suggested that a reference to the police might well be valuable but 'not, of course, conclusive'.[45]

Bosanquet agreed that it would be a 'good idea to ask [the police] whether they could give us any details about FUCHS in view of his important employment'. Dykes must have done so as the chief constable wrote to him on 28 July, and attached a three-page report on Fuchs that had been supplied at the time of his naturalization. The response came that there was 'nothing to [Fuchs'] detriment'. Once again, the fact that the information about his being a communist originated from the German consulate rendered it 'possibly biased'.[46]

Nonetheless, MI5 decided to intercept Fuchs' post to see whether he was getting 'any letters of interest'.[47] This revealed nothing, literally – a fortnight passed without a single letter. Fuchs was not a social being. Now in his thirties, he had no girlfriend (the trysts with Sonya were of course a sham), nor did he appear to have any friends at all other than his inner circle of scientific colleagues. In short, he was a loner. Today such a profile could be enough to attract attention; in 1943, however, MI5's naïve conclusion was: 'It seems unlikely that he is in close touch with anyone of interest.' A handwritten postscript from Hugh Shillito – head of MI5's Russian desk in the counter-espionage section – endorsed this view. Shillito had experienced major success during the war in breaking a GRU spy ring, but on this occasion he made what must be one of the worst judgements in MI5's history: 'I do not regard Fuchs as likely to be dangerous in his present occupation.'[48]

His 'occupation' was as Peierls' assistant in establishing what was needed to make an atomic bomb. By the end of 1943 the British team was sure that it had defined the best large-scale combination of parts and configurations for the enrichment of U235 in a diffusion factory. Peierls had directed work on the mathematical physics of the actual bomb's explosion – the propagation of blast and shock waves, the efficiency of the explosion, and how best to achieve a super-critical configuration of uranium from subcritical pieces.[49] Much of this had been done with Fuchs' assistance; all of it was known and understood by Fuchs.

By this stage Fuchs had been passing information to Moscow for two years, first via Kremer and now, actively, via 'Sonya' – Ursula Kuczynski (Beurton). Although MI5 already had a file on Ursula – sister of a leading communist – no one made the connection between them until years later after Fuchs had been arrested and she had fled to East Germany.[50] Once again he had slipped through their net.

SECRETS AND STALIN

In addition to all this top-secret work for the British government, Peierls had continued to do his public duty as an auxiliary fireman. As early as 1942, however, the demands of Tube Alloys were already causing him to attend meetings away from Birmingham at short notice, such as his secret visit in January 1942 to the United States, which interfered with his fire duties. On 22 July the divisional officer of 'C' Division of the National Fire Service sent Peierls a letter about irregular attendance on NFS duty, pointing out that he had been present in June for only thirty-five hours, below the stipulated amount of forty-eight. On 24 July Peierls replied to explain that he was 'very fully occupied on work of national importance involving frequent absence from Birmingham, and work that often has to be carried out at night'. Peierls had explained this to the then commander when he joined, and offered his resignation at the very beginning 'if he felt that the limited amount of duty I was still able to do was of no use to this service'. Peierls added that he was 'surprised to discover from your communication that in June this amounted to as much as 35 hours'.

Now Peierls offered his resignation again, if he were unable to achieve the required forty-eight hours. He added: 'The future development of my work may quite possibly make it necessary for me to be released from NFS duty altogether in a few months time, but I was trying to remain as long as possible so as to be available for any serious raid occurring before then.'[51]

Peierls had been aware since the start of 1943 that development of an atomic bomb would be a vast industrial project, which would involve the construction of nuclear reactors, electrical power stations and diffusion plants hundreds of metres in length. Keeping the infrastructure out of reach of German aircraft, and maintaining secrecy, would require moving the British effort to the United States. On 19 August 1943 Churchill and Roosevelt signed the 'Quebec Agreement' in which the United States agreed to resume collaboration with the British on the bomb. Britain was very much the junior partner, however, as in order to forge the agreement Churchill had given America a veto on the development of nuclear power in the United Kingdom.[52] The fundamental truth was that United States taxpayers were footing the bill for the Manhattan Project, and this dictated the terms. Whereas in January the British had ignored American proposals that it give up commercial rights to atomic energy after the war, now the United Kingdom was at a disadvantage. The positive for Churchill was that Roosevelt had committed, in writing, to allow the involvement of British scientists in the Manhattan Project.

James Chadwick, the scientist who discovered the neutron and now oversaw Tube Alloys research, was a realist. He saw that the United Kingdom could never compete with the United States and that it was vital to 'acquire the fullest possible knowledge and experience of the project' so that when work eventually started post-war in England, the UK could benefit from the American experience.

Within hours of the Quebec Agreement being signed, Peierls and a handful of senior Tube Alloys scientists arrived in the United States in 'indecent haste' to discuss progress with their American counterparts in preparation for a move.[53] (The accusation of 'indecent haste' is apposite: Peierls had been making preparations to visit the USA as early as 10 August,[54] a week before Churchill and Roosevelt had met to sign the agreement.[55]

The two nations agreed in September that a number of British scientists should transfer to the United States to assist the Americans.[56] As to the duration of this secondment, there was no certainty other than it was 'expected to be long'. As a result the scientists were allowed to take their families. On 17 November the Department of Scientific and Industrial Research submitted applications by teleprinter for Rudolf Peierls to travel as part of the official mission, and for Genia to accompany him. These were approved the next day.[57] There is no evidence that Peierls was vetted by MI5. It would appear that his continued work on Tube Alloys, which had been vouched for by his university vice-chancellor and Mr Perrin on his previous visit to the USA in August, implicitly assured the authorities of his reliability.[58]

With their eyes on the post-war era, Churchill and Roosevelt decided to keep all aspects of the atomic bomb and their collaboration a secret from the Soviet Union. Stalin had been aligned with Hitler until the summer of 1941. The German invasion of the Soviet Union had forced him to make an alliance with the United Kingdom, and later with the United States, but in Churchill's opinion this was but temporary political expediency. Communism remained an evil, but for now a lesser evil than National Socialism.

Not only did Stalin know exactly what the Western allies were up to, of course, Moscow Centre knew that their prime source of insider information was Klaus Fuchs. There were other scientist atomic spies, notably the chemist Engelbert Broda in Cambridge – whom Fuchs had recommended to Sonya in April 1943[59] – and Alan Nunn May at a nuclear reactor in Canada, but none matched Klaus Fuchs, not least because his association with Peierls placed him at the heart of the project. Fuchs' assignations with Sonya were destined to come to an end, however, when in November 1943 preparations were made for him to move with the British scientific mission to New York and ever closer to the heart of the Manhattan Project.

One of Sonya's final acts in England was to arrange a means for Fuchs to continue passing information from within the United States. She had lived in New York for a few months in 1928 and tried hard to remember some landmarks in order to arrange a location for him to meet a Soviet contact there. She chose the Henry Street settlement, at 256 Henry Street, where she had worked. It was a popular street for poor Jews on New York's East Side near where she had lived. She chose the settlement, found methods of identification and code names, briefed Fuchs, and forwarded the details to Moscow.[60] In return, Fuchs gave her instructions for contacting him through his sister Kristel, who lived in Cambridge, Massachusetts.[61]

'IT WILL WIN THE WAR'

Major Leslie Groves was a big man, nearly six feet tall, and very solid. His hips invisible beneath his ample girth, Groves' trousers resisted gravity through friction with his rotund midriff. By September 1942 Groves had spent two years in Washington DC in charge of all US Army construction in both the continental United States and its offshore bases. He had even overseen construction of the Pentagon building. Preparations were now in hand for Operation Torch – the British-American invasion of North Africa and the first major operation that the United States would undertake in Europe in the Second World War, and Groves was eager for service abroad, in charge of combat troops. On 17 September he learned that the Secretary of War had selected him for a very important assignment, and the President had approved. Groves, intrigued and excited, asked, 'Where?' only to be deflated by the reply: 'Washington'.

Prepared to be posted overseas and see some real action, Groves had no desire to stay at a desk-job in Washington. 'If you do the job right,' he was told, 'it will win the war.' As a further hint of the importance of the still-secret task, Groves learned that he would be promoted to Brigadier General.

His role would be to organize and coordinate the construction of an atomic bomb on behalf of the 'Manhattan Engineer District', which was the formal title of what has become known as the Manhattan Project. The background was explained to him as if the enterprise were a fait accompli. Groves was assured: 'The basic R&D are done. You just have to take the rough designs, put them into final shape, build some plants and organise an operating force and your job will be finished and the war will be over.' Groves recalled, 'Naturally I was sceptical,' but it was only later that he realized how over-optimistic the projections were.[62]

Optimistic indeed. The plans were that by March 1943 facilities would be in place for a nuclear reactor to breed plutonium, and for three plants to separate U235 – by centrifuges, by electromagnetic methods and by gaseous diffusion.[63] Groves described this as 'utterly unrealistic' because the basic research was so primitive that there were not even general design criteria to hand.

Groves' first meeting with Vannevar Bush was not a success. In Bush's opinion Groves didn't have 'sufficient tact' for the job and, Bush summarized: 'I fear we are in the soup.'[64] Bush need not have worried, however, for Groves was well chosen for the task: he was military through and through, a bulldog disciplinarian who would do whatever was needed to build an atomic bomb and win the war. Fortunately, from this nadir Bush and Groves rapidly became a formidable pair, and Groves' appointment of physicist J. Robert Oppenheimer to be Scientific Director proved to be an inspired choice.

Groves insisted that secrecy would be paramount and not even families were to know the nature of the work. His son, for example, was a cadet at West Point and was told to reply to any questions from his colleagues with a flat 'I never know what he's doing.' Groves realized that this might be a problem if an officer who knew him persisted; in such a case, Groves said his son could elaborate solely with 'I think it's something secret.' Like the families of many who were sucked into the Manhattan Project, Groves' own family first learned the nature of his work three years later, when the bombing of Hiroshima was announced to the world.

In his memoirs, Groves recalled, 'No one at the time anticipated a cost of billions of dollars' and added that in peacetime such a project would have been 'reckless in the extreme'. Groves had realized after that first meeting with Bush that this was a project for which no one had any experience and he would have to create the rules. As he remarked years later: 'Normally haste makes waste; for the Manhattan Engineer District, however, haste was essential.'

PART THREE

Manhattan Transfers: 1944–6

7

The New World

For General Groves, the goal of the Manhattan Engineer District – MED –
Project was the successful delivery of an atomic weapon before the enemy
themselves created one. Were the enemy to get wind of the project, steal
its knowledge by espionage and win the race, utter disaster could result,
so from the very start Groves fixated obsessively on security. This even
included control of the press.

The Office of Censorship would ensure that no sensitive information
leaked out in official and personal correspondence, but Groves worried
that even bland news could be of use to a well-informed member of the
enemy. He ordered nothing be published that might attract attention to
any phase of the project. On the one hand, censorship of local newspapers
near MED sites might draw notice and be counter-productive, but a news
blackout was especially important for any magazine or national newspaper
that was likely to be read by enemy agents or by people whose knowledge
of scientific progress would enable them to deduce what was going on. He
wanted no mention of places such as Oak Ridge* or Los Alamos, nor any
reference to the Manhattan Engineer District. Names of scientists that
might arouse the interest of foreign agents were also to be avoided.

Groves was wise to have anticipated this danger, but was unaware that
Russians had already deduced what was going on simply from checking
the open physics literature. At the start of 1942 the physicist Georgi Flerov
was in the Soviet army, about 300 miles from Moscow. One day, with a
few hours to spare, he went to the local university physics department to
see their magazines and learn what progress had been made with nuclear
fission. He flipped through the pages of the available Western journals
and found papers on a variety of topics, but surprisingly there was nothing
at all on fission. That was only half of it: not only had all mention of

---

* The Oak Ridge site was originally known as Clinton Engineer Works. The name Oak Ridge
did not come into use until after the war, but I shall use this familiar form to avoid confusion.

fission disappeared, but the leading nuclear physicists had also – Enrico Fermi, Niels Bohr and other luminaries had published nothing for several months. The explanation for the absence of papers, Flerov quickly realized, was that American research on fission had become secret. This also explained the disappearance of the nuclear scientists: they were working on a nuclear weapon.[1]

Flerov mused that at least the Americans and Soviets were on the same side in the war, but he worried that German scientists might have come to the same conclusion. Moreover, Germany had the means to enrich uranium. Flerov sounded the alarm by writing to Stalin in April 1942. What he didn't know, of course, was that Stalin was already aware of the state of the Allied programme thanks to Klaus Fuchs. This independent information probably convinced the paranoid leader that the GRU reports from the British scientist were genuine. And to complete the mockery, Fuchs was now en route to Groves' fiefdom.

'SECURITY WAS AN ESSENTIAL ELEMENT'

For the first year after Groves took responsibility for the Manhattan Project, internal security was supervised by Counter-Intelligence in the United States War Office, under the direction of Major General George Strong. In February 1942 Strong and Groves agreed on their responsibilities. The War Office undertook security for its civilian employees and all who were on any property under military control. The Manhattan Engineer District came under this heading.

The FBI, on the other hand, had focused during the 1930s on criminal gangs, notably bootleggers during Prohibition and bank robbers who crossed state lines. By 1940 the spectre of communist subversion increasingly concerned the Bureau. Early in 1943 this led to the first potential hiccup with maintaining the secrecy of the Manhattan Project.

The FBI had been investigating a scientist at Berkeley as part of its surveillance of Communist Party leaders in the San Francisco Bay Area, and through this enquiry had got wind of the Manhattan Project. General Strong asked the FBI to cease surveillance of the scientist, and had to tell FBI Director J. Edgar Hoover of the Project's existence, though not its object. Hoover was informed of the Army's plans to protect the Project, and agreed with Strong that the Army should continue with responsibility for MED security. Groves stressed, 'Security was an essential element, but not all-consuming.'[2]

As MED expanded and matured during 1943, the centralized

counter-intelligence focus in the War Office became unsuitable for maintaining MED security. A dedicated security force of MED 'creeps' was
formed, still ultimately responsible to the army, and by the end of the war
this corps was 485-strong. Throughout the war there was the fullest cooperation with the FBI. This was vital because the FBI had reams of valuable
background information on individuals, and in return MED was uncovering information that interested the FBI.

For Groves and the MED counter-intelligence force there was the question of whom they were to protect against. Of the enemy, Japan and Italy
were judged not to have the industrial capacity to construct a bomb, and
their intelligence channels to Germany were deemed poor, so it seemed
logical to protect MED from German espionage. Very soon after Groves
started, however, he learned from the FBI that the only known espionage
was by the Soviet Union, which was using American communists to infiltrate the Berkeley laboratory. The Russians were trying to get military
information, including intelligence about the Project, which led the FBI
to monitor the activities of Soviet Embassies and Communist Party groups.
Groves now made it his top priority to examine the communist sympathies
of MED staff.

During the next three years the Manhattan Project involved many
thousands of people, from world-famous scientists through technical staff
to office clerks, truck drivers, cleaners and more besides. It was utterly
impossible to make thorough checks on all of these. New people were kept
on non-secret parts of the work until hurried investigations could be
completed. Those without classified access were subjected to police checks
and their fingerprints compared to those on FBI files. Workers with access
to secrets were more carefully vetted, and in some cases their history was
examined back to childhood. Those employed in restricted areas filled out
security questionnaires, and if these raised any doubts a more thorough
investigation ensued. The Army made all of these first-level checks, the
FBI being consulted about fingerprints and in the cases where more
detailed examination was deemed necessary.

If there was an FBI record on any individual, it was compared with
that admitted to by the employee when hired. Most were no more than
traffic violations or drunkenness, but any discrepancies would lead to an
interview. Depending on the individual's attitude under questioning and
the need for their speciality, the candidate was then either retained or
discharged. There was an absolute rejection of anyone who had been
convicted of rape, arson or narcotics offences; such people were suspected
of having 'weak moral fibre' and to be liable to blackmail.[3]

Scientific workers came predominantly from the academic world. Those raised in the United States had been students during the years of the Great Depression when communist sympathies were prevalent, while scientific refugees from Europe were uniformly anti-fascist, a cause that had also attracted many to communism, as in Fuchs' case. These historic links made Groves worry that many scientists at the heart of the project – be they from Europe or America – might be sympathetic to the ideals of the Soviet Union. When he reviewed the personnel files, he found that a number of people in the Project had not received proper security clearance, even though some had been involved for several months. Among those whose employment was essential for the Project's success, Groves made a distinction between 'those whose use might be dangerous and [those] whose use would probably not be'.[4] He paid considerable attention to the length of time they had espoused communist sympathies and their closeness to the party line. In particular he assessed their reactions to the 'twists and turns of Soviet relations with Germany' and in doubtful cases this 'was a deciding factor'.

The FBI was Groves' backstop in vetting American scientists who would have the most sensitive access to the heart of the enterprise.* The arrival of twenty-three scientists from the United Kingdom, however, created a fresh difficulty, highlighted when Klaus Fuchs passed through all of these filters. Groves himself admitted later: 'Our acceptance of Fuchs into the Project was a mistake. But I am at a loss when I try to determine just how we could have avoided that mistake without insulting our principal war ally, Great Britain, by insisting on controlling their security measures.'

General Groves' paranoia about sharing information, even among the Project's scientists, added to the apparently secure firewall around the Manhattan Project and its eventual centre at Los Alamos, New Mexico. Yet neither Manhattan Project Security nor the FBI ever had a suspicion about Fuchs, nor the other spies, until the war was over and the damage had been done. Years later, after Fuchs' espionage had been exposed, Groves, the FBI and MI5 all disputed who was to blame for his admission to the Manhattan Project in the United States, and members of the US Congress fought over Groves' role in this failure. Groves was to insist that 'the British [never] made any investigation at all'. The British authorities had assessed Fuchs, but there was clearly a breakdown of communication between them and General Groves, which sadly included rank duplicity. This is what took place insofar as available documents allow the saga to be reconstructed.

---

* This was far from perfect as the later exposure of machinist David Greenglass and physics prodigy Theodore Hall, both at Los Alamos, along with numerous Americans at other centres of the MED, would reveal.

When Groves received the names of the British scientists coming to the United States he noticed that there was no mention of their reliability. Groves claimed in his memoirs that he told an (unnamed) British official he 'must have assurance that all have been properly cleared'.[5]

The British assessments of Fuchs were, with hindsight, fatuous. When Fuchs began work of a 'particularly secret nature' in the United States in 1944, MI5 re-examined his file. This began almost by accident in November 1943 when MI5 learned that Fuchs had applied for an exit permit. This had already been granted on 18 November and recorded in his file when Milicent Bagot's photographic memory revealed an anomaly in the paperwork: the exit application testified that Fuchs had been granted a certificate of naturalization fifteen months before, in August 1942.[6] Recall that her colleague Daphne Bosanquet had spent the summer of 1943 investigating Fuchs' communist affiliations, and her evidence had included a letter from the Chief Constable of Birmingham, which referred to Fuchs' application for naturalization. Now that Fuchs was a British citizen he would come under the watch of Michael Serpell – an expert in communist subversion from section F.2.a., whose responsibilities included monitoring the Communist Party in Great Britain. Bagot now drew his attention to the police chief's note. In a rare display of emotion in establishment minutes she commented, 'we knew that [Fuchs'] application for naturalisation was under consideration, but the [chief constable's] report did not say it was a fait accompli'.[7]

Serpell contacted Major Garrett to find out how long Fuchs would be in the United States.[8] (Fuchs was now in mid-Atlantic.) Garrett replied that Fuchs' name had not been on the DSIR's (Department of Scientific and Industrial Research) original list of workers going to the USA, and appeared to have been 'added at the last minute', but even so he assumed Fuchs would be there for several months at least, like the others. Serpell needed to be sure and asked Garrett to get a definite answer.[9] This was on 3 December, the same day that the British naval transport ship HMT *Andes* docked in Newport News, Virginia, with Peierls, Fuchs, and the rest of the British team on board.[10] The scientists then took a train to Washington, where General Groves briefed them about security, stressing that they must not discuss their work with anyone else in the Project other than their immediate team, and certainly not with their families. Lest they needed reminding, they were now subject to the law of the United States, where the penalty for committing espionage could be execution by electric chair. Suitably chastened, the scientists continued by train to New York.

Meanwhile, back in London, Garrett had passed Serpell's enquiry about Fuchs' status to Michael Perrin, who as Akers' assistant in the DSIR was the administrative head of Tube Alloys and the person best placed to know how long Fuchs would be in the United States. Perrin too was unsure but conjectured that Fuchs would probably be one of the scientists who would remain.[11]

That was the state of play on 8 December, by which time the British team members were settling in. The matter of security remained unresolved. Groves regarded British responses to his enquiry about clearances as inconclusive and in his memoirs written years later he recalled that he asked for 'a more definite one'.[12] FBI files confirm Groves' memory, as he requested 'formal assurance that all members of the British Tube Alloy organisation, who are now in the [United States], have been cleared by the British Security organisation for work on this project'. In response, Wallace Akers wrote to Chadwick – head of the British Mission – on 10 December to say that he could inform Groves: 'Special clearance is required in England for anyone who is brought into this work, even though they may already have been cleared for work on ordinary secret war projects.'[13] He then listed twenty-three names that had been so cleared, including those of Chadwick himself, Peierls and Fuchs. The following day this letter was forwarded to Groves, with a covering letter on behalf of Chadwick that assured Groves, 'all members of our present parties have been cleared by the British Security organisation in Great Britain'.[14] Groves was satisfied and in his memoirs summarized the reply as implying 'each member had been investigated as thoroughly as an employee of ours engaged in the same work.'[15]

Although Groves' memory two decades later was accurate on these issues, he glossed over one embarrassing matter. First, Groves' memoirs don't record that on 4 July 1951 he was criticized by Senator McMahon for 'fail[ing] to check the certificate of clearance given by the British when Groves admitted Fuchs to the project'.[16] Nor was Akers' response on 10 December the end of the investigation, for the British continued to look into Fuchs' background during January, and there were communications to and fro between Groves and the FBI over several weeks before the British scientists were finally cleared at the end of March.

Meanwhile the British had got down to physics immediately, long before Fuchs' clearance was completed. The urgency that Peierls had showed back in 1941, when Fuchs was deep into top-secret research for Tube Alloys many weeks before his security clearance came through, was now repeated in the United States. From 10 to 17 December, Fuchs and Peierls had meetings with American scientists at Columbia University in Manhattan and the Kellex Corporation* – a chemical engineering

---

* The name derived from Kell for Kellogg and X for secret.

subsidiary of the Kellogg Company in Jersey City – which had been developing the diffusion programme in the USA. They discussed specific
mathematical problems that were related to the control of the diffusion
plant. In addition, they arranged a symposium on the British treatment of
the equilibrium time – the time the enrichment of U235 takes to reach
equilibrium when the gas of isotopes diffused through the membranes –
and designs for the layout of the plant. On 14 December Fuchs gave a
lecture about his work at Birmingham.[17] On 21 December they spent
the whole day comparing the British and American results. Fuchs then left
to spend Christmas with his sister Kristel in Boston.

The New Year started with a plenary conference on 5 January, attended
by the full delegation of British scientists and their American colleagues.
General Groves presided and seems to have had no qualms about the presence
of any British delegate. The discussions covered all aspects of Oak Ridge's
construction, including the production schedule, the instrumentation
required, and the training of personnel.[18] As soon as this had ended, there
was a specialized conference on the control of the plant, and Fuchs 'dominated
the discussions because of his greater experience with gaseous diffusion'.[19]

Peierls, who was due to stay in the United States indefinitely, decided
that Fuchs' long-term presence would be invaluable and so he sent a telegram to Michael Perrin asking permission for Fuchs to remain there with
him. Perrin was aware that MI5 at one time had 'slight doubts' about
'some of Fuchs's connections', so on 10 January he asked Garrett for 'your
latest and most detailed views on the question of Fuchs, from a security
angle'. Perrin added that this was a 'very important matter vis-à-vis the
Americans and I want to be sure that we do not slip up in any way'.[20]

General Groves always insisted that the vetting of the British scientists
in the team 'was a British responsibility'.[21] In the case of Fuchs, Garrett
must have made enquiries, because a week later he received the advice from
which the fateful decision to keep Fuchs in the United States indefinitely
would emerge. The source is obscure; the memo, which originated on 16
January in Garrett's division, D.2 – Security and Travel Control – contains
an indecipherable signature, and mentions someone named 'Clarke'.[22]*

Garrett's informant first recommended that 'a full picture of FUCHS'
communist activity can be obtained from Serpell, F.2.a'. The rest of the
brief note deals with the opinions of Clarke. In the first of these Clarke
assessed: '[Fuchs] is rather safer in America than in this country and for

---

* The reference may be to David Clarke, who was in section F.2.a around this time and an
expert on the British Communist Party: see Christopher Andrew, *Defence of the Realm: The
Authorized History of MI5* (Allen Lane, 2009), p. 278. The signature is not that of Daphne
Bosanquet; contrast Mike Rossiter, *The Spy who Changed the World* (Headline, 2014), p. 119.

that reason [I am] rather in favour of [Fuchs] remaining in America', where he would be 'away from his English friends'. This judgement could have had some merit if the goal were to make life easier for people in MI5's British headquarters, but Perrin needed to assess Fuchs 'vis-à-vis the Americans'.

Clarke's second opinion parodically assessed, 'It would not be so easy for FUCHS to make contact with communists in America,' before adding presciently, 'In any case he would probably be more roughly handled were he found out.' In essence, Clarke's Anglocentric judgement amounted to: 'We [in the UK] have no reason to be concerned.'

Groves' reaction to this vetting would have been withering if he had learned of it, but Perrin never told him, and that was because Perrin himself was unaware of these manoeuvres. Instead, Perrin had received the following précis from Garrett: 'I have consulted the department which deals with such matters. It is considered that there would be no objection to this man remaining in the USA as he has never been very active politically, and recent reports endorse the good opinion you have of his behaviour in this country.'[23] Garrett's message to Perrin continued with a cosy assurance: it was 'unlikely that [Fuchs] would attempt to make political contacts in the United States'. Small wonder that Perrin took this as assurance that the Security Services had no reasons to oppose Fuchs' transfer to the United States.* Unsatisfactory as this was, it was as nothing compared to Garrett's outrageous closing statement, with which Groves and the FBI could have hung MI5 out to dry, had they ever been aware of it. Garrett told Perrin: 'It would not appear to be desirable to mention [Fuchs'] proclivities to the authorities in the USA.'

On 20 January there was a meeting in Washington between representatives of the FBI and the Manhattan Project. The FBI asked for a list of individuals whom the British had sent to the United States. They were promised a copy of the names but Groves warned the FBI, 'protocol prevented an inquiry into [their] backgrounds as they were sent to work in this country as a result of an agreement between President Roosevelt and Churchill'. Nothing happened, and on 25 February the FBI asked Groves once again. Finally on 28 March the FBI received a list of British scientists together with a letter stating 'all had been cleared by the British'.[24]†

Fuchs was now persona grata in the United States; for the next six years

* The judgement that Fuchs would be 'of less danger to security on the other side of the Atlantic' was later described with bureaucratic understatement as 'rather unsatisfactory'. (Michael Serpell, 11 November 1946, TNA KV 2/1245, minute 49; see also chapter 11).
† In a 1953 review this letter received a handwritten comment by Hoover: 'This case should serve to alert us re thorough handling of all [underlined] angles of matters in the future.'

his access to scientific conferences there would be based on that clear-ance.[25] At the very moment Garrett and Perrin were giving Fuchs' posting the all-clear and keeping the Americans in the dark, the atom spy was preparing for his first assignation with his new courier, who would be his intermediary with the Soviets for the next two years.

HARRY GOLD

In order to help maintain security, Fuchs and Peierls were given offices in the British Supply Mission, a government organization that occupied the twenty-fifth floor of a skyscraper at 37 Wall Street. Peierls later remarked that he 'felt like a real New York businessman, one of the crowd streaming into Wall Street every morning'.[26] For Klaus Fuchs, the committed com-munist, this location at the heart of capitalism must have been piquant.

Upon arrival in New York in December 1943, the British group stayed at the Taft Hotel on the corner of 51st Street and Seventh Avenue. Within a few days Fuchs moved to accommodation where he could have more privacy, at the Barbizon Plaza (today, the 340-apartment condominium known as Trump Parc) on the south side of Central Park. He expected to be there for at most a few weeks. However, by the middle of January 1944 Peierls' request that Fuchs stay and be part of the team in North America had been agreed. At the end of February, Fuchs moved into a furnished first-floor apartment in a four-storey dwelling at 122 West 77th Street.[27]

For someone used to the privations of England during the war, with its nightly air-raids, blackouts, and rationed food and fuel, New York in 1944 was a revelation. Street markets were adorned with fruit, vegetables and real meat; neon lights shone bright in Times Square; central heating was common; everywhere evoked a feeling of optimism and freedom. Meta-phorically as well as literally the war felt thousands of miles away. Yet the opulence appears not to have disturbed Fuchs' commitment to the com-munist cause: at the beginning of 1944 he followed Sonya's instructions and made contact with his new courier.[28]

The rendezvous was to be outside the Henry Street Settlement House on the Lower East Side of Manhattan, on 5 February at 4 p.m. Fuchs, no doubt mindful of General Groves' admonitions, avoided all risk. So cau-tious was he that he would not even ask directions from total strangers. Instead, he bought a map and worked out how to get to Henry Street by subway from the Barbizon Plaza.[29] Having successfully navigated sub-terranean New York, Fuchs climbed the steps from East Broadway subway station and emerged into the chill of a late afternoon in winter. Whereas

East Broadway itself was a reasonably well-lit main thoroughfare, Henry Street, a block to the south, was gloomy with a seedy air. In summertime, an avenue of leafy trees helped mask its run-down appearance, but in February their barren skeletal forms added to the sense of foreboding. The Settlement House was about three blocks east, and as Fuchs made his way along the sidewalk he must have presented a strange sight because while clothed smartly in a tweed overcoat, hat and scarf, which made sense in the cold afternoon, Fuchs prominently carried a green book and a tennis ball. A short stocky American approached him. The man was wearing gloves but also carried a second pair. Tennis balls and gloves: the match was made.[30]

The man, who suddenly appeared to be lost, asked Fuchs: 'What is the way to Chinatown?' Fuchs replied: 'I think Chinatown closes at 5 o'clock.'[31] The contact introduced himself as 'Raymond'. In reality Raymond was Harry Gold, a chemical engineer who was the son of Russian Jewish immigrants to the United States. Gold had turned to communism during the Great Depression, and had been recruited for industrial espionage by the Soviet Union in 1934. When the United States entered the war in December 1941, Gold had been assigned to the Soviet Union's military endeavour, which is how he came to be the contact for Klaus Fuchs. The pair walked a short distance along Henry Street, took a ride on the subway, and then Gold hailed a taxi. They drove uptown to 49th Street in the vicinity of Third Avenue where they had dinner at Manny Wolf's restaurant.[32]

Over dinner they spoke little, with Fuchs limiting himself to generalities about where he worked and lived. After they had eaten, it was dark. They took a short walk together and now, with more privacy, Fuchs gave 'Raymond' more information. Fuchs had no documents with him, he had after all only just started work in New York, but he filled in the details of the atomic project and the basic ideas of gaseous diffusion by which the Allies planned to enrich U235.

Fuchs knew nothing of Raymond's background, of course, let alone that his identity was really Harry Gold. Nonetheless, Fuchs deduced that his contact had a scientific background, or at least was already well informed, because Gold sought no clarification when Fuchs referred to 'atomic energy' or 'atomic bomb'.[33] They agreed to meet 'in two weeks' and parted. Gold also reported to Moscow that at that meeting Fuchs 'will have information for us'.[34]

Ten years later, Gold retained clear memories of this next meeting where Fuchs handed over his first package: 'It was cold and we both wore overcoats.'[35] Fuchs had brought with him some fifty pages of documents covering the team members' work on diffusion since their arrival in New York. To minimize the risk, the meeting place, on Madison Avenue in the 70s, was a short walk from Fuchs' apartment.[36] Gold recalled that they 'immediately turned into one of the dark deserted streets toward 5th [Avenue], and the transfer of information took place there. The whole affair took possibly 30 seconds or one minute, and I immediately walked ahead of KLAUS and down 5th Avenue toward 57th Street and 6th Avenue, where approximately 15 minutes later I turned over the information to JOHN.' 'John' was Anatoly Yatzkov, based at the Soviet Consulate in New York. Gold's meeting with Yatzkov was also brief, 'possibly a minute or so'.[37] Yatzkov then went to the Consulate and used the information as the basis for coded signals that were sent to Moscow.

The one important unknown about this meeting is the date. Gold remembered this as the third rendezvous, but at ten years' remove his memory seems to have inverted the second and third. KGB records have Fuchs transferring fifty pages at the second occasion and then at a meeting on 11 March asking Gold, 'How has [this] initial material been received?' So the handover appears to have been in mid-February, in line with their earlier agreement to meet 'in two weeks', and that of 11 March is the third.[38]

Gold replied that what Fuchs had given the Russians was 'completely satisfactory, but with one flaw: it lacked references to previous material pertaining to an overall description of the process, and what we needed was a detailed plan or scheme of the whole set-up.' Fuchs, not surprisingly, was 'not very pleased with this'. Not only had he already given this information back in England but he thought it 'would be dangerous if such explanatory material were found in his possession because his work [in New York] has nothing to do with such materials'. What Fuchs didn't know was that in his transition from Sonya to Gold he had moved from the control of the GRU to the KGB. Presumably the GRU had not passed over Fuchs' original material to his new masters. Nevertheless, Fuchs agreed to give Gold what he requested 'as soon as possible'.

On 11 March[39] it was already dark when they met at the corner of 59th and Lexington. Gold had specified the northeast corner where there was 'a bank with very tall colonnades, and . . . a subway entrance in the bank building itself'. They met 'directly under one of the first colonnades'.[40] Gold originally planned that they would walk across the Queensborough Bridge to Queens, but the bridge was closed, so they walked underneath it and continued uptown, initially along First Avenue and then beside the East River for about half a mile to the vicinity of 75th Street. The surroundings here were more downmarket than where they started. They made 'several passages on the dark deserted streets between 1st and 2nd

Avenue between 55th and 70th Street'. Fuchs, with understatement, described it as 'anything but an exclusive area'.[41] Had he and Gold been actors in a Hollywood thriller, the background scenery could hardly have been more appropriate. While walking along First Avenue, the real-life spy now told his contact about the work in isotope separation, only for Gold to start proffering ideas of his own.[42]

Unknown to Fuchs, Gold had once written a dissertation on thermal diffusion, the very method that Otto Frisch had tried in Birmingham in 1940. This had been deemed inefficient and superseded by two lines of attack – magnetic separation (being pursued at Berkeley in California) and gaseous diffusion, which would be the agenda for the British team in New York. Fuchs knew nothing of thermal diffusion, however, and airily dismissed Gold's intervention.[43]

Gold said no more about it, but he had inadvertently revealed his scientific background and experience in this arcane technique. Years later this would lead to his downfall.

Fuchs, by now more used to espionage, found Gold's behaviour too casual. Fuchs later admitted, for example, that he was irritated by the 'very obvious manner in which [Gold] looked back to discover whether we were being followed'.[44] Furthermore, in Fuchs' opinion, the meetings lasted too long, which added to the chance of him being compromised. He and Gold would meet, walk the streets together, and even spend time in restaurants. In a strange city, in an unknown country, and risking death by electric chair, Fuchs was not comfortable. Yet Gold was the only person in whom Fuchs could confide, and during their meetings Gold learned about Fuchs' family, including that his sister Kristel had left Germany and now lived in Cambridge, Massachusetts.

Fuchs recalled that at this and each of his subsequent meetings with Gold he passed over 'two or more' of the latest papers on diffusion.[45] His ability to do so was because of a flaw in the security of production of the team's top-secret reports. When Fuchs completed a piece of work, he would produce his draft manuscript in longhand. After Peierls had approved its contents, a secretary would type the official version, which would then be duplicated and all copies numbered individually. These would then be distributed around the team, with numbers matched against individual recipients; were any report to go astray, this reference number would reveal the original owner. This plan had a weak spot, however. In addition to his official copy of the duplicated reports, Fuchs retained his original longhand version and also a carbon copy. As for reports that originated with other members of the team, Fuchs could copy these at leisure in his apartment.

DESIGNING OAK RIDGE

The basic mathematical ideas of gaseous diffusion had been solved in the United Kingdom; now, in New York, Peierls' team moved on to practical plans for a diffusion plant that would operate on an industrial scale. In the United States, the Kellex Corporation was charged with designing and building a large-scale plant, with research based at Columbia University in New York. However, Kellex wasn't happy with the Columbia theorists who, in Kellex's opinion, were interested more in the mathematical subtleties rather than the practical goal of design.[46] Peierls and Fuchs, by contrast, had studied the construction and stability of a plant in great depth. In Birmingham they had formulated the equations that described the separation of different isotopes through a single filter, and then iterated them to simulate the repetitive filtering of the gas and its consequent enrichment in the U235 isotope. In New York their investigations matured, and Kellex relied on their theoretical work to design a practical facility. The result, a diffusion plant built at Oak Ridge in Tennessee, was a mile-long complex with over 250 buildings, and eight electricity power stations, whose construction was an immense project of civil engineering, involving more than 20,000 workers.

Diffusion is simple in principle; the problems lie in the variables of the pressure, temperature and volume of the gas of uranium hexafluoride. The gas must pass through a filter, which will separate the different uranium isotopes, enabling enrichment of U235 at the expense of the initially dominant U238. The first stage will enrich the mix slightly; the next stage more so, until after enough iterations – one of the many questions to resolve was: how many? – it is enriched to the required level. In reality, however, the gas is not uniform. The surroundings will introduce fluctuations in its temperature, while the pressure of the gas and the volume flowing though the membranes between successive sectors will also be unsteady. So the team had to understand how the efficiency of the plant varies when fluctuations are taken into account. It would be a paper on fluctuations that, years later, led to Fuchs' downfall.

Furthermore, in common with any complicated machinery, a realistic plant with a large number of components would rarely operate at 100 per cent efficiency. For example, the fundamental principles of a car are the ignition of gasoline, which by a series of links transmits rotation to the wheels and hence linear motion to the vehicle as a whole. The car requires periodic servicing: oil leaks, tyre-wear, inefficient brakes can all be ignored for a while, but at some point the machine will break down entirely if these are not repaired or replaced. For a diffusion plant, too, individual components have to be removed for maintenance. The effects of periodically withdrawing these sections had to be assessed by the designers. There were practical questions, such as deciding on the optimal strategy for servicing: does one replace components in a continuing cycle and let the plant run at less than 100 per cent efficiency, or is it better to close down sections, or even the whole machine, only when essential components fail? One piece of information needed to decide this question is: If the machine is shut down, how long will it take before it reaches working efficiency again?

Peierls' time was split between this design work in New York, political administration with the British director James Chadwick in Washington, and scientific contacts with other parts of the Manhattan Project in Chicago, Oak Ridge and eventually Los Alamos.

Diffusion would produce the raw material for the uranium bomb, but there remained intricate problems concering the weapon's assembly. The plan was for an atomic bomb, to be known as the 'gadget', to be constructed at 'Site Y' – Los Alamos, 7,500 feet above sea level on the mesas of New Mexico, and some 30 miles from the nearest town, Santa Fe. Barbed-wire fences surrounded the entire campus. The belligerent General Groves continued to restrict the flow of information even among the scientists within the venture. Los Alamos was the most security-conscious place in the war. J. Robert Oppenheimer, an ascetic theoretical physicist from the University of California at Berkeley, was given charge of the whole scientific research and development programme.

By April the British team had made huge progress on the practicalities of diffusion, and Peierls possibly visited Oak Ridge that month to discuss the engineering of the diffusion factory.[47] Fuchs held the fort except for one 'wet and chilled night' when he went to the Bronx to update Gold.[48] They met in front of a large movie theatre on the Grand Concourse near Fordham Road. The main goal on this occasion seems to have been to arrange for a second transfer of documents, which they agreed would be at their next meeting, in Queens.

At their Bronx meeting, Fuchs had a 'bad cough', which may have been an example of the nervous stress that Genia Peierls would later associate with his spying activities. Gold was concerned and in the rainy conditions 'did not wish to expose [Fuchs] to the elements any more than was necessary'. So after agreeing the details of their next meeting, Gold took Fuchs to dinner. They discussed a number of personal matters, including music and chess. They also concocted a fiction as to how they met, so that if they were ever seen together by a friend, or questioned about this, they had a credible answer.

Meanwhile, tensions were growing over the future cooperation between the British and Americans. Fuchs brought Gold up to date on these developments together with information about American plans to build the diffusion plant. Fuchs did not yet know its location (Oak Ridge, Tennessee), but Gold recalled later that Fuchs told him it would be 'Somewhere in the south, perhaps Alabama or Georgia'. Fuchs added that in the summer he would leave New York, probably to work on a diffusion plant in England as their design for the American diffusion facility was essentially complete.[49]

A drizzle was falling when they left the restaurant, so 'we took a cab and went downtown to the neighbourhood of Madison and the 80s' on the east side of Central Park, diametrically across from Fuchs' apartment on West 77th Street. But first they went into a small bar that contained tables, and at one they had 'several drinks'. They then left the bar and Gold 'put Klaus in a cab'. Gold recalled the reason for doing so was because 'Klaus lived on the other side of Manhattan and direct public transportation through Central Park late at night was very difficult.'[50]

Their next meeting was in Queens, when Fuchs handed over twenty-five to forty pages of information. Years later, Gold remembered 'clearly' that the documents were filled with 'very small but distinctive writing, in ink, mainly mathematical derivations'. Further along in the report there was some 'descriptive content'. Gold got lost near Queens Plaza, took a cab, and when he arrived, Fuchs was already waiting for him.[51] This meeting was 'not more than three or four minutes'. Fuchs told Gold that Peierls had just returned from his three-week visit to 'Camp Y', and promised to report to Gold about that next time. He then handed over the documents, which Gold would transfer to Yatzkov later that day.

In that brief moment the fruits of months of intense research, which had advanced diffusion from theory to a practical design, were passed to the Soviets. Thanks to Fuchs, the Soviet Union now had the complete set of instructions needed for the first stage of building a uranium bomb. Neither Fuchs, nor Peierls, nor anyone outside Los Alamos yet knew that a plutonium bomb was the new priority.

POLITICS AND PLUTONIUM

On 11 February 1944, General Groves met the head of the British scientific delegation, James Chadwick. The two bonded extremely well; Chadwick accepted that Groves had a job to do, and respected his openness and obvious determination to succeed. He also immediately understood

Groves' agenda. In a memorandum of the meeting, Chadwick observed that the Quebec Agreement between the two national leaders had been drawn up so informally that 'Groves had no compunction about slipping through every one of the loopholes.'[52]

Groves believed his instructions were to build an American bomb. Its history was irrelevant for him, so he knew nothing of Peierls and Frisch's contribution and viewed the arrival of the British as merely some political agreement between President Roosevelt and Prime Minister Winston Churchill. The British presence was an additional security headache, so he didn't intend to involve them in the details of the Manhattan Project beyond the minimum necessary.

By the spring of 1944 victory over Hitler was probably just a matter of time, so long as the Nazis didn't themselves get an atomic bomb. Given that the vast resources of the Manhattan Project – both in engineering and scientific brilliance – far exceeded what Germany in isolation could muster, and the fact that even so an Allied atomic bomb was still a year away, the implication was that there was no immediate threat from the enemy on that score. The invasion of Normandy was being prepared and the Nazi defeat by the Allied forces was confidently anticipated without need of an atomic bomb. Work on the weapon proceeded urgently, nonetheless, as the agenda subtly shifted. Eventually, of course, the war ended after the atomic bombs were dropped over Hiroshima and Nagasaki in Japan, but already in 1944 the British and Americans were planning for the post-war era. Their visions encompassed the opportunity for the industrial exploitation of atomic power, preservation of control of the impending atomic bomb, and eventually the possibility of Soviet aggression in Western Europe.

So while the United States and the United Kingdom had a common goal – defeat of the Nazis and Japan – tension between the Allies was growing. In order to get Roosevelt's agreement to British participation in the Manhattan Project, Churchill had given the President a veto on the development of nuclear power in the United Kingdom. Churchill judged that British scientists had to be in the Project to learn how to build an atomic weapon after the war. By mid-1944 the British began to suspect that America planned to restrict the flow of information to them during the final stages of atomic bomb design and construction, with the intention of establishing global hegemony over atomic weapons post-war.[53]

Nonetheless, the British assessed that being frozen out of uranium technology would not be serious so long as they could make plutonium. Recall that in 1940 Egon Bretscher and Norman Feather deduced that in theory plutonium should fission (in part because it has odd numbers of constituents – 239, like 235, being key). Whereas before Peierls' arrival at Los Alamos the British had viewed a plutonium weapon as a remote theoretical possibility at best, by 1944 Manhattan Project physicists had established that plutonium should behave similarly to uranium in its ability to fission, liberate nuclear energy, and be a potential explosive.

The act of producing power in a nuclear reactor converts some of the uranium fuel into plutonium. Whereas a uranium bomb requires a high proportion of U235, and the vast infrastructure of diffusion plants to produce it in necessary quantities, the uranium for a nuclear reactor needs only marginal enrichment. British post-war strategy would be based on plutonium, as this could be made in a reactor without the need for the ultra-pure enrichment of uranium to a level necessary for a nuclear explosion. Their goal therefore would be to design and eventually build in the United Kingdom an 'LSP' – Low Separation Plant. This would enrich uranium sufficient to operate a nuclear reactor, though not enough to make a uranium bomb. The reactor would then enable them to produce plutonium, which could fuel a weapon. After consultation with Peierls, Chadwick identified Fuchs as the ideal individual to drive this forward in the United Kingdom. Peierls agreed, and by the spring of 1944 it seems that Fuchs also saw this as his intended future.

As we have seen, at his meeting with Gold in the Bronx, Fuchs had told him about the conflict with the Americans, and that he would probably be returning to England to work on a diffusion plant there. However, he added, the Americans regarded any independent British initiatives to be contrary to the agreements between the two governments. Gold passed this information to Yatzkov, and on 15 June the Soviet Embassy sent a coded message to Moscow. Years later, the successful decryption of this message would lead to Fuchs' downfall. It said that the British planned to build a diffusion plant in the United Kingdom, but the Americans were angry because this would be 'in direct contradiction to the spirit of the [Quebec] Agreement', which gave the Americans a veto on the development of nuclear power in Britain.[54] It mentioned agent 'REST', the KGB's code name for Fuchs at that time, but also gave details that compromised his secret identity. First, it revealed that James Chadwick was deciding whether REST's future would be in the United States or at the new facility back home. REST meanwhile expressed doubt that he could remain in the USA without raising suspicion and, damning by its explicitness: 'REST assumes he will have to leave in a month or six weeks.' And, fatally, it mentioned Fuchs' paper on fluctuations.[55]

On 29 and 30 May, Peierls and Fuchs visited Montreal, where a team of British scientists was collaborating with French and Canadians on the design of a nuclear reactor. Peierls was at Los Alamos from 2 to 21 June. His expertise would be invaluable in the final stage of the bomb's construction, but also for the British politically. At the end of June 1944 he prepared to move to Los Alamos with his family. Fuchs, meanwhile, anticipated a return to the United Kingdom.

8

Trinity

Peierls moved to Los Alamos at the end of June 1944. While his primary goal was the race to beat Hitler to an atomic weapon, Peierls was alert to the political manoeuvring behind the scenes. The British agenda was to cooperate with the United States on the joint project and gain experience that would eventually create a pay-off for the United Kingdom. Aware of the United States' strategy to monopolize atomic energy post-war, James Chadwick, the head of the British Mission, and Peierls, the lead theorist, manoeuvred to get British scientists deeper into the Manhattan Project, for if they remained outsiders they would have to work out for themselves the practicalities of making atomic weapons after the war.

Already during his three-week visit to Los Alamos early in June, Peierls had learned that the war aims had changed radically: a bomb made of plutonium now seemed a better option than one of U235.[1] The plutonium would be made in nuclear reactors elsewhere in the United States and shipped to Los Alamos for assembly.

Plutonium is an element that does not occur naturally, so although its potential as a nuclear explosive was clear in theory, how it could actually be used would only become clear when the first samples were made in nuclear reactors. The goal was to release the greatest amount of energy before the explosion destroyed the lump itself, but to do this a quantity of plutonium greater than the critical mass would be required. The theorists first needed to determine the size of this optimum amount, and then design and engineer a means whereby individual small samples came together into a super-critical explosive ball. To begin the explosive reaction, a plutonium bullet is fired at a target, also made of plutonium, at a speed of about a kilometre per second. During the spring of 1944, however, the scientists discovered that plutonium was so unstable that even at this supersonic speed the two pieces degraded before they had a chance to join. They now had to find an ingenious means of making a critical mass of the element so rapidly that it would explode to order and not detonate partially. The solution – 'implosion' – involved a blast spread evenly around a hollow sphere of plutonium so that the shell would collapse inwards, uniformly, to form a dense central ball.*

First there is a puzzle, whose solution is well known today to anyone who has seen a soccer ball: How do you cover the surface of a sphere with shaped thin strips of high explosive? The mathematician Leonhard Euler had discovered a theorem around 1750 on how to do so with polyhedrons; Euler's formula shows this can be achieved with twelve pentagons and an unlimited number of hexagons. The original Trinity bomb used twelve pentagons and twenty hexagons, which is the same as a modern soccer ball. Much of this remains classified, but the brilliant mathematician John von Neumann worked on implosion at Los Alamos and it is likely that he was the inspiration behind this unusual configuration.

Having assembled this array of explosive charges, the ignition of each of them would have to occur within less than a millisecond for the implosion to be uniform, and the concentrated lump thus formed should then explode spontaneously. The idea of implosion was excellent in theory, but would it work in practice? One problem was that the blast waves from the individual explosive charges around the surface of the sphere created turbulence and interfered with one another. As of mid-1944 there was no guarantee that this would be solved. If that remained the case, the plutonium bomb would be impotent, so work on the uranium bomb continued as a hedge.

Theoretical analysis of implosion – in effect a shock wave travelling inwards to the centre of the plutonium shell – was at the limits of mathematical possibility. Yet when Peierls was consulted about this problem during his first days at Los Alamos in June, he noticed that the equations for implosion were similar to those for blast waves in air, which he and Fuchs had studied in Birmingham two years previously. Peierls realized that Fuchs' experience, and his natural mathematical ability, would be invaluable to the project: solving the problem of implosion for a plutonium bomb at that juncture appeared to be key to the success or failure of the entire mission to build practical atomic weapons. So having brought Klaus Fuchs into Tube Alloys in May 1941, Peierls now prepared to suggest to Hans Bethe – head of theoretical physics at Los Alamos – that Fuchs join him and a handful of other British physicists in the collective enterprise at Los Alamos.

On 13 June, however, London asked Peierls whether Fuchs should

---

* The plutonium isotope relevant for fission is Pu-239, which can be obtained by chemical extraction from spent fuel in a uranium-filled reactor. However, some Pu-240 is also present, which undergoes fission spontaneously, and very quickly. This causes unwanted pre-detonation before the two pieces of plutonium combine. Hence the need for an ultra-fast method of combination – implosion.

return to England to work on the Low Separation Plant (LSP). On 24 June, Peierls agreed that if the LSP were a serious project then Fuchs would be well placed back home, but he commented that Fuchs would also be welcome at Los Alamos. For Chadwick, who saw a British LSP as part of the strategic future, this created a problem. If General Groves were to ask for Fuchs to move to Los Alamos, Chadwick obviously could not say: 'No; he's needed in the United Kingdom for non-war work.' He wanted to ensure that if Groves were to consult Hans Bethe, Bethe would say that Fuchs would not be especially useful at Los Alamos. As Bethe and Peierls were old friends, Chadwick asked Peierls to contact Bethe tactfully and steer him away from Fuchs by doing 'what is necessary by suggestion rather than direct action'. Chadwick had made the first move in this chess game by saying that 'Fuchs could be useful [at Los Alamos], but his special qualifications are not on the nuclear side but on the diffusion plant'.

Fuchs' future was thus uncertain when early in July, after Peierls had left New York on his long-term secondment to Los Alamos, Fuchs again saw Gold by the Metropolitan Museum of Art adjacent to Central Park.[2] They had a leisurely walk through the park during which Fuchs said that he would probably go back to England or to 'somewhere in the south-west' but that 'nothing was certain on his departure'. On 14 July he went to Washington to discuss his future with Chadwick. He wrote to Peierls three days later to say that his position was rather 'difficult' and that he 'had better leave it to Chadwick to tell you about our discussion'.[3] Chadwick, meanwhile, had written to Peierls immediately after the meeting and noted: 'Fuchs feels that he has a special contribution to make in England, whereas in [Los Alamos] he would be one of a number and can make no really significant difference to the work.'[4] Chadwick told Peierls that he agreed completely with Fuchs' view and hence asked Peierls to reaffirm, via Bethe, that there would be no request from Los Alamos for Fuchs' services.

Chadwick's letter portrays Fuchs as actively proposing a return to the United Kingdom and not merely agreeing to a prior suggestion from his boss, which suggests that Fuchs – the spy – was reluctant to go to Los Alamos. Why? Was he looking for a way out of espionage, or did Moscow judge the United Kingdom to be more interesting?[5]

The FBI Director J. Edgar Hoover later assessed that Fuchs' professed wish was part of a Soviet strategy, for around this time Yatzkov proposed that Russia encourage Fuchs' return to the United Kingdom.[6] Scientists in the Soviet Union – based on the collective input from Fuchs and other spies, and as yet unaware that a plutonium weapon was now the goal – thought that the path to a uranium bomb was a straightforward if intensive engineering project. In the United Kingdom, by contrast, Fuchs would be singularly well placed to keep Moscow informed of nuclear developments in Western Europe.

On 21 July letters between London and Chadwick in Washington recognized Fuchs' wish: 'it looks as if Fuchs would return to the United Kingdom rather than to Los Alamos'.[7] Fuchs' anticipated return to Britain, which would have changed the course of events profoundly, became a mere footnote when a fortnight later he was ordered to join Peierls at Los Alamos. Why this was decided, and so quickly, was probably for two reasons. First, Chadwick cooled on the urgency of the LSP research in the United Kingdom. Second, Peierls, by now at Los Alamos, realized that Fuchs' special skills really could be crucial for completing the atomic bomb.

TWO-THIRDS OF THE TEAM

On 14 August 1944 Fuchs completed a train odyssey aross the United States to Santa Fe, New Mexico. He first reported to an inconspicuous address in the centre of town, and was then transferred to an army staff car to be driven northwest for about an hour into the desert country. The vehicle then negotiated a hair-raising unmetalled road up the wall of a canyon until it reached a plateau full of pine trees. On this isolated mesa, surrounded by canyons, scrub and desert, Fuchs saw at last the secret laboratory where the atomic bomb would be constructed.

It was only upon his arrival at Los Alamos that Fuchs discovered the immense scale of the Manhattan Project. There, quarantined from the outside world, was a small city of army huts, and row upon row of drab prefabs for living accommodation, where muddy streets with duckboard pavements connected laboratories and workshops. Chemists and metallurgists prepared and tested materials while nuclear physicists and explosives experts performed experiments to optimize construction of what was called the 'gadget'. This industrial infrastructure was, in effect, the campus of a huge university whose faculty members were many of the most outstanding scientists in the Western world, assembled to work out how to beat Hitler in the race to building an atomic bomb. They were young and almost exclusively male: Fuchs at thirty-two was slightly older than the average age of thirty; Peierls at thirty-six almost a patriarch. Names that Fuchs had previously only seen in books, research papers, or in the announcements of Nobel Prizes were manifested as living colleagues. The talent was remarkable. Existing or future Laureates in Physics among the throng included Enrico Fermi, Niels Bohr, Isidor Rabi, Richard

Feynman, Hans Bethe, Norman Ramsey, Fred Reines and Roy Glauber. In addition Joseph Rotblat, the only physicist to quit the project when the Nazis surrendered, later won the Nobel Peace Prize.[8]

The freedom of human society could depend on the scientists' success or failure, and in the first half of 1944 'failure' seemed the more likely outcome. One Los Alamos resident recalled being isolated from the rest of the world, with formal entertainment being 'movies three times a week, admission 10 cents', and the scientists 'were producing babies more efficiently than anything else'.[9] Families consisted of wives and young children. Peierls by then had two – Gaby (aged ten) and Ronnie (aged eight) – and Fuchs was a ready companion when they went for picnics, hikes and ski trips. Secrecy prevented the scientists talking about work with their wives. With the exception of the movies, entertainment was mostly self-made and consisted of a continuous round of parties, playing games and drinking, together with outdoor pursuits.

Fuchs went to the parties and enjoyed playing charades with the others. He wore the same brown sports coat and slacks every day, but there was a general feeling that his austere exterior masked deep emotions and care for his fellows;[10] the wives liked him – and he was in demand as a babysitter. To the Peierls' two children he was like a big brother; Genia would happily leave them with Fuchs if she and Rudolf had some function of senior staff to attend, and the Peierlses trusted him with their children's care on extended camping trips in the surrounding countryside. Their daughter Gaby remembered him as 'very nice to us, perhaps one of the few grown-ups who didn't talk down to us'.[11]

Among Fuchs' new colleagues at Los Alamos was William Penney, a British mathematician with a rare gift for visualizing the meaning of equations, which had made him an expert on waves – in solids, liquids and gases; he had made a particular study of how pressure waves spread after explosions underwater. Early in 1944 Penney had been doing scientific work to prepare for the D-Day landings, designing ways to stabilize Mulberry Harbours – the havens for landing craft at the Normandy beaches – against the ebb and flow of the sea. Then in the spring of 1944 he got the call to Los Alamos. The atomic bomb would generate supersonic shock waves in the atmosphere and on the ground on an unprecedented scale. Penney had the experience necessary to analyse how best the bomb be deployed and to estimate its likely damage. Two years older than Peierls, Penney was made head of the British delegation. When asked why he was suddenly leaving for some unidentified destination in the United States he replied: 'I'm not allowed to say but I hope that nothing comes of it.'[12]

At Los Alamos, Penney, Peierls and Fuchs were members of Hans

Bethe's Theoretical Physics Division. Fuchs and Penney spent considerable time together analysing the problem of plutonium implosion, where Penney's expertise helped Fuchs study how an arrangement of explosive charges on the surface of the bomb could produce waves that converged to a point at its heart.

Fuchs was the Theoretical Division liaison with the team responsible for conventional explosives by which implosion of plutonium would be triggered. He looked at all aspects of these chemical explosions, especially what effect instabilities in the shock waves would have, and what would happen when the pressure waves converged at the heart of the bomb. What was the best radioactive source to have within the device in order to initiate the nuclear explosion, at the instant of the plutonium's critical mass having been attained?

Peierls and a member of his group, Robert Christy, made a key breakthrough on the formation of the critical mass itself. The idea was for the heart of the bomb to have a solid core of plutonium, which was about 95 per cent of a critical mass. In this situation, the plutonium does not detonate. The critical mass depends on the density, and is smaller for more compact material. If the solid core is suddenly compressed it becomes super-critical and with a suitable supply of neutrons will explode.[13]

In an authoritative history of Los Alamos, Peierls and Fuchs were credited as being 'two-thirds of the team which handled the hydrodynamics in the theory division which made implosion possible'. Furthermore, 'they both contributed heavily to all phases of the weapon development including implosion and the Super'.[14]* Penney's expertise helped Fuchs and Peierls answer questions such as once the explosion began, what would the shock waves rushing outwards be like? How would they spread through the atmosphere? How large, indeed, would the explosion be? In a nutshell, Fuchs and Peierls played key roles in the design and nuclear physics of the plutonium bomb, while Penney computed the blast effects of the explosion. In particular he advised on the optimum height at which the bomb should be detonated to maximize the amount of damage.

FROM KRISTEL TO CHARLES

As in Birmingham and New York, Fuchs was now again at the centre of the action. However, to transmit what he was learning to the Soviet Union

---

* 'Super' refers to the hydrogen bomb developed after the war, exploiting know-how from the atomic bomb project.

from within the confines of Los Alamos, with its barbed-wire fences, intense security and censored mail, would be an utterly different business from before. Los Alamos, an hour away from the nearest significant town and isolated at the top of a ridge, was the most security-conscious place on Earth. For two years Klaus Fuchs nevertheless managed to carry out the most extensive and far-reaching feat of espionage in history. From August 1944, for the duration of the war and beyond, Fuchs successfully kept the Soviets so well informed that Stalin knew more about the atomic bomb than did the vast majority of those fighting as his allies; those not in the know included the British and American Security Services themselves.

At Los Alamos, General Groves' security staff censored outgoing mail and examined all incoming mail for any hints of coded messages. For scientists at Los Alamos, security was an irritant, which inspired some of them to devise ways round what they saw as petty bureaucracy. They were not primed to suspect that any of their clan could willingly breach security, other than as a harmless game. The idea that anyone would pass on information from Los Alamos to anyone other than a colleague within the larger Manhattan Project never seems to have crossed most of their minds. When Richard Feynman, an arch prankster as well as one of the smartest physicists of the century, joked with Klaus Fuchs as to which of them was more likely to be a spy, they agreed that it would have to be Feynman because he made frequent trips away from Los Alamos to see his wife in hospital in Albuquerque.[15]

Fuchs and Gold had arranged to meet again in Brooklyn that August, but Fuchs – now 2,000 miles away – didn't turn up. They had a fallback plan for such an eventuality, which was for Gold to go to an agreed rendezvous by Central Park West near Harlem a week or so later. This was in an area where muggings often occurred and when Fuchs once again failed to appear, Gold became worried that the slightly built scientist might 'seem an inviting prey'.[16]

Gold reported Fuchs' non-appearance to Yatzkov. They discussed the implications for two hours, trying to gauge what the problem might be. This boiled down to a single question: was Fuchs still in New York or had he left?

Gold and Yatzkov met next in late August, near Washington Square. Yatksov had good news: he had found Fuchs' address on West 77th Street. He told Gold to go to the apartment and find out whether Fuchs was there. Cleverly Gold took a book in which he wrote Fuchs' name and address, as if the book was Fuchs' property. His story, if necessary, would be that Fuchs had lent him the book, which he was now attempting to return.

Gold came up to New York from his home in Philadelphia and made his way to the west side of Central Park, about a mile above its southern end. On West 77th Street he found an avenue of trees in the full leaf of summer. Number 122 was built of 'white stone, newer and better kept than the other buildings on the same block'.[17] He arrived in front of the building, went up some steps to the vestibule, and among the nameplates was relieved to see: Dr Klaus Fuchs.

Gold pressed the buzzer, but there was no answer. The door leading from the vestibule to the main hall was unlocked, so he went in and started to look for Fuchs' apartment. A door opened across the hall and an old woman peered out. At that moment her husband, the janitor, appeared from the street where he had been clearing garbage and asked Gold whether he was looking for someone. A conversation ensued which revealed that Fuchs was no longer there. They had no idea where he was except that they were sure it would be impossible to find him because he had 'left for somewhere on a boat'. Fuchs was sharing atomic secrets with the Russians but was rigorously adhering to the demands of security by withholding any clue to his Los Alamos destination from the janitor of his apartment.

Gold explained that he was a friend of Fuchs, that he wanted to return the book, and left. He went immediately to see Yatzkov at a rendezvous near Columbia University. They walked along Riverside Drive and discussed what to do. Perhaps Gold should write to Fuchs in West 77th Street in the hope that the letter would be forwarded? This idea was quickly dismissed as too risky, and for the moment they decided to 'sit tight'.[18]

When Fuchs first went to North America, the KGB had noted his sister Kristel Heineman's address as an emergency means of contact.[19] Gold was instructed to visit her in Cambridge, which he did at the end of September, but she was away. The housekeeper told him that Kristel was on vacation and would return in a week or two. Gold went back to New York to report to Yatzkov, who then sent a message to Moscow on 4 October: 'REST's [Fuchs'] sister has not yet returned home. [Gold] should make his next trip to visit her on 12 October.'[20]

Yatzkov's report of Gold's next visit, transmitted to Moscow at the time, confirms Kristel's involvement.[21] Gold arrived in Boston early, at 8 a.m. on 12 October, and went to Kristel's house about two hours later so that her husband would not be at home. He rang the doorbell and a young woman appeared. She confirmed that she was Mrs Heineman. After introducing himself as a friend of Klaus, Gold 'gave her the [pre-arranged] message . . . She knew the answer.' Gold entered, stayed for about half an hour, and chatted about Klaus. Kristel told him she thought her brother had returned to England.

Gold came back again, on Thursday 2 November. This visit was also made during the day while her husband was out, and now Kristel had good news: Klaus had called from Chicago.[22] He had 'been there on business from New Mexico where he was stationed'. She said she was happy that he was now in the United States as they were very close and he was fond of her children. Kristel said that Klaus would likely be in Cambridge for Christmas, as he 'usually made a great event of bringing presents for the children'.[23] Gold said he was 'so overjoyed that I stayed for lunch'.

In the meantime, as added security, the KGB changed Fuchs' code name from REST to CHARLES. On 16 November the Soviet Embassy informed Moscow that Gold's 'visit to CHARLES' sister revealed that he had not returned to the UK but had moved to Camp2 [Los Alamos]'. The message added that Gold is 'taking steps to liaise with CHARLES while he is on leave'.[24] Gold had told Kristel that he would return in about a month 'to make sure of everything'.

He duly returned on 7 December. Kristel – he reported to Yatzkov – had remembered more of Klaus' phone call. He was entitled to four weeks' vacation but didn't expect to get it all. He was certain, however, of at least two weeks. She asked him how long he would have with them, and Klaus had replied that he might have to spend a day or two in New York. Gold was excited as this implied 'Klaus expected us to get in touch with him.'[25] So Gold gave her a sealed envelope to pass on to Klaus when he arrived. This contained instructions that he should call a certain phone number any morning between 8 and 8.30 and say: 'I have arrived in Cambridge and will be here for [some number of] days.'[26]

KRISTEL IS COMPROMISED

Commitments at Los Alamos meant Fuchs was unable to visit his sister at Christmas but he managed to do so in February near one of the children's birthdays. She told him that Gold had visited. This disturbed him, because he didn't like the idea of Gold visiting Kristel's home; nonetheless, Fuchs 'accepted it'.[27] Gold eventually met him there on Wednesday 21 February 1945.[28] Kristel answered the door and called out to Klaus, who was in his room upstairs. It was about 10 a.m.

Kristel was aware of Gold's existence – that was unavoidable – but Fuchs didn't want her husband to meet him too, so he and Gold went for a walk away from the house during which Fuchs outlined the situation at Los Alamos. He also assured Gold that he had made a careful check and was certain that he was not being watched. They returned to the house around 1 o'clock and had a 'very fine lunch' with Kristel.[29]

Gold and Fuchs were thus reunited at the start of 1945, thanks to Kristel, but at a price: Fuchs had involved his sister in his activities. Unknown to Kristel, the Soviet GRU had approved her as a contact back in 1943 before Klaus was transferred to the United States.[30]

The KGB recognized Kristel's role and gave her the code name ANT.[31] Yatzkov warned Moscow that it was paramount not to alert Kristel's husband, as 'we do not know her husband well and we would not want to get an extra person involved'.[32] Fuchs must have known that he had taken a dangerous gamble to use Kristel in this way. But he judged this to be the only practical way for the Soviet Union to receive his news, which was in a different league to anything that he had been able to reveal before. After lunch Fuchs and Gold went up to Fuchs' room where he was now able to tell Gold the inside story of Los Alamos, and he handed over a full report on their research into a plutonium bomb. This information would turn out to be among the most significant in all Fuchs' espionage. Until this juncture the Soviets knew only of the uranium bomb, which would be ignited by the 'gun method' – ramming two pieces of sub-critical metal together like a bullet hitting a target. Inspired by Fuchs' news about plutonium, Igor Kurchatov, leader of the Soviet atomic bomb programme, 'chose the plutonium implosion bomb as his primary goal'.[33]

Fuchs told Gold that when he arrived at Los Alamos in August 1944 there were only 2,500 to 3,000 people, but 'now it has expanded to 45,000!' These included physicists, mathematicians, chemists, and engineers of all varieties: civil, mechanical, electrical, chemical, and 'many other types of technical help as well as a US Army Engineer Detachment'. He explained that they were manufacturing the actual atomic bomb and 'expected to go into full-scale production in about three months'. Fuchs was 'hesitant about this date and said he would not like to be held to it'.[34]

He told Gold also of an idea to build a 'Super' or hydrogen bomb, a device of almost unlimited power, far greater even than the uranium and plutonium 'atomic' bombs. The hydrogen bomb was just an idea, he added, and not a priority. One Soviet physicist later recalled how the news arrived in Moscow. 'In March 1945 the Soviet Intelligence Service received a report that [Hungarian émigré physicist Edward] Teller was working on a superbomb at Los Alamos', investigating whether with 'a small quantity of $U235$ or $Pu239$ as the primary source, a chain reaction could be initiated in the less scarce deuterium'.[35] If this were the extent of the detail, the Soviets would have been alerted to little more than that the United

States was pursuing a new direction. But Fuchs' report gave the Soviet Union its first inkling that nuclear thinking had expanded further.

The question 'Who was the father of the H-bomb?' has no simple answer: 'In a laboratory there is constant interplay between people. And then the way is found.'[36] Enrico Fermi is traditionally credited with having been present at the conception, with a chance remark in 1942, but he was not the first to make the seminal suggestion that would ignite the quest.

The energy source of a hydrogen bomb is the fusion of isotopes of hydrogen – of deuterium, a heavy hydrogen nucleus, which consists of one neutron and one proton, and tritium, a nucleus of super-heavy hydrogen, consisting of one proton and two neutrons. These combine – fuse – to produce a nucleus of helium and a neutron that carries away most of the energy. To force the nuclei together you need very high temperatures such as occur in stars where fusion reactions provide the energy.

In May 1941 a physicist at Kyoto University named Tokaturo Hagiwara remarked that an explosion of U235 could create temperatures high enough to start a thermonuclear reaction between hydrogen atoms.[37] Hagiwara's observation was before serious work on an atomic bomb had begun; his idea appeared theoretical with no practical consequences, and was forgotten if indeed it was even noticed at the time. Enrico Fermi seems to have been unaware of Hagiwara's suggestion when Edward Teller visited him at Columbia University in 1942 to discuss atomic weapons. Fermi casually remarked that an atomic explosion might generate temperatures akin to those in stars: 'Their conversation foreshadowed the advent of the H-bomb 10 years later.'[38]

Teller, who at that stage was preparing to work on atomic weapons at Los Alamos, became obsessed by Fermi's idea, to the extent of believing that the focus of the Manhattan Project should be on this fusion device rather than the uranium or plutonium bomb. This obsession never left him and led to an infamous spat with Robert Oppenheimer both during the war and after. To appease Teller, in the autumn of 1943 Oppenheimer had created a special division at Los Alamos in which Teller and a small group could work on the 'Super'. Teller's departure left a gap in the Theoretical Physics Division, and when Peierls joined Los Alamos he took over Teller's role there.

All of this information about Los Alamos' interest in the Super was sent by Fuchs to Moscow. In addition Gold told Yatzkov that when he tried to give Fuchs money, Fuchs had refused to accept it but did make a request. He foresaw the end of the war against Germany and the possibility that the Allies might soon have access to the Gestapo's files on his past and wanted these destroyed. Yatzkov told Moscow, on 19 March, '[Fuchs] is positive that the English [do] not know about his past [communist] activities and that this was the only reason why they let him work on ENORMOS [the Manhattan Project].' He added, 'CHARLES asked us to make sure that when the Gestapo archives in Kiel and Berlin are seized, his files are confiscated and do not, under any circumstances, get into the hands of the Islanders [British].'[39]

Fuchs didn't know when he would next have any leave, but he insisted to Gold that in any event there were to be no further meetings at his sister's home. Their meeting lasted until about 3.30 p.m. He told Gold the exact location of the laboratory, said that he could find an excuse to get out of the Los Alamos camp and visit Santa Fe once a month, and that any future rendezvous would have to be there. Fuchs gave Gold a street map of the town, together with a bus timetable, and they agreed to meet in Santa Fe in early June. By then the designs for the atomic bombs – of uranium and plutonium – should be complete and ready to be passed to Moscow.

Oppenheimer wanted the plutonium bomb tested to be sure that they had solved the problem of implosion. Peierls and Fuchs were at the heart of this mathematical analysis. These, and a host of other problems, were gradually solved through the first half of 1945.

On 8 May, however, Germany surrendered. This gave the Allies victory in Europe, but also rendered redundant the original motivation for the bomb – as a defence in case Nazi Germany built one first. The war against Japan, however, still needed to be won. In a judgement over which controversy has resounded ever since, the decision to proceed with the atomic bomb was taken. Only Joseph Rotblat quit the Manhattan Project at that point; the majority of those who remained wrestled with the implications for the rest of their lives.

BLUEPRINT FOR A BOMB

The test of the plutonium bomb was planned for 16 July 1945. It would take place before dawn in the desert, about 230 miles south of Los Alamos. Oppenheimer chose the code name: Trinity.

On the afternoon of Saturday 2 June, Fuchs drove 'a dilapidated old two-seater car' out of Los Alamos, down the thirty miles of mesa slopes into Santa Fe.[40] On Alameda Street, near the Galisteo Street Bridge, he saw Gold at 4 p.m., as agreed, sitting on one of the benches beneath the trees. Gold got into the car with Fuchs, and after driving across the river bridge they 'turned left into a lane which terminated at a gate'.[41] They talked in the car, and Fuchs told Gold that the bomb would soon be tested. Fuchs had examined official classified documents at Los Alamos in preparing a report, which Gold described later as 'a considerable packet of information'.[42] Fuchs had written this all in longhand while in Los Alamos, and driven out of the camp with it in the car.[43] Years later, Peierls observed that this was remarkably easy: 'Nobody examined the papers we were carrying, so it would have been physically possible to smuggle documents.'[44]

By then the designs of bombs made of uranium or plutonium were complete, and Fuchs provided a full description of the plutonium bomb to be tested at Trinity,[45] including a sketch of the bomb and its components with important dimensions indicated, information as to the type of core, a description of the initiator and details of the tamper.[46] He gave Gold orally the names of the types of explosives to be used in the bomb, the approximate size of the Trinity test, and he told Gold, 'the atomic bomb, according to his calculations, would be vastly greater in its explosive force than large quantities of TNT'.[47]

This information was encoded at the Soviet Embassy and sent to Moscow on 13 June. Thus, even before the Trinity test had taken place, the Soviet scientists knew what to expect. This 'virtual blueprint for the Trinity device' was 'the most important information that Fuchs gave the Soviets'.[48]

On 12 April, President Roosevelt had died suddenly following a brain haemorrhage. Vice-President Harry Truman was called urgently to the White House and sworn in as Roosevelt's successor that evening. His first briefing included the news that the Allies had developed an atomic bomb: the Manhattan Project was so secret that even the Vice-President had not known of it – but thanks to Klaus Fuchs, Stalin had known about it before the new American President. By the time of the Potsdam Conference on 24 July, two bombs had been prepared, a fact that was also known to the Soviet Union, thanks not least to Klaus Fuchs. When President Truman proudly informed Stalin that the Americans had 'a new weapon of unusual destructive force', Stalin showed no sign of surprise. He merely said he was pleased to hear it, and hoped that it would be used against the Japanese.

9

The Destroyer of Worlds

On the evening of 15 July 1945 a fleet of military buses drove down the winding roads from the laboratory and into the desert. They were filled with scientists, who tried unsuccessfully to sleep on the uncomfortable seats as they headed south into the wilderness. Shortly after 2 a.m. the convoy reached its destination and disgorged its passengers, by now cold and stiff, but also in a state of high excitement as they prepared to see the fruits of their work. In the darkness the scientists could discern the faint glow of floodlights some twenty miles distant across the valley floor. These illuminated a tower, which housed the 'gadget'. The test itself was still two hours away.

Even at this late stage, remarkably little was understood as to the likely outcome. Several scientists half feared that the bomb would ignite the Earth's atmosphere. This was because the temperature within the explosion would be millions of degrees, similar to those in the sun, and Edward Teller had calculated that at such temperatures nuclear reactions might be triggered in nitrogen, a key element in the air. One scientist had said that if the chance were 'more than 3 in a million' he would not proceed, for 'even the horrifying prospect of a Nazi victory' was not worth this.[1]

Teller's calculation was flawed, however. He had forgotten to take into account that heat would be lost from the explosion to the surrounding cooler air. The extreme temperatures needed to fuse atoms of nitrogen and destroy the atmosphere would not happen. Hans Bethe had redone the calculations independently and assured Oppenheimer that all was fine, with a vast safety margin. Teller had concurred with Bethe's new calculation.

So everything was ready to proceed, but General Groves remained deeply worried because what might happen was in the last resort unknown. He called the Governor of New Mexico to give him a set of code words by which Groves would alert him to the seriousness of a potential disaster and how much of the state would need to be evacuated.[2] The *New York Times* journalist William Laurence was the sole member of the press authorized to witness the explosion. Groves told him to prepare three press releases.

One was to announce a successful explosion without casualties or damage; the second release was to announce severe damage; the third was to include 'obituaries of all present at the test, including Laurence'.[3]

About an hour before dawn, a flare briefly illuminated the darkness to mark a minute's countdown. Everyone now put on welder's goggles, and lay flat on the sand to avoid any blast waves. No one present was really sure what to expect. The scientists had laid bets on the size of the blast. Hans Bethe wagered that it would be equivalent to 8,000 tons of TNT; Oppenheimer – cautiously pessimistic – chose 300 tons; others, with less riding on the outcome, guessed up to 50,000 tons. There was a faint glow heralding dawn in the east, which enabled them to see their immediate neighbours very dimly. Then suddenly there was an enormous flash of light, which was 'the brightest anyone had ever seen' and which 'bored right through you'. Night was instantly turned into day. One of many descriptions compared it to 'like opening heavy curtains of a darkened room to a flood of sunlight'.[4] The blast was later calculated to have been equivalent to about 20,000 tons of TNT. Isidor Rabi, who had won the Nobel Prize for Physics in 1944, now won the Los Alamos pool with his bet of 18,000; he had chosen this value simply by going through the book of bets and looking for the biggest gap with no bet.[5]

The dazzling intensity was not the most impressive thing, however. Until that moment the scientists had been lying chilled in the cold desert night, but with the flash came 'scorching heat on [our] faces, like opening a hot oven with the sun coming out like a sunrise'.[6] A fireball grew in silence, the first time that the soon-infamous shape of a gigantic mushroom cloud had been seen on Earth. The shockwave took five minutes to reach them, and then there was a bang, which echoed from the valley walls like thunder, rolling back and forth. All the while the cloud rose higher, its colour changing as it grew, until its light subsided and in the east the red glow of the real dawn took over.

NUCLEAR REACTIONS

The knowledge that matter is made of atoms whose nuclei house powerful forces was barely thirty years old. Even Ernest Rutherford, who discovered the atomic nucleus, had as recently as 1933 asserted that it would be impossible to mine this store of energy.[7] He had not anticipated the discoveries of fission, and of the chain reaction, which provided a route to the explosive release of energy from within the nucleus of an atom – in theory. Ever since Peierls and Frisch had recognized the possibility in 1940, physicists had been certain that their speculations were correct, but to engineer machines capable of releasing that unique source of power had required the assemblage of the brightest scientific talent in the world, and success was never guaranteed. When that ball of light, brighter than the midday sun, filled the sky – 'like sunrise but in the south'[8] was how one scientist described it – even those closest to the undertaking saw the reality far exceed their imagination. Rabi eloquently described his feelings: 'A new thing had just been born; a new control; a new understanding which man had acquired over nature.'[9] J. Robert Oppenheimer famously exclaimed: 'I am become death, the destroyer of worlds.'[10]

Initially the observers of the blast were euphoric. The experiment had worked. Humanity had achieved the Promethean dream. Then a month later, on 15 August 1945, the Second World War ended after the detonation of two atomic bombs. The first bomb, made of uranium, exploded over Hiroshima on 6 August; a mere three days later, a second bomb, made of plutonium, blasted Nagasaki. Now the fuller implications of their creation overwhelmed the scientists. Tens of thousands of innocent civilians had died at Hiroshima, a massacre hastily repeated at Nagasaki. The horror of what they had made affected them profoundly.

When Peierls conceived the atomic bomb the goal had been to defeat Hitler, but Germany had surrendered in May with no atomic weapon deployed and none to show. The overriding fear that had motivated the project had not been necessary. For Peierls, the realization of his vision was now especially painful. His ability to quarantine emotion and analyse logically led, years later, to his assessment of the awesome events:

> Nobody could look at the reports and the pictures about Hiroshima and Nagasaki with anything but horror, and nobody would feel any pride at having a hand in bringing this about. But this was war, and in war death, suffering, and destruction are unavoidable.

Then Peierls made a logical comparison with the awful fire-bombings of Tokyo, which had killed similar numbers to the atomic bombs:

> It is not the scale of the destruction that gave war a new dimension with the introduction of the atomic bomb; what was new was the ease with which the weapon could be used, with a single plane creating the kind of destruction that could previously have been achieved only by a massive military operation.[11]

Here was both the proof and also the disproof of Peierls' vision, which he had articulated in March 1940. Fewer than 2,000 days had elapsed from conception to demonstration that the bomb worked with the irresistible force that he had foreseen. His new fear was of the ease with which the weapon could be used, amplified by the overturning of his belief that the atomic bomb would not be used by a civilized nation.

Peierls had originally conceived the weapon as a form of defence. He now had to live with the implication of his creation, and resolved to educate the public, from policymakers to citizens at large, about the reality and opportunities of atomic power. This could have great benefits if the energy produced by nuclear reactors could provide clean power for peaceful use. He would also lead the fight against proliferation of nuclear weapons themselves. The bomb could not be un-invented, but Peierls would devote the rest of his life to promoting his original vision of it as a deterrent, and trying to ensure that it would never be used again.

ENRICO FERMI AND THE SUPER BOMB

The Los Alamos experience determined that U235 was a costly and industrially intensive way to make atomic weapons. The practical route to an arsenal of bombs was to breed plutonium in nuclear reactors. By the end of the war, American reactors had produced enough plutonium for several weapons. Yet with Japan defeated, and the Second World War over, a new threat to American hegemony had appeared – their former ally, the Soviet Union. Fuchs was worried by the prospect of an atomic bomb in the possession of the Americans alone.* He continued his espionage and stayed close to post-war research into atomic weapons.

Terrible though the atomic devices were, their power was nonetheless limited. That was why, as Klaus Fuchs told Harry Gold in January 1945, the scientists at Los Alamos were already contemplating an even more terrifying weapon, of unlimited power, potentially even capable of destroying life on Earth: the hydrogen bomb.

Two key requirements of a fission bomb – atomic bomb – are that there is enough material present to make a chain reaction explosive, and that there remains enough for the process not to fizzle out. The key reason for this is that the neutrons liberated by each individual fission reaction must find unused atoms of uranium or plutonium if they are to initiate further repetitions. In a large lump of the element this is possible; in a small lump, however, the neutrons are more likely to escape from the surface than to hit an atom within. Hence the concept of the critical size, or 'critical mass',

* The United Kingdom had no atomic bomb until October 1952.

of material below which fission cannot continue and the sample is harm-less. By contrast, above this mass, the level known as super-critical, the fissions grow exponentially and an atomic explosion can happen.

For this reason an atomic bomb made of uranium or plutonium has to be assembled from separate units, each of which is less than the critical mass. The engineering challenge of bringing these units into an explosive mix itself limits the bomb's size. Furthermore, when a fission bomb explodes, its material disassembles. Thus even if a huge amount of mat-erial is assembled the act of explosion destroys the mix, creating sub-critical pieces, which immediately stops the chain reaction. The magnitude of a fission bomb, made of uranium or plutonium, is thus in practice limited to about a megaton of TNT. The fission bombs that exploded over Japan were equivalent to about 20 kilotons.

The hydrogen bomb is on a qualitatively grander scale to the atomic bomb. In essence it brings the power of the sun to the Earth. The sudden liberation of vast amounts of energy in a fusion reaction is similar to what happens in fission, but there are also dramatic differences, which are key to the greater destructive power of the hydrogen bomb and to the technical difficulties of designing an effective weapon.

First, fission involves the nuclei of heavy elements, uranium and pluto-nium being among the heaviest of all, whereas deuterium and tritium, as used in fusion, are isotopes of the lightest element, hydrogen. This is the reason for the colloquial reference to such weapons as 'hydrogen bombs'. Here nuclei of deuterium (D) and tritium (T) merge – 'fuse' – to make a nucleus of helium and a neutron. The mass of the latter pair is less than the total in the deuterium and tritium, and so (following Einstein's equiva-lence of mass and energy, $E=mc^2$) energy is liberated. This energy appears in the kinetic energy of the products. An atom of plutonium or uranium is roughly fifty times heavier than the combined mass of a single atom of deuterium and tritium, so a kilogram of fuel for a hydrogen bomb has about fifty times as many atoms as the same weight of plutonium. The energy released per fusion of hydrogen may be smaller than that from a single fission of uranium, but there is more energy per kilogram in a fusion bomb because there are more atomic nuclei present.

The second feature is this: the more deuterium and tritium you start with, the more fusions can occur. There is no disassembly or critical mass constraint, as in the case of fission. For a hydrogen bomb, the limit is the amounts of fuel that can be brought together and once ignited remain hot enough for fusion to continue. The power of a fusion bomb is therefore in earthly terms boundless.

The proof is blindingly obvious, quite literally: the sun is a fusion engine and it is vast. The sun burns very slowly, with half of its hydrogen fuel still unused after 5 billion years; a terrestrial hydrogen bomb, however, must burn its fuel within a millionth of a second, so while the sun shows that thermonuclear fusion can happen on a vast scale, it gives no clue as to whether the process can be sped up a billion trillion times faster.* If this can be done, and the burning maintained, there is no limit to the power of such a bomb. At Los Alamos the leading enthusiast for the hydrogen bomb, Edward Teller, was already aware that it would be possible to envisage a single fusion bomb with enough power to destroy all life on Earth. Such a bomb would be too big to deliver by plane, but there would be no need: as it could kill everyone, there would be no need to move it from the construction site. Teller disarmingly called it the 'Backyard' weapon.

The third difference proved to be the biggest challenge for the designers of a practical fusion weapon: how is the device to be ignited, and once lit, made to stay alight? We know that matter is robust in the ambient world, and spontaneous nuclear explosions do not occur. The nuclear reactions that drive the sun, and all stars, operate at temperatures of millions of degrees and to make an explosion in a hydrogen bomb such extremes of heat must first be attained and then maintained. The basic idea was that a long pipe full of liquid deuterium would ignite if the temperature were high enough. A fission explosion at one end of the tube would create these hellish conditions and set off the fusion reactions.

After the conversation with Enrico Fermi in 1942, which had inspired his messianic interest, Teller had developed an outline design for the 'Super'. His original concept was deceptively straightforward in theory but impossible in practice. Liquid deuterium in a cylindrical pipe – the 'tube' – would be the thermonuclear fuel. Place it next to a fission bomb, made of uranium, so that the heat of the fission explosion ignites the deuterium.† Once lit, the fuel would burn, the power of the resulting H-bomb being determined by the amount of deuterium, in effect by the length of the tube. The longer the tube, the bigger will be the bomb – *if* the deuterium can be ignited and then continues to burn. The problem was how to make the fuels hot enough for ignition to occur and be self-sustaining.

---

* The temperature at the heart of the sun is about 10 million degrees, which is tepid on the scale needed for fusion, and limits the rate of solar burning. To speed up the rate, as in a hydrogen bomb, exceedingly higher temperatures are required.
† In 1942 the idea of plutonium implosion had not yet been developed.

ENRICO FERMI'S SUPER LECTURES

During the war the goal had been to build an atomic bomb, although as we have seen, Teller continued to work on the Super – the hydrogen bomb. The successful experiment at Trinity inspired Enrico Fermi also to think again about the Super for which the ignition system – an atomic explosion – had now been demonstrated.

On 2 August 1945, two weeks after the Trinity test and four days before the atomic bombing of Hiroshima, Enrico Fermi gave the first of six lectures at Los Alamos on the 'Super'.[12] The title of Fermi's opening lecture was 'Ideal Ignition Temperature' – in essence, the temperature the thermonuclear fuel must attain if it is to continue to burn and generate heat faster than heat is lost to the surroundings.[13]

First, Fermi calculated that if deuterium is heated (by an atomic explosion for example) to a million degrees, the deuterons (the positively charged nuclei of deuterium atoms) will have enough energy to overcome their mutual electrical repulsion, bump into one another, fuse, and generate heat.* As the temperature rises, the rate of fusion increases, and at first sight the conditions for an explosive release of nuclear energy seem at hand. However, energy also leaks into radiation, mainly due to electrons being accelerated as they pass the electrically charged deuterons in this infernal atomic mix. Fermi calculated the rate of this heat loss, using standard textbook equations known to any competent physicist. The rate of energy production in fusion, however, depends on the magnitude of the cross section for deuterons to fuse, which has to be determined by experiment. This magnitude is important, and Russian scientists at that time had no accurate data for it, so this information – passed on by Fuchs – would have had some value to them. Fermi calculated that the ignition temperature in this simple model would be a vast 295 million degrees, which is very high and would be a huge challenge to achieve. Fermi referred to the figure in his lecture.

His second lecture was on 7 August – one day after the atomic explosion over Hiroshima. In this talk he extended the simple model to include the effect of secondary reactions.[14] Specifically, when two deuterons (D) fuse, tritium (T) is produced, which opens the possibility of this newborn tritium fusing with the abundant deuterium, to create helium and a neutron. This

---

* In the energy units familiar to physics this is technically $kT=100eV$; room temperature corresponds to about $1/40eV$, and so 1 eV corresponds to about 10,000 degrees, and 100 eV is about a million degrees.

adds to the overall energy production and makes ignition easier, but to calculate precisely how much easier requires knowing the cross section for 'TD fusion'. The Soviet Union knew nothing about this quantity in 1945, but the Americans did: the fusion between deuterium and tritium has unique characteristics, and is about one hundred times more likely to occur – its 'cross section' is larger by this amount – than between two nuclei of deuterium; in effect, a TD mixture will ignite at a lower temperature than pure deuterium. Fermi estimated that the fusion of this newborn tritium would reduce the ignition temperature to 200 million degrees.*

Fermi's third lecture, on 18 August – three days after the Second World War ended – was titled 'The Addition of Tritium'.[15] The fact that tritium produced in the fusion of deuterium would bring down the ignition temperature so much convinced Fermi that the best fuel for a hydrogen bomb would involve tritium.

But this is easier said than done, as tritium is 'not one of the most easily available isotopes': it is radioactive, difficult to handle, and expensive to manufacture. Fermi noted that a few cubic centimetres of tritium gas had been made in the nuclear reactor at Oak Ridge by directing neutrons at an isotope of lithium – Lithium-6, where three protons are joined with three neutrons.[†] He calculated the ignition temperature as a function of the amount of added tritium, and for a concentration of 0.5 per cent, for example, found that the ignition temperature came down to about 100 million degrees.

In this lecture Fermi also calculated the time taken to reach the ignition temperature. This frustratingly turned out to be of the order of hundreds of microseconds, which he deemed was too long for a practical reaction 'since inertia would not hold the system together for so long'. Mathematical analysis during the following year showed the amounts of tritium required for this basic 'Super' to be impractically large.[16]

---

* For fusion to happen, two nuclei must first come into contact. The repulsive electrical force between the protons in each nuclear pack resists this, however. This repulsive force is stronger the nearer the protons approach one another. In tritium or deuterium, if the nuclei are by chance oriented such that their protons are 'at the back' with neutrons at the vanguard, the relative remoteness of the charged protons reduces the electrical repulsion. This makes it easier for the nuclei to encroach, whereby one of the neutrons in the tritium touches the neutron in the deuterium nucleus, and ignites the fusion reaction. As there are two neutrons to do the shielding in tritium, its proton can be further away from the target than in the case of deuterium alone, which has only one neutron to hide behind. This makes it easier for tritium to fuse than deuterium. Tritium is hard to come by and is unstable, however, which is a reason why deuterium is important.

† The process is n+ Li6 -> T + He4. Remarkably two years would elapse before Teller proposed using Li6 (in molecules of lithium-deuteride) within the bomb itself, so that tritium could be made in situ.

On 11 September Fermi gave his fourth lecture: 'Time Scale and Radiation Cooling'.[17] Producing tritium in the DD fusion was all well and good, but it came at the cost of depletion of the deuterium. Furthermore, some of the neutrons this produced would escape from the production device. When Fermi accounted for this he found that it pushed the ignition temperature back up again. To add to his problems, his model of cooling up to this point had assumed that energy was transferred to radiation only as a result of electrons being accelerated as they passed charged deuterons. However, he noted a counter-intuitive effect where electrons could cool faster in the presence of radiation than if there were none, namely that in Compton scattering, where an electron has more energy than a photon, on average the electron loses energy. He concluded that this could alter his estimates of the ignition temperature by more than 50 per cent.[18]

The fifth lecture was on 17 September.[19] The route Fermi had been outlining to a practical Super seemed to be doomed unless some way could be found of reducing the cooling. In this lecture Fermi examined the cooling mechanisms in fine detail, and discussed the possibility of a magnetic field cutting down conduction of heat to the walls. This helped, but not enough. Fermi had covered everything in detail, and concluded that he could not see how to make a hydrogen bomb work. A problem was that although you could use a fission reaction to provide the spark to light the thermonuclear fire, only some of the deuterium and tritium would be ignited and the reactions would peter out. By analogy, this would be 'like trying to light a log fire with a match'.[20] In practice, some intermediate kindling is needed.

Fermi's sixth and final lecture was in October. He calculated the mean range of neutrons produced in DD and TD reactions.* This would also affect the way energy was shared in the plasma, but it did not affect his main conclusions. Fermi concluded with a wry dig at Teller, whose optimistic proselytizing for the Super was a source of amusement in Los Alamos. Fermi used his own nickname – 'The Pope' – in his remark. He said: 'Teller who has been in charge of most of the work reported is inclined to be more optimistic than is the lecturer. The procedure that has been adopted in trying to resolve the practicability of the Super is that Teller shall propose a tentative design which he considers somewhat over-designed, and the lecturer will try to show that it is under-designed.' And Fermi's punchline: 'This makes the Pope the Devil's Advocate!'[21]

---

* They have energies of DD (2.4MeV) and TD (14MeV) and in consequence a different ability to penetrate the gas.

THE VERSIONS OF P. D. MOON
AND KLAUS FUCHS

Dr Moon, a member of the British delegation, produced a four-page summary of the main points, which were later delivered to James Chadwick in Washington for transmission to the United Kingdom. Meanwhile Fuchs had made assiduous notes himself, which he was about to pass to Gold.

Moon's notes[22] give the main formulae and essential numbers under a set of headings, which cover the basic questions of physics. These are mainly for reference as it is not straightforward to calculate the numbers for oneself. So, for example, 'Generation of Energy' gives a formula for the production of energy as a function of temperature, asserts that this depends on the fusion cross section, and gives the empirical values. Next is 'Transfer of Energy to Radiation', where a formula for this rate is quoted, and then under 'Critical Temperature' there is merely the (essential) information that the ignition temperature is '27keV' (295 million degrees). The notes of Fermi's lectures that reached Russia contain more pedagogy. For example, Fuchs quotes a formula for the 'critical temperature', with identical symbols to those in Fermi's notes, enabling readers to verify for themselves the value for the ignition temperature.

Moon's discursive summary appears to be a considered brief prepared from the detailed information in Fermi's lectures. Fuchs' notes, by contrast, follow Fermi's path more closely and quote his formulae with the same notation, with some intermediate steps that do not appear in Fermi's notes but we can infer were included by Fermi during his actual presentation. Fuchs' notes also include a rough schematic of the weapon, two concentric circles representing the atomic explosion, surrounded by a tamper of beryllium oxide, adjacent to a mixture of tritium and deuterium, which fronts a cylinder of deuterium. This figure does not appear in the available official record of Fermi's lectures, nor is it in Moon's notes. It appears either to be a gratuitous 'extra' that Fuchs has added for the Russians' benefit, or it has been redacted in the available American and British records.

On 19 September, two days after Fermi's fifth lecture, Fuchs had a rendezvous with Harry Gold. To get out of Los Alamos, Fuchs volunteered to drive to Santa Fe to buy drinks for a party that the British delegation was planning for its American hosts. As Genia Peierls told me in her idiosyncratic staccato style: 'I remember I thought Klaus away long time!' She was right, for Fuchs had taken a detour into the desert where he could write a report for Gold, which included all the details of the Trinity explosion together with seven pages of formulae and notes about Fermi's lectures.

On this occasion Fuchs carried much of the information in his head. As he would later explain: 'En route . . . I stopped on the way in the desert, drove off the highway to a solitary place, and wrote a part of the paper . . . which I planned to deliver.'[23] While at first sight this might appear to imply a prodigious feat of memory – there is some anecdotal evidence that he had an eidetic memory – in Fuchs' circumstances it was perhaps not so remarkable, at least as far as the plutonium bomb was concerned.[24] That project had for him been a full-time activity, the details of which were always near the centre of his attention. Nonetheless, knowledge was continuously evolving. A colleague believed that 'every evening at Los Alamos Fuchs wrote out what he had done during the day. He had the correct numbers for everything and you don't carry that in your head for long.'[25]

Having prepared his report, Fuchs then met Gold in Santa Fe and gave him his dossier with information on the explosion at Trinity, and all the details of the bomb's construction.[26] This was especially valuable because it described a practical atomic bomb – one that was known to work. The papers also provided information from which the Soviets deduced how quickly the Americans could build a stockpile of plutonium weapons.

Fuchs told Gold about the different crystalline forms of plutonium, each of which has unique properties. The most familiar example of an element having different solid forms is carbon; configured as diamond it can have great value, as soot it is mere waste, whereas for the recently discovered form known as graphene, the possibilities are still being worked out. In the case of plutonium, Fuchs explained, some forms are brittle, others malleable and soft. The element can burn and crumble in air, or disintegrate to powder at room temperature. Some forms of plutonium will contract when they are heated, a property that is unique among the chemical elements. These facts are not of immediate relevance to an atomic explosion, but are nonetheless crucial to anyone who plans to store and use the substance. Fuchs had given the Soviets a crash course in the metallurgy of this novel element, which it would have taken them many months to discover for themselves.

To complete this goldmine, Fuchs handed over his notes on Fermi's lectures about the hydrogen bomb. I doubt that this material relied on memory, however. The formulaic identity throughout, even to the extent of the order of symbols in equations, suggests that the basic maths had been written out already. There is a considerable amount of instructional material, which makes this report more of a primer on the physics than a straightforward report on the outcome. This distinguishes Fuchs' record from Moon's notes, and suggests that what Fuchs prepared en route was the pedagogic explanation, based on formulae that he had already written down.

Fermi's lectures were on what today is known as the 'Classical Super'. This was not the 'secret of the hydrogen bomb' as some breathless descriptions claim, because there seemed at that stage no means to make the idea work. Indeed, the key breakthroughs that led to hydrogen bombs in both the United States and the Soviet Union came only after 1950. Even so, Fuchs' information was invaluable. It revealed at the very least that the Americans now had a programme to develop this new breed of weapon, together with the fundamental ideas, and the theoretical work that had exposed the difficulties around them. In any event, it is clear that what Fuchs prepared for Moscow was far more detailed than the notes of Moon, which Chadwick received (see chapter 10).[27] Their quality, in both the clear logic of the argument and its exposition, also confirms the widely held opinion that Fuchs' lectures – given later in the United Kingdom – were exemplars of the form.

Thanks to Fuchs, Stalin now had a deep insight into the United States' strategy, and a means to assess his rival's strength. The Russians now began to research the hydrogen bomb for themselves. The arms race would have begun eventually in any scenario, but Fuchs' notes on the Classical Super, passed to Moscow via Gold on 19 September 1945, were an enormous stimulus to the Soviet Union starting its own programme.[28]

A GOLD MEDAL FOR SECRECY

Klaus Fuchs had now added nearly two years of espionage in North America to his already impressive CV as an agent in the United Kingdom. After MI5's cosy assessment of Fuchs' threat in January 1944, they took no interest in him until after the war had ended, when he returned to work at AERE Harwell, the United Kingdom's new Atomic Energy Research Establishment near Oxford. Nor was he identified by the FBI, initially in New York, or then within the confines of Los Alamos itself. Fuchs' most damaging espionage was performed in the United States, a fact that MI5 would cling to later when harangued in 1950 by J. Edgar Hoover, head of the FBI.*

---

* At least, this was the public perception when Fuchs was exposed. We now know that there were other spies inside Los Alamos, such as the young physicist Ted Hall, whose information complemented Fuchs'. I shall argue later that Fuchs' Harwell period of espionage, when Russia was an enemy and he alone was the primary source at the heart of the British nuclear programme, may have been more dangerous still.

There was almost nothing to indicate that Fuchs was actively involved in espionage, and even if he had been suspected it would be hard to find proof short of catching him in the act of gathering the information or of passing it on. Fuchs was obtaining the information he passed to the Soviets in the course of his work; indeed much of it was the product of his own brain. As for catching him in the act of transfer, he only met Gold sporadically, and although in Fuchs' opinion the meetings ran on too long, he controlled the risk by transferring documents only at the very end. If federal agents had found Fuchs with secret scientific documents in his possession, he could at least offer some explanation for them and as long as the conspirators took basic precautions the odds were in their favour.

After Fuchs handed information to Gold, they would immediately part. Gold would pass it on to Anatoly Yatzkov, the resident at the Soviet Embassy. Within a short space of time, therefore, Fuchs' information was securely in Soviet hands, with Fuchs and Gold in the clear. FBI and MI5 tactics at this time were to monitor the embassies of unfriendly nations and gather whatever intelligence they could in the hope that at some point in the future a nugget would fall towards them. But no connection was made between Yatzkov and Gold, let alone at this stage between Gold and Fuchs. If there was a weak point in the Soviet Union's espionage operation in North America it was that the information, however obtained, had to be passed on to Moscow. The Soviet Embassy did so in coded telegraph cables in which Fuchs was referred to as 'REST', or later 'CHARLES'. The messages were transmitted over open commercial telegraph lines. This would turn out to be the Achilles heel of the entire operation.

Back in February 1943 the United States had worried that Stalin might make a secret peace deal with Hitler. The US State Department initiated a programme whereby transmission of Soviet cables to Moscow was temporarily delayed so they could be copied. These copies went to the security agency of the United States Army, at which point the FBI had access to them. Among the avalanche of messages, therefore, the FBI had copies of the missives from the Soviet Embassy to Moscow containing Fuchs' information about atomic bomb research.

The FBI had a mountain of data, but until 1948 no solid information. The insurmountable problem was that the encoded messages were based upon 'one-time pads', which makes them impossible to crack. There are two parts to this unbreakable code. First is a codebook, which is like a reverse telephone directory with a list of five-digit numbers, each of which corresponds to a different letter, word or phrase. For example, 11042 might correspond to CHARLES. In 1945 a charred copy of a Russian codebook was salvaged from a battlefield in Finland. This was not enough to enable the Americans who obtained the copy to read messages, however, because there is a second part to the encryption, which involves 'additives', key to encoding and decoding the message.

An 'additive' is a random five-digit number, known in this case only to Yatzkov and Moscow. Suppose this is 12124, for example. Yatzkov adds this to the number in the codebook, which means that to transmit CHARLES the five-digit code is 23166 (that is 12124 added to the codebook's 11042). When Moscow receives 23166, they subtract 12124 from it, giving 11042, which the codebook reveals corresponds to the word CHARLES.

If the same additive were applied to every string of five throughout the message, however, the result would be vulnerable. An ingenious modification makes the message totally secure: change the additive randomly from one string to the next. Whereas encoding and decoding the message required the sender and recipient to know the value of a single additive, now they need to know the string of pentagrams to make up the whole set.

A huge book of strings of random numbers, grouped in fives, lists the additives used to prepare and decode Russian messages. During the Second World War Moscow had produced a vast number of these pages – or pads – one set remaining in Moscow, the others being taken under strict security to Soviet embassies. Each coded message would begin with an instruction as to which pad number had been used to prepare it, which Moscow would then use to unscramble the strings. So long as a pad was used only once, there was no means to decode the message. If a pad were employed more than once, however, it would be potentially vulnerable, as the second key would contain the same sequence as the first one and no longer be random.

Even had the contents somehow been translated, the reader would have learned only that information about the atomic bomb was leaking out of New York, from a source code-named 'REST' or 'CHARLES'. So Klaus Fuchs' identity was doubly protected. The FBI built up a library of these encoded Russian messages in case someday a means was discovered to bring them to life. In the absence of such a miraculous resurrection, Fuchs was safe.[29]

On 5 September 1945, three days after Japan formally surrendered and a fortnight before Fuchs' meeting with Gold in Santa Fe, there was a shocking development. Igor Gouzenko, a cipher clerk at the Soviet consulate in Ottawa, defected and exposed a Soviet atomic spy ring in Canada. This revelation led to the arrest of the British physicist, Alan Nunn May, and Israel Halperin, a professor of mathematics at Queen's University in Kingston, Ontario – the same Halperin who had supplied Fuchs with scientific journals during his internment in Canada during 1940. Nunn May was convicted of violating the Official Secrets Act and sentenced to ten years' imprisonment. Halperin was more fortunate, as a crucial witness withdrew his testimony and the case collapsed. Meanwhile, when the Canadians examined Halperin's diary they found that it contained over 700 names.[30]

Among the names were those of Klaus Fuchs, and his sister Kristel, resident in Massachusetts. Although MI5 seems to have been aware of Halperin's diary, it apparently remained unaware until November 1949 that it contained Fuchs' name. Had MI5 officers been aware of this discovery at the time, they might have examined Fuchs more critically in 1946, when he was preparing to return to Harwell and to take a pivotal role in the top-secret design of the British atomic and hydrogen bombs.[31]

When Fuchs met Harry Gold on 19 September, two weeks after Gouzenko's defection, Gold gave him instructions on how to make contact with a Soviet courier in London after his return to England.[32] Fuchs added that he might visit his sister in Boston again around Christmas and that she might be a means to let Gold know where Fuchs had moved. With that, they parted.

Transmission of Fuchs' news was delayed, however. Gold had to take the sensitive package with him all the way across the country, by train, to his home in Philadelphia. From there, he went to New York the next day, 22 September, intent on passing the information to his Soviet controller, Anatoly Yatzkov. Yatzkov failed to appear, however, because he, along with others in Soviet espionage, was lying low following Gouzenko's exposure of the Soviet spy ring.

Gold and Yatzkov met eventually on 12 November. When Gold saw Fuchs in September, Gold had suggested that they meet in Boston and that Kristel should decide the date.[33] Now Yatzkov told Gold that he should not see Fuchs directly. Instead he should 'go to CHARLES' sister', tell her that Klaus should not see him but 'instead [Klaus] should leave materials' with her and that Gold would collect them 'later'.[34] Kristel would be told to display a signal visible from the street to indicate when the coast was clear so that Gold could collect the documents. To ensure that Gold would not accidentally meet Fuchs at her house the signal will not be displayed 'if Fuchs is home'. The goal was clearly to ensure that there would be no direct contact between the courier and the Soviet Union's most valuable atomic spy. Kristel was of course unaware of the reasons for this machination, but by agreeing to provide signals she was becoming more deeply involved in her brother's intrigues.

The first stage of Fuchs' espionage had been in England, at Birmingham; the second in the United States in New York and Los Alamos; and now in England once more, at Harwell, he began his third.

PART FOUR

From Trinity to the Soviet Atomic Bomb: 1945–9

Harwell, Hydrogen and Plutonium

The United States and Great Britain had built the atomic bomb, which had ended the war. Their ally the Soviet Union celebrated the defeat of Nazism, but at a huge price: its territory and industry were devastated, and millions of its citizens dead. Its factories were destroyed, its transport infrastructure in ruins. In the middle of the twentieth century most of Russia was once again an agrarian society, struggling to survive.

Stalin's control was absolute. In the dozen years before the war he had brutally usurped power, through assassination, deportation to the Gulag, by genocide. His empire now extended throughout Eastern Europe. In March 1946 Winston Churchill described the new reality graphically as an 'Iron Curtain' that had descended across the continent, with many of its ancient capitals – Budapest, Prague, Berlin – on the Soviet side of the divide. For Stalin this was partly a security blanket, which put Moscow further from its external enemies, the United States and its allies. He may have decided on this strategy long before Trinity and Hiroshima, in which case Churchill and Roosevelt were wise to have withheld intelligence from him. They had not reckoned, however, that thanks to Fuchs and other spies, Stalin knew of his wartime allies' duplicity.

Stalin realized that the atomic bomb, which had closed the war, would be the trump card in the new world order. He suspected that the United States would now use its nuclear monopoly to extend its influence, or even make a pre-emptive strike on his industrial wasteland. The Soviet leader wanted an atomic bomb himself. Klaus Fuchs was as yet unaware that his espionage had already pointed Stalin towards achieving that goal. With Germany and Japan defeated, Fuchs continued his efforts to ensure that the USA did not have sole ownership of the new weapon.

General Curtis Le May, who was now the US Air Force Chief of Staff in the Pentagon, openly advocated pre-emptive strikes against the Soviet Union with atomic bombs so that the United States could establish global hegemony.[1] The idea that a million innocent civilians might be murdered merely because geography placed them in Stalin's fiefdom typified the distorted morality of the new atomic era. Cooler heads thankfully held sway and the subsequent development of an atomic arsenal by the Soviet Union created a balance of terror – mutually assured destruction (MAD) – that has now lasted for seventy years. From this perspective it may be that Fuchs' sharing of atomic knowledge with the Soviet Union has affected history for the better – or the less bad – and helped to maintain Peierls' original 1940 vision of the atomic bomb as deterrent.

The awesome effects of atomic bombs had been demonstrated by the explosion of a uranium bomb at Hiroshima and a plutonium bomb at Nagasaki. American strategy was now to develop a whole arsenal of weapons and to understand their effects. Because the data on plutonium explosions from Nagasaki and the Trinity Test were not consistent with each other, nor with the theoretical expectations – either the Nagasaki explosion had been over-estimated or the Trinity Test had been inefficient in some way – this would involve bombing a fleet of decommissioned naval vessels at Bikini Atoll in the South Pacific so proper measurements could be taken. As many American scientists were returning to universities, and as Fuchs had been central to the theory of the plutonium bomb, he remained at Los Alamos until the middle of 1946, working on the discrepancy between the magnitude of the explosion over Nagasaki and that of the Trinity Test, and also preparing for the upcoming tests at Bikini Atoll.

The difficult wartime marriage between Great Britain and the United States, where collaboration had been for a common goal but with different long-term objectives – for the USA to establish itself as leader of the free world, for the UK to maintain at least some of its global position – now faded. During the war the British had led in intelligence and decryption, while the Americans dominated the atomic partnership following the Manhattan Project. Even though the conception of the atomic bomb had been with Peierls and Frisch in Birmingham, and the early work on enrichment had been in the United Kingdom, the US Congress regarded the bomb as an American invention, any British involvement being a perturbation at best. The work had been done in secret, and the true credits would not become clear until later; what was indisputable was that the US government had spent around $2.6 billion on atomic research during the war. For Congress, answerable to American taxpayers, the cost defined the reality: 'Great Britain or Canada did not give us any material aid in discovering this bomb' and 'The work of twenty-five or thirty [British] scientists' was 'so inconsequential' that the British could 'not claim a property interest in the formula of the bomb', wrote Senator Kenneth McKellar to President Truman in September 1945.[2]

The atomic bomb changed the character of war. The Americans had enough uranium to build an arsenal of weapons and although a few British scientists, especially Klaus Fuchs, were regarded as marginally useful, the post-war American programme had no overwhelming need of them. The goal of the United States was to ensure security with an arsenal of atomic weapons whereas the United Kingdom's long-term vision had been towards the development of nuclear power. This had led the British to construct an experimental nuclear reactor in Canada, which as we have seen was infiltrated by Soviet espionage. The bomb was a symbol of great power, however, and the United Kingdom could not risk being without one. Within days of the explosions over Japan, British Prime Minister Clement Attlee set up a committee to examine the feasibility of Great Britain developing nuclear weapons. The United States, meanwhile, was the sole nuclear power and 'anxious to remain so'.[3] On 1 August 1946 the McMahon Act forbad the transfer of data on nuclear power or weapons from the USA to any foreign country, including Great Britain. The penalty for violating this edict included 'death or imprisonment for life'.[4]

There were two reasons why the Americans placed their principal ally out of bounds. First, the Americans distrusted the efficiency of British security following the Nunn May espionage debacle, and so believed that this would better guarantee security. Second, and more direct, was that the United Kingdom was best placed to build a weapon of its own, and rival American hegemony; Washington saw no advantage in helping them do so. If the UK were to develop an atomic weapon, it would have to do so alone. Foreign Secretary Ernest Bevin's blunt opinion about a British nuclear weapon was, 'we've got to have this thing over here, whatever it costs . . . we've got to have a bloody Union Jack flying on top of it'.[5] A British bomb was essential, both as a deterrent (in the era before NATO) and as a dowry whereby the Americans might rethink their opposition to atomic collaboration. Thus Fuchs' presence at Los Alamos and the Bikini Atoll tests could have great long-term advantages for the United Kingdom.

This paid dividends very quickly when in April 1946 Fuchs attended a conference at Los Alamos on the 'Classical Super', or hydrogen bomb. As we have seen, in 1945 he had heard Enrico Fermi's lectures in which this greatest of physicists demonstrated that the bomb would cool before all its fuel ignited. Edward Teller, still obsessed with the idea of the 'Super', was convinced that there must be a solution. The 1946 conference would be Teller's attempt to start a dedicated programme to develop the weapon.

GRANDFATHER OF THE
HYDROGEN BOMB?

Had the ignition of a hydrogen bomb remained an insuperable problem, the age of thermonuclear weapons would not have happened. It would take five years before this difficulty was overcome. The first stage towards the solution was found in 1946 by an unlikely duo in the form of Klaus Fuchs, the committed communist, and the Hungarian-born American mathematician John von Neumann, a diehard conservative.

Fuchs was primarily a physicist who was a powerful manipulator of equations; von Neumann was one of the smartest mathematicians of the twentieth century but also had deep insights into how nature works. During the war, von Neumann together with Fuchs and Peierls had been central to solving the problem of implosion, which had threatened to derail development of the plutonium bomb. The contrasting capacities of these two very different personalities now combined to design an improved mechanism for igniting a hydrogen bomb. On 28 May 1946 Fuchs and von Neumann filed a patent, but the details of their work remain classified in the West.[6]

Prior to the conference, Fuchs had been investigating ways to make the Super operable by building on an idea of von Neumann's. To initiate an atomic explosion powerful enough to ignite a sustainable thermonuclear fire, von Neumann proposed in 1944 a simple change in the arrangement of the ingredients: place a deuterium-tritium mixture *inside* the uranium or plutonium of the atomic fission mixture.

When this assembly explodes, the contents vaporize, which creates a gas of electrically charged particles – electrons and the nuclei of atoms of deuterium, tritium and the heavy uranium or plutonium. When two materials with different numbers of electrons in their atoms are ionized – as here – a pressure difference ensues between the remnants of heavy and light atomic elements, whereby the heavy material squeezes the lighter elements. As a result, von Neumann argued, the light deuterium and tritium will become highly compressed by the atomic explosion. This is known as 'ionization compression'.

In 1944 von Neumann realized that the heating and ionization compression would activate thermonuclear reactions between deuterium and tritium. These would release fast neutrons, which in turn would trigger further fissions in the rapidly dissembling atomic bomb and enhance its yield. This boosted atomic fission explosion would further heat and compress the thermonuclear fuel, making it easier to ignite. This idea 'foreshadowed the later development of boosted bombs' – fission bombs

whose yield was enhanced by the presence of limited amounts of deuterium and tritium – and became a key concept in the development of more
powerful atomic bombs, after the war.[7] However, it did not move forward
the problem of making a genuine large thermonuclear explosion.

In the early months of 1946 Fuchs had been investigating whether an
initial atomic explosion 'boosted along the lines of von Neumann' could
ignite the Super.[8] It was during the Los Alamos conference that Fuchs
appears to have made the pivotal proposal that while deuterium-tritium
mixed with the uranium could boost the *ignition*, the chance of a thermonuclear *explosion* could be further increased if one used a deuterium-tritium
mixture also placed *outside* the U235 in a tamper of beryllium oxide. The
result would be a four-stage device: a fission bomb as detonator, with a von
Neumann booster, and a primer to ignite the main fuel.

First, the detonator – a fission bomb of the Hiroshima type where a
piece of U235 is fired at another lump of the element, but supplemented by
a 'booster' of deuterium with a 4 per cent admixture of tritium. Each piece
of uranium is small and harmless on its own, but their combined mass
forms a super-critical lump, which explodes. In so doing the deuterium-
tritium booster is ignited, producing neutrons that feed the fission reactions
and generate a more powerful blast in the uranium. This far is essentially
what von Neumann had already suggested in 1944. The novel features of
Fuchs' suggestion now come into play. This exploding mass is in motion
and slams into the 'primer' – a solid shell of beryllium oxide containing a
50:50 mixture of deuterium and tritium, which is adjacent to a cylinder of
deuterium: the 'main charge'. The goal is to ignite the main charge and for
it to continue burning.

Fuchs reasoned that X-rays from the uranium explosion would reach
the tamper of beryllium oxide, heat it, ionize the constituents and cause
them to implode – the 'ionization implosion' concept of von Neumann but
now applied to deuterium and tritium contained within beryllium oxide.
To keep the radiation inside the tamper, Fuchs proposed to enclose the
device inside a casing impervious to radiation. The implosion induced by
the radiation would amplify the compression caused by the atomic explosion's material shock wave and increase the chance of the fusion bomb
igniting. The key here is 'separation of the atomic charge and the thermonuclear fuel, and compression of the latter by radiation travelling from
the former', which constitutes 'radiation implosion'.[9]

This separation of fission spark from the fusion fuel, and use of radiation and ionization compression, became a feature of H-bombs developed
in the United States, the Soviet Union and Great Britain in the 1950s. The
Fuchs and von Neumann invention improves the ignition significantly, as

was demonstrated later in the Greenhouse George test of 1951. However, it is not sufficient to ignite a megatonne thermonuclear explosion, for which compression of the 'main charge' also is required. The latter would involve a further invention, by Stanislaw Ulam and Edward Teller in 1951, some aspects of which appear to owe their inspiration to Fuchs' 1946 exploitation of radiation implosion.*

Fuchs and von Neumann's invention was the state of the art in H-bomb research at Los Alamos in mid-1946, albeit briefly, when Fuchs returned to England. Fuchs' epiphany to use the radiation implosion principle was 'far ahead of its time'.[11] The mathematical modelling of the physical processes would have been relatively straightforward if modern computers had been available in those days, but in 1946 a precise analysis was impossible. Even so, one conclusion was clear: the amount of tritium needed would be so large as to be impractical.

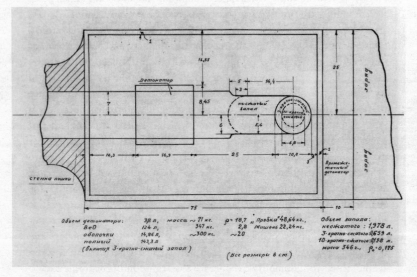

This Soviet schematic is probably based on the von Neumann–Fuchs 1946 patented device for igniting a hydrogen bomb, probably transmitted to the USSR by Fuchs in 1948. At the left is a gun-type uranium fission bomb, which ignites a capsule of deuterium and tritium on the right.

---

* The details of this also remain classified, which makes an assessment of Fuchs' implicit contribution controversial at best. In any event, Ulam–Teller came later and lies outside the present narrative.[10]

Fuchs and von Neumann had made a key breakthrough, but one that would remain theoretical unless a means of creating large amounts of tritium was invented. Teller's ingenious idea would be to include the solid substance 'lithium deuteride' in the weapon, because when neutrons hit this compound, tritium is produced within the device itself. Teller had this insight shortly after Fuchs left Los Alamos and returned to the United Kingdom. Five years would pass, however, before he and Stanislaw Ulam developed the 'enormous conceptual potential' of radiation implosion. By then, Fuchs' ability to influence events was over.[12]

Fuchs' idea of radiation implosion underlies much of what subsequently developed in both the United States and the Soviet Union. The British hydrogen bomb, which was developed in the 1950s, also involved separation of the atomic blast and fusion fuel.[13] An informed history of the Soviet hydrogen bomb concludes that Fuchs' insight was seminal there too.[14] Edward Teller has been dubbed the father of the hydrogen bomb. Whatever the parentage of the Soviet bomb, 'Klaus Fuchs must be its grandfather.'[15]

SPYING FOR BRITAIN

At the end of 1945 Rudolf Peierls returned to academic life at Birmingham University. He was deeply troubled. He had originally conceived the atomic bomb as a means of defence against Hitler, only to see it used in anger against Japan. Had he remained at Los Alamos for a further year like Fuchs, and seen the emerging enthusiasm for a hydrogen bomb, his worries would have been even more acute. Back in England, however, and as yet unaware of this even greater horror, Peierls became a founder and chairman of the Atomic Scientists Association, or ASA. Its role was to educate both politicians and the general public about the reality of atomic energy and the dangers of the proliferation of nuclear weapons. The ASA was an impetus for the later Campaign for Nuclear Disarmament, CND, in the United Kingdom, and soon drew the attention of the Security Services, which perceived it as a communist front. Peierls, meanwhile, advised Harwell and was briefed about the nuclear developments there.

The main intention at Harwell was to design the first nuclear reactor in Western Europe. The stated goal was to produce energy for the civilian use of industry and the domestic well-being of British citizens, but a covert agenda was also to develop the means for enriching uranium to a level suitable for a specialized reactor that could then convert the uranium into plutonium. That plutonium, in turn, would be the raw material for an arsenal of atomic weapons.*

Klaus Fuchs would be the fulcrum of the British quest for its own atomic bomb and in June 1946 he was recalled from Los Alamos to head the Theoretical Physics Division at Harwell. In his final weeks in the United States, Fuchs withdrew from the Los Alamos archives everything that they had on the hydrogen bomb and, in the opinion of a subsequent US Congressional inquiry, held it 'for an inordinate amount of time'. There was 'no question, but that these [documents] went to the Soviets', though only after he had delivered copies to James Chadwick for the British: on 18 June he wrote to Chadwick and enclosed copies 'of some notes' that he wanted to speak about 'on Thursday', 20 June.[16] Where Peierls had wanted to neuter the horror of the atomic and, later, the hydrogen bomb by public awareness and the prevention of nuclear proliferation, Fuchs decided to share the knowledge, a strategy that would result in the high-risk game of mutual deterrence.

At the end of June 1946 Fuchs returned to England in a British bomber. He flew, rather than taking a ship, because Harwell needed him urgently for a meeting on 1 July.[17] Fuchs made his way from Los Alamos to Montreal via Washington, where he saw Chadwick, and then he visited his sister Kristel in Boston. In Washington the information on the hydrogen bomb he had gleaned from the Los Alamos archives was given to Chadwick. This included calculations on deuterium and tritium interactions, which were fundamental to understanding the conditions in which a fusion explosion could occur. This information summarized the state of the art at Los Alamos at the time of Fuchs' departure.

Thus Fuchs' last 'espionage' before leaving Los Alamos was in aid of the British.† Did Fuchs have a last-minute assignation with Harry Gold, or someone from the Soviet Embassy, to update them about the last of Enrico Fermi's lectures, which took place after his meeting with Gold on 19 September, or to brief them about his idea with von Neumann, or about all that he had taken from the Los Alamos archives? A clue that an urgent rendezvous may have taken place is that Fuchs was delayed by a day, and his explanation was bizarre. In the rush from Washington to Montreal via his sister in Boston, Fuchs the brilliant scientist with the logical brain claimed that he had made a basic error. In a letter about his travel expenses,

---

* Harwell was experimenting with the design of nuclear reactors. Windscale in the north-west of England became the site for dedicated production of plutonium.
† Fuchs managed by a few weeks formally to avoid adding espionage on behalf of the British literally to his CV, because the McMahon Act, which forbad sharing atomic information with other allies, including the British, did not come into force until 1 August.

written at his sister's home on 27 June, Fuchs blamed his delay on 'a mix up between standard time and daylight saving time'.[18] Fuchs' flight on 26 June was due to leave at 3 p.m. daylight-saving time. When he saw 3 p.m. in the timetable he said he assumed this to be standard time, as 'I assumed that all timetables are on standard time but the one I used was an exception.' Thus Fuchs assumed that during daylight-saving time his departure was at 4 p.m. In those days air flight was more relaxed than today and one could arrive at the airport at the last moment and still make the flight. Fuchs duly turned up at the airport after 3 o'clock, prepared for a 4 p.m. departure, only to discover that the flight had just departed. As a result, he spent another day at his sister's home.

Fuchs eventually left Boston on 27 June,[19] stayed overnight at the Windsor Hotel in Montreal, and flew to England. He arrived in London on 29 June, and after another night in a hotel he completed his journey by train to Didcot, the nearest station to Harwell. On 30 June, although exhausted, he was back in England for the first time in three years, and ready for the Harwell meeting on 1 July. Fuchs had not seen Peierls for a year, so on 2 July he visited his friend and mentor in Birmingham. There they brought one another up to date on scientific developments, although Fuchs assiduously kept from Peierls information on the hydrogen bomb that was classified, even though content to share it with the Soviets. Peierls now brought Fuchs up to date with some news of his own.

CONFIDENTIAL INFORMATION

In March of that year, while Fuchs was still in Los Alamos, Peierls had received a letter from G. P. Thomson, the former chairman of the Tube Alloys committee who was now Professor of Physics at Imperial College London. Thomson's letter contained ideas for generating nuclear energy by the fusion of isotopes of hydrogen. Today Thomson's breakthrough is remembered as a key step in developing fusion power, but originally he saw its potential for breeding plutonium. This led to his work being classified secret.[20]

Thomson was less concerned whether the scheme would be a self-sustaining energy machine than that the basic idea was sound. Thomson was an experimentalist who won the Nobel Prize for his experiments on electrons. Thanks to his skills, he could develop the apparatus, but the theoretical underpinning would require specialist knowledge. He therefore consulted Peierls. Correspondence between the pair over the following months identified some technical problems, but these were solved.

Thomson's original letter to Peierls, however, reveals that he had foreseen another potential application of his idea: he had realized that fusion 'would [also] be a formidable source of plutonium using very little uranium [which] would be cheaper than a pile and would have at least political importance'. He made the coy remark about 'political importance' because in 1946 plutonium was seen as the key element needed for an arsenal of nuclear weapons.

Thomson's insight was that fusion would produce not just energy, but also neutrons. These neutrons emerged with enough energy, moreover, to be especially effective as a means to convert uranium to plutonium. Although today Thomson's insight is remembered as a key step in developing fusion as a power source, in 1946 it was its potential implications for breeding plutonium that generated political and scientific excitement.

Peierls had realized the implications of Thomson's idea as soon as he read his letter. In his reply on 12 March, Peierls wrote, 'I find myself in a very peculiar situation when I try to comment on this problem. The reason is that I am in possession of a great deal of information obtained on these topics by work at Los Alamos . . . which is regarded as particularly secret.' He was so worried about the sensitivity of his reply that he added a postscript: 'Please also regard as confidential information that I know aspects of this problem that are specially secret, since it is not too hard to guess what these aspects might be.'[21]

Klaus Fuchs was one of the world's leading experts at that time, and Peierls respected his mathematical abilities implicitly. What's more, Fuchs had security clearance – by July 1946 at a higher level than Peierls – and Harwell's secure facilities made it an ideal place to test Thomson's concept. So it would have been perfectly natural for Peierls to have discussed it with him when they met on 2 July. There is no record of what was said but it seems exceedingly likely that this was the moment. Fuchs would then have been fully briefed about the opportunity that fusion might offer for the production of plutonium.*

Two days after replying to Thomson's letter, on 14 March 1946 Peierls wrote to a young research student, Jerry Gardner: 'I do not want to have secret work carried on [in Birmingham], but it is very likely that there may be problems in connection with the applications to power production

---

* Peierls was a consultant at Harwell, but had had no involvement with the work at Los Alamos for nearly a year. He would have been unaware of developments in the British atomic bomb programme, for example, if he even knew of its existence. Given Fuchs' level of security clearance, there was no reason for Peierls to hold back. The subsequent programme of research at Harwell confirms that Thomson was in accord with his insight being shared.

which are not covered by secrecy orders.'[22] There is no doubt what was on his mind.

Peierls and Thomson exchanged several letters during the spring, which refined Thomson's idea into a realistic scheme.[23] It had been known for over a century that when electric currents flow through two adjacent wires, the wires are forced towards one another. Thomson's inspiration was that a similar effect would occur when electric currents flow in plasma: a magnetic force would push the two streams towards one another. This so-called 'pinch' could force electrically charged particles into close proximity, and increase the chance of a fusion reaction between them.

At the start of May, Thomson and Peierls met in London to talk. Thomson's idea appeared to be excellent, but the question remained what the optimum structure of the magnetic field would be and how to create it in practice. They discussed various possibilities of shapes and intensity, their analyses filled with arcane mathematical terms from topology. Peierls was now interested in 'anchoring electrons to toroidal space by means of a magnetic field of which the lines of force are circles', but that would be difficult to implement. He calculated that in Thomson's device the electrons would be 'anchored radially but not axially'.[24]

Later that year Gardner was due to begin his Master of Science project on the motion of electrons in magnetic fields, the property that Peierls and Thomson had discussed and is key to fusion engineering. Gardner's work was clearly inspired by Thomson's letter to Peierls. On 2 July an excited Peierls, still of course completely unaware of Fuchs' duplicity, told him about Thomson's idea for nuclear fusion, together with its potential for production of plutonium. Fuchs also learned that Peierls had a new research student: Jerry Gardner. Peierls said he hoped that Gardner could consult Fuchs about the project; Fuchs, naturally, agreed.

Security at Los Alamos had been overbearing but incomplete. Fuchs was surprised by the contrast at Harwell, whose affable security officer, Henry Arnold, seemed a gentleman amateur. As Arnold would later remark, 'I am sure that he thought I was pretty harmless'.[1]

The new laboratory was fifteen miles south of Oxford in a rural backwater near the picture-postcard village of Harwell and not far from the main road from Oxford to Newbury. The red-brick functional buildings of the laboratory on a former airfield were a blot on a landscape once known for its extensive orchards. King Alfred's birthplace, Wantage, was five miles to the west; the other nearest town, Didcot, was on the Great Western Railway, a similar distance to the north. Between these two, Harwell was isolated in the open Berkshire countryside. Most of its scientists were housed in prefabricated bungalows in the fields surrounding the laboratory, or in a handful of small villages and market towns nearby, but with intermittent access to Oxford and London by train from Didcot.

That Harwell was so relatively remote suited the needs of security. From the lone access road, the site – a decommissioned airfield – appeared pleasantly countrified. Colonial-style detached houses built of brick, which had formerly been the homes of the highest-ranking Royal Air Force officers, stood behind tall beech hedges on South Drive. These became homes for Harwell's most senior staff with families. The hillside adjacent to the laboratory rapidly filled with prefabricated single-storey living accommodations that could be erected in a matter of hours. The bleak rows of white 'prefabs' littering the hillside appeared to one resident as 'like a penal colony'.[2] Fuchs' boss, Herbert Skinner, the head of physics, lived with his wife Erna and their eleven-year-old daughter, Elaine, in one of the substantial houses, at 3 South Drive. Fuchs' deputy, Oscar Bunemann, his wife Mary and their two infant sons lived in one of the semi-detached brick houses, separated from South Drive by fences, as if a metaphor for the social hierarchies of 1940s England. The bachelor Fuchs initially lived in a bed-sitting room in the imposing Ridgeway House, which had accommodated pilots and general staff during the war – two storeys high, with two wings, and fronted by three arched porticos. A large room, which could be used for public events, gave way to linoleum-floored corridors of bedrooms. A bar with a snooker table doubled as the staff social club. The building's exterior brick walls were still daubed with grey and green camouflage.

The majority of the scientists were young, many of them less than thirty years old. They were an odd mix gathered from the Manhattan Project, from the national reactor programme in Canada, from universities in Britain and the Commonwealth, and thrown together for a common purpose, the details of which were known only to a few.

Fuel was still rationed in those post-war years (and would be until May 1950) and buses linked Harwell to Didcot only twice a week. The fewer people scientists saw other than those working at the laboratory, the easier conversations could be. All social life was in a bubble where the atomic scientists, privy to secrets, cut outside interactions to the essential. But whereas those working on the project had a purpose in this rural cage, their families could either die of boredom or create their own entertainment. There were few cars, and one resident remembered that in the open views across the prefabs 'everyone could see whose car was parked outside whose house and for how long'. An incestuous society developed where social and official lives merged, with the security officer, Henry Arnold, at its nucleus.

Fuchs was now head of the Theoretical Physics Division. Oscar Bunemann, like Fuchs a political refugee from Nazi Germany, had come to Harwell from the Manhattan Project at Berkeley. He and his wife were both liberal socialists, a fact already noted by MI5 in their files. Of all Fuchs' Harwell colleagues, Bunemann's background most closely mirrored his own. Both were non-Jewish refugees from Germany, and they came from austere, intensely moral families. Bunemann was vehemently anti-Nazi, had been imprisoned by the Gestapo in 1933, fled to the United Kingdom, and like Fuchs was then interned in Canada; the two were released at the same time. Yet with so much in common, Mary Bunemann noticed that Fuchs was reluctant to talk to Oscar alone other than in closely controlled discussions of theoretical physics. Only later did she become aware of Fuchs' pathological need to protect his covert life, so he would not allow himself to be in a situation where, by chance, his real story might leak out.[3]

Herbert Skinner had also spent the war in the Berkeley team, which

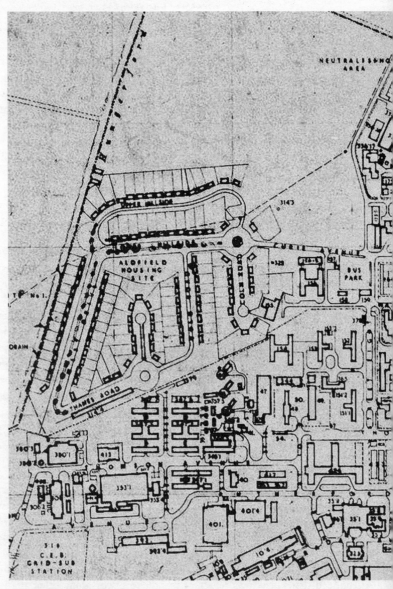

Site plan of Harwell. Cockcroft and Skinner's houses are at the upper right, labelled respectively 133 and 135. Fuchs' prefab is at the upper left, at the extreme left of Lower Hillside at the loop from Upper to Lower Hillside. Fuchs' office was in building 329, to bottom left of the Sports Ground. The social and residence section of Ridgeway house is building 142 between Curie Avenue and the Sports Ground.

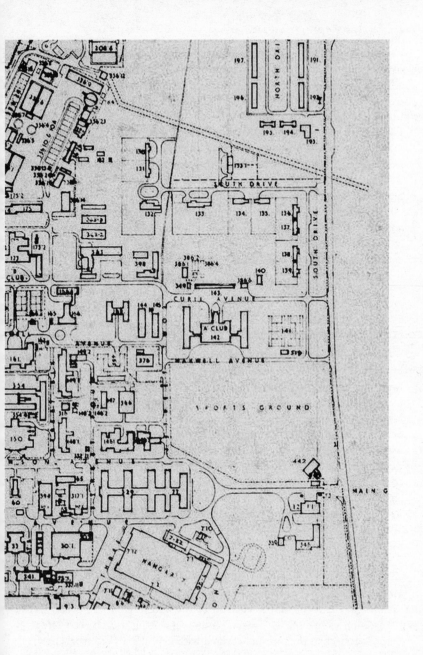

had studied magnetic separation of isotopes and investigated the physics of plutonium. A lean man with tousled hair, he and his wife Erna shared a bohemian outlook. She had grown up in Berlin between the wars. Both were socialists, like many of the scientists who had worked on the atomic bomb programme, but they also had a cosmopolitan circle of friends in London, all of which interested MI5. Erna was forty, dark haired and vivacious, with a neurotic fear of being alone, and 'very needy of attention'.[4] 'One man had never been enough for Erna,' in the opinion of Mary Bunemann.[5] Herbert's response seemed to be pragmatic: if this kept Erna happy, he was relaxed.

The Skinner house became a social centre for a small group of scientists and their families. At their parties alcohol flowed freely, thanks to friends in London who had access to supplies. This was in marked contrast to the entertainment at the home of the director and his wife, Sir John and Lady Cockcroft. The Cockcroft parties were more formal, marked by economy and temperance (although sherry was served to guests on arrival). In the Cockcroft residence, at 1 South Drive, lights would be turned on or off as rooms were occupied and vacated; by contrast, the Skinners' house blazed with illumination as if Erna was afraid of the dark.

The marriage of Mary and Oscar Bunemann was in difficulty. Harwell's inwardly turned society exacerbated their problems and within two years Mary was involved in an extra-marital affair with Brian Flowers, a junior member of Fuchs' theoretical physics group. This would generate a full-blown crisis. In what Genia Peierls described to me as 'a game of musical beds', the social whirl sucked in the Skinners also. When Herbert Skinner was away, Mary frequently called upon Erna, and felt 'delectably naughty' as Erna offered drinks from her copious supply. Erna was desperate for companionship and Klaus Fuchs would become one of the ports in her continual storm. Later, Mary Bunemann and Erna Skinner would each unwittingly become central players in the final scenes of Fuchs' tragedy.

HENRY ARNOLD

Henry Arnold, the security officer, was a dapper retired Wing Commander who had been shot down in the First World War. Now he oversaw the erection around the site's perimeter of high wire fences, with concrete posts bent back at the top, and covered with helical coils of razor wire. Although common today, this was novel in 1946.

Arnold's adopted persona of gentleman amateur was key to his armoury. A generation older than the young Harwell scientists, Henry Arnold had

1. Klaus Fuchs on his British Registration Card in 1933, aged 21.

2. Rudolf Peierls, aged 24, visiting the Theoretical Physics Institute at the University of Leipzig in 1931. Peierls is seated on the left next to Werner Heisenberg, one of the founders of quantum mechanics. The members of Heisenberg's group behind Peierls and Heisenberg are (left to right) George Placzek, G. Gentile, Giancarlo Wick, Felix Bloch, Victor Weisskopf and F. Sauter. Victor Weisskopf would later be innocently caught up in the FBI's investigations surrounding Fuchs' espionage; Felix Bloch won the Nobel Prize for Physics in 1952.

3. An international physics conference at Bristol University in July 1935. Peierls is seated fifth from the right; Fuchs' head is visible third from the left in the back row. Other notable participants include Edward Teller (sitting cross-legged at the right of the front row) and Herbert Skinner (seated at extreme right, four places from Peierls).

4. The 24-year-old Fuchs in Bristol, 1936.

5. Genia and Rudolf Peierls shortly after their arrival in New York, 1943.

6. The Lawn Road Flats ('Isokon Building') in Hampstead. Flat number 6, the residence of Jürgen Kuczynski, is on the ground floor hidden by the wall in the foreground.

7. Jürgen Kuczynski, brother of 'Sonya', in the 1950s. Kuczynski first introduced Fuchs to his Russian contacts in 1941.

8. Ursula Beurton – 'Sonya' – with her children, in Oxford, 1945. Sonya, the GRU's chief illegal in the UK, was Fuchs' contact from October 1942 to November 1943.

9. Jane Sissmore-Archer, MI5's first female officer and brilliant expert in Soviet counter-intelligence, who had qualified as a barrister in 1924.

10. Guy Liddell, Deputy Director General of MI5 during the pursuit of Fuchs.

11. William Penney, Otto Frisch, Rudolf Peierls and John Cockcroft after the award of the US Presidential Medal of Freedom on 1 May 1947.

12. The Los Alamos theoretical physics building, containing Fuchs and Peierls' offices, *c.* 1945.

13. Major General Leslie R. Groves (right), Chief of the Manhattan Project in which the first atomic bomb was developed, and Robert Oppenheimer, the Scientific Director, examining the base of the steel tower two months after the Trinity explosion on 16 July 1945. The intense heat of the bomb melted the tower, and seared the surrounding sands into jade-green glass-like cinders.

14. The physicist Norris Bradbury sits next to the 'Gadget', created by scientists to test the world's first atomic bomb, at Trinity Site. A matrix of conventional explosive charges initiated the implosion of the central plutonium to ignite the atomic bomb.

9.0 SEC.
N

⊢——⊣ 100 METERS

15. A fireball begins to rise, and the world's first atomic mushroom cloud begins to form, about 6 miles distant, nine seconds after Trinity detonated.

spent the Second World War working for Military Intelligence. At Harwell his role was to have a friendly acquaintance with everyone. He was a superb mimic, a capable amateur actor, artist and cellist. Outgoing and with an easy manner, it was impossible not to like him. With his greater age and experience he was also a ready source of advice for all, on political and social issues, and on life in general. Klaus Fuchs soon became a frequent visitor to his bungalow.

Arnold was a far more effective security officer than Fuchs ever suspected. Lorna Arnold, the distinguished historian of the British hydrogen bomb (no relation to Henry), described him as 'the perfect intelligence officer', because 'his unobtrusive build and his personality helped him merge into the background. He was very observant and tuned into people'. Lorna completed her brief portrait with what, she believed, was the key to his success: 'He was very good at understanding the psychology of suspects, winning their confidence and then destabilising them.'[6]

Henry Arnold joined the establishment very nearly at the start, in August 1946, just one month after Fuchs. He made it his business to get to know all members of the staff, some of whom were from alien backgrounds of which he knew very little. It was, however, reassuring that the Ministry of Supply had cleared each of them. Many had been employed on the American and Canadian projects, where they had been trusted with very highly classified data. This was only a year after the dropping of the atomic bombs on Japan, so it was small wonder that those closely associated with the project in America were looked on by the authorities at that time as entirely reliable.

Nonetheless, Arnold thought it essential that a security clearance of each individual employed at AERE (Atomic Energy Research Establishment) Harwell should be satisfactorily completed. He always maintained that a security officer must never, for a moment, assume that persons previously cleared are in consequence free from suspicion. His mantra, as he later wrote, was: 'I accept no form of clearance and am only satisfied if I am able to form my own opinion of each person who comes under my charge.'[7]

His method was to familiarize himself with his charges' official and private lives, the names of their friends and associates, and what Arnold regarded as 'more difficult to assess': their 'outlook on life'. Some subjects stood out immediately, as 'they differ from the accepted normal person and cannot be judged from normal standards'. Arnold put people of alien origin in this category, 'since their outlook and behaviour is influenced by that hidden part of their life spent in the country of their origin, where moral and political standards differ widely from our own'. These definitely included Klaus Fuchs, which is why Arnold found him interesting and 'began to cultivate him'. Fuchs' extreme reserve meant that Arnold found getting to know him intimately a 'difficult and lengthy process'.

In the early days of Harwell, Arnold found Fuchs 'odd', 'somewhat lonely' and 'unapproachable'. The 'strangely silent' Fuchs seldom spoke, except when a question was put to him, and in response he would answer 'in a monosyllable'. This contrasts with Genia Peierls' description of Fuchs as 'penny in the slot': silent until spoken to, and then transformed into eloquence. Combined with his intense love for theoretical computation, these are the traits of autism – or perhaps of Fuchs playing a role to convince Arnold that he was harmless.

Arnold at this stage was groping for a means to deal with those 'who might possibly be amongst us' whose loyalties lay with 'communists and the Soviet'. He had studied Karl Marx and other communist literature. These led him to conclude that communists believed 'lying is permitted to achieve an end', that 'there is no scope for individual conscience in achieving victory for the cause', and that their loyalties were to the 'cause [rather than] to individuals'. To counter this, Arnold decided that the most important part of his work was to 'inspire in the individual a personal loyalty and affection' for him. He hoped to 'awaken a conscience in the minds of such persons', which in Arnold's opinion was 'in contradiction to the communist ideologies in which there is no scope for the scruples of the individual's conscience'. Arnold regarded the second part of his work to consist of recording 'any unusual instance' that occurred during his association with 'persons selected for study'.

At that time, in the late summer and early autumn of 1946, Arnold did not consider Fuchs a spy. However, he had already noticed that Fuchs reacted differently from other senior staff to certain 'outlandish suggestions', such as that when Fuchs was away from Harwell he should give Arnold the keys to his office safe. When the other scientists were asked, they expressed astonishment: they had ultimate responsibility for the security of the contents and refused, politely. Fuchs alone was willing to hand over his key; no other member of staff agreed to cede to Arnold the control of documents in their charge. Arnold suggested that he would 'like to keep an eye on Fuchs when he was away from Harwell', in effect, to assign Fuchs a bodyguard. In Arnold's judgement, Fuchs agreed 'all too willingly', even supplying Arnold with a list of all his movements. Fuchs struck Arnold as overly conscientious, even giving unnecessary levels of detail, as on 29 September when Fuchs reported to him: 'I expect to attend a meeting of the Physics Club on October 5 in the Royal Society Lecture Room' and included the times of the lectures and the names of the speakers.[8] Arnold had no means of verifying that Fuchs had told him every movement. Fuchs 'kept it up for sometime until I eventually called it off'.

As the security officer, Arnold made regular reports to MI5. From the outset he recalled, 'Fuchs [is] beginning to attract my attention, and to stand apart from the others.'[9] On 1 October he wrote to Colonel Collard of MI5, 'After one month's experience here I am becoming even more of the opinion that certain scientists have to be nursed and educated in Security consciousness.' Then, moving from the general to the particular, he continued, 'I am meeting with a great deal of co-operation from Dr. Fuchs [who] has agreed to let me know of his movements when away from [Harwell].'[10] Arnold enquired whether Collard 'would like to receive such information'. Collard replied a week later to say he wasn't clear whether Arnold was using Fuchs 'as an informant' or whether Arnold was 'doubtful about Fuchs' integrity'.[11]

On 10 October Collard issued a memo with two purposes. One was to notify section B.1.c – the research section of the Counter-Espionage Division – of the news that Fuchs was back in the United Kingdom and engaged on atomic energy work 'of extreme importance'.[12] He was also aware that Arnold had spoken to T. A. 'TAR' Robertson, head of Soviet Counter-Espionage at MI5, and Collard wanted a record of Robertson's views on Arnold's letter about Fuchs.

Robertson's record on 15 October of his meeting with Arnold shows the first glimpse of concern: 'I assumed that [Fuchs] had been vetted and that he was regarded by us as being all right. Now I gather Arnold realises from some quarter that Fuchs has or had a Communist background.'[13]

A COMMUNIST BACKGROUND

This is what appears to have happened. In the course of getting to know the staff at Harwell, Arnold had spoken with Herbert Skinner, Fuchs' immediate boss. Skinner and his wife Erna had known Fuchs back in Bristol, where Erna and Klaus had been members of the Soviet Cultural Society. There is no evidence that Herbert had been active in that group himself – the list of its members in 1941 mentions Erna but not Herbert[14] – and Arnold seems not to have marked Herbert Skinner for special attention (though Erna would become a *cause célèbre*, as we shall see later). It would be natural for Arnold to have asked Skinner about Fuchs' time in Bristol and from that to have learned about his link with the Cultural group; as Fuchs' boss at a secure government laboratory, Skinner would have been ill advised to hide such information.

The image of Fuchs as some goody-two-shoes overly keen to please yet with an undeclared interest in the Soviet Union worried Robertson. His report continued with both a call for action and a political comment. As for action: 'In view of this Communist background it is for [section B1a] to assess the value of information against FUCHS and, if you think fit, to have further enquiries made about him and his activities in this country.' Then, perhaps in anticipation of a political reaction, Robertson continued with great foresight: 'It would undoubtedly be said, if FUCHS proves to be a dangerous customer, that his technical ability is such that Atomic Energy Research would suffer very considerably if he were removed from his present employment.'[15] Robertson suspected that unless MI5 presented indisputable evidence of serious malpractice, the national interests could trump any negative report.

His note included an ambiguous comment inspired by Fuchs' willingness to cooperate: 'It is, of course, possible that Arnold is having his leg pulled and that FUCHS may be passing vitally important information, which he has in his possession by virtue of his work, through various channels to the Russians.'[16] Quite what Robertson meant here is hard to gauge. On the one hand this remark might have been intended as one of sarcasm at Arnold's expense. MI5 officers in London regarded Arnold as an excitable 'amateur' sleuth: he was useful as an ear at the laboratory, but the 'professionals' would handle anything serious, and there are derogatory remarks elsewhere in the files that describe Arnold's views as 'unbalanced'.[17] If Robertson's remarks on this occasion were intended to display scorn, then Aesop's story of the boy who cried wolf comes to mind. Still, many a true word is spoken in jest and Robertson was probably intuitively suspicious of Fuchs, not least because Robertson's own history had sensitized him to duplicity. During the Second World War he had been one of those responsible for the Double Cross operation, which turned captured German spies and used them to send false information to Germany.[18] Thus 'TAR' Robertson was singularly positioned to perceive Fuchs' cooperation for what it was: a ploy to lull Arnold into a false sense of security.

Robertson felt unable to decide, however. Nonetheless, his report guided the research team on how to continue: 'If you [B.1.A] wish to have further enquiries made about FUCHS, would you approach Arnold at Harwell through Collard of [section] C.2.'[19]

On 13 November the first review of Fuchs' history appeared in MI5 files, written by Michael Serpell, an expert in communist subversion.[20] Serpell recalled that the experience with Alan Nunn May had led the Security Service to recognize that they had made some errors when vetting atomic scientists. When the Canadian espionage case broke in September

1945, MI5 attempted to recollect a number of cases of communists or communist suspects employed on the Tube Alloys project. This led to the rediscovery of the January 1944 memo, with its judgement that Fuchs would be less danger on the other side of the Atlantic. MI5's revised opinion, as Serpell now admitted, was: 'I am afraid the Canadian case has shown this argument to be quite unsound.' Serpell continued: 'There was, however, some difficulty in 1943 in persuading DSIR of the dangers inherent in the employment of such people as FUCHS. I presume that the position is now considerably altered and that whatever the value of a refugee scientist's work may be to atomic research, his possible danger to security will be considered as a prime issue.'[21] In a nutshell: while the risk could be lived with in wartime, times had changed.

Fuchs' youth in Nazi Germany, where he had evaded the Gestapo and lived undercover in extremely dangerous times, had hardened him for the secret, lonely life of espionage. Except for the period in the United States when he involved his sister Kristel, Fuchs' activities were completely invisible to anyone other than his immediate Soviet contacts. And all communication from them to Moscow referred to Fuchs only by a code name. As his transfer to Harwell had taken place without a hitch, Fuchs felt sure that his secret past was secure, and that any Gestapo files about him in Kiel or Berlin had not fallen into British hands.

As part of the post Nunn May re-examination, Serpell now reviewed Fuchs' history: 'The facts of this case seem to be that FUCHS in his youth acted as a communist penetration agent in [Nazi Germany]. That he should have begun his political career in this undercover style seems to me to be of considerable significance at the present time. It is also apparent that as late as 1942 he was engaged in some communist activities in a refugee group at Birmingham.'[22]

MI5 had whiffs that Fuchs was more than an historical communist, but at this stage they had 'not conclusively established' that FUCHS was the same 'Claus [sic] Fuchs that had been a close friend of KAHLE' in the Canadian internment camp (see pages 44 and 55). Nonetheless, the identification was regarded as 'probable' and as such 'potentially dangerous, since KAHLE is known to have acted as a CGPU representative [in the UK]'. Now Serpell identified a fundamental flaw in some previous arguments: 'The quietness of FUCHS' political behaviour here [is irrelevant] if FUCHS is to be considered a potential Soviet agent.'[23] Serpell continued:

Except as 'cover' for serious security investigation, I find it difficult to see what useful purpose can be served by Wing Commander Arnold's arrangements with FUCHS [to notify him of his movements for security reasons].

I agree with the suggestion [that Arnold is having his leg pulled by Fuchs] but I suggest that 'leg-pulling' should go no further. The present arrangement may already have made proper investigation difficult since it must be supposed that FUCHS regards Arnold's interest as a warning.*

Serpell concluded his review by resurrecting the link with Peierls:

It will be seen that FUCHS is a close friend of PEIERLS. While FUCHS himself is highly placed in atomic research work, I gather that PEIERLS may be even more important. In view of their association it may be as well to point out that PEIERLS himself has a Russian wife and is known to have visited Russia in 1937. If proper investigation is to be made of FUCHS' activities and contacts, I suggest that action would be taken at the same time with regard to PEIERLS.[24]

The head of Counter-Subversion, Roger Hollis, responded to Serpell's review with his usual caution: 'I consider that present action should be limited to warning W[ing]C[ommander] Arnold about the background of Fuchs and Peierls.'[25]

When Arnold visited MI5 the following week, Collard told him about Fuchs' communist past in Germany. Collard's record of the meeting was succinct: '[Arnold] had recently invited Fuchs to his house but had found him extremely difficult to talk to!'[26] Arnold's own account of their meeting was more colourful.[27] He told Collard that his campaign of befriending the staff included Arnold and his wife inviting scientists, one at a time, to their home for coffee and drinks after evening dinner. Fuchs was due at 8.30 one evening that November, but was late. Arnold went outside to look for him. The dark campus was empty, save for a man and woman coming up the hill. Arnold returned indoors, but almost immediately there was a knock at the door. His wife answered it, and found two strangers – the aforementioned couple. The man was a scientist of Austrian extraction, whom Arnold hardly knew. Neither of them had been invited, but the woman explained to Mrs Arnold that they had been looking for the bungalow 'in order to bring some cheese, which they had received from Canada'.

---

* I have retained the capitalization, as in the original, as this shows names for which MI5 has a file, and illustrates that they were interested in KAHLE too. Moreover, Serpell noted that there was no direct proof on file that Fuchs' internment was in Canada or that he met KAHLE, even though Serpell judged this as 'probable'. This uncertainty would make no sense if Serpell had known of the two FBI items mentioned in note 22. The content of Serpell's extensive (fifty-five line) memorandum is consistent throughout with him, at least, being unaware of these two pieces of information.

Arnold thought this odd, but invited them in. Soon afterwards Fuchs arrived. Since the couple and Fuchs were all living in the Staff Club, Arnold felt that the whole thing had been engineered. He certainly 'found it difficult to believe' that the couple had spent time looking for his bungalow, for he had seen them coming up the road from the direction of the Staff Club, and they had found his home without any delay. Arnold decided that Fuchs had organized it this way because he 'did not want to come alone to see me on that first occasion'.

It is of course possible that Fuchs wanted to avoid a personal inquisition, and that the strategy of expanding the guest list was the solution, but also we have Fuchs' personality: uneasy in company, perhaps very slightly autistic, and shy. For such a person, a social visit to the Arnolds' home could have been a trial even were Arnold not the security officer.

As Arnold's account was written five years later, after Fuchs' secret was in the open, it is possible that he read more into the events with the benefit of hindsight and did not reveal this detail at the time. Collard's memo made no comment that Fuchs acted suspiciously, but this might have been because he regarded Arnold's version as fantasy.* It seems that Collard's parting shot was to draw Arnold's attention to Peierls, who 'occasionally visits Harwell in a consultative capacity'.

ARCHER ON TARGET

Collard's boss, 'Joe' Archer, the head of section C2 and responsible for vetting, reviewed the whole saga. Archer's analysis has either been lost or suppressed, but the remarkable conclusion is on record: 'FUCHS is a possible (I would prefer to say *probable*) Russian agent, and obtained their [KGB] consent to his remaining where he is.'[28]

John Oliver (J. O., hence the sobriquet 'Joe') Archer was the husband of the talented Jane Sissmore. As we saw earlier, Sissmore was a veteran of the Security Services, who had been responsible for Soviet Intelligence in MI5 until she was moved in 1941 to MI6, where her boss was the infamous double agent and traitor, Kim Philby. Philby quickly recognized her talent and years later in his memoirs he wrote: 'After Guy Liddell, Jane Archer was perhaps the ablest professional intelligence officer employed by MI5. She had spent a big chunk of a shrewd lifetime studying Communist

---

* Guy Liddell in his diary described Arnold's views as 'unbalanced' – (TNA KV 4/469, December 8, 1947) – and this story might have helped fuel that view. If Arnold told Collard this version in 1946, Arnold's intuition might have been nearer the truth than Collard gave him credit for.

activity in all its aspects.'[29] For Philby, having Jane Archer in MI6 was a 'nasty shock'. Her interrogation of the Soviet defector Walter Krivitsky had revealed 'a scrap of information' about a traitor, which pointed towards Philby and, as Philby himself recalled, 'here she was, plunked down in my midst!' He set out to neutralize her by 'keep[ing] Jane busy' with a 'considerable amount' of wireless traffic from Eastern Europe, which would leave no time for mulling over tidbits from Krivitsky.

It was not Jane who signed off this opinion, as the signature is clearly that of J. O. Archer, her husband, but the penetrating conclusion has the hallmarks of her singular forensic mind. Whether it was he or she who examined the files and drew the – correct – conclusion is perhaps secondary, except for the historical record of giving credit where it is due. If the pair discussed this case – and in the circumstances it would seem likely, as they were both cleared and shared expertise on Soviet espionage – Jane probably deserves credit for the analysis; this may also explain the absence of any paperwork to back up the stark conclusion.[30]

Archer described this judgement to be the 'first important result from [my] survey of potential danger points in long-term secret munitions'.[31] He added: 'I cannot agree that this case should be dealt with by the traditional method of leaving the suspect alone and hoping to catch him red-handed unless we have informed the Atomic Energy Directorate of the facts set out in [Serpell's note].' Archer recommended that Fuchs be 'divorced from all contact with Atomic Energy' and that 'PEIERLS should not be used any longer as a consultant'.

Different analysts in MI5 had thus come to contrary conclusions.[32] J. Allen, the Director of C Division – responsible for vetting[33] – noted in a direct reply to Hollis the 'considerable difference of opinion' between on the one hand the critical warnings of Michael Serpell and of Archer, which both raised serious worries,[34] and 'your' [Hollis'] response[35], which merely advised that Arnold should be alerted. Allen recommended that they inform the Director of Atomic Energy, Sir John Cockcroft, of Fuchs' background and state the risk, leaving Harwell to decide whether to continue to employ him. Allen asked Hollis for his opinion on both Fuchs and Peierls.[36] This excited a flurry of activity.

On 3 December[37] Hollis learned from his deputy, Graham Mitchell, that Fuchs' release from detention in Canada in 1940 followed intervention by the Royal Society, which had included Fuchs in a list of mathematicians and physicists whom they wanted released urgently. The Home Office duly identified Fuchs as 'a man to be repatriated to this country if he were willing to come'. Hardly any of those sent to Canada were released as early as January 1941, and Fuchs – 'an exceptional case' – was 'one of the very first to be sent back', Mitchell informed Hollis. This confirmed to MI5 that Fuchs was hugely talented and that by now he must also be very important to the British atomic programme. By implication, therefore, his knowledge would have great value for the Soviet Union. Fuchs' communist leanings together with the importance of what he knew should have raised the alarm with Hollis.

Instead of heeding Serpell and Archer's warnings, Hollis seemed bent on defending his judgement to Allen. In so doing he introduced a false premise, which would continue for the next four years to plague MI5 perceptions of Fuchs' relation to Hans Kahle. On 4 December Hollis side-lined this link with the following claim. 'It should be borne in mind that detainees sent to Canada in 1940 were supposed to be ardent Nazis. It is known that some mistakes were made and that anti-Nazis were sent among the Nazis. This clearly occurred in the case of KAHLE and FUCHS and it is not altogether surprising that the two should have become friendly, surrounded as they must have been by Nazis who would have been un-congenial to them.'[38] Hollis concluded that he saw 'nothing in this file which persuades me that FUCHS is in any way likely to be engaged in espionage or that he is any more than anti-Nazi'. As for Peierls: 'the only significant point I can see in his case is that he married a Russian wife'.

Hollis' judgement might appear to be reasonable given the information available to him: Fuchs was anti-Nazi, but unambiguous proof of a commun-ist affiliation was missing and otherwise his record was exemplary. On the other hand, Hollis had based this opinion on a belief that Fuchs and Kahle's friendship was nothing more than a natural result of two anti-Nazis finding themselves kindred spirits in a crowd of Nazi sympathizers, for which he presented no evidence. Hollis then remarked with a hint of sarcasm that if Lord Portal, the wartime chief of the Air Staff and now head of Atomic Energy at the Ministry of Supply, wished to exclude people with records such as those of Fuchs and Peierls, it would 'lead to a considerable purge' including 'many very highly placed British scientists'. Hollis is certainly correct in this last remark, but given the analyses by Serpell and Archer his reaction overall seems remarkably unconcerned.[39] In the circumstances, Chapman Pincher's accusation that Hollis had blind-eyes seems appropriate.

Archer was clearly both confident in his advice and chagrined that Hollis had dismissed his candid appraisal. His immediate superior, Allen, the Director of C Division, also appeared concerned, as on 5 December he sent a terse memo to the Deputy Director General of MI5, Guy Liddell, via the Director of B Division, Dick White: 'D[irector of Division] C would like to discuss this case. Would you please consider and let me know a date and time.'[40]

Archer's assessment brought Fuchs to the attention of Guy Liddell, who had become the Deputy Director General earlier that year. That Liddell had previously been unaware of him shows how unremarkable Fuchs' file had been within the morass of MI5's concerns to this point. Fuchs had been but one scientist among many whose backgrounds merited examination by the Security Service. But by 1946 two events had occurred that would redefine the relationship between the scientists and national security. First, the discovery that Alan Nunn May had passed atomic information to the Soviet Union showed that not all of the atomic scientists were heroic. Second, the Soviet Union was fast becoming a threat, and communists were now the perceived demons. Meanwhile Klaus Fuchs had become central to the United Kingdom realizing its atomic ambitions; the need for him to be part of the national team was thus great, and the wish to approve him compelling. Yet the worry that he was a closet communist was now beginning to nag. While there was nothing conclusive against him, the case officers in MI5 were sounding alarms and passing decisions up the chain of command. From now on, Liddell would become increasingly involved.

On this first occasion, however, he stumbled. Sixteen years after his initial encounter with the Gestapo, Liddell's scepticism remained: 'The case against FUCHS would appear to rest on a statement by the Germans in 1934.' (So much for Archer's – or the Archers' – clear assessment.) Liddell concluded: 'I agree with B.1. [Roger Hollis] that as it stands there is really nothing of a positive nature against either FUCHS or PEIERLS.' He summarized:

> The case against FUCHS would appear to rest on (a) a statement by the Germans in 1934 when they 'made no distinction between Jews, Communists or Social Democrats' which asserted that FUCHS belonged to a Communist Movement and was involved in anti-nazi activities. (He himself said that he belonged to a Left Wing Socialist Movement). (b) In Canada he associated with a well-known Communist, Hans KAHLE in the internment camp (This, as pointed out by [Hollis] is not surprising if all the other members of the camp were Nazis). (c) A rather vague suggestion that although FUCHS was not active in the Communist Movement, he did engage in a certain amount of propaganda in Birmingham (no details).
>
> The case against PEIERLS is based on his association with FUCHS, his Russian wife and his visit to Russia in 1937.[41]

Liddell's repetition that Fuchs' association with Kahle 'is not surprising if all the other members of the camp were Nazis' suggests that he had taken Hollis' statement as fact, and that he deemed their collegiality to have been 'because' they were lone anti-Nazis. Basic police work could have shown that the majority of the aliens in the camp were in fact refugees from the Nazis, and included many Jews. Instead, Liddell's endorsement of Hollis' judgement created the received wisdom within MI5 that the internees were all Nazis, such that Fuchs and Kahle's collegiality had no deep significance.

Liddell sent a note to White and Hollis 'for action'. While he appeared to side with Hollis, he nonetheless hedged: 'I do feel there is a prima facie case for investigation of both Fuchs and Peierls', and added that with such 'important issues at stake we cannot possibly afford to leave matters as they are. I think it would be unwise to make any approach to the Ministry of Supply [Fuchs' employer] until we know more about these people.'[42]

As there was no live information on Fuchs or Peierls' activities, on 14 January 1947 MI5 began to intercept all mail and bugged their phone calls, 'in view of the secrecy and importance of the work on which [they are] engaged.'[43] The warrant on Peierls asserted: 'This man, a German by birth, is engaged on scientific work of the utmost secrecy. He has Russian associations and it is desired to learn more of his contacts and activities.'[44]

Meanwhile, Liddell explained to Sir Alexander Maxwell, Permanent Under-Secretary at the Home Office, why this action was regarded as so significant:

> They are both concerned in atomic research and are close friends. Both are Germans of the refugee type and FUCHS, at any rate, at one time was fairly near to the Communist Party. We are carefully reviewing the cases of all such people employed on highly secret projects, since the circumstances in which they were taken on during the war have very considerably changed. There is nothing really positive against either. The only thing we know against PEIERLS is that he visited Russia in 1937 and has a Russian wife. We hope by means of these HOWs [Home Office Warrants to intercept mail and monitor phone calls] to get a better idea of the circles in which PEIERLS and FUCHS move, and of the contacts they make, in order that we may advise the Ministry of Supply as to whether they can be safely kept on.[45]

By 2 April 1947 the bugging had revealed nothing, and was abandoned. Guy Liddell reviewed the evidence and concluded: 'I feel that in the absence of any further facts which may be brought to our notice, we have no case on which to make any adverse recommendation to the Ministry of Supply.'[46]

It was MI5's misfortune that their first close watch on Fuchs coincided with him taking a sabbatical from espionage. Following the exposure of the Canadian spy ring, the Soviets reduced contacts with their agents for nearly a year, until July or August 1947. If this is why Fuchs lay low during his first year at Harwell, it still does not explain why he had failed to make a rendezvous with his Soviet controller in Mornington Crescent, London, in August 1946, four weeks before the order was issued.[47] The simplest explanation is that Serpell was correct: Fuchs was wary of Arnold. Fuchs' 'too good to be true' behaviour could have been over-compensation by someone who did not want to disturb the unstable equilibrium between his covert life and the responsibility of being head of theoretical physics in the nation's atomic energy programme. In these circumstances, and having been alerted by Arnold's initial approach, Fuchs kept his head down until he was more certain about the security situation and Arnold's role. True, Arnold had befriended Fuchs, and Fuchs had reciprocated, but Arnold was a relatively novice security officer and Fuchs an experienced spy. Arnold was testing Fuchs, along with all the staff; Fuchs, for his part, was assessing Arnold and using him as an indicator of his own security.

Only after a year of inactivity, during which Arnold would have formed his baseline opinions of the Harwell staff, did Fuchs reactivate his Soviet alliances. Throughout this period MI5 maintained its interest in Fuchs. He may also have become aware of this activity, either subliminally from Arnold's behaviour or, according to conspiracy theories, due to some well-placed Soviet mole in MI5.[48] In any event, Fuchs seems not to have had any role in espionage during the period when MI5 were watching him, from November 1946 until April 1947, and would only return to espionage once MI5 were off the scent. For the moment, Fuchs was dormant, and in the clear.

SUSPECT PEIERLS

Meanwhile, as part of the 'Nunn May review', Peierls' history and background were re-examined.[49] Genia's Russian background was noted, as always, but now his post-war activities with the Atomic Scientists Association drew attention. Peierls was chair of the Association; the ASA was lobbying against the harsh sentence of the convicted atomic spy, Alan Nunn May; its members included several prominent left-leaning scientists. Peierls was the articulate public voice of the 'subversive' ASA.

Although the ASA lobbied government on scientific matters, they sometimes did so in ways that crossed the boundaries of what others deemed the province of lawyers or politicians. The exposure of a Canadian spy ring as a result of Igor Gouzenko's defection revealed that Nunn May had passed samples of rare uranium isotopes to the Soviet Union during the war. This led to his arrest, conviction, and vilification by the media as a traitor, even though technically he had not dealt with the enemy, as the Soviet Union was at that time an ally of the United Kingdom. But when the ASA argued vehemently that the maximum sentence was unjust, their voice became an irritant for the British government, and MI5 began to regard it with suspicion.[50]

Peierls enjoyed a love-hate relationship with the Security Services. Sceptical about their efficiency, he was confident of his own ability to take care of security without the need for what he perceived as bureaucratic interference by the state authorities. He also knew full well that his consultancy with Harwell caused many secret papers to come into his possession. These were held securely in a locked safe in his physics department office at Birmingham University. Construction work in the department forced him to move into a temporary office, which was a 'hut' adjacent to a public road.[51] When he became concerned about the security in this building, where passers-by could look in through a window and see his confidential papers and safe, he alerted the authorities almost, one feels, for the pleasure of winding them up. The response from MI5 was to send a Captain Bennett to assess the situation and offer advice.

The letters between Peierls and Bennett ooze with mutual antipathy. Bennett acted as if giving advice to a child, and found Peierls to be a 'shifty and rather oily individual'.[52] Peierls' responses exhibit a similar respect for Captain Bennett's mental qualities. Bennett's opening move was that it was straightforward for Peierls to make the safe secure: 'have it moved into the cleaner's closet'. Peierls immediately rejected this trivial solution: 'the safe is too large', he explained, even if they were prepared to 'forgo the use of the closet for other purposes'. Bennett, miffed at the nature of Peierls' rejection, now suggested that the safe be housed in the Nuffield Science Building, near the hut. Peierls dismissed this: it would have to be 'in a room already set aside as a laboratory'. Furthermore, it would be 'highly inconvenient' for Peierls, as any time he was interrupted by a visitor or had to attend a meeting he would have to take the papers across to the other building. The logical scientist delighted in pointing out to the security expert that the latter had overlooked basic human nature: 'I would have to resist the obvious temptation to stick the papers in any handy filing cabinet and dispose of them later in the correct manner.'

Peierls continued: 'The more I consider the security advantages of such a course, the stronger my conviction that one would not really gain, since the safe is quite strong enough to resist the curiosity of the casual passer-by and the only danger to be considered is an attack by someone determined to go to the trouble of breaking into the safe. I cannot help feeling that a person who really wants the contents of the safe as badly as that would have no difficulty in discovering the location of the safe wherever it is within the university, and in breaking down the necessary internal doors that prevent access to it.'

Peierls now escalated the conflict: 'I think it would be proper to ask for guidance from Director of Atomic Energy [Sir John Cockcroft] and I am therefore sending a copy of this letter with a further explanation of the position to Air Vice Marshal Davis.'

Convinced that national security was in the hands of a dimwit, as Bennett's responses became ever more bureaucratic, Peierls announced a solution to the security issue himself, namely to have the bottom panes of his windows obscured. He added a dry comment: 'While for this purpose only one window would have to be treated, I am having it done to several windows in the building in order not to draw attention to the purpose.'[53]

Peierls was clever – too clever for the comfort of Bennett and the Security Services. In their view he was suspect, an independent-minded thinker who seemed to delight in outmanoeuvring them. Additionally he had colleagues who had allegedly expressed left-wing sympathies, such as Cecil Powell of Bristol, and Patrick Blackett of Imperial College London, prominent socialists and campaigners against nuclear proliferation, both of whom would later win the Nobel Prize. MI5's conviction that the ASA was a left-wing organization caused their names along with those of other distinguished scientists to go on file. Peierls' colleague, Klaus Fuchs, also went on the register – because of his link with Peierls.

How ironic that MI5 was obsessed with the 'subversive' aspects of the Atomic Scientists Association when – until Henry Arnold's realization about his communist background set the hare running – they were relatively dismissive of Fuchs, who had been passing information about the atomic bomb for five years. Although Fuchs was on a sabbatical from espionage, he was even now preparing to send information about Britain's own weapons' development to the Soviet Union. This highlights the tensions of the immediate post-war period, when the political establishment and international strategy relied heavily on nuclear scientists, whose work the politicians did not understand even though they had to administer it. Some officers in the Security Services saw these over-powerful scientists as potential threats to the stability of the state; others, such as Hollis, weighed the national interest to be paramount unless they were confronted with unambiguous evidence that a scientist might also be a spy.

12

1947–9: Resurrection

For over a year Klaus Fuchs stopped spying and settled in to work at Harwell, which was designing the first nuclear reactor for the generation of electrical power. This was largely teamwork built around regular discussions between scientists from Harwell, administrative chiefs in London, and consultants from the universities. Fuchs' diary testifies to the regular schedule, which included meetings in London on Fridays, intermingled with visits to universities in Oxford, Cambridge and Birmingham. This would be the core of his activity for the next three years. There is no sign in this schedule of his secret life – not of espionage, for the Canadian exposé had put that career into quarantine, but of his official secret life as guru to a British government project whose very existence was top secret: the United Kingdom planned to 'go it alone' and build an atomic bomb.

In the United Kingdom, for the handful who knew of Clement Attlee's decision, the McMahon Act confirmed the correctness of Fuchs' strategy. A search for a project leader had begun as early as November 1945.[1] Four names were proposed: Rudolf Peierls, Otto Frisch, Klaus Fuchs and William Penney – the armaments expert who had worked at Los Alamos on the blast effects of the atomic weapon.

Penney and Peierls were the two senior physicists. Peierls had conceived the weapon and helped build the atomic bomb from the beginning. Given his experience in the intricacies of bomb design, his role in inspiring the British to initiate Tube Alloys, and his leadership, Peierls would have been the natural choice. However, he was already back at his university whereas Penney, fresh from Los Alamos, was still in government service. Besides, Peierls was surrounded by a host of political disadvantages. He was involved in public campaigning for international control of atomic weapons and for official openness on all atomic matters. Moreover, xenophobia was prevalent in the Britain of the 1940s and Peierls, although naturalized British, was by birth German and his wife Genia came from Russia.

Perhaps most relevant was that his strong views about the use of his brain-child were well known. He wasn't approached and for years remained unaware of the project's existence. The task was given to Bill Penney.

By 1946, when Penney got the call to develop a British atomic bomb at Fort Halstead – a Ministry of Supply research centre near Sevenoaks in the south-eastern suburbs of London – he knew everything about conventional explosives and had seen the effects of atomic bombs at first hand in visits to Hiroshima and Nagasaki. But about their nuclear physics and design he knew little. On the other hand, Fuchs' knowledge of atomic weapons – including the top-secret concept of a hydrogen bomb – was unique in Britain. Recall that at Los Alamos he had studied the implosion mechanism thoroughly and liaised with the team responsible for conventional explosives, by which implosion would be triggered. He knew all about these key components in constructing a plutonium bomb, which the United Kingdom would need to develop itself. Fuchs had also helped design the initiator – the device setting off the fission reactions at the heart of the weapon. In his final months at the laboratory he had studied alternative configurations to that used at Nagasaki, with the goal of designing more efficient weapons. So Fuchs was an encyclopaedia of knowledge for the physics and engineering of a plutonium bomb and became Penney's chief advisor.

In Los Alamos, Fuchs had not only been at the centre of the atomic bomb's development, he had also participated in the intense assessments of the problems of the hydrogen bomb. His extended time at Los Alamos after the war, and his work with John von Neumann, meant that when Fuchs left there in the summer of 1946 he knew more about the construction of the atomic bomb and the conception of a hydrogen bomb than anyone in the United Kingdom and all but a handful in the world. Within weeks of Fuchs' arrival at Harwell, Penney visited him to discuss atomic weapons. In December 1946 Fuchs sent him a copy of one of his and Peierls' reports, 'The Equation of State of Air at High Temperatures', which is relevant for the propagation of the blast wave from a nuclear explosion, and how the damage correlates with the size of the weapon.[2] Now he became key to the British plans for their own nuclear deterrent, and Penney consulted him on a regular basis.

Prime Minister Attlee informed only five trusted colleagues when he took the decision, on 8 January 1947, to build a British atomic bomb.[3] Other members of Attlee's cabinet left in the dark included the Chancellor of the Exchequer (Hugh Dalton), Lord Privy Seal (Arthur Greenwood) and President of the Board of Trade (Sir Stafford Cripps), at a time when Britain was 'almost at its darkest economic hour'.[4] In the close-knit community of nuclear physicists even Peierls, father of the atomic bomb and Fuchs' closest friend, knew nothing of the British project, let alone of Fuchs' involvement. Close colleagues at Harwell too were unaware of his role, and wondered at his frequent absences from the laboratory;[5] any visits to Fort Halstead were surrounded by cloak-and-dagger arrangements intended to conceal their destination from Fuchs' colleagues. There is no mention, not even a hint, of such trips in Fuchs' travel log. This official secrecy would also provide cover later for his clandestine meetings with Soviet contacts when he returned to espionage.

At the start of April, Fuchs joined Rudolf and Genia Peierls and their two children for a ski vacation in the Alps. Tony Skyrme, a colleague from Los Alamos who was now working at Birmingham with Peierls, accompanied them. Fuchs, a workaholic, took some persuading. First, Peierls' daughter pleaded with him to join them, and then Rudolf Peierls simply made all the travel arrangements and booked the tickets.[6] This was Fuchs' first vacation since leaving the United States, when over a year earlier he had visited Mexico with Rudolf and Genia. In the Alps they hiked and skied together for five days. The Peierls' son, Ronnie, remembered later one of Fuchs' habitual acts of kindness. After an overnight ski trip with a guide a tired Ronnie had fallen behind, and as his parents pressed him to hurry up, Fuchs 'had quietly stayed with him'.[7] Skyrme, an enthusiastic photographer, recorded the relaxed intimacy of the group of friends, comfortable in one another's company (see Plates 22 and 23). All too soon the idyllic days were over. Peierls and Skyrme returned to Birmingham, Fuchs to Harwell and the new challenge of designing a British atomic bomb.

Fuchs shared Peierls' fears about nuclear weapons and, like him, saw deterrence as their sole rationale: but their divergent paths to this goal continued. Whereas Peierls led efforts to make the public aware of the atomic reality, Fuchs revived his mission to achieve a global balance of power by ensuring a maximal spread of information.

By the summer of 1947 Fuchs had been out of contact with the Soviet Union for a year. He was now desperate to tell the Russians that the British were developing an atomic bomb, and that in addition to the experimental work on nuclear reactors at Harwell, a large nuclear reactor to breed plutonium was being built at Windscale on England's north-west coast.[8]

Through his communist friends in London, Fuchs made contact with the Soviet Embassy, which in turn passed on news of his availability to Moscow. To one of these friends, Hannah Klopstech, the German communist whom he knew from 1941, the Soviets gave details of how contact would be made with Fuchs. On 19 July, Fuchs met her in Richmond, a posh suburb in the southwest of London; he was in his car and they drove to Hampton Court. During a walk around the park, Hannah told him to go to the Nag's Head public house, near Wood Green underground station in north London, at 8 p.m. on Saturday 27 September, where he would meet his Soviet contact. Recognition signals were agreed.

WHEN 'SONYA' MET SKARDON

As Klaus Fuchs prepared to renew contacts with Russians on British soil, he might have had second thoughts had he known that the Security Services were at that moment in pursuit of his controller from 1943: Ursula Beurton – *nom de guerre*, 'Sonya'. On 13 September 1947 two MI5 officers called on her at home in Great Rollright, an isolated village in the Cotswolds south of Banbury.[9] By 1947 Beurton had been the Soviet Union's top 'illegal' in the United Kingdom for five years. One of the MI5 pair was William 'Jim' Skardon, who would later become famous for his lengthy questioning of Fuchs; his companion was Michael Serpell.

Skardon had until recently been an inspector in Scotland Yard's Special Branch. Promotion to Chief Inspector was clogged, however, and in June he was poached by MI5.[10] The interrogation of Beurton would be his first major test in his new job; he failed dismally.

Ursula Beurton lived with her bigamous husband, Len, at The Firs, a stone farmhouse adjacent to a road, with double gates leading to a yard and barn outhouses. Skardon and Serpell arrived there shortly after lunch. According to Skardon's account, he went 'straight into the attack' telling her, 'We have a vast amount of information in our possession and require your cooperation in order to clear up ambiguities.' She 'made it quite clear from the start of our interview that she did not think she could cooperate and stated that she did not intend to tell lies and therefore preferred not to answer questions'. Skardon's opinion was that by her stand she 'tacitly admitted that she had worked for Soviet intelligence'.[11]

Sonya's version, not surprisingly, paints a different picture, though it is clear that Skardon wasted no time.[12] She recalls a knock at the door; two men greeted her politely and had hardly entered the room before Skardon said rapidly, 'You were a Russian agent for a long time, until the Finnish war disillusioned you. We know you haven't been active in England and we haven't come to arrest you but to ask for your cooperation.' She regarded this 'psychological' attempt to take her by surprise as 'funny and inept'. If Skardon expected to throw her off balance he failed, as she 'almost burst out laughing' and contained herself by offering them a cup of tea. In response to her demand, the pair identified themselves 'somewhat sourly'.

They focused on Sonya's time in Switzerland, which convinced her that a former colleague had betrayed her. They repeated 'again and again' that they knew she was disillusioned since the 'invasion of Finland by the Soviet Union', and that she was a 'loyal British subject'. As she therefore had 'nothing to fear' there was no reason for her not to cooperate with them, they said, and tell them about her time in Switzerland.

She confirmed her loyalty and said that she was quite prepared to talk about her time in England but not in Switzerland, as that was before she had become a British citizen. Skardon parried: She had 'recognised the real worth of communism', so why did she refuse to say anything? Sonya assessed her situation. She took the party newspaper, and was a party member; her father was a known left-winger and her brother Jürgen's political books were also well known. She agreed with Skardon that she had suffered disappointments after Finland but this did not make her anti-communist. And then she trumped them: 'There is no contradiction between being a loyal British citizen and holding left-wing views.'[13]

It would seem that Skardon and Sonya were 'remembering with advantages the feats they did that day'.[14] That she outwitted the security men does seem agreed, however, as Skardon admitted that her performance impressed him as a 'credit to her earlier training, for every possible piece of cajolery, artifice and guile that could be, was employed without any success whatsoever'. In effect she outwitted them by 'sheltering behind the rock of non co-operation'. Despite using 'every conceivable argument' with her, they left at 4 p.m. undertaking to call again the next day 'in the hope that upon consideration she would change her attitude'.

Given Sonya's dominance of the contest during that Saturday afternoon, Skardon's report is a paradigm of how to bury bad news by understatement: 'Our hopes were not fulfilled.' They proposed to her that her refusal to talk 'might be a positive disadvantage to some of her connections' who, Skardon suggested, 'might be under some suspicion which could be removed if she were frank'. However, he reported afterwards, she 'preserved a Slav-like indifference' to Skardon's line of argument. Sonya recalled that Skardon left 'calmly and politely but empty-handed'. As he did so he remarked how beautiful it was in Great Rollright and that he 'shouldn't mind living here'. Sonya replied, 'That could be arranged. I am letting rooms.'

Skardon and Serpell returned the next day, a fact that Sonya's subsequent account glosses over. Their purpose was to highlight that her marriage was bigamous, so if she did not cooperate her British citizenship could be revoked and she would have to revert to her original German nationality. Skardon claimed that towards the end of this second inter-rogation 'she was psychologically at her lowest ebb, but she suddenly became possessed of an excess of resistance which she made manifest'. In a nutshell: 'We got little positive information.' She was 'clearly anti-fascist' and 'disappointed with the Russian policy in 1939/40'. She had commented though that 'Many people lose faith in Governments, but retain their political beliefs.' Skardon came away 'confirmed in our belief' that she was a Russian agent, but had got nowhere in proving it. Dick White, head of Counter-Espionage, was not impressed. This would be but the first occasion when Skardon – who in White's opinion was 'all image and style' and overrated – was fooled when confronted with the 'committed sincerity of an ideologue'.[15]

On 18 September Sir Percy Sillitoe wrote to the Chief Constable of Oxfordshire that 'There is no reason to suspect them [Ursula Beurton and her husband Len] of present or even recent espionage activities although both are communists.' In October Skardon and Serpell reported they had given 'considerable thought . . . to re-interrogating Ursula Beurton' but nothing had arisen to make such an effort likely to be more productive. They decided not to pursue this line further as it would only 'underline the fact that we had no substantial stick to wield on this matter'.[16] So while Sonya's account may be a self-serving version of events, there is no doubt that Skardon failed.

Sonya would continue to outmanoeuvre MI5 for another two years. Meanwhile, on 27 September Fuchs began his third phase of espionage. None of the players in this act foresaw that Jim Skardon would make his name by becoming Fuchs' nemesis.

'WHAT CAN YOU TELL ME ABOUT THE TRITIUM BOMB?'

The Nag's Head opposite Wood Green underground station was a classic Victorian London pub, with sturdy dark wooden tables, high ceilings, and large windows set in stone. It still exists but today is named The Goose – coincidentally the KGB's code name for Fuchs' previous contact, Harry Gold. There is a large and popular sports bar adorned with flat-screen television but no plaque to commemorate its moment in history. On 27 September 1947 the plan was for Fuchs to enter the bar, sit at a table in a corner, and drink something while reading *Tribune*, a socialist magazine. His contact, who would arrive at 8 p.m. carrying a red book, would bring a glass of beer over to the table and say, 'Stout is not so good, I prefer lager.' Klaus was to reply, 'I think Guinness is best', then leave and go outside, towards a park. The contact would follow and say, 'Your face looks familiar to me.' Klaus would answer, 'I think we met in Edinburgh a year ago.' The stranger would then ask 'Do you know big Hannah?', to which Fuchs' affirmation would complete the overture.[17]

His contact, Alexander Feklisov, began preparations earlier that afternoon. A highly experienced KGB officer, thirty-three years old and solidly built, Feklisov had worked in the United States during the war until he was recalled to Moscow in 1946 after the Canadian spy-ring exposure. He was sent to London on 10 September as number two to the KGB Resident at the Soviet Embassy. The prohibition on contacts with agents, which had been in place for nearly a year, had barely been lifted and this liaison on 27 September would be the first meeting with their most valuable source. The utmost care was called for.

With the aid of two other Russian colleagues, Feklisov checked for signs of surveillance by MI5. He got on and off buses, walked in and out of department stores, doubled back on his tracks several times, and only when satisfied that all was clear did he get into a car. Now another agent drove while Feklisov and a third officer continued to monitor. After about thirty-five minutes, Feklisov was satisfied that they weren't under surveillance, and he alighted near Wood Green station. He then spent another half an hour familiarizing himself with the streets and the park before conducting the conversation with Fuchs.[18]

At 8 p.m. Feklisov entered the bar and saw Fuchs already sitting at a table, drinking beer. It was Saturday night, the pub was busy, and several other people were near to Fuchs. Feklisov passed the 'first half of the oral password'. Fuchs left, and after a short interval Feklisov followed him outside 'where the second half of the oral password was exchanged'.[19] Feklisov began the conversation by asking after the health of Fuchs' father, his brother – who suffered from tuberculosis – and Kristel. Pleasantries over, and certain that they weren't attracting any unwanted attention, Feklisov asked Fuchs where he was working, what he was doing, and the names of other scientists at the laboratory.

The Russian learned from Fuchs of the British decision to go ahead with an independent programme to build an atomic bomb, under Penney's leadership at Fort Halstead. Fuchs informed him further that a small experimental reactor was under construction at Harwell, and a large one, to breed plutonium, at Windscale. Feklisov recalled that Fuchs gave him forty pages of notes 'in tiny but legible handwriting', and information about plutonium production 'including documents he had been unable to obtain in America'.[20] It is likely that these included Thomson's idea for enabling nuclear fusion to produce intense beams of neutrons with which plutonium could be made.

Feklisov offered Fuchs £100. Whereas Fuchs had declined payment from Harry Gold in February 1945, he accepted the money from Feklisov 'as a symbolic payment signalling [my] subversion to the cause'.[21] This appears to have been a one-time payment, but it was nonetheless sufficient to disturb Fuchs' vision that his spying was purely voluntary, driven only by his belief in the righteousness of communism. Feklisov had also memorized some technical questions and asked Fuchs to provide written answers at their next meeting. The 'first [question] concerned the superbomb [H-bomb]'.[22] Fuchs told him that Edward Teller and Enrico Fermi were working on this in Chicago. He described some 'features of [the bomb's] structure and principles of its operation, and mentioned the use of tritium alongside deuterium'. Fuchs said that the superbomb was 'feasible' but didn't know if R&D on a real bomb was underway in the United States. He explained that he could only give an approximate description because Feklisov was not a physicist, but agreed to provide written information at their next meeting.

It isn't clear how Fuchs obtained this information on the superbomb. He had left Los Alamos in July 1946, and would not have had access to any results of Fermi and Teller because the McMahon Act had ended atomic cooperation between the United States and the rest of the world immediately afterwards. However, Fuchs was close to Teller, who recalled 'Fuchs talked with me and others frequently in depth', and 'it was easy and pleasant to discuss my work with him'.[23] Teller even admitted that he 'learned many techniques from [Fuchs]'. So it is possible that Teller told Fuchs privately or that Fuchs worked out steps for himself from incidental information.*

Whatever its source, Fuchs' news about this work stimulated the Soviets to direct attention to Chicago. Within a month Moscow learned of a remarkable breakthrough – Teller had found a new way to make tritium. The trick was to use lithium deuteride (Li6D) in the weapon itself with a specific isotope of lithium – lithium-6, which consists of three protons and three neutrons. When neutrons from a fission explosion hit lithium-6, this produces tritium (see Appendix, p. 429).[24] So tritium is made inside the

---

* Fuchs passed more information about the H-bomb after a visit to Chicago in November 1947 and this seems to have involved intelligence gained from Teller, see p. 194. It is possible that at the 27 September meeting he briefed Feklisov about Fermi's lectures and assumed that his own work with von Neumann had made the bomb feasible. He handed over details of the Fuchs–von Neumann idea at a rendezvous in March 1948.

bomb itself, and in the presence of deuterium – in the Li_6D – provides the thermonuclear fuel. This would become one of the key connections that led eventually to a working thermonuclear bomb.

This information did not come from Fuchs, but was nonetheless a direct result of his news about Fermi and Teller. This focused Soviet interest on Chicago, which was where their wartime agent Ted Hall was now based. Although there is no certain evidence, it appears that the Soviets now reactivated Hall in the city and learned about this novel idea.[25] They quickly realized its importance; the chief architect of the Soviet bomb, Andrei Sakharov, later referred to the Li_6D suggestion as the 'second idea' on the way to their own eventual hydrogen bomb.[26]

Fuchs and Feklisov agreed to meet in London bars on Saturday nights at intervals of three months. By now he had moved out of Ridgeway House and lived for more than a year in Lacies Court, an impressive mock Elizabethan-style mansion in Abingdon. Today Lacies Court is the residence of the headteacher of Abingdon School, but in the post-war years it was a communal lodging for scientists and their families. The landlady remembered Fuchs' other-worldliness: 'While he understood Einstein, he could not tie a bow tie'.[27] The young son of one scientist had a model electric train set, which he would lay out in his room. The space was limited as the lad had to share the room with his brother, so Fuchs let him set up the trains in his own rooms at weekends whenever he was away.[28]

One question from Feklisov at that first meeting had surprised Fuchs: 'What can you tell me about the tritium bomb?' Fuchs had mentioned Fermi's lectures to Harry Gold back in September 1945, but that was the last information on this topic that Fuchs had passed to the Russians. As we have seen, the Fermi lectures gave the basic principles of a Classical Super bomb, a design that had been superseded by April 1946. Yet, from Feklisov's questions, it appeared that the Russians were already aware that there had been progress, which suggested to Fuchs that he had not been the only source of information in Los Alamos.[29]

On reflection this was perhaps not a complete surprise. In the febrile period before the war when fascism was confronted by anti-fascism, many intellectuals had followed the Red Flag. During the war the Soviet Union had been an essential ally, and many scientists were uncomfortable at its exclusion from the Manhattan Project. Four out of five German soldiers killed in the Second World War were on the Russian front – a full 80 per cent. The Soviet achievement was huge, as were its losses with millions of its own soldiers dead, and but for their sacrifice the war might well have been lost by 1942. Thus active support of the Soviet Union up to 1945 was hardly likely to have been an article of faith for Klaus Fuchs alone. This is now well known; in 1946 the arrest of Alan Nunn May and the exposure of the Canadian spy ring was already some evidence for it.

By 1947 allegiances were changing. The Nazis had been defeated; in many quarters the Soviet Union was regarded more as the new enemy than as a recent ally when rigged elections turned Eastern European countries into Soviet satellite states. Sharing information with the USSR after the war was a different issue entirely from what had gone before. Fuchs was aware now, more so probably than ever before, that this was a dangerous game; he was no longer sharing information with an ally and would only make assignations and pass information when he was completely sure that it was both safe and, in his mind, justified.

The next meeting with Feklisov should have been in December, but Fuchs didn't make it. The end of the year was an intense period for him. In the second half of November he went to the United States for twenty days to take part in a conference, which discussed the 'de-classification' of documents on nuclear energy and weapons technology. He had much work to do in preparation for the meeting, and then again after it in light of the decisions at the conference. Fuchs had gone there with the explicit assignment from the Russians to obtain information on the current state of nuclear reactors and 'new types of atomic bombs'.[30] Preparing answers for Feklisov and ensuring a safe rendezvous created difficulties – petrol for Fuchs' car was rationed, and a casual visit to London without some sound reason was, at that time, perhaps enough to raise suspicions. Instead, Fuchs decided that the meeting would be aborted and the next would be on Saturday 13 March 1948, as per their agreed schedule.

Did Fuchs alert Feklisov to the sudden change of plan, and the singular opportunity that his visit to the United States had presented? Guy Liddell's diary records that in the middle of November, MI5 intercepted two calls to the Soviet military attaché, one on his office phone and the other at his home.[31] The caller, from Harwell, said he must see the attaché urgently, and an appointment was made for Monday 10 November. MI5 called Henry Arnold in hope of identifying the voice, but without success, as no further action was recorded. If this was Fuchs trying to make an urgent connection before his visit to the USA it was a remarkably dangerous gamble, as it is unlikely he could have disguised his Germanic accent, which still remained, and not been recognized by Arnold. It is possible that this was some prankster as the level of risk was out of character for Fuchs, and there is no other known candidate.

For the meeting in March, Fuchs achieved two goals in a single absence from Harwell. First, he contacted William Penney, whose laboratory was in Fort Halstead, and suggested that on Friday 12 March he brief Penney's team about the plutonium bomb and implosion, which was key to its operation. This gave Fuchs a valid reason to go through London, and pass information about the H-bomb to his Russian contact on the Saturday evening.

The McMahon Act had cut Penney off from all developments around the atomic bomb, so Fuchs' experience and memory were essential to British success. During 1948 and 1949 Fuchs prepared for Penney written summaries of the design of the Trinity weapon, as he remembered it. Two mathematicians in Penney's team, John Corner and Herbert Pike, had discussions with Fuchs 'on three or four occasions'. Fuchs visited Fort Halstead several times during those two years and his lectures about the weapon, in which he 'could pack a lot of detail into a few sentences', were remembered as having been 'a star turn'.[32]

At some point in this series Fuchs also addressed future longer-term questions. His experience of the hydrogen bomb convinced him that this was 'an important field and [he] was anxious to see some research begun in Britain'.[33] It is tempting to suppose that he included all of these topics during his visit on 12 March 1948, as they would have been at the front of his mind. He wrote to Penney on 2 March saying that he intended to talk about a specific problem, but he also gave other possibilities. 'If you like I could also give another lecture. Perhaps I might talk in greater detail about the implosion and the considerations that have led to the particular designs which we believe to be the most favourable. Alternatively I might talk about the methods of determining critical sizes.'[34] The letter reminds us of Fuchs' wide range of experience and singular importance for Penney's atomic weapons programme. It also shows his cunning. This meeting with Penney was top secret and is hidden in Fuchs' travel claims at Harwell as a visit to 'Cambridge'.[35] Then, having created a legitimate reason to be away with his car on the Friday, he was able to stay over and on the Saturday evening meet Feklisov once again.

This time the venue was the Bull and Bush in Golders Green. Fuchs explained to the Russian how radiation led the superbomb to cool and become impotent, thus the 'Classical Super', as in Fermi's lectures, would not work in practice. He then handed over diagrams of a fusion bomb, with a U235 fission bomb as the fuse, and the idea of X-ray implosion, which he and von Neumann had patented (see p. 158). The Russians thus learned how a mixture of deuterium and tritium in a pellet of beryllium oxide could be blasted both mechanically and also by X-rays from the uranium bomb. Fuchs also handed over the computations that Bretscher and Teller had made for deuterium and tritium fusion.

On his visit to the United States from 11 to 30 November 1947, Fuchs had also learned about American progress, the McMahon Act notwithstanding. The quality of what Fuchs wheedled out of the Americans during this visit is remarkable, as the KGB report of his meeting in March confirms: 'He managed to obtain highly valuable information on the structure of existing types of atomic bombs, including a hydrogen super-bomb. Upon his return from the USA he passed these materials to our operative, Major A. S. Feklisov.'[36]

How did Fuchs obtain all this information? Teller is an obvious possibility given their closeness and Teller's own admission that he enjoyed discussing physics with Fuchs, who had made 'several impressive contributions during discussions' on the hydrogen bomb in 1946.[37] During the classification conference the attendees were invited to a party at Teller's house. This much was in line with normal social practice, but Fuchs was also a special guest of Edward Teller and his family for Thanksgiving. There is no doubt that the pair enjoyed their time together during Fuchs' extended visit.[38]

The Russians were so advantaged that in April, Lavrenti Beria, Stalin's henchman and enforcer of the atomic weapons programme, ordered Soviet scientists to develop a hydrogen bomb, with a target date of June 1949. This would have been impossible to achieve even had the hydrogen bomb idea that Fuchs had given them worked. The Americans tested some features of his and von Neumann's idea later, but the weapon as eventually developed relied on a further advance by Teller and Stanislaw Ulam in 1951. Although Fuchs did not give the Soviets the key to the hydrogen bomb, his information of March 1948 alerted them that the Americans were taking the idea seriously, that some basic problems had been identified, and that the first of a series of solutions had been found.

The next assignation with Feklisov was due in May 1948, but once again Fuchs failed to turn up. Between March and May much had happened.

FUCHS' ESTABLISHMENT

In December 1947 Fuchs' name had again come up in MI5 discussions, in connection with his employment at Harwell. Fuchs had been appointed in 1946 on a temporary contract, and now Harwell wanted to employ him long-term. For this he had once again to be vetted. On 19 November Harwell contacted MI5 and emphasized that there is 'only one other person in this country who possesses the qualifications and experience of Dr Fuchs', which was of course Peierls. MI5 responded quickly to say that they did not have sufficient grounds to advise against Dr Fuchs being placed on the permanent establishment of AERE Harwell.[39] However, it seems that they then had second thoughts.

Martin Furnival Jones, of Protective Security in MI5, recommended that the Ministry of Supply should be given a full statement about Fuchs. He pointed out that Arnold was 'in the picture' and that back in 1944 Michael Perrin (then of the Department of Scientific and Industrial Research, or DSIR) had been given some information about Fuchs, but 'I do not think the Ministry of Supply have ever been given the full story.'[40] This quickly moved upwards within MI5. Upon receipt of Furnival Jones' memo, Hollis contacted Dick White: 'In my opinion there is really nothing we can usefully give the Supply Ministry and I should be inclined to answer only that we have no objection to the establishment of Fuchs.'[41]

White's response to Hollis' letter was to write to Deputy Director General Guy Liddell on 2 December. Although White was 'inclined to agree' with Hollis, in view of Liddell's previous interest in the case he would like Liddell to see the papers before action was taken.[42]

Both MI5 files and Liddell's diary reveal a sense of serious disquiet, even suspicion, about one or both of Fuchs and Peierls, but recognition that there was no hard evidence. Once again the exchanges show the caution within MI5. Should it later transpire that either of the two scientists was a Soviet agent, then it would be better that any decision had been made high up the chain of command, hence the escalation from Hollis to Liddell via White.

On 8 December 1947 Liddell called a meeting with White, Collard, Furnival Jones and Hollis to frame a policy on Fuchs. The power of this gathering can hardly be overstated: White, Hollis and Furnival Jones were all destined to become Director Generals of the organization. The group was concerned that 'Some slight risk attaches to the employment of FUCHS' because of his alien origin, the Gestapo report from 1938 – though that of course had been dismissed as unreliable – and his association with Hans Kahle during his internment in Canada in 1940. Hollis' report of this meeting maintains the fiction, for the third time: 'The detainees sent to Canada were supposed to be ardent Nazis though occasionally, owing to a mistake, anti-Nazis were sent among them. This clearly occurred in the case of KAHLE and FUCHS and it is not altogether surprising that they should have become friendly in such uncongenial surroundings.' Their discounting of the Gestapo report was now joined by the same attitude to the Kahle connection: 'Records indicate only that FUCHS held anti-Nazi views and associated with Germans of similar views. The security risk is very slight.'[43]

Nonetheless, Liddell recorded in his diary that 'although our information was entirely negative, we should tell Atomic Research what we know and express the opinion that in our view the information does not really amount to anything'. Liddell's diary reveals also how he viewed Arnold's opinions about Fuchs: 'The alternative was to say nothing, which seemed to me undesirable – the more so since Henry Arnold the security officer at Harwell, would be putting in his comments which might be somewhat unbalanced.'[44]

This therefore was their attitude to Arnold, who had alerted MI5 to his concerns about Fuchs on at least two occasions and, it seems, now continued to brief them about other security problems at Harwell. For MI5, through Arnold's eyes and ears, had become aware that three members of the Harwell staff had communist links. Fuchs was not one of these, but his behaviour led Arnold to suggest that 'Fuchs was running an espionage organisation in Harwell'.[45] It is unfortunate that this over-excited interpretation can't have helped MI5's opinion of Arnold's judgement.

This particular fancy came to light when Colonel Collard of C Division – responsible for vetting – visited Harwell on 18 March 1948. Collard's scepticism is apparent from the start of his report that Arnold 'told me an elaborate story complete with diagrams, concerning the activities of SEATON-BULL [one of the alleged communists] and Dr. FUCHS'.[46]

Arnold had alerted Dr Egon Bretscher, the head of Seaton-Bull's department, about his record – Collard adding parenthetically, 'without, incidentally, any reference to this office'. Arnold told Collard that early in March he had been sitting near Fuchs at a classified discussion on a problem to do with uranium convened by Sir John Cockcroft. Bull and Bretscher were also present. Towards the end of the meeting, Bretscher left his seat, strode up to where Arnold was sitting, and 'in a loud voice' proclaimed 'I hope Bull is enjoying this.' Arnold noted that this was 'undoubtedly heard by Fuchs', who 'moved not a muscle'.[47]

Near the end of the talk, Arnold left the hall and from a balcony observed the audience's departure. He noticed 'Fuchs elbowing his way through the crowd to speak to Bull.' Having reached him, 'the two scientists remained in a close huddle for a few minutes under the undetected observation of Arnold'. Arnold concluded that Fuchs was 'acquainting Bull with Bretscher's remark at the back of the hall', which Arnold took as supporting his 'theory that Fuchs is running an espionage organisation in Harwell'. Arnold found further grounds for attributing sinister motives to the Bull–Fuchs conversation because he had never known them exchange 'verbal intimacies on any previous occasion, despite their long association at Harwell as colleagues'.[48]

Collard told Arnold that he 'could not attach very much importance to this story or his suspicions', but he 'would be sure to pass them on to the proper section of the office'.[49] The suspicions about the communist scientists didn't remain secret, however. The journalist Chapman Pincher somehow learned about them and on 23 March he published an article in the *Daily Express*. When the Soviet Embassy in London saw Pincher's article they informed Moscow, who in turn sent a warning letter to Stalin and Beria.[50]

Fuchs wasn't one of the named scientists and he continued to lead a charmed life. There is no evidence that he knew of Skardon's visit to 'Sonya' back in September, but he was made aware of MI5's interest in the Harwell communists when in May and June 1948 'three junior researchers were fired'.[51] Fuchs became badly scared. He therefore cut the meeting that he and Feklisov had planned for May, a failure that was communicated to Beria along with news of MI5's interest in Sonya. Moscow was concerned, but when Fuchs met Feklisov next, on 10 July 1948, Fuchs claimed that there was no problem. Instead, he said, he had missed the assignation because the Harwell reactor had been in a 'pre-launch phase' and his presence at Harwell had been required throughout. This seems to have been an invention designed by Fuchs so as not to lose face, for there is no hint in Fuchs' travel records of any change in his routine: throughout this period he had continued with a normal round of meetings in Oxford and London. Another possible explanation for his non-appearance was that he was ill with a recurrent dry cough – a condition that Genia Peierls recalled later seemed to be brought on by stress.[52] Given the circumstances, this seems more believable than Fuchs' lame excuse that his boss required his permanent presence at Harwell. At the meeting in July, Fuchs gave Feklisov the lattice design for the Windscale nuclear reactor, the design rate for plutonium production at Harwell, and details of how to extract plutonium from rods of uranium.[53]

Meanwhile MI5, unaware of all this background, advised the Atomic Energy authorities as the question of Fuchs' professional future came to its climax. On 1 January 1948 Major Badham of MI5 told the Ministry of Supply the standard mantra on Fuchs: namely that the Gestapo report was discounted – Fuchs 'himself stated that he was chairman of a Socialist Students Society'; the affinity with Kahle in the Canadian internment camp was again excused on the false grounds that the pair were singular in being anti-Nazi; and MI5's conclusion remained: 'the security risk is very slight'.[54]

The wheels turned slowly in Whitehall and not until 14 August 1948 was Fuchs' permanent establishment at Harwell approved. The letter to MI5 from the Ministry of Supply stated that, in response to MI5's letter back in January: 'It has been decided that the advantages gained by Harwell through the undoubted ability of Dr Fuchs outweigh the slight security risk.'[55] Fuchs was duly established as a permanent member of Harwell's staff, head of the Theoretical Physics Division, member of the central scientific management team – and very lightly paid informant for the Soviet Union.

Apart from formal notes about scientific visitors to Fuchs from abroad, and a minute in April 1949 that his father planned to visit him that summer, there is no mention of Fuchs in MI5's files for the whole of 1948 and much of 1949.[56] Although MI5 had relaxed, Fuchs continued with espionage from July 1947 until the spring of 1949. He met Feklisov on three more occasions: in November 1948, February and April 1949. The rendezvous on 12 February 1949, at the Spotted Horse Pub near Putney Bridge, was the only occasion where Fuchs' travel reports contain a trifling record of his duplicity. He was due to visit Cambridge to see Sir James Chadwick and two other scientists, a journey by car of between two and three hours at most. He set out from Harwell on 12 February at '12 a.m.' and returned home at 11 p.m. the next day. The journey via Putney would involve a detour of perhaps 20 miles. Fuchs appears to have overlooked this and prepared his travel claim of 200 miles from his odometer; his visits to Cambridge in March and July 1948 showed the direct distance to have been 180 or 182 miles respectively.[57] The possibility that this mild discrepancy could have opened up Fuchs' double life to view is akin to the hoodlum Al Capone having been convicted for errors in his tax return.

By the end of these meetings, Fuchs had given the Russians his calculations of the American nuclear tests at Bikini Atoll and information about the hydrogen bomb, plus details on the British atomic bomb and reactor programmes, including the rate of plutonium production at Windscale. This information enabled the Soviets to deduce how rapidly the British could stockpile atomic weapons. Through Fuchs they could now estimate the strength of the American nuclear arsenal and monitor the progress of Britain's own weapons programme.[58]

JERRY GARDNER: FROM HARWELL TO RUSSIA

Meanwhile Peierls' student Jerry Gardner made good progress with his research and by March 1948 Peierls had recommended to Fuchs that Gardner work with him at Harwell. This letter to Fuchs included the statement: 'You are familiar with his work on orbits in magnetic fields.'[59]

Fuchs' familiarity with Gardner's work was because, as leader of the Theoretical Physics Division, he was fully informed of Thomson's idea about fusion, and had been actively involved throughout his time at Harwell. We know this thanks to a personal memorandum that Thomson made. At the outset he had consulted Peierls, who in turn had assessed the implications with Fuchs, and then for the full development of the secret idea Harwell's expertise had become involved. Thomson's notes included a chronology of his interactions with others in order to establish priority for patenting his invention, and he maintained a record in the subsequent years.[60] These show that once his initial discussions with Peierls had satisfied him that the idea was sound, Thomson presented a paper, 'Atomic energy from Deuterium', at Harwell on 15 January 1947.[61] Fuchs then assigned his deputy Oscar Bunemann a lead role in working with Thomson. Later that year and into 1948 there was a dedicated programme of collaboration, on whose progress Fuchs was informed. Shortly before Fuchs' arrest, Thomson circulated in January 1950 a paper titled 'Thermonuclear reactions'.[62]

Not only was Fuchs fully briefed on this physics, but also it seems that he shared the ideas with the Russians, if what now happened to Jerry Gardner is not merely coincidence. Following Peierls' letter of recommendation, Gardner had an interview with Fuchs on 1 April 1948, who agreed that Gardner would join him at Harwell after completing his Master of Science thesis. The only problem was that its subject – the behaviour of electrons in magnetic fields – was so near to the classified fusion area that Peierls checked with Fuchs to ensure the firewalls between open and classified work were not breached. Although the inspiration behind the interest in the behaviour of electrons in magnetic fields was classified, the fundamental questions about their motion were not, and this enabled Gardner to publish his research in the open literature.[63] The circumstances, and what happened next, are intriguing.

By 8 October 1948 Gardner prepared for publication a paper: 'Confinement of Slow Charged Particles to a Toroidal Tube'. Oscar Bunemann was 'somewhat worried' whether the last section of Gardner's draft could be published or should be classified secret, so Peierls suggested that Gardner change some words, in order to set the context differently, and checked that Fuchs was happy with it.[64] Gardner continued to do good work, Peierls submitting a paper by him to the Physical Society for publication in June 1949. Once again, Fuchs cleared it with the authorities, and on 21 June he gave Peierls the go-ahead to publish. The Physical Society paper also formed the basis of Gardner's thesis.

By now it seems that Fuchs had identified Gardner as a worthy scientist, as he asked Peierls to send a formal statement about him. On 20 September Peierls did so and noted that of his own initiative Gardner had changed over to a problem in nuclear physics. 'I think you will find that when he joins your department he will pull his weight as a fairly senior worker and certainly with a maturity quite out of proportion with the short time he has so far spent on theoretical physics proper,'[65] Peierls told Fuchs.

All must have been well because on 25 October 1949 Gardner joined Fuchs' group as a scientific officer. Three months later, on 11 January 1950, Gardner wrote to Peierls to say that he had found a paper in the Russian literature, which covered 'substantially the same ground as my thesis but which was published a year before my work.'[66] Fortunately Gardner had already independently submitted his own paper, and included it in his thesis.

Peierls interpreted the Russian paper, which had anticipated Gardner, as one of the vicissitudes of research. It is not unknown for ideas to develop independently, and that may be the case here too. The circumstances and timing, however, suggest that at some point in the preceding year Soviet scientists had been tipped off about Thomson's work. Thanks to Fuchs, the Soviet Union was now aware that the British were looking at nuclear fusion as a possible route to the production of plutonium for weapons.[67]

THE MAN WHO LOVED ENGLAND

Where Peierls in 1942 had thought of the atomic bomb as the ultimate deterrent, Fuchs' unique position in spreading knowledge to all participants was inadvertently helping to achieve that end. However, during his time at Harwell his world view was beginning to change. During the war his motivation had been clear, and the risks worthwhile. Now, Soviet ideals appeared tarnished as they annexed states in Eastern Europe, and Stalin began to appear in Fuchs' eyes less as a flag-bearer for the communist ideal than a murderous tyrant little different from Hitler. Furthermore, Fuchs was happy in rural Harwell, in a peaceful country that welcomed him, and in which he had found companionship. Now too, Erna Skinner and Klaus Fuchs' lives became profoundly emotionally entwined. According to Henry Arnold their 'very close friendship' started about the end of 1947 and 'became more intimate as time went on'.[68] From that point on, Fuchs' commitment to espionage began to become fragmentary.

Recall that he aborted a rendezvous in November 1947, made one on 13 March 1948, but in May 1948 had again failed to turn up. At their next meeting, in July, the Russians put in place a plan for emergency revision to the schedule in the event of a rendezvous being dangerous or missed for any reason.[69]

In the event of any rendezvous failing, Fuchs was to make fresh arrangements by writing a prospective place and time on the tenth page of the magazine *Men Only* and dropping a copy into the garden of 166 Kew Road at the corner of Stanmore Road. The sequence of events and the relative locations all suggest that Fuchs would arrive at the leafy oasis of Kew Gardens railway station, one stop from the District Line terminus at Richmond. On the southern side of the station forecourt at Kew Gardens in Station Parade there is a group of shops, with a narrow passage between two of them – Etherington's furniture shop at number 14 (now The Glasshouse restaurant) and a butcher's. Fuchs would first check the wall of the passage to see whether someone had inscribed a small cross in chalk: the presence of such a mark would indicate it was dangerous to make the magazine drop. If the coast was clear, and Fuchs made the drop in Stanmore Road, about ten minutes' walk away, he would then make his way back to the station and en route would place a chalk mark on a fence on the north side of Holmesdale Road by the junction of Ennerdale Road.[70]

Fuchs never had need for this clandestine minuet, however, as he and Feklisov met again in November 1948, and on 12 February 1949 without trouble. Fuchs would later claim that this was their final rendezvous, but KGB records list one further meeting, in April 1949.[71] The unsatisfactory nature of meeting in public places clearly troubled the Russians as in April Fuchs' contact was keen to know whether Fuchs knew any girl in London whose apartment could be used as a safe rendezvous. Fuchs said he 'spends time with various girls he comes across' – the Russian 'got the impression that they are prostitutes' and concluded there was no safe meeting place. Fuchs gave verbal information on this occasion and promised to provide written notes at their next meeting, which was arranged for 25 June.

Fuchs was now entering the eighth year of his double life, and the strain finally proved too much. Immediately after meeting his Russian contact, Fuchs visited Paris for a few days in April with the Skinners. The vacation was a failure as Fuchs was 'very ill' throughout, was nursed by Erna Skinner, and had barely half an hour to himself.[72] The friends returned to Harwell and Fuchs was fit enough to work. But when the time came for his next meeting with the Russians, on 25 June, illness struck again. KGB records state simply 'Didn't show'.[73] Nor did he appear at the back-up meeting on 2 July. At some point during the spring or summer of 1949 Fuchs decided to cut his ties with the Soviet Union.[74]

Fuchs' illness and his failure to meet the Russians might have been a reaction to news that he received from his father in March. Father and son had not met for many years when out of the blue Emil told Klaus that he would like to visit him that summer, at Harwell. Klaus' nephew, Klaus Kittowski, the son of Elizabeth who had committed suicide, would accompany Emil. While Klaus was keen to see his father again after many years, the visit would be fraught with danger. Emil knew Klaus' political history, of course, and one careless remark by his father could ruin Klaus' carefully guarded secret. The pair planned to visit for 'four weeks' from 'about 14 June'.[75]

When Fuchs learned of his father's plans, he was still living at Lacies Court, in Abingdon.[76] In preparation for his father's visit, he quit Abingdon and moved to a place of his own: a modest prefab, 17 Hillside, on the barren slopes adjacent to the Harwell laboratory. Fuchs' whole existence now focused on the Harwell site. The move was undoubtedly inspired by the impending visit of his father, who would stay with the Skinners in their substantial house on the Harwell site, near to Klaus' prefab.

By the summer of 1949 Fuchs was comfortable in England, whose way of life he had begun to love. Having broken with the Russians, he now had the chance of a peaceful, settled life, and contemplated the possibility of adopting his nephew. Peierls nominated him for Fellowship of the Royal Society. Fuchs' future in Britain seemed assured.

Three events then disturbed his equilibrium. First, his father brought news that Klaus' sister, Kristel, was mentally ill. Klaus – all too aware that he had involved her in his espionage – feared that she might commit suicide, as had their other sister, Elizabeth, and their mother and grandmother. The visit itself was continuously stressful as Klaus had to ensure that his father did not inadvertently give the game away. There was one occasion when the mask nearly slipped. Hanni, wife of Egon Bretscher, recalled a dinner party, which the security officer Henry Arnold also attended. There is no record of what was said, and it is possible that memory was recovered with hindsight after Fuchs' duplicity became public, but she was adamant that Fuchs 'acted strangely'. Of perhaps greater significance, this was 'the first clear indication for Arnold that Fuchs had something to hide'.[77]

Whether Fuchs' broken contact with the Russians that summer was due to a change of heart, as he later claimed, or enforced by the presence of his father and nephew, is impossible to judge. In any event, Fuchs then got wind that the Russians were not going to let him break off contact easily. In what MI5 would later describe as an 'inspired move' the KGB brought pressure on Klaus Fuchs by arranging the offer of a professorial chair to his father at Leipzig, in the Eastern part of Germany under the sway of the Soviet Union.[78] Klaus learned of this in a letter from his father a few weeks after Emil returned home. The Security Services were rightly concerned at the potential for the Soviet bloc to exert pressure on, or even to blackmail, individuals who had close relatives living in the East. Anyone who had access to top-secret papers, such as Fuchs, was obliged to alert the authorities if any of their relatives came in this category. Fuchs duly told Henry Arnold. Arnold told MI5.

By that summer of 1949 Fuchs could have imagined his life in espionage was behind him. The only clouds were his father's future, and his sister Kristel's fragile mental health. The prefab in which he now lived with complete privacy was minimal but functional: a small living room of no more than 10 square metres with a coal fire, and a single bedroom with built-in furniture, were supplemented by a kitchen with an electric cooker, a spare room and a bathroom. This was fine in summer, but in winter the sills of the aluminium window frames were notorious reservoirs of condensation, while the lack of insulation required constant stoking of the coal fire. Fuchs chose to remain there after his father and little Klaus had returned to Germany, at least partly because it was less than half a mile from number 3 South Drive, which enabled him to visit Erna Skinner easily whenever her husband Herbert was away.

THE FIRST CRACK

MI5's Deputy Director General, Guy Liddell, took his 1949 vacation at the end of August and returned to the office on 13 September. His diary for that day reveals a profound development that had taken place during his absence: 'A serious case has blown up with regard to atomic energy. [The Americans] have discovered that one of the British team working in America in 1944 was giving information to the Russians.'[79]

The source was the most secret breakthrough in counter-espionage: the Soviet diplomatic codes had been cracked, revealing that a member of the British delegation in Los Alamos had been a spy. Liddell summarized the situation: 'There is not much clue to his identity except that he had a sister. The suspicion falls on one FUCHS and to a lesser degree on PEIERLS whose cases were looked into here some time ago but with negative results. A mention of FUCHS' sister apparently appears in the diary of the Russian [sic] HALPERIN, who was connected with the GOUZENKO case in Canada. An intensive investigation is being made into the affairs of both FUCHS and PEIERLS but the problem is by no means an easy one.'[80]

Steps were already being taken to place both Fuchs and Peierls under surveillance. To add to the pressure, within days the fruits of Fuchs' secret life became apparent. A shocked Liddell wrote in his diary: 'The explosion of an atomic bomb has occurred in Russia.'[81] The news had been given at the weekly meeting of the Joint Intelligence Chiefs on 16 September under 'a melodramatic bond of secrecy'. First, the room was cleared of secretaries. Next, all remaining were told 'if there is anybody present who can not keep what is going to be said to themselves, would they kindly leave the room. All wondered what was coming! It was then announced by Perrin of Atomic Energy that the explosion of an atomic bomb had occurred in Russia, somewhere in the vicinity of Lake Baikal.'

Liddell then summarized what was known about the detection of the blast, and also aired his doubts about the accuracy of the information:

Apparently for some time both the Americans and ourselves have been doing aerial reconnaissance; the aeroplanes carry a kind of filter which will catch any particles of radio-active substances, which can subsequently be identified. They were patrolling somewhere in the North Pacific in September and obtained particles which have been definitely identified as plutonium. On discovering this, we sent out patrols somewhere in the vicinity of Norway and obtained similar results. It is, I believe, alleged by the scientists that they can more or less date and locate the explosion from these particles, and that the evidence is entirely convincing.

There appears still to be some slight doubt as to whether the scientists are right in their conclusions, and even whether all of those most qualified to speak have had the opportunity of examining the evidence. Knowing absolutely nothing about the matter, but with a certain experience of scientists and their tendency to go back on their theories, I cannot help being slightly sceptical about the whole thing.[82]

In a separate entry to his diary that day, Liddell reinforces this false hope: 'Dick [White] saw Victor [Rothschild] last night. The latter shares my scepticism about the Russian atomic bomb. He also takes the view very strongly that a resurgence of Right Wing parties in Germany is the most serious menace at the moment. He thinks it might well lead to a tie-up with the Russians. Winston [Churchill], I gather, takes a contrary view.'[83]

After the announcement of the Joint Intelligence Chiefs:

... there followed a discussion as to what should be done about informing those most concerned. 'C' [Sir Stewart Menzies, Director of MI6] seemed to think that only the Chiefs of Staff should be told, under a bond of the utmost secrecy. The D.G. [of MI5] thought that the P.M. ought to be told at once. This was at first shot down, but ultimately agreed by the Committee. 'C' said that as he had in the first instance obtained the information through his contact with atomic energy in the U.S., he would be prepared to go down to Chequers immediately with Perrin. There were various developments during the following week. 'C' discovered on visiting the P.M. that he had already been in telegraphic communication with Truman, who was anxious to disclose the information to the American people. We were apparently opposed to this, at any rate until the evidence had been more closely sifted.[84]

The clincher, which decided that the information should be announced in public, came when Perrin 'told us on Friday that it had been impossible to hold the Americans and that Harwell, including FUCHS and PEIERLS, would now know how the information had been obtained'. Perrin thought Liddell and MI5 might like to know this 'in case we got any reactions'.[85]

As for the identity of the spy, who now had much to answer for, the key was to find the identity of the sister. This might not be so straightforward, however. On 20 September Liddell concluded his diary: 'It has now been discovered that both FUCHS and PEIERLS have a sister in the US. The bidding lies heavily on FUCHS whose sister's name is in HALPERIN's diary.'[86]

To solve the mystery of CHARLES' identity, and of his Soviet contacts, would require the combined efforts of both British and American Intelligence. In the United Kingdom, cryptanalysts at the Government Communications Headquarters (GCHQ)* collaborated with MI5; their link with the United States was through the British Embassy in Washington where MI5's representative, Geoffrey Patterson, liaised with the FBI and with his MI6 counterpart, Peter Dwyer. In the United States, Army cryptanalysts shared information with the FBI, but MI6's American cousins, the CIA, remained unaware of this activity, having been frozen out by byzantine inter-agency politics at the highest levels of US Counter-Intelligence. The egotistical and paranoid Director of the FBI, J. Edgar Hoover, would haunt the denouement of the Fuchs affair and its political fallout on both sides of the Atlantic.

---

* GCHQ at Cheltenham is a descendant of the GC&CS, Government Code and Cypher School, which had been based at Bletchley Park during the war. Shortly after the war the name was changed to GCHQ and the operations were located at Eastcote in northwest London. In 1950 GCHQ transferred to Cheltenham, the move being completed early in 1954.

PART FIVE

The Haunting: 1949–50

13

The VENONA Code

THE FIEFDOM OF J. EDGAR HOOVER

In the years after 1945, when the war against fascism morphed into a Cold War with the Soviet Union, J. Edgar Hoover began an egomaniacal war of his own. Anti-communism and subversion became *bêtes-noires* in the United States, and Hoover unashamedly exaggerated the threat to gain funding for the FBI. Under his direction, the Bureau pursued Americans who were not criminals but who did not live up to Hoover's idea of an acceptable citizen.

Congressman Don Edwards, Chair of the House Committee on Civil and Constitutional Rights, later described the FBI's obsession as 'a blot on our claim to be a free society'.[1]

Director Hoover had become a popular hero during the 1930s when FBI agents used fast cars and firepower to arrest notorious bank robbers and bootleggers, and he used the press to maximize publicity for the Bureau. He developed intelligence with files of fingerprints, not just of convicted criminals but of anyone interrogated, and established a highly professional national police force. But power corrupts, and after two decades in charge of national secrets Hoover was also using his position to accumulate dossiers of scandal on leading figures. Much of this was tittle-tattle and smear, material ideal for blackmail. Hoover collected this intelligence as a potent armoury, which he did not hesitate to use to further his ambitions.

Following Roosevelt's sudden death in April 1945, Harry Truman became President. Along with the stupefying news of the atomic bomb, Truman was alarmed by what he learned about the FBI, which had become 'bloated in size and power'. In a memo to himself on 12 May he mused that the FBI was tending towards a Secret Police or Gestapo, 'dabbling in sex life scandal and plain blackmail when they should be catching criminals'. Hoover, who had become used to having direct access to President Roosevelt, looked for someone in the FBI known to Truman who could act as liaison to the White House. The chosen agent duly told the new President, 'Mr Hoover wants you to know that he and the FBI are at your personal disposal and will help in any way you ask.' Truman was incensed and boomed. 'Any time I want the services of the FBI, I'll ask for it through my Attorney General.'[2]

Assistant Director William Sullivan recalled that when Hoover received this message his 'hatred knew no bounds'. Hoover had been put in his place and lost his direct line to the seat of power. He was by then twenty years into a tenure that would last nearly half a century, until his death in May 1972. Hoover's lengthy immersion at the heart of government enabled him to hold sway over transient presidents by selective use of information. Truman and Kennedy, apparently, were the only ones who kept some distance. A considerable amount of Hoover's energy would be devoted to finding a way 'to draw the Truman White House into his web'.[3]

Sensitive information, including political innuendo from wiretaps, was sent to the White House on untraceable paper with no FBI letterhead and no watermarks. Titbits of political intelligence, such as advance news reports critical of the President, or rumours of scandals, were leaked to Truman. Hoover was in effect running a political espionage service and Truman appears to have accepted it.[4] The intention was that Truman would be beholden to Hoover.

It seems, however, that Truman was less concerned about the blurring of conventional norms than Hoover, because Hoover felt insecure and paranoid that his job was at risk. Hoover's own private life contained skeletons too. After the war there were rumours that he was homosexual, fuelled in part by his behaviour at a dinner attended by senior lawmakers. A female singer at the function performed her routine while moving among the diners. Pausing by Hoover's table, she honoured the FBI Director by sitting on his lap, at which Hoover, overwhelmed with embarrassment, fled the room. The story was around Washington like wildfire. Worried about his homosexuality he visited a psychiatrist, but ended the consultations because he was afraid to trust the doctor. He attempted to muzzle the rumours by using FBI agents to threaten the press.

He reinvented himself as 'J. Edgar Hoover, American hero' by identifying a new foe to fight: communism. The Cold War provided a perfect backdrop, even while Hoover's spying on American citizens was often indistinguishable from the totalitarian regimes he despised. The real level of the perceived threat is almost farcical when examined rationally. Hoover himself credited the United States Communist Party with fewer than 80,000 members at its peak, and that was during the war when the Soviet Union was America's ally. This amounted to less than 1 in every 2,000 citizens, and of these only a minority were industrial workers capable of creating economic trouble. Even so, Truman felt he had to appease the right wing and introduced vetting, or loyalty tests, for civilian employees of the federal government. Truman deliberately snubbed Hoover by entrusting this task to the Civil Service Commission rather than the FBI.

Hoover fought back, and in testimony before the House un-American Activities Committee he made remarks about liberals, clearly aimed at Truman. Hoover's face appeared on the front cover of *Newsweek* promoting an article on 'How to Fight Communism'. Thus establishing himself as the nation's chief crusader against the communist menace, Hoover gained full control of the loyalty investigations.

This was not enough for Hoover's insatiable ambition, however, and he manoeuvred for the FBI – an American national force – to have a larger remit, a grandiose pan-global 'FBI Special Intelligence Service'. President Truman, worried that Hoover was building a 'Gestapo' at the FBI and was 'getting too big for his britches', in September 1947 approved the creation of an extra-national organization, the Central Intelligence Agency, which would be responsible to the President through the National Security Council, with no role for Hoover. Hoover was so furious 'that he gave specific instructions that under no circumstances were [agents of the FBI] to give any documents or information to the CIA'.[5]

Hoover's relationship with the CIA was petty from the start and would be destructive throughout his entire career. His encyclopaedic files on high-profile Americans were now expanded to include dossiers on the CIA Directors. One of these, General Walter Smith, had a head-on clash with Hoover, reminding him it was 'mandatory' that the FBI give the CIA full cooperation and failure to do so would lead to a fight 'all over Washington'. On this occasion Hoover backed down but wrote puerile comments on Smith's file – 'Smith is a stinker'.[6]

Such was the confused and conflicted state of American intelligence and counter-intelligence when the case of Klaus Fuchs and his contact 'GOOSE' blew up in 1949.

THE VENONA BREAKTHROUGH

Code-named VENONA,* the decryption of the Soviet diplomatic codes, which led to the unmasking of Klaus Fuchs in the summer of 1949, was the United States' greatest intelligence secret. Hoover kept VENONA

---

* VENONA was an invented word with no specific meaning.

intercepts in a locked safe in his office. He didn't tell President Roosevelt or President Truman, the Attorney General or the Secretary of State; nor, he ensured, did the existence of VENONA reach the ears of the CIA.

The story begins in 1939 when the US Army Signals Intelligence Service – now the National Security Agency – started to collect Soviet diplomatic telegrams sent from the United States to Moscow on commercial telegraph lines.[7] In February 1942 Winston Churchill had informed Roosevelt that British cryptographers had broken the codes and ciphers used by the US State Department, enabling them to read US diplomatic messages, adding 'now that we are allies I gave instructions that this work should cease'. Having thus intimated the ability of British code-breakers and alerted the President to the 'danger of our enemies having achieved a similar amount of success', he offered to 'put any expert you nominate in touch with our technicians', adding that the whole matter was so secret that 'you should burn this letter when you have read it'.[8] In May 1943 the United States and the United Kingdom formally agreed to exchange expertise on cryptanalysis and intelligence.*

Churchill and Roosevelt were worried that Stalin might be planning to negotiate a separate peace with Hitler, so in 1943 the Americans assigned code-breakers to work on decryption of their Soviet diplomatic messages at Arlington Hall, Virginia, in the suburbs of Washington DC. During the war the British had primarily focused on German messages, of course, but had also been collecting traffic of the Soviet GRU.[9] This provided experience that became invaluable later during the VENONA collaboration, when American analysts discovered that their Soviet communications were concerned not just with diplomatic subjects but also with espionage. From 1945 to 1946 members of the British cryptographic unit at GCHQ were briefed on the American programme;[†] it was not until the following year that the FBI was informed. Meanwhile Meredith Gardner – Arlington Hall's principal translator and analyst – explained his progress to his British colleagues, and early in 1948 the UK was formally indoctrinated into VENONA.[10] Collaboration between US Army Signals Intelligence and their British colleagues was almost seamless. The UK assigned full-time analysts to Arlington Hall, and in 1949 Joan Malone Callahan crossed the Atlantic to become the first American analyst and linguist to work at Eastcote. When she returned to Arlington Hall in 1954 to become project supervisor she was replaced in Britain, at GCHQ's new centre in Cheltenham, by Gardner.[11]

---

* The BRUSA agreement of 1943 was officially enacted in March 1946, and later extended to include Canada, Australia and New Zealand.
† On the history of GCHQ, see chapter 12, footnote on p. 207.

Meredith Gardner was a lean and gangly American linguist who had taught himself Russian during the war and it was his work from 1946 that had brought the VENONA project to life. The Soviet messages formed strings of apparently random numbers, and were almost impenetrable. Real progress only occurred after the summer of 1946 when Gardner began analytically to reconstruct the Russian codebook.[12] In December that year he made a breakthrough when one message turned out to contain the names of the leading scientists in the Manhattan Project. Here was the first clue that the Soviet Union had monitored the construction of the atomic bomb.

Gardner continued to chip away at the coded messages and through 1947 managed to read tiny fragments, but their interpretation was confused as the identities of the Russian agents were hidden behind cover-names. Gardner gradually collected several KGB monikers and in October 1948 the FBI – alarmed at the possible extent of Soviet espionage, and alert to the likelihood that it was still ongoing – assigned agent Robert Lamphere to liaise with Gardner with the aim of identifying these individuals.

In Washington, Assistant FBI Director Mickey Ladd liaised with Peter Dwyer, who was the representative of both MI5 and MI6 at the British Embassy. This was mirrored in London where US Legal Attaché John Cimperman visited MI5 and MI6 freely. When the FBI first learned about the deciphered KGB messages, Ladd informed Dwyer, and assigned Lamphere to talk with Dwyer but to be careful. Ladd was concerned because Dwyer was also MI6, which had good relations with its US counterpart – the CIA. Ladd, who was FBI 'through and through', and as such party to Hoover's anti-CIA bent, worried that the CIA might get wind of this top-secret project. Ladd's instruction merely formalized the FBI agent's natural caution, however, because in Lamphere's opinion MI6 were horse-traders who would tout small pieces of information to try to get a lot in return. Dwyer was so adept at this game that Lamphere didn't trust him.[13]

Lamphere told Dwyer that he would be happy to share anything 'where there's a British interest'. The MI6 man responded tartly that he had been promised no restrictions and asserted, 'you can't tell in advance whether there's a British interest'. Dwyer threatened to go over Lamphere's head directly to Mickey Ladd to get what he wanted, which in Lamphere's opinion was 'everything in the cupboard'. Early in 1948, MI5 decided they wanted their own representative in Washington and the new arrival, Dick Thistlethwaite, diplomatically smoothed things over with Lamphere.[14] The FBI agent then shared with them one piece of information that was indisputably of 'British interest' – fragments of KGB messages that indicated someone in the British Embassy in Washington in 1944–5 had passed the KGB information about cables between the United States and Great Britain.* The British pair were startled by this news, which showed that communications between the British and American governments had been compromised at the highest level.

At the end of 1948 Thistlethwaite returned to London and was replaced as MI5 liaison by Geoffrey Patterson. Then in the late summer of 1949 Dwyer told Lamphere that he was leaving; his replacement as MI6 liaison would be – Kim Philby. The Soviet Union's double agent at the heart of the British Intelligence Services was about to move to centre stage in the next dramatic breakthrough – the discovery of a British spy at the heart of the Manhattan Project.†

In the meantime, and following on the discovery of the KGB message about the mole in the British Embassy, the British used the agreement between the United States and themselves to get direct access to the deciphered material. They did so by outflanking the FBI: British cryptanalysts were already working with their American colleagues at Arlington Hall, and GCHQ made a formal request to share in the analysis of KGB traffic. The result was that by the summer of 1949 the British had direct contact with Meredith Gardner, the controlling officer in London being Arthur Martin, MI5's liaison with GCHQ. The specialist code-breakers at GCHQ, collaborating with Gardner, were to prove invaluable to the decryption.[15]

It was in the summer of 1949 that Gardner made the decryption which unearthed Klaus Fuchs. Fuchs, who for eight long years had been so careful – first learning spycraft from Sonya in the anonymous English countryside, then in New York taking precautions to cover for Harry Gold's casual arrangements, and finally only going to rendezvous in London when he judged everything to be favourable – had been let down by his masters, who had used a one-time pad twice, and thereby given Gardner an entrée into their labyrinth of secrets. At first there were only fragmentary clues from a partially decoded message, sent to Moscow Centre in June 1944. The enigmatic note, when eventually deciphered,‡ was as follows:[16]

---

* This was later established to be Donald Maclean.
† In 1949, Philby was in charge of the MI6 station in Turkey, based at Istanbul's British Embassy. He was recalled to London for briefing during September, where he learned about VENONA and of its exposure of two spies – later revealed to be Donald Maclean and Klaus Fuchs.
‡ The taxonomy of VENONA decrypts is discussed in chapter 22, note 22.

FROM: NEW YORK
TO: MOSCOW
NO: 850
To VIKTOR.

[1 group unrecovered] Received from REST the third part of report MSN –
12 Efferent Fluctuation in a Stream [37 groups unrecoverable]. Diffusion
[a] Method – work on his speciality.

R[EST] expressed doubt about the possibility of remaining in the COUN-
TRY without arousing suspicion. According to what R[EST] says, the
ISLANDERS and TOWNSMEN have finally fallen out as a result of the
delay in research work on diffusion. The TOWNSMEN have told the representative of the ISLAND that construction of a plant in the ISLAND 'would
be in direct contradiction to the spirit of the agreement on ENORMOZ
signed together with the Atlantic Charter'. At present the ISLAND's director
in CARTHAGE is ascertaining the details of the transfer of work to the
ISLAND. R[EST] assumes that he will have to leave in a month or six weeks.

15th June [1944][17]

The VENONA project decrypted other messages, none of which
referred to 'diffusion' or 'efferent fluctuation', whatever that might mean,*
but from them Gardner was able to translate some of the code names.
Thus he knew that VIKTOR was Lieutenant General Pavel Fitin, head
of Soviet Intelligence in the United States. He was able to identify COUN-
TRY as the USA; TOWNSMEN as the Americans; CARTHAGE as
Washington DC; ISLAND as Great Britain; and ENORMOZ as the
Manhattan Project. However, the all-important identity of REST, the
informant, remained an enigma.

By 1949 the presence of spies in Canada had been known for three
years. This intercepted message now revealed that there had also been a
spy in the British atomic mission, at the heart of the project in the United
States, who worked on diffusion. The message suggested that in July 1944
this person thought that he would return to the United Kingdom.

There were only a handful of scientists who worked on diffusion and
would fit the bill. With forensic investigation there was probably enough
detail already to focus on Fuchs, as records of his 14 July meeting with
Chadwick – the 'ISLAND's director in CARTHAGE' – and the expectation that Fuchs would soon return to the United Kingdom, could eventually
have singled him out. That would be for future analysis, however, as when

---

* 'Efferent' turned out to be a miscoded 'Effect of'.

Gardner first decoded VIKTOR's telegram there was nothing more specific to pinpoint the spy's identity. The net began to close when two further messages were partially decoded, which revealed more about REST.

The first, which had been sent on 4 October 1944, said: 'REST's sister has not yet returned home. It is planned that GOOSE should make his next trip to see her on 12 October.'[18] So REST has a sister, but where?

The second was a message sent the following day, 5 October 1944, which revealed that REST's code name would henceforth be CHARLES. His contact, GOOSE, would become ARNO. This new vocabulary brought a previously innocuous message of 16 November 1944 to life:[19]

On ARNO's last visit to CHARLES' sister it became known that CHARLES has not left for the ISLAND but is at Camp No. 2. He flew to Chicago and telephoned his sister. He named the state where the camp is and promised to come on leave for Christmas. [ARNO] is taking steps to establish liaison with CHARLES while he is on leave. The assumption that CHARLES had left for the ISLAND – [and then frustratingly]: 40 groups unrecoverable.

So REST and CHARLES (as he would from now on be named) were one and the same. This quartet of messages revealed that there was a spy – CHARLES – in the British atomic mission, who worked on diffusion, who in the latter half of 1944 had moved to Los Alamos – 'Camp No. 2' – visited Chicago, telephoned his sister, and promised to come on leave for Christmas. Meanwhile, in October of that year, CHARLES' sister had probably met his Soviet courier.*

The new lexicon, where GOOSE is identical to ARNO, would later give significance to a message of 20 December 1944:[20]

FROM: NEW YORK
TO: MOSCOW
NO: 1797
To VIKTOR.
We have been discussing his cover with ARNO. ARNO's note about setting up a laboratory was sent in postal despatch No.8 on 24 October. As the subject on which to work ARNO chose 'Problems of the Practical Application Under Production Conditions of the Process of Thermal Diffusion of Gases.' In his note ARNO envisages concluding agreements with firms . . . A detailed report on KRON's office was sent in postal despatch No. 9.

---

* But see also chapter 8, note 22.

Here was information about CHARLES' contact, if of nugatory value. Part of the art of counter-intelligence, however, is to collect such trifles, to store them and continue to bear them in mind, because occasionally what at first appears worthless can be turned into gold.

'THIS WILL PROVE GRAVE MATTER'

In August 1949 Peter Dwyer was nearing the end of his tenure at the British Embassy in Washington as the MI6 liaison with the CIA. He and his MI5 colleague, Geoffrey Patterson, assessed Gardner's news about the British spy. On 16 August Dwyer sent a telegram to Maurice Oldfield, MI6's deputy chief of Counter-Espionage and his supervisor in London: 'We have discovered material which, though fragmentary, appears to indicate that in 1944 a British or British sponsored scientist working here on atomic energy or related subjects was providing Russians with policy information and documents.' Dwyer continued: 'On one occasion he handed over through a cut-out a report described as "MSN 1 [sic, see also note 17] (part 3)" the subject of which appears to be in part, fluctuations in a stream or ray.' He assessed the situation with prophetic resonance: 'I do not wish to cause undue alarm at this stage while fragmentary material is still being worked on [but] my present opinion is that this will prove grave matter.'[21]

Patterson amplified the news in a letter that same day to his boss, Sir Percy Sillitoe, the Director General of MI5: 'Our first problem is to decide the nationality of [CHARLES]. Your guess is as good as ours but we clearly cannot exclude the possibility that he is British.' Patterson added that he and Dwyer might have a good chance of resolving the issue 'once we have access to certain files here'.[22] After a fruitless week of searching, however, Patterson admitted to London that their hopes of identifying CHARLES from files in Washington had drawn a blank, and he requested 'assistance from someone closely associated with the project in 1944'.[23]

Dwyer and Patterson's communications reveal how much in the dark these members of the British Embassy were about atomic energy matters. And their colleagues in London were initially no better placed. On 29 August Maurice Oldfield and Colonel Valentine Vivian of MI6 met with MI5's Arthur Martin and John Marriott, deputy head of Counter-Espionage. At this stage they did not even know the scientific project on which the spy had been engaged. They had a garbled title of the scientific report communicated by CHARLES, and nothing more; no one in MI5 or MI6 – more at home with politics and philosophy than matters scientific – had any idea as to its meaning, nor could they identify it. The reference to the Atlantic Charter, however, was nearer to their experience. Martin honed in on this, and asked: 'What agreement governing scientific projects was signed at the same time as the Atlantic Charter?'[24] After discussing who might be best placed to answer these questions, Roger Hollis agreed that Dick White, head of Counter-Espionage, should speak with Michael Perrin at the Atomic Energy Authority, 'and tell him as much of the story as was necessary', but not to divulge the source.[25]

In the United States, according to Robert Lamphere's memoir written years later, it was he who 'found a fragment in a newly deciphered KGB message', which 'seemed to have come directly from inside the Manhattan Project'.[26] This was the first of the messages above, with its reference to a paper 'MSN12'. Lamphere asked the Atomic Energy Commission (AEC) for a copy of the paper, and also obtained the names of all British mission scientists. Lamphere's memoir recalls, 'In two short days we had learned that Klaus Fuchs was author of the paper.' The FBI informed the British.

In Lamphere's account, the FBI were drivers of the investigation, able to identify Fuchs 'in two short days' and, having alerted MI5, they received an answer 'within a few weeks'. This version certainly chimes with J. Edgar Hoover's later claims that the FBI should take the credit. We can establish that the British learned that the FBI had identified the British report mentioned in VENONA, and that its author was Klaus Fuchs, on Friday 2 September, as Geoffrey Patterson sent a telegram from Washington, which arrived on that day.[27] However, the same telegram widened the inquiry with news that there were 'two British scientists in New York' whose movements corresponded with CHARLES. One was Fuchs; the second was identified as Rudolf Peierls: 'FUCHS' close friend'.

The Security Services now had to consult with the Atomic Energy people in the United Kingdom to assess the full significance of this news. Immediately after the weekend, on Monday 5 September, Dick White briefed Michael Perrin.

CHARLES IS FUCHS – OR PEIERLS

Michael Perrin, who during the war had been a leader of Tube Alloys, was by 1949 'Deputy Controller of Production, Atomic Energy (Technical Policy)'. This bureaucratic mouthful hid his singular importance. Whereas Viscount Portal of Hungerford had become administrative head of the post-war British Atomic Project, Perrin was the hands-on expert, in all but name the CEO, responsible for ensuring that government policy in the field of atomic energy kept in step with scientific and technical developments. Perrin was well known in Whitehall, and was a familiar presence in the London clubs where government officials lunched or did business after hours.

It was Perrin's job to interpret the science to politicians and civil servants. He was privy to research on the atomic bomb – both during the war and now at Fort Halstead – and was watchful for the security implications of the work. So it was to Perrin that White turned to understand the meaning and seriousness of the VENONA message. There is a piece of folklore that Perrin responded: 'It looks like Fuchs has been working with the Russians.'[28]

Perrin returned to Shell Mex House on the Strand, headquarters of the Ministry of Supply, the next day, 6 September, where he and White met with Arthur Martin and Colonel James Robertson of the Counter-Espionage Branch. Once the identity of CHARLES was established, it would be Robertson's section that would take responsibility for the everyday aspects of the investigation. This would be Robertson's introduction to a case that he would manage full-time for the next six months, and would become the defining investigation of his career.*

Perrin was able to confirm to the security men that the 'compromised document' was 'MSN 12: Effect of Fluctuation in the Flow of Nitrogen', which had been 'written by Dr FUCHS while he was in the U.K. [sic] and was published on 6 June 1944'.[29] He explained that diffusion was the subject under discussion by the British team in New York at that time, in the preliminary stages of the Manhattan Project. Perrin also remarked that the British had been considering setting up a diffusion plant in the United Kingdom and that Fuchs was one of the scientists whose name was suggested for transfer to it. Perrin agreed to obtain a copy of 'MSN 12' to 'ascertain its circulation and the present whereabouts of all copies'.

He was also asked to help with yet another matter, not to do with CHARLES but with the Soviet contact, code-named GOOSE (or ARNO). MI5 was aware from the decoded message of 20 December 1944 that GOOSE had written a scientific document titled 'Problems of the Practical Application . . . Thermic Diffusion of Gases'. As a possible route to establishing the identity of CHARLES' contact, Perrin was asked to try and identify this document.

The identity of GOOSE/ARNO would be primarily a problem for the FBI. In London the urgent question was to identify CHARLES. Diffusion; New York; the dates: Peierls and Fuchs alone filled the frame.†

---

* James Robertson bears no relation to 'TAR' Robertson.
† Two other British scientists, Tony Skyrme and Christopher Kearton, were candidates but were quickly eliminated.

Perrin briefed White and Robertson about the two scientists and their relative significance for security. He explained that while Peierls had been a leader in the atomic bomb research from the 'ground floor', and as such well placed to have passed information to the Russians, he was now at Birmingham University and removed from the centre of classified research. If CHARLES were Peierls, at least the threat to defence of the realm was in the past. The possibility that CHARLES was Fuchs, however, was for Perrin a nightmare. Fuchs was head of the Theoretical Physics Division at Harwell and intimately involved in the British development of nuclear power. That much, at least, Perrin could tell White. Perrin, however, was one of a small number of individuals who also knew that the United Kingdom was designing its own atomic bomb and that Fuchs was the key advisor to William Penney on its construction. If CHARLES was Fuchs, the United Kingdom's secret development of an atomic weapon was now an open book in Russia.

14

Father or Son? September 1949

Immediately after the briefing at Shell Mex House – headquarters of the
Ministry of Supply – Colonel James Robertson of the Counter-Espionage
Branch called a meeting at MI5 headquarters – Leconfield House on
Curzon Street in Mayfair – to plan the investigation. He and Arthur
Martin, MI5's liaison with GCHQ, were joined by Martin Furnival-Jones
and Colonel Collard of C Branch – vetting – and by Ronnie Reed and Jim
Skardon, colleagues of Robertson in B Branch, Counter-Espionage.

The situation was extremely delicate politically, not least because
CHARLES appeared to have spied in the United States. This could
embarrass the United Kingdom, which had sponsored him during the war.
The alert about CHARLES also had come from the Americans, so the
British Security Services were under pressure to prove their worth. The
case was also of course critically important because their prime suspect
was even now handling top-secret information daily. Consequently when
Colonel Robertson drafted his planned strategy, he reviewed it with the
Director General, Sir Percy Sillitoe.[1]

Mindful of the secrecy of the VENONA source, all liaisons with the
FBI were made through Patterson; even the FBI's representative in London, John Cimperman, was excluded because the British were not sure
that he had been cleared to handle VENONA. Cimperman's ignorance
would later cause problems with his boss, J. Edgar Hoover, for both himself and the British.[2] MI5's ears and eyes on the ground at Harwell,
Security Officer Henry Arnold, was simply told that there had been some
unspecified security leak, and of several suspects Fuchs was the only one
at Harwell.[3] Robertson was so concerned about the abnormal level of
security needed that when his application to intercept Fuchs' communications was approved, he took the unusual step of checking the 'bona fides
of the GPO staff involved at the local post office, including postmen'.[4]

Fuchs would be watched in London by MI5's foot-soldiers. Observation
in Harwell, however, would be risky and, Robertson judged, 'unlikely to

produce results of any value'. He ordered that Arnold should check the layout of Fuchs' home to see whether there were any places where a microphone could be hidden, and whether he had any means there of photocopying documents.[5]

Arnold was told to say nothing of this to anyone else in Harwell, and not to make any enquiries of his own unless told by MI5 to do so. For now, what Robertson wanted from Arnold was 'what is already in his head about such matters as, for example, Fuchs' habits, regular movements, friends, personal description, present address, telephone extension number etc.' Robertson decided that Jim Skardon would be the officer responsible for liaison with Arnold. And as a final layer of security, 'It was agreed that as little as possible of the information Arnold will be supplying should be put on paper': Arnold was to visit MI5 headquarters and report verbally.[6]

The Director General endorsed the plan, but added a warning. 'I think the plan for investigation is good. It is about as complete as it could be which I agree is essential for it to have any chance of success but with one word of caution. By the very virtue of its completeness the more the chance of a Russian [(?) illegible] spy (if he is one) or criminal 'feeling' he is being watched, and I am sure therefore the greatest care will be exercised by all. In the meantime I shall anxiously await developments.'[7]

MI5's focus on Fuchs intensified following a communication from Maurice Oldfield on 8 September. Oldfield informed Arthur Martin that in the 1930s Klaus' brother, Gerhard Fuchs, was known by MI6 to have been an active communist in Switzerland and editor of a party magazine, *Mahnruf*.[8] The next day, 9 September, Martin received news from Peter Dwyer in Washington about CHARLES' sister. This focused attention directly on Fuchs: 'FUCHS sister almost definitely identified as Kristel HEINEMAN whose name appears amongst papers of Israel HALPERIN of [Canadian espionage] case.'[9] Dwyer was confident enough to add: 'Please inform C' – Sir Stewart Menzies, head of MI6.

Meanwhile, MI5 had re-examined its fifteen years of files on Fuchs and discovered that their surveillance of him in 1947 had revealed something after all: Fuchs had received a letter back then from 'Mrs K F Heineman of 9 Lake View Ave, Cambridge Mass signed KRISTEL.' Martin cabled Washington on 10 September: 'Identification agreed.'[10]

MI5 now knew that Fuchs had a sister in the United States. Absence of evidence of Peierls' sister seems, at this stage, to have been treated as evidence of absence; Robertson proceeded as if CHARLES and Fuchs were now known to be one and the same. MI5 officers now watched their target round the clock and produced a daily log of his activities. They noted coyly that Fuchs 'chooses to sleep more often than not with his close friends the SKINNERS at Harwell. He is on more than usually friendly terms with Mrs Skinner.'[11] MI5 knew that the Skinners were planning to move to Liverpool in about six months, when Herbert Skinner would devote his time about 'half and half to Liverpool and Harwell'. As Fuchs spent a considerable amount of his social time with the Skinners, plans were made to bug their phone.

Arnold gave Robertson a description of Fuchs as a 'very reserved man, and mentally tough. Nevertheless he is fond of both whisky and women and can take a large amount of alcohol without being affected. He is a man who is not only brilliant intellectually, but also extremely shrewd from a practical point of view.' He added that Fuchs had recently been ill with suspected TB during which time Mrs Skinner nursed him.

One problem for observation would be 'the small Harwell community, with its closely packed residential quarter immediately outside the perimeter of the main establishment', which would present 'very considerable difficulties'. The head of Counter-Espionage, Dick White, now added, echoing the Director General, 'While it is necessary to press on our enquiries with the utmost speed and urgency, you should at every point take the greatest care to avoid detection by F[uchs]. Speed may therefore sometimes have to be sacrificed for safety.'[12]

Michael Hanley, a rising star in White's B Branch,* reviewed the case and remarked, 'The possibility that FUCHS' communications may lead into the Soviet Embassy in London should not be overlooked. In a matter of such secrecy and importance a short line of communication might seem to be preferable. It is possible, indeed likely, that someone of very little significance could be the cut-out between FUCHS and the Soviet Embassy in London. It must be stated once more that women have often been used by the Soviets for this purpose and that some connected with the Soviet Embassy in London (if this thesis is true) may be utilized as a cut-out from the London end.'[13] This led to interest in female contacts that Fuchs and Erna Skinner established in London.

Hanley now made a key observation about Fuchs: 'If this man is a spy, he is by now an experienced one and therefore well versed in the security measures used by Soviet Intelligence' – in other words, Fuchs would be expert in counter-surveillance. Hanley's conclusions were sober and perspicacious: 'Consequently it is unlikely that a [mail-intercept] or phone check will be of *direct* [Hanley's emphasis] assistance in solving the case. The fact that FUCHS has not recently been heard to express Communist

* Hanley rose through the ranks to become Director General of MI5 in 1972.

views and has appeared to his superior (Sir John Cockcroft) as punctilious about security precautions is not in our opinion significant.'[14]

MI5 officers duly geared their efforts towards Klaus Fuchs, but they were almost immediately diverted when an article in the *Sunday Express* of 11 September threw Rudolf Peierls back into the centre of attention. Entitled 'Scientists Warned No Hotel Talk' the newspaper report mentioned that Peierls would be one of the British representatives at an international atomic conference at Chalk River, Canada, between 26 and 28 September. This created some consternation inside MI5. It would seem that they were unaware of this excursion, and having concentrated on Fuchs they now worried lest Peierls was actually the spy, and might disappear in Canada.

They discussed whether there might be any way to alert the Canadians without 'going much further than is just or safe'.[15] To cover all bases they instigated a mail-intercept on Peierls too, in which the request to the Home Office included the 'Russian' angle once again: 'This man who has a Russian born wife, is engaged on highly secret work of national importance, and it is desired to investigate his activities and contacts.' The MI5 internal memorandum added: 'As in the case of Fuchs it is necessary to pay the closest attention to security.'[16]

Geoffrey Patterson now sent MI5 a message that 'Peierls may have married sister living in United States.' This further reinvigorated interest in Peierls and MI5 advised that the FBI's 'first priority' should be to 'identify PEIERLS' sister'. Meanwhile MI5 intensified its preparations to cover the upcoming visit by Peierls to Canada, which would include time in the USA. One worry was how MI5 might interact with the Canadian Police (RCMP), while protecting its most sensitive source, the VENONA decrypts. On 20 September MI5 duly alerted Patterson: 'No Repeat No intention to alert RCMP', but 'FBI may be told if you think it necessary'.[17] The next day Patterson responded: 'We shall push ahead [with Peierls but] we still feel that FUCHS is a much more likely candidate.'[18]

In R. J. Lamphere's memoir, it was only now, around 20 September, that he became centrally involved in the Fuchs affair – after learning of the Soviet bomb test, which sensitized him to the possible presence of a major spy in the Manhattan Project. While it is possible that the passage of time conflated the order of events in his memory,[19] it is nonetheless true that the FBI records of this affair develop only in the final weeks of September, although they contain the results of some sturdy earlier investigations.[20] An FBI memo for the director at that time mentions 'a Soviet agent who used the cover name of REST or CHARLES in 1944 and who is believed identical with Klaus Fuchs'. The 'work on his speciality' had led the FBI to focus on the paper's author – Fuchs – though technically there is no reason to make such an inference. That someone in the FBI had had exchanges with MI5 is clear from the remark that MI5 'has also suggested' the names of Peierls and two others as candidates for CHARLES. This initial FBI activity appears to have been supervised by H. B. Fletcher, head of the Philadelphia Station, who made a summary for Assistant Director Mickey Ladd at the end of the month.[21]

The FBI had focused on Fuchs, first because he was not only the author of the leaked paper but also the subject of two 'derogatory pieces of information' about him on their files: his name appeared in the diary of Israel Halperin (who the FBI had on file as a Soviet agent) and also in a list of leading German communists that had come into their possession at the end of the war.[22] On 26 September Lish Whitson, the head of Counter-Espionage, sent a draft summary to Fletcher, with the instruction that – 'if you approve' – this memorandum on Fuchs should be passed to 'Special Agent R J Lamphere who will, as in the past, personally deliver it to [REDACTED]'.[23] This is probably referring to Dwyer or Patterson, as these were at the fulcrum of exchanges with MI5.*

In any event, Patterson by now was concentrating on Fuchs, but he devised a way to obtain information on both Peierls and Fuchs without raising their suspicion: 'Thanks to the conference which is being held here we hope to be able to obtain the personal files for these scientists without arousing undue comment. Those on FUCHS and PEIERLS should be far more illuminating now that we know more about them and may possibly enable us to spot the man we want.'[24]

CASTING THE NET

On 20 September, Colonel Robertson visited Harwell and saw Henry Arnold at his home in the village of Marcham nearby, to make plans to monitor Fuchs.[25] Arnold told Robertson that Fuchs had invited him to drive his car whenever he needed one, and this would enable him to keep note of the mileage. Robertson asked about Fuchs' next-door neighbour as a potential eavesdropper who might be able to provide information, but Arnold did not rate the man, an engineer, to be 'a very good bet'.[26]

MI5's interest in Fuchs had grown for a pragmatic reason: Peierls was now involved in classified work only very indirectly, whereas Fuchs

---

* It is likely that Lamphere focused on Fuchs after uncovering the two pieces of 'derogatory information', but his chronology and timescales, with their implicit criticism of MI5 playing catch-up, seem memories distorted by the passage of time.

was completely immersed in top-secret research and development. To identify and punish CHARLES for past misdemeanours was desirable, but to stop present or future espionage was a commanding necessity.

Whereas VENONA implied that Fuchs was probably active in the United States in 1944, it was impossible to estimate the chance that he was active in Great Britain in the 'different world conditions of 1949'. Robertson judged: 'In 1944 he might have felt justified in passing to the Russians, then our ally, a part of the product of his own brain. The arguments, which in 1944 might have supported such an attitude, do not now apply. The impulse to treachery may therefore no longer exist in Fuchs' mind. He may on the other hand have long and secretly been a convinced communist, considering himself justified in aiding the Soviet Union in the conditions of 1944 or in those of the present year.' The principal object of the present investigation was therefore 'to prove which of those hypotheses is true – to obtain evidential proof as to whether Fuchs is or is not still a spy. It will not be easy to prove either, and to prove the negative will perhaps be even more difficult than to prove guilt.'[27]

The fundamental difficulty for the investigation was the delicacy of the VENONA information about the 1944 leakage. As Robertson understood, and emphasized throughout: 'At no stage in the investigation can action be taken which might in any way compromise the security of the source involved.' The sharing of VENONA information was restricted even within MI5: 'This means that the many investigators who, in their different special fields, have to cooperate in the enquiry, must necessarily act while in possession of only a part of the story, and with the greatest caution. They are handicapped from the beginning.'[28]

If MI5's sole evidence for a prosecution came via VENONA, they would be impotent. Not only would the source be withheld from the judiciary, a competent defence counsel would undermine its claim to be hard evidence. Evidence that Fuchs was CHARLES was circumstantial, but convincing; actually incriminating statements about CHARLES, however, relied totally on the decryption. The actual messages consisted of strings of symbols, in effect gobbledygook; that they referred to an agent CHARLES, with characteristics that led to Klaus Fuchs, was completely the work of the code-breakers.*

To be guaranteed success, MI5 needed to catch Fuchs in the act. This led to their second difficulty. MI5 were bothered because the number of

---

* In the USA, VENONA led to the identification of several spies who managed to escape prosecution because VENONA was the only proof of their guilt. The Los Alamos atomic spy Theodore Hall, who refused to confess, is one example.

possible ways in which Fuchs could pass information to the Soviet intelligence services 'is almost limitless'. The method could be through an intermediary who was in touch with a professional officer. MI5 assessed that the go-between could be a domestic servant at Harwell, or some casual acquaintance based in London or, indeed, in any other place to which Fuchs travelled. Their conclusion: 'It follows that we shall only be able to satisfy ourselves that Fuchs is or is not a spy by accounting for his every act throughout 24 hours of the day.'[29] By the end of September, MI5 had a watch on Fuchs and Peierls, together with Fuchs' lady friend Erna Skinner and her husband Herbert.

This included the use of listening devices from the start. The diary of activity in Fuchs' home records on 21 September 'movement and clatter', which revealed that he and Erna Skinner had lunch there. Afterwards, conversation in the room often sounded 'distant and indistinct'. Their voices were distinguished easily, and 'odd indistinct remarks from [Erna] met with no audible responses from [Fuchs]'.[30]

Three days later, Henry Arnold seems to have made his first attempt to trip up Fuchs when on that Saturday morning he visited Fuchs at home 'because of the news' that the Russians had exploded an atomic bomb. On this occasion Arnold's attempt to be an agent provocateur and amateur sleuth had little success. He first confirmed that Fuchs had seen Skinner the previous day and was fully informed about the news. 'I don't know what to make of it, do you?' he asked, to which Fuchs replied, 'Well, we don't – I mean, we want to know the details.' Arnold then conjectured that it might not have been an atomic bomb but a 'runaway' – some accidental disaster at a nuclear physics centre – and suggested, 'Probably their precision work might not be so good as ours.'[31]

If he hoped that Fuchs might let slip some unguarded comment about Russian know-how, Arnold was disappointed, as the conversation became more social. Arnold offered Fuchs a cigarette: 'Or are you still not smoking?', to which Fuchs made an 'inaudible' response. Arnold commented that Fuchs' room was 'quite cosy'. He then brought the conversation back to his main goal by asking how Fuchs felt about the balance of power in light of the Soviet bomb. Fuchs replied he had 'spent a lot of time yesterday trying to find everybody' so that when the news of the Russian bomb was announced in the press, 'they would not associate [Harwell] with that particular announcement' – in other words, to ensure that staff were assured that Harwell was not building atomic weapons. Fuchs said that although people 'very definitely' should not talk about the announcement, 'there's a grave risk they will, once the papers get their teeth into this'.[32]

Arnold changed the subject, asked how Fuchs managed for meals, and suggested that Fuchs 'take a housekeeper or a wife'. At this point a woman, whom they addressed as Marjorie, arrived. She said she would not stay but would clear up Fuchs' breakfast things. Arnold and Fuchs talked about cars for about five minutes, by which time Marjorie's work was done and she left with Arnold. The exercise proved that it was possible to listen in to conversations in Fuchs' living room, although on this occasion nothing of importance had resulted.

Robertson had focused attention on Fuchs, but the Director General, Sir Percy Sillitoe, urged caution. On 30 September he wrote to Patterson in Washington, whose letter of 21 September had moved Fuchs into the position of prime suspect. While agreeing with Patterson's assessment of the two candidates 'in general terms', Sillitoe said that 'there is a danger in placing too much significance on dates'.[33]

This refers to the information from VENONA, which hinted that CHARLES had expected to return to the United Kingdom in late July or August – namely 'in a month or six weeks' after 15 June. This appeared to fit with Fuchs' agenda and not that of Peierls; the FBI, for example,

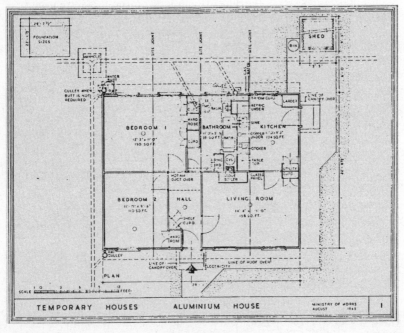

Plan of Fuchs' prefab.

regarded it 'as unlikely that there could have been talk of [Peierls] visiting England in July immediately after his posting [to Los Alamos].'[34] In Sillitoe's opinion, this was tenuous and needed more certain evidence before it could be regarded as definitive.

Sillitoe, who was still suspicious about Peierls, continued: 'We are hoping to obtain a sight of certain files at this end which might clear up this point.' Sillitoe's position was that MI5 must 'attempt to cover both suspects and must continue to do so until we can positively eliminate one or the other'.[35]

The following morning, Saturday 1 October, Robertson put Sillitoe's strategy into motion, with a priority list. Fuchs was in first place, and Peierls was in fourth after Mrs Skinner and one Elieser Yapou, the Israeli press attaché who had journalistic contacts 'in the Russian colony in London'. The reasons for highlighting Erna Skinner were 'the obscurity of her past history' (she came from Austria), 'her intimate association with FUCHS, and the fact that she visited with FUCHS the flat of YAPOU on 20.9.49'.[36]

To watch Yapou the next day, Sunday, created a problem. He lived in Lancaster Close, a quiet district very near to a Russian residential area. MI5 was concerned by the considerable risk of watchers being noticed by 'some Russian if not by Yapou himself'. So Robertson instructed his teams to suspend observation on the Sunday unless something untoward happened in the meantime. Skardon and Robertson prepared to be ready over the weekend for telephone consultation if necessary. On 4 October a telephone check was mounted on Yapou, who in fact was irrelevant to the case. The net was getting wider and MI5's resources were being spread ever thinner.

Peierls meanwhile was at the Chalk River conference in Canada, and MI5 awaited information about the time and place of his return to the United Kingdom the following week, for if he came through London en route to Birmingham, it should be possible to detach one or two men to get a sight of him. Skardon gave Inspector Burt of Special Branch a description of Peierls with a very precise assertion that he was '5 foot 7 ½ inches tall'.[37] MI5 hoped to have details of his flight, but should he arrive at London Airport without prior notice, they asked that Burt tell them and find out Peierls' intended destination.

In popular perception, surveillance of a suspect involves a team of watchers who are always one move ahead of their quarry, their movements coordinated like the players in a symphony orchestra who have rehearsed to perfection. The reality is more often subject to the vagaries of human frailty – as on this occasion. When MI5 checked the passenger lists on BOAC and discovered that Peierls would leave New York, fly to Prestwick in Scotland, and then continue to London Airport, at Heathrow, Robertson was told to expect Peierls in London on Wednesday 5 October. Had they followed this information, they would have been a day early – it seems that the informant had given the day of departure from North America, and MI5 analysts had failed to take account that the flight would be overnight. Fortunately this was updated to 'Thursday 6th' with Peierls expected home by midday.[38]

Even now their information was awry, as on 6 October, Special Branch officers recorded Peierls as he passed through immigration at Prestwick, having arrived from New York at 11 a.m. He took the midday flight to London. They informed MI5 headquarters that Peierls was already in the country and would be arriving at Heathrow on an internal flight. MI5 managed to detach one or two men to get a sight of him, and at last the operation began to run smoothly. These foot-soldiers reported that Peierls was dressed in a 'shabby waterproof trench coat with a belt, dark grey soft hat with a black band and the brim turned up all round', 'clean shaven, Jewish appearance wearing spectacles,' and confirming that he was '5 foot 7 ½ inches tall'. They tracked him from Heathrow to Victoria coach station, where he collected 'a battered suitcase'. From there he went to Paddington station, where he was observed to have taken 'a bath in the gentlemen's washroom on platform 1' before boarding a train for Birmingham, which 'left two minutes late'.[39]

Peierls was home, unaware of the silent watchers who followed his movements like twitchers obsessed by some exotic bird. He had made no clandestine liaisons, picked up no secreted documents, nor deposited contraband for others to find. Nor had he met Fuchs. In summary, he had made a perfectly normal journey home after a long trip.

Robertson now drew up plans for surveillance over the weekend of 8–9 October, with sufficient numbers of men to cover any 'sortie on the part of FUCHS'. As the goal was to catch Fuchs in the act of espionage, and to identify any contacts, Robertson built a matrix of alternative possibilities. The planning, at least, was superbly efficient, with Robertson the conductor of an orchestra of watchers. He briefed the team on the overall strategy: 'The main objective is to keep a 24 hours watch on FUCHS himself. On occasion however, it may happen that an identified contact of FUCHS will be of such interest as to merit an even higher priority than FUCHS. When FUCHS himself is observed to make a contact, observation of the contacted person will be maintained only for so long as is necessary for identification.'[40]

Robertson then visualized how events might develop, and planned for each potential outcome. First, if the contact met Fuchs again, they were to become priority 1. However, if after twenty-four hours there had been no such contact, attention would again concentrate on Fuchs himself.

Robertson insisted that a general overriding priority should be given not only to Fuchs but also to 'any of his contacts that are under investigation. Thus PEIERLS will be a secondary priority as compared with these. If however PEIERLS is observed to meet FUCHS, the priority for keeping watch on him will be decided in accordance with the principles applying to any other contact, as set out above.'

As things turned out, none of these contacts took place. Robertson's complex plan was never needed, which is perhaps just as well as there were so many tricky manoeuvres in its choreography. He seems to have remained suspicious of Peierls, and this notwithstanding the fact that during the first two weeks of October a series of communications from Patterson in Washington had put Fuchs clearly in the frame. The timing of Fuchs' travel and transfer to Los Alamos in 1944 undoubtedly fitted with those of CHARLES; Peierls' did not. Sillitoe's worry about dates was removed.

Patterson recorded that he had 'carefully studied' the files in Washington on 'our two favourites and two outsiders'.[41] He had found Peierls' travel expense claims from the spring and summer of 1944. These revealed 'PEIERLS left New York for Albuquerque New Mexico on 2nd June. He returned on 20 June and between those dates was in New Mexico. Files also show that Peierls' posting to Los Alamos was decided at end of May 1944 and would take place in early July.'[42] This did not mesh with CHARLES, who in mid-June was still uncertain of his future other than it would entail a move in 'six to eight weeks'. Also, the paper 'MSN 12', which Fuchs had written, was dated 6 June and hence had not been completed before Peierls left, and was handed over to the Russians in New York while Peierls was elsewhere.[43]

Furthermore, in what with hindsight was perhaps the key breakthrough, on 5 October, MI5 received from Patterson two pages of notes on Fuchs' movements in the United States. Coincidentally, Patterson had sent this on 30 September, the same day that Sillitoe had written to him with the recommendation to be cautious 'about dates'; the two messages seem to have crossed in the mail, as Patterson's long letter makes no reference to Sillitoe's. Patterson now included the news that on 'July 14, 1944, [Fuchs] visited Chadwick [in Washington].'[44] This was almost like finding CHARLES with a smoking gun registered to Klaus Fuchs, because the first VENONA message, sent to Moscow on 15 June 1944, had mentioned that CHARLES – 'in four to six weeks' – expected to return to the United Kingdom and that Chadwick was at that time deciding on CHARLES' future. It seems that it took a few days before this connection was noticed, as it was not until 10 October that MI5 asked Perrin to ascertain 'the purpose of Fuchs' meeting with Chadwick on 14 July'.[45]

THE GAMBIT OF FUCHS' FATHER

That Fuchs was CHARLES was now reasonably solid. On 11 October London received from Patterson a lengthy résumé of information that Washington had accumulated about Fuchs. First, Patterson reported a link of Klaus not only to his sister, Kristel, but also to the Canadian espionage case of 1946. Patterson wrote: 'The FBI have an address book of Israel Halperin, which they found at the time of his arrest in February 1946 in the Canadian spy case. It contained the entry: "Klaus Fuchs, Asst to M Born, 84 Grange Lane, University of Edinburgh, Scotland Camp N. Camp L Internment operations – Kristel Heineman 55 Carvel Road, Watertown".' The phrase 'camp L' was circled. FBI records showed that Kristel was Fuchs' sister, and that she had lived at that address before January 1941. 'In other words, Halperin has an address for Kristel Heineman that was five years old at the time of his apprehension.'[46]

FBI records showed that Kristel's husband, Robert Heineman, had been a communist of long standing since at least 1941. Patterson also reported that the FBI had discovered that the Nazis had Klaus Fuchs' name – he was described as a student of philosophy – on a list of people to be identified during the invasion of Russia in 1941; so much for Fuchs' hope that this file would not fall into American hands. This document belatedly reinforced the Gestapo's claims, of 1938, that Fuchs had communist associations. Patterson's dossier provided undoubted evidence that Klaus Fuchs had not only the opportunity to have passed atomic secrets to the Russians, but also established a motive: his hitherto secret communist past was now in the open.

A comment in the final paragraph of Patterson's message would later have huge resonance: 'The local MI6 representative is sending the gist of the above to his HQ.' This would have been one of Peter Dwyer's last acts as he was in the final week of his posting as MI6 representative in the British Embassy in Washington. That very day his replacement arrived: Kim Philby – the double agent whose real masters were in Moscow. Philby had been alerted to VENONA, and how there was a spy at Los Alamos, in his briefing by Maurice Oldfield during September in London. He was now confronted with the facts as soon as he arrived in the United States on 10 October, for Dwyer's welcome to Philby was his telegram to London that CHARLES was most likely to be Klaus Fuchs.[47] This information was received by MI5 on 11 October, by which time, thanks to Philby's treachery, Moscow too was probably aware that Fuchs was in trouble.[48]

MI5 was watching Fuchs but with no chance of catching him in an act of espionage because he had ceased contact with the Soviets six months earlier. Following Philby's discovery that both the FBI and MI5 were pursuing Fuchs, Moscow would have cut off contact even if Fuchs had not already ended it of his own accord. Although MI5 was by now certain that Fuchs was the scientist known as CHARLES, it had no idea what information he had passed to the Russians nor how he made contact with them. The Security Services thus needed to identify Fuchs' contacts, and assess their backgrounds.

These defining breakthroughs took place, as we just saw, in the first week of October, and were in MI5 files on 11 October. Within two days* – either by coincidence or following a tip-off – Fuchs approached Henry Arnold, out of the blue, and told him about his father's move to the Russian Zone of Germany. Fuchs expressed the worry that the Russians might use his father's situation to put pressure on him at Harwell. When Fuchs intimated that Arnold might offer him advice, Arnold hedged, and proposed that they discuss the subject further 'in a few days' time': Arnold, caught unawares by Fuchs' news, needed time to consult MI5.

Robertson had arranged that Arnold should visit him at Leconfield House every Monday, and on 17 October Arnold broke the news about Fuchs' father. They decided that Arnold should certainly tell Fuchs that he would be 'ill advised, if he had any control over his father's movements, to allow him to move to the Russian Zone of Germany'. The reason, if any were needed, would be that of which Fuchs had already shown himself aware – namely that such a move on the part of the father would place 'a hostage in the hands of the Russians of which, having regard to Fuchs' own position, they might be tempted to make use'.[49]

As a result of this development Robertson arranged for the immediate imposition of outgoing checks on all letters addressed by Fuchs to his father.

Three days later, Arnold and Fuchs met again in Arnold's office. Arnold asked Fuchs whether he had given any further thought to the 'problem of his father's affairs', adding in explanation: 'The security authorities regard it as highly important that those who are engaged in places and on work covered by the Official Secrets Act should have no close ties to those countries dominated by Russia.'

---

* On 17 October, Arnold told Robertson this took place on 13 October, whereas Arnold's handwritten statement of 24 October gives the date as Wednesday 12 October. Arnold and Fuchs met again on 20 October.

Arnold now applied a small amount of pressure. He pointed out that Fuchs' father was seventy-three years old: Did Fuchs not find it a surprise that he should 'suddenly' be offered a chair in Leipzig at that age? Fuchs admitted that the idea had occurred to him. In view of this, Arnold asked – might Fuchs' father be induced to turn down Leipzig if it could be arranged to offer him a similar type of chair in the British or American Zones? Fuchs replied that he did not think his father would do so, as he was 'disillusioned' by the administration of the Western Zone of Germany.

Fuchs and Arnold then discussed other matters for a time, but they returned to their original subject later when Arnold asked whether Fuchs did not fear that pressure might be brought to bear on him through his father's arrest, for example. 'What would your reaction be if that happened?' Fuchs replied: 'At present I don't think I would be induced to cooperate, but of course it's impossible to say how I might feel under altered circumstances.' Fuchs then asked Arnold the pivotal question: 'If my father accepts this post, should I resign?' Arnold told Fuchs that it was for the 'administration people' to decide.

When they parted, Arnold suggested that Fuchs would probably like to think it over further before they spoke about it again. However, Arnold was 'left with the impression that Fuchs does not intend to do so unless I approach him'.

Fuchs gave this information to Arnold 'in the strictest confidence'.[50] Arnold duly passed it on to MI5 in the same manner.

15

Private Lives: October 1949

Today we know that MI5's surveillance of Klaus Fuchs from October 1949 had no chance of catching him in an act of espionage. It did give insights into Fuchs' life and relationships, however, which frame the momentous events soon to overwhelm him. The daily record of reports from the foot-soldiers who shadowed Fuchs, from the eavesdroppers on his phone line, and of meetings at MI5 headquarters where the information was analyzed, reveals the reality of security work, in contrast to portrayals of spooks by fiction and film. But as in any fictional mystery tale, the Fuchs affair too had its fair share of false trails.

Although Colonel Robertson was by now fairly certain that Fuchs was the scientist known as CHARLES, he had no idea how or what information had passed to the Soviets. Robertson needed to identify Fuchs' contacts, which led him to review Fuchs' first arrival in England, and relations with his sponsor, Ronald Gunn. With the benefit of hindsight, a litany of missed opportunities emerged.[1]

Gunn was a British subject, born in 1899, and Security Service records showed that he had made two visits to Russia, one in 1932 and the second in June 1936. Gunn had sponsored Fuchs' immigration in 1933, and Gunn's address permeated Fuchs' file, yet neither Bristol police nor MI5 made the connection between Gunn and the Soviet Union in 1934 when they received the Gestapo report on Fuchs' communist background.

By 1941, when Fuchs' suitability for the top-secret Tube Alloys project was first assessed, Gunn's history on MI5's files was even richer. He had come to the attention of Bristol police in May 1940 for having 'leanings towards either Communism or Nazism' – at a time when the Soviet Union and Germany were allies. In 1941 he again attracted attention by his association with local communists, and because he was under suspicion of having organized the Bristol Air Raid Precaution Campaign Committee, which was thought to be communist-sponsored. In the course of that year he was dismissed from his employment as an air-raid warden.

Thus Gunn was a natural conduit for a communist refugee from the Nazis to have entered the United Kingdom. Gunn's background should have raised questions once again in 1943 when Fuchs' transfer to the United States and the Manhattan Project were on the line. But beyond the discredited Gestapo report, and the association with Gunn, there had been nothing to incriminate Fuchs.[2]

LIFE WITH ERNA

MI5 would be slow in unmasking Fuchs' espionage, but much quicker in exposing his private life: 'Fuchs has a relationship with Erna Skinner. Age about 37, plump, short (5 foot 4 to 5.5) dark [and] attractive type of Jewess. Generally well dressed though inclined to be untidy.'[3] Telephone conversations between Fuchs and the Skinner house were monitored at the Newbury exchange, and the records are full of titbits from the start. On 20 September: 'At 16.37 Fuchs rang Mrs Skinner. He then asked if she needed his support and [added] that Herbert would not be back before 6 p.m.' When Fuchs said he might call in to see her about 5 p.m., the eavesdropper commented: 'Fuchs [appeared to be] taking the opportunity to see Mrs Skinner while Skinner was out of the way.'[4] The following day bugging equipment in Fuchs' living room listened in on the pair's lunchtime date, the first of many such snoops into their private lives.[5]

Whereas Fuchs appears to have been unaware that his privacy was invaded, MI5's records contain implicit clues that within a few weeks Fuchs knew that he was being watched from the world outside. MI5 were learning on the job and, it appears, revealed more than they intended.

When Skardon and Robertson first assessed Harwell back in September they immediately realized that the community was tightly knit and that MI5 personnel could not merge into the scene unnoticed. That was why Arnold was chosen as the resident source of information. Nor would it be practical to follow Fuchs by car due to the scarcity of traffic. The plan therefore would be to have Arnold monitor Fuchs' requests for travel warrants, and advise MI5 if he would use a car or train. If by train, they would try to start their observation at Didcot station, and continue to the terminus or address of his destination. If by car, watchers would wait for him on the most likely trunk road according to his advertised destination.

Three MI5 staff members were seconded to the Newbury telephone exchange to monitor calls to Fuchs and Skinner. As cover story they claimed to be making a statistical survey of calls passing through the exchange. They prepared a complete paper record daily of phone intercepts and of activity overheard in Fuchs' home. A courier collected these each evening and took the report to London by car. Urgent matters would be communicated by phone.* To aid security on the open line, code names were assigned to relevant towns. With wry humour, Slough was then named POOLE, and Maidenhead VIRGINIA, while some Oxford graduate must have inspired the decision to refer to Cambridge as BACKWOOD.[6]

The first test of their plan came with Fuchs' visit to the General Electric Company in Wembley on 22 September. The previous day, a conversation between secretaries was overheard saying that Fuchs and Skinner would go there the next day by car, 'probably Fuchs' but conceivably Skinner's'.[7] Arnold didn't know the time but his 'guess' was that it would be about 11 a.m.

On 22 September the eavesdroppers noted Fuchs left home at 9.25 a.m. – 'No sounds since that time.'[8] Then he and Skinner were heard together in an office around 11 o'clock, and at 11.35 Arnold phoned in to say that two cars had just left: Skinner was driving a Riley saloon, accompanied by one passenger, and the other was Fuchs' MG, in which he was on his own.[9] Arnold confirmed that they were heading for Wembley. At MI5 headquarters Mr Storrier, in control of the watching team, was informed. Immediately he put into action the plan to have a car ready on the outskirts of Henley-on-Thames, at the acute junction between the Oxford and Marlow roads,† about half an hour's drive from Harwell.

In 1949 cars in rural Berkshire were not frequent. At 12.10 p.m. watchers saw Skinner's Riley approaching Henley along the grand Fair Mile Road.[10] They remained where they were as the vehicle slowed almost to a halt, before making the sharp left turn onto the Marlow Road. But of Fuchs' MG there was no sign. Twenty minutes passed before Storrier received an update from Arnold: Fuchs had left his car at Skinner's house and was now travelling with Skinner. There is no record of how, or even if, the Henley watchers were told. Meanwhile, five minutes later, and unaware of this news, another team waiting at the Hillingdon Roundabout on Western Avenue in the London suburbs saw Skinner's car with three people inside. Fuchs was at last under surveillance.

No harm had been done on this occasion, but lessons had been learned. Arnold's initial information had been misleading, and by the time he had the facts correct an hour had elapsed. Fortunately other watchers had

---

* Witness the speed with which Robertson on 26 September knew of Fuchs' absence the previous night, p. 240.
† These are the Fair Mile Road, A4130, and the Marlow Road, A4155.

found Fuchs – by chance. Meanwhile the intelligence from the phone intercepts had worked.[11]

Arnold and Robertson's next meeting, on 26 September, was both a post-mortem and a preparation for Fuchs' next sortie. The timing was fortuitous because that very morning Robertson had received word from the Newbury snoopers that Fuchs had disappeared the previous night. On Sunday evening, at about 7.40 p.m., the recording picked up the 'noise as of a key in the lock' followed by the sound of a car 'revving up'. Then there was silence in Fuchs' home until his return was overheard – 'at 4.08' on the Monday morning.[12]

Losing contact with the prime suspect, and so early in the investigation, worried Robertson. He raised this with Arnold and received his first insight into the tittle-tattle of incestuous Harwell life: 'Arnold thinks it possible that Prof SKINNER was away from Harwell on the night in question, travelling by sleeper to Liverpool. If so, FUCHS may have spent the evening and part of the night with Mrs SKINNER.'[13]

Apparently satisfied, Robertson turned to the haphazard nature of their first attempt at external surveillance. On balance he felt that the first test had been 'satisfactory enough'. However, for the next forty-eight hours they would have to be on their toes as Fuchs was due to attend two days of meetings at the Royal Institution, off Piccadilly in London, at which 'Top Secret matters will be discussed' about the atomic bomb.[14] The conference would undoubtedly give Fuchs new information that would merit passing to the Russians, and so presented a strong likelihood that Fuchs would initiate contact with his courier.

The first piece of intelligence about Fuchs' likely movements for that event came from the eavesdroppers in the Newbury telephone exchange when they intercepted a call from Fuchs' secretary. She ordered 'two travel vouchers, both returns (1st class) for Fuchs from Didcot to Paddington, one for tomorrow Tuesday and one for Wednesday'.[15] Fuchs' plan was to travel alone on the train to London and back on each of the two days. MI5 activated a major surveillance operation. In addition to having a watcher at Didcot station from 4.30 a.m., as well as back-up at Paddington and outside the Royal Institution, they were concerned at the possibility that Fuchs might make contact with someone at Reading station, en route, and so had extra officers watching for activity there also.

Unknown to MI5, however, at the last moment Fuchs changed his plans.

'FUCHS IS A NERVOUS DRIVER'

In an uncanny replay of what had happened the previous night, at 9.24 p.m. on the Monday evening the eavesdroppers heard Fuchs' front door slam shut and then a car engine start. His house remained quiet all night and at 5.30 the next morning the report – perhaps influenced by Arnold's discussion with Robertson the previous day – concluded lamely, 'It was presumed [Fuchs] had spent the night away from home.'[16]

Henry Arnold's suggestion that Fuchs and Erna Skinner had 'spent the evening and part of the night [of the 25th] together' was, at the least, prescient for Fuchs' disappearance on this second occasion: Erna later confirmed that in the 'early hours of the morning' of 27 September, after Fuchs had been debating whether to go by train, 'they decided to go by car'.[17] Once again, MI5's watchers were frustrated; they had focused their resources on the Great Western Railway, but Fuchs was nowhere to be seen. Nevertheless, as on 22 September, they reconnected fortuitously when their agent in Albemarle Street noticed Fuchs marching into the Royal Institution, mid-morning.

At lunchtime Fuchs came out of the Royal Institution's front door, went over to the Albemarle Post Office and made two phone calls. MI5's observer must have been very close to Fuchs, because he recorded the first number as that of the Great Western Hotel and the second was later identified as that of a private residence in Herbert Crescent. Then Fuchs hailed a taxi, which headed off into Piccadilly, with his MI5 shadow in pursuit in another. The two vehicles drove west past the Wellington Arch at Hyde Park Corner into Knightsbridge. Fuchs' taxi then diverted into smaller streets and after about a mile he alighted in Herbert Crescent. His shadow stayed in the vicinity for about an hour, until Fuchs reappeared and returned to the Royal Institution for the afternoon's business.

MI5 now mounted a watch at Herbert Crescent. At 2.30 p.m. a man left and was followed on foot to Imperial College where he entered the science laboratories. He was later identified as Dr Wallace Harper, a professional colleague of Fuchs, but in the circumstances he was escalated by MI5 into a potential contact.

At 5 p.m. the Royal Institution meeting ended for the day and MI5 took up the pursuit again. The reason for their failure to see Fuchs on a train that morning now became apparent, as he went to a garage and collected his car. Fuchs' shadows managed to follow him again as he drove to Herbert Crescent, removed a suitcase from his car, and entered the house. Forty-five minutes later, at 7.45 p.m., he and Erna emerged together with Dr Harper and his wife. They all got into Fuchs' car, and the limpets prepared for more action.[18]

Fuchs was followed as he drove about a mile through central London to Chelsea Embankment and the Blue Cockatoo restaurant,* a favourite haunt of artists, scientists and the bohemian glitterati of London society in those days.

Among patrons recorded in the Blue Cockatoo's autograph book was William Joyce – the traitor known as Lord Haw Haw – but no record remains of Fuchs' presence in the restaurant that night beyond that of MI5, which merely notes that the quartet had dinner and emerged an hour or so later. MI5 then trailed them back to Herbert Crescent, where the two women got out. Fuchs and Dr Harper then drove to a garage in Brompton Road, left the car and returned to Herbert Crescent, about half a mile away, on foot. All very ordinary.

Fuchs and Erna spent the night at the Harpers' home.

The next morning the Newbury eavesdroppers called in to say that (unsurprisingly) they had heard nothing of Fuchs at his home that night.[19] Meanwhile in London the watchers were in place at 7.30 a.m. and maintained vigilance for nearly three hours until Fuchs emerged after 10 o'clock. They followed him by bus and foot to Piccadilly and the Royal Institution. At lunchtime they were fully alert once more as he emerged with William Penney, with whom he lunched at the Buttery in the Piccadilly Hotel. Then it was back to the Royal Institution for the afternoon and the conclusion of the meeting.

Once again Fuchs emerged from the entrance hall of the Royal Institution, flanked by its Corinthian mock-Grecian columns, and set off along Albemarle Street. He walked alone, while being shadowed by two of MI5's footpads all the way to the garage, where he recovered his car, drove to Herbert Crescent, and collected Erna. They did not drive home, however, but visited friends of Erna in Bayswater. Only at 7.25 p.m. did they finally set off for Harwell, followed by MI5's car along Western Avenue.

Could MI5 have succeeded in such detailed and intensive surveillance, for so long, without Fuchs noticing? On his return journey, at least, the watchers were more circumspect and implemented the strategy of not following continuously on the open road but of checking at various times en route. Even so, they noticed that Fuchs stopped several times, first to fill his car with petrol near Uxbridge, then once more in the country for

* A brief history of the Blue Cockatoo and an oil painting of the restaurant from that period may be found at: http://www.masterart.com/Christopher-Sanders-Wakefield-Yorkshire-1905-1991-The-Blue-Cockatoo-PortalDefault.aspx?tabid=53&dealerID=8929&objectID=664577.

about twenty minutes near Wycombe. This smacks of counter-surveillance, not least because MI5 remarked, 'Fuchs is a nervous driver.'[20] There is no record that anyone else recalls Fuchs to have been a nervous driver. His colleagues seemed prepared to be passengers in Fuchs' car. Furthermore, he had plenty of experience. While at Los Alamos, for example, he had driven his car on a trip to Mexico City, accompanied by Rudolf and Genia Peierls.[21] Augusta Teller, wife of Edward, accompanied them, Edward being happy for her to take the trip because Fuchs was 'a good driver'.[22] At Harwell, his travel records show that he regularly made short trips into Oxford, and periodic longer trips to Birmingham and Cambridge (including, as we have remarked, one that included a diversion to Putney to meet his Russian contact). In December 1947 he had driven to Southampton 'to fetch Herbert Skinner from the Queen Elizabeth'.[23] The 'nervous' behaviour remarked on by MI5 seems more likely to have been a consequence of keeping an eye on his shadows while he was driving through the streets of central London.

Fuchs and Erna now drove on to Henley, where they pulled in to the Bull Hotel. From 9.30 p.m. for nearly an hour they were 'drinking double gins'.[24] (MI5's close attention to detail can hardly be faulted – unless it further alerted Fuchs to their interest.) Whether multiple 'double gins' made Fuchs less nervous as a driver or increased the risk of an accident, they arrived safely back at Harwell 'at 11.15 p.m.', the record confirming that MI5 had shadowed him for two whole days.

MI5 was unaware that Fuchs might be suspicious and they missed the clues once again, on 7 October, when Fuchs was back in London for his weekly Friday scientific meeting at Shell Mex House in the Strand. During a walk along the Strand after lunch he parted from his colleagues and visited Dolland and Aitchison's photographic store to ask about Kodak films. He looked into shop windows and then made a 'hurried tour' and visited 'four other photographic supply shops in the vicinity of Trafalgar Square'. MI5 verified that he had asked about 'a film for a cine-camera or a very small film'.[25] The dipping in and out of shops lasted for about forty minutes, by which time Fuchs had worked his way back to Shell Mex House. MI5 were suspicious, naturally, and when Arnold came for his weekly meeting on the Monday morning following, Robertson asked him whether Fuchs was 'in possession of a camera, probably of the 35 mm. or other miniature type'. Arnold 'did not know for certain' but 'did not think [Fuchs] had one'.[26] No explanation for Fuchs' behaviour was ever forthcoming, other than as a classic manoeuvre of someone attempting to identify a shadow.

That he was already feeling the pressure on 28 September is apparent from Erna's reaction when they reached home: she said that Fuchs 'looked unwell' and she 'sent him straight to bed'.[27] His behaviour seems to bear out Genia Peierls' experience that he would become unwell whenever confronted with the pressure of betraying his friends, although on this occasion a succession of demanding meetings and nights out, rounded off with an hour downing double gins, could have played a role.

On 10 October Herbert Skinner was at a meeting in Oxford. Telephone taps and bugs on site revealed that Fuchs and Erna passed the afternoon in Didcot, and after having a 'late tea' they returned to Fuchs' prefab where they spent the evening together. From 10 until after 11 p.m. that night the bug in Fuchs' home recorded activity that seemed to originate away from the living room. It picked up 'practically no conversation': Fuchs 'could not be heard at all' while 'Mrs Skinner made odd inaudible remarks.'[28] At 23.26 Herbert phoned to ask when she was coming home. Just over half an hour passed before she left, on the stroke of midnight, accompanied by Fuchs. He returned home, alone, twenty minutes later.[29]

As to whether Fuchs and Erna Skinner were having an affair, MI5 was initially ambivalent. In November, Robertson judged Fuchs to be 'fond of women': as for Mrs Skinner: 'We have no proof that she is, in the complete sense of the term, Fuchs' mistress. My own impression is that she is not.'[30] Three months later, after constant surveillance had confirmed that Fuchs seemed to spend more time with Erna than he did alone in his own prefab, and bugs had overheard their conversations, Robertson's opinion had changed: 'It has been established that she has been his mistress for some time', and when he reviewed the saga three years later, he asserted positively, 'Erna Skinner – who was of course Fuchs' mistress.'[31]

Klaus Fuchs and Erna Skinner were closer than many married couples in the intensity of their mutual support, but whether they were lovers 'in the complete sense of the term' is unknown, and probably secondary to their emotional relationship. Fuchs was a loner, a bachelor with an intellectual intensity that bordered on autism; Erna Skinner, with her chronic fear of solitude, appears as a mother-hen, who in taking charge of another lost soul helped fill the vacuum of her own life. Her profound emotional insecurity was common knowledge at Harwell. MI5 intercepts report that she suffered from 'anxiety neurosis'. Genia Peierls chastised Erna for her flirtatious way with men: 'If you must blow soap bubbles, don't use scented soap.'[32]

Because Erna's husband, Herbert, was in the process of transferring from Harwell to take up a professorship at the University of Liverpool, he was frequently away from the laboratory, so there were many empty hours for Erna, which she would pass with Fuchs. On one occasion, however, she accompanied Herbert to Liverpool; a letter that she wrote from there to Genia Peierls reeks of depression: 'I am pretty desperate. Personal atmosphere gloomy in the extreme. Just shoving off panic as best I can.'[33]

Unlike Erna, Fuchs was (as Henry Arnold had assessed) mentally tough – a minimal requirement for one who had been living a double life for eight years. But the accumulated stress had taken its toll. He was often ill, and suffered from exhaustion around the times of his assignations with his Soviet couriers. He suffered serious dental problems, and wore a plate containing false teeth – a lifetime reminder of his treatment by Nazi thugs – requiring regular visits to his dentist. His consumption of alcohol and addiction to cigarettes were not unusual for those times, but would be regarded as excessive today. His huge – legitimate – workload would have tested the constitution of a healthy thirty-year-old let alone one nearer to forty and under the extraordinary pressure he was. Fuchs would calculate deep into the night on behalf of William Penney and the British atomic bomb, a responsibility that he carried in secret on top of his overt duties at Harwell. He took no holidays, and Genia Peierls became increasingly concerned for his welfare. It is possible that his decision to break contact with the KGB in April 1949, followed that summer by a rare vacation with the Skinners, had been in part to prevent a complete breakdown.[34]

By mid-October, MI5 had a fairly detailed picture of Fuchs' lifestyle, though nothing yet to incriminate him. They recorded that he was absent from Harwell on comparatively few occasions, and these were almost exclusively for official business. His leisure hours were almost always spent in the Harwell residential area with one or other of a limited circle of acquaintances. His closest friends were 'undoubtedly' Professor and Mrs Skinner, 'with whom he has more often than not spent his evenings'.[35]

On a Sunday typically Fuchs might spend the morning at home, while the afternoon and evening, until midnight, would be with the Skinners. This intimacy exemplified the nature of Harwell society. Professional life was built around secrets. Social life thus revolved around those who were party to the secrets. Harwell was also remote, a bubble of scientists working together to an end that only they could know or mutually discuss. In a way, this was something that Fuchs shared with his watchers. For the staff of MI5 too, the boundaries between the safe closeted world of state secrets and the world of those outside the Official Secrets Act had to be maintained; full relaxation was impossible unless one's social colleagues were all privy to the same constraints as oneself. Thus atomic scientists in one closed bubble formed a set of mutually agreed values, while those in the Security Services swam in the same pond as their own peers, and tested their ideas only within this restricted group.

For the MI5 foot-soldiers it seems that the only relief from the tedium of watching Fuchs lay in his private life. On 12 November 1949, MI5 again commented on his relationship with the Skinners: '[His] most intimate friend is without question Mrs Erna Skinner, and it is possible that she is his mistress, a fact which does not seem to have prevented Professor Herbert Skinner himself as regarding Fuchs as a friend – at least until very lately, when it has been reported that the relationship between the two men may have deteriorated to some extent.'[36]

This piece of gossip refers to a report about Fuchs' and Skinner's behaviour during a business trip to London. MI5's watchers were in place at Didcot station ready for the London-bound train, when at about 8 a.m. Skinner drove up to the forecourt and parked his car. Five minutes later, Fuchs arrived on the Harwell Establishment bus. Both changed their travel warrants for tickets, but did not greet one another on the platform, 'although each had obviously seen the other'. They travelled to London's Paddington terminus in the same first-class coach 'but sat in different compartments'. They joined up at Paddington and travelled to Shell Mex House together on the Underground, but 'were not seen to speak and in the Underground sat apart even when adjacent seats were available'.[37]

Diverted by the relationship between Fuchs and Skinner's wife, MI5 interpreted this extra-marital liaison to be the cause of the two scientists' behaviour. However, Skinner seems to have tolerated Erna's flirtations, and even encouraged them. MI5, as yet unaware of Fuchs' long experience in espionage and counter-surveillance, seem not to have considered another interpretation: Fuchs had sensed that he was being watched and was teasing out his protagonists. Indeed, as he would later tell Jim Skardon, he had assured his Russian contact in London that he 'knew how to make sure' that he was not followed.[38] His decision to sit away from Skinner on the train may well have been a strategy to stretch and expose any watchers. As I know from personal experience, even until the 1980s Didcot station was an up-country location where regular passengers were familiar and the appearance of new faces noticeable. Back in 1949, Didcot was a small town at the centre of sporadic tiny villages, and it would have been even harder for MI5's watchers to remain inconspicuous. Fuchs, after eight years of espionage, would have been especially sensitive to his surroundings.

THE WOMAN WITH A CROOKED NOSE

The Security Services had nothing detrimental recorded against any of Fuchs' contacts. His friendship with Erna, however, gave rise to 'certain doubts' about her. The reasons seem primarily to have reflected MI5's prejudices: 'Mrs Skinner's Austrian origin'; she had been married and divorced 'at some place unknown in Europe', and her cosmopolitan friends had 'left-wing sympathies'.[39]

MI5 noted two of Erna's friends in particular had records on their files, which showed them to be 'of left-wing views' and even 'decidedly pro-Russian'. These were Edith Yapou, wife of the Israeli press attaché, whom MI5 regarded as part of the Israeli intelligence services, and Tatiana Malleson, an actress who was of interest to MI5 for being 'strongly Communist in her views' and 'a firm admirer of the Soviet Union'. She was known earlier that year to have attended a Soviet Embassy celebration of the Thirtieth Anniversary of the Revolution.[40]

The only contacts that Fuchs had 'of any interest', in MI5's opinion, were associates 'rather of Mrs Skinner than of Fuchs himself'. So MI5 begin to suspect that Erna – married to one division head at Harwell and, Robertson was increasingly certain, the mistress of another – might be a conduit for classified material.

On 13 and 14 October Fuchs was again in London for an official meeting, and once again Erna went along too. The visit is interesting for two reasons. First, it was contemporaneous with Fuchs having alerted Arnold to his father's move to Leipzig, and within three days of the notorious double traitor, Kim Philby, taking up residence in the Washington Embassy, where he monitored FBI and MI5 interest in Fuchs. Second, MI5's records of movements during the two days illustrate the resources devoted to the Fuchs affair.

As usual, MI5 knew in advance that Skinner and Fuchs planned to go to London. Fuchs said he would collect 'the car' and then pick up Erna. MI5 were thus unaware of whose car this would be, and whether all three would travel together or whether one of them would take the train.

To cover both possibilities, MI5 put in place what was by now a standard procedure: lookouts at both Paddington station and on the road to London at Western Avenue from 8.30 a.m. Even so, Fuchs was not seen until 3.35 p.m. when he was followed in his MG car to 10 Devonshire Place near Regent's Park. He was accompanied by Erna, and by a woman whom the watchers did not recognize; they named her 'B' in their report.

At 4.40 p.m. Fuchs, Erna and 'B' left and Fuchs drove the short distance to Oxford Circus where 'B' alighted. Two MI5 officers watched all this. One, David Storrier, now followed Fuchs and Erna around the West End to the Ley-One restaurant. Storrier parked and watched until they emerged two hours later. With remarkable efficiency Storrier somehow managed to confirm both that Fuchs paid the bill and then to follow Fuchs' car out of London. Only when it reached Uxbridge, en route back to Harwell, was observation withdrawn. This far was similar to the previous sortie in September.

Meanwhile, when Fuchs had stopped his car to let 'B' alight, Storrier had done likewise. Storrier's colleague, now on foot, followed the woman, 'B', down the steps to the Underground. What ensued reads like a script for a Cold War thriller. 'B' was in her early fifties, about 5 feet in height, her dark hair cropped and greying, a 'crooked nose' and slightly built. She wore a black costume with a velvet collar and white blouse. The matronly look was completed with 'horn-rimmed glasses with thick lenses'. Finally, she walked with 'a pronounced limp'. She travelled south of the Thames by Underground and then continued by bus to Southwark. She completed the journey on foot to the St Alphege Clergy House in Pocock Street where a man 'in clerical attire' opened the door, and 'B' entered. The time was 5.15 p.m.

Storrier's colleague hung around, trying to remain unnoticed, until 6.30 p.m. when 'B' emerged and walked to St Alphege Church, an Anglo-Catholic shrine on the corner of King James Street and Lancaster Street. 'B' went 'up to the altar, left almost at once and was traced to 122 Kennington Road [about a mile away] where she opened the door with her own latch key at 6.50 p.m.'

Soon after she entered, a light was switched on in the top-floor room. The MI5 man checked the names on the doorjamb and found the top flat to be that of 'Miss Peto'. He continued to watch the house until 9.30 p.m., but B did not leave.

The next day, Fuchs was in his office. As usual, Newbury telephone exchange meticulously logged all calls, in and out. Meanwhile, in London, Storrier joined his colleague early and continued to watch 'Miss Peto's' house. Nothing of interest happened until 11.15 a.m. when the front door opened, 'B' appeared, and set off along the street.[41] She was followed to a shop ten doors away, where she paid a bill. Storrier, who seems to have been the senior of the two MI5 shadows, questioned the owner and learned the bill was in the name of Miss R. Peto. 'B' returned home twenty-five minutes later. At midday she came out again, went to various food shops and returned home, only to reappear a few minutes later carrying two suitcases. She took a taxi, which MI5 followed to Paddington station.

At Paddington she boarded the 13.20 train to Didcot. Storrier phoned Robertson and passed on this news, and told him that his colleague had boarded the train with 'B'. As MI5 had no means of contacting their man en route, Storrier suggested that Robertson call Arnold and give him a description of 'B', so that Arnold could go to Didcot and watch for her arrival himself. If Arnold recognized the woman, he could tell the MI5 man to cease observation.

Shadowing is portrayed in popular fiction and on film as a well-oiled machine; here in reality it now veered towards farcical. First, Arnold was away from his office and Robertson could not reach him. So Robertson contacted a Mr Woodhouse, one of Storrier's team who was present at headquarters. They agreed that it would be inadvisable to arrange for any contact between Arnold and the watcher, since neither Arnold nor the watcher knew one another, and there 'might be a muddle'. No harm would be done, however, if Arnold were to be at Didcot station to meet the train, with the object of identifying any passenger known to him.

Robertson reached Arnold, eventually, at 14.15 and gave him the information. By now time was short, as the train was due to arrive at Didcot station, about five miles from Harwell, at 14.28. Arnold agreed that the best thing would be for him to meet the train, and establish whether he knew any of the passengers. He rushed from his office to get his car and precious minutes passed as he drove the country roads to Didcot. As Arnold approached the station forecourt he saw the semaphore signal rise, and clouds of smoke from the engine billowed above the buildings as the train began to pull out. A handful of people were already exiting the station as Arnold pulled up. He could not be sure that he saw every passenger that alighted, but he recognized no one. There was no official car awaiting any Harwell personnel and he was quite sure that 'there was no transport provided for or used by any woman'.

In his haste, however, Arnold had overlooked an obvious further option: the local bus. The MI5 watcher, whom Arnold did not know, had seen 'B' get on the Number 30 bus to Harwell, which left at 2.40 p.m., ten minutes after Arnold arrived. What Arnold was doing during this period isn't known, but 'B' must have waited at the stop for some minutes with her suitcases on the ground because MI5's watcher had managed to read the labels on her baggage: 'Owner Pohl; address 3 South Drive, Harwell'. When asked by a luggage porter whether she needed any help, she replied: 'No thank you. I live here at the AERE [Harwell].'[42]

Shortly thereafter MI5 received a message from an intercept of the phone at the Skinners' home: 'A woman named Vera Pohl has just arrived at Harwell, and is with the Skinners at their house.' So two days of considerable effort, involving several watchers, concluded with the realization that they had been chasing the Skinners' housekeeper. The news of Fuchs that evening was no more significant: he had gone to see *Kind Hearts and Coronets* at the theatre in Oxford with friends, and had made a lunch assignation for the next day with Mrs Skinner.[43]

These three examples typify a daily diary of surveillance of Klaus Fuchs that eventually extended over four months. That he was aware of being followed seems very likely. That MI5 was chasing someone who was not going to be pinned down is certain. Already by the end of October 1949 it was clear that vast resources were being devoted to a wild goose chase. Some change of strategy was required.

That Fuchs had told Arnold about his father's move to Eastern Germany implied that he might cooperate with the Russians, if they pressured him via his father. In the judgement of Dick White, Director of Counter-Espionage and Robertson's line manager, this intervention within weeks of the Soviet atomic bomb test seemed planned. With the benefit of hindsight we can ponder whether Fuchs' action within days of Philby alerting Moscow was mere coincidence or prompted.* In any event, on 26 October White decided that Fuchs' move confirmed their suspicions that he was indeed the agent CHARLES, but the evidence from VENONA was so sensitive that it could not be used in any prosecution. MI5 had been focusing all possible resources on watching Fuchs in the hope of catching him red-handed, but without success, and by November it had reached a dead end. Somehow they would have to pressure Fuchs into making a fatal error or catch him in the act of passing information. White recommended that Fuchs now be interviewed.[44]

---

* It is certainly intriguing that a similar tactic would be used by one of Fuchs' communist colleagues at Harwell, Bruno Pontecorvo, when six months later Philby got wind that the FBI were interested in him. Pontecorvo defected to the Soviet Union in September 1950. See Frank Close, *Half Life: The Divided Life of Bruno Pontecorvo, Scientist or Spy* (Basic Books and OneWorld, 2015), p. 152.

16

Guy Liddell's Pursuit: November and December 1949

If Guy Liddell had not gone to Nazi Germany in 1933, and formed his negative opinion on the value of information from the Gestapo, their reports about Klaus Fuchs might have been taken seriously, none of this story would have happened, and the course of world history would have been changed. Instead, on 31 October 1949, Liddell, by now Deputy Director General of MI5, was discussing the Fuchs affair with his boss, Director General Sir Percy Sillitoe.

Sillitoe was a heavily built man with an imposing physical presence, but lacking in self-confidence. Formerly Chief Constable of Police in Kent, he had become Director General of MI5 in 1946 when Sir David Petrie's 'uninspired leadership' ended.[1] Guy Liddell was the internal favourite for the post, but the collapse of his marriage, by which his children were taken to America by their mother, had left him 'aggrieved and morose'. Whether it was because of his personal situation, or Whitehall dissatisfaction with MI5's performance during the war, Liddell was passed over for the job. Old-timers, such as Liddell, regarded Sillitoe as an outsider who had been foisted on them by a government intent on curbing MI5's autonomy. Sillitoe, on the other hand, felt that he was surrounded by men who were 'more intelligent and better educated', and he openly distrusted the 'Oxbridge types' who, he was convinced, made fun of him in conferences by 'quoting Latin epigrams that he could not understand'.[2] Liddell, his deputy, had also formerly been a policeman, but after twenty years in MI5 he was known and respected by all the main players. Although Sillitoe was the Director General and so formally responsible for representing MI5 to government – and for overseeing the fraught relations with his opposite number in the FBI, J. Edgar Hoover – within MI5 it was Liddell to whom officers would look for advice, and whose judgement carried weight.

Dick White's proposal that Fuchs be interviewed created a host of problems. First, MI5's evidence originated in the United States, so it needed the FBI's approval to interview Fuchs on the basis of this material, without disclosing its source. Liddell posed the fundamental issue: 'What precisely do we want to achieve?'

Here, 'we' could refer to any of MI5, the Atomic Energy Authority (AEA), or the government. If Fuchs had indeed passed information to the Soviet Union, this violated the Official Secrets Act, for which the law would demand retribution. Yet Fuchs was even now of considerable value to the AEA and the national effort. A charitable view might be that to have shared classified information with an ally might not be so objectionable as to require the elimination of one of the nation's star scientists from the Cold War that was now looming. And a worse outcome threatened if Fuchs, alerted by MI5's pursuit, chose to take his skills and knowledge to the Eastern Zone of Germany, or to Russia.

Liddell debated his own question: 'It seems to me even questionable whether we want him to make a confession: were he to do so he could hardly be allowed to remain in Atomic Energy and he would clearly feel that there was no future for him either here or in the USA; the urge would therefore be to go to the Russians.' Ever the pragmatist, Liddell then outlined his preferred strategy: point out to Fuchs that, 'on the basis of his statement about his father to [Henry] Arnold, it would be embarrassing both for us and for him if he remained in Atomic Energy'. This could move Fuchs out of harm's way, and an inconvenient piece of history might be swept under the rug. Liddell added, 'We would do our utmost to find him other suitable employment.'[3]

For the Director General, Percy Sillitoe – who had the reputation when a policeman of being a crime-buster – the objective was to obtain evidence for a conviction, not to make pragmatic deals with the guilty. He was never comfortable with moves of expediency, by which suspected spies were removed from classified work but otherwise allowed to continue with their lives. Liddell shared his own thoughts with his diary: 'I should agree if I felt that such evidence would be forthcoming.'[4]

PREPARATION

A week later, this was still the 'FUCHS and PEIERLS case'.[5] Whereas it had proved possible to eliminate other candidates for CHARLES among the British delegation fairly easily, on 8 November Liddell recorded: 'considerable enquiries were necessary before it was possible to be satisfied about PEIERLS. While PEIERLS had a sister, there is no certainty that she was in America at the material time, and his movements did not coincide with what we know of the movements of the suspect.' In fact Peierls' sister Annie (Krebs) had been living across the river from New York City all along, in Montclair, New Jersey, and it was the dates of Fuchs' and Peierls' movements that proved decisive.[6] The accumulated evidence led Liddell to summarize that he was 'morally certain that FUCHS is the man'. Two delicate pieces of politics were needed before the next stage: 'The Americans have been asked whether under certain safeguards we can interrogate him. Meanwhile, Atomic Energy have been asked to state exactly what they want to achieve.' In Liddell's judgement: 'It seems fairly definite so far that they are anxious whatever the outcome of the case, to get FUCHS out of atomic energy.'[7]

Permission to interview Fuchs was granted by the 'owner' of VENONA: Admiral Earl E. Stone, Director of US Armed Forces Security. The FBI confirmed to Geoffrey Patterson that they had no objection to Fuchs' interrogation but that under no circumstances was the origin of the source material to be made known.[8] The intense secrecy surrounding VENONA had to be preserved at all costs.

On 16 November MI5 planned a 'high-level meeting with Atomic Energy'. The day before, Liddell, Colonel Robertson and other senior officers met to 'try and clear [their] minds'. The investigation of Fuchs was perhaps the most sensitive of all MI5's work in the early Cold War and they agreed that they could not go on indefinitely, as it was 'too expensive, too much of a burden, and too unprofitable if it was to be maintained on the present extensive scale'.[9] The round-the-clock monitoring of Fuchs, and attempts to identify his Soviet contact, had stretched the agency's resources. Finally there was the permanent fear that Fuchs would get wind of their investigation, by some careless or inadvertent leak. Examples of possible holes in their security net now began to appear.

For example, a fault developed on Fuchs' phone. This had nothing to do with the investigation, but Fuchs needed it to be repaired. The senior engineer at Harwell, who normally oversaw the telephone interception, was away at the time, so in his absence a junior engineer dealt with the fault. Henry Arnold overheard this youth remark to a colleague that 'the fault was probably connected with the link-up'. Robertson spoke about this with Major Albert Denman, who had been directly involved with the installation of the phone taps. Denman confessed: 'in a small establishment like Harwell it is impossible to disguise from the three or four line engineers the fact that certain unusual circuits had been installed'. Denman judged, however, that even if one or more assistant engineers was aware of these special circuits, the method in which the wiring had been carried out would be such that 'no particular attention would be drawn to any one person at Harwell'.[10]

By mid-November, MI5's eavesdroppers had been at work for nearly two months. They had gathered a fairly detailed picture of Fuchs' lifestyle, though nothing yet to incriminate him. That the investigation seems to have been so watertight, and that Fuchs appears not to have been alerted to it, at least from Harwell, is remarkable. It seems unlikely, however, that he had remained oblivious to his shadowy limpets.

Preparations to interrogate Fuchs continued, but the authorities were nervous about the implications. Liddell, by now beginning to despair of ever catching Fuchs in the company of a Soviet contact, wrote: 'On the whole I felt it might be better to try and edge FUCHS out and find him some other suitable job, rather than make any attempt to get him to confess, but this must be a question for Atomic Energy to decide. When we know the objective we shall be better able to advise them.'[11]

Two weeks later, on 28 November, little had changed. The belief that Fuchs was guilty had hardened, but nothing substantial had been found. Liddell summarized that day's meeting: 'The only conclusions we have reached were that it was essential for D.At.En. [Cockcroft and Atomic Energy] to be quite clear as to what they were going to do with FUCHS after his interrogation. They ought to have some job ready for him at once, if this is necessary.'[12]

His diary entry hardly does justice to the intense, and worried, debate that Fuchs' proposed interrogation was generating. MI5 'lacked trained interrogators' and so for Fuchs they called in Jim Skardon – the same Special Branch officer who, two years earlier, had been outmanoeuvred by Fuchs' erstwhile handler, Ursula Beurton ('Sonya'). Skardon discussed tactics with Robertson at length and the meeting with Liddell and others was long.

The original plan was for the inquisition to take place in London, at Shell Mex House.[13] The first question that concerned them was, what would Fuchs do afterwards? They judged that if Fuchs were still a spy he would attempt to make contact with his accomplices, notwithstanding the risk. They decided to arrange for Arnold to drive Fuchs back to Harwell afterwards. This would impress upon Fuchs that the Security Services were keeping an eye on him, and give him a further opportunity to 'unburden himself before he had relaxed from the mental tension produced by the interrogation'.[14]

Next was the possibility that Fuchs might try to flee the country. They debated whether to demand his passport at the time of his grilling, as a psychological deterrent in the event that he was making plans to leave. In addition, Fuchs' photograph and description should be circulated to 'selected Special Branch officers at ports'.[15]

November turned into December. On 5 December, Michael Perrin visited Liddell once again to discuss the Fuchs case. Liddell records: 'We tried to envisage every possible situation that might arise. I made it clear to Perrin that in our view the chances of his getting the answer he wanted were extremely remote. One might have a lucky break, but it seemed on the whole more likely that we should be left in a state of uncertainty if not positive suspicion.' Liddell recommended that 'efforts should be made now to explore the ground for alternative work, since it would be undesirable to have any hiatus between the interview and FUCHS' ultimate disposal'.[16]

Given the seriousness of the situation, some of the practical issues were rather banal. As Fuchs was a civil servant, any dismissal could cause industrial disputes, and 'lead to protests from the appropriate Union or from FUCHS' own colleagues'.[17] So with the question of Fuchs' interrogation still unresolved, Liddell agreed to explore the legal position about getting rid of a civil servant, while Perrin would make enquiries about a possible university job for Fuchs.

A greater worry was that the Fuchs affair would generate questions in the House of Commons, or even lead to demands for an inquiry. Liddell was politically astute, and sensed where this might be heading. In the privacy of his diary he wrote: 'It was [my] experience that when Ministers found themselves in difficulties of this sort they were inclined to say that the Intelligence Services had let them down, unless they were allowed to tell the House of the facts.'[18] Worried that a minister might be forced to reveal his source, Liddell judged it more important to maintain the secret of VENONA than to act on Fuchs. At this stage, of course, all that MI5 suspected was that Fuchs had passed on a limited piece of information, on possibly just one occasion, six years ago.

Ten days later, on 15 December, there was a full-scale gathering of senior MI5 officers. The one-line summary in Liddell's diary that evening encapsulated the fragility of their position: 'We talked all round the case of FUCHS and came back more or less to where we started.'[19] One decision was taken, however: Jim Skardon would interview Fuchs on 21 December at Harwell. They agreed the script: the news that the suspect's father would be in the Soviet Zone had created a security risk, which required Klaus Fuchs to be removed from secret work at Harwell. Perrin commented that Herbert Skinner was about to move to Liverpool University, and that a transfer of Fuchs to Liverpool might be arranged through Skinner, who would probably welcome Fuchs' presence there. Someone added dryly that Mrs Skinner presumably would too.

Meanwhile Fuchs must have become aware of MI5's interest. By

December his behaviour was becoming erratic. The Skinners and Fuchs were due to go to Birmingham to see Rudolf and Genia Peierls on 10 December, but the day before Fuchs suddenly cancelled. Erna phoned Genia and explained, 'Klaus has completely ruined himself' because of 'some idea that keeps himself awake till 4 in the morning and he's just like a log. He says he doesn't think he can possibly get up.' The tension was perhaps becoming unbearable. MI5 made a note to check with Henry Arnold.[20]

JIM SKARDON

According to MI5's official history, Skardon, a former detective inspector from the Metropolitan Police, was the 'foremost exponent in the country' of the interrogation of suspects.[21] This is reminiscent of MI5's positive portrayal of Skardon in the aftermath of the Fuchs case, based on Kim Philby's description of Skardon's 'scrupulously courteous' approach to interrogation. Philby knew Skardon's approach at first hand because he outwitted him on no fewer than ten occasions. Skardon's record includes failures against two other double agents: Anthony Blunt, who convinced Skardon he was innocent 'by upper class bluster', and John Cairncross, who upon being cleared by Skardon 'promptly left the country'.[22] Ursula Beurton/Sonya is already on this sorry list, so Philby's positive reference was less an unbiased testimonial for Skardon than self-congratulatory, designed to advertise his own cleverness at having duped MI5's best. Nonetheless, it helped sustain the image of Skardon as the grand inquisitor. In Philby's version, Skardon 'wormed his way into Fuchs' confidence' until Fuchs cracked.[23] This contrasts with the view of Dick White, who was unimpressed by Skardon and remarked later, 'Skardon's interrogation taxed my wits.'[24]

Skardon's role required him to stay out of the public gaze. A rare photo of him and Henry Arnold, entering the Old Bailey in 1950, shows a lean man with a neat oblong moustache. On 19 December he met with Liddell, Dick White and Roger Hollis to discuss tactics. Skardon knew the substance of MI5's evidence, of course, but not its source. In particular he knew nothing of VENONA and its implications for Fuchs' guilt. The plan was for Skardon to focus on Fuchs' time in New York in order to convince him that MI5 knew he was a spy. Liddell and White agreed that this was essential, for otherwise Fuchs might reason that the explosion of an atomic bomb in Russia had led the security authorities to suspect a leak and were pouncing on him in view of his communist past. In effect, Fuchs might assume that MI5 was really running a bluff, and so would say nothing.

Skardon was given free rein on the exact form of the interview. If, however, Fuchs seemed ready to make a confession and required some form of assurance, Skardon was authorized to say to him that 'his position can only be improved by complete frankness'.[25]

Having carefully positioned the pieces on the board for the interrogation on 21 December, MI5 had failed to brief all of the players. Shortly before 10 o'clock, Sir John Cockcroft summoned Arnold and asked him to tell Fuchs, 'someone would be coming down this morning to talk to him on the subject of his father's presence in the Soviet Zone of Germany'.[26] Arnold now realized that he was unsure as to how much he should say, so he immediately called Robertson to check.

Robertson was adamant. It was 'most undesirable that Fuchs should be given any prior warning of the interrogation. It would be infinitely better if he learned nothing of it until Skardon had arrived and he had been summoned to the Director's office'. Now suitably prepared, Arnold met Skardon at Didcot station, took him to Harwell, and introduced him to Cockcroft. Skardon then told Cockcroft his strategy for the interview.

Skardon explained that he planned to keep the two parts of his enquiry in watertight compartments. On the one hand was the matter of Fuchs' father; on the other that of Fuchs' espionage. The location of Fuchs' father in the Soviet Zone of Germany posed a security risk, which was being actively considered by the Ministry of Supply, and for this MI5 was 'giving advice'. Matters relating to Fuchs' espionage activities, on the other hand, were known only to MI5.

Sir John Cockcroft 'was satisfied with this division of responsibility' and asked Arnold to bring Fuchs to meet Skardon in Arnold's office. Shortly after 11 o'clock the surveillance log recorded Arnold arriving in Fuchs' office with Cockcroft's message. Arnold reminded Fuchs, 'he had said a few days ago that the case of FUCHS' father was to be investigated'. He added 'someone has come down to see you'.[27] Skardon was introduced to Fuchs as 'Mr Seddon', a *nom-de-guerre* that was used to hide the presence of an MI5 interrogator on the site. Arnold then left them.

THE FIRST INTERVIEW

'How do you get them to break down, the traitors and spies who have been carefully trained with cover stories?' Commander Leonard Burt of Scotland Yard asked rhetorically at the time of the Fuchs affair.[28] The experienced spy has rehearsed an answer to every difficult question that can be thrown at them, yet mastery of the investigation can break them so they 'tell all'. The key, according to Burt, is 'psychological insight' where a subtle variation in tone can reveal the lie. The technique is not to begin with interrogation but instead to have a 'man-to-man conversation'. Basically, you want your suspect to talk. If guilty – as Skardon expected Fuchs to be – Fuchs' main interest would be to find out how much Skardon already knew. At some point Skardon would have to reveal his hand, but it was crucial that Fuchs didn't turn the tables and use the interview to discover the extent of Skardon's evidence.

Burt's second axiom was that once a suspect gets talking, he often does your work for you. Therefore, don't ask probing questions right away; appear indifferent if a potentially important piece of detail is mentioned. In such circumstances even an intelligent suspect such as Fuchs might unwittingly try to explain. Once he knows that you suspect him, he will be 'bursting to justify his action'.[29]

Burt's experience that the suspect often does the police's work was confirmed in the Fuchs case. Fuchs had asked Arnold for advice within weeks of the Soviet atomic bomb explosion. Did Fuchs hope that Arnold would suggest his resignation, with the consequence that he could leave Harwell in the clear, his misdeeds passed over if they surfaced? Whatever his reasons, the result was that Fuchs had provided the authorities with the perfect excuse to interview him.

Skardon's report and Liddell's diary reveal that the interrogation was like a poker game, in which Skardon bluffed that he had a strong hand. He set traps, but Fuchs cleverly avoided them.

Skardon followed Burt's formula: start with a friendly chat. Skardon explained that Fuchs was there for an interview because of the presence of Fuchs' father in the Soviet Zone of Germany, which posed a considerable security risk in view of Fuchs' position and standing in the 'extremely secret work' he was doing. Fuchs confirmed that he understood this. Skardon added, 'I want to ask you numerous questions, some of which you might find impertinent, but it is necessary that I should do so in order that we might fairly assess the risks involved.'[30]

Fuchs concurred, and Skardon continued with the standard gambit in Security Service inquiries: establish the family background of the suspect.

Early in the interview, Skardon verified that Fuchs recognized his Oath of Allegiance to the United Kingdom to be a serious matter, and 'a thing to be observed'. At the same time, however, Fuchs claimed freedom to act according to his conscience 'should circumstances arise in the United Kingdom comparable to those which existed in Germany in 1932 and 33'.

In such an extreme case, Fuchs said, he would 'act on a loyalty which he possesses to humanity generally'.[31]

Here was the first glimpse that Fuchs wanted to 'explain' himself. He continued to reveal nuggets within the superficially friendly conversation. Skardon learned that Fuchs and his father had been members of the Social Democratic Party in Germany, and that Klaus had been associated with the Communist Party in his activities against the Nazis. After Hitler came to power, Fuchs went to Paris. Here he took part in an International Congress in August 1933, which was organized by the 'United Front'; Fuchs said, 'today it would be called a Communist Front'.

He confirmed what Skardon already knew about his flight to England and his time in Bristol, with the addition that he claimed to have taken no part in politics except when he joined a committee for the defence of Spanish democracy. He said that he was 'extremely grateful for the hospitality that the United Kingdom had extended him, and for his naturalisation'. Then he moved on to describe his internment in Canada.

He admitted that he had taken part in political activities in the camp, but said these were no more than domestic issues relating to the camp and internees. He had associated with Hans Kahle, whose activities were to convince the camp authorities that they should not exchange internees for Canadian prisoners of war in Germany. As Fuchs explained, the majority of the internees were Jewish refugees, although Fuchs himself was not, and there was a 'general anxiety lest these people be given back into Hitler's hands'.[32]*

Fuchs explained how he had lived with Peierls during his time in Birmingham, and as he was working on a matter of extreme secrecy, he had 'give[n] up his association with Kahle and other people like him who had returned at about the same time from internment'. He said that the only contacts with them had been before he went to Birmingham. They had seen him in Edinburgh, early in 1941, and he had visited Kahle once in London. Fuchs' version of this fateful trip, in April 1941, was that Kahle took him to a Free German Youth organization, which had a restaurant in the Hampstead area. Fuchs had no idea of Skardon's hand, and in case Skardon was aware of any contact between himself and Jürgen Kuczynski, Fuchs cleverly covered himself by adding that 'one of the refugees', whom Fuchs met on this occasion, later attempted to renew his acquaintance in Birmingham, but 'I shook him off.'

---

* This detail of 'Jewish refugees' seems not to have registered with Hollis and others, who continued to believe that the camp had been predominantly for Nazis, Fuchs and Kahle being there by mistake.

As for his time in the United States, initially in New York, Fuchs gave his addresses and said he had 'very little time for social activities'[33] because his work occupied him full time. He did, however, manage to visit his sister and her husband in Cambridge, Massachusetts, at Christmas 1943, and again during the following April or May. He did not mention the visit early in 1945 at which he also met Harry Gold.

They had been talking for over an hour and Skardon now came to the point: 'While you were in New York, I allege that you were in touch with a Soviet official, or a Soviet representative, and passed on to that person information bearing on your work.'

Fuchs' jaw dropped. His mouth opened as if surprised, and then quickly relaxed into a smile. He played for time and 'took his glasses off and polished them'.[34] Then he shook his head: 'I don't think so,' he said.

Well, had he, or hadn't he? Skardon looked Fuchs in the eye and said: 'I am in possession of precise information which shows that you have been guilty of espionage on behalf of the Soviet Union. For example, during the time that you were in New York, you passed to them information concerning your work.'[35]

Fuchs had but a moment to think. He knew that his covert career in espionage spanned seven years on two continents with locations ranging from Birmingham to Los Alamos via New York and then to Harwell, a vast panorama out of which Skardon had challenged him on New York. Was that the extent of Skardon's knowledge or did Skardon's 'for example' imply this was just the opening bid? Fuchs had to hold his nerve now or the game was up. Again he replied: 'I don't think so.'

Skardon said that this was an ambiguous reply, but in so doing he lost the initiative; his failure to follow up with a penetrating thrust enabled Fuchs to gather his wits. Skardon's approach had the hallmarks of someone on a fishing expedition. Fuchs stood his ground: 'I don't understand. Perhaps you will tell me what the evidence is. I have not done any such thing.'

Skardon tried to regain control of the skirmish: 'I am not really questioning you; I am stating a fact. I shall, however, want to question you on how you gave the information, how you made contact, and determine the full extent of your guilt.'

While this might have unnerved a novice, Skardon was here confronted with a hardened spy who must have prepared himself for such a moment, as Burt theorized. Skardon's generalized threats with lack of detail would not work on a committed and highly intelligent foe such as Fuchs who, outwardly calm, maintained his innocence: 'I cannot assist you, and I strongly deny that I have ever been responsible for such a leakage.'

Fuchs now tried to dismiss the whole idea as nonsense, saying that he had been doing everything he could to help win the war. Skardon noted the ambiguous nature of this remark. A disingenuous defence might claim the passing of atomic information to an ally as consistent with an aim to 'win the war'. So he asked Fuchs whether he was aware that a decision had been taken to exclude Russia from sharing the information.

Fuchs now had a decision to make. If Skardon had solid proof of his espionage, this might be the moment to claim he was unaware that Russia, even though an ally, was off limits, in the hope of mitigating his crime from potentially high treason to a regrettable misunderstanding. However, Fuchs was canny enough to know that this tactic was doomed. The absence of any consultation with Russia had been self-evident to everyone at Los Alamos. It would be easy for Skardon to demonstrate that Fuchs was lying, and this would be tantamount to a confession. So Fuchs confirmed: 'I know quite well that a decision had been taken to exclude Russia from sharing the information. And I think this was quite a good idea from a scientific point of view since the Americans were well equipped to make all the necessary experiments. Anyway, I was not concerned with the political motives underlying that decision.'

Skardon decided to move on to more specific evidence, and asked Fuchs why his name appeared in the diary of Israel Halperin, who had been accused of spying in 1947, before being cleared. Fuchs denied knowledge of Halperin's name. Then Skardon told Fuchs that Halperin's diary contained Fuchs' name next to that of his sister, Kristel Heineman.

Skardon's introduction of Kristel into the tussle must have been a shock to Fuchs. Now he remembered, as if for the first time, that it was during his time in internment that his sister had made representation to Halperin, a mathematician, to send Fuchs copies of *Physical Review* and other scientific journals for him to read in the camp. Fuchs added that he had never met Halperin.

By this stage, nearly two hours into the interview, Skardon had not confronted Fuchs with any damning evidence, or with anything of much substance at all. Furthermore, Fuchs knew that he had passed secrets for seven years, so he must have wondered whether Skardon's focus on New York was because MI5 was ignorant of his full story, or whether this was a ruse to trap him. Fuchs now asked Skardon: 'Is all your evidence of this same kind?' Skardon responded by saying that he could not break faith with his informants and that it was only by being trustworthy in this respect that he could carry out his duties. At the same time, Skardon pointed out that he would not break faith with Fuchs either, and that if Fuchs should 'care to make a clean breast of the matter he could trust [Skardon] to ensure that his actions were presented in the most favourable light'.[36] This was the first of what Skardon described as giving Fuchs 'many opportunities to confess'.

Skardon knew that Fuchs was not going to crack, at least not yet. He returned to his initial strategy of friendly inquiry and turned to the British Mission in New York – its composition, duties and security arrangements. He wanted to understand the operation in order eventually to see how Fuchs – or someone – could extract key documents for the Soviets. Fuchs knew nothing about how the junior staff had been recruited and suggested that if Skardon wanted to know more about the administrative details he would do better to consult Peierls. Maintaining the fiction of someone keen to help Skardon's inquiry, he added that he thought it unlikely that any of the half dozen scientists, including Peierls, were engaged in espionage. All of these would of course have said much the same about Fuchs.

Skardon moved on and asked Fuchs about the security of the papers produced by members of the mission. Fuchs said that in the early days these were duplicated within the office, but at some stage the stencils were sent out for duplication. Fuchs told Skardon that he could probably confirm the date of this change in the routine by referring to his own copies of these papers.

It was now about a quarter before one o'clock. Fuchs took the opportunity 'while his secretary was away' to go to his office, which was in the same building as Arnold's, and collect the papers. Skardon and he must have discussed these for about a quarter of an hour, as Fuchs was heard returning them to his office at ten past one.[37]

The documents showed that the change in practice was in February 1944, at about the same time as Fuchs arrived at the British Mission in New York. Between January and July 1944, of the seventeen papers produced there, ten were the work of Fuchs alone. To Skardon their 'abstruse mathematical calculations' confirmed Fuchs' story that during this period he 'worked from dawn to dusk'. His main contact outside the British delegation was Dr Karl Cohen, head of the Mathematical Physics department at Columbia University, the acknowledged expert on isotope separation.[38]

Fuchs agreed that he habitually carried some papers with him to study at home. He also did so when moving from place to place, and thought he might have taken some with him when he visited his sister. He did not think this would have given her any opportunity to pass information to some third party. He agreed with Skardon's suggestion that his brother-in-law 'was of Communist tendencies', although he did not believe him to be a member of any party.

These seemingly minor remarks sowed doubts in Skardon's mind. He knew little about Fuchs beyond MI5's belief that he had passed some information to the Russians in New York. He knew no details of Fuchs' work, nor of the circumstances in which he did it. Skardon could not eliminate the possibility that someone had masqueraded as Klaus Fuchs. This individual could have been a member of the British technical mission, a secretary with access to documents, someone involved in the official duplication process, or Israel Halperin in collaboration with Fuchs' sister. Could Klaus Fuchs be an innocent dupe?

It was by now 'about 1.30 pm' and they broke for lunch until 'just after 2 pm'. Skardon let Fuchs eat alone in order to 'think about what he had said'. If Skardon had any serious hope that Fuchs would have cracked, he was disappointed when they continued half an hour later. The actual start of the afternoon session was delayed as Fuchs had more urgent matters to deal with: his dental plate had broken and was very uncomfortable. At five past two Fuchs called his dentist and made an appointment for 23 December. He was certainly back with Skardon by two thirty as Fuchs' secretary told a caller that he was 'at a meeting'.[39]

Skardon continued to apply pressure, but the lunch break seems to have strengthened Fuchs' resolve. By mid-afternoon he had successfully called Skardon's bluff and turned the tables. Skardon had nothing to pin on Fuchs. He prepared to close the meeting by saying that the knowledge that Fuchs had been engaged in espionage was shared with no one outside Skardon's department, and that any decision about his future would be taken solely on the issue of his father's situation. Then Skardon confusingly said if he gave the Security Services a favourable report this might have the effect of keeping Fuchs at Harwell, where Fuchs said he would be most happy to stay.[40] Skardon's offer unwittingly gave Fuchs the impression that MI5 regarded anything that he had done to be at most some minor indiscretion, which could be cleared up if he admitted it. This was the second time that Skardon gave Fuchs an 'opportunity to confess'. Later, after Fuchs' arrest, such remarks by Skardon, which amounted to an inducement to Fuchs to confess, would create problems for the prosecuting counsel.

It is not clear what Skardon expected to achieve by this offer, other than to keep contact alive. Fuchs could hardly admit to espionage and expect a favourable report to ensue. Conversely, what could Fuchs say to ensure that Skardon went away in a positive frame of mind? For four hours Fuchs had admitted nothing while Skardon had twice asserted that he had committed espionage, as if there was no debate about the fact, yet Skardon had provided no solid evidence to back it up.

Fuchs responded: 'In the absence of any evidence being produced against me, I am utterly unable to help your enquiry.'[41]

This was a fair point, even allowing for Fuchs' duplicity. His innocent play was that if Skardon was genuinely trying to get to the bottom of some mystery, which vaguely pointed to Fuchs but might have been due to some mistaken identity or someone having stolen papers from Fuchs' possession, then Fuchs would be only too happy to help, but he could only do so if Skardon was more specific.

Nonetheless, it was now obvious to Fuchs that the Security Services were concerned about him, even if this was only because of his father's situation. In such circumstances, Fuchs recognized that he might 'upon reflection think it quite impossible to work at Harwell'. He continued: 'If I come to that conclusion, I shall offer my resignation.' [42] He thought that there would be no problem in getting a post at a university, nor would there be any financial disadvantages. However, Fuchs made it clear that his current work at Harwell was where his interest lay.

The meeting ended at about a quarter to four[43] and had lasted just over four hours. In preparing to part, Skardon told Fuchs: 'I am the only person that you know who can discuss the espionage angle of this case with you. If you think of any useful information, or change your mind, you can reach me at any time through Henry Arnold.'

Skardon ended by referring again to the security problem raised by Fuchs' father. 'Why had you thought it proper to bring this fact to the attention of Wing Commander Arnold?'

Fuchs replied: 'I thought it quite possible that the Russians would seek to make political use of the fact that my non-Communist father was working peacefully in the Soviet Zone. I also worry that my father might get himself into trouble on his own account. Although he is impressed by what he finds there at present, the day may come when he will disagree, and will say so quite strongly.' Fuchs added that he had not considered the likelihood of pressure being brought to bear on himself through his father, until Henry Arnold had suggested it. Skardon replied that he thought this was an important matter to consider and 'was not a very remote possibility';[44] Fuchs agreed.

AN EXTREMELY AWKWARD SITUATION

After this interrogation, Skardon was unsure whether Fuchs was guilty or innocent. His report, written the next day, 22 December, reveals his dilemma. '[Fuchs'] demeanour during our interview could have been indicative of either condition. If he is innocent, it is surprising that he should receive allegations of this kind so coolly, but perhaps this squares with his mathematical approach to life.' This says more about Skardon's attitudes than about mathematicians; he was nearer the truth with his conclusion: 'It could also be argued that he is a spy of old standing and was prepared for such an interrogation.'[45]

MI5 alerted its eavesdroppers that Fuchs had been interrogated and that Colonel Robertson would be 'particularly interested from now onwards in any indication that they might obtain about Fuchs' reaction to it'.[46] In particular they were told to report immediately if they received any hint that Fuchs intended to move from Harwell at any time.

Fuchs, however, remained cool. Guy Liddell closed his diary for 21 December: 'Fuchs' demeanour throughout was wholly consistent with guilt or innocence. We are, therefore, left with an extremely awkward situation on our hands'.[47]

How did Fuchs react? His secretary had just taken a phone call from Shell Mex House at 3.46 p.m. on 21 December when Fuchs, at that very moment, returned to his office from the interrogation by Skardon, and took the call himself. The conversation referred to a detail in one of his physics papers.

Fuchs 'seemed to be pre-occupied', but was cut off by another call. This one, which originated in Reading, turned out to be a wrong number. He then took tea at 4 p.m., a custom that he had picked up from Peierls in Birmingham, and returned to his home.

Alone, he could now weigh the significance of Skardon's visit. The stated reason had been his father's move into the Soviet Zone, but Skardon had made an allegation which Fuchs knew to be correct. On the other hand, Skardon seemed to be casting a fly. Fuchs' best hope was that the Soviet atomic bomb test had made the Security Services suspect that someone might have passed information to them, but that they had no idea who this was. If this was true, Skardon was bluffing.

Now followed a sequence that could fit into a spy novel. Two hours after the erroneous phone call, at 6 p.m., the phone rang again in Fuchs' prefab. MI5 recorded 'wrong number' for the second time that afternoon. Shortly after: 'The door slammed. It was afterwards quiet. FUCHS had gone out.' At 9.15 a knock on his door was unanswered. At 11.59 the log for that day ended lamely: 'FUCHS had not yet arrived home.' It would appear that he was out until the small hours. Wherever he was, it was not with Erna Skinner, because the following morning at 10.45, she phoned him and said: 'You're a heavy sleeper. I phoned you for 1 ½ hours last night until 2 a.m.'[48]

That night of 21 December 1949 was the longest of the year, and dry.[49] It was also just two nights after the new moon, however, and the remote countryside around Harwell would have been pitch dark, hardly ideal for a contemplative walk on the Ridgeway. After months of pursuit, at the very moment when Fuchs might make contact with the Soviets, or in extremis might have panicked and defected or even attempted suicide,* MI5 had no idea where he was.

The next day, 22 December, Liddell and Perrin discussed the case and agreed that the most urgent issue was Fuchs' 'disposal'. Perrin advised they should meet with Lord Portal, Head of Atomic Energy at the Ministry of Supply, and Sir John Cockcroft, Harwell's director, to decide on Fuchs' future. Even though he was confronted with a crisis with international ramifications, Liddell was told that Portal wasn't available before Christmas.[50] The meeting was duly arranged for Wednesday 28 December at 10 a.m.

So three days after Christmas, Liddell, Dick White and Skardon on behalf of MI5 met with Perrin and Sir John Cockcroft; Portal took the chair. Arthur Martin, MI5's liaison with GCHQ, was also present. Liddell went over the basic information, Skardon gave an account of Fuchs' attitude during the interrogation, and they concluded that what Fuchs had said was consistent with either guilt or innocence. At last alive to the profound depth of the Fuchs affair, Portal showed sound judgement, concluding the meeting by saying it was too risky to keep Fuchs at Harwell. But first he wanted to reflect, and ruled that MI5 should 'think of some pretext for a further talk with Fuchs in case he showed any signs of breaking'.[51]

The meeting had one further outcome that would turn out to have far-reaching consequences. GCHQ had been cooperating with Robert Lamphere in decoding the wealth of Soviet messages; this may be how MI5 had learned of GOOSE's link with a paper on thermal diffusion back in September. Now Martin suggested, 'GCHQ should request from Washington the [VENONA] worksheets about the agent REST [CHARLES]. This will enable GCHQ to examine these messages themselves and possibly fill in some of the gaps.'[52]

FRIDAY 30 DECEMBER 1949: THE SECOND INTERVIEW

On 30 December 1949, nine days after the previous interrogation, Skardon returned to Harwell. In preparation, Arnold visited Fuchs at 10 o'clock that morning to discuss some laboratory business and then remarked, as if in an afterthought, that 'the man who talked to you before' had phoned to ask whether Fuchs could see him again that day. To hide that this was the purpose of his visit, Arnold continued the conversation with some

---

* Later Fuchs did intimate to Erna Skinner that he had contemplated suicide; see chapter 19.

discussion of whether scientists should take security papers home. Arnold said that he did not like the idea; Fuchs was 'non-committal'.[53]

Arnold called Fuchs again at noon to confirm that Skardon would arrive early that afternoon. Fuchs lunched with Erna, and returned to his office; Skardon arrived shortly before 3 p.m.[54]

First, Skardon asked whether Fuchs had thought of anything that would be of assistance.[55] When he replied 'No', Skardon asked directly: had he decided to make a clean breast of his espionage work on behalf of the Russians? Fuchs, who struck Skardon as calm and self-possessed as he answered 'No' again, added that he had given a lot of thought to Skardon's allegations, but could think of no way to account for them.

Skardon now moved to his main task and questioned Fuchs at length about his sister, Kristel. This served two purposes: first, if CHARLES was indeed Fuchs, to add to the pressure on him by appearing to have lots of background information, but second, help him to decide whether CHARLES was Fuchs or someone masquerading as him. Kristel, whose name was in the diary of one alleged spy – Israel Halperin – was an obvious possibility: for example, Klaus could have been careless with documents in her presence, enabling her to have copied them. So Skardon set out to establish the movements of Kristel and her husband, and to assess the significance of her name in Halperin's diary.

Fuchs described how Kristel had gone to America in 1936, travelling via England. He was an irregular correspondent – only one or two letters a year passed between them – and he claimed to know little about her life in the United States. In particular, he had no idea how she had made contact with Halperin. He confirmed that he had made two visits to her, but deliberately gave the impression that his visits to Kristel had been from New York and made no mention of the one in January 1945, during his time at Los Alamos, when he met Harry Gold.

Fuchs said that his sister had not visited him in New York, and he knew of nobody there who could be described as a mutual friend. Kristel had three small children, who took up considerable time, he said. Fuchs believed that she only left her home for a holiday at the coast in mid-1944.

Any possibility that Kristel somehow had adopted Klaus' identity as cover for espionage looked most unlikely to Skardon. He asked Fuchs whether Kahle had made contact with him in New York. Fuchs replied that he had had no contact with anybody connected with his earlier life, 'either directly or indirectly'.

Skardon returned to a question from his first interview: whom did Fuchs know in New York? Fuchs confirmed that his sole university contact was with Columbia, where he knew Dr Cohen – 'the only person in New

York with whom he struck up any sort of friendship'. He deemed his departure to Los Alamos to be most secret, and accordingly had been careful not to tell anyone about it. He said that when asked by Dr Cohen where he was going, he 'dissembled'.[56]

As they drew to a close, Skardon told Fuchs that the Ministry of Supply would undoubtedly dispense with his services, since his father's presence in Leipzig created a substantial security risk. Skardon also said that he would need to interview Fuchs again, and Fuchs promised to be available. Fuchs throughout was 'not in the least discomposed by the interview or any questions'. The only sign of nervousness was Fuchs' 'parched lips', which Skardon noticed when he left the office. Nonetheless, Fuchs' sincerity was so convincing that Skardon told Dick White: 'You're barking up the wrong tree. Fuchs is innocent.'[57]

Arthur Martin's suggestion that GCHQ examine partially decoded VENONA transcripts had an unexpected consequence. Within a week Martin had 'delved' into British files ,'which have just been made available to us,' and noticed 'several references to US Navy Department research into the Thermal Diffusion process'. He wrote to Patterson in Washington and remarked, 'You will remember [this] was the subject of a paper written by [GOOSE].'[58] Martin dug further and noticed that in 1944 there had been work on thermal diffusion at Columbia University by Dr Cohen – the very same Cohen that Fuchs had mentioned to Skardon. The university had collaborated both with Fuchs and Peierls at the time in New York and, Martin pointed out, Cohen had been 'Fuchs' opposite number' in this work. Moreover, Fuchs had told Skardon that Cohen was 'the only American with whom he had regular contact'.

So VENONA had highlighted a link between GOOSE and thermal diffusion. This had put the investigation on the right track to identify Fuchs' American contact. Unfortunately, in focusing on the name of Cohen, the quest – for now at least – was pointing in the wrong direction.

SATURDAY 31 DECEMBER 1949: THE SKINNERS' NEW YEAR'S EVE PARTY

Erna had been planning her New Year's Eve party for weeks. Designed to celebrate the maturing success of Harwell, and its launch as the nation's great hope for a new atomic age in the second half of the twentieth century, the great and the good had been invited. Rudolf and Genia Peierls were due to arrive from Birmingham, and Klaus Fuchs had reserved a room for them at Ridgeway House. The guest list included the Simons from

Oxford – back in 1942 Franz had been the experimental guru for Peierls' and Fuchs' theoretical designs for the uranium diffusion plant. The presence of Sir John and Lady Cockcroft honoured the moment in the history of Harwell – Lady Cockcroft agreed to bake the meringues. Klaus Fuchs would, as usual, play the role of deputy host, pouring drinks but otherwise keeping in the background.[59]

Mary Bunemann, wife of Fuchs' deputy Oscar Bunemann, helped Erna with the preparations. On 29 December Mary phoned to tell Erna of an 'amputation in her life'. For over a year Mary had been in a tempestuous affair with Brian Flowers, a younger member of Fuchs' group, and after wrestling with her conscience between the choice of her husband Oscar and children on the one hand and her passion for Brian Flowers on the other, Mary had 'done the right and noble thing' in a last attempt to save her marriage. Not surprisingly, at the party itself she was under immense strain and had too much to drink.

The origins of what happened that night lay in other events that had gripped the community during the previous fortnight. By chance, a few days before the party the journalist Chapman Pincher had published a story about a leak of information from Harwell. Arnold had tried to identify Pincher's source, and even talked to Fuchs about it, but without success. Fuchs, of course, had problems enough already, but with the media speculating freely about leaks, there was plenty of tension around. Mary recalled later that she was certain her phone was being tapped: 'We had a manual exchange, and there was from time to time an "open" or echo sound, followed by a soft click, temporarily interrupting conversations.'[60] Mary was probably recalling her regular calls to Erna Skinner, whose phone was indeed tapped. If her memory was accurate, we must assume that Fuchs too was aware of all this – his home and office phones and those of the Skinners, of course, having been monitored by this stage for several weeks.

Against this background, and in the presence of the distinguished gathering, Mary – 'a little the worse for alcohol, but not so far gone that I cannot remember exactly what I said or did' – decided to tease Klaus Fuchs. She sidled up to him, and in a voice that was audible around the room, said: 'Why do you give all those secrets to the Russians?' Fuchs, who 'never as much as batted an eyelid', said: 'Why should I?' Years later, according to her account, old friends would recall, 'I was there when you told Klaus Fuchs he was a spy.'

17

Chasing the Fox: January 1950

SUNDAY 1 JANUARY: GUY LIDDELL

For Guy Liddell, a new year meant a new diary. The implications of atomic weapons occupied his mind as he began to write: 'The event of [1949] has been the explosion of an atomic bomb in Russia, which has thrown everyone's calculations out of date.' In August 1945 two atomic bombs had reduced Hiroshima and Nagasaki to rubble. Instead of a period of Western dominance, the unexpected detonation of a Soviet bomb now meant that an arsenal of atomic weapons might soon threaten British security. Liddell wrote, 'It is clear that by 1957 the Russians should have sufficient bombs to blot this country out entirely.'[1]

MONDAY 2 JANUARY: MI5

The national importance of the Fuchs affair was formally confirmed on the first day of business of the new decade, when on Monday 2 January, Liddell went to 10 Downing Street to give the Prime Minister, Clement Attlee, a summary of the state of play. He told Attlee how 'by a process of elimination' MI5 had decided to interrogate Fuchs. Liddell explained how Fuchs had given MI5 an opening with the news that his father was living in the Soviet Zone in Germany, and this created security issues that could interfere with his continuing at Harwell.

Next he gave Attlee a 'rough outline' of the interrogation and that Fuchs' remarks were consistent with 'either guilt or innocence'. He reported that Lord Portal took the view – 'although no final decision had yet been reached' – that Fuchs could not continue at Harwell, as this was too big a security risk. The tactic would be that 'some post should be found for him at one of the universities'. Liddell added: 'We [would] be holding a further meeting with Lord Portal before any action was taken.'

He closed his diary entry: 'The PM said that he presumed Lord Portal would be informing him of his official decision.' Liddell now prepared to meet with Portal and Cockcroft to plan the next moves. [2]

WEDNESDAY 4 JANUARY: MI5

On Wednesday 4 January, Liddell, Cockcroft and Portal debated how to remove Fuchs from Harwell without inducing him to defect. That Fuchs had given the Russians information about the atomic bomb was already a huge embarrassment; if their actions now caused him to take all his knowledge and experience directly into the Soviet atomic project it would be a disaster. [3]

They agreed that Cockcroft should first speak with Herbert Skinner. The story here would be that 'as FUCHS' father has accepted a position in the Eastern Zone it is impossible to retain him at Harwell, and the Security authorities are quite adamant on this point'. [4] Cockcroft was sure that Skinner would find an opening for Fuchs in one of the universities.

Next, Cockcroft would speak to Fuchs himself. His brief here too was to cite the problem of Fuchs' father in East Germany, and to say that the Security Service was adamant that Fuchs must leave Harwell. Fuchs would perhaps have to stay until Easter, while an 'orderly' move could be arranged. This was a risk MI5 was prepared to accept. Their judgement recognized reality: 'It would be little short of madness on his part to attempt to extract any documents. For as long as he is alive, the possibility of his transmitting to the Russians all that he knows up to now will remain, whether he does it here or elsewhere.' [5]

MI5 discussed whether there might be one more chance for 'FUCHS to come clean'. Liddell noted that the key could be 'suggesting to him that he had up to now been reluctant to do so in view of his sister being implicated. This might be followed by a guarantee that anything he told us would not be passed to the Americans.' [6] Plans for Skardon to interview Fuchs for a third time would have to wait until Harwell's director, Sir John Cockcroft, had told Fuchs that he could not remain at the laboratory.

THURSDAY TO TUESDAY, 5–10 JANUARY: HARWELL

Cockcroft, however, seemed in no hurry to act. When he met Fuchs the next day he said nothing about Fuchs' status, possibly because he wanted to speak with Skinner first. Instead, they discussed a physics paper which Cockcroft had to give later that afternoon.[7]

On Tuesday 10 January, Cockcroft met with Fuchs at 9.30 a.m.[8] and later with Skinner, as planned. Even at the best of times Cockcroft was withdrawn and difficult to talk to. He would remove his spectacles and wipe them, while looking vaguely into the distance. He was especially ill at ease on this occasion, as he disliked confrontation, and skirted around the main issue.[9]

With Fuchs, Cockcroft said that he would help him find a university post and suggested that Professor Skinner might be able to take Fuchs on at Liverpool, adding that there was also a theoretical physics post at Adelaide in Australia. Cockcroft, embarrassed, could not stop himself from talking to fill any silence: the reference to Adelaide ran counter to the strategy for Fuchs to remain within reach, both so his expertise would be readily available and so the Security Services could constrain him, should events ever require it. MI5 subsequently described Cockcroft's introduction of Adelaide as a 'grave complication'.[10] Fortunately Fuchs said that he had no desire to move to Adelaide, even though for some time he had had the idea that he would like to move to a university. He said he wished to defer any move until the fast reactor at Harwell, on which he had been working, produced results. That, however, would be many months away and Cockcroft knew it would be outside any timetable with which MI5 would be comfortable.

Cockcroft said that only he, Portal, Perrin and Arnold knew of the decision, and that the only chance of the Security Service changing its opinion would be if Fuchs provided full information about himself, his life and background. With this extemporization, however, Cockcroft muddied the waters. Fuchs' heart was in Harwell, and Cockcroft had inadvertently implied that there might be a deal, subject to Fuchs' cooperation.

Cockcroft may have overstepped the mark when he spoke to Skinner too. Cockcroft was the only scientist in Harwell who knew the full seriousness of Fuchs' position. Arnold, as security officer, knew that Fuchs was under suspicion, but not the what and the why. Skinner at this stage knew nothing and was supposed to be told only that Fuchs had to leave because of his father's compromised position in East Germany. One way or another, Skinner learned 'considerably more about the Fuchs affair than he is authorised to know', and in consequence decided to take steps to ensure 'partly for personal reasons', that Fuchs stayed at Harwell.[11] MI5 labelled Cockcroft, perhaps vague about the constraints of secrecy, as the culprit but it seems more likely that the leak to Herbert Skinner came from Fuchs himself, via Erna. The train of events that led to this knowledge and to the denouement of the Fuchs affair began on 10 January, after his interview with Cockcroft. This is what happened.[12]

TUESDAY 10 JANUARY: FUCHS AND ERNA

Erna Skinner was desperate, in need of a break from the claustrophobic isolation of life at Harwell. Herbert's move to Liverpool University was difficult for her as he was away about half of the time, and buried in Harwell business for the remainder. On Monday, the day before Fuchs met Cockcroft, Erna had two telephone calls with wives of other scientists in which she talked about visiting London. By the Tuesday morning she was overheard in a long conversation with Eleanor Scott, wife of Dr John Scott in Herbert's division. Their chat began with Erna musing about visiting London in the next few days, and escalated, first into a desire to 'go away for a month' and next 'until the end of February'.

They discussed the possibility of going skiing. When Eleanor asked: 'Does Klaus still have any holiday?' Erna replied with a laugh: 'Oh, endless amounts!' For Herbert, however, the mix of Liverpool and Harwell meant that he 'could not even take a weekend off'. During the whole of January, for example, he would be 'almost solidly in Liverpool'.

Fuchs and Herbert Skinner were both workaholics. During seven whole years, apart from the road trip with the Peierlses to Mexico in 1945 and some days with them and with the Skinners in France and Switzerland, Fuchs had taken only a handful of days of holiday. But whereas Herbert Skinner appears to have been robust enough to suffer occasional exhaustion without serious illness, Fuchs was forever on the edge of collapse. His dental plate caused him chronic trouble, and around Christmas his cough had returned for a few days, probably brought on by the stress of Skardon's interrogation. The toll must have been immense, Erna describing Fuchs as 'swollen eyed and green faced'.[13]

While Erna was dreaming of escape that Tuesday morning, Fuchs was in conclave with Cockcroft, discussing his future. After leaving Cockcroft's office, Fuchs met Peierls, who was visiting the laboratory that day in his role as Harwell consultant. Even so Fuchs managed to find time before lunch to telephone Erna Skinner. In the previous days, he had come to terms with his two Skardon interviews and seemed much better, but now suddenly Erna found him 'all wonky again'.[14]

His tension must have been evident as Erna immediately asked: 'Are you starting something?' His ups and downs were a 'mystery' to her; 'What,' she asked, 'is going on?' Fuchs explained it away: 'I've just had a long meeting.'

He told her that the meeting would continue for another hour after lunch, and that Peierls would then leave for Birmingham. Erna asked whether Fuchs would then be free. In response to Erna's query, Fuchs asked: 'How do you feel?' Erna replied that she was 'flat out' and 'could not take responsibility for everything any more'.

It would appear that Fuchs and Erna had discussed her need for a break, as each manoeuvred to gauge whether they might go away together. Erna added that she: 'could go, but I don't want any sacrifice or any misery'. Having hinted at the possibility, she gave Fuchs a means to excuse himself: 'I don't know how busy you are.' Fuchs made it clear that he was constrained for the rest of the afternoon, and this seems to have convinced Erna that her daydream was out of the question: 'I suppose we'd better wash it out.'

Suddenly Fuchs took the initiative. 'How about next week?' he asked, and then, completely out of character, announced: 'In fact, I think I'll take off the whole week!'

Erna, surprised: 'Why? Because you're so tired?'

Fuchs hesitated, uncertain what to say. Erna pressed: 'Why? Tell me. Are you fed up?'

Fuchs replied, defensively: 'No, it's just so I get my leave.'

This wild deviation from the norm for Fuchs – the 'ascetic theoretic' – appears to have come as a result of Cockcroft's ultimatum.[15] Fuchs, as was his habit, had worked without a break for months and accumulated a considerable amount of leave. During his time at Los Alamos, likewise, he had taken very little time off, so much so that Peierls became concerned about his health. When Fuchs was due to start at Harwell, in 1946, Peierls had urged that Harwell allow him time off before he began work. Fuchs had not taken any, but had started at full tilt from day one. Were he to leave Harwell, as now seemed likely, he would forfeit up to six weeks of leave. Fuchs now decided to break free, if cautiously: three days in London with Erna Skinner.

They agreed that Elaine, the Skinners' fifteen-year-old daughter, could 'take care of herself for two days' before school restarted. Erna then decided: 'We could go up on Monday night, or something. Would you rather do that?' Fuchs replied: 'I think I would', to which Erna replied: 'All right!'[16] The tryst was agreed.

FRIDAY 13 JANUARY: THE THIRD INTERVIEW

More in hope than expectation, MI5 arranged for Jim Skardon to interview Fuchs for a third time. Skardon was sceptical. Following the second interview he had told Dick White that he believed Fuchs to be innocent. White, who knew of the evidence from VENONA, instructed Skardon to 'Go back and continue the questioning.' As yet unaware Skardon had been duped by Ursula Beurton back in 1947, White nonetheless had formed a cogent opinion of Skardon's weakness, and admonished him: 'Sincerity is a wonderful disguise.'[17]

White, who before his time at MI5 had been a schoolmaster, always preferred to 'create understanding rather than [demand] obedience'. He recalled later, 'I wanted Skardon to understand and agree to what was worth doing.' Meanwhile Arthur Martin, who as MI5's liaison with GCHQ also was aware of VENONA, urged Skardon on enigmatically: 'I know he's guilty.'[18] So on 13 January Skardon set off for Harwell.[19] When he arrived at the laboratory he 'lost no time' in telling Fuchs that he had come to discover Fuchs' New York address.[20] Fuchs immediately replied: 'Oh yes, the Barbizon Plaza.' Skardon then pointed out that although he was interested to know the name of the second of the two hotels at which he had stayed, it was the address of Fuchs' apartment that he required.

Fuchs said that he might be able to locate it if he had a map. Skardon had come well prepared. He produced a map of New York, which Fuchs then proceeded to study carefully. Eventually he decided that his apartment had been on West 77th Street, near Central Park, in the middle of the block between Columbus Avenue and Amsterdam Avenue. Fuchs promised to search among his records to recover the precise address, and proposed to pass it to Henry Arnold.

Fuchs denied once again that he had ever passed any information to the Soviets or their representatives. Skardon replied that if Fuchs were speaking the truth it was his, Skardon's, duty to make such enquiries as would clear him and it would be to Fuchs' advantage to help him. Skardon maintained his persona of 'Mr Nice' and asked Fuchs, almost socially, about his present position. Fuchs said that he had been told that he must leave Harwell, but that there was nothing very urgent about it and he had not yet made any positive enquiry to find another job. He thought it would not be too hard.

The hands-off style of interview now turned into more direct confrontation. In an attempt to destabilize his opponent, Skardon asserted that a Russian contact called at Fuchs' apartment in New York after his departure. Fuchs was 'not in the least alarmed' and said he 'thought it extremely unlikely that such a visit had occurred'.[21]

Skardon noted: 'Fuchs was completely composed.' This was hardly a surprise: Skardon had asked few penetrating questions and focused on such a limited piece of Fuchs' vast oeuvre of espionage that Fuchs had no reason to be unduly concerned. What's more, as Fuchs had never used his apartment for illicit activities, he knew that if this was the sum of MI5's concerns he had nothing to fear.

After this, the third interview, Fuchs could even now think that MI5 was ignorant of what he had done. Skardon had adopted a scattergun approach, with occasional barbs but lack of clear follow-through. He had, supposedly, come to check on Fuchs' address in New York; his claim that a Russian had called there was, Fuchs knew, no threat to him.

From Fuchs' perspective, one explanation of Skardon's questions was that 'Raymond' – Gold – had been arrested and news of Raymond's visit to Kristel had somehow leaked. Skardon had beaten around the bush to such an extent that Fuchs may have suspected that Kristel was the focus of FBI interest, and that the Security Services knew nothing of his real involvement. But this too worried him. Their grandmother, mother and a sister had committed suicide, and a few weeks previously, Klaus had learned that Kristel herself was now severely disturbed mentally. His father had alerted Klaus in mid-October that he had 'no good news from Kristel. Things do not seem to be better', and at the end of the month Klaus received a letter from Kristel herself. She was in a psychiatric unit and desperate because her children were kept from her, which gave her 'a terrible heartache. I simply got to see them very soon.' Her letter showed that her mental state was delicately balanced. Fuchs now began to fear that Kristel might harm herself if the FBI put pressure on her.[22]

The eavesdroppers lost track of Fuchs once again. From 5.30 on that Friday evening, when 'Door slammed. Fuchs went out', until 11.15 the next morning, when Erna called and advised him to 'stay in bed all day', MI5 had no record of him.[23]

It is likely that Fuchs had spent some considerable time at the Skinners, and returned home, unheard, after midnight. Erna's instruction hints that Fuchs was emotionally exhausted after Skardon's interview, and that she was concerned by the stress to Fuchs.

MONDAY 16 JANUARY–THURSDAY 19 JANUARY: KLAUS AND ERNA'S TRYST

From 16 to 20 January, Herbert Skinner was away.[24] He spent two days in Liverpool, and then went to a meeting at the Royal Society in London. Erna Skinner and Klaus Fuchs filled Herbert's absence with their tryst. Fuchs' leave would begin after lunch on Monday 16 January; Erna told Eleanor Scott on the phone that she would be away, leaving 'not before 4 or 5 o'clock' and had 'no idea where I shall be'. In the meantime, the housekeeper, Vera Pohle, would look after the Skinners' daughter, Elaine, rather than have her left alone.[25]

Fuchs informed his secretary that he would be 'going away for a few days'. MI5's watchers overheard all of this, yet it would appear that no attempt was made to follow him. Only later was MI5 able to piece together his movements, and even then they had no idea of who else he might have met or, more significantly, what he said to Erna Skinner about his situation.

It was already turning dark as the two of them left in Fuchs' car. They drove about 30 miles to Maidenhead, on the River Thames. There they checked in to the Riviera Hotel as 'K. Fuchs, Dr. and Mrs., 17 Hillside, Harwell.' They 'were shown to their room and remained there until the following morning'.[26] MI5's sole record of Fuchs at this time was: '23.20: Still quiet in the pre-fab'.[27]

In the morning, after a cooked breakfast, they checked out. They continued towards London, where they spent the following two nights together at the Palm Court Hotel in Richmond, a suburb in the west of London, which Fuchs knew from his espionage contacts.[28] Contrary to later claims by Elaine Skinner that her mother was always chaperoned by Vera Pohle when away with Fuchs, Pohle was not with them.[29] The tryst was planned with a level of deception on Erna's part that influenced MI5 later to assert unequivocally that she was Fuchs' mistress.

The records of the phone conversations at the Skinner residence showed that on 17 January Mary Bunemann called Erna, only to discover from Vera that Erna 'would be away until the end of the week'.[30] Later that evening, Erna called and spoke to Vera, who told her that Elaine had gone to the cinema and that Eleanor Scott, whose marriage was also in difficulties, was sleeping at the house that night. Vera then mentioned a party at Harwell 'that night', and Erna replied that she 'did not think she would be able to go to it'. She then added: 'If you want to ring Klaus it's the Palm Court Hotel, Richmond 0066.' Erna added that this was in case of emergency, which she 'did not expect to arise'.[31]

Far from being a chaperone, Vera Pohle was more like a conspirator, because Erna then completed the deception by telling her that if Herbert telephoned, Vera should 'tell him that I am at the cinema and will be late back'. She told Vera to say that Erna was 'all right and would ring him at the Royal Society on Thursday [19th] at lunch-time'. She concluded by saying that she would not ring Vera again, but would see her on Thursday night.

Klaus Fuchs and Erna Skinner spent 18 January in London,[32] while Vera Pohle continued to take calls at the Skinner residence.[33] That evening Fuchs called Vera, from London, to enquire about a 'strange message about Eleanor [Scott]', which suggested that she had 'a nervous breakdown'. Fuchs, for all his appearance as an archetypical 'boffin' who was socially limited, was nonetheless intensely interested in the welfare of his group, especially the marital turmoils of two of his team – Oscar Bunemann and John Scott. Vera confirmed that Eleanor had had a bad night, seemed cheerful today, and would come up to London, arriving in Paddington at 6.50 p.m. Fuchs asked Vera whether she had given Eleanor 'our' (*sic*) telephone number. Vera said yes, and added that Eleanor would come to London and 'hoped to see you tonight'. Fuchs' reaction, according to MI5, was as if he thought this to be 'a practical joke'. Vera then asked how Erna was, but Fuchs 'evaded the question'.[34]

Two months later, following press reports that Fuchs had stayed overnight at a hotel in Maidenhead with Erna Skinner, the Director General of MI5 was incandescent. Had Colonel Robertson been unaware that a spy had gone away with the wife of Professor Herbert Skinner, deputy to Sir John Cockroft of AERE Harwell? Why had the DG not been informed of such a singular breach of security, and at a time when Fuchs was supposedly being watched around the clock? In response, Robertson produced the following revisionist account:

> FUCHS' leave from Harwell with Mrs SKINNER took place ... at a time when it was thought that the next development in the case would be his resignation from Harwell, and we were in the process of gradually reducing the extent to which he was being kept under observation. At this particular time, it being known that his absence from Harwell was for the purpose of leave and that he was in the company of Mrs. SKINNER, it was decided that he should not be watched. This decision was reviewed and confirmed on January 17th, when it was established from the telephone check that he was staying at an hotel in Richmond.[35]

Robertson added, gratuitously, 'It is known that Mrs SKINNER has for some time been his mistress. She is a woman whose unfaithfulness to her husband is a matter of common knowledge in Harwell.'[36]

These three days and nights included much intimate conversation, which seems to have led to a crisis and confession by Fuchs.[37] Erna was aware that 'a man' from London had interviewed Klaus about his father's move to the Russian Zone. She might well have thought that removal from Harwell was a severe punishment for having a father in the Russian Zone of Germany and jumped to the conclusion that the authorities had doubts about Fuchs' personal integrity, or perhaps Fuchs told her of Skardon's accusations: what he and she discussed in detail during their assignation stayed with them. What we do know is that at lunchtime on 19 January, Erna phoned Herbert at the Royal Society 'in distress' and told him that Fuchs had 'confessed' to her.[38]

According to Erna, Fuchs told her about his impending departure from Harwell. She must have pressed him about Skardon's interest in his father, because Fuchs 'agreed [sic] there was something else', but he did 'not consider it very serious'.[39] He then revealed to her that he had shared his work on the diffusion plant more widely than the authorities allowed.

Two years later, Herbert Skinner claimed in a letter to Henry Arnold, 'Klaus confessed to Erna about the diffusion plant', but 'F. denied the bomb to E.' How reliable was Skinner's recall?[40] His remark, 'F. denied the bomb to E.', is explicit and only has contextual meaning if there has been some prior discussion about Fuchs' part in its development. It is possible that Fuchs made some self-serving remarks, which were restricted to his early work – Skardon, after all, had focused totally on New York, at which time only diffusion was on the agenda. This would be consistent with Herbert Skinner's memory that Fuchs had mentioned diffusion, and had dismissed his behaviour as 'not very serious'.

We can also be sure of the date when Erna told Herbert of this. She had called him 'at the Royal Society' on 19 January. On that day the Royal Society considered Fuchs for election to the Fellowship. Peierls had nominated him and although this application had been unsuccessful the previous year, by 1950 there was a wider realization that Fuchs was the nation's leading full-time theorist in atomic energy.[41] Herbert Skinner was on the Council and present at the Society's headquarters in London that day, so the date in Skinner's diary – 'January 19' – is assured. Erna's 'distress' suggests that the full import of Fuchs' 'confession' had come to her late during their time in London.

There is no record of this crucial phone call, which suggests that Erna phoned Herbert during the day, from a London phone that was not monitored by MI5. Herbert, aware of his wife's neuroses, did not inform the authorities immediately and probably agreed with her that they talk about this together once he was back home. The natural person to inform was Henry Arnold, but he was away from Harwell as his mother had just died.

Erna Skinner never revealed what took place between herself and Klaus Fuchs and the nature of his 'confession'. Over thirty years later, Fuchs gave an insight into his personal turmoil at that time. He recalled that Herbert Skinner – 'a close personal friend' – told him: 'Klaus, there are charges against you but if you tell us there is nothing to it, then all of us will be behind you and fight it together with you.' Fuchs thought that he had prepared himself for every eventuality, with a ready answer for any question, but he recalled that this was a moment 'he wasn't ready for'. As a spy, he 'should have been happy' to accept this support, but as a human being, 'to have so close relations with your friends that they give you their complete trust [was too much.] I couldn't lie. In this moment I confessed.'[42]

Fuchs arrived home at Harwell that evening at 8 o'clock. At 9.30 p.m. his phone rang. It was his deputy, Oscar Bunemann, who was calling about a 'personal matter', which he couldn't discuss over the phone.[43] His wife Mary's resolution to break off the affair with Brian Flowers had foundered.

Fuchs was about to go to the Skinners and did not want to make a pastoral visit to Oscar at such a late hour. Yet Fuchs was a complex man, always concerned about the welfare of his subordinates: 'If it is very important I must come if there is anything you think I can do tonight, if there is anything wanting help . . .' Oscar cut in: 'No it's not that urgent.' They agreed to discuss it the next day, but only after Fuchs had checked: 'Are you sure you are all right?'

MI5's eavesdroppers noted, 'The matter at issue was local scandal' and more bluntly, 'the misbehaviour of BUNEMANN's wife'.[44]

FRIDAY 20 JANUARY–SUNDAY 22 JANUARY: ARNOLD RETURNS

Fuchs was woken at 10.45 the following morning by a phone call from Oscar. Fuchs arranged to see him ten minutes later. The visit was bugged and MI5 noted that Fuchs and Oscar talked for nearly an hour about Oscar's 'private problems'. Along the way MI5 learned that Oscar Bunemann wanted to leave Harwell, and was asking Fuchs to help him get a job elsewhere. Fuchs, already in turmoil over his own future at Harwell, was now involved in a similar crisis for one of his staff.

The fallout from Fuchs and Erna's intimate conversation began on 20 January. Henry Arnold returned from his mother's funeral and found a communication from Herbert Skinner waiting for him.

Skinner had learned of Fuchs' interviews with Skardon and with Cockcroft. He was aware that Fuchs was very worried, and would probably be leaving Harwell; he asked Arnold to see him that morning to discuss all this. Arnold was now in a quandary. During his absence, events had moved out of control, and he urgently needed to be properly updated. So he delayed until 5 p.m. so that MI5 could brief him on what he should and should not say.

As yet unaware of Erna's tryst with Fuchs, Arnold suspected that Cockcroft might have given Skinner a hint, by some such remark as he 'wished Fuchs had been more co-operative'.[45] This news alarmed MI5 headquarters. As a safety-first policy MI5 decided that if Skinner asked Arnold any questions, Arnold should admit to the standard three facts only: Fuchs recently had a visit from the Security Services; this was because of his father's situation in the Soviet Zone of Germany, as previously reported to the authorities by Arnold himself; the authorities took a serious view of his father's situation and that in consequence Fuchs would be resigning. Arnold was to warn Cockcroft that Skinner would be calling him and that he should take the same line. Arnold agreed, and said he did not plan to let Skinner know of Fuchs' resignation unless it became apparent that Skinner already knew about it.

In the pre-dawn of Saturday, Erna phoned Fuchs three times between 4.50 and 5.15, but either Fuchs didn't wake up or chose not to answer. At 10.50 she got through and told him that she had had the most terrible toothache in the middle of the night. She had telephoned but he had not replied. Fuchs apologized, and when Erna said that Herbert was showing someone around Harwell, Fuchs said he would come round now.

Fuchs did not go anywhere else that day. It would seem that he spent time weighing up his options.

When Klaus Fuchs had been a child, Sunday morning had meant church in the household of Pastor Emil Fuchs. Now nearly forty, he awoke to the cold silent Sunday solitude of a Harwell prefab. Churchgoing was long gone. On the slopes of the Ridgeway there were no church bells within earshot, no companionship other than the closed society of the isolated laboratory, whose brick buildings scarred the landscape like an industrial site. Fuchs had nothing to do but replay the interrogation by Jim Skardon, and assess its implications.

Shortly before noon he called the Skinners. Erna said that her toothache felt a little better and asked whether Fuchs had fixed up anything with Henry Arnold. This suggests that their conversation in Richmond had debated whether Fuchs should talk to Arnold about his future. Fuchs said he had not. He declined the offer of lunch but was persuaded to come for 'a little pudding'.

At 1.37 Fuchs called Arnold to say how sorry he was to hear about the death of his mother, and said he would like to see him sometime. Arnold's first impression was that this was to talk about Oscar Bunemann, but then he sensed that it might be more significant. They agreed to lunch the next day at noon. Fuchs said he would go to see Oscar and he and Arnold then discussed 'the affaire Bunemann'. Arnold said that with both Fuchs' deputy, Bunemann, and the young star, Brian Flowers, in emotional crises, there was a danger of Fuchs' division being 'mucked up a bit' and that the best solution might be 'to have Brian [Flowers] removed'.[46]

MONDAY 23 JANUARY:
'A LONG QUIET TALK'

At 10 a.m. Arnold called Leconfield House. He told Robertson that Fuchs wanted to have a 'long quiet talk' with him, and so they had arranged to have lunch together that day. Arnold also mentioned Mary Bunemann. He explained that Fuchs, in his capacity as head of the Theoretical Physics Division, and also as a friend of Bunemann, was worried about him and had mentioned it to Arnold.

Robertson rhetorically wondered whether Arnold was a social worker or a security officer. Arnold explained that he viewed his role as ensuring the most efficient secure operation at Harwell, and the personal crisis in Fuchs' group threatened that already. Were Fuchs to leave Harwell this combination of shocks would be catastrophic for the laboratory and for the entire national atomic research programme. Arnold stressed that he was quite certain, however, that this was not the prime reason that Fuchs wished to talk with him. His sense of looming crisis was amplified by the fact that Erna Skinner, while asking Arnold to call on her 'this afternoon', had also made a passing remark that she intended to discuss Fuchs and his 'integrity'.[47] Arnold therefore anticipated that she would ask about the 'Fuchs affair'.

Arnold assured Robertson that he would tell Erna he was unable to discuss it but would listen to what she might have to say, because 'it might throw some light on the Fuchs affair from our point of view'. Arnold also remarked ominously: 'News of Fuchs' impending resignation, and of its connection with the presence of his father in the Soviet Zone, is now beginning to spread in Harwell.'[48]

Robertson replied that a plan would be formed in MI5 on what Arnold should say, and Robertson would get back to Arnold 'later that morning'.

Arnold now went to see Fuchs to arrange their lunch date. As he was not yet briefed on how to proceed, he focused on the Bunemann affair. At about 11 o'clock Arnold called Skinner from Fuchs' office and said that he would come over to see whether Mary Bunemann was fit to travel with him to her parents. Fuchs then called Bunemann and told him to come to his office.

Skinner, by now aware that in addition to problems with Fuchs there was a looming crisis with Bunemann, postponed a trip to Liverpool with Erna until the following week. He booked a hotel in Liverpool for the night of 31 January.

Arnold returned to his office where, almost at the last possible moment, he received Robertson's call outlining MI5's brief for Arnold's lunch with Fuchs. First and foremost, he stressed, Arnold must reveal no knowledge of the circumstances surrounding Fuchs' resignation, other than the link with his father's move to the Soviet Zone. He advised Arnold to hear Fuchs out, and to encourage him to tell everything that was on his mind. If Fuchs were to say anything new, Arnold was to say that he would report it to the authorities – Robertson was acutely aware that there must be no opportunity for any suggestion of coercion that could prejudice any eventual trial. However, Arnold must postpone any statement to this effect until the latest possible stage of the conversation.

MI5 worried that Fuchs might try to get some advance guarantee of immunity in the event of frankness, and so Robertson emphasized: 'On no account commit [yourself] to a guarantee of any kind, or make any promise whatever to Fuchs.'[49] If pressed, Arnold should say that he had no authority to do so, and that his own knowledge of the whole affair was too limited. Having received his instructions, at 12.15 Arnold then went to meet Fuchs.

Arnold and Fuchs went to eat at The Old Railway House Hotel, a pub restaurant in Steventon, near Harwell. Over lunch, Arnold maintained the persona of counsel and confidant. His friend – for that is what Fuchs had become over four years, notwithstanding their professional relationship – appeared 'under mental stress' and 'might now be ready to make a confession'.[50]

Arnold had met Fuchs' father during his visit to Harwell the previous summer and now, following the recent death of Arnold's mother, they talked about family history. Arnold then moved the conversation gently towards politics; the British Labour government had come to the end of its allotted term and a general election was due in just over three weeks.* With Emil's appointment in the Russian Zone of Germany being the spectre at the feast, the discussion moved to politics more generally. Fuchs then said that he disagreed with communism – 'as it was practised in the

---

* The general election was announced on 11 January.

Soviet Union'. This implied to Arnold that Fuchs found the principles of communism to be generally acceptable; in any event the qualification struck Arnold as significant.[51]

Arnold then raised the issue of Fuchs' meeting with 'Mr Seddon', the pseudonym that Skardon had used. This seems to have breached Fuchs' defences. In reply he asked for a further talk with Skardon, and requested that this should take place at his own home.

As soon as Arnold was back at Harwell after lunch, he called Robertson to say he had seen Fuchs, who had asked for a further talk with Skardon. Arnold said he felt that Fuchs wanted 'very much to talk, and to talk a lot' and possibly might be ready to confess. The interview was scheduled for the next morning in Fuchs' house at Harwell. This would be the fourth interview.

TUESDAY 24 JANUARY: THE FOURTH INTERVIEW

Skardon arrived at Fuchs' home at 11 a.m. When the door opened, Skardon made no greeting of 'Good morning' or 'How are you?' This was no social chat. Instead he announced himself with 'You asked to see me and here I am.' Fuchs replied: 'Yes, it's rather up to me now.'[52]

They sat in the living room, facing each other in Fuchs' two armchairs, one either side of the coal fire which warmed the spartan accommodation. Fuchs began to talk but seemed reluctant to take the plunge. For two hours Fuchs hedged as he gave Skardon the story of his life. Skardon had heard the raw details at their first interview, but now Fuchs began to reveal more of his inner self. Picking up from his tête-à-tête with Arnold, Fuchs talked about his work for the communist underground in Germany, and his fight against the Nazis; he had not felt that any country except Russia was really sincere in their efforts to defeat them and all they stood for. He had to some extent been reinforced in this view when he was arrested on the outbreak of war and deported to Canada, at a time when he would have liked to take a more active share in the efforts of the United Kingdom.

By this stage it seems that Fuchs had already gone further than in his lunchtime talk the previous day with Arnold. Whether it was because he felt more at ease in his own home than in a public restaurant, or that Arnold's friendship had made him relax and created the circumstances in which he could now confess, is hard to divine. Certainly Skardon seems to have done nothing up to this point other than listen. Had Fuchs been in the analyst's chair, and Skardon been the counsellor, this would have been standard fare. Skardon deduced that Fuchs was 'under considerable mental stress'.

So far, the interview fitted well with Commander Burt's thesis – the guilty party will open up and explain their motives. There comes a point, however, when some closure is needed. Eventually Skardon interjected: 'You have told me a long story providing a motive for acts, but have told me nothing about the acts themselves.' Fuchs continued his monologue, but to Skardon's frustration made no admission of any espionage activity. Skardon suggested that Fuchs should 'unburden his mind and clear his conscience by telling me the whole story'. Skardon's attempt to play the role of confessor, however, drew a blank, as Fuchs retorted: 'I will never be persuaded by you to talk.'[53]

By now it was 1 o'clock and they went off for lunch.[54] Fuchs drove the two of them to Abingdon, where they ate at The Queen's Hotel, on Market Square. In those days the Queen's was Abingdon's grandest hotel, famed for its linen tablecloths, its waiters dressed in dark suits and starched collars.[55] During the meal Fuchs was 'considerably distracted' and in Skardon's opinion 'seemed to be resolving the matter'. This was the second day in a row that Fuchs was dining in a public restaurant with a security officer. His lunch with Arnold had brought him to the decision to see Skardon and now 'here they were'. Fuchs had encouraged the meeting but seemed unable to carry it through.

Some epiphany must have occurred, however, as Fuchs suddenly seemed to have come to a decision and suggested that they should 'hurry back to his house'. Skardon judged Fuchs to be 'anxious that the interrogation should be continued immediately'.

Back at Harwell, Fuchs told Skardon he had decided it would be 'in his best interests to answer Skardon's questions'. He remarked enigmatically that he had 'a clear conscience at present but was very worried about the effect of his behaviour upon the friendships which he had constructed at Harwell'.

Fuchs had just performed the overture to an opera but not yet sung. Skardon intuitively sensed Fuchs' vulnerability, and now pressed his advantage home, asking him directly: have you passed information to the Russians? Fuchs replied that he had been engaged in espionage from 'mid-1942 until about a year ago'.[56]

To that moment no one had suspected that Fuchs had spied throughout seven years. With the single member of his audience rapt, Fuchs' story unfolded. Skardon discovered 'there was a continuous passing of information relating to atomic energy at irregular but frequent meetings'. Fuchs told him that he had begun on his own initiative, no approach having been made, and described how the first rendezvous and future meetings were arranged. Skardon, alone in Fuchs' living room, was discovering the extent and importance of Fuchs to the Russians.*

Fuchs said he had begun by passing the products of his own brain (in Liddell's judgement this had 'obviously eased his conscience at the outset'), but 'ultimately had passed everything he could lay his hands on down to details of the atomic bomb'.[57]

Fuchs described the nature of his meetings, which had generally been quite short. He explained how he would pass documentary information and the other party would then arrange the next rendezvous. At times some questions would be asked of him, but he felt these had come from some other quarter and did not originate with his contact. Fuchs said that the worst thing he had passed to the Russians was 'the manner of making the atomic bomb'.

Even for Skardon, who knew nothing of nuclear physics but was fully aware of the impact of Hiroshima and Nagasaki, this confession must have been a shock. As if in excuse, Fuchs said it would have been impossible for him to do more than explain the general principles, and that the infrastructure for the weapon would still have required development on an industrial scale by the Russians. Fuchs added that he was 'somewhat surprised' when the Russians detonated their atomic bomb in August 1949, for whereas he believed they might be sufficiently scientifically advanced, he 'did not believe they would be up to it from a commercial and industrial standpoint'.[58]

Fuchs stressed that his sister Kristel knew nothing of his illegal activities. If she had seen anything in Boston she would probably have thought it was 'merely a continuance of his underground activity in which she earlier joined in Germany'. By admitting to espionage covering seven years, Klaus Fuchs had reduced Kristel to a minor role, and saved his sister from prosecution. He implied as much in the letter to Kristel: 'We take a good deal on and have to pay for it [and it is] characteristic that we do not complain [about] the price.'[59]

Now, hesitatingly, Fuchs began to explain why he had chosen to confess. Echoing what he had said to Arnold, he now explained to Skardon: 'I still believe in communism, but not as it is practised in Russia today.'[60] He had decided 'fairly recently' that he could 'only settle in England'.

---

* Even though arrangements for installing a microphone in Fuchs' home and office had been discussed by Robertson and Arnold, and evidence from bugging permeates the files, any record of this climactic conversation is either lost or withheld.

England had given him refuge. He respected its liberal ideals. His colleagues respected him, as he did them. Rudolf and Genia Peierls had taken him into their home and treated him as one of the family. Fuchs was very worried about the effect of his behaviour upon these friendships. Subsequent events suggest that he might have added that he was bewitched by Erna Skinner and had already confessed to her. If so, MI5 did not advertise it: this was to be Skardon's triumph.*

Skardon, reeling from the extent of Fuchs' confession, said he would want some more detailed information, and they agreed to meet again on Thursday 26 January. MI5's published records do not reveal who paid for lunch.

Skardon now called MI5 and told Colonel Robertson that Fuchs had made a 'full confession of espionage on behalf of the Russians from 1942 until February 1949'.[61] Robertson's shock can be imagined: VENONA had pointed to a single event in 1944, and here Fuchs was admitting to seven years of espionage, including his time in Harwell. He listened with increasing astonishment to the fact that Fuchs had admitted to having supplied the Russians 'with all the information in his possession about British and American research in connection with the atom bomb'. Skardon ended the call by saying that Fuchs had not implicated any other person, and claimed not to know the identity of any of his contacts. In particular he did not name the person in the United Kingdom who had first introduced him into the Russian espionage system 'in 1942'.[†]

Skardon agreed to give a detailed report in the Director General's office at 10 the following morning.[62]

After Skardon left Harwell, Arnold noticed that Fuchs had been arranging a considerable number of documents in neat piles on his desk in his office. Arnold had seen him doing the same thing the previous afternoon, but it did not occur to him as significant. He now thought it necessary to report the matter, since it might conceivably be an indication that Fuchs was planning a 'get-away'. On the other hand, it was also possible that Fuchs was putting his affairs in order for an eventual successor.

---

* Later, in 1952, letters between Skardon and Herbert Skinner suggest that Fuchs had told Erna that MI5 were pursuing him, and something of the reason why (TNA KV 2/1259).
† On 24 January Fuchs told Skardon that he started espionage 'in 1942'. On 26 January he said it was 'a little later than October 1941, when [I] was cleared for Top Secret work . . . that [I] indicated to a friend that [I] wished to pass over secret information to the Russians'. Fuchs has translated the timetable for his early espionage about six months later than in reality. This incorrect chronology was never challenged by MI5 and became part of Fuchs' folklore. It seems that Fuchs was deliberately hiding his 1941 espionage, probably because his initial contacts were made dangerously near to the time when the USSR was allied with Germany – up until June 1941.

Arnold decided that if the opportunity arose, he should enter Fuchs' office to ascertain what types of papers Fuchs had been sorting out and for what purpose. If, however, he saw Fuchs in his office after working hours, he would enter and ask what he was doing. This was a normal course of action for Arnold anyway.

Meanwhile, at 8.10 that evening Robertson alerted the eavesdroppers to listen for any sounds of movements in Fuchs' office during the night. Half an hour later they called back with news that Fuchs was paying a lot of attention to the fire in his house.* He might have been destroying papers but 'this was only guesswork'. Robertson decided to alert Arnold, but he was 'absent at Harwell and unobtainable on the telephone'. At 10 o'clock that night Robertson reached Arnold, but on an open line, which restricted conversation. Arnold said he might be able to enter Fuchs' house the next day but would take extreme care to avoid any risk of detection.

---

* This suggests that bugging of Fuchs' home was still in operation (see footnote, p. 286).

18

Closing the Net: 1950

WEDNESDAY 25 JANUARY

The following morning at 10 o'clock the chiefs of MI5 gathered at Leconfield House to hear Skardon's report. By the time he was finished, the room was in shock. The scale of Fuchs' treachery and its implications were staggering.

The meeting lasted an hour. All agreed it was essential to ensure that Fuchs remained in his present state of mind to give a formal interrogation the best chance of success and enable the preparation of a legally valid case. Guy Liddell's diary for the day reveals how MI5's second-in-command saw the unfolding drama. He was puzzled as to why Fuchs had suddenly confessed, and in such a grand fashion:

> It is difficult to say what the deciding factor was in FUCHS' mind when he asked for the interview . . . Cockcroft had said to him, when he was told that he would have to leave Harwell, that it was a pity that he had not been frank with the security authorities. [I think] that he had made some conversation with Skinner, his immediate superior at Harwell. Meanwhile his somewhat intimate relations with Mrs Skinner had come out. All these factors, coupled with a certain amount of erosion due to his earlier interrogation by Skardon, may have caused him to unburden himself.[1]

Meanwhile, at Harwell, Henry Arnold had half an hour's conversation with Fuchs, who apologized for having been 'secretive' with him.[2] Fuchs also intimated that he believed Arnold to know 'far more than he had admitted'. 'Arnold gave nothing away.'[3] Liddell's narrative from his position at the centre of MI5's universe of espionage reveals his ignorance that Fuchs' confession was a result of years of patient cultivation by the outsider Arnold. Arnold had become Fuchs' confidant, which bore fruit when they lunched together on 24 January; Arnold had used the forthcoming general election as his entrée and Fuchs had then revealed his political allegiances. Skardon had to complete the task, and this required considerable skill, which Liddell recognized. He continued in his diary: 'In the light of what [Fuchs] has said, it is clear that vanity plays a great part. For two hours he tried to explain his mental make-up, without saying anything about what he had done as a result of it.'

'In his conversation he made it perfectly plain that in his view he was quite indispensable at Harwell, his services should be retained. He evidently thinks that he can, without too much difficulty, persuade the authorities to retain his services. This is, I think, where his vanity and megalomania come in.'[4]

'Vanity and megalomania' were convenient labels with which MI5 could denigrate its quarry, and while Fuchs undoubtedly exhibited such characteristics they do not truly describe his situation. Fuchs fully understood his singular importance to the United Kingdom's atomic strategy. First, he knew what MI5 did not: Britain was building its own atomic bomb, and he was the project's lynchpin. He was one of the most knowledgeable experts on the weapon in the world, and there is no doubt that by 1950 he knew more about the atomic bomb than anyone in the United Kingdom, including its father, Rudolf Peierls. What's more, Fuchs was also uniquely knowledgeable about thermonuclear weapons – the hydrogen bomb. Klaus Fuchs was indispensable not merely to the civil nuclear project at Harwell but to William Penney and his team at Fort Halstead in their quest to make the UK an international nuclear weapons power.

Unaware of this scientific and geopolitical background, Liddell decided, 'FUCHS is clearly about as good an example of completely muddled thinking that it would be possible to find. Psychologically the case is of very great interest as showing the type of person we are up against.' Next, Liddell turned to assess the major question for MI5: had they made obvious errors in the past which allowed Fuchs to slip through the net? And most importantly from a pragmatic standpoint: what might they do to avoid a repeat in the future?

Hindsight is a wonderful teacher, of course, but from the outset the directors of MI5 seemed set on showing that whatever had led to Fuchs' treachery, they could not reasonably have done more to prevent it. Liddell started this *non est mea culpa* in his diary that same day:

> Dick [White], Roger [Hollis] and I have been reviewing [Fuchs'] disclosure from the point of view of the action that we have taken in this case and in many others. During the war, when FUCHS was sent to America . . . even Winston [Churchill] took the view that anti-Nazism was a positive asset.

It was in this atmosphere that FUCHS had been taken on. When he returned he was already in Harwell before we were asked to vet him. There was a considerable amount of argument and we finally decided it was our duty to inform Atomic Energy of what we knew, and to say that in our view it did not add up to anything positive. All that we did know at the time was that FUCHS had been associated with some youth movement, which was fighting the Nazis in Germany, and that when he was interned in Canada he had associated with the Communist Fritz KAHLE in the camp. This did not seem surprising, *since a large number of the other inmates were pro-Nazi* [my emphasis]. It would, of course, have been possible for us to have taken a stronger line about FUCHS' [employment] at Harwell, but I am quite certain that in view of his past services to atomic energy and the importance of the position he held in the whole project, it would have got us nowhere. If we always took a completely rigid line, Government Departments would merely get into the way of saying: 'Oh well, of course the Security Service would turn a case of this sort down', and ultimately any advice we gave would be disregarded. On the counter-espionage side, I think there is no doubt that if we had turned the heat on to FUCHS when he came back to this country, in the same way that we have been doing in the last six months, we should undoubtedly have bowled him out. But it is difficult to see in the light of the information available why we should have made him the subject of special investigations any more than many others whom we have got on our books.[5]

The latter point was certainly true. However, much of the rest was fanciful. First, to say that in Nazi Germany Fuchs was associated with 'some youth movement' was euphemistic in the extreme; information given to MI5 – notwithstanding that it was tainted by its Gestapo origins – correctly stated that he had been in the communist underground. Next, as Fuchs had explained to Skardon during his first interview, the inmates of the internment camp in Canada were largely German Jews and certainly not 'pro-Nazi'. Fuchs' association with Kahle was not insignificant, contrary to Hollis' persistent interpretation. Liddell seemed unaware too that Jane and John Archer had regarded Fuchs as a 'probable' spy in 1946. Finally, and most disturbing, is Liddell's assertion that Fuchs was in Harwell 'before we were asked to vet him'; Liddell seems to have forgotten that Fuchs had been – or should have been – vetted for transfer to the United States in 1943, when MI5 deliberately withheld information from the Americans about his 'proclivities'.

Having assessed the lessons from the past, Liddell ended with his assessment of the present. Perhaps optimistically, given that the case was by no means watertight, he concluded: 'It is now possible for Fuchs to be charged.'[6] Fuchs had confessed, yes, but in circumstances that smacked of inducement. He had not been cautioned, nor had he signed a written statement, so the authorities still had nothing of legal value to condemn him. MI5 were now sure of their quarry, but as yet they had nothing with which they could bring him to court.

THURSDAY 26 JANUARY

Two days after the conclusive interview at Harwell, Jim Skardon saw Fuchs again in the hope of getting something onto paper. This was the fifth interview, but Fuchs had yet to be cautioned. Earlier that morning Fuchs had called on Arnold, who asked him directly, 'Have you disclosed very important information to the Russians about atomic research?' Fuchs admitted that he had. Arnold pressed him and Fuchs confirmed that the information 'was secret'.[7] Skardon arrived mid-morning and he met Fuchs, as before, in Fuchs' living room.[8] Fuchs cooperated but was vague about his contacts; MI5 suspected that he was protecting people. Fuchs had confessed to protecting his sister; the unwritten code of espionage now required silence to protect his contacts with Moscow.

Skardon started at the beginning: where and how did Fuchs' espionage start? Fuchs said he thought that it was a little later than October 1941, after he was cleared for top-secret work with Professor Peierls in Birmingham, when he indicated to a friend that he desired to pass over the important information to the Russians. In reality, of course, Fuchs had begun during the summer of 1941, and his first manoeuvres were earlier still.[9]

Fuchs told Skardon freely about times and places – though when questioned about these on subsequent occasions, details changed – but was consistently vague on the people. So, for example, he said that the first meeting took place in a private house in London on the south side of Hyde Park where he met a man whom 'he believed to be Russian' and who 'may have been in uniform'. This might have been confusion on Fuchs' part after nine years, or deliberate disinformation: if you walk for five minutes northwards from the house in Lawn Road, the verdant pastures of Hampstead Heath spread before you. As for his meetings with 'Sonya': 'meetings took place with a foreign woman in a country road near Banbury'. Fuchs' version of events in New York was that he had 'three or four meetings' with a man 'who was probably a Russian'. In reality, of course, he met Harry Gold – an American – more than half a dozen times. Following this there were 'possibly' two more meetings in Santa Fe before his return to England in 1946.

Fuchs was 'most anxious' that his future should be resolved as soon as possible. Ironically he wondered whether the authorities would 'clearly understand his position', even though he seems not to have appreciated the seriousness of the situation his confession created. Skardon used Fuchs' desire to be understood as an opening to ask whether he would like to make a written statement, 'incorporating any details that he thought ought to be borne in mind'.[10] Fuchs concurred and they agreed to meet in London the next day, Friday 27 January.

Immediately following his meeting with Skardon, Fuchs devoted himself to the welfare of his team of theoretical physicists, where another drama was playing out. During those fateful days, as we shall now see, his actions reveal his innermost thoughts as he prepared to face his Calvary. Recall that Mary Bunemann's attempt on New Year's Eve to save her marriage, by breaking with Brian Flowers, had failed. This had come to a crisis with Mary experiencing a nervous breakdown, which led to her admission into Oxford's Warneford Hospital, in those days a psychiatric establishment of controversial reputation. As the MI5 files record, in the brutal style of that time, Mary was in a 'lunatic asylum' because she was 'mentally deranged'.[11] Henry Arnold drove her to the hospital; Mary recalled later that he was 'distressingly preoccupied'.

On 24 January, Brian Flowers visited her, coincidentally at the moment Fuchs was making his confession to Skardon. When Fuchs saw Flowers the following morning and heard about Mary, he offered to drive him on his next visit to the hospital as Fuchs felt that he could give her some useful advice. This he did on the afternoon of 26 January, after his interview with Skardon. Before he went, however, he called Erna. Their conversation reveals his inner turmoil.[12]

Erna remarked that Fuchs sounded fragile and hinted that he was taking on too much with this social work. He replied, 'Just now, I'm in the habit of taking things in my own hands.'

'Well, that you MUST NOT do,' Erna admonished, 'I'm much stronger and more sensible.'

She asked whether Klaus could find someone else to take Brian to see Mary, but Fuchs insisted on doing this himself. Then, in a remark that had huge resonance, she challenged him: 'Well! Can you drive? Because if you're going to drive as you've driven me lately . . . !'[13] Erna was echoing the observation of the MI5 pursuers that Fuchs – the experienced safe motorist – had been driving strangely. Without doubt, Fuchs must have known for some time that he had been followed, and Erna's observation

I do not know that I shall be able to do anything that might in the end give them away. They are not inside the project but they are the intermediaries between myself and the Russian Government. At first I thought that all I would do would be to inform the Russian authorities that work upon the atomic bomb was going on. They wished to have more details and I agreed to supply them. I concentrated at first mainly on the products of my own work but in particular at Los Alamos I did what I consider to be the worst I have done namely to give information about the principles of the design of the plutonium bomb. Later on at Harwell I began to be concerned about the information I was giving out and I began to sift it but it is difficult to say exactly when and how I did it because it was a process which went up and down with my inner struggles. The last time when I handed over information was in February or March 1949. Before I joined the project most of the English people

K.F. I had met with whom I had made personal contacts were left wing, and were

"F. affected to some degree or other by the same kind of philosophy. Since joining the

K.F. project coming to Harwell I have met English people of all kinds and I have

K.F. come to see in many of them a firm deep rooted firmness which enables them to lead a decent way of life. I do not know where this springs from and I don't think they do but it is there.

I have read this statement and to the best of my knowledge it is true   Klaus Emil
Klaus Fuchs

Statement taken down in writing by me at the dictation of Emil Julius Klaus Fuchs at War Office on 27th January 1950. He read it through made such alterations as he wished and initialled each and every page.
Wm. Skardon

Skardon's transcription of Fuchs' confession, confirmed by Fuchs.

demonstrates that his attempts at counter-surveillance were less than perfect.

There was no need for a tail when Fuchs took Flowers to see Mary in hospital. Later she recalled that Fuchs was 'kind and tender'. His remarks carried an eerie insight into his state of mind as he advised her to make up hers and stand by her convictions. He said his upbringing had taught him to follow a course of action, if 'one was beyond any doubt it was right', and to disregard any opposition. Fuchs said, 'everyone has their own conscience to live with and must obey its commands'.[14]

That day Mary Bunemann and Klaus Fuchs resolved their individual crises with unselfish decisions. Mary decided that she must put her children's needs ahead of her own and remain with her husband. Fuchs decided that he must protect his sister's future above his own.

FRIDAY 27 JANUARY

The next morning Skardon was at Paddington station in good time to meet Fuchs at 10.45 and accompany him to room 055 at the War Office. This was the sixth time that Skardon and Fuchs had talked, and only now was he cautioned. If Fuchs clammed up now, the Security Services would be sunk; Fuchs would be removed from Harwell, certainly, but not prosecuted. Skardon asked whether Fuchs still wanted him to write down his statement. This was a key moment. Fuchs said: 'Yes, I quite understand and I would like you to carry on.'[15] With that a sequence of events began which would lead not just to Fuchs' imprisonment but also to the decimation of the Soviet spy network in North America, and the execution of Ethel and Julius Rosenberg.

In an echo of what he had said the previous day to Mary Bunemann, Fuchs dictated: 'There are certain standards of moral behaviour which are in you and that you cannot disregard. That in your actions you must be clear in your own mind whether they are right or wrong.'[16] At the conclusion Fuchs said he was most anxious to discover what his future was to be and did not want to waste any time in getting the matter cleared up. Fuchs seemed to think that by having told all, he now had a clean slate with his friends and that uncertainty about his career, whether at Harwell or a university, could at last be settled. Fuchs told Henry Arnold later that he had written his confession 'for several people and you are one of them'.[17] As for Fuchs' future at Harwell, Skardon hedged, saying that it was 'under active consideration'. In his statement Fuchs offered to provide all technical information that he had passed to the Russians. Skardon was prepared to see him on Saturday 28 and Sunday 29 January to follow this up, if he so wished, but 'thought a rest would do him good'. Fuchs asked for a rest, and agreed to meet Michael Perrin, the scientific expert responsible for atomic energy at the Ministry of Supply, on Monday 30 January to impart full details of his technical disclosures. Perrin wanted to know not only precise particulars of the scientific intelligence that he handed over, but also the details of any questionnaire that Fuchs may have received from the Russians, as this could give clues to the state of Soviet know-how.

Fuchs now returned to Harwell. Erna had been to the theatre in Oxford and at 10.30 p.m. phoned to ask whether Fuchs 'was coming round or should she come to the pre-fab?' Fuchs said he would come round. He did not return home until 4.15 the next morning.[18] His demeanour and enthusiasm for telling Skardon so much suggest not only that he had a weight off his mind, but also that he didn't understand the seriousness of his situation.

At Leconfield House, Skardon's news was regarded to be of 'over-riding importance', as the possibility of getting a successful prosecution now began to appear 'by no means out of the question'.[19] Dick White reminded Perrin that the Security Service would have to inform the FBI, perhaps 'today or tomorrow'.[20] White also remarked that in the interrogation Fuchs 'refused to recognise the fact that espionage is properly to be considered an offence, in which connection he had drawn attention to the information he himself had supplied to the British, after obtaining it in the United States'. Fuchs here referred to information on the hydrogen bomb, for example, which he had obtained in the USA and had 'shared' democratically with both the United Kingdom and Russia.

Liddell's summary in his diary that evening revealed the satisfaction at having exposed Fuchs, but he also began to recognize the profound legal problems that could now arise:

FUCHS has made a statement to Skardon which incriminates him fairly well. This will be supported [in any legal process] by statements from Arnold and also from Cockcroft. The difficulty is to avoid any accusation of inducement of a temporal kind, e.g. if he could say that he was told he could remain at Harwell if he made a complete confession and that he acted on that motive in making his statement both to ourselves and to Arnold, a prosecution would be extremely difficult if not out of the question.[21]

Here Liddell identified the weak spot in MI5's case. He seems worried that Skardon might have gone too far in order to get Fuchs to confess and offered Fuchs inducement, if only implicitly. In the hands of a competent defence team, Fuchs could possibly undermine any prosecution. Fuchs' actions all seem consistent with him being deluded, thinking what he had done to have been a minor transgression, which by cooperation could be consigned to past history and forgotten. Liddell weighed up how to respond to this and assessed the counter-arguments:

> If, on the other hand, he was merely urged to get the whole thing off his chest and put himself right with his employers whom he had been deceiving, the case would be a clear one. In fact, in his statement he has very much stressed the moral side, although I should be inclined to think that his motives may well have been mixed. It could, of course, always be said that if any suggestion were made of his continuing to work at Harwell it only applied to a confession that during the war years he had let his enthusiasm run away with him, and that such activities had ceased when he joined Harwell. In fact, of course, he now tells us that he was active up to February, 1949.[22]

In these last two sentences Liddell all but admits that there had been inducement, otherwise why go to the trouble of contemplating a defence? Fuchs' admission that he remained active in espionage after leaving the United States could be used by MI5, in extremis, to claim that 'yes, we agreed to write off the wartime transgression, but Fuchs then elevated his crimes to a new level'.

Three tasks now remained. The first would be to learn the technical details of what Fuchs had transmitted to the Russians; that would require an interview by Michael Perrin. To this end, MI5 arranged Perrin's interview with Fuchs to be on the Monday, 30 January, at the War Office. Second, it was necessary to prepare a case for prosecution with legal advice, and move towards an arrest of Fuchs if this was deemed legitimate. And third, but of most immediate importance, it was crucial to watch Fuchs carefully to ensure that he did not disappear, or destroy any evidence.

SATURDAY 28 AND SUNDAY 29 JANUARY

With the goal of reeling in Fuchs now in sight, MI5 became increasingly nervous. At 6.45 on the Saturday evening the Newbury eavesdroppers alerted Colonel Robertson that Fuchs had been in his office for twenty minutes and it sounded as if he was clearing up. Robertson called Arnold, who explained that there had been a significant number of visitors to

Harwell that day. Fuchs in consequence had to receive several of them in his office and so might have had to tidy up afterwards. Arnold remarked: 'if Fuchs appeared in his office on Sunday, this would be more unusual'.[23]

A similar saga happened the next day. Fuchs was heard to get up at about 10 a.m., stoke the fire, and then return to bed. MI5 seem to have not recorded any actions by him all day. When contact was eventually restored, shortly before 6 p.m., the eavesdroppers reported that Fuchs had been heard in his office, and appeared to be 'tearing things up'. This continued for about an hour.

Robertson called Arnold who, this time, found it unusual for Fuchs to be in his office. Arnold decided to visit Fuchs' office the next morning, before the cleaners arrived, and check the wastebasket 'on the chance of being able to discover what Fuchs had been doing'. Robertson reminded Arnold to be careful as Fuchs himself might be up early the next morning in his office since he had an appointment at the War Office at 11 a.m.

MONDAY 30 JANUARY

Fuchs was heard in his prefab '08.13 to 09.00' and then he rang for a car to take him to Didcot station. Arnold checked Fuchs' desk and wastepaper baskets and then phoned Robertson at 9.45 a.m. to say that, as far as he could ascertain, there was no cause for alarm on the grounds of Fuchs' presence in his office the previous evening. Arnold confirmed that Fuchs was now on his way to Didcot station en route to meet Skardon in London.

The same sequence of events took place as on the Friday: Skardon was waiting at Paddington station as Fuchs' train pulled in at 10.45, and they travelled together to the War Office, once again to room 055, but this time to see Perrin.

Before Perrin arrived, Fuchs told Skardon that he had something to say to him. Fuchs indicated that he thought during his contact with the Russians there was some other person passing information to them. Moreover, Fuchs indicated that the final rendezvous, which he failed to attend, had been fixed for the Spotted Horse public house in Putney, or another one near – he believed – Wood Green underground station. Fuchs' behaviour was consistent with a desire to please, as if he might yet make amends by being cooperative. In reality, he was naming places which no longer had any significance, while adding nothing to help identify his associates.

Perrin and Skardon had taken notes, while Mrs Grist, a secretary with

MI5's surveillance staff, had the task of transcribing a recording of the meeting. When Robertson heard the recording, however, he realized that it included highly secret matters beyond Mrs Grist's level of security clearance. He took the pragmatic course: he 'warned Mrs Grist to keep knowledge of the recording within the smallest possible circle'. Robertson discussed this with Dick White, after which he sharpened the order: 'The records, and any notes which may have been made during the recording, are [to be] kept by [Mrs Grist] in a safe place.' To avoid raising suspicions she was told this was because 'a transcription might be needed at short notice' at some future time.[24] This concern for security was somewhat farcical because even if Mrs Grist had understood the concepts of plutonium, implosion, and neutron absorption cross sections, Fuchs had already given all the information to the Russians.

Perrin divided Fuchs' admissions of espionage into four periods, the first of which lasted from '1942 [sic] to December 1943'.[25] Perrin recorded that at this time Fuchs thought the atomic project would 'at best' be a 'long term possibility for the production of power' and intended to hand over only his own work. He copied documents from the 'MS series' from Birmingham.

The 'Second Period' was in New York, from December 1943 to August 1944. During this time Fuchs told Perrin that he learned about the US programme to build a large gaseous diffusion plant. He had no real knowledge of plutonium. He made one visit to Montreal and knew that a heavy-water reactor was under construction. He had no real interest in that, as he believed it to be a project for long-term nuclear power and not linked directly to a weapon. In Fuchs' memory, he told nothing of this to the agent. Fuchs got the impression that 'the Russians had a great general interest in the project and appreciated its importance'.[26]

Perrin's 'Third Period' was the two years at Los Alamos, from August 1944. Only when Fuchs arrived there did he realize the full nature and magnitude of the venture. He learned about the importance of plutonium and of plans to create it in a pile at Oak Ridge. He told Perrin that he handed over information about plutonium and a sketch of the Trinity bomb to a man who he deduced was an engineer but not a nuclear physicist.

Fuchs left Los Alamos in July 1946, which brings us to the 'Fourth Period: Summer 1946 to Spring 1949'. Fuchs was now at Harwell, by which time, he claimed, he had 'increasing doubts about passing information'. Fuchs said that when he was asked by the Russians about the 'tritium bomb' in 1947, he was surprised.[27] Fuchs said also that in 1948 he was asked for a specific Chalk River report, which he had never seen. Fuchs claimed: 'All these questions confirmed [my] opinion that the Russians

Reg. No: **994** Name **K. Fuchs** Prison **Brixton**

①

Meetings

First contact: London. Meetings arranged to suit my convenience. Usually weekends. Evenings. First meeting in house. Later in street, quite residential street, or busy bus stop. Contact left and arrived on foot, but on one occasion he had left private car in neighbouring street. Location different each time. Information consisted primarily in spare copies of my own papers, which at that time I was typing myself. In envelope or wrapped in packing paper.

Second contact.

Always country road just outside Banbury. (On one occasion she came to Birmingham and we met in café opposite Snow Hill Station). Weekends. Time arranged to suit trains from Birmingham. Usually afternoon. Information as above, though later I used original manuscript. Contact arrived by train and left.

Third contact, New York.

In street, quiet residential. Evening. Date arranged to suit his convenience. Place varied each time. Sometimes lonely street sometimes busy square. Usually Manhattan. Would arrive on foot. Information as above. Would walk from meeting place and leave through streets.

Boston: Busy street, somewhat off the main centre, mixed residential and business. Arrived and left on foot. Don't remember second place. Time between two meetings probably a day. Information: Notes written between two meetings.

Fuchs' handwritten notes for Skardon and the FBI exhibit the quality of writing implements in Brixton Prison.

had access to information from another source or sources.' Perrin high-lighted this in the margin of his report.

Whether these sources were at Chalk River, Los Alamos or Harwell wasn't clear, but Fuchs' remarks to Perrin reinforced what he had said to Skardon in the car, and made MI5 suspect that other spies were at work, possibly within Harwell.[28] In February and March 1950, MI5 duly made checks into potential leaks at Harwell and enquiries into communist asso-ciations of its employees. This led Bruno Pontecorvo, a world-class scientist at Harwell, and colleague of Fuchs, to approach Henry Arnold in April and inform him of 'communist relatives', and later (September 1950) to defect to the Soviet Union.[29] Fuchs also told Perrin that he was surprised when the Soviets exploded their atomic bomb in August 1949. He judged it was 'too soon' if his information had been all that had been available to them. This was further proof that Fuchs was not alone.

The meeting took four hours, with an interval for lunch. Skardon arranged to see Fuchs the following day to identify his Russian contacts. Fuchs had already told Skardon that his meetings all took place between 6 and 8 o'clock on Saturday evenings, so MI5 decided to watch the pub in Putney and in Wood Green every Saturday night for a month, as from that weekend. They also planned to question the publicans about 'any aliens they have seen in their saloon bars on Saturday evenings at the time in question'.[30]

Fuchs returned to Harwell and at 8.50 p.m. rang Erna Skinner, who asked why he had not done so earlier – she had been 'waiting for hours' – and why he had not come straight to see her? Fuchs told her he had gone home to attend to his fire but would come on his bike to see her now.

They spent a couple of hours together. MI5 noted that Fuchs 'returned to the prefab at 22.46. He retired at 23.35.'[31]

TUESDAY 31 JANUARY

Fuchs was up around 9 a.m. The eavesdroppers at the Newbury exchange overheard him moving about in his prefab until about 9.30, after which he was tracked in his office all morning. At 12.40 he was to be picked up at the main gate of Harwell to go up to London for his afternoon meeting with Skardon.

Although no one at Harwell knew the extent of the crisis about to overwhelm Klaus Fuchs, there was a sense that all was not well. The stress on the Skinners was evident. Erna called Fuchs at 10.30 and said Herbert was in bed with exhaustion. She asked him to come straight to see her on his return from London.

She then enquired: 'How did you sleep?'

'Oh – er fair,' Fuchs replied.

Erna, resigned, sighed: 'That's what I always fear.'

Fuchs, to reassure her, said that he was 'all right'. Erna's maternal instincts now took charge.

'You *are* all right?' she pressed.

When Fuchs said yes she asked again:

'You're quite all right to go [to London]?'

Fuchs assured her that he was: 'Yes, quite all right.'

'Well then I'll see you tonight.'[32]

Having seen Skardon, Fuchs was back home by 7 p.m. where he was overheard moving about for two hours before going to see Erna Skinner to tell her about his day. He returned home at midnight, but at 1 a.m. his phone rang and Erna asked him to come back. He stayed the night and returned to his prefab just before dawn.

Fuchs' interview with Skardon that afternoon had lasted from 2.30 until 4 o'clock. He was shown about a thousand photographs of 'Russian men and women who are at present in the U.K. or have been'. These included 'Soviet Diplomatic Couriers', 'Members of Soviet Embassy and Soviet Trade Delegations' and 'Russians in the U.K. '46 to March '49'. This exhausting list was not exhaustive, however, as neither Simon Kremer nor Anatoly Yatskov was included. From the crowd of Russian faces, Fuchs selected twenty-four as being 'familiar'.[33] MI5 had also collected some forty photographs of 'British Communists' and a couple of dozen individuals, 'many of them English', who were 'known or suspected of being engaged in Intelligence activities'.[34] Fuchs had described one of his contacts as a 'woman, an alien – although she spoke good English – short, unprepossessing in her mid 30s' whom he had met 'in a country lane near Banbury'. This sounded to MI5 like Ursula Beurton, whom Skardon had interviewed unsuccessfully back in 1947. MI5 had never subsequently been able to confirm their strong suspicion that she was, or at least had been, a Soviet spy. Their files record enigmatically that she was 'touch not'; a pencilled annotation added to the typed memorandum explained that this should be a 'tough nut'. Robertson included a photograph of her in Skardon's collection.

As well as Ursula Beurton there were photos of Hans Kahle and Jürgen Kuczynski. We do not know the order in which Fuchs was shown the various photographs, nor how tired his eyes were when this trio of images turned up, but whereas he found 'familiarity' in some faces that, as far as we know, he had never personally encountered, he did not select any from the trio who had played such central roles in his early espionage. Fuchs preserved the spy's code of silence. MI5 concluded rather lamely: 'Although FUCHS has been shown a large number of possible photographs, he has been unable to identify any of them as that of the woman in question, and without further information it seems improbable that this contact will be identified.'[35]

Even with the benefit of hindsight, this seems a remarkably defeatist reaction. We now know that Beurton left Britain for East Germany around the time of Fuchs' arrest, probably as a result of a tip-off from Kim Philby.[36] Later that year, MI5 officer Evelyn McBarnet posited that the 'Woman from Banbury' was consistent with Beurton, and advised that her photograph be shown to Fuchs again. That Fuchs was withholding information in January seems certain as in November 1950 he immediately identified Beurton from the very same photograph that he had rejected before.[37] By this juncture Beurton was safely out of the United Kingdom; it is not clear how or if Fuchs was aware of this.

On 31 January, however, Fuchs was not yet ready to betray those to whom he had passed his secrets. By 4.30 he was on his way to Paddington station for his train home, and Skardon had joined Liddell and others to meet Commander Burt of Scotland Yard's Special Branch.

The Security Services have no powers of arrest. That final act would therefore be in the hands of Special Branch, and Commander Burt would now become the main player. Liddell gave him the story about Fuchs, 'in the presence of Dick [White], John [Marriott], James [Robertson], Skardon and Bernard Hill [MI5's legal advisor]'.[38]

MI5's official minutes blandly state: 'The remainder of the meeting was taken up with discussions of the legal aspects of FUCHS' possible prosecution.'[39] This is classic committee obfuscation designed to remind those present of what took place while obscuring the full debate from outsiders. Liddell's personal diary, however, reveals the turmoil when Burt realized there was a danger the case would be 'thrown out on the grounds of inducement'. MI5 then went over Fuchs' full statement with Burt.

Their entire evidence came from a secret source that was inadmissible, and from Fuchs' confession, which seemed less robust the more they examined it. Burt offered to take another statement from Fuchs. This was potentially very risky, however. Liddell and his colleagues:

> . . . realised that if it was the kind of statement we wanted, namely, that it was principally his desire to put himself right with his friends and to make retribution that had caused him to come clean, there would be considerable advantage in the course proposed. If [on the other hand] he refused to make a statement, it would not really matter, but if he accepted the proposal and

then said that he confessed owing to a suggestion made to him that if he did so he might possibly remain at Harwell, we should be very awkwardly placed indeed.

Once again we see Liddell's private thoughts revealing the ever-present fear – invisible in the official minutes – that Skardon had gone too far. Liddell's ten-word summary is eloquent: '[Burt] thought that we ought to get away with it.'[40] Given the uncertainty, however, Burt said that he would like to take legal advice. He would come and see the group again the following morning.

WEDNESDAY I FEBRUARY

Burt might well have said to Liddell that he thought they could 'get away with it', but the next morning doubts remained. Liddell concluded that the best course would be to hear first the views of the Director of Public Prosecutions (DPP), and 'if he was not satisfied with the case as it stood, then we should be very grateful for Burt's offer to take a further statement'.[41] Arrangements were made for Bernard Hill and Skardon to see the Director that afternoon.

Hill's formal memorandum records that 'Mr Hill pointed out to the Director that there was an element of inducement in this case, namely the inducement made by Mr Skardon on the 21st December 1949, and repeated by Sir John Cockcroft at his interview with Dr Fuchs on the 10th January 1950.'[42]

This adds weight to Fuchs' claim, later, that Skardon had stated he was:

> . . . authorised to assure me that, if I admitted the charge, I would not be prosecuted and would be allowed to retain my position at Harwell. If I denied the charge, I could not be prosecuted, but he would advise the Ministry of Supply that my father's residence in East Germany was considered to be a security risk and I might be asked to resign. Major Skardon was anxious that I should not consider this a threat and in fact offered his assistance to find alternative employment in another Government Department.[43]

It is not clear what 'Department' Skardon had in mind that would be relevant to Fuchs and for which Skardon had influence, but Fuchs' claims here are notable in that there is no mention of them in Skardon's report, yet they are consistent with the concerns about inducement that permeate the prosecution's worries prior to the trial.

This central problem was admitted in MI5's 'Report on Emil Julius Klaus Fuchs', written before Fuchs' arrest, which spelt it out explicitly:

> Dr FUCHS, in dealing with the inducement made by Mr Skardon at his interview on 21 December, said – 'I was given the chance of admitting it [espionage] and staying at Harwell or clearing out. I was not sure enough of myself to stay at Harwell and therefore I denied the allegation and decided to leave.'[44]

MI5 and the prosecution team were relieved when the DPP 'expressed his strong view that the inducements mentioned would not prevent the voluntary statement being admitted in evidence' and judged that 'a successful prosecution could take place'. Authorization would be needed from the Attorney General, Sir Hartley Shawcross, but he was currently in Cardiff. Liddell delightfully records that the DPP left for Cardiff, 'without even collecting his pyjamas'. Confident that at last Fuchs could be called to account, MI5 planned that he should be arrested the next day, 2 February.

Although convinced that Fuchs was their man, suspicion of Rudolf Peierls remained, and Robertson arranged for surveillance on him to be renewed.[45] As for their main target, the plan was for Perrin to summon Fuchs to London the next day, for a meeting at 3 p.m. at Perrin's office in Shell Mex House. Meanwhile, Commander Burt would arrive there at 2.30 p.m. so that when Fuchs arrived, Burt would arrest him.

At Harwell, on that Wednesday morning, Fuchs asked to see Henry Arnold. Arnold, who was aware that momentous events were taking place but knew no details of them, or what economies he should make with the truth, telephoned Robertson at noon for instructions. Robertson advised him to listen without comment. If asked any 'leading questions' – about Fuchs' future at Harwell or possible prosecution – Arnold should 'profess ignorance' and tell the MI5 office what was said, 'especially if there should be any mention of prosecution'.[46]

When they met that afternoon, Fuchs asked if Skardon had told Arnold anything about the interrogation. Arnold said that he had 'no clue' and feigned lack of understanding of Fuchs' question. Fuchs told Arnold that he was expecting another visit from Skardon on Thursday afternoon and would be 'very busy with meetings' until then.[47]

As the Fuchs affair reached its denouement, with uncanny timing the fruits of his espionage continued their impact when on 31 January, in response to the Soviet atomic bomb test, US President Harry Truman directed the US Atomic Energy Commission to 'continue its work on all forms of atomic weapons, including the so-called hydrogen or super-bomb'.[48] The next day, MI5 intercepted a call from Otto Frisch. Years before it had been the breakthrough on the atomic bomb by Frisch, with Peierls, that had been the overture for Fuchs' spiralling descent into espionage. Now, following fast on Truman's announcement, Otto Frisch had been asked to give a talk on Friday 3 February about the hydrogen bomb, and was consulting Fuchs – of all people – on the security implications.

Frisch's worry was whether he was likely to say anything that would break the bounds of secrecy. He had spoken to Cockcroft, who 'thought it would be in order but had suggested that he get in touch with Peierls or Fuchs'.[49] Frisch was due to attend a meeting of nuclear physicists in London on the Friday, and hoped to see Fuchs then in order to discuss the hydrogen bomb in secrecy. Fuchs said that Peierls would be there but Fuchs himself was 'not sure whether he would be going'.

Frisch agreed that it would be best to 'discuss it with a responsible person [at Harwell] who knew the security problems'. Fuchs then said that it would be better if he could discuss it with Peierls, but if not then Frisch 'should get back to him [Fuchs]'. Frisch said he would do that; Fuchs then repeated, as if in afterthought, that he was 'not sure whether he would be going to London on Friday'.[50]

THURSDAY 2 FEBRUARY

As if he didn't have enough problems of his own, Klaus Fuchs remained intensely preoccupied by the welfare of his physics group at Harwell. In a desperate attempt to save his marriage, Oscar Bunemann had asked Fuchs to help him get a job away from Harwell. Oscar told Fuchs that he 'wished, with Mary's consent, to give up the house'.[51] This would create both personal and administrative problems. As if Fuchs' own troubles were not enough, he was now to be a wise counsellor in a crisis for one of his staff.

Somehow, Fuchs' professional life continued, and in Newbury the eavesdroppers diligently recorded his last hours of freedom.[52] They next logged a call 'at 10.36' from Peierls about the hydrogen bomb talk. Otto Frisch had taken Fuchs' advice and discussed this with him; now Peierls too was consulting Fuchs on the security implications.

During their conversation Peierls told Fuchs that he 'had heard by accident that Fuchs would not be going to the meeting tomorrow'. Peierls said he too could not be there, explained that he had to go to the technical committee 'today' and had to be in London again on Saturday (4 February).

In addition Peierls had invited Dr Maurice Pryce, a former colleague of them both, to present a colloquium at Birmingham University on Friday, so he was overstretched.

Peierls asked: 'How's everything?' Fuchs answered: 'Fine.' Then at 11.07 came a call from Perrin, which began the chain reaction: 'Could [Fuchs] come up [to London] by 15.00?' Fuchs supposed he could 'if the matter were really urgent'. Perrin assured him that it was. Fuchs, apparently under the impression that this was to arrange administrative details of his future at Harwell, or a transfer to a university, agreed to make the trip.

MI5 recorded the final acts in Fuchs' Harwell career. At 11.40 his secretary booked a taxi to take him to Didcot for the 13.05 train. He remained in his office for the next hour; at 12.40 a car from the laboratory transport department collected Fuchs at the main gate and he left Harwell for the last time. The driver taking Fuchs to the station had been told to ignore the black car following them, but he recalled later that he saw 'the occupants board the carriage immediately behind Dr. Fuchs'.[53] He had a travel warrant for a return ticket to London and, ever punctual, headed to Perrin's office for his three o'clock appointment.

Lord Portal now realized that the Fuchs affair could have far-reaching implications for Anglo-American cooperation in the atomic field. Portal wanted it made clear to the American authorities at the outset that Fuchs had committed espionage in both the United States and the United Kingdom. He emphasized, 'If this were not done, it was certain that Fuchs' arrest in the United Kingdom would cause an outcry against British security, and that even though subsequent disclosures would make it plain that the major leakage took place from Los Alamos, a good deal of the original mud was likely to stick.'[54] To meet that potential problem, two separate charges were framed. One related to Fuchs' activities in the USA, and one to those in Britain.

The Security Services, however, wanted the American charge to be omitted, since 'it might embarrass the FBI in the investigation of the American end of the affair', and create tensions between the two agencies. So, at this eleventh hour Guy Liddell and Dick White visited Roger Makins in the Foreign Office to discuss Portal's point and decide how to frame the charges against Fuchs. Michael Perrin, by now anticipating Fuchs' imminent arrival and arrest, was also present for this discussion.

The Foreign Office, while expressing a certain anxiety that the American charge might 'savour of political manoeuvring', felt that the point made by Portal was an overriding one and agreed to allow the American charge to go in. A telegram would be sent to Geoffrey Patterson, MI5's representative at the British Embassy in Washington, 'instructing him to inform the State Department of the broad facts and of the charges which were being made, but in dealing with the Press to say merely that the whole matter was sub-judice and could not therefore be disclosed'.[55]

When Liddell returned to his office, however, he discovered that the Director of Public Prosecutions, for legal reasons, was anxious to leave out the American charge, whereas for political reasons the Foreign Office and MI5 had just agreed to include it. The DPP and Liddell now presented one another with their arguments until eventually the DPP found a compromise: there would be two charges, but the British one would go first with the American one appended. Liddell recorded that 'this could be properly explained by the fact that the second charge needed additional proof of Fuchs' British nationality'.[56]

In the American charge, the DPP removed the reference to Boston, Massachusetts, as the place of Fuchs' meeting with the Russian agent and substituted vaguely 'in the USA'. Liddell then spoke to Sir Roger Makins and gave him clearance for his telegram to Washington. Commander Burt was informed that everything was now in place for Fuchs' arrest. However, owing to delays in framing the charges against Fuchs, Burt was already too late to make his 2.30 p.m. appointment with Perrin.

Perrin was alone in his office when his phone rang at 3 p.m. His secretary, in the outer office, informed him that Fuchs had arrived. Perrin told her to inform Fuchs that Perrin was delayed at a meeting, and that he should wait. Burt eventually arrived, some fifty minutes late for his appointment with Perrin and, aware that Fuchs was probably in the secretary's office, entered Perrin's office directly from the corridor, avoiding the anteroom with Fuchs and the secretary.

Perrin and Fuchs had been colleagues, and Perrin did not want to be there when Fuchs was arrested. So, with Burt at last present, Perrin phoned his secretary, and asked her to invite Fuchs to come in. He then slipped out into the corridor, seconds before Fuchs entered by the other door.

Fuchs had been waiting patiently in the anteroom in the expectation that he was about to be offered some deal to remain at Harwell. He now walked into Perrin's office to be confronted by a complete stranger, who announced that he was under arrest and was charged with communicating information that might be useful to an enemy in violation of the Official Secrets Act. Fuchs, in shock, 'staggered into Perrin's chair' and 'was in a poor state' and seemed 'stunned by events'.[57] Fuchs' version was more positive: 'I was so mad at [Perrin]. He just opened the door of his office for me to face the inspector and disappeared without a word. I had to give him a few uncomfortable minutes by calling him back and saying the first words that came into my mind.'[58] Perrin now entered from the secretary's office by the same door that Fuchs had just used. Fuchs confronted him: 'You realise what this means?' Perrin said: 'I realise that it means we shall be deprived of your services at Harwell.' Fuchs blurted out: 'It means more than that – Harwell will not be able to go on.'[59]

'Harwell' here was code for the United Kingdom's nuclear effort. Britain was building its own atomic bomb for which Fuchs was the leading expert. But he was unable to play this trump card, for this was a secret that even MI5 didn't know.

Irony upon irony. Fuchs had served the Soviet Union for eight years. By 1950 his continued use to the Russians would have been limited at best, but his value to the United Kingdom was potentially immense. With his arrest, MI5 was unwittingly depriving Great Britain of its most valuable atomic scientist.

In its quest for supremacy in atomic weapons, the Soviet Union had thus won a double victory – firstly in obtaining from Fuchs the intelligence that allowed them to build their bomb, and then in seeing the United Kingdom deprive itself of the ability to outrun them.

In anticipation of Fuchs' arrest, Robertson had prepared the groundwork for potential repercussions. At 2.15 he set up a 'close watch for any significant reaction on the part of any of the Russians whose telephones [MI5 are monitoring]'.[60] Next he called Arnold and told him to keep a particularly close watch on other Harwell staff who had attracted MI5's attention as possible suspects. In general, Robertson advised, Arnold should 'keep his ear close to the ground'.[61]

Robertson called Arnold again at 4.30 to say that he expected to hear soon that Fuchs had been arrested, and would inform Arnold once they had the news. Commander Burt would then go to Harwell to make a search, but would be unlikely to arrive before about 6 o'clock. Arnold should meet him at the main entrance, and arrange for him to gain access without his name becoming known and 'in such a way as to attract the minimum of attention'.

Burt would have the key to Fuchs' safe. The search would be to gather evidence for the police. Robertson added that after they had taken away any documents, the residue 'might be of interest to the Security Service'. In this respect MI5 wanted Arnold to act on their behalf, and to collect Fuchs' 'private letters, diaries, old notes or jotting pads, and any indications of his movements at any time, whether official or otherwise. This applied not just to his time at Harwell but to time in the USA or the UK.'[62]

At 5 o'clock Robertson called Arnold to confirm that Fuchs had been arrested and that Burt would therefore soon be on his way to Harwell.

No publicity was expected until the next day at the earliest, and 'more probably the evening than the morning'. This gave added reason for Arnold 'doing what he could to keep things quiet at Harwell, and prevent any premature leakage.'[63]

On the evening of 2 February MI5 had no record of calls on the Skinners' phone. Erna expected to see Klaus, but he was no longer there.

PART SIX

Endgame: 1950

19

Arrest

HOMELAND INSECURITY

The news of the Soviet atomic bomb test in August 1949 had taken hold of public attention at a juncture when FBI Director J. Edgar Hoover was under intense pressure. For over a year he had been pursuing a vengeful strategy against President Truman, intent on exposing communists in the administration. In March 1949, however, the President had learned of Hoover's homosexuality. Of itself this caused Truman little concern – he remarked 'I don't care what a man does in his free time; all that interests me is what he does while he's on his job' – but he was appalled three months later by Hoover's hypocrisy when the FBI pursued two of the President's aides for supposed sexual misconduct.[1]

Any lingering presidential support for the FBI Director was sorely tested that summer when Hoover was publicly humiliated. Soviet espionage at the heart of government was not confined to the United Kingdom: Judith Coplon, an employee in the Justice Department, was caught in June 1949 with Valentin Gubitchev, a Soviet diplomat, her bag stuffed with twenty-eight summaries of FBI reports.[2] At her trial the judge ordered the FBI to produce the originals so as to establish their authenticity. This would be the first time that raw FBI files were made public, and Hoover was worried – less by any secret information they contained than because of their mass of unverified gossip collated from unauthorized wiretaps, and showing evidence of the FBI's political bias. Hoover unsuccessfully lobbied the President to intervene, and production of the files in court proved a huge embarrassment. What's more, the trial exposed the FBI for having bugged privileged conversations between Coplon and her attorney. Compounding the scandal, the FBI then destroyed the records and tapes, 'a cover-up that could only have happened with Edgar [Hoover]'s approval'.[3] Truman came close to firing Hoover, who was now twenty-five years into his tenure.*

Not used to such overt criticism, the increasingly insecure Hoover became convinced that the Washington establishment was waging a vendetta against him. That autumn, an article in *Harper's Magazine* by Bernard de Voto, a prominent defender of civil liberties, criticized the FBI's actions. Hoover's response was to have his agents investigate de Voto's background.

The FBI began to infiltrate college campuses and influence academic appointments by feeding derogatory information on candidates to the university authorities. Hoover also fed information to Senator Joe McCarthy and helped fuel the communist witch-hunt that became known as McCarthyism. The news in September of the Soviet atomic bomb test, and the suspicion that this was the product of communist spies in America – correct as it turned out – helped fan the growing hysteria that freedom and the homeland were under threat. When in that same month VENONA revealed that a British spy had worked undetected at the heart of the Manhattan Project, and undoubtedly enabled the Soviet Union to build its own weapon, Hoover immediately focused on two goals: first, to show that this undetected espionage in the United States was the fault of others, not the FBI; second, to maximize credit for the Bureau and consolidate his personal power and influence once the spy, Klaus Fuchs, was brought to justice.

Hoover's blinkered view that his FBI 'furnished the lead' in solving the atomic spy 'crime of the century' overlooks the role of other players, not least the US Army Signals Intelligence Service, which owned and deciphered VENONA.[4] Indeed, it was the USAS Director Admiral Stone from whom MI5 had requested permission to interview Fuchs, in November 1949. He had agreed, with the condition 'the source must be protected under any circumstances'.[5] Meanwhile, cryptanalysts at Britain's GCHQ had liaised with the US Army Signals for some time as part of the agreement between Britain and America, and helped decipher some of the codes, which led to exposure of Fuchs and his courier, Harry Gold.[6]

The excessive secrecy surrounding VENONA enabled Hoover to make claims of FBI successes that could not be publicly refuted, and his paranoia threatened to derail cooperation between the FBI and MI5. Less than a week before Fuchs' arrest, Hoover was upset that London had not sent

---

* The Coplon case eventually collapsed after she was twice acquitted on legal technicalities. The FBI was hampered because it was unable to reveal the VENONA source of its evidence – see R. J. Lamphere and T. Shachtman, *The FBI–KGB War: A Special Agent's Story* (Random House, 1986), chapter 6.

16. Building B329 at Harwell included the offices of Klaus Fuchs and Henry Arnold.

17. The senior scientists at Harwell, 1948. Klaus Fuchs stands at the left with the head of the General Physics Division, Herbert Skinner, seated. The Director, Sir John Cockcroft, faces them, seated. The balding scientist seated with his arm resting on the table is Egon Bretscher, Head of Nuclear Physics. The other scientists are B. Chalmers, H. Tongue and R. Spence.

19. View of the Harwell prefabs from Hillside, close to Fuchs' home, *c.* 1950. This is roughly what Fuchs would have seen when he looked out of his window.

18. Aerial view of part of the Harwell estate *c.* 1950. One resident referred to its appearance as 'like a penal colony'. Fuchs' prefab is circled.

20. Rear view of Klaus Fuchs' prefab, 17 Hillside, immediately after his arrest in February 1950.

21. A picnic near Harwell during Emil Fuchs' visit in the summer of 1949. Fuchs at the left is making calculations; his father and nephew are at the right. The young woman is Elaine Skinner; the woman next to her is her mother, Erna Skinner. To the rear is Dr Scott, a member of Fuchs' theoretical physics team; the man standing, whose legs alone are visible, may be Herbert Skinner.

22. Weary hikers in Switzerland, April 1947. Rudolf Peierls is in the foreground followed by Genia, in dark clothing. Klaus Fuchs is on the extreme left, in dark trousers and white top, encouraging Ronnie Peierls to keep going. Gaby Peierls is at the right.

23. Klaus Fuchs on skis followed by Genia Peierls, on the same holiday.

24. A party to celebrate the inauguration of Harwell's BEPO Reactor, 5 July 1948. Fuchs is third from the right, Skinner seventh, Bunemann ninth, Cockcroft tenth, Peierls twelfth and Bretscher fifteenth. Cross-legged in the front, third from the right, is Henry Arnold; the boy next to him, fourth from the right, is Christopher Cockcroft. The tall man immediately behind Peierls is Christopher (later Lord) Hinton, who supervised the construction of Calder Hall, the world's first large-scale commercial nuclear power station.

25. William 'Jim' Skardon of MI5, and Henry Arnold, Security Officer at Harwell, arrive at the Old Bailey on 1 March 1950, the opening day of Klaus Fuchs' trial.

26. Harry Gold has his handcuffs removed by Deputy US Marshal John D. Leahy as Gold arrives at the US District Court in Philadelphia, on 7 December 1950. Gold was sentenced to thirty years imprisonment for espionage, and paroled in May 1966.

27. The man who loved England? Klaus Fuchs in the German Democratic Republic reading the story of his release from prison in *The Times* of 24 June 1959.

him reports of Skardon's first three interviews of the suspect, and he accused MI5 of being 'cagey' with intelligence. On 1 February Sir Percy Sillitoe wrote to Patterson and told him to explain that there was 'no intention on our part to withhold information. The truth is [we have] nothing that the Bureau did not already know.' The Director General continued with a hint of Fuchs' impending arrest: 'However events have clearly overtaken your request and you will of course continue to receive all information derived from the later interrogation which will we hope dispel any suspicions the FBI may hold.'[7]

On 2 February, as soon as he received confirmation of Fuchs' arrest, Hoover moved into action. First he called Admiral Sidney Souers, special consultant to the President, and told him he had 'gotten word from England' that one of their top scientists who had 'worked over here' had confessed that he 'gave the complete know-how of the atom bomb to the Russians'. Hoover then commented, 'The Admiral might want to pass this information to the President.' Very much shocked, Souers stated that he would do just that, to which Hoover quickly added that Fuchs, who had 'been in the employ of the Russians since 1941', had entered the United States in 1943 and 'of course had been cleared by the British'. Hoover then put a self-serving spin on the crisis when he volunteered to the admiral: 'Of course we have had Fuchs under investigation for some time and it was as a result of information that we had gotten over here and which we gave to the British that they picked him up.' By getting his retaliation in first, Hoover intended to avoid blame for allowing a foreign undercover agent to infiltrate the Manhattan Project, and had started his campaign to claim all the credit for his subsequent exposure.[8]

Hoover continued, 'Several of Fuchs' associates are still working in this country and we are of course checking on them.' He added that he would be sending Lish Whitson, head of the FBI's Counter-Espionage section, to London to 'assist in the interrogation' of Fuchs. Hoover's strategy was for Fuchs to lead him to GOOSE, which in turn might expose other Soviet agents in the United States; Souers, meanwhile, sensed that Whitson's secondment could create an exciting opportunity for espionage by the Americans. A short while later Souers called back to tell Hoover his idea. Fuchs was a 'very eminent scientist in his own right', Souers pointed out, and might have information about the state of British atomic science. The admiral spelled out his vision: FBI interrogation of the scientist could assess British knowledge about the H-bomb and atomic weapons in general. Hoover agreed, and boasted that federal agents would be able to interview Fuchs, because it was thanks to the FBI that he had been identified.[9]

Hoover next spoke to Admiral Lewis Strauss, a member and future chair of the Atomic Energy Commission, an intellectually arrogant man whom many regard as the architect, four years later, of the case against J. Robert Oppenheimer.[10] Hoover had informed Strauss of Fuchs' impending arrest by letter and Strauss saw in this both threats and opportunities. He was bullish about news of the arrest being published, as this would 'reinforce the hands of the President' on what Strauss in plain code termed 'the decision he made a few days ago' – in other words, that the United States should develop the hydrogen bomb. When Strauss had first heard Hoover's news, he examined what Fuchs had been working on and to his dismay discovered that the spy was fully informed about the hydrogen bomb, at least up to the time of his departure from Los Alamos in 1946. Hoover's memo records Strauss' coded reference to Fuchs' 'research on this very last word that we are so concerned about'.[11] The coincidence between Fuchs' arrest and the President's public announcement of the hydrogen bomb was a huge concern to Strauss who, unlike Hoover, knew the extent of Fuchs' involvement in that field.

Strauss believed that publicity about Fuchs' arrest could be a way to bully other scientists into being 'careful what they say publicly'. He told Hoover that he wanted to know the names of Fuchs' scientific contacts during his visit to the United States in 1947, and specifically, whether an FBI agent in Princeton could find out whether Fuchs visited the Institute for Advanced Study that year. Strauss was a trustee of the Institute and had been instrumental in appointing J. Robert Oppenheimer as its director in 1947. In 1949, however, the pair had a disastrous rupture, when Oppenheimer testified at a hearing of the Congressional Joint Committee on Atomic Energy. Strauss, who was an amateur physicist with an inflated opinion of his expertise, had made some proposal with which Oppenheimer disagreed. Oppenheimer – who never suffered fools gladly – subjected Strauss' opinion to 'lacerating ridicule' in the full glare of the media. Strauss was furious, his demeanour 'showing a look of hatred that you don't see very often on a man's face'.[12] From that moment onwards, Oppenheimer was Strauss' *bête-noire*. Strauss knew of Hoover's fixation that Oppenheimer had communist leanings and by implication was therefore a Soviet spy.[13] His curiosity about Fuchs and Princeton suggests that he already had Oppenheimer's ruin in his sights and saw political advantage – for both Hoover and himself – if mud from Fuchs could be attached to Oppenheimer.

As Fuchs prepared for his first night in custody, in Washington political intrigues were already afoot.

'A STORM AMONG THE SCIENTISTS'

For twenty-four hours in the United Kingdom, Klaus Fuchs' arrest remained a secret. The next day, 3 February, Peierls was hosting Maurice Pryce's research talk in the physics department at Birmingham University. As the audience gathered afterwards for tea and biscuits, Peierls' secretary entered and said that someone wanted to speak to him urgently on the phone. The caller turned out to be a journalist who 'out of the blue' gave Peierls the 'most traumatic experience'. Peierls learned that Fuchs had been arrested and charged with giving secret information to the Russians. 'Do you have any comments?' the journalist asked. 'No,' replied Peierls.[14]

Peierls first telephoned home and his daughter Gaby answered. He asked that Genia call him as soon as she got back. Then he phoned Harwell, but Skinner wasn't there. Peierls managed to speak to Perrin, who could say little other than to confirm that Fuchs had been arrested and charged with violating the Official Secrets Act as a result of information received from the FBI. For Peierls, this dashed any hope that the news reporter had either misrepresented or misunderstood the situation.

At the second attempt Peierls made contact with Genia. MI5, already prepared, intercepted the call and recorded it.[15] Peierls went straight in: 'Terrible things are happening. I had a message from London that Fuchs has been before a police court today charged with violating the Official Secrets Act.'[16]

Genia cut in with astonishment: 'Fuchs?'

'Yes. Charged with giving away information, it says, to the Russians.'

'Good God!' she exclaimed as Rudolf continued, 'I've phoned everyone at Harwell but nobody is there. I got hold of Perrin who of course couldn't tell me anything and I'm trying to reach Skinner who is in Liverpool and probably doesn't know anything about it yet.' He told her how he had learned from the Associated Press, 'who wanted [me] to make [some] comment about it'.

Genia exploded: 'I think it's complete nonsense!' When Rudolf confirmed that there was no doubt that Fuchs had been charged and that it was as a result of information from the FBI, she exclaimed 'Good God in Heaven. Who could have done this?'

Rudolf said he must go to London to see Fuchs, who would otherwise feel 'everyone has dropped him'. Genia was convinced that some third party had 'done this dirty thing' and that Fuchs had been arrested 'since FBI demanded it'.[17]

Rudolf's news tested Genia's world view. For both of them, Klaus Fuchs was a trusted friend who had lived for some years as part of their family and was regarded 'almost like a son'.[18] For Genia, the idea that this quiet, polite, reliable colleague had been arrested as a result of information from the FBI raised spectres of malevolent forces at work. Experience from her Russian past made her cautious about the power of the state, and suspicious as to its motives.[19] In Russia, members of Genia's family had been incarcerated on the whims of the authorities (see chapter 1). News of Fuchs' arrest renewed nightmares, which now made her afraid that the same might be possible in Britain. Rudi's news that he planned to visit Fuchs in prison unnerved her: extrapolating from experience of what went on in totalitarian states, the awful sequence could be: Fuchs in jail, Rudi visits him, Rudi disappears into the labyrinth too. Speaking in Russian she urged caution, and said, 'But my dear, you are in the same danger yourself!'

Rudi said he wasn't. She challenged him: 'How [can you be sure]?'

He replied, 'I don't know but I can't care less now anyway.'

Genia insisted, 'It isn't all the same to me.' Convinced that there was some malevolent hand at work she mused, 'Who could have done this dirty thing?' Then in Russian, 'Oy, oy, oy! What can it be? When was he last in USA? Who sank him?'

Rudi, thinking back to the 1930s and Fuchs' time in Germany, theorized 'It may be the old communists who are now out to trip everybody.'

Genia, reacting like a mother who trusts their child implicitly, asserted, 'But he doesn't know a single Russian.'

Rudi, ever logical, responded, 'Can you prove it?'

They agreed that they needed to establish all the details and to ensure that Fuchs had an expert legal representative. Rudi said he would 'put a call through to Brixton [Prison]. I'll find out what time I'm allowed to see him.'

'Yes, go tonight,' Genia urged, 'then you'll have the whole of tomorrow to get a solicitor.'

She offered to call Harwell because she expected that Erna would be 'in complete hysteria'. Then, hardly less hysterical herself, she offered rash suggestions without thinking them through: they should phone Robert Oppenheimer; they must 'raise a storm among the scientists'.

Rudi urged caution. 'No. You can get yourself in jail.'

'Nonsense. It must all come from America.'

'Yes, but it must be done in accordance with the wishes . . .' Genia butted in with 'Why? Can't I say that the man is . . .'

Unfortunately here the testimonial for Klaus Fuchs was never recorded because in Genia's excitement her words were 'not clear'. She wanted action, chastized Rudi for being 'so cool' and, the listener recorded, 'became quite incoherent'.[20]

Rudi calmed her and then, aware that his seminar speaker and guests were waiting for him, said he must go. They had planned that the speaker, Maurice Pryce, would come and dine at their house that evening, but if Rudi were to go to London that would have to be cancelled. Genia meanwhile would call the Skinner residence and hope to get a message to them as they were in Liverpool.

Just after 4.30 p.m. Rudolf called Genia again to say he would go to London on the 6 o'clock train and not wait for Skinner to call. He would stay at the Athenaeum club and Genia should cancel the dinner with Pryce. Shortly before he left for London, however, Herbert Skinner called him to say he had heard the news, and then added enigmatically, 'You can imagine what's been happening in the last fortnight.'

Peierls was flabbergasted, and Skinner continued, 'We've known about it for a fortnight. Vaguely. We've only known a few facts and had to guess the remainder.'*

Skinner amplified, 'Well I didn't think it would come to this but – well, it has and presumably it's serious.'

When Peierls pressed, Skinner backed off: 'There's nothing much to discuss you see – as I haven't known anything – I've only known small and vague things of what's been going on.'

Peierls replied that he thought they wouldn't take action without 'some – at least on the face of it – serious evidence'. Skinner agreed.

Peierls explained that rather than ring the prison governor from Birmingham and ask to see Fuchs, he would go in person. One urgent thing, he said, was to get Fuchs a good lawyer.

Skinner said, 'He's behaved marvellously these last few weeks, going about his normal business.'

Peierls, surprised, asked: 'He knew in fact something like this would happen?'

'Oh yes. For goodness sake, he's known it for months. I didn't of course but he did.'

'But you don't know exactly what's alleged?'

'No. I can only guess.'

'Does he?'

'I think so, yes.'

---

* Two years later it would be contended within MI5 that Fuchs admitted to Erna that he had told the Russians about diffusion but denied the bomb. Skinner's remark in this telephone call suggests that he had made at least the first of these admissions.

Peierls now re-evaluated the situation and explained to Skinner, 'I pictured this as if he'd been taken completely by surprise and so . . .'

Skinner cut in with 'No. Nothing of the kind! No, really, I can assure you of that. There's no surprise whatever.'

Erna then came to the telephone and told Peierls ominously, 'Klaus has promised me that he won't do anything, but if you see him do remind him.'

Peierls, stupefied and needing to be sure what she was implying said, 'I don't understand.'

'Just think about it,' Erna replied.

So Fuchs had perhaps contemplated suicide; if so, and Erna was aware of it, that would explain why she had called Herbert 'in panic' a fortnight earlier.

Peierls excused himself, as he had to go for his train. Herbert closed the conversation saying, 'Very terrible thing.'[21]

When MI5 analyzed this call they judged that Skinner's reaction showed he knew beforehand Fuchs had something to hide, but the extent of his knowledge was hard for them to gauge.

'WE LIVE AND LEARN'

In London, Peierls took a room at the Athenaeum and at 9.15 p.m. called Special Branch at Scotland Yard to ask for permission to see Fuchs. He was asked to call back in the morning. Commander Burt discussed the request with MI5 and it was agreed that the meeting should take place, 'but that suitable arrangements should be made for it to be covered'.[22]

When Peierls called again on Saturday morning, Burt suggested that Peierls 'might care to come to see him', and 'They talked in Burt's office for about an hour.'[23] Burt asked whether Peierls (who himself was still suspect, though he did not know it) was prepared to tell everything he knew about Fuchs and whether he had any objection to a written note being made of what Fuchs said when they met. Peierls said he had no objection.

Burt asked also whether Peierls would be willing to assist the authorities. Peierls replied that this would depend on whether he could be satisfied that Fuchs was guilty of the charges against him and he would not agree to do anything that would make Fuchs' position worse than it already was. If, however, he was satisfied of Fuchs' guilt he would certainly pass on to Burt anything that Fuchs might say about other persons involved.[24]

Peierls' meeting with Fuchs at Brixton Prison on 4 February started at 2.15 p.m. and lasted just a quarter of an hour. Police Sergeant Smith of Special Branch was present, but Peierls and Fuchs spoke in such low tones that much of what they said was inaudible and no notes were taken. The deputy chief warder, who was also present, reported that they seemed embarrassed, their conversation slow and difficult. Peierls made an attempt to draw Fuchs as to why he had acted as he had. The answer, which the detective overheard, was that he felt 'knowledge of atomic research should not be the private property of any one country but, instead, shared with the world for the benefit of mankind'.[25]

Peierls thought that Fuchs must have had a breakdown. Fuchs told Peierls 'with some pride' that the case against him 'rested entirely on his own admission'. As Peierls recalled the next day: 'I was haunted by the thought that if this was true one could believe he had cracked up mentally and now imagined things he had not done, or exaggerated or distorted things he had done.' He continued, 'It is important to find out whether one should believe him since presumably one has to rely on his own statement for an estimate of what exactly he did give away, and this is most important. For the last two years he has been working extremely hard, practically without a break, and has been seriously ill.'[26]

Immediately after seeing Fuchs, Rudi called Genia and spoke in Russian. After it was translated, Colonel Robertson got his first indication of the profound effect these events were having on the Peierlses.

Rudi opened by confirming that he had seen Fuchs and 'the case is very serious'.[27] Then, in English, he repeated three times, 'We live and learn.' Genia realized that Rudi was very worried and asked whether he had seen Fuchs alone.

'No, there was another man present. I advise you not to mention any of this. I learned it all from his own mouth – he told me everything. He came to realise the evil of it all.'

Genia bluntly replied, 'Do you mean he didn't realise it before?'

'No, no – he knew very well what he was doing.'

'He must have changed his views then,' she responded, and when Rudi confirmed once again that Fuchs admitted everything she asked, 'Did the thing go very deep?'

Rudi replied sadly, 'Oh yes. Very deep indeed.'

Genia asked whether the Soviet bomb test success had been due to Fuchs. Rudi first said he didn't know, and then, on reflection admitted: 'Probably. I'll tell you everything when I get home.'

'It seems to me he is finished,' she said, to which Rudi agreed: 'Certainly.'

Genia now anticipated the international implications: 'Imagine the reactions in the USA.'

'Indeed,' Rudi replied, and then Genia asked a penetrating question: 'Why didn't he do it [give himself up] before?'

Rudi said he didn't know, and repeated 'all the information was volunteered by Fuchs', who 'didn't know whether the authorities knew anything or not'.

Genia asked, 'How will it affect you?'

Rudi ended the call, down in the mouth: 'I don't know yet. I feel myself a complete idiot. Let's not talk about it any more.'

The listener added a note to the transcript: 'PEIERLS sounds most upset at the whole thing.'[28]

FIRST REACTIONS

When Peierls was back in Birmingham he called the Skinners. He told them that Fuchs could have only one visitor a day so they should make arrangements through Commander Burt. Herbert thought they might go on 'Monday or Tuesday'. Peierls explained that Fuchs was in the hospital, not because he was unwell but 'because the accommodation was better'. He said that at the start of their meeting Fuchs had seemed 'quite as usual, but towards the end had been a bit upset'. Erna asked what Klaus had said when Peierls had given him her message about going to see him. Peierls said that Klaus had said 'she could come if she liked' but 'had not seemed to regard it as very urgent'. Herbert thought this might be because 'Klaus hesitated to impose on Erna'. Peierls explained that there was always a third party present and Skinner responded, 'One has to be fairly careful therefore.' Erna said she would 'try and sleep tomorrow so that she would be all right [to see Klaus] on Monday'.[29]

Immediately after Peierls's visit, Klaus Fuchs wrote his first letter from prison; it was for Erna and Herbert Skinner – addressed 'in strict alphabetical order'. He began, 'I did not dare to write before, but I have just seen Rudi and it has helped a bit.' His handwriting was almost illegible thanks to the rudimentary tools provided by the prison service. With a random variation of dark and light, thick and thin, Fuchs scratchily covered the sheet of poor-quality paper. Parts of the opening lines teetered on utter incomprehensibility but as he gradually mastered the technique the letter became more readable. Aware of its likely impact, and in an attempt at being light-hearted, he urged them not to worry – 'Please do not think the handwriting is an expression of my state of mind. It is due to somewhat inferior writing utensils.'

Fuchs then alluded to some conversation that he had had with Herbert, probably after Erna's panicky call to her husband on 19 January. 'Do you remember, Herbert, when you told me I was taking myself too seriously?

Yes, I was only thinking of myself, and the easiest way out for me. All I had to do was to keep quiet, and not to care what you and other people thought about me, and walk out.'

Fuchs then attempted to present himself in a positive light: 'Since that evening I have done what I thought would be best for Harwell. I used nothing but the truth and I believed that I convinced [Skardon]. But the decision was not his.' By the 'decision' here Fuchs appears to be referring to his future at Harwell, and that by confessing to Skardon he expected to save his career and continue to work at the laboratory – the 'best for Harwell'. Fuchs then admitted that he had contemplated suicide – in his words 'there was one other way out' – 'as a last resort'. He had not done so because he had thought that his future was assured, until 'the smart Perrin got me unsuspecting'. Fuchs continued enigmatically, 'Now I only want that Harwell shall know the whole truth and that is why I shall defend myself.'

His long letter asked the Skinners to tell their daughter Elaine that 'some people grow up at 15 and some at 38 and at that age it is a much more painful process'. Then he returned to his arrest and apologized for that 'silly question to Perrin'. Fuchs had been 'so mad at him. [Perrin] just opened the door of his office for me to face the inspector [Commander Burt] and disappeared without a word. I just had to give him a few uncomfortable minutes by calling him back and saying the first words that came in my mind. Silly isn't it?'

Towards the end he lightened the mood with an allusion to his addiction to cigarettes. 'I can buy cigarettes but have to ask for a light each time I want to smoke. Helps to cut down consumption and I suppose that is the reason for this regulation.'

In his final sentences, Fuchs returned to his innermost feelings and revealed his love for Erna: 'Smile please Erna when you think of me. I am trying to when I think of you, though usually the tears get in my way. But I'll learn to smile just as I learned to cry. Don't be too hard on me Herbert. I deserve it but I couldn't take it just now.'[30]

When news of Fuchs' arrest became public on 3 February, the sense of disbelief among his friends was total, including those who, unknowingly, had been watched by MI5 during the previous months. The actress Tatiana Malleson phoned the Skinners first thing on the morning of 4 February, and spoke to 'Grace', who was looking after the house in the Skinners' absence. Tatiana said she was 'so upset, I can't tell you, I haven't slept all night'. Grace, who found it 'perfectly dreadful', said that she 'didn't believe a word of it'. Neither did Tatiana: 'It is utter nonsense; they just pick on someone because he is foreign.' Grace echoed this, saying, 'If they knew him as well as we do they would know that he couldn't possibly do anything like that.' Tatiana agreed and added, 'it must be so dreadful for his friends – poor little man'.[31]

The reactions from the scientific community to news of Fuchs' arrest were almost uniformly incredulous, as if they had just learned of a sudden death, but not everyone was surprised by his communist affiliation. Max Born's son Gustav lodged with Franz Simon's family in Oxford. When Born read the news of Fuchs' arrest in the newspaper he came into the room 'with a very white face', considerably shocked. He exclaimed to Simon that he could not understand how the authorities had been unaware of Fuchs' communist sympathies, 'when this was widely known in Edinburgh University'.[32] This might be dismissed as being wise after the event, but there is evidence that Fuchs' sympathies with Russia were well known, if not his active communism. Recall that Gustav's father, Max Born, had written to Fuchs back in 1942: 'You must be gratified that your belief in the Russians is so much justified now.'[33]

For Edward Teller, Fuchs' arrest was an epiphany. Teller had worked closely with Fuchs at Los Alamos, and been inspired by some of his ideas on the hydrogen bomb, but outside of their collaboration on physics Teller had found Fuchs 'taciturn to a pathological degree'. When Teller heard of Fuchs' arrest, he is said to have exclaimed, 'So that's what it was!'[34] Teller also thought back to his last meeting with Fuchs in the late autumn of 1949, at a conference on the safety of nuclear reactors held at The Cosener's House, a pleasant mansion on the Thames in Abingdon. The gathering had been considering the possibility of a nuclear accident resulting from sabotage of a reactor, and Teller had remarked that he considered it improbable. The speaker disagreed, saying 'There may even be a traitor sitting here at this table.' Teller recalled, 'Klaus Fuchs was sitting right next to [me]. If he flinched, I didn't notice.'[35] For others, such as Mary Bunemann, the news lifted a veil. Still overwhelmed by the crisis in her marriage she made no public recorded inferences at the time, but later realized the significance of Fuchs' reticence to talk about his German past with her husband Oscar.

On Monday 6 February Peierls sent a letter to Maurice Pryce: 'I am sorry I walked out on you on Friday and I am also sorry that the afternoon was such a mess, but I am sure you understand. I cannot say more about the problem at the moment but it is all very distressing . . . I hope there will be an opportunity for you to come again when we can talk in more reasonable circumstances.'

Pryce replied to the effect that there was no need to apologize: 'I feel most deeply for you in this matter. I have just been listening to the news on the radio of what happened at Bow Street today.' And then Pryce encapsulated what all of Fuchs' colleagues must have felt: 'What an unhappy life poor Klaus must have been leading these last years.' Klaus Fuchs was loved by many of his colleagues even though he had in fact betrayed them.[36]

GENIA'S LETTER

On the evening of 5 February, Rudolf Peierls phoned 'Whitehall One-Two-One-Two' – in those days the well-known number of Scotland Yard – and asked to speak to Special Branch. When he was connected he said that he had a letter he would like to reach Commander Burt by the following morning. He did not want to rely on the post and suggested that he give it to the guard of the train from Birmingham to London; could someone meet the train at Euston station and collect the letter? The train would be the 5 o'clock from Birmingham, due to arrive in Euston at 7.55 p.m. The receptionist at Scotland Yard left the telephone for a while and then returned to say, 'it would be all right – the letter would be collected from the guard'.

Peierls clearly was satisfied of Fuchs' guilt, as he told Commander Burt in his letter: 'I now undertake to help you in any way you wish, without reservations.' He continued: 'You will have understood my reasons for not committing myself to this before I knew what, if anything, I would be told in confidence.' Nonetheless, Peierls was 'still puzzled by a number of things that do not hang together. I can believe now that he may have had so much self-control as to deceive all those who believed themselves to be his friends. But even granting this, some things he said did not sound right.'[37]

As an example, Peierls commented on Fuchs' claimed attitudes to communism. Peierls had asked whether Fuchs 'really believed in the superiority of the Soviet system', to which Fuchs replied, 'You must remember what I went through under the Nazis.' Peierls told him he understood but was surprised that Fuchs 'continued to believe in all that while we were in America'. Fuchs confirmed that he did, but tried to explain himself by adding that he intended 'when the Russians had taken over everything to get up and say what he thought was wrong with the system'. This struck Peierls as utterly out of character, a level of 'naïve foolishness' that did 'not fit him at all'. Peierls added that Fuchs' surprised reaction to Perrin at the moment of his arrest suggested it 'sounds as if he expected to get away with it'.

With great insight, Peierls now interpreted these events as possibly showing that Fuchs 'has NOT changed his views; that he has until recently been mixed up with agents, and is now trying to protect them, once his own position has become untenable.' In Peierls' judgement Fuchs was 'still acting a part and a pretty tough one at that. [This] would explain why the picture does not look right. It would also explain his anxiety to assure the people that he has not given away any secrets recently.'[38]

Peierls had tried to persuade Fuchs to tell 'everything he knew'. Fuchs replied that he had talked freely before his arrest but would not say any more now because 'it would look as if he wanted to buy himself off'. Peierls thought that illogical, as it would have looked more like that before his arrest than afterwards.

Fuchs had given MI5 details of what he told the Russians, but revealed nothing of his contacts. Peierls concluded that it was likely that Fuchs' contacts were people 'whom none of his colleagues ever met'. Peierls added, 'I did not want to try and bully him – one cannot all at once re-adjust one's attitude to a man that has been such a close friend. However my wife, with whom I share my knowledge of these matters, and who in the past has had great influence on Fuchs, has written him a letter. We believe that if anything [will], this letter has a chance of moving him.'

As part of Rudolf Peierls' offer to help Commander Burt find the missing pieces of the puzzle, Genia Peierls would now apply her own special pressure. Genia's letter would turn out be one of the most significant actions of her life. Peierls included Genia's letter in his note to Burt, because 'you ought to know what we are doing, and also because I hope you can arrange for it to reach him with the least delay, and perhaps without being seen by too many people on the way'.[39]

Peierls delivered the two letters to the guard at Birmingham station, then returned home and called the Skinners. Genia also spoke to Herbert and asked, 'How long have you known?' 'Two weeks,' he replied. He also confirmed that Fuchs had passed information voluntarily, without being coerced, though when pressed by Genia he agreed that this was his and Erna's inference and not certain.

Genia then told Herbert, hesitantly, 'I wrote a letter.'

After some tentative back and forth, Herbert sensed the depth of her unease and proffered, 'Hmm – was it a nasty letter?'

Genia first denied it, and then opened up more: 'No. Well, sort of. If you like – appealing – to come all the way out.'[40]

She was clearly now very worried about the effect her letter might have on Fuchs, but it was on its way to London and beyond her power to call back.

Meanwhile, in Brixton Prison, following Peierls' visit, Klaus Fuchs had begun to write a letter on 6 February to Genia. He started by saying how wonderful Rudi's visit had been and then, with mock bravado, wrote, 'although I couldn't do anything to cheer him up'. Fuchs' inner turmoil is apparent as after an hour of writing all he managed to add was: 'Sometime I shall try and describe to you what went on in my mind. But you will have to be very patient.'[41] It was at this moment that Genia's letter to him arrived.

Genia Peierls had a profound intuitive understanding of human nature, and Klaus Fuchs was 'almost like a son' to her. First, she disturbed any defences he had erected with her remembrance of their shared freedom:

> I am writing to you in front of our sitting-room fire, where we so often talked about so many things. This is a hard letter to write, perhaps even a harder one to read, but you know me well enough not to expect me to mince my words.

Nor did she:

> I am taking it all much easier than everybody else, because my Russian childhood and youth taught me not to trust anybody, and to expect anyone and everyone to be a communist agent. Twenty years of freedom in England softened me, and I learned to like and trust people, or at any rate some of them. I certainly did trust you. Even more, I considered you the most decent man I knew. I do that even now. This is the reason why I am writing to you.

She now pricked his conscience:

> Do you realise what will be the effect of your trial on scientists here and in America? Specially in America where many of them are in difficulties [with McCarthy witch-hunts] already. Do you realise that they will be suspected not only by officials but by their own friends, because if you could, why not they?
>
> For your cause you did not <u>have</u> to be on such warm personal relations with them, to play with their children, and dance and drink and talk. You are such a quiet man that you could have kept yourself much more aloof. You were enjoying the best of the world you were trying to destroy. It is not honest.
>
> In a way I am glad that you failed in this, because these people taught you the value of humanity of warmth, of freedom. What did you do to them, Klaus? Not only that their faith in decency and humanity is shaken, but for years to come they will be suspected of being involved in this with you. Perhaps you did not think about it at the time, but you must think now.

*

Fuchs had told Rudolf that he didn't want to reveal the names of his contacts because this might be construed as an attempt to curry favour and thereby buy a lighter sentence. To this Genia gave short shrift in her letter:

> Klaus, don't be a child! This is the schoolboy code of honour. Impressions don't matter. You personally do not matter. The issues are too important for that. And you know it, otherwise you would have taken the only easy way out for you personally – to take your life. Thank you for not doing that. You could not leave all this terrible mess for others to sort out. This is your job, Klaus.

The emotional intensity of Fuchs' betrayal for her, and of her sadness at his situation, then led to the climax of her appeal:

> Oh Klaus, my tears are washing away the ink. I was so very fond of you, and I so much wanted [y]ou to be happy, and now you never will be.
>
> I still think that you are an honest man. It means that you do what you think right, whatever the cost. [Now] do the right thing. Try to save as much as you can of the decent and warm and tolerant, this free community of international science, which gave you so much these last ten years. You are now going through the hardest time a man can go through, you have burned your god [*sic*, small g]. God help you![42]

Fuchs, deeply troubled, now continued with his own letter, which the receipt of Genia's had interrupted: 'I have told myself almost every word you say, but it is good that you should say it again.' He tried to explain how he was able to maintain friendships even as he betrayed their trust, and claimed it to be 'controlled schizophrenia'. Except 'I didn't control the control, it controlled me.' He admitted, 'It is my job to try and clear up the mess I have made. I am afraid I did shirk it at first, and that made the mess even worse.' The letter continues with his belief that he could have cut a deal with the authorities who, he claimed, 'gave me an easier way out: I could have left Harwell to go to a university a free man, free from everything, free from friends, with no faith left to start a new life.' What's more, Fuchs wrote, 'I could even have stayed at Harwell', if he had admitted 'just one little thing [the espionage in New York, which VENONA had exposed] and kept quiet about everything else'.

Hints of his despair come through where he explains, 'I bungled the "take your life" stage; yes, I went through that too, before the arrest.' His letter has a postscript: 'Sorry I haven't got anybody to type this for me. I

62

In replying to this letter, please write on the envelope:—

Number....044.... Name....Fuchs K.......

.............Brixton..Prison

Dear Genia,

It was wonderful of Rudi to visit me on Saturday, although I couldn't do anything to cheer him up. On the contrary it is up to you.

Do you mind if I talk of other things? Some time I shall try and describe to you what went on in my mind. But you will have to be very patient.

I have been sitting here for an hour trying to think what to write next, when your letter arrived. I have told myself almost every word you say, but it is good that you should say it again. I know what I have done to them and that is why I am here. You ask "Perhaps you did not think about it at the time." Genia, I didn't, and that is the greatest horror I had to face when I looked at myself. You don't know what I had done to my own mind; and I thought I knew what I was doing. And there was this simple thing, obvious to the simplest decent creature, and I forgot it. didn't think of it.

No. 243   (21442–3-11-42)

Fuchs' handwritten letter to Genia Peierls

hope you can read it. And don't worry if you don't see the tears. I have learned to cry again. And to love again. K.'[43]

Genia's appeal cut Klaus Fuchs to the quick. He now agreed to see Jim Skardon again and, later, two FBI agents. But he had a new dilemma. On the one hand he had to assuage his conscience and protect his former scientific colleagues and their families from suspicion and prosecution by the Security Services, yet on the other he still felt he could not reveal information that might incriminate any of his contacts.

FALLOUT

Herbert and Erna Skinner had planned to visit Fuchs on Tuesday 7 February but the previous evening they were besieged by 'a scandal press phone call'. Fearing a press barrage they decided that their housekeeper, Vera Pohle, should apply for the visit and they would then hope to be able to come on Wednesday without the press being alerted. Herbert acknowledged, 'We got your touching letter today. I can only say I believe you, I had realised it before. But there remains the past I'm afraid. In haste, Herbert.'

Erna's letter, which accompanied Herbert's, was more encouraging. She said she would come 'as soon as I can', but Rudolf had gone first to find out Fuchs' personal needs as 'I might break down and be useless.' She endorsed Herbert's news, 'Now the press makes it very hard for us but we shall come as soon as we can. Do smile for me.' She added a postscript: 'And please keep on writing.'[44]

Instead of the Skinners, a cousin of Fuchs visited him on 7 February. The warder who listened in recorded that most of their conversation concerned their health, and 'if he wanted anything sent in etc.' The only noteworthy item was that Fuchs said, 'If you write to my father, tell him that I have only done what I considered to be right.'[45]

This apparent calm was disrupted, however, when the Skinners eventually visited him on 8 February. Now Fuchs caught his first glimpse of the unexpected fallout from his actions. Erna had received a cable from her father in the United States, telling her that he was seriously ill and asking her and Herbert to visit him there. This family imperative was frustrated, however, because MI5 stepped in and through Henry Arnold said it was 'in the highest degree undesirable' that the Skinners go to the USA where they would be 'besieged by Press reporters and subjected to considerable pressure to make statements about the FUCHS case'. Herbert nonetheless felt they ought to go, but was then bullied by the authorities, who reminded him 'that he was a Government Servant subject to the Official Secrets Acts, and therefore precluded from imparting any information whatever about matters which [he had learned through his employment], and this with particular reference to anything connected with FUCHS'. In addition he was 'warned that his wife should regard herself as being in the same position, since her knowledge derives from him'.[46]

This news had arrived immediately before they visited Fuchs in prison and must have framed their meeting. Afterwards, Fuchs wrote to them to say he had been 'looking forward to your visit but not prepared for the news you brought. It stunned me and I didn't know what to say.' Nothing mattered, apparently, 'except that I had hurt you both so terribly'. This left him with a 'terrible feeling of helplessness – which I tried to hide'. He asked that they 'don't worry too much about me', and as he was only allowed one visit a day, to let him know as he didn't want to 'use up this privilege on anyone else'. He ended, 'And please smile – through the tears – for me.'[47]

Herbert replied two days later with the good news that Erna's father was somewhat better, so there was no need for them to visit the United States after all. However, Skinner spelled out his feelings: 'We may visit you again one day but at the moment I think there is no point in heart to heart conversations.'[48] A week later, on 19 February, Erna's letter showed the ebb and flow of her turmoil as she began, 'I could not write last week because I would have been very bitter and have hurt you.' The three barely legible pages urged him not to worry about rumours that might appear in the newspapers, such as 'that I am your sister' and that 'Herbert and I have fled the country'. She included some cod philosophy on the nature of life, and promised to 'try and come to see you again as soon as possible'.[49]

That second visit took place on Saturday 25 February. Fuchs seems to have begun to adjust to the reality of his changed circumstances, for when he wrote to the Skinners two days later he admitted, 'when I was waiting, I wished you would not come, but afterwards I was glad you did'. After this promising start the letter rapidly fell apart. There followed two pages on the nature of friendship, written in abstract generalities with little personal resonance for the Skinners, which included mention of an unnamed past lover from a time when he had been 'idealistic and immature'. Fuchs and this mystery woman were 'left-wing intellectuals', working 'for the same thing' and 'an ideal partnership for the Devil and the Devil she was'. She had left him, he wrote, and with that news Fuchs went to bed, for the letter restarted, 'It is Tuesday morning now' and 'I shall just babble a bit and then stop.'[50]

The self-indulgent epistle showed no contrition. Its tenor suggests Fuchs was deluded, believing their friendship had suffered merely a minor blip. His bumbling suggestion that he might 'salvage a little bit of self-respect out of all this' showed a complete lack of empathy for the Skinners' feelings.

Two weeks passed before Erna sent a brief reply. She began, 'One day I may be able to write to you more fully' – but not yet, obviously. 'I feel that you do not yet understand the extent of dismay you have brought to all of us,' she wrote, and if he needed any pointers towards understanding, her descriptions of being 'so flagrantly deceived', 'wounded', and 'will prove difficult to heal' would have been a start. Herbert added some lines at the end of Erna's note, which did nothing to ease Fuchs' anguish: 'It will take a long time to get over the fact that you deceived us so grossly.' Herbert pointed out that Fuchs had done damage to 'the country as a whole' and 'in joining Harwell, although you did much to help in building it up, you have involved it in some of the consequences of your crime'. While Herbert offered a small olive branch by saying that he had 'not written in anger [but] with affection still left', he let there be no doubt that he was cut to the quick: 'There is no excuse for what you have done, and, try as I may, I cannot understand it.'[51]

Fuchs' arrest made the departure of 'Sonya' (Ursula Beurton) from England 'an urgent necessity'. She wondered at once how far the discovery of Fuchs' activities concerned her. She was sure there was no evidence of their assignations as they had never visited each other's homes, and were professional enough to know that their meetings in the countryside had not been observed. She decided that the only risk to her was betrayal by Fuchs or if MI5 associated the link – German communist, known to her brother. The British press then announced that Fuchs had 'met a foreign woman with black hair in Banbury'. Sonya now expected her arrest 'any day'.[52] She decided that if that were to happen, she would refuse to make a statement.

She left England on 28 February, the day before Fuchs' trial began, flying from London to Hamburg and on to East Berlin.[53] She never knew whether MI5's failure to connect her with Fuchs had been incompetence, or whether they had allowed her to get away 'since further discovery would have increased their disgrace'.[54] If it was the latter, conspiracy theorists have long debated whether it was to 'let sleeping dogs lie' and not add to the uproar – as would later be the case with Kim Philby's defection – or whether there was someone in MI5 working for the Soviet Union who protected her. This question has never been resolved.

20

Trials and Tribulations

Fuchs had been arrested on 2 February 1950 and would be held in Brixton Prison pending appearance at Bow Street Magistrates' Court on 10 February. On 8 February the prosecution team and main witnesses – Jim Skardon, Henry Arnold and Michael Perrin – met with the Director of Public Prosecutions (DPP), Sir Theobald Mathew, and Mr Hill, the Security Services' legal advisor. The gathering took place at teatime in the Temple Gardens chambers of the prosecuting counsel, a barrister with a name that could have graced a Dickensian novel, Mr Christmas Humphreys. In addition to the normal issue of establishing the guilt of the accused person there were two other concerns of national and international interest. First, the Security Services were party to evidence so secret that they could not share it with the prosecution let alone with the court; for this reason Fuchs' confession would play a singular role in the trial. This could raise problems, both with the nature of Skardon's dangerous hints of inducement to Fuchs but also because it could lead to a public perception that MI5 was incompetent in having overlooked Fuchs' duplicity for seven years. Second, there was the delicate issue for the Foreign Office of relations with the Americans; much of Fuchs' espionage had been committed in the United States and his role had been exposed thanks to VENONA evidence. Future relations between these one-time atomic collaborators would be seriously tested by the proceedings.[1]

These delicacies soon showed themselves when Mr Humphreys presented a draft of his intended opening statement. Hill made some modifications to bring it into line with the attitude the Foreign Office was taking on the matter; Perrin then made further suggestions to cover aspects from the Ministry of Supply's position.[2] Perrin's directive from the British government made his task difficult: the government would 'not admit that the Russians had exploded an atomic bomb' nor even that they had one, so no mention could be made of Fuchs having supplied the information that had enabled them to do just that. The most the government would concede was that 'the Russians had caused an atomic explosion' of unspecified origin. Perrin thought that if it came out in open court that Fuchs had given the Russians full details of the first plutonium bomb, this 'would create alarm and despondency both here and in America'. This decision was politically motivated: the United Kingdom was in the middle of a general election campaign, and polling day – 23 February – was but two weeks away.

The DPP and Mr Humphreys accepted this argument and agreed the final form of the opening speech with Perrin. Hill asked for an extra copy of Humphreys' opening remarks, as he had 'promised one copy to the representative of the FBI who is now in the UK cooperating with us on the case'.[3] The meeting next considered Skardon's evidence, upon which the main case would rely.

AT BOW STREET

Two days later, Klaus Fuchs was brought from Brixton Prison to the Bow Street Magistrates' Court for his initial arraignment. Sir Laurence Dunne, the Chief Magistrate, presided. No. 3 court, on the second floor, was a small mahogany-panelled room that could seat about twenty-five people. Two hours before the doors opened, however, about sixty reporters – 'many of them American' – waited outside the court. No members of the general public were allowed in; the few seats were filled and the remaining reporters 'scribbled their notes in a huddled crowd'.[4]

Fuchs later recalled his own memory of the occasion.[5] To reach the court from the cells beneath, he walked up some stairs that led to a fenced-off bench for the accused. His defence lawyer asked, 'Do you know what the maximum sentence is?', to which Fuchs replied, 'It looks to me like death.' 'No!' replied his counsel, 'It's 14 years.' Fuchs recalled, 'It was a shock. For someone who has come to terms with the end of his life, suddenly you are told you will continue to live – you have to get used to the idea. Fourteen years: How many days, how many hours, what do you do for that time?' Fuchs next either showed his humanity, or possibly re-invented himself later, claiming he decided that to pass this length of time, 'I must help others in jail. You have to live with them. Many are unhappy people who somehow got there, and [doing so] helped me get through by keeping busy.'

That, at least, is what Fuchs recalled years afterwards. Christmas Humphreys rose and announced to the court that there were two charges under Section 1.1(c) of the Official Secrets Act, 1911. The first that 'on a day in 1947, for a purpose prejudicial to the safety or interests of the State, [Fuchs] communicated to a person unknown, information relating to atomic research which was calculated to be, or might be, directly or indirectly useful to an enemy'. He added: 'That offence took place in England.' The second offence was that Fuchs 'being a British subject' did something similar, 'on a day in February 1945 for a purpose prejudicial to the safety or interests of the State, in the USA'.[6]

The prosecution was focusing only on Fuchs' espionage after 1945, while at Los Alamos and at Harwell. Fuchs' espionage in Birmingham was not on the charge sheet.

Humphreys, a lean man with a hawk-like nose and piercing eyes reminiscent of Sherlock Holmes, cut an impressive figure in his silk gown and wig. He promised to call three witnesses, to each of whom Fuchs had 'made statements, orally, which amount to a confession of these two charges'. Fuchs made a written statement to Skardon, 'all due precautions having been taken to ensure that [it] was made voluntarily and without threat or promise'. As we have seen, and as the prosecution team continued to worry, the claim that it was made 'without promise' was debatable. The evidence of the three witnesses and the written statement would constitute the case for the prosecution.

Humphreys gave a brief description of Fuchs' early life where he 'joined the German Communist Party' and came to England as a refugee – 'so he says' – from Nazi oppression. Humphreys mentioned Fuchs' internment and continued, 'In 1942 [sic] atomic research was being intensified in more than one country, certainly in England.'* He then summarized the reason for hiring Fuchs at this crucial juncture of the war: 'The very finest brains available were needed to assist in that research and such brains as Dr. Fuchs possesses are very rare indeed.' Fuchs, he said, was one of the 'finest theoretical physicists living', his 'great brain was harnessed to atomic research' with Rudolf Peierls at Birmingham University 'after very careful examination of his background and mental make-up'.

Humphreys produced evidence of Fuchs' oath of allegiance of 31 July 1942 and his naturalization as a British subject, in which he had sworn 'to be faithful and bear true allegiance to His Majesty, King George VI, his heirs and successors, according to law'. Now in full rhetorical flow, Humphreys told the court that although Fuchs had always impressed his

---

* This mention of 1942 was the first public utterance of a date in the trial of Fuchs and has become incorrectly established in the received wisdom as the year in which Fuchs began his espionage. The *Daily Telegraph* of 11 February 1950, for example, headlined 'Jekyll and Hyde Betrayal since 1942' and referred to 'the first meeting ... in early 1942'. TNA KV 2/1263, s. 29a.

superiors as being a thoroughly security-minded person, 'it is now clear that such an oath of allegiance meant nothing whatsoever to a man whose mind was irrevocably wedded to communist principle'. Before Fuchs was naturalized, Humphreys asserted, 'He signed the usual security undertaking.'[7] Humphreys narrated Fuchs' career of espionage in which 'for a long time he confined the information he gave to the product of his own brain, but as time went on, this developed into something more'. Fuchs confirmed that his contacts were 'certainly Russian, but often other nationalities', and Humphreys pithily summarized the pressure on Fuchs: 'He said he realised he was carrying his life in his own hands, but had done this during his underground days in Germany.'

The prosecution wanted to ensure there was no question about the goal of Fuchs' espionage. 'Lest there be any doubt, Sir, that his communications were to the USSR and not merely to a vague and unspecified agent of a foreign power, he told Mr Skardon before making his written statement that the first meetings were in London and at one stage he visited the Soviet Embassy in Kensington Palace Gardens.'

Humphreys said it was 'undesirable and unnecessary that I should here reveal how much of the information' passed to the Russians were the 'results of his own research and how much [was] acquired from his colleagues'. Nonetheless 'you will hear evidence from experts that what he did reveal was of the highest value to a potential enemy'. Humphreys then remarked, 'He did receive money.' This referred to Fuchs having accepted expenses in the early days of his espionage and 'to taking the sum of £100 shortly after returning to England in 1946'. This was but a 'symbolic gesture signifying his subservience to the [communist] cause'. However, 'his real motive, as shown by his statements, reiterated many times, was undoubted, unswerving devotion to the cause of Russian Communism'.

Now Humphreys laid on the sarcasm as he exploited Fuchs' claim to have separated his mind into two. 'The mind of the accused may possibly be unique and set a new precedent in the world of psychology,' he opined. One half of Fuchs' mind, he said, was 'beyond the reach of reason and the impact of facts. The other half lived in the world of normal relationships and friendships with colleagues.' Fuchs' self-description of this as 'controlled schizophrenia' was the 'classical example of that immortal duality in English literature – Dr Jekyll and Mr Hyde'.

Humphreys compared Fuchs' Dr Jekyll – 'a normal citizen, happy in the use of his magnificent brain in the cause of science' – with 'Mr Hyde, [where] he was betraying week by week his oath of allegiance, his vows of security, and the friendships of his friends. Outwardly he appeared to be, to all about him, a loyal Englishman by adoption. Inwardly, unknown to all about him, he was a political fanatic on the pay-roll of a foreign power.' His 'sudden' contact with Arnold, at which he 'volunteered news of his father', was, Humphreys hinted, possibly because he suspected enquiries were already being made.[8]

Arnold was now placed at the heart of Humphreys' narrative. Humphreys explained how Fuchs had told Arnold about his father's status in eastern Germany, at which Arnold alerted MI5; Fuchs was then questioned by Skardon. After 'point blank denials of point blank accusations of treachery he suddenly volunteered to answer questions'. Then, in Humphreys' narrative, 'Finally on January 26 of this year [Fuchs] had clearly reached a mental crisis. He confessed to Mr Arnold that he had communicated a great deal of information.'[9] Following this, Fuchs made a written confession to Skardon, which would have been produced in court. Humphreys then read an abbreviated version of Fuchs' statement to the court and added that Fuchs had also made a statement of technical information to Mr Perrin, who would testify that this was 'information of the greatest possible value to a potential enemy'.

The three witnesses were then called.[10] First was Commander Burt, who presented the Attorney General's 'fiat consenting to the proceedings', which became exhibit 1, and Fuchs' certificate of naturalization and oath of allegiance, dated 31 July 1942, which became exhibit 2. No evidence that he had signed the Official Secrets Act was presented.

The next witness was Wing Commander Henry Arnold. He testified that he had always impressed on Fuchs the need for secrecy and safeguarding official information and that Fuchs appeared to be 'a most security-minded scientist'. He continued, 'On 26 January, 1950, this being the morning that Dr FUCHS was seeing Mr. Skardon, Dr FUCHS came to see him (Arnold).' When Arnold then 'asked Dr FUCHS whether he had in fact disclosed certain very important information to the Russians about atomic research', Fuchs confirmed that he had and 'ended up by saying that this information was secret'.[11]

The news media duly reported that Fuchs had made his confession first to Arnold.[12] In court Arnold was not cross-examined; the next witness – Skardon – was cross-examined, but there is no correction of the impression given in Arnold's testimony nor, apparently, did Skardon claim that Fuchs had confessed to him on 24 January. Fuchs' counsel, Mr Halsall, asked about Fuchs' cooperativeness and Skardon said that 'from the afternoon of the 24th January 1950, Dr FUCHS had been cooperative with him and had helped all he could'.[13] The tactic seems to have been to play as if the first confession to Skardon, potentially tainted with inducement, never happened. Skardon produced the original voluntary statement which he had taken down at Fuchs' dictation on 27 January, and this became exhibit 3. He also confirmed that the handwriting on the certificate of naturalization was that of Fuchs.

The last witness was Mr Perrin. He said that Fuchs had passed information during his time in Birmingham 'of great use to a potential [sic] enemy'. Perrin made similar assessments about Fuchs' espionage in the United States, and post-war at Harwell.*

Exhibit 4, which was 'later produced' by Perrin, was the 'security undertaking that Fuchs signed in 1944'.[14] This was prior to his secondment to the United States. Again no evidence was presented that he signed the Official Secrets Act in 1941, and there is no evidence that Perrin ever satisfied the request made for this document by Hill on 6 February. As we have seen, the charges against Fuchs related only to the USA in 1945 and to the United Kingdom in 1947; the omission of his earlier espionage in the charge may be because of the lack of evidence that he had signed the Official Secrets Act before 1942. Perrin's evidence, nonetheless, included Fuchs' espionage during that period.

The press, meanwhile, asked for a copy of exhibit 3 – Fuchs' statement to Skardon. This, however, was declared secret and was retained by Commander Burt. Thus it was not possible to compare what Fuchs actually said in court with what he was reported to have said when he confessed. One consequence was that the phrase 'of use to a potential enemy' became part of the public perception of Fuchs' transgression.

Sir Laurence Dunne, the Chief Magistrate, was unsurprisingly satisfied that there was a case to answer, and formally charged Fuchs. Throughout the proceedings Fuchs 'did not utter a word' and 'showed no sign of emotion'.[15] Mr Halsall, Fuchs' defence counsel, pleaded 'Not Guilty' on his behalf, and reserved his defence. Fuchs was committed for trial at the Central Criminal Court, the Old Bailey, at the sessions commencing 28 February. He would appear in front of the Lord Chief Justice, Lord Goddard, who would be both judge and jury.

GRAVE CRITICISM OF MI5

On 18 February Sir Hartley Shawcross, the Attorney General, wrote to Sir Theobald Mathew, the Director of Public Prosecutions, enclosing a

---

* Russia was at no stage an enemy of the United Kingdom during Fuchs' Birmingham period but had become so by 1950. Fuchs' espionage at Harwell, which was on the charge sheet, is consistent with Perrin's description.

letter from Brigadier Telford Taylor, who had been the US Chief Counsel at the Nuremberg trials. This gave an early clue of the fallout in North America from the Fuchs affair. The news had broken there 'close on the heels of the wide publicity about the H-bomb'. This had helped to make it a 'great sensation' in the United States, and things took a 'very unfortunate turn' when *The New York Times* carried a big story that 'Fuchs has a long background of Communist sympathy which the FBI uncovered with no special difficulty.' A prominent Senator had 'declared himself unable to throw light on the fact that the British apparently had not learned of this background, while Dr Fuchs worked for years in atomic matters'.

Taylor commented with the unfortunate pun, 'this whole episode has explosive possibilities'. He was concerned about its implications for Anglo-American relations, as it was already 'being seized on by those misguided people who think that secrecy and security are invariably synonymous, and who oppose any kind of international collaboration, even with our most trusted allies in the field of secret weapons'. Taylor recommended that if there are 'any facts which can be disclosed and which would put the British in a better light on this matter, the time for such disclosure is now, before preconceptions take hold, which nothing can eradicate'.[16]

Shawcross was also an MP, and preparing to fight in the general election. He now advised the DPP in a letter sent from his constituency office in St Helens, Lancashire: 'Whoever succeeds me in my present office and conducts the Fuchs prosecution will want to be very fully briefed on the circumstances.' He then came to the sharpest potentially damning puzzle: 'I am afraid it does seem to me the most amazing thing that a German refugee who, not being a Jew, was presumably a refugee on account of Communist sympathies, should have been given a post of such high security and should have remained undetected for so long.' He then gave a warning: 'I am afraid there will be grave criticism of MI5 and I think it may be desirable for the Attorney-General [himself] to make some statement either in his opening if the man pleads guilty or after conviction if he is convicted about the circumstances in which MI5 failed to discover his Communist sympathies.'[17]

Two days later the DPP rang Hill, the Security Service legal advisor, to say that Shawcross had received letters from 'two Members of Parliament' about MI5's perceived failure to have spotted the 'Communist' Fuchs and recommended that a statement be made at the trial. Hill hedged, saying that 'no quick decision could be given', and arranged that the DPP write formally to Liddell.[18]

Liddell discussed this with his division heads and with Hill on 22

February. They judged that there was no need to make a statement at the trial because 'the matter had been adequately covered in the opening made by Mr Humphreys at the Magistrates' Court'.[19] Nonetheless they recognized that 'questions would be asked in the House as to why FUCHS had been allowed to remain at Harwell, and why his espionage activities had remained so long undetected'. They agreed that their Counter-Espionage Division should prepare a statement to answer three questions.

First, 'Why was FUCHS passed and vetted for his job at Harwell?' They agreed that the Ministry of Supply must answer that. Second, 'Why were his espionage activities not detected earlier?' Third, 'Was it a fact that the FBI knew about the Communist activities of FUCHS before the Security Services?' The directors thought that if a statement was prepared along these lines and agreed with the Ministry of Supply, it would be the basis for any questions which it 'could reasonably be foreseen would be put on this case'.[20]

Liddell then explained to the DPP that MI5 had decided not to make a statement at this time.

THE EVE OF TRIAL

The date for Fuchs' trial at the Old Bailey had been set for 1 March. On the evening of 28 February Sir Hartley Shawcross called a conference to consider the points that might arise the next day.[21]

Perrin opened by saying that he had discussed the case with Lord Portal and Sir Archibald Rowlands, the Permanent Secretary at the Ministry of Supply. There was a possibility that Fuchs might recant his confession: the sole evidence. Rudolf Peierls' comment about Fuchs possibly having had a nervous breakdown worried them; what if Fuchs were to claim to have committed at most some minor misdemeanour and blame his extended confession on the product of a fevered imagination? At no stage had there been a legal advisor present when Fuchs made his statement, and MI5 now worried that a canny defence counsel might create problems.

Perrin said that Portal and Rowlands were both of the opinion that not enough had been said in the Magistrates' Court about the extent of the information which Fuchs had passed to the Russians. They knew the extent of Fuchs' espionage spanning seven years, whereas the charge sheet focused on a subset where the prosecution had evidence of his perfidy in the form of his 1944 agreement to secrecy. Perrin presented a paper on what they felt should be said. In summary, this stated that while in Birmingham Fuchs had revealed the method for separating U235, which might be used in an atomic bomb. Next, in New York he had worked closely with a section of the American organization responsible for the design and construction of one of the production plants at Oak Ridge. This plant used the same process for separating U235 as Fuchs had studied at Birmingham. Perrin added that any statement should include that the information passed by Fuchs in these two periods 'would have been of great value to Russia under two heads. First, in disclosing the fundamental principles on which one method of separating the uranium isotopes was based; secondly in showing the importance attached to the project by the British and American Governments, and in confirming speculation, current at the time, that it would probably prove practicable to design and make an atomic bomb using pure U235.'

The litany continued, covering much of what we have already seen, but now with the expert assessment of the implications of Fuchs' treachery. Perrin indicated that Fuchs' information about plutonium would have saved the Russians 'a long period of research and development' in producing this 'explosive ingredient in an atomic bomb' and, without explicitly saying so, left the clear implication that the Soviet atomic bomb test of a few months earlier had been a direct result of Fuchs' espionage.

After Perrin described the impact of Fuchs' treachery during the war, his continued espionage at Harwell seemed relatively minor, except when it became apparent that by giving details about plutonium production at Windscale together with American data, he had enabled the Russians to infer Western ability to defend itself against a nuclear threat. Arguably Fuchs' post-war espionage was the most dangerous threat to the United Kingdom. In the Second World War there were other spies whose information corroborated and duplicated Fuchs; furthermore, Russia was at that time an ally. At Harwell, Fuchs gave information to a Cold War enemy at a time when Stalin, as was now known, had designs on Western Europe. Through Fuchs, the Soviet Union knew the state of both US and UK readiness. Finally, Perrin said that Fuchs had told his Soviet contact the general principles underlying the H-bomb.[22]

He proposed that this evidence be presented by the Attorney General in his opening statement, or by Perrin in the witness box. No doubt this would convince the court of Fuchs' extreme perfidy, but Sir Roger Makins of the Foreign Office balked at such 'sensational information being discussed at the trial, which would provide the American Press with further sensational news to publish'.[23] They agreed that none of this could be presented in open court, and that it was highly undesirable for any part of the proceedings to be held in camera, if it could be avoided. The conference therefore decided not to adopt Perrin's suggestion.

Shawcross now raised the concern about MI5's perceived failure, which he had previously raised with Liddell but to little effect. In Shawcross' opinion the Lord Chief Justice was likely to ask how Fuchs came to be employed at Harwell, when he was a known communist 'from 1942 onwards [*sic*]'. He stated that the authorities knew that Fuchs was a communist and that this 'appeared in Home Office files'. Dick White immediately contradicted this by pointing out that MI5 'had no knowledge that FUCHS had ever been a member of the British Communist Party'. All they knew was the Gestapo report, which 'had never been confirmed by Police reports in this country'.[24]

If there was any further debate, the minutes do not show it. The prosecution would rely totally on Fuchs' confession, and assessed that his defence would question its nature and legal validity. Now at the eleventh hour there was a violation of procedure that could have influenced the outcome had it been known, and had the trial been overseen by a less prejudiced judge. The Director of Public Prosecutions had somehow learned that Fuchs' defence counsel, Mr Curtis-Bennett, believed that Fuchs had indeed invented the whole story. Peierls' conjecture seemed to have struck home with the defence, or perhaps the fragments that MI5 had picked up from eavesdropping had raised the spectre in their minds. In any event, the DPP was worried that at the Magistrates' Court, Fuchs had entered a plea of 'Not Guilty'; if he were to maintain this plea in the trial at the Old Bailey, and in addition claim that his confession was nothing more than a figment of his imagination, it would be necessary for the prosecution to present highly sensitive evidence in court. That would undermine the strategy to avoid proceedings in camera. So on the eve of the Old Bailey trial, in a complete violation of procedure, 'arrangements were accordingly made for Mr Perrin to meet Mr Curtis-Bennett later that evening' with the express hope that Perrin would 'convince him that [Fuchs'] story is genuine'.[25]

Perrin was successful. Curtis-Bennett was prepared to accept that Fuchs' statement was indeed factual, and he would not contest it. All was at last in place for Fuchs to condemn himself. Four months later, Fuchs added a remarkable postscript to the machinations between the prosecution and his counsel. In his remarks about Skardon's 'bargain' – that his admission would enable him to remain at Harwell and not be prosecuted – Fuchs remarked: 'Although [these] facts would have been of great value in a plea for mitigation, I agreed through my Counsel not to mention these facts during my trial', and then in a remarkable explanation as to why he made this decision, 'since in the opinion of the prosecution this might have been prejudicial to the interests of this country'.[26]

THE FINAL VISIT

On 28 February, the day before Fuchs' trial, Rudolf and Genia Peierls visited him in prison to ask about some of the things they simply could not understand. He drank, and although always sober, how could a spy take such a risk? He was about to adopt a nephew – the son of his sister who had committed suicide under the Nazis. Fuchs' father, Emil, had been looking after the boy but was getting old; how could Klaus tie a child so closely to himself when there was this awful secret in his life? Fuchs was unable to offer explanations for any of this, but he did convince them that the charges were justified.

It was the only time Genia saw Fuchs in jail, and the last time that the trio of friends would meet.

THE HANGING JUDGE

Rayner Goddard was the last of the hanging judges and a domineering, malevolent bully who delighted in donning the black cap before announcing a death sentence. According to his clerk, Goddard's perverse pleasure in having this power was so extreme that he would ejaculate when condemning a prisoner to death, and 'a fresh pair of trousers had to be brought to court on those occasions'.[27] Luckily this valet service was not required when Goddard sat in judgement over Klaus Fuchs, because passing secrets in wartime to an ally – which was the status of the Soviet Union, at least after June 1941 – was not a capital offence. Nonetheless, Goddard's frustration at being unable to have Fuchs executed for treason is all too clear in the proceedings.

At the Old Bailey, Fuchs' espionage now divided into four charges. Their substance was essentially the same as at the Magistrates' Court, but the first charge referred to 'a day in 1943 in the city of Birmingham'; second, 'on a day unknown between 31 December 1943 and 1 August 1944 in the city of New York'; third, 'on a day unknown in February 1945' at Boston, Massachusetts; and finally, 'on a day in 1947 in Berkshire'. Any fear that Fuchs might contest the case evaporated as he pleaded 'Guilty'.[28]

The Attorney General, Sir Hartley Shawcross, appeared with Mr Christmas Humphreys for the prosecution, Fuchs being defended by Mr Curtis-Bennett, assisted by Mr Malcolm Morris. Shawcross had a pleasant, genial face, his half-moon spectacles giving him a bookish appearance. He described the case to be 'of the utmost gravity' and 'as serious as any which has ever been prosecuted under this Statute'. To press this point, he explained that although Fuchs had communicated information 'extending over, perhaps, seven years', the indictment would relate to just 'four specific cases'. And – preaching to the converted in Lord Goddard – he emphasized that 'the country to which the information is conveyed need not be an actual or present enemy. It is enough that the foreign country be a potential enemy, one which, owing to some unhappy change in circumstances, might become an actual enemy, although perhaps a friend at the time that the information was communicated.'

As the Attorney General paused to draw breath, Lord Goddard helped the prosecution case by commenting, 'Or might never become an enemy.' Shawcross responded, 'My Lord, in this case the information was in fact conveyed to agents of the Government of the Soviet Union.' Aware that the case would be reported widely, he added that Britain's relations with Russia left 'much to be desired but they are not those of enmity'; however, to ensure his case against Fuchs retained maximum power, he continued, 'but none the less it must have been quite obvious to the prisoner that the information he was conveying to the agents of that Government would have its maximum value if, as he apparently thought might be possible, that country ever did become an actual and open enemy'.

Next, in 'fairness to the prisoner, and as a warning to others', Shawcross said 'a word or two about motive', because this would 'make explicable facts which in the absence of expressed motive might be most difficult to understand'. He began, 'The prisoner is a communist, and that is at once the explanation and indeed the tragedy of the case.' With high rhetoric Shawcross assessed those 'indoctrinated with the communist belief' as 'misguided', and because this desire to 'build a new world' would inexorably mean 'a world dominated by a single power' – the Soviet Union – Fuchs had done 'great harm to the country that he adopted and which adopted him'.

He outlined Fuchs' early life to the point where he left Germany in 1933, at which Goddard made his second intervention: 'Do you know whether he left Germany because of the fear of persecution?' to which Shawcross answered 'Yes, My Lord' and expanded on the background. He then came to Fuchs' time in England and his work in Birmingham.

At this point Shawcross' prosecution becomes error prone. First, he asserted that Fuchs was interned in Canada 'until the beginning of 1942'. Yet, as we know, he was working with Peierls from May 1941 and already making assignations with the Soviets that same year. When he was released, Shawcross had him at 'Glasgow' rather than Edinburgh University. These slips do not give confidence in the next bizarre claim in Shawcross' narrative where for the first time he presented, as exhibit 4, 'a document in which attention was drawn to the security nature of his work, and indeed, to the provisions of the very Statute under which he is now prosecuted'. This clear reference to Fuchs having signed the Official Secrets Act is dated '18 June 1942 [sic]'. This date is not a typing error, for Shawcross continued, 'In the following month (sic) he applied for naturalisation as a British subject' – Fuchs signed the Oath of Allegiance on 31 July 1942.[29] Unless Shawcross here was compounding his mistakes, it would appear that Fuchs had been working with Peierls for over a year and, we now know, in contact with Soviet agents for a similar time, without having completed the bureaucracy of National Security. For a trial of such huge significance, these are hardly trifling issues. If Shawcross was wrong about when Fuchs took the Oath of Allegiance, it raises questions about when he signed the Official Secrets Act, or whether he did so before 1944. Its implications for Fuchs' relations with Peierls and the secret MAUD research in 1941 are at the least muddied.[30]

Shawcross then went through Fuchs' statement and history, along similar lines to what transpired at the Magistrates' Court, until he came to a delicate point: 'I [Fuchs] was then confronted with evidence that I had given away information in New York. I was given the chance of admitting it and staying on at Harwell or in clearing out. I was not sure enough of myself to stay at Harwell and therefore I denied the allegation and decided that I would have to leave Harwell.'

Lord Goddard now intervened: 'Does he mean this was in his own mind?' Goddard here seems to be establishing whether Fuchs has been induced to confess or has taken a decision of his own volition. Shawcross replied: 'My Lord, that is what he seems to have understood. It is not a correct account of what happened but that is what he appears to have understood. What he was being confronted with were the incidents in America. His whole course of conduct had not at that time been discovered.'

It is moot whether Shawcross was telling the whole truth with this reply. In any event, Fuchs' counsel raised no question, and by stressing that Fuchs' 'whole course of action' had yet to be discovered, Shawcross had cleverly opened an escape route for MI5: were the defence to claim that an offer was made to Fuchs, Shawcross could respond that this was before they realized the extent of Fuchs' espionage.

Next Shawcross attacked Fuchs' morality. Fuchs, he said, had breached 'the loyalty that he would, one would suppose naturally, feel towards the country which had befriended him, which had enabled him to complete his training and to become a great scientist'. The loyalties that Fuchs owed to the king, 'who had granted him the privilege of British nationality', had been 'cast aside in favour of his loyalty to the spurious ideology of Russian Communism'.

The general election had taken place just a week earlier and Shawcross'

Labour Party had been returned with a slender majority. With a shrewd political eye to the future, Shawcross now created a myth for the attendant media – and through them, the British public – that Fuchs' treachery had not left Britain's cupboard of atomic secrets bare. 'My Lord, as to the value of the information which he did convey, it is perhaps not in the public interest to say more than this: There were, of course, many fields of atomic research and of the general and experimental and developmental work in regard to atomic energy which were being carried on, which were unknown to him, and these fields were consequently protected against his betrayal.'

While it is true that there was work in atomic and nuclear structure taking place, of which Fuchs would have been more spectator than practitioner, this was mainly published in the open literature. In the field of concern to the trial – atomic energy and nuclear weapons – Fuchs was at the vanguard of research and everything of real significance that he could have passed on, he had. Having offered this placebo, Shawcross ensured he did not undermine his case and emphasized Fuchs' disclosures were 'very grave indeed'.

Finally, for the benefit of international consumption, he reminded the court that Britain did not induce 'sinister confession extracted in one way or another after a long period of secret incarceration incommunicado, and by methods that one knows not of, which have become a characteristic of proceedings in certain foreign countries'. Fuchs' confession was made 'whilst he was still a free man, able to come and go as he chose, to consult with his friends, to take the advice of his lawyers, that upon his arrest he was immediately brought to trial and that at that trial before your Lordship, in open Court, he has pleaded guilty to the charges that have been brought against him'.

Lord Goddard helped amplify the Attorney General's point: 'It might perhaps be known that this man was arrested as recently as February 2nd, was committed for trial on February 10th, and is being tried on the 1st of March.' To which Shawcross added: 'With the assistance of a legal adviser of his own choosing, he comes before your Lordship after this very short period of delay.'

These were the facts, he said, and he did not propose to call any evidence. Mr Curtis-Bennett, for Fuchs, now asked that Mr Skardon be called to give evidence. He told the court that he had seen Fuchs on several occasions and upon being asked by Curtis-Bennett, agreed that 'before he took a statement from Fuchs, there had been no evidence upon which [Fuchs] could have been prosecuted. Fuchs had made a long and absolutely free statement to [Skardon].' Lord Goddard checked that 'on 21st and 24th of January, [Fuchs] was not under arrest', to which Skardon replied 'No, My Lord.'

Skardon said that he had not 'pressed' Fuchs 'in any way'. He now became in effect a witness for the defence as he confirmed that Fuchs had done 'everything to co-operate with [him] in trying to minimise the wrong he had done'.

Fuchs' defence counsel, Mr Curtis-Bennett, convinced by Perrin that Fuchs' story was genuine, never questioned the nature of Fuchs' confession. His sole defence was built on two strands. First, that as the only evidence against his client was Fuchs' voluntary confession, he hoped for a lenient sentence. To that end he presented a long description of Fuchs' early life, his life under the Nazis, the anti-fascist movement, and then Fuchs' escape to England. But he then overplayed his hand with a claim that Fuchs had not hidden his communist affiliations in England. Lord Goddard cut in: 'I don't know whether you are suggesting that [his association with communists in this country] was known to the authorities?'

Curtis-Bennett haltingly replied, 'I don't know – but making no secrecy of the fact.'

Goddard riposted: 'I don't suppose he proclaimed himself as a communist when naturalised or taken into Harwell, or when he went to the USA?'

Curtis-Bennett tried to keep some initiative, 'If I am wrong, Mr Attorney will correct me. It was on his record in this country at the Home Office that he was a member of the German Communist Party.'

Shawcross stepped in: 'It was realised when he was examined by the Enemy Aliens Tribunal at the beginning of the War, that he was a refugee from Nazi persecution because in Germany he had been a communist.' He explained that there was no evidence of Fuchs being involved with the British Communist Party and all investigations tended to show he was immersed in his academic studies and taking no interest in politics at all.

Curtis-Bennett stood his ground, and made the point that Shawcross himself had raised with the Director of Public Prosecutions: 'It was known in Germany that he had been a communist. I make no more comment on it. I state a fact. I think it was pretty plain that this man who becomes a British subject in 1942 could never have achieved that without it being known what his political allegiances were in Germany.' He then continued that for Fuchs, a 'known communist', it was obvious 'as anyone who has read anything of Marxist theory must know that any man who is a communist, whether in Germany or Timbuctoo, will react in exactly the same way when he comes in possession of information. He will almost automatically, unhappily, put his allegiance to the communist ideology first.' The passing of secrets was therefore 'not to hurt this country' but 'because it is the right thing to do in his mind'.

Having introduced the nature of the communist Fuchs' mind,

Curtis-Bennett now moved to his second argument and submitted that Fuchs was under severe mental stress – Fuchs having described his ability to separate his secret and professional lives as 'controlled schizophrenia'. Lord Goddard would have none of it. He interjected to say that he could not understand this 'metaphysical philosophy or whatever you like to call it. I am not concerned with it. I am concerned that this man gave away secrets of vital importance to this country. He stands before me as a sane man and not relying on the disease of schizophrenia or anything else.'

Curtis-Bennett desperately tried to make his plea: 'If your Lordship does not think the state of mind of a man acts under is relative to sentence . . .', but he was interrupted by the judge: 'A man in that state of mind is the most dangerous that a country could have within its shores.'[31]

Fuchs' defence was trapped. Fuchs had confessed, yet at no stage did Curtis-Bennett pursue a defence that this was the result of inducement. At no point did anyone draw attention to Fuchs' sworn statement that 'I was given the chance of admitting [that I had given away information in New York] and staying at Harwell or of clearing out.'[32] At no point did Curtis-Bennett challenge the accuracy of dates and locations of the charges. Instead he made a last-ditch attempt to plead that Russia had been an ally of Britain throughout Fuchs' espionage. He pointed out that this was true in 1943, and in 1944 and 1945, but in so doing he was inadvertently reminding Goddard – not that he needed any prompting – of the extent of Fuchs' perfidy. When he concluded this with the remark that Fuchs 'was giving assistance to the Russians because he believed in communism', Goddard interjected, 'And he was giving it according to his own statement up to the time of victory and to March, 1949.'

Curtis-Bennett didn't give up. He reminded the court that the indictment covered times uniformly when Russia was our ally and 'if that is not important on the question of sentence on these three counts, then I have made a mistake'. He made a brave, but hopeless case, for Fuchs to be treated leniently. He asked that Goddard 'understand what was acting in [Fuchs'] brain as a result of what happened in 1932 and 1933'. Finally he made a vain attempt to flatter Goddard that the British courts were famous as the 'fountain of all justice' and that the sentence to be imposed on Fuchs would be 'tempered by the mercy which your Lordship always shows in every case you try'. Had he been pressed about it, Curtis-Bennett would have struggled to defend this piece of desperate flattery.

Within ninety minutes the trial was over. Upon being asked whether he wished to say anything before sentence was passed, Fuchs said little. 'I have committed crimes for which I am charged, and I expect sentence. I have also committed some other crimes which are not crimes in the eyes of the law – crimes against my friends – and when I asked my counsel to put certain facts before you I did not do so because I wanted to lighten my sentence. I did it in order to atone for those other crimes. I have had a fair trial and I wish to thank you and my counsel and my solicitors. I also wish to thank the Governor and his staff at Brixton prison for the considerate treatment they have given me.'

In contrast to this humble and contrite statement, Lord Goddard now rounded on Fuchs, as if from a pulpit above the courtroom. He said that Fuchs had 'taken advantage' of Britain's gift of asylum and 'betrayed the hospitality and protection given to you by the grossest treachery'. He seemed to understand Fuchs' espionage to have begun only in 1942 as he remonstrated Fuchs, because 'in return' for gaining British nationality he had then 'started to betray secrets of vital importance'. Fuchs had attempted to 'further a political creed' which was 'held in abhorrence by the vast majority in this country'. He had 'imperilled the right of asylum' for others: 'Dare we now give shelter to political refugees who may be followers of this pernicious creed and disguise themselves and then treacherously bite the hand that feeds them?'

Remarks more likely to upset Fuchs were that he had betrayed the work of his colleagues and 'caused the gravest suspicion to fall on those you falsely treated as friends and who were misled into trusting you'. Perhaps with an eye to the intense American interest in the proceedings, Goddard saw also the political consequences that Fuchs had 'imperilled the good relations between this country and the great American Republic with which His Majesty is aligned'.

Then Goddard demolished Fuchs' statement, which, he said, 'shows to me the depth into which people like yourself can fall. Your crime to me is only thinly differentiated from high treason. In this country we observe rigidly the rule of law, and as technically it is not high treason, so you are not tried for that offence.' He then assessed what sentence he should impose, as the lack of high treason excluded capital punishment. 'It is not so much for punishment that I impose it, for punishment can mean nothing to a man of your mentality. My duty is to safeguard this country and how can I be sure that a man, whose mentality is shown in that statement you have made, may not, at any other minute, allow some curious working of your mind to lead you further to betray secrets of the greatest possible value and importance to this land?'[33]

Had the law permitted, Lord Goddard would have surely sentenced Fuchs to death by hanging. As it was, a freely given confession notwithstanding, he gave Fuchs the maximum sentence allowed: fourteen years' imprisonment.

PART SEVEN

Fallout: 1950–59

21

Going for Gold

After Fuchs' arrest and eventual conviction, both the British and the Americans were deeply concerned about the implications of his espionage for the balance of world power. But beyond that their goals in relation to him diverged. In the United Kingdom the authorities had two main agendas. First, there was the problem of national security and the possible continued presence in Great Britain of Fuchs' Russian contacts, both from his time at Birmingham before he moved to the United States and during his post-war espionage out of Harwell. Second, if they could be obtained, the reactions of Fuchs' contacts to his information and the questions that they asked him might give clues to the state of the Soviet Union's expertise in atomic physics. The British government was concerned by public reactions at home, and also the implications of the Fuchs' affair for its political relations with the USA, on whose soil a British citizen had performed a devastating betrayal.

From the perspective of the United States the concerns were similar, but their priorities differed. The politics in America was about to be overtaken by Senator McCarthy's communist witch-hunts. The discovery that the atomic scientists who had won the war included active communists would cast a long shadow, leading in 1954 to the infamous persecution of J. Robert Oppenheimer, the scientific leader of the Manhattan Project. By February 1950, VENONA had exposed evidence of many spies, most known only by Soviet code names, though none (at least yet) appeared to have been as dangerous as Klaus Fuchs.* Recall, J. Edgar Hoover's agenda was to ensure that the FBI came out of this with maximum credit and with himself the hero. To these ends, the FBI's immediate goal was to

---

* The most significant of these was probably Ted Hall, a young science prodigy based at Los Alamos. His story is told in J. Albright and M. Kunstall, *Bombshell: The Secret Story of America's Unknown Atomic Spy Conspiracy* (Times Books, Random House, 1997).

identify the agent that from VENONA decrypts they knew as GOOSE –
the contact in New York whom Fuchs had known as Raymond.

The secrecy surrounding VENONA caused problems for Hoover and
relations with his senior staff. FBI agents in the United States were called
upon to make specific enquiries but were unaware of the vortex around
which their investigation swirled. Even John Cimperman, 'legal attaché'
in London's American Embassy and the normal conduit for secret intelligence, knew nothing of the pursuit. So it is ironic that when Hoover
failed to obtain details of Fuchs' confession, he berated Cimperman.
Cimperman was aghast and told Hoover that he had never heard of Fuchs
until the time of his arrest. The first hint that something 'of great magnitude' was breaking had been a cable from Hoover to Sillitoe to say that
Hoover planned to send his head of Counter-Espionage, Lish Whitson, to
London. The first details had come to Cimperman the evening of Fuchs'
arrest – and he had learned them from MI5! He couldn't make any enquiries to them about Fuchs' confession because the British deemed the case
to be sub judice. As Whitson was on his way over to Great Britain, Cimperman assessed that this was in hand at the most senior level and his role
was to assist but not to interfere.

Hoover was irate to learn of Cimperman's ignorance and now blamed
his deputy, D. M. 'Mickey' Ladd, and Washington's Special Agent in
Charge, H. B. Fletcher, for the 'atrocious handling'. He berated them,
'While I was kept in ignorance I didn't think Cimperman was also.' This
suggests that Hoover himself had been remote from the day-to-day
VENONA decryption.* The case escalated when Ladd defended himself
by accusing Cimperman of lying; according to Ladd, Cimperman had been
sent a 'large number of memos'. Hoover responded, 'This is amazing', and
he called Cimperman to Washington on 21 February.[1]

If the ensuing arguments are recorded, they do not appear in available
Fuchs files. The episode illustrates some of the misunderstandings that the
carefully controlled 'need to know' rule for VENONA engendered, and
the intense pressure that Hoover felt he was under. While Hoover could
bully his way in Washington, he was unable to exert control so easily over
the United Kingdom. He quickly discovered that he would have to respect
the legal processes and political sensitivities of what he characterized as
'the sly British'.[2]

Hoover's plan to control the politics required him to have Fuchs'

---

* Robert Lamphere recalls he 'wrote a memo to Hoover, who initialled that he had seen it,
but made no significant mention'. Available FBI files show no evidence of any active interest
by Hoover until after Fuchs' arrest (R. J. Lamphere and T. Shachtman, *The FBI–KGB War:
A Special Agent's Story* (Random House, 1986), and FBI FOOCASE files 65-58805, vol. 1).

confession on file. He had led his Washington political colleagues to believe that obtaining this would be a trivial matter, but instead it turned into a quagmire when Whitson informed his chief that the British were denying him access to Fuchs and also were unwilling to hand over copies of Fuchs' interviews. Hoover's reaction is not recorded but can be imagined, as Sillitoe judged it required direct contact, chief to chief, and telegraphed a reply headed: 'Personal for Mr Hoover.' He explained that while 'earnestly wishing to co-operate to the full I cannot furnish these statements because I am bound by British legal procedure. FUCHS' statement will be made exhibit of the Court next Friday [10 February] and therefore will be subject to Court direction.' In essence, the British Attorney General advised that if the court learned that there had been discussion of Fuchs' confession, it would be inadmissible as evidence and the trial would collapse. What's more, to pass copies of this confession could be deemed an illegal act and the case would be dismissed.[3] Nonetheless Sillitoe made every effort to avoid the legal constraints by adding that he would ensure that Whitson received 'any individual items of information' that he judged likely to be helpful to the FBI.[4] In the meantime, MI5 arranged for Whitson to attend the trial, incognito under diplomatic cover, to ensure that he was not called as a witness.

WILD GOOSE CHASE

The FBI suspected, correctly as it would turn out, that identification of GOOSE might crack a ring of Soviet spies. The FBI therefore badly needed to talk to Fuchs and the British agreed that this could be done once his trial was over. In the meantime, Skardon would interview the prisoner and also pose questions on behalf of the FBI. Meanwhile in the United States, on 2 February 1950, the same day that Fuchs was arrested, two FBI agents took the first step in the quest to identify GOOSE: they visited Fuchs' sister Kristel and her husband Robert Heineman in Boston.

By this stage, Kristel had been confined at Westboro State Hospital in Massachusetts for some months, suffering from schizophrenia.[5] On 2 February she was deemed by the hospital to be 'completely rational' and was duly interviewed. When asked about Klaus in the period following Hitler's rise to power, she said that she had not seen a great deal of her brother but 'remembered seeing him in Germany in 1933 and again in 1935 after his expulsion from Germany'. She claimed to know nothing of his activities back then but 'recalled that after his expulsion he went to France'. She explained that while Klaus was in the Canadian internment camp he was befriended by Israel Halperin, who 'furnished him with cigarettes' and physics papers. According to Kristel, the link to Halperin had been a Boston physicist, Wendell Furry, who was 'a member of the same Communist Party club to which her husband belonged'.[6]

Robert Heineman was also interviewed that same day. He admitted that he had been active in the Communist Party 'in the past' and that he knew Klaus Fuchs but had 'been away from home on several occasions' and did not know how often Fuchs had visited his wife. He offered to go through his papers to see whether they contained any information about Fuchs.

Re-interviewed on 3 February, Heineman admitted former membership of the Young Communist League, but 'not since 1941'. The FBI officers' scepticism showed in their report, which commented: 'despite evidence to the contrary'. He had no useful information about Fuchs and claimed to have been absent 'on almost every occasion' that Fuchs had visited. This is a strange description if Fuchs only visited on two occasions, as he claimed, though Heineman's recall of events at five years' remove might be wayward.

The FBI agents appear to have considered seriously the possibility that Robert Heineman was a link in Fuchs' chain of espionage. They noted that Heineman was 'reluctant to identify his associates, was not fully co-operative, and definitely appeared to be lying'.

They returned the following evening, 4 February. At this third interview Heineman finally admitted that he was 'an active member of the Communist Party' and added that party meetings were held at his home. He refused to give names of other communists but was 'willing to give any information that might be of use in connection with espionage activities'.

The agents then asked him directly about anyone who had called to see Fuchs while he was visiting his sister. Heineman mentioned a scientist by the name of Martin Deutsch, who had been a colleague of Fuchs at Los Alamos, and volunteered the information that in 1946 Fuchs and Kristel had borrowed a car from the physicist Victor Weisskopf to visit another former Los Alamos colleague, Hans Bethe, in Schenectady.* These two innocent liaisons spawned further trails of investigation by the FBI, which led nowhere. Deutsch, for example, had been the FBI's original suspect as contact for Fuchs, until they discovered from Los Alamos records that Deutsch had been 'present at the laboratory during the relevant period in February 1945 when FUCHS was in touch with his contact in Cambridge,

---

* Hans Bethe was based at Cornell University in Ithaca, but he was a consultant at the General Electric Company and met Fuchs in Schenectady: TNA KV 6/135, s. 163a.

Mass.' Victor Weisskopf, who later became a distinguished Director General of CERN, was hounded for a simple act of generosity.

Robert Heineman then provided the breakthrough. He described 'an unknown individual who had visited their home on three different occasions in 1945'. With some excitement, the FBI agents realized that this might be Fuchs' Soviet contact and took a description: 'Full face with fine features, stocky, hair dark and thinning with impression of baldness, 5 foot 8 inches aged about 30 (in 1945)'.[7] Kristel, interviewed again on 10 February, agreed with that but gave his age as 'in the forties'. She recalled that the man had arrived by foot and that he had 'come into the city by train'. She thought he had a name like Roberts or Robinson. He had mentioned a wife and children, and that he was a chemist.[8] The FBI now had something to go on.

In London MI5 had collated information on Fuchs' American contact, drawn not only from their interrogation but also from a decrypted VENONA message.[9] This was passed to Lish Whitson, Hoover's newly arrived emissary, on 4 February. In addition to information about GOOSE's physical characteristics and the agenda of his meetings with Fuchs, the summary included the news – from VENONA – that GOOSE was probably connected with the 'practical implementation' of a US Navy project on 'Thermal Diffusion' in 1944, and concluded that he had probably considered setting up his own laboratory.[10] Harry Gold had asked Fuchs about thermal diffusion during one of their meetings, but Fuchs had never heard of it – the British had dismissed it as a viable process before Fuchs had started work in 1941. Gold, however, had told Fuchs that he had worked on it. Find a paper with the title 'Problems of the Practical Application under Production Conditions of the Process of Thermal Diffusion of Gases' and its author would reveal the identity of GOOSE.

The FBI had a lead on GOOSE back in September 1949. Decryption of VENONA at that time was still patchy.[11] Meredith Gardner's team at Arlington Hall had decoded enough to reveal that in October 1944 GOOSE had given the KGB's representative in New York information about an agent with cover name CONSTRUCTOR. The decoded message said, 'According to GOOSE's latest advice CONSTRUCTOR has stopped working at the Chemurgy Design Company', and further referred to CONSTRUCTOR 'at his lab at 114 East 32nd Street . . . where he has organized [sic] his own company and in the course of two or three weeks proposes to finish work on Aerosol and DDT'.[12]

There was plenty of information here that enabled the FBI to conclude that CONSTRUCTOR 'has been identified as Abe Brothman'.[13] Brothman had a history with the FBI, and it was through him that Harry

Gold – as well as others – was on their register. Furthermore, Brothman was a chemical engineer. From the start of their quest for Fuchs' American contact, the FBI focused on Brothman as either a conduit to GOOSE or as the phantom itself.

If every storm begins with a single raindrop, the seeds of Harry Gold's demise and its awful far-reaching consequences for the lives of several individuals can be traced back to a day in 1945 when Elizabeth Bentley, an American who spied for the Soviet Union, quit and handed herself in to the FBI. The deal was that she bought freedom in return for becoming an informer. She named scores of individuals, including Abe Brothman.

Brothman had been involved in industrial espionage for the Soviets, and Bentley had been his contact. In 1941, long before Gold met Fuchs, the Soviets decided that Brothman would be more effective if his contact had technical knowledge (Bentley was a graduate in Italian literature) and so they replaced Bentley with Harry Gold. Gold became Brothman's courier until the end of 1943, when he was told to 'drop completely his association with Abe Brothman and never to see him again'.[14] This was when Gold learned he was to be courier for Klaus Fuchs.

Move forward to 1946, when Fuchs returned to England. Two events now conspired to entrap Gold. First, in the post-war climate companies were trimming their staff and Gold was made redundant. He quickly found a new job – with Abe Brothman's 'Chemurgy Design Group'. The Canadian spy exposé had led the Soviet Union to put agents into cold storage for about a year, and it is possible that this is why Gold lost focus and violated a fundamental law of spycraft: his covert life as an anonymous Soviet courier mingled with his real life as Harry Gold.[15] In any event, the result was that Brothman now knew his former courier by name: Harry Gold. In 1947, when Brothman faced a Grand Jury, he named Gold, whom the FBI then questioned. None of Bentley's allegations stuck, however, with the result that no action was taken against Brothman or Gold. But the pair now had files at the FBI, which identified them – Brothman especially – as possible Soviet couriers.

In hindsight, the route to Gold via Brothman and VENONA might seem direct, but at the time it was hard to see. VENONA had revealed a link between GOOSE and thermal diffusion; the link with CONSTRUC-TOR and Brothman was more tenuous. At the time of Fuchs' arrest the FBI lamely summarized 'there are various suspects' of whom the 'principal one' was a former partner of Brothman named Gerhard (Gus) Wollan.[16] The KGB hid its agents' identities better than to give a code name GOOSE to one already named Gus, however, and Wollan was soon eliminated. So the FBI saturated efforts on a systematic search through its files for politically suspect chemists and engineers, and trawled through scientific journals for a specific paper. According to Robert Lamphere, the trawl for politically suspect chemists and engineers generated over one thousand individuals.[17] If true, this illustrates both the extreme level of political paranoia at that time and the magnitude of the task facing the Bureau.

The FBI painstakingly worked its way through lists of possible experts on diffusion based at Columbia University in New York and the Kellex organization, each of which had been involved with the British team back in 1944, and also examined Atomic Energy Commission (AEC) files of Oak Ridge staff members. Dr Karl Cohen of Columbia University, whose name had already arisen in Skardon's interrogation of Fuchs, became an early suspect. The editor of *Journal of Chemical Physics* – Joseph Meyer – was investigated; he was the husband of Marie Goppart Meyer, a future Nobel laureate in nuclear physics – a chance correlation that at the time seemed suspicious. Their lives were raked over, gossip collected, political leanings and statements weighed for signs of malicious – communist – activity. Ultimately none of this led to anything significant in the search for GOOSE, although in the rapidly brewing storm of McCarthyism the accumulated documentation remained on file latent with future menace.

SKARDON – THE GO-BETWEEN

On 8 February, two days before his appearance in the Magistrates' Court, Fuchs had asked to see Skardon.[18] They met in Brixton Prison for about half an hour and Fuchs told him the name of the Russian whom he saw at the embassy was 'Mr ALEXANDER'. He added that he had no idea whether that was the man's real name but when he asked for that name, 'he saw the man to whom he had originally been introduced in the house on the South side of Hyde Park'.* Fuchs also told Skardon that 'in 1946

---

* The description 'South side of Hyde Park' does not fit with any other description of Fuchs' meeting with Kuczynski. All other evidence is consistent with this having been at Lawn Road, south of Hampstead Heath. See footnote, chapter 2, p. 46, for the possibility that, nine years later, Fuchs' memory – or deliberate deception to protect his partners in crime – has conflated a visit to Kremer at the Soviet Embassy in Hyde Park with Lawn Road. If we adopt this hypothesis, events would become consistent with Chapman Pincher's unsourced claim that Fuchs was introduced to Kremer at the party in April 1941 (Chapman Pincher, *Treachery: Betrayals, Blunders and Cover-Ups: Six Decades of Espionage against America and Great Britain* [Random House, 2009]). Further support for the thesis that Fuchs was deceptive is that MI5 took Fuchs by car from Brixton Prison to identify the locations of the dead-letter boxes in the vicinity of Kew Gardens that he had described to Skardon. This he did. MI5 also offered to take him to identify the house south

or 47' a Russian contact gave him an address in Paris where 'it might be profitable for him to go to' in order to be put in touch with people 'who had technical knowledge and would be able to discuss his disclosures more fully'. This address was repeated at his last meeting in 'February or March 1949', but Fuchs never made use of it. MI5 duly investigated the French connection, but without success.[19]

Fuchs confirmed his previous description of GOOSE, adding that he was 'fairly broad with a round face' and 'possibly a first-generation American'. Their meetings took place in the street and Fuchs said he might be able to identify locations if he were shown a map of New York. However, he declined to tell Skardon the name of his original introducer. Fuchs indicated only that it was 'a man, an alien, and not living in Birmingham. He was a Communist, but may have changed his views and want[ed] to come to this country as a refugee'. This appears to have been disinformation by Fuchs, or a misunderstanding on Skardon's part, as Jürgen Kuczynski had migrated to the United Kingdom before he met Fuchs. Skardon recorded: 'He implied however that the man was out of our reach.'

Fuchs now gave more information about Kuczynski, which Skardon noted and would later use as a means to wheedle more out of Fuchs. Skardon recorded that this first contact 'was a decent man and [Fuchs] believes that had [Kuzcynski] known that FUCHS was going to indulge in a series of meetings he would not have been a party to the arrangement at all'. Fuchs claimed that Kuzcynski had asked specifically whether he intended to meet the Russians on more than one occasion, and Fuchs had said, 'No!' Fuchs amplified that 'at the time his intention was merely to let the Russians know that there was work going on in atomic research'.[20]

Fuchs added that his examination of the photographs 'last week' was done 'quite faithfully' and asked to be able to look again at those he had selected as being familiar. Fuchs' appearance as cooperative was an act, however. He looked again at selected photographs, none of which were significant to the case, but did not re-examine the rest, including that of Ursula Beurton.*

---

of Hyde Park where Fuchs said he had first met Kremer. Fuchs, however, claimed it would be 'useless to drive in that area'. He prevaricated, saying it was 'only an impression of his that he went south of the park'. MI5 recorded that 'in spite of intense questioning' they found it 'impossible to get him to recall any detail which would serve to locate the house' (Skardon report, 4 December 1950, KV 2/1256, s. 762a).

* 'Minute on interview [by Skardon] with Klaus Fuchs, 8 February 1950', TNA KV 2/1251, s. 479b. Ursula Beurton's picture was among those shown to Fuchs. In May 1950 this was copied into Beurton's file, TNA KV 6/43, s. 224b, with the added note: 'The photograph of Ursula Beurton was not among those he placed on one side.' Colonel Robertson came very

Two days later, on 10 February, Skardon managed to speak with Fuchs at the end of his appearance before the magistrate. On a map of New York, Fuchs identified the Henry Street location of his first meeting with Gold. Skardon also had a map of the Kew Gardens area, by which Fuchs indicated a house on the corner of Kew Road and Stanmore Road as the place where he was supposed to throw the marked magazine; he identified a fence on the north of Stanmore Road where he would then make a mark to alert the Russians, and the passageway in the parade of shops fronting Kew Gardens station where the chalk mark would denote danger.

Skardon showed Fuchs three photographs provided by the FBI. None of these included Harry Gold, and Fuchs confirmed that none of them looked like his American contact. Next Skardon handed him a list of FBI questions about his contact and methods of making a rendezvous but 'as time was short' Skardon asked Fuchs to complete his answers later. He also showed Fuchs 'selected photographs with a view to identifying his contacts in the United Kingdom';[21] Fuchs now picked out the photograph of Colonel Kremer as the man he knew as Alexander.

Once again, Fuchs was being selective with his information. His identification of Kremer came at no cost to him. He knew that Kremer was long gone from the United Kingdom, of course, as it had been Kremer's departure in 1942 that had forced Fuchs to change his contacts with the Russians that year. From the perspective of MI5, on the other hand, this added to the perception of Fuchs as a willing helper.

Skardon returned to see Fuchs at Brixton Prison on 15 February. Having positively identified Kremer as Fuchs' contact in the first phase of espionage, MI5 was now chasing the Russians who had controlled Fuchs between 1946 and 1949.[22] Skardon showed Fuchs photographs of members of the Russian Embassy staff and trade delegations, from which he selected three possible matches. Skardon then took Fuchs through photographs of people listed by the FBI as candidates for GOOSE, but he failed to recognize any of them. The photos included one of Abe Brothman but none of Harry Gold.

Next Skardon pressed Fuchs on his Boston rendezvous. The FBI had told MI5 that Fuchs had met GOOSE at his sister's home, but Fuchs claimed to have 'no recollection of this event'. Nor, he claimed, did he remember his sister telling him 'of the visits of the man ROBERTS or ROBINSON to make enquiries about him'. He insisted to Skardon that he was 'quite

---

near to nailing her on 20 May 1950 when he proposed that she be interviewed again about 'her espionage activities', as 'she may have been impressed, and possibly alarmed, by the arrest of FUCHS' (TNA KV 6/43, s. 228). However, MI5 were even now unaware that she had left England for East Germany soon after Fuchs' arrest.

positive that no meeting took place with him at his sister's residence'. Having confessed in part to deflect attention from his sick sister, Fuchs' strategy was to distance her as much as possible from his activities.

Finally Skardon returned to Fuchs' first contact and attempted to bluff him into revealing more about that person. Skardon first told Fuchs that – 'as he would suspect' – MI5 had been pursuing enquiries and were 'gradually piecing together a story which seemed to indicate that his friend had played only a small part in effecting his introduction'. In reality, Skardon knew no more than Fuchs had already told him, and was making a minimal inference from Fuchs' earlier claim that Kuczynski had been less than totally enthusiastic. Skardon then introduced the name of one Jimmy Shields, a communist who had died the previous year and who, according to Skardon, 'formed one link in a chain which was set up for the purpose of introducing Fuchs to the Russians'. Why Skardon said this is a mystery as there is no mention of Shields elsewhere in the relevant files, and he played no role in the Fuchs affair whatsoever. Nonetheless, Skardon built on this to make the fantastic suggestion that 'his friend was almost an innocent party and we were most anxious to discover for ourselves to what extent he was in fact involved'. He continued, expectantly, 'In those circumstances FUCHS would not feel the same reticence in mentioning his name.'

Fuchs explained that he had not given this information before because Skardon 'had not specifically asked the question'. Fuchs then claimed to 'believe' this to be 'the only matter that he had withheld'. Skardon reported back to MI5 that he 'left Fuchs to turn the matter over in his mind' and proposed that Fuchs 'let me have his decision when next we met'.[23]

On 23 February Skardon learned more about Fuchs' contact with the Russians when he returned to England in 1946. Fuchs explained that back in the United States he had been given instructions for a rendezvous in North London's Mornington Crescent, but he never kept it. His relations with Soviet Intelligence 'were broken off until the end of 1946 or early 1947'. During 1947 he wished to resume contact and attempted to locate 'the individual' who had first introduced him to the Russians – Fuchs continued to withhold Kuczynski's identity. He failed to find this individual, and so – Skardon reported to Robertson – he next 'approached a woman of whose identity he is uncertain [Hannah Klopstech] but whom he believes to be either German or Czech and to have been a member of the Communist Party, and asked if she could find his original introducer [Kuczynski]'.[24] Klopstech was unable to do this, so Fuchs admitted to her that he wished to resume contact with the Russians. She agreed to help and contact was re-established. Fuchs said that when he resumed meeting with the Russians, he was admonished for having made contact through the Communist Party. Fuchs refused to give Skardon Klopstech's identity.

Meanwhile in the United States, Harry Gold's identity had gradually filtered out of the morass. He first appears as one of many potential candidates for GOOSE on 11 February, after a search through the FBI New York files. When FBI agents interviewed the Heinemans at the start of the month, they had been told that the name of the mystery man might have contained 'Rob' in it. So chemists with the names Robin, Robbins and Roberts were also scrutinized.

On 24 February Lish Whitson sent MI5's John Marriott a summary of the FBI meeting with the Heinemans. In addition he attached 'for display to FUCHS' one photograph each of four suspects. One of these pictures was of Harry Gold.[25]

On 28 February Skardon saw Fuchs for the last time before his trial, which would take place the next day at the Old Bailey. Did Skardon see this as his final opportunity to lean on Fuchs? Possibly, though if Fuchs thought that by cooperating he might reduce his sentence he was to be sadly disappointed. Once again Skardon showed Fuchs a series of photographs supplied by MI5 together with the four that had just arrived from the United States via Whitson. And once again Fuchs claimed not to recognize any, including, for the first time, the one of Harry Gold.

Skardon now raised the question that he had left with Fuchs at their previous meeting, namely whether he had 'considered the matter of telling me the names of his introducers'. Fuchs now agreed to do so on condition that Skardon undertook not to harm these people if this were the only act of which they were guilty, and that Skardon would 'keep their names from any foreign intelligence organization'.

Skardon agreed to this condition. Fuchs then gave the names of Hannah (Joanna) Klopstech, the communist whom he had known in Scotland, and added that she had helped him make contact in 1947 with Jürgen Kuczynski, 'who is at present a professor at Berlin University'.[26] Fuchs had solved his dilemma because by this stage both Klopstech and Kuczynski were out of reach of the Western Security Services, living in the Eastern Zone of Germany. The identity of his American contact and the 'girl from Banbury', however, remained undisclosed.

FUCHS SOWS CONFUSION

When the trial was over, copies of Fuchs' confessions were sent to the United States along with transcripts of the court proceedings.[27] The FBI's hopes of interviewing Fuchs, however, were once again postponed. Initially their interview was to be after the time for Fuchs to make an appeal had passed, but the date was further delayed until questions in Parliament about the case had been concluded. Hoover was convinced that the British were stalling and had no intention of allowing the FBI to interview Fuchs.[28]

Skardon continued to be their go-between. On 6 March the FBI sent sixteen questions for him to put to Fuchs, along with twenty-seven photographs. On 10 March they sent five more questions. In the meantime on 8 March Skardon visited Fuchs again, now imprisoned at Wormwood Scrubs, and showed him the photographs.

Fuchs examined the pictures and rejected them one by one. Then he retained one, looked at it 'carefully for several minutes' and said: 'There is something familiar about this man.' This was not Harry Gold but a man by the name of Joseph Arnold Robbins, who seems to have been selected because he was a chemist with 'Rob' in his name. Fuchs covered the forehead with his finger, considered the image afresh and said, 'I cannot swear, but I am pretty sure that this is the man I met in the USA.' Skardon asked Fuchs to look at the photograph carefully while at the same time thinking about his contact in Manhattan. Fuchs did so and confirmed, 'I think that this is the man.'[29]

Meanwhile, Fuchs had heard gossip from fellow prisoners that MI5 was looking for the woman with whom he stayed in Maidenhead on the night of 16 January. He told Skardon that he was concerned lest this brought her into trouble. Skardon told Fuchs – 'frankly' – that 'we knew who she was' and named Mrs Skinner. Fuchs agreed that this was so, and was relieved when Skardon told him that MI5 was not interested in 'that sort of adventure'. Fuchs might have been less sanguine had he learned the extent of MI5's knowledge, and their opinion that her 'unfaithfulness to her husband is well known in Harwell'. He assured Skardon that Mrs Skinner was not involved in any form of espionage, but her friends included some who were 'roaring communists' and might easily be suspect. This opinion was already shared by MI5, whose records drily stated that Erna Skinner's 'reputation and reliability leave something to be desired'.[30]

In Hoover's opinion Skardon was to blame for the FBI's inability to interview Fuchs. MI5's interrogator felt that he had a good relationship with Fuchs, and now wanted to re-establish that following Fuchs' extreme sentence of fourteen years in jail. He told Fuchs that the FBI wanted to interview him. For Fuchs this raised again the spectre of his sister Kristel's well-being. Fuchs said that he wanted Skardon – and especially the FBI – to understand that the Heinemans were not implicated. He added that his sister had been an 'active undercover Communist in Germany' and she may have deduced that the contact was 'continuation of his underground work in Germany'. Concern for Kristel's welfare seems to have been paramount for him throughout. Soviet Intelligence had noted Kristel's time in Germany and kept her on their files, with the code name ANT.[31] Her brother probably knew nothing of this.

Skardon assured Fuchs that there was no compulsion for him to meet FBI interrogators; when Hoover learned of this he was outraged, 'after all the cooperation we have extended to the British over the years'. In his opinion, Skardon had 'too much pride and too little ability' and probably wanted to make the breakthroughs and get maximum credit for himself.[32]

By the middle of March, Hoover was on the warpath. In a letter to the US Attorney General, J. Howard McGrath, he referred to 'delaying tactics' by the British that 'have seriously impaired our efforts to completely identify the American contacts of Fuchs and have hindered [our] investigation'.[33] He urged McGrath to lobby Secretary of State Dean Acheson to bring pressure on the British. Next, Hoover wrote to Admiral Souers and blamed the delay on Sir Frank Newsam, the Permanent Under-Secretary in the British Home Office. According to Hoover, Newsam was 'violently anti-American' and had 'accused Americans of being barbarians'.[34] As for the FBI's relationship with MI5, Hoover asserted 'this so-called collaboration is just a load of hog-wash'.[35]

He ordered that the FBI no longer 'volunteer information to the British' about the case, and urged Admiral Lewis Strauss to do likewise in the field of atomic energy, through the Atomic Energy Commission. Strauss agreed that the Commissioners should terminate the exchange of information with the British 'until and unless' they provided the FBI with material on the Fuchs case.

The British also worried about the longer-term 'ownership' of Fuchs. On 9 March Geoffrey Patterson judged that once the identity of GOOSE was known, 'the FBI will want Fuchs to testify in the USA, [which] would lead to congressional enquiries and a media storm'.[36] Sir Percy Sillitoe was adamant that this would not happen and assured Patterson: 'There is absolutely no precedent for allowing a person in legal custody to leave the jurisdiction. If Fuchs' evidence is required it can be obtained here on commission – a procedure which would have to be invoked by the State Department through the Foreign Office.' Sillitoe added that the Home Office and Attorney General would raise 'every sort of objection to Fuchs appearing in the USA', and concluded that the whole idea was 'entirely out of the question'.[37]

For now, at least, Skardon would continue to be the go-between, acting in London on behalf of the FBI. On 16 March he visited Fuchs again in Wormwood Scrubs to show him further photographs that had arrived from the FBI. The photograph of Robbins, which Fuchs had previously identified as a possible candidate for GOOSE, had been taken in 1943. The new set included a photo of the same man, taken but a few days before. This looked very different from the one that Fuchs had seen before, and Fuchs now agreed that he would 'never have identified this man as his contact'.

He then worked his way slowly through the rest of the photographs and picked out two of a James J. Robbin (no connection with the previous Joseph Robbins other than having been caught in the 'Rob' trawl). He said there was not enough information in the pictures for him to express a view one way or the other. He asked to see a better photograph of the man.

Skardon passed this request on to John Cimperman at the US Embassy, for transmission to the FBI. The Americans' frustration at this long-range bouncing to and fro via third parties is apparent as they continued to press for more information and better access.* Confidential transcripts continued to be sent to Hoover, along with Fuchs' responses to questions put by Skardon on behalf of the FBI.

On 20 March the CIA's liaison officer at the American Embassy in London asked MI5 for results of their interrogation, especially 'operational details', and details of the extent of Fuchs' 'divulgement of atomic energy information to the USSR plus the British estimate of the extent of compromise resulting there-from'.[38] The final question contained a catch – British judgement on this could also reveal to the Americans the state of British know-how in atomic energy, four years after the Americans had cut off sharing information with the British.

Guy Liddell cleverly side-stepped that pitfall by responding 'this was not the direct concern of this department' and then reminding the Americans that 'it had been agreed' that the British Embassy in Washington was sharing information with the State Department 'for the latter to forward to the US agencies concerned'.[39] He recommended that the Americans raise this with their own State Department.

Senator McMahon, chair of the Joint Committee on Atomic Energy, believed that the British had done a 'bad job' and were 'fearful that we will secure information that will prove embarrassing to them'. He undertook to raise the matter with the British ambassador. Hoover increased

---

* FBI files also reveal that Fuchs' identification of Robbins was ruled out because he didn't write any paper on thermal diffusion (Fuchs FBI FOIA file 65-58805-1156; 30/3/50).

the tension further by telling McMahon that the British had 'two more' spies in the United Kingdom but 'didn't know that'. Hoover continued, 'I have advised my representative to inform the British of this though he was not to give the source or state how reliable it was, though it was of the utmost reliability.' Hoover was at least honest enough to admit to McMahon that 'we ourselves do not know who they [are]'.[40]

VISITS BY THE FBI

In April the Home Office decided against any FBI interview of Fuchs for fear of setting a precedent. Sir Percy Sillitoe was so worried at this that Geoffrey Patterson was instructed to see Hoover personally and explain that Sillitoe was urgently attempting to have this restriction overthrown.

This hardly assuaged the irascible Hoover. The FBI had files on numerous communists, real or suspected, and assorted evidence of espionage. Hoover was concerned that news of the arrest might have alerted Fuchs' contacts in the United States to impending danger, which would frustrate his investigations. He continued to pressure MI5 by informing Patterson that he was to testify before the Joint Committee on Atomic Energy. This powerful body could block collaboration with the United Kingdom, so there could be devastating consequences if he were to tell its members that MI5 was not cooperating.[41]

Hoover further hassled the British by implying that even if they agreed to grant the FBI access to Fuchs, 'little could be expected in view of the extended delay'.[42] He also cleverly turned the threat into an opportunity by telling Senator McMahon that there were several individuals who the FBI were watching in the United States in connection with the Fuchs case, but that his efforts were being thwarted by the British. The unstated implication was that if the FBI failed to find GOOSE, the British were to blame.[43] The pressure through McMahon paid dividends as on 8 May the British Home Secretary, James Chuter Ede, decided that due to the 'exceptional circumstances', FBI agents would be permitted to interrogate Fuchs.[44]

The FBI prepared to interview Harry Gold and Abe Brothman simultaneously in early May. Plans were put on hold, however, when on 6 May a 'bag-job'* on Brothman's office produced results. In the coy words of the FBI files, 'a confidential source with access to Brothman's office'

---

* 'Bag-job' is American slang for a covert, often illegal, break-in by a law officer to gather information.

provided a 'typewritten document' whose contents 'referred to the industrial application of a process of thermal diffusion' and 'appeared to coincide very closely with the topic' that GOOSE had chosen.[45] The document did not bear the name of its author, however, nor was there any way to identify the individual. At least the discovery proved that in focusing on Brothman and Gold, the FBI were on the right track.

Gold lived in Philadelphia, and on 15 May FBI agents Brennan and Miller interviewed him at the Bureau's office in the city. When shown a photograph of Fuchs, Gold said that he recognized the face because he had seen it in *Newsweek*. When they asked about Gold's travels 'out west', he denied ever having travelled west of the Mississippi. They agreed to meet again in about a week.

On 18 May FBI agent Robert Lamphere came over to London together with FBI Assistant Director Hugh Clegg. Accompanied by Skardon, they saw Fuchs in Wormwood Scrubs Prison over several days at the end of that month. They applied pressure by telling him that they had interviewed Kristel, but did not reveal any details of what had transpired.

En route from Washington to New York, in their journey to London, Lamphere and Clegg had picked up a cinematograph film of Harry Gold, taken while Gold was under surveillance in Philadelphia. They had some still images made from this film and brought these, along with images of other potential suspects, with them on their first visit to Fuchs, on 20 May. This was primarily an introductory meeting, in which Clegg explained that he had come to England 'to lend the weight of Mr Hoover's authority' to the investigation and to enable decisions to be taken 'on his own authority without reference back to the USA'. He told Fuchs that he was not obliged to answer any questions, and expressed appreciation that Fuchs had agreed to see them.

Clegg and Lamphere asked Fuchs for a description of his contact, and then showed him 'a number of photographs'. Fuchs 'rejected all but five': two pairs, which were 'stills' from a cinematograph film, and a single full-length photograph of the same sort. Skardon recognized these all to be of Harry Gold, 'a passport photograph of whom FUCHS rejected when shown to him at an earlier date'.[46] Fuchs now said he could 'not exclude' this individual from consideration.

On 21 May, in Philadelphia, agents Brennan and Miller met with Gold again and interviewed him for four hours. He continued to deny knowing Fuchs, but did admit that he was interested in thermal diffusion and hoped to open a laboratory for its industrial application. He allowed them to take his photograph and also to make a short motion picture; finally he agreed to a continuation of the interview at his home the following day.

On 22 May the FBI was active on two continents. First, in the morning, London time, Lamphere and Clegg showed Fuchs the cine-film of Gold, which had been taken surreptitiously while he was under surveillance. (The film that Brennan and Miller had taken with his permission the previous day was of course still in the USA.) At about 11 a.m. a projector and a screen were set up in Wormwood Scrubs Prison, the windows of the room were blacked out, and Fuchs watched the film twice. The film of Gold had been taken in the street, which made it obvious to Fuchs that the FBI was actively shadowing Gold. As far as Fuchs knew, it was possible that Gold was already under arrest, but if so, why were the FBI agents going to all this trouble now? Fuchs could not risk being the one who confirmed Gold's role to the FBI, even as he was sure that GOOSE was the same man – 'Raymond' – that he had met six years before. The giveaway was that GOOSE kept looking over his shoulder as if being followed, the same mannerism that had bothered Fuchs when he had met Raymond in New York. Fuchs hedged and said, 'I cannot be absolutely positive but I think it is very likely him.'[47]

The interview ended in London at 4.30 in the afternoon. At about the same time, late morning in Philadelphia, FBI agents were searching Gold's home. Gold had, of course, taken care to remove any obvious documents that could incriminate him, but as in any classic crime thriller he had made one fatal error. Behind books on his shelves the agents found a map of Santa Fe, on which was an X to mark the spot where he had arranged to meet Fuchs. This was the very map that Fuchs had given Gold for their rendezvous in 1945. Gold was now trapped as he had previously claimed that he had never travelled west of the Mississippi.

The FBI duo suggested to Gold that he 'might as well come clean'.[48] By now exhausted, Gold had no energy left to escape from the hole that he had created. Instead, as if to show how important he really was, he defiantly admitted he was the one to whom Fuchs had passed information on atomic energy. The FBI satisfyingly completed the trail of evidence when agents at its Albuquerque office located a registration card at the town's Hilton Hotel in the name of Harry Gold, for the night of 19 September 1945 – the date of his rendezvous with Klaus Fuchs in Santa Fe.

In London the next day, 23 May, Clegg and Lamphere returned to see Fuchs. At first they said nothing about Gold's arrest, and asked Fuchs about Israel Halperin, whose name was in Kristel's diary. Fuchs was now disoriented, concerned at the FBI's continued interest in his frail sister, and unaware still of what, if anything, she had told them. He stonewalled.

The FBI pair came back again on 24 May. Clegg now announced that

Gold was under arrest, had confessed, and had given details about his meetings with Fuchs.[49] In the meantime the new film and photographs of Gold had been rushed to London in the care of the captain of American Overseas Airlines flight 176. This arrived in London at 9.45 that morning, to be met by Cimperman who collected the documents and sped them to Lamphere and Clegg.[50]

In Skardon's presence, the FBI agents showed Fuchs the new cine-film of Gold, taken at his home on 21 May. Only now, when given clear proof that Gold had been caught – for example Gold had mentioned to the FBI that at their first meeting he had carried a green book and Fuchs had a tennis ball in his hand – did Fuchs agree, 'this was the arrangement'.

There can be no doubt that Fuchs was (at the very least) being economical with the truth throughout this later interrogation. In February, when Skardon showed Fuchs a photograph of Gold, Fuchs had disclaimed any recognition. On 20 May the FBI showed him an enlargement, at which Fuchs hedged and said on this evidence 'he could not exclude Gold from consideration as his US contact'. On 22 May the FBI showed a cine-film taken before Gold's arrest, which Skardon thought 'provided a very fair opportunity for identification' and Fuchs gave a tentative confirmation, although 'he could not be absolutely positive'. Not until 24 May, after learning of Gold's arrest, was Fuchs ready 'to state with certainty that Gold was his US contact' and sign a statement to this effect on 26 May.[51] Prompted by the FBI, who had already got the information from Gold himself, Fuchs then 'remembered that his American contact had been known to him as Raymond'. Yet in earlier statements to Skardon, Fuchs had claimed 'he had never been given a name by his contact'.

Even now, Fuchs was careful not to reveal information needlessly. For example, he 'had no recollection of two meetings between "Raymond" and himself in September 1945'. The FBI suggested the meetings 'took place on September 1, and there was a second meeting in Santa Fe the same month'.[52] Clegg concluded by saying that he would prepare a written report of their interviews and present it to Fuchs to read, approve and sign. This would take him 'a little time to prepare', so the next meeting would be the following afternoon, 25 May.

On this occasion Clegg showed Fuchs a rough draft of his report, which Fuchs verbally approved. In addition Clegg asked about the exact location of Fuchs' meeting with Gold in Queens. The following morning, 26 May, the FBI pair met with Michael Perrin to discuss the propriety of introducing statements about the technical information that Fuchs had transmitted. Perrin advised that the Atomic Energy Commission might be unwilling for such detail to appear, so Clegg arranged to prepare a separate document on this aspect and to omit any such technical detail from the statement to go before a Grand Jury in the proceedings against Harry Gold.

That afternoon Fuchs signed the statement and confirmed that Harry Gold had been his contact in the United States. Although the FBI continued for a few days to ask Fuchs specific details about his contacts with Gold, trying to determine whether Fuchs had information about other potential spies of interest to them, their primary purpose had been achieved: Harry Gold had been identified as Fuchs' courier, and with Fuchs' signed statement the FBI had enough to bring Gold before a Grand Jury as the precondition to an eventual trial.

On 9 December 1950 Harry Gold was sentenced to thirty years in jail. For the KGB this was the start of a catastrophe, as their networks in North America were decimated. Gold's arrest led to the exposure of further Soviet agents, and culminated in the execution of Julius and Ethel Rosenberg by electric chair in June 1953.

Fuchs had held back information, and had only given it up when he knew it was already known. Nonetheless, for the KGB, Fuchs' failure to keep secret his contact with Gold was unforgivable, and the case was filed away for the moment.

Fuchs' exposure led to the discovery, and dismemberment, of Soviet spy rings in the United States. In the United Kingdom, by contrast, his contacts had fled and the authorities' interest was focused more on the international implications of his espionage – how much had the Soviet Union gained from his input, and what damage had been done to Britain's fragile atomic relationship with the USA? The Foreign Office was all too aware of the threat to British–American relations. The Fuchs affair was hugely embarrassing for them already, but this was compounded when within a year it became but the first in a chain of such embarrassments for the British establishment.

First, in the atomic sphere, Bruno Pontecorvo's sudden flight to the Soviet Union in October was a direct consequence of Fuchs' conviction. Pontecorvo, one of Fuchs' Harwell colleagues and a closet communist, disappeared along with his family, eventually to resurface in the Soviet Union. Whereas Fuchs had passed information, and was no longer of use to the USSR, Pontecorvo was a scientist of Nobel Prize quality, one of the world's leading experts on nuclear reactors, on tritium, and on ways of using nuclear physics to locate minerals, such as uranium. At a time when the Soviet Union was in desperate need of raw materials for atomic and hydrogen bombs, Pontecorvo would be invaluable.[1]

These events were soon followed by the defection of the British diplomats, and Soviet agents, Donald Maclean and Guy Burgess, in May 1951. The activities of John Cairncross, Anthony Blunt and Kim Philby – the other three members of the so-called Cambridge Five – came to light later, although there were suspicions, blind-eyes and rank cover-ups within the United Kingdom establishment throughout the 1950s.

The political implications of these events played out differently on the two sides of the Atlantic. In 1950 the Republicans had been out of the White House for nearly two decades, and so had a perfect opportunity to portray the espionage exposures as a failure by the Democrats. In Britain, the saga spanned the full range of politics and neither of the main parties could claim the high ground. Before the Second World War, when the Cambridge Five began their treachery, the Conservatives had been in power; during the war, when Fuchs was hired, there was a coalition government; his post-war recruitment to Harwell was under the aegis of Clement Attlee's Labour government. In the United States the Republicans oversaw a communist witch-hunt whereas in the United Kingdom there was no political appetite to exploit the espionage debacle. There was 'remarkably little public debate [about] espionage and security', nor did Britain 'descend into the chaotic cacophony of accusations and counter-accusations by ambitious demagogues and beleaguered public figures that characterised McCarthyism'.[2]

THE RECRIMINATIONS BEGIN

For General Leslie Groves, the arrest of Fuchs was devastating. Having wanted compartmentalization in the Manhattan Project, which the scientists at Los Alamos had fought against on the grounds that it inhibited debate and free discussion, Groves had put in place what he thought was a foolproof system of security only for one of those scientists to undermine it.[3] In need of a scapegoat, Groves blamed the British Security Services. 'I never believed that the British made any investigation [of Fuchs' background] at all,' he wrote, and continued, 'It was said that each member [of the British Mission] had been investigated as thoroughly as an employee of ours engaged on the same kind of work.'[4] Here Groves implied that the more efficient American investigative procedures would have identified Fuchs as a security risk early on, for if the British had 'given me the slightest inkling of his background, which they did not, Fuchs would not have been permitted access to the project'. Groves touches here on potentially the most egregious failure by MI5 – the decision to hide knowledge of Fuchs' 'proclivities' in 1944.[5]

General Groves combatively brooked no dissent: 'It was a British responsibility [to vet the British scientists]. As partners in the atomic field each nation had to be responsible for its own personnel. The United Kingdom not only failed us, but herself as well.'[6] Whatever the rights or wrongs, Groves was forced to blame the British because the FBI was implicitly criticizing him for the failure. Whereas in the United Kingdom MI5 had been responsible for advising on the political reliability of those employed in Tube Alloys, and subsequently the British contingent in the Manhattan Project, their American counterparts, the FBI, had ceded all responsibility for Manhattan Project security to the Army at the War Office's request in 1943 (see chapter 7). So when Fuchs, the Los Alamos machinist David Greenglass, and later Ted Hall were all shown to have been spies in Los Alamos, the FBI escaped significant criticism. In Great Britain, by contrast, MI5 faced censure.

'As a result of the discovery of a Russian spy among Britain's atomic team, few Government departments within living memory have suffered such a headlong fall from public favour as MI5. Until recently MI5 was regarded as the most efficient organization of its kind in the world. Today its name is in disgrace.' So wrote 'A Former Agent' in the British *Sunday Dispatch*.[7] The author, perhaps with a nod to former colleagues, then excused MI5 who were only 'advisory'. The writer blamed the Ministry of Supply,* as 'it is perfectly clear that Fuchs' Communist background must have been revealed to the Ministry in his Home Office papers, his immigration papers, and his naturalization papers'. Except, as we have seen, that they were not.

MI5 began a counter-offensive, with Colonel James Robertson preparing a list of responses and explanations in case of scrutiny.[8] The central accusation was that MI5 had failed to detect Fuchs' espionage. To counter this, Robertson recalled that Fuchs had made contact with the Russians on his own initiative and – 'as is now known' – after considerable experience in 'underground' activities in Nazi Germany. Thus in August 1941, when the question of Fuchs' suitability first came to MI5's attention, he had already acquired 'the habits of self-discipline and the ability to lead a double life'. There had been no period of 'prolonged recruitment' during which the Security Services would have had their best chance of detecting his activities. This was a fair comment. Robertson was on weaker ground, however, when he continued with the excuse that Fuchs' initial espionage had been during the war when 'attention of both the British and American security authorities were directed primarily against German agents'. Here Robertson ignored MI5's concern about communist activity and finessed its deliberate suppression of Fuchs' 'proclivity' from the Americans in 1943.

One important point in Robertson's assessment was that Fuchs abandoned espionage six months before investigation by MI5 began. This defended the Security Service against the accusation of having been slow to catch him once they had been alerted to his espionage; nonetheless, it

---

* While the Ministry of Supply took the decision, it was based on recommendations from MI5. Roger Hollis in particular favoured Fuchs being employed, because of his singular importance and because there was no conclusive proof that he had communist affiliations.

left open the issue of culpability for having hired an active communist in such a sensitive post.

Here Robertson noted, 'The work for which he was required in August 1941 was of the greatest importance to the war effort and no other person was available with suitable qualifications.' The memo recalled that 'the responsible employing department' – in this case the Ministry of Supply – made the decision after 'weighing the adverse information then available against the lack of confirmatory evidence obtained during his residence in Britain'. Robertson stressed that Fuchs' case was kept under periodic review but that assessment moved in his favour by 'the growing confidence felt in him by his colleagues and by the outstanding contribution he himself was making to the Atomic Energy project'. This was also fair.

Finally, Robertson addressed the irritant: 'Why is it that the Americans appear to have known all about Dr FUCHS' Communist history but not the British?' He denied the premise outright: 'There is no official evidence to suggest that the Americans possessed any information which would have modified the British assessment of Dr FUCHS' security record.' He noted that if the Americans had any such knowledge about Fuchs they would have warned the British. 'No such warning was received.'[9]

Here Robertson touches on one of the murky aspects of the Fuchs affair. FBI files contained what agent Robert Lamphere deemed two 'derogatory pieces of information' about Fuchs.[10] First was a captured Gestapo document, which had been found at the end of the war, hence after Fuchs' time in the United States. This said: 'In 1933, one Klaus Fuchs had been identified as a German Communist to be arrested when and if the Gestapo found him.' This was the very document that worried Fuchs, and which he had asked Harry Gold to tell the Soviet Union to destroy if it ever came to light. The second 'derogatory mention of Fuchs' was his name in the address book of Israel Halperin, whom the FBI knew to have been 'one of the GRU agents in Canada' during the Gouzenko affair.

The American history of what happened is relatively clear. On 15 June 1945 the FBI's man in London, John Cimperman, obtained from US Army Intelligence a roll of film with a list of individuals 'of interest to [Nazi] intelligence'. This had been drawn up in the spring of 1941, prior to the German invasion of Russia. It included names of German communists whom the Nazis deemed enemies of the Reich. One of these was Klaus Fuchs, identified as a 'German communist of relatively important character'. The film was printed and photographs were sent to the FBI's Philadelphia Office for translation. This was completed by March 1946, and the results went into the possession of FBI supervisor Bill Harvey, a man with a chequered history in the organization, who 'resigned' – more enforced than voluntarily – in the summer of 1947. It was only following his dismissal that the German document and the Halperin data were properly recorded, though at that time they had no particular significance – Fuchs was no longer in the United States nor were there any particular reasons to be concerned about him. Only in September 1949, when Fuchs' name came into focus after the VENONA discovery of CHARLES, did the FBI discover the two items. They judged that the 'failure to act more promptly' was that of 'former Special Agent Supervisor William Harvey'.[11]

This explains why the intelligence gathered from Germany does not appear in MI5's records. As for Halperin's address book, however, the fault appears to lie with the British. The Royal Canadian Mounted Police (RCMP) had specifically mentioned four British names, including that of Fuchs, but Robertson's statement categorically denies knowledge of them. How this oversight occurred has never been established. Available MI5 files say nothing. FBI files, however, do. According to them, the RCMP was 'cooperating very closely with Peter Dwyer of MI6 who was then in Canada in connection with the [Gouzenko] case'. For this reason the FBI made no attempt to investigate any of the 'over 700' people named in the book who were resident in Britain. The Gouzenko case was a Canadian affair and as such primarily the responsibility of the RCMP and, according to the FBI, 'the RCMP offered the Halperin data to Peter Dwyer but he did not take it'.[12] Why he declined the data remains obscure. Chapman Pincher claimed that this mishandling of intelligence was because Roger Hollis was a Soviet mole in MI5. While MI5's released files do reveal Hollis to have been singularly relaxed and liberal in his assessment of Fuchs' threat (and, indeed, of other subsequently confirmed spies or defectors), there is no evidence to confirm Pincher's theory, nor, if the FBI account is correct, does it explain why MI6 failed to act.[13] Whatever the reasons, MI5 was unaware of these aspects of Fuchs' history.[14]

Meanwhile in the United States, Fuchs' arrest caused a public outcry. Five months previously, in September 1949, the explosion of a Soviet atomic bomb, earlier than expected, had dominated the news.* Now Fuchs' arrest revealed a likely reason for this Russian advance. Editorial comment around the United States was consistent: the lightness of the sentence imposed was regarded as disproportionate to the gravity of the offence. A few writers even considered that the death penalty would not have been excessive. They recognized, however, that fourteen years was the maximum sentence allowed by British law and approved of the speed with

---

* The test took place on 29 August 1949, but the news only became public in mid-September.

which the proceedings were completed, in contrast to the USA where the tempo would have been much slower.

The *St Paul Dispatch* wrote: 'He stabbed in the back the country that took him in when he came there in 1933 to save his body and soul from Hitler.' For the *Tampa Tribune*, Fuchs' 'staggering ingratitude and treachery betrayed, in effect, all Western civilization'. In the emerging McCarthyism the *Washington Evening Star* saw the case as demonstrating the power of communist ideology 'even upon men of brilliant mind' such that 'no Communist anywhere may safely be regarded as other than a potential traitor'. The *New York Herald Tribune* drew a conclusion that has been confirmed by the passage of time: 'The coils of suspicion, secrecy and security close more deeply around us. Therein lies the greatest of Fuchs' betrayals of the free world.'[15]

General Groves was never slow to advertise his opinion that the fault lay with the United Kingdom's Security Services; J. Edgar Hoover, meanwhile, took every opportunity to gain maximum credit by claiming unashamedly that the FBI were responsible for having uncovered Fuchs' activities.

Sir Percy Sillitoe's frustration with Hoover's opportunism, and his own inability to make a public response – not least as the true source had been VENONA, whose decoding had intimately involved Britain's GCHQ, but also because of his own service's anonymity – spilled over in a note to the Prime Minister, Clement Attlee: 'The public has been left with the impression that a notorious Communist was negligently cleared by Security Service for work in one of the most secret branches of Defence research, and that he would have been there to this day had it not been for the perspicacity of the FBI.'[16]

Questions were tabled for the Prime Minister to address in Parliament on Thursday 9 March. Brigadier Frank Medlicott MP asked that the PM make a statement, 'in view of the public disquiet', while David Gammans MP asked that he 'in particular, state how this leakage was detected by the American Secret Service and not by our own'. This was a perfect example of MI5's hands being tied, Dick White advising that it would 'not be in the public interest to discuss sources of intelligence available to either the Americans or to ourselves'. Meanwhile, Raymond Blackburn MP asked the Ministry of Supply to explain in what circumstances 'a member of the Communist Party and a former alien' was 'screened by the police and permitted to hold security appointments'.[17]

MI5 briefed the Prime Minister with a rose-tinted history of Fuchs permeated with errors that obfuscated the truth. First it attempted to shift any blame by pointing out that while it is the duty of the Security Service to point out the risk, 'the final decision' on whether to employ Fuchs 'rests with the employing Department'. MI5 then listed five occasions on which Fuchs had been reviewed, starting with 'October 1941 (grant of an A.W.S. [Aliens War Service] permit)'.[18] The Prime Minister was not alerted that Fuchs had worked with Rudolf Peierls since May that year, which MI5 knew. MI5 was not then aware that he had been privy to secrets in meetings at Cambridge in June, and had passed them to Russia in August. The lateness of the AWS review was hidden behind the false claim that Fuchs left Edinburgh 'in August 1941'.[19]

MI5's self-generated reference worked. The Prime Minister gave them a clean bill of health: 'I do not think there is anything that can cast the slightest slur on the Security Services; indeed I think they acted promptly and effectively as soon as there was any line they could follow.' He conveniently assured the House of Commons that there was no blame attached either to the present government or previous governments, 'or to any of the officials'. He concluded, 'I think we had here quite an extraordinary and exceptional case.'[20] Sadly, within six months the disappearance of the Harwell physicist Bruno Pontecorvo would show this was not so.

VENONA: THE REAL HERO

But for the VENONA decryption project, it is plausible that Fuchs would have continued to work in British nuclear physics for the rest of his career, with no one suspecting that he had been anything other than a dedicated patriotic scientist, driven by hatred of the Nazis, and then by love of his adopted nation. It was VENONA, not the FBI and not MI5, which gave the first clue to a spy in the British Mission in New York, and it did more: it made the link between GOOSE and the paper on thermal diffusion, but for which Harry Gold might never have been identified.[21] VENONA revealed that GOOSE was also linked to another American espionage source, known to Moscow as CONSTRUCTOR, whom the FBI had identified as Abe Brothman, the chemist who had been 'outed' by Elizabeth Bentley. As we have seen, the thermal diffusion breakthrough about GOOSE appears to have come from the British GCHQ, Meredith Gardner's team at Arlington Hall meanwhile having discovered the link to CONSTRUCTOR. However the credits are apportioned, the profound collaboration between the two cryptographic agencies belies Hoover's version of an FBI triumph.[22]

Large swathes of FBI files show that from February 1950 the FBI mounted an intense surveillance operation on Brothman in the hope that this might lead them to GOOSE. They had identified Harry Gold as a candidate for GOOSE back in February, but were led into a maze by Fuchs' failure to identify him, compounded by his selection of Robbins' photograph. In addition to mounting round-the-clock surveillance on Abe Brothman, the FBI checked their files on hordes of other candidates, and compared their movements against Fuchs' descriptions of his meetings with GOOSE before finally returning to Gold and settling on him.

VENONA had also revealed the code names and links between Soviet agents in the United States in sufficient detail that the FBI had trails to follow. This was in marked contrast to the United Kingdom, where the only source for Fuchs' contacts was Fuchs himself. Throughout his inter-rogations Fuchs was economical with the truth, and he followed the spy's charter of not revealing the identities of colleagues who were still free and within reach of the authorities. He confirmed Gold's identity only after it was clear that Gold was under arrest and had admitted his role. Fuchs held back on Ursula Beurton ('Sonya'), Jürgen Kuczynski and Hannah Klopstech until all were safely within the Eastern bloc. The one person whom he gave up to MI5 was himself; the other person whose secrets he withheld assiduously was his sister, Kristel.

KGB files now confirm that Kristel was a significant player in the Klaus Fuchs affair. Fuchs had given Kristel's details to 'Sonya' back in 1943 in preparation for his move to the United States. The Soviets put her on file, as agent 'ANT'. She was involved in her brother's espionage to the extent of being a holding agent for documents, and presenting signals in the window of her home to alert Harry Gold when it was safe to call and collect them. It is possible that Fuchs' bizarre failure to make his flight on his final day in the USA was because he was held up with last-minute information to pass via Harry Gold. In any event, Fuchs would have to have been naive not to realize that he had involved his sister in his treach-ery, and that in the United States she might face capital punishment. The price of ensuring that his mentally ill sister Kristel remained in the clear, and did not commit suicide like their mother, their grandmother and their sister Elizabeth, or even face the death penalty for espionage herself, was for Fuchs to confess to his own involvement. And by announcing that his espionage had extended over eight years in three different episodes, he succeeded in portraying Kristel as a bit player, a walk-on part in but one scene of his three-act play.

VENONA had exposed Fuchs and pointed to Harry Gold, but as its existence was known to a mere handful, Hoover was well placed to pro-mote the triumphal myth that netting Fuchs and Gold was entirely due to his FBI. This was supremely opportunistic – even though the success in identifying Harry Gold, bringing him to justice, and breaking other espionage networks indeed involved much hard graft by his agents. Hoover was so successful in ensuring that credit flowed to his organization that the American media failed to comment that Fuchs had managed to pass information from the heart of the Manhattan Project for two years without the FBI being aware of the fact.

This contrasted with the relatively low-key approach of the British Security Services, which left them open to accusations of incompetence. However, MI5 was all too aware of a real danger that Fuchs would defect to the Soviet Union; that he did not is a credit to their investigation. The same cannot be said about their enquiries into his contacts, however. All Fuchs' contacts in the United Kingdom were out of reach by the time MI5 identified them, and in each case the Security Services only learned their names when Fuchs himself told them; and he invariably did so when the information was no longer any use. MI5's failure to consider Ursula Beurton as a candidate, and the ease with which she outmanoeuvred Jim Skardon and Michael Serpell in 1947, do not reflect well on the service.

Meanwhile, as Hoover exploited public ignorance of VENONA to claim credit for the FBI, and MI5 was unable to reveal the role of the British, not least GCHQ, in exposing Klaus Fuchs, the Russians were equally ignorant about the cause of Fuchs' 'failure'. Still unaware that identification of Fuchs was because VENONA had broken their codes, Moscow set out to identify a human traitor within its ranks.

SOVIET PARANOIA

Moscow learned of the unfolding disaster for its master spy in a terse message from their London Embassy. 'On 3.2.50 the London evening newspapers ran articles about Klaus Fuchs' arrest. Two charges were brought against him during the arrest. (a) of passing information pertaining to atomic energy that could have been useful to the enemy to an unknown person in 1947 (b) passing information in the USA in Feb. 1945.'[23]

For Moscow Centre the urgent questions were: How had Fuchs been exposed, was there a traitor in their midst, and how much were KGB operations compromised? Unaware that the culprit was the Soviet Embassy's own diplomatic telegrams, the KGB looked for clues among their agents. Their first suspicions focused on Harry Gold – 'Arno'. The immediate task was to check whether Arno had been arrested.

The Russian military attaché in their New York Embassy was informed that Fuchs had been arrested, and that the press reported he had given materials to an 'unknown person'. Arno was due to meet another contact on 5 February. Fearing that his cover might be compromised, and that the FBI might be using Harry Gold as bait, the KGB ordered the contact not to go to the rendezvous. However, another agent, whom Gold would not recognize, was sent to watch to see if 'Arno' turned up, and if so, whether he behaved normally. Arno was seen to arrive; there was no sign of any surveillance of him by the FBI, and the observer reported: 'Arno seemed to be at ease.'[24]

So Harry Gold was in the clear – for now. The KGB, however, were convinced that he had betrayed Fuchs, because Gold was the only person to have met Fuchs in the United States who knew the nature of Fuchs' material. A KGB analyst assessed the situation:

> Considering that Charles was charged with passing materials on the assembly of the atomic bomb in the USA in February 1945, which did in fact happen, it may be presumed that the reason for Charles's failure was connected to his work while he was in the USA. Because A. is the only person with whom Ch. was connected in the USA, as well as the only one who knew the nature of the materials that were passed, it may be presumed that A. betrayed Ch. to American counterintelligence.[25]

This was but the first KGB pointer to Gold. Their suspicions were further excited because a mole had told them that MI5 had asked French Intelligence questions about Anatoly Yatzkov – 'John', to whom Gold had passed on Fuchs' material in New York. Fuchs knew nothing of this. As Yatzkov never worked in England, the KGB deduced correctly that 'the interest of the English in him can only be explained by the investigation of Arno [and] Charles. Not even Ch. himself knew about Yatzkov's involvement in Charles's case, and the only person who could have said anything about this was A. whom [Yatzkov] handled in 1944–45.'[26]

This was deemed so serious and conclusive that Deputy Foreign Minister and chairman of the Intelligence Committee of Information, Valerian Zorin, sent notice direct to Stalin. 'Although Arno has said he did not give evidence against anyone to the FBI, an analysis of the circumstances of Ch-s's arrest and of A's behaviour at meetings gives reason to suppose that Ch. was exposed by the latter. We are carefully investigating Ch-s's arrest with the aim of determining in detail the reasons and circumstances surrounding his failure.'[27] Quite what the reference to Gold's 'behaviour at meetings' means is not explained. That day, their agent had merely confirmed that Gold came to the planned rendezvous and that he acted normally. Possibly the writer deemed that it would be wise to create a cover from Stalin's retribution by providing some 'evidence' to give an illusion of being in control.

In any event, the thesis of Gold as sole suspect could not long survive the inherent paranoia of Stalin's Russia. When the KGB reviewed Fuchs' file, more suspicions arose. They recalled that their rival, the GRU, had recommended Fuchs to them back in 1943. During his time with the GRU he had been in contact with their station chief in the United Kingdom, 'Sonya' – Ursula Beurton. The KGB now grew concerned about the visit of Jim Skardon and Michael Serpell to Sonya in September 1947. 'Two counterintelligence officers came to see S., told her that they knew about her work for Sov. Intelligence in Switzerland and asked her to tell them about this work. However S denied everything and did not give any evidence.'[28] So Sonya had insisted that she had given nothing away, but was this true? The sceptical KGB duly added Sonya and her brother Jürgen Kuczynski – 'Karo' in KGB files – to their 'possible reasons for failure'.[29]

A further suspect was Kristel: 'Charles's sister suddenly came down with a nervous disorder. It is possible that her illness might have resulted from her being interrogated by Amer. Counterintelligence.'[30] Meanwhile an order was sent to the Russian arm of the KGB in Berlin to 'launch an investigation of Jurgen Kuc-ski and Hanna Klopstock [sic] who live in the Sov.-occupied zone of Berlin'.[31] This pair had been instrumental in recruiting Fuchs and in maintaining contact with him back in 1942, and Hannah had helped again in 1947, but they were otherwise bit players in the saga.

With the help of Fuchs' father, Emil, the Russians hatched a cunning scheme to hire an experienced lawyer for Fuchs' defence. The idea was that a skilled defence could force British counter-intelligence to call as witnesses 'individuals whom they had used to investigate Charles in the USA and England' and thereby help determine 'the real reason for Charles's failure'.[32] As the trial lasted only two days and was over by 1 March, there was no time to hire a suitable defence lawyer, so the plan was stillborn.

A new plan was drawn up: Emil would try to have the case reviewed with the aim of reducing the sentence, as a gambit to tease out the information from MI5 during the review. Even in the unlikely event that this proved successful, an intervention by TASS created a problem. Sir Hartley Shawcross' statement in court that Fuchs had passed atomic secrets to Soviet agents was described by TASS to be 'a gross fabrication, since Fuchs is unknown to the Soviet government and no Soviet government agents had association with Fuchs'.[33] TASS's unwelcome intervention put paid to the KGB's scheme. This was because Emil was 'not bound to [the KGB] in any way and therefore [Russian] interest could become known to his

English Quaker acquaintances and the counterintelligence which will undoubtedly use this for an anti-Soviet campaign, especially after the refutation of TASS'.[34]

On 28 February 'Sonya' was ex-filtrated from Great Rollright in Oxfordshire, the heart of England, to East Berlin, as it was deemed 'dangerous to stay in England' (see above, chapter 21).[35] On 18 March she reported to the KGB in Berlin on her work with Fuchs, and described him politically as 'weak'. In her judgement, his entire confession stemmed 'not from malicious intent, but from political short-sightedness'. She felt that the KGB should spend more effort on 'educational work' with its agents. In a confident if risky move, she asserted, 'if Charles had been handled by [me, I] would have found time for his political education, and this affair would not have ended so regrettably'.[36] Sonya was highly regarded in Moscow, and her advice was heeded. Plans to 'educate' agents were drawn up.

The KGB now teetered on desperation with a proposal to recruit Fuchs' brother Gerhard. Their wild idea was that once Gerhard was their agent, he could go to England, meet with his brother, and 'find out from him the circumstances surrounding his failure'.[37] The plan was hatched by the KGB in mid-March, although it seems that it was not carried out. Instead the subsequent files record merely that 'Kin' – the code name for Gerhard – 'died of tuberculosis in Berlin in January 1951'.[38]

By the end of May 1950 information about VENONA appears to have percolated through the Soviet system, and the true culprit identified. 'To Comrade J. V. Stalin. As a result of checking and investigating the circumstances surrounding the failure of our agent Charles . . . The following has been established.' There followed what must have been a difficult memorandum to send to Stalin, which could have become a suicide note. It told him:

> . . . the American decryption service had worked for a long time on one of the telegrams from New York's KGB station dating from 1944–45 during Charles's stay in the USA. Unable to decode this telegram in its entirety, *the Americans sent it in 1949 to Eng. Counterintelligence* [my emphasis], which was able to decode it completely and ascertain that Ch. was a Sov. Intelligence agent, who had passed us important information about work at Amer. and Eng. Atomic centres, where he worked. This cipher telegram was processed using a one-time pad that had been used for a different cipher telegram, which is what allowed counterintelligence to decode its text.[39]*

* KGB files point to the crucial breakthrough having involved the key role of GCHQ in England, contrary to J. Edgar Hoover's self-serving claims for the FBI (see also chapter 13, note 21). That Moscow had this level of detail illustrates the efficiency of Kim Philby in monitoring the VENONA programme.

This was a damning admission that the procedure for use of one-time pads had been violated – the whole essence of a 'one-time pad' of course being that it is used but once. 'Our experts allow for the possibility that the English have decoded telegrams of ours that were processed with a used one-time pad.'[40] As to the further implications of this debacle, and what the KGB planned to do about it, Zorin continued:

> On the basis of Charles's testimony, on 24 May of this year [five days previous to the letter] Harry Gold – our long-time agent 'Arno' – was arrested; he had received materials from Ch. on the atomic bomb in 1944–45, and we stopped using him to receive material in December 1945. At the beginning of 1950, in the interest of preventing employees of the Committee of Information from being compromised, we recalled Feklisov, an employee of the London station who had handled agent Charles, and Kamenev, an employee of the New York station who had handled agent Arno. At present there are no Soviet workers in England or the USA whom these agents might know. Measures have also been taken to get out from the USA four agents who had previously been connected with Arno, and who are threatened with failure if the latter confesses.[41]

Success in protecting their North American espionage rings was limited, however. First, Harry Gold identified another source at Los Alamos – a machinist named David Greenglass. Greenglass was arrested in June, and confessed to having given Gold secret information about the explosive lenses used to initiate implosion. Under questioning, Greenglass led the FBI to the heart of the Soviet spy ring in the United States, his brother-in-law, Julius Rosenberg.

Rosenberg was a spy under the charge of Feklisov. Back in September 1944, Rosenberg had suggested to Feklisov that he recruit his sister Ruth and her husband David Greenglass. Greenglass, an avowed communist, was in the army and had been posted to Los Alamos. In November 1944 Ruth visited him in Albuquerque and asked him to forward information on the project. So it was that Gold would meet not just Fuchs but also Greenglass on his visits to Santa Fe.

Following Harry Gold's information, the FBI interviewed David Greenglass. He agreed to confess to his own activities and to testify against Julius and Ethel Rosenberg in exchange for immunity for his wife, Ruth. As part of this deal, which has been mired in controversy ever since, Ruth testified that the Rosenbergs had urged her to recruit David in espionage.

David Greenglass was sentenced to fifteen years in jail; in 1960 he was released after nine and a half years – a similar incarceration to that of Klaus Fuchs. They were relatively fortunate. For others caught in the fall-out of Fuchs' arrest and confession, the penalty would be extreme: on 19 June 1953, Julius and Ethel Rosenberg were executed by electric chair. The saga thus exhibited one of the features of American justice – those who confess and name co-conspirators escape with relatively light penalties, whereas the last person in the chain who refuses to confess or to name others receives the maximum punishment, even though being no more guilty. Without question the information that the Rosenbergs received through David Greenglass was trifling relative to that which Harry Gold passed on from Klaus Fuchs, yet only the Rosenbergs – who refused to confess or name names – paid with their lives.*

BRITAIN'S ATOMIC FALLOUT

Moscow's losses were the FBI's gain, as the arrest of Fuchs and ensuing convictions of Soviet spies helped to reinvent J. Edgar Hoover as an all-American hero, as he intended. For the atomic ambitions of the United Kingdom, however, Fuchs' arrest could not have happened at a worse time.

Fuchs' expertise had been crucial to William Penney since 1946 when Britain had been forced to 'go it alone'. Termination of the – always informal – atomic agreement between Roosevelt and Churchill by the United States in the 1946 McMahon Act was because the US Congress viewed the atomic bomb to be 'United States property and not to be given away'. Churchill loved to stress the 'special relationship' between the 'English-speaking peoples', but this was a rhetorical invention. In reality, 'American nuclear policy was based on retaining a monopoly over the atomic bomb and excluding all other nations, including the British.'[42]

Doubts about British security that originated in 1946 with the revelation of the spy network in Canada had provided a convenient cover for this agenda. The inclusion of the United Kingdom in the McMahon Act was given apparent legitimacy by General Groves, who opined that the British scientists 'did not advance the date of the bomb by a single day'.[43] In reality, as we have seen, the émigré scientists were essential to the Manhattan Project; Peierls and Fuchs' contribution to the critical issue of plutonium implosion alone is testament to that. Without them, the atomic

---

* Fuchs' arrest led to eight further arrests and forty-five new espionage cases, according to F. M. Szasz, *British Scientists and the Manhattan Project: The Los Alamos Years* (Macmillan, 1992), p. 86, based on a report by A. Belmont to Mr Ladd 28/2/51, FBI 65-58805, vol. 41, s. 1457–1500.

bomb would have been significantly delayed, and very probably would not have been available before the end of the war.

Following the McMahon Act in 1946, the United Kingdom was forced to develop its own atomic weapon, but meanwhile put in diplomatic efforts to restore cooperation with the United States. There were two cards in British hands. First, back in 1944 when Roosevelt and Churchill promised 'full and effective cooperation', the agreement had also included a right for either country to veto use of the atomic bomb. After the war, several influential US Congressmen were shocked to discover that Britain held this power over them, and were keen for some new agreement to free American atomic policy. Second was an urgent practical issue. Global supplies of uranium were shared by agreement, and the United States' growing needs outstripped those available. In 1948 the two nations signed a 'Modus Vivendi': the United Kingdom would drop its veto, allow the United States a larger fraction of the uranium supply, and in return the Americans would allow some exchange of atomic information.[44] By the end of 1949, with the Soviet Union having unexpectedly exploded an atomic bomb in August, the United Kingdom found support within the Atomic Energy Commission (AEC) and the State Department for discussions about restoring collaboration. A technical hurdle would be support of Congress for amendment of the McMahon Act. Nonetheless, at the start of January, the British Cabinet was confident that some deal could be achieved.[45]

It was on 9 February, exactly one week after Fuchs' arrest, that Senator Joseph McCarthy launched the paranoia named after him in a speech at Wheeling, West Virginia.[46] McCarthy ruthlessly exploited the gift of Fuchs' arrest with accusations of a communist plot, and claims to have a list of 205 communists in the State Department. The timing of Fuchs' arrest was also unfortunate for British hopes because in America as in Great Britain 1950 was an election year. Congressional elections in the United States implied 'It would not be possible to put draft proposals for any agreement to this session of Congress, particularly because this is an election year and Congress will presumably be breaking up too early for it to be possible to produce proposals in suitable form for them.'[47]

Meanwhile General Groves was 'angry at what he considered lying to him by the British delegation about clearance on Fuchs'.[48] These feelings were perhaps reasonable, as the British had not told the whole truth about Fuchs, but his vision of the bomb as an American creation was rather myopic and resonated with some United States politicians. Three days after Fuchs' arrest, Republican Senator John W. Bricker of Ohio stated: 'I've always opposed the use of foreign scientists on atomic projects. The arrest of Fuchs makes me even more certain that I'm right about it'.[49] The espionage factor, which had been exploited back in 1946 at the birth of the McMahon Act, now threatened to undermine restoration of co-operation in 1950.

Nonetheless, by the summer of 1950 British hopes of success in the coming year had grown. First, the American programme was short of uranium, which the British could provide as a dowry. Second, US Defence Secretary Louis Johnson – who opposed collaboration with the United Kingdom – was replaced with the more anglophile General George Marshall, the inspiration behind the 'Marshall Plan' for rebuilding post-war Europe. The Americans drafted a proposal for cooperation, which would include British scientists working on weapons research in the United States. Michael Perrin was very excited at the prospect, as it seemed that only the hydrogen bomb would remain off limits.[50]

Meanwhile at Harwell, the fallout from Fuchs' conviction led to renewed interest in rooting out any communist staff. It was now that Fuchs' colleague Bruno Pontecorvo feared that his closet communism would come to the fore, and he fled to Moscow in August. Suspicion of British reliability erupted again in the United States and British hopes for renewal of collaboration were dashed. Alec Longair, of the United Kingdom Atomic Mission based in Washington, was forthright in his recollections:

> The American xenophobes went rampant, include a son-of-a-bitch called (Adm.) Lewis Strauss, a Commissioner who eventually [1953] became Chairman of the US Atomic Energy Commission. All hopes of *effective* exchange of scientific information on the project really became minimal until about 1954 when the British work had advanced so far that it was to the US advantage to know what was going on.[51]

A TRUCE

Meanwhile, the Security Services of both countries had to face their failures. Tension continued between the FBI and MI5. In the Washington Embassy, MI5's Geoffrey Patterson transmitted to London: 'the attitude of FBI towards both the MI6 representative [Philby] and myself' has become 'somewhat adolescent' as relations became 'strained over repercussions of the Fuchs case'. It is perhaps ironic that although Bruno Pontecorvo's defection temporarily killed off the cooperation in the atomic field, it brought some form of truce between the FBI and MI5. MI5 had covered up their information about Fuchs' communist 'proclivities' in

1944, and the FBI had been careless with the same knowledge about Pontecorvo. He had lived in the United States from 1940 to 1943 and then worked in Canada, on the Anglo-Canadian reactor programme within the Manhattan Project, even though he had been a communist since 1939. This 'proclivity' was known to the FBI, but it had unaccountably failed to inform the British when the latter vetted him in 1943.

Eventually the FBI and MI5 agreed to a mutual cover-up of errors they had both made. The two agencies withheld the full story from their governments, even though they exchanged information freely with each other. MI5's records show that a letter, sent to Gordon Arneson in the US State Department, omitted a crucial paragraph, and thereby hid errors by both agencies. An annotation in the minutes says: 'It is naturally desirable that these facts should not become public'.[52]

This cover-up reached the highest levels in the two agencies. Sir Percy Sillitoe saw J. Edgar Hoover in the autumn of 1950 and the two agreed 'Neither [would] make press statements about the other's office without first clearing with the other.' In part, this was in order to mend fences, where the media in the United Kingdom and the United States had been fed quotes by the respective agencies to spin versions of events that favoured one nation at the expense of the other. The report within MI5 of Sillitoe and Hoover's meeting reveals a darker agenda, however: 'It [is] important that nothing be said that gives any indication that the FBI had not passed on their information [about Pontecorvo's 'proclivity'] to the British authorities.'[53] This was an outrageous statement implying that the FBI's failure, which was probably no more than a bureaucratic oversight, was on a par with the deliberate act perpetrated by the British Security Services. What is indisputable is that MI5 was fortunate that the depth of its own calumny remained hidden. Its recommendation in 1944 that 'it would not appear to be desirable to mention [Fuchs'] proclivities to the authorities in the USA' was unknown to Hoover – and remained secreted in classified files for half a century.

J. EDGAR HOOVER'S LEGACY

Hoover continued to annoy MI5 with his claims that the GOOSE case was solved as soon as the FBI had access to Fuchs. The dual implications were that the British had been unable to extract the information and that Harry Gold would have been identified sooner had the British not been so perfidious. Geoffrey Patterson wrote to Sillitoe to establish the record as he saw it.[54] The original leads had come from VENONA – while the link between GOOSE and thermal diffusion appears to have originated with GCHQ and with Fuchs' remark to MI5 that his contact had asked about that subject. The VENONA information had been passed to Lish Whitson on 4 February; the FBI's search for a chemist interested in thermal diffusion had arisen from that. The FBI did not interview Gold until 15 May, just one hour before they heard from London that Fuchs had positively identified him from a photograph. Patterson concluded by pointing out that at no time had the FBI intimated to him that Gold was their prime suspect and made his remark that the attitude of the FBI was becoming 'adolescent'.

None of this was public knowledge at the time, of course, nor would it be for more than thirty years. So for decades the perception persisted that Hoover's leadership of the FBI was the key to cracking the case. By 1951 his reputation had soared, his persona that of the Guardian Angel who had rescued the nation from a British-made spy disaster, and but for whom the United States might already have been overrun by communist subversion. There had been Democrats in the White House for nearly two decades, and some prominent Republicans urged Hoover to run for President in the upcoming election. Hoover declined, claiming to be above politics, though he probably felt that the skeletons in his own closet were safer if he retained the key by remaining in control of his army of snoopers. Instead, he threw his considerable prestige behind war hero Dwight D. Eisenhower, and as his running mate a young congressman whose scurrilous fabrication of smears against a rival had impressed Hoover by its ruthless efficiency. Hoover, who had shamelessly bugged the premises of 'enemies' while circumventing due process, and covered up evidence by destroying records – as in the Coplon case – endorsed as candidate for Vice President, Richard Milhous Nixon.

FUCHS AND THE BRITISH HYDROGEN BOMB

Following Fuchs' arrest and Pontecorvo's defection, cooperation between Britain and the United States in atomic energy stopped.* The secret British project to build an atomic bomb, overseen by William Penney, now faced

---

* This remained the case for eight years. The Mutual Defence Agreement between the United States and United Kingdom was signed on 3 July 1958. The Soviet Union had launched Sputnik on 4 October 1957, and the British announced they had successfully tested a hydrogen bomb on 8 November 1957. Britain was also a world leader in detection and analysis of debris from bomb tests, know-how that the USA desperately needed to access.

an existential crisis as with Fuchs' imprisonment Penney had lost 'his finest theorist'.[55] Desperate for a means to improve plutonium production, Penney remarked that there were only four people in the United Kingdom who had the 'knowledge and ability' to discover how to do so. One was Penney himself, and 'two of the others are university professors who are unwilling to do more than give advice'. And the fourth 'is now in prison'.[56]

By the spring of 1952, Britain's first atomic weapon had been assembled ready for shipment on 5 June to its test site in Australia, its plutonium core based on the design that Fuchs had inspired.[57] Penney had been 'combing over Fuchs' work up to the time he was arrested' and become concerned that Fuchs seemed not to have been asked how much of his Harwell work he passed to the Russians. Apparently Fuchs had 'merely answered specific Russian queries'. Penney now wanted this matter clarified, 'in light of recent developments'. To do so, on 28 May he sought permission from Guy Liddell to visit Fuchs 'in his cell'.[58] In June 1952 Penney went to see Fuchs in Stafford Prison.

Although the contents of their long meeting have never been revealed, at first sight its date suggests Penney wanted to consult Fuchs about the upcoming atomic bomb test. However, Liddell's response only came on 10 June, by which time the bomb had left England. Liddell also made clear that permission would be needed from the governor of Stafford Prison, where Fuchs was now incarcerated, so this appointment wasn't likely to be fixed immediately. There is no sense of urgency, and by the time Penney achieved his consultation, any modifications to the upcoming atomic bomb – now on the high seas – would have been impractical.* It is possible that Penney had some last-minute thoughts on how effective Russian monitoring and analysis of fallout would be, and hoped to discover whether Fuchs had given them details of Harwell's expertise in that field, but here too there seems little of practical relevance that would merit seeing Fuchs after so long.

There was, however, another 'recent development' for which an urgent consultation with Fuchs could prove invaluable. The Atomic Energy Board, with an eye to the future, had decided to begin investigation into the hydrogen bomb, for which Penney and Sir John Cockcroft had been asked to present a paper on 15 May.[59] Britain's atomic bomb, now en route to Australia, was out of Penney's control for two months and this new development – the H-bomb – took centre stage. The level of ignorance

---

* The plutonium core was still to be flown out to the test site, but if Penney had worries about that it seems remarkably late to be seeking Fuchs' advice when this could have been done at any time.

about hydrogen bombs was vast in the United Kingdom in 1952, with some thinking it to be merely 'a large re-designed A-bomb'.[60] On balance it seems likely that Penney wanted a basic tutorial, and the natural source for such a briefing would be Klaus Fuchs.

Penney destroyed his papers on retirement, and any records of Fuchs' involvement in the British atomic and hydrogen bombs have been withheld from public view. The official history of Britain's nuclear deterrent poses a cogent question: 'If Fuchs' information was of such value to Soviet scientists, how much did he also give to the British and how important was it?'[61] When Fuchs' papers were examined in 1950, they were found to contain some information on the hydrogen bomb, but nothing of importance was found in his safe. Brian Flowers, Fuchs' successor, remarked, 'What he did with his Top Secret documents, which is what the safe was for, God only knows.'[62] Possibly this explains the report to Arnold on 29 January 1950 that Fuchs had been overheard tearing up papers and stoking his fire.

There are some indirect clues that support the thesis that Penney consulted Fuchs about the hydrogen bomb. On 9 February 1953 Sir Freddie Morgan, Controller for Atomic Energy, wrote to Penney, 'Fuchs is continuing to collaborate in various other matters.'[63] When that same month Prime Minister Churchill asked about the feasibility of a British H-bomb, he was told, 'Lord Cherwell is already consulting Penney.' In April Cherwell informed Churchill that Fuchs had told Russia 'all he knew about the [H-] bomb'.[64] Fuchs' interview with Perrin on 30 January 1950 gave no such assurance, and Lord Cherwell's statement suggests that the question posed in Penney's letter to Liddell had now been answered.

The general consensus among respected scientists and historians of the atomic era is that Fuchs played a pivotal role in the early phase of the hydrogen bomb project.[65] If, as Cherwell attested, Fuchs had told the Soviets all he knew, it is unlikely that he would have told the British any less. As to his role overall, Lorna Arnold, official historian of the British H-bomb project, made a pithy comment to me: 'The parentage of the British, Russian and American hydrogen bombs has long been debated, but I suspect Klaus Fuchs was grandfather to them all.'[66]

23

Father and Son

THE FATHER'S TALE

Embarrassed by their failure to have caught Fuchs while he was still active in espionage, MI5 now became obsessed by Peierls. They convinced themselves that he was sympathetic to the goals of the Soviet Union more than of Great Britain. In the United States fear of communism was being fanned by the rise of McCarthyism and active pursuit of communists, real and imagined. Although the extreme persecution of socialists and 'fellow travellers' did not reach the United Kingdom, suspicion of leftish intellectuals caused MI5 to target the Atomic Scientists Association (ASA) – described in a dossier as a 'communist front organisation' – and especially its chair: Rudolf Peierls.

The ASA had three main roles: to educate British citizens about nuclear energy, to give the government advice on nuclear matters, and to promote international control of nuclear weapons. In a world where the nature of these terrifying inventions was not yet widely understood, cautions from experts in the ASA were viewed with suspicion. In his capacity as chair of the ASA Peierls wrote articles that raised hackles in Whitehall. In one, for example, he commented that 'we would be in a better moral position if the Allies had dropped a demonstration bomb' away from Japan's major cities.[1] This opinion was recorded in MI5's files, and in the United States was used by the FBI to confirm its prejudice that the ASA is a 'communist front organisation'.

Official paranoia about Peierls burned slowly throughout 1950, fuelled by rumour, innuendo and analysis reminiscent of times when witches were dunked. This began with an article by him in the *Daily Worker*, a British communist newspaper, which by chance appeared on the same day as Fuchs' arrest, 2 February 1950.

Eleven atomic scientists issued a statement calling for the 'utmost attempts' to be made now 'to eliminate atomic warfare'. The reason for their plea, and its timing, was the news that the United States planned to develop a hydrogen bomb, a device whose genocidal implications were apparent to atomic scientists, but were not yet understood by politicians, let alone the general public. The scientists urged what today would be deemed relatively mild: 'The utmost efforts must be made to eliminate atomic warfare either by a new effort to solve the problem of the effective control of atomic energy or by a new contribution to the wider problem of international relations.' Signatories included the Nobel laureate in physics G. P. Thomson and Peierls, who had done so much to create the early British momentum for the atomic bomb. In the febrile atmosphere of 1950, however, this statement in a left-wing newspaper put the Security Services on alert. A copy was abstracted to Peierls' file.[2]

The phones of the Atomic Science Association were tapped. Its secretary was heard reading a letter from Peierls that mused 'maybe the lesson [of the Fuchs and Nunn May cases] is that the best security system in the world cannot work on a project the size of the atomic energy project unless one is prepared to go the whole way and establish an Iron Curtain, an atmosphere of suspicion as has been done in Russia. If the price to be paid for Security is to establish a similar atmosphere, is it worth the price?'[3]

Enquiries into Peierls' history and Genia's family background spread. Sir Percy Sillitoe wrote to Chief Constable Dodd of Birmingham Police for anything he might know but stressed 'No direct enquiry please'. Sillitoe enclosed a bald summary of Peierls' CV that read, '1934 arrived from USSR. 1950 thought to hold Left wing sympathies', the first of which was certainly wrong – he arrived from Germany in 1932 – and the latter seemed to rely on his caution about atomic weapons, as expressed in the *Daily Worker*.[4]

Dodd's perspective seems to have been influenced by Sillitoe's concise resumé, as his response added fuel to the fire: 'I have received some information of late regarding this former alien, all of which tends to confirm that his political views are more extreme than moderately left.' He gave no details or explanation other than 'My source of information has always proved reliable in the past and I have no reason to doubt its authenticity so far as PEIERLS is concerned.'[5]

Sillitoe wrote back asking for more details, but received no reply. Two months passed and Sillitoe wrote again, on 30 August. Two more weeks elapsed before Dodd responded, and the 'reliable information' began to unravel. The informant had 'based opinion' on 'numerous small incidents and snatches of conversation', which pointed to Peierls being 'on friendly terms with known communists at the university'. Peierls was also a friend of a Professor Pascal, for example, whose wife was a 'fervid' champion of Russia.[6]

That might have been the end of it had not a new crisis erupted within days, when Bruno Pontecorvo, who had worked alongside Alan Nunn May in Canada during the war, and had been a colleague of Klaus Fuchs at Harwell for the last two years, defected to the Soviet Union. As well as creating further strains in an already fraught relationship between Britain and the United States, the flight of Italian-born Pontecorvo focused attention on émigré scientists, such as Peierls, who worked on atomic energy in the United Kingdom. The media storm included an article in the *Sunday Express* on 29 October. Headlined, 'Perturbed Men', it announced with xenophobic fervour, 'Foreign-born atom experts, working on top secret atomic research in Britain, are profoundly disturbed by the disappearance of Professor Pontecorvo and its effect on public opinion.' According to the article, 'Some of the perturbed scientists feel that as a token of their loyalty they should surrender their British passports and not go abroad.' Peierls was highlighted with a photograph, captioned to suggest that any allegiance was fickle: 'German Born. Three years in America. Now British.' As one of the supposed 'perturbed men', Peierls wrote to the editor to expose the article as a product of its author's imagination with little or no basis in fact, but the damage was done.

The questioning of Peierls' loyalty continued apace in exchanges between the British Security Services, their American counterparts, and the Ministry of Supply – overlords of the British Atomic Energy programme. Chief Constable Dodd put in his four-pennyworth, writing to alert Sir Percy Sillitoe, in case this had slipped below MI5's attention, 'Peierls was an intimate acquaintance of Professor Pontecorvo whose departure from this country has been the subject of considerable Press comment.'[7]

MI5 now prepared a carefully written draft weighing Peierls' loyalty and his risk to national security. Peierls had visited Russia in 1931, spent a holiday in the Caucasus in 1934, and attended a physics conference there in 1937. It cogently assessed that the close friendships of Rudolf and Genia Peierls with 'communists and sympathisers in Birmingham' was not unnatural in view of 'common professional interests', the 'Russian origins of three of these friends', and (added as afterthought) 'in view of the Russian origin of Mrs PEIERLS'. The information 'suggests that they are honest and loyal citizens'. Nonetheless, unable to prove a negative – that Peierls was not disloyal – the assessor chose to have a safe pair of hands with a convoluted conclusion: 'Such associations must raise a doubt whether some degree of security risk does not arise from PEIERLS' access to secret information.'[8]

Meanwhile, in December Peierls was one of four members of a scientific delegation making a three-week visit to India, and a telegram was sent to

New Delhi: 'PEIERLS Friendly with communists and fellow-travellers. Has a Russian wife.'[9]

An MI5 minute that month noted: 'The Americans have their eye on PEIERLS and suspect him of being a bad security risk.'[10] The result of this ongoing saga was that MI5 consulted Perrin about Peierls, in particular whether Peierls had access to secrets shared with America. While MI5 knew about Peierls' background and lifestyle, it knew nothing about his specific contributions to atomic energy and the national programme. Perrin gave the suspicions short shrift and stood up for the scientist.[11] He asked for the 'full facts and precise reasons' for doubts about Peierls. Upon hearing MI5's assessment, Perrin expressed surprise and said the reports were 'completely out of character with the man'. He then explained what Peierls had done, describing him as 'one of the few men who knew the atomic energy project from A to Z'. Perrin, constrained by the Official Secrets Act, said Peierls had 'built the ground floor of the atomic project' and was 'one of the most clear-minded people [Perrin] had ever met'. In Perrin's view, Peierls was always 'two moves ahead of everybody else', so to discontinue him from classified research would make little difference to Peierls' knowledge as he could 'anticipate any progress made in the next five years' for himself. Therefore, Perrin explained, the nation had 'quite a lot to gain and little to lose in retaining his services'.

Perrin, who had known Peierls well for nearly a decade, was sceptical about the aspersions made against him and asked whether the Americans had any basis for mistrust. He was told that it was 'by nose more than fact'. Perrin made clear that in the absence of concrete evidence he wasn't prepared to accept this. Cockcroft and Penney also supported Peierls as an invaluable expert and said that if they decided to terminate his contract as a Harwell consultant, they would have to face 'considerable publicity'. Lord Portal was emphatic: 'MI5 should extract from the Americans with all the force in our power such information about PEIERLS as they have. If such information is no more than suspicion, they should be made to say so.'[12] It seems the reason that the FBI suspected Peierls was because he 'introduced Fuchs to Atomic Energy'.

Peierls was hugely regarded by leading research scientists in atomic energy, but his style and cleverness had also made him some powerful enemies. Churchill's scientific advisor, Lord Cherwell, was one such, and he contributed to the perception of Peierls as a closet communist: 'Peierls announced that he would be unable to attend an important meeting of a committee to which he belonged "since he had to go to the Soviet Embassy".' In another example Cherwell commented that: 'Peierls frequently behaves like a silly ass in matters of security and appears to go out of his way to advertise the fact that he considers security to be nonsense. This may be an extremely clever piece of bluff on the principle that no-one who behaved as foolishly could be suspected of anything sinister.' In a further piece of completely unjustified character assassination, Cherwell said Peierls 'could not be trusted and that should circumstances change, Peierls would certainly desert this country if he was satisfied that it was to his personal advantage to do so'.[13] This contrasted with the positive opinion of Sir Charles Darwin – Director of the National Physical Laboratory and grandson of the famous naturalist. Darwin quoted the late Ernest Rutherford, Lord Rutherford, who had said, 'Peierls would make a good Englishman.' Darwin attributed Peierls' attitude to security as 'a result of a liberal outlook, characteristic of the ASA of which Peierls is President'.[14]

Pressed by the British, the FBI presented their report on Peierls, which Geoffrey Patterson forwarded from Washington.[15] Federal agents had interviewed several people, but the interpretation of their evidence seems to have been influenced by a preconception that Peierls was to be deemed a threat. For example, Edward Teller gave balanced and carefully argued support for Peierls. He said that he had first met Peierls in Leipzig, in 1928, and explained that the Communist Party was perfectly legal in Germany at that time, so if Peierls had any communist sympathies he would have had no reason to hide them. Teller added that Peierls had no marked political interests and had indicated no communist sympathies.

The FBI called Teller's testimony into question, however, because an Edward Teller had been on the roster at the Communist Workers' School in New York City in 1941, as a teacher of political economy. Whoever this was, it was not Edward Teller the physicist, who 'emphatically denied' being this man, not least as he had 'absolutely no background or qualifications which would entitle him to teach at the workers school'.[16] Suspicions grew, however, because Mrs Teller was on a 'membership list' of the 'League of Women Shoppers' in Washington DC, which was described by the House Un-American Activities Committee as a communist-controlled front organization.

None of this specious noise would prevent acceptance later of Teller's damning testimony against J. Robert Oppenheimer in 1954; in 1951, however, it seems to have negated his support for Peierls. Positive remarks by Victor Weisskopf, who had known Peierls before the war and throughout the atomic project, were neutered because Weisskopf was reported to have said, 'Russia was making a greater sacrifice in attempting to keep the peace than the USA, and he suggested the USA destroy its stockpile of bombs for peace.'[17]

The FBI report noted that in 1946 Peierls had been a member of the committee of the British Association of Scientific Workers – the committee 'included Dr A. Nunn May'. Given that the majority of leading atomic scientists had at one time or other worked alongside Nunn May, or Fuchs, or Pontecorvo, the entire cast could be damned by association. Peierls had produced more direct self-damnation in his remarks of April 1949, in the *Bulletin of Atomic Scientists*. He had written, 'One hears a good deal of talk about scientists who hold subversive views of one kind or another, and this, fortunately, is not taken very seriously in this country. I believe most of you know that in the United States things are rather more difficult in that respect.'[18] In the rampant McCarthyism culture of the United States, this statement classified Peierls as 'subversive'.

Peierls felt the effects of surveillance, though unaware that it was happening. Trips that he had planned to the United States, for instance, were curtailed due to visa problems or because the American or the British government removed his name from invitation lists without explanation. In August 1951, for example, when Peierls was named among a British delegation due to visit the United States for a closed discussion on atomic energy, his visa request was refused because the United States Atomic Energy Commission 'raised further objections to Peierls'. These included Peierls' role as a vice-president in the ASA – a 'Communist Front organisation' – though Lord Cherwell, among others, was also a vice president. The British Cabinet Office described some of the objections as 'pure McCarthyism' – for example, 'Peierls' membership of a delegation petitioning the Home Secretary to ameliorate the sentence of Alan Nunn May' and the citation of the article in which he had written that we would be in a better moral position if the Allies 'had dropped a demonstration bomb on Japan'. MI5 commented, 'all of [them] were shown to be either untrue or of no significance'.[19]

After British protests, the visa was granted, but on 30 August there was a hiccup. A top-secret telegram from Washington announced that the Atomic Energy Commission are 'most anxious that UK holds up press release with names of the delegates because although the AEC has no objection to Peierls participating, the *Chicago Tribune* has attacked Peierls name as being "unreliable". This would cause the AEC great difficulty if Peierls' presence in the UK team were publicly announced.'[20] The delegation set off for the United States with what had been hoped would be limited publicity. The *Daily Mail*, however, trod dangerously near the bounds of libel on 5 September with Peierls' name as its lead for the article: 'Peierls Leaves for USA. American Press Attacked Him. Atomic scientist labelled as a fellow traveller by some American newspapers leaves London today with an official party of British atomic scientists for talks on September 14–16 on means to protect atomic information.'[21]

This inspired a series of what Peierls' lawyer described as 'grossly defamatory articles'.[22] For example, that month *Intelligence Digest* mentioned Birmingham University, 'an establishment under powerful Communist influences – where there is one professor (an expert in nuclear physics) of great importance, who entertained Fuchs in his house for a year or so'. Emboldened, the rag went further in October. Under the headline 'People Who Must Be Removed', it opined, 'The very fact that a close friend of Professor Fuchs has recently been given a top-secret job, shows that the dangers have never been greater. This man (a foreigner by birth) can only have been passed by the Security Services because unreliable men remain in the service. A near relation has stated that this man's wife is a Communist. Yet the man has just been given what is, at the moment, one of the most secret jobs in the world.'

Intelligence Digest threw all caution to the winds in its next edition with 'Friends of Traitors Not to Be Trusted'. Under this banner it asked, 'Is it common sense to trust a friend of Fuchs, a man whose origins are foreign, and whose wife is a Communist? One would have thought that, even without evidence beyond that, such a person should be confined to less important work, and not trusted with our top secrets. It is to be feared that at the very highest levels there are powerful officials who sympathise with those of Communist associations, and refuse to admit the implications of the cases of Nunn May, Fuchs, Pontecorvo and the diplomats.'[23]

While its bald assertion about Genia Peierls was potentially a libel, the article cleverly used Peierls' situation to argue that the real rot was with 'powerful officials' at the 'highest levels' who were blind to the perceived threat. Although suspicions about Kim Philby's duplicity were already present in the Security Services, another decade would pass before he too defected to the Soviet Union, and later still before the extent of his treachery became known, including attempts to tip off Nunn May and Fuchs, an intervention in August 1950 that probably led to Pontecorvo's defection, and his role in the flight of Guy Burgess and Donald Maclean.[24]

The trigger for these polemics was, in Peierls' view, the nationally read *Daily Mail*. His lawyer confronted its editor: 'Your article clearly states that our client is a traitor to this country and the article plainly implies that he is going to the US with reputable British scientists and will probably misuse his scientific knowledge to the detriment of this country. The mischief of your article is that although you yourselves merely repeat these suggestions you in no way dissociate yourselves from them.'

The *Daily Mail*'s editor had to climb down, distancing the newspaper if not fully withdrawing the innuendos: 'The *Daily Mail* wishes to dissociate itself completely from these attacks on the reputation of Professor

Peierls. We deeply regret any impression which may have been given that in recording the attacks we were in any way supporting them.'[25]

Peierls also resisted political interference in intellectual life, such as his statement to the ASA that he was 'uncompromisingly opposed to the application of political tests to candidates for academic appointments'. This too was noted. In the 1930s Peierls, Fuchs and other scientists had escaped fascist persecution; two decades later Peierls now began to help left-wing scientists fleeing from another right-wing persecution – the McCarthy witch-hunts in the United States. Gerry Brown, for instance, an American who was later one of the leading nuclear theorists in the world, was blacklisted in the USA before he joined Peierls' team in Birmingham in 1954. This led to a note by MI5: 'We sense that the FBI is by no means satisfied that PEIERLS' connection with FUCHS was innocent, that their suspicions have been renewed by this contact with BROWN and that their proclivity for seeing security risks in terms of black and white will lead them to place PEIERLS among the blacks.'[26]

With his phone and mail continually monitored, Rudolf Peierls became part of the communist witch-hunt until 1954. Only then, after the continued inability of MI5 to reinterpret facts to fit with their preconceived beliefs about Peierls' trustworthiness, did the Security Services close their file on him. The *mea culpa* conclusion by MI5: Peierls was found guilty by association; (i) He was a close personal friend of Fuchs, but Fuchs' arrest came as a shock to him; (ii) Peierls and his wife are close personal friends of communists, but this is not unnatural in the context of science and his wife's Russian origins (iii) His wife was born in Russia.[27]

For several more years, nonetheless, Peierls continued to be under suspicion. In 1957, for instance, his consultancy at Harwell was threatened when he received a letter saying that he would no longer be able to see classified documents 'for reasons of administrative convenience'. Peierls found the letter 'odd' and asked whether it was routine or whether 'there was more behind it'. He was told it was 'routine' and common for all senior consultants whose contracts were up for renewal. This Orwellian logic couldn't be faulted, as Peierls' was the first and at that stage the only such contract due for renewal.

Peierls told me that he had subsequently learned that the United States had asked the British Department of Atomic Energy that he be given no access to American secret documents. Peierls' reaction was that while the USA had that right, Harwell had tried to deceive him. In 1957, as a result, he resigned his consultancy.

Peierls had become collateral damage in the Fuchs affair. From time to time, scurrilous stories appeared in the media, which implicitly accused Peierls of being a traitor like Fuchs. In this vein, in 1979 the popular historian, Richard Deacon, made what Peierls described as 'damning and unjustified' statements about him, under the mistaken belief that he was dead – there being no libel in English law against the dead. The error was discovered shortly before Deacon's book was published, but by this time a few copies had been sold. Peierls received a substantial sum by way of damages. In response to a journalist's question about his reaction to the statement that he was dead, Peierls replied: 'It is about as accurate as the rest of the book.'[28]

Back in 1941, when he had hired Fuchs in the United Kingdom's hour of need, Peierls had unwittingly brought a Trojan Horse into the nation's war effort. As a result, Peierls, the British father of the atomic bomb, was pursued by the Security Services in the United Kingdom, and shared some of the agony of his American colleague, J. Robert Oppenheimer, who in 1954 was destroyed by political forces in the United States. While Peierls' professional life survived, and the nation later recognized the importance of his work, the trauma of being betrayed by his closest friend was devastating for both Rudolf Peierls and his family.

In 1952, two years after he had first been imprisoned, and visited by William Penney, Klaus Fuchs' British nationality was revoked, an event that left him 'in tears'.[29] Having paid the maximum price and, it appears, continued to provide advice to the nation, Fuchs felt that he was being punished twice.

As a model prisoner Fuchs received full remission for good behaviour. His release date was set for 23 June 1959. The news made headlines, created a furore in the British Parliament, and renewed questions about the efficiency of the Security Services. His impending release also highlighted the anomaly of Fuchs' role in the country, now that his citizenship had been revoked. Where would he go?

After his conviction, Fuchs had made no attempt to contact Peierls. On 15 June 1959 Peierls wrote Klaus Fuchs the following, brief letter:[30]

Dear Klaus

I see from the papers that you are soon going to be released. If you need any help in getting started in life, financial or otherwise, or if you need advice, please let me know. I shall do what I can.

Yours sincerely
R E Peierls

The sense that the British had betrayed him when they revoked his nationality had affected Fuchs deeply. He ignored Peierls' offer and didn't reply to his oldest friend. Fuchs made no attempt to communicate with Rudolf and Genia Peierls, or with Erna Skinner, for the remainder of his life.

THE SON

In the summer of 1957, Klaus' father Emil and nephew – little Klaus – visited him in prison. With remission, he could hope to be released within two more years. He explained that his future prospects were bleak, however, because he was discredited in the United Kingdom and was unlikely to be wanted in socialist countries. His father disagreed and insisted that Klaus would be well received in the German Democratic Republic. It seems that the Security Services in the GDR had already interviewed Emil, because KGB files record that he had assured Klaus he would 'find a suitable job for himself in the GDR'.[31]

The following January, the *Daily Express* ran a story that the British Security Services would try to stop Fuchs leaving for the GDR because he knew atomic secrets. This was a bizarre claim as he had been out of research for nearly a decade and by now was well behind the state of the art. TASS picked up the *Express* article on 28 January 1958, and Moscow Centre asked Berlin whether Fuchs' father knew anything. Emil, however, hadn't heard from Klaus 'for two months'.

The Fuchs saga went quiet for fifteen months until April 1959 when the authorities in East Germany and in Moscow became active following articles in the British press announcing that Fuchs would be released within three months. Furthermore, he was apparently planning to join his father in Leipzig and work as a 'philosophy instructor in the worker-peasant faculty'.[32] The KGB now put pressure on their East German counterparts, and berated them for lack of information; the sole source of news for Moscow apparently at this stage was the open British press. The KGB now spelled out what they expected: 'In view of [Fuchs'] imminent release it is essential to take all possible measures – through his father and through German friends – to make sure he moves to the GDR and gets a job.' Nearly a decade after Fuchs' arrest, the KGB desperately wanted to know 'what he was charged with, what was known to English counter-intelligence about the details of our work with him, and the reason for his failure'.[33] Fuchs' confession had rankled with them for years. In 1953 the KGB had recorded that Fuchs 'betrayed his courier', that the 'Rosenbergs' failure happened as a result of Fuchs' betrayal', and 'the reasons for Fuchs' failure have not been precisely identified to this day'.[34] With Fuchs' release now imminent, the KGB wanted him in the GDR for two reasons. First, in order to have an opportunity to interview him about his 'failure'. The other, remarkably, was to reel Fuchs in as their agent in East Germany, in line with their policy of never letting an agent go free. The Soviet agenda was for Fuchs to take a senior scientific position in East Germany, on the grounds that his experience would have 'positive and important implications'. The political agenda would be to lobby the GDR to pursue this singular opportunity, but 'without telling them that [Fuchs] is our agent'.[35]

Emil petitioned the Central Committee of the Socialist Unity Party of East Germany (SED) for Klaus to become a citizen of the GDR. This was granted and Emil received the papers, but now he couldn't decide what to do with them. He didn't want to trust them to the mail, and considered sending his housekeeper with the papers to see Klaus. Klaus eventually received the news by a circuitous route. Emil's eighty-fifth birthday was 13 May 1959 and in celebration he was awarded 'the gold order for service to the fatherland'.[36] This gave an excuse for a meeting between Emil and journalists from Germany and the West, at which he mentioned that Klaus had been granted East German citizenship. This was reported in the British media and presumably is how Klaus first learned of it.

A month later, on 23 June and just released from prison, Klaus Fuchs duly flew to East Berlin. In so doing, he fulfilled the dreams of those who had enabled him to escape the Nazis in 1933, namely that 'after the revolution in Germany, people with technical knowledge will be required to build Communist Germany'. At the airport on arrival he was met by a delegation of members from the Central Committee of the SED. Among them 'at the gangway' was the widow of the former chief of the press division of the GDR's Ministry of Affairs – Grete Keilson.[37]

Keilson held an official post on the Central Committee, and now aged fifty-three had been a hardline member of the Communist Party since her youth. She was none other than the Grete who had met Klaus in Paris in 1933 when they were fleeing Hitler's regime (see chapter 2). Fuchs' nephew, Klaus Kittowski, had brought her to the airport, and then drove the three of them, pursued by hordes of reporters, to Klaus' father's weekend cottage by Wandlitzsee.[38] There is no record of any contact between them in the intervening quarter-century, yet within four months, on 9 September, they married. Given the KGB's continued interest in Fuchs, and Grete's high office in the Communist Party, it is not impossible that the KGB were the matchmakers.[39]

There may be a more innocent explanation, however. Klaus Fuchs was a hero in East Germany, especially so for someone with Grete's background. When aged twenty-seven, she had known him as a twenty-one-year-old student as they shared the terror and excitement of the underground fight against Hitler. The highly publicized reappearance of this lean, intellectual and highly principled man must have been a powerful attraction for Grete, who had been a widow for six years. As for Klaus, he had always needed the presence of women, older women – Erna Skinner, Genia Peierls – as if surrogates for his own lost mother. Whether it was the KGB or the media that brought them together, their story appears to be another secret in Klaus Fuchs' collection.

More than a decade earlier Fuchs had told his Russian contact of his dream: 'I'd like to help the Soviet Union until it is able to test its atomic bomb. Then I want to go home to East Germany where I have friends. There I can get married and work in peace and quiet.'[40] Fuchs had helped the Soviet Union create an atomic bomb, and was now back in East Germany, married. His dream of peace and quiet, however, would not be so easy to achieve.

FUCHS' FAILURE

By the end of 1959, Fuchs was Deputy Head of the GDR's Central Institute for Nuclear Research in Rossendorf (Dresden) and professor at Dresden Technical University. After a decade's absence from professional contact, he was again contributing to nuclear physics. Now, for the first time since 1941, he was able to pursue his scientific passion, freed from the stress of leading a double life. However, he was less free of that past than perhaps he realized. On 14 December 1959 the KGB's representative in Berlin discussed with Moscow the idea of 'a meeting between our representative and Fuchs to learn about the testimony Fuchs once gave to the English'. They also wanted to assess Fuchs' current political reliability and his 'views on Soviet science' with a view to 'establishing conversation with Soviet scientists on a trip to the Soviet Union'.[41] The first step would be a meeting in Berlin between the KGB's 'operative' and Fuchs.

Early in March 1960 a Soviet Embassy employee in Berlin talked with the head of the science division of the Central Committee of the East German Communist Party. He proposed that Fuchs should be invited to the Soviet Union in order to visit the major laboratory at Dubna and to 'familiarise himself with the USSR'.[42] The Soviet Embassy thought this would be 'expedient'. On 17 May the Central Committee of the Soviet Union's Communist Party 'gave consent' to invite Fuchs as a member of a GDR delegation to a conference in May of the Academic Council of the Joint Institute of Nuclear Research – a Warsaw Pact analogue of CERN.

The KGB's memorandum then recaps Fuchs' great work for which he was arrested and cites this as the reason for him to partake in a twenty-day expenses-paid trip across the Soviet Union 'so that he can see Moscow, Leningrad, Kiev and Sochi and familiarize himself with the open work being done [there]'. Their real agenda, however, was that this extended visit was 'with an eye to carrying out the assignment to study him'. Then came the sting: 'During this trip we will take steps to find out tactfully from Klaus Fuchs the circumstances of, and possible reasons for, his arrest.'[43]

The delegation, which included Klaus and Grete, left for Moscow on 24 May. The planned twenty-day visit, however, was cut short by Fuchs after a week, supposedly because 'business require[d] that Fuchs be in the GDR at the beginning of June'. This may be true, though the belief among some physicists at Dubna is that there was a sudden decision to abort the visit; the KGB records confirm that Fuchs arrived on 24 May but that the itinerary was 'cut short' and he went home on 31 May.[44]

The visit to Dubna confirmed, for some at least, that Fuchs' itinerary was tightly controlled. In the audience for his seminar at Dubna was Bruno Pontecorvo, Fuchs' former colleague from Harwell. Recall that six months after Fuchs' arrest, Pontecorvo and family had vanished, to reappear in the Soviet Union. A Dubna scientist remembered Fuchs' talk as 'rather tedious' but a 'very excited' Pontecorvo commented, 'Enrico Fermi was very severe in estimating scientists but he considered Fuchs a star of the first order.'[45] If that is an accurate description of Fermi's opinion, it must reflect his valuation of Fuchs' contribution, with John von Neumann, to the hydrogen bomb at a time when Fermi had demonstrated that the original design was flawed: Fuchs' other work, though first rate, was not singular compared to other theorists at Los Alamos, nor did his published oeuvre make radical contributions to the field of nuclear physics. Fuchs was a supreme manipulator of equations – if you wanted a mathematical problem solved, Klaus was the person to do it – but he was not an innovator, he created no new pathways nor inspired a school of followers. But Pontecorvo clearly held Fuchs in high regard, based on their two years together in England. This gives some significance to what happened at the end of the seminar, which was, in sum, nothing. As they left the hall, Pontecorvo was 'agitated'. He was an extrovert – 'hail fellow, well met!' – always first to put out his hand and give welcome. On this occasion, Pontecorvo made no effort to meet Fuchs, or say hello to his former colleague. The interpretation of a fellow attendee was that Pontecorvo had been ordered not to speak to Fuchs, the KGB having placed restrictions on any contact, other than what had been formally agreed in advance.

While we cannot verify the truth of that, nor the idea that 'business' in the GDR was a convenient face-saving excuse for the unexpected termination of Fuchs' trip, Fuchs was discomfited by his discovery that two 'scientists' assigned to him were in reality KGB plants.

The KGB files reveal that the delegation visited Moscow, and that at the welcome party Fuchs became concerned by the behaviour of his two aides. Whether or not this was indeed the case, Fuchs seems to have been uneasy if the report of 'Hans', the delegation's leader is any guide. 'Hans', who Fuchs knew as a scientist, was 'an agent of the ... KGB ... in the GDR'.[46] The KGB had hopes of using Fuchs as an informant, but needed first to establish whether he was still reliable. To this end, in a conversation with Hans, a Soviet Embassy official 'nonchalantly brought up [the name] of Dr Fuchs'. Moscow's dream that Fuchs, their star agent in the United Kingdom and then the United States, would now be reborn in East Germany, began to unravel when Hans said that, in his opinion, 'Fuchs has not yet recovered from the moral trauma' of his arrest and imprisonment. He was 'closed off', 'taciturn', and 'never discussed the past with anyone'. What's more, he 'didn't even share his impressions of his stay in Moscow' with Hans.

Hans, following the party line, said that Fuchs had received 'a fantastic offer' in the form of a sponsored trip with his wife. The nature of the interaction between Hans and the Russian official suggests that Hans was already aware that Fuchs would not go through with the trip.

The key event that determined Fuchs' decision appears to have been on 28 May when a meeting with 'Comrades' L. R. Kvasnikov and D. N. Pronsky 'made a big impression on him'. That, at least, was the judgement of the KGB, by whom the comrades were employed. Immediately after this meeting Fuchs pulled out of the visit, on the grounds that 'he felt unwell'.[47]

The meeting, which lasted over two hours, took place at a Chinese restaurant in Moscow at a time when the establishment was practically empty. The pair introduced themselves as 'representatives of the organisation for which he had worked'. They began by expressing gratitude to Fuchs for all he had done during a 'difficult time' for the Soviet Union, and expressed regret that 'circumstances had put an end to this collaboration'. They apologized for 'having to bring up difficult memories' and then asked Fuchs to explain the 'circumstances connected with his failure' and 'his conduct during the investigation'.

Part of Fuchs' statement to them reveals his agenda and duplicity back in 1949 when interrogated by Jim Skardon. He explained to the two Russians that 'it soon became obvious that the English suspected [me] of intelligence activities, though they did not have any evidence against [me]'.

Fuchs judged, moreover, that 'the matter would have gone no further than this conversation, had he not confessed of his own free will'. Prior to his arrest he had told MI5 that he had ceased espionage because of his doubts about the correctness of Soviet policies in Eastern Europe. At the time he had described the reasons for this change of heart, and told his British interrogators that his heart now lay with the British way of life and the friendship he had found. Now, a decade later, he told the two Russian comrades a different tale. To them he claimed that his doubts had come as a result of having been exposed to 'bourgeois propaganda and his detachment from sources of truthful information'.[48]

He also emphasized that the only person whose identity he had confirmed was Harry Gold. Fuchs described the circumstances. He had been shown two filmstrips of Gold, he said, in the first of which Gold appeared to Fuchs 'like someone in a state of nervous agitation who felt he was being followed'. Although he knew this was his one-time contact, Fuchs said he 'did not admit to knowing Gold after this strip'.[49]

In the second strip, Fuchs claimed that Gold was filmed 'when he was already in jail'. According to Fuchs, he 'looked here like someone who had just gotten a big load off his chest'. Only now, when it was clear to Fuchs that Gold had been apprehended, did Fuchs identify and testify against him, he said.

Fuchs admitted he had told the British that he had passed atomic secrets, but claimed the British were not aware that he had passed information about the hydrogen bomb. With this fabrication, Fuchs was trying to regain some respect from the Russians: he had not let MI5 know the vast extent of his work for the Soviets. This was utterly false, of course, as in 1950 Perrin understood Fuchs to have revealed 'all he knew of the general principles of the hydrogen bomb'.[50]

Not surprisingly, no one was being entirely straight in this interchange. The comrades 'thanked [Fuchs] once again for helping us in the past, wished him success in his future life and work and told him that in the future he can turn to us for friendly support if ever he has any problems'. Within a month a critical report of Fuchs' history landed on the desk of Premier Nikita Khrushchev. The KGB interrogators had debriefed Fuchs more effectively than Skardon and Perrin, it would appear, and the head of State Security formed a poor opinion of Fuchs' behaviour. The head's report highlighted that 'in spite' of the British having 'no direct evidence against him', and with no danger of being arrested or exposed, Fuchs had 'confessed to intelligence activities on behalf of the Soviet Union' entirely on 'his own initiative'. Despite having been 'under no serious pressure from the English', Fuchs had testified about his collaboration and 'identified the agent through whom he used to pass us intelligence in the USA'. In short, he had violated the code of espionage and in so doing had wreaked havoc on KGB operations in North America.

The comrades ended with self-congratulation, which revealed the motives behind their conversation with Fuchs, and the KGB's verdict on their great atom spy: 'At the start of the conversation Fuchs had felt very unsure of himself and [was] guarded, [so] we used a certain amount of tact in finding out about matters that were of interest to us[: we] expressed our gratitude to him for helping the Soviet Union in the past. At the same time, we expressed great regret that at the time his confessions led to a major failure.'[51]

Epilogue

SPIES, REAL AND IMAGINED: FUCHS, KAHLE AND HOLLIS

Media interest in Fuchs' story brought him to the attention of the public at large, including many who had tales to tell. MI5 received communications from people who were convinced that they had seen Fuchs with mysterious strangers in various locations, some of them rather cranky ideas. One contact, however, was especially interesting: a former internee in the Canadian camp from back in 1940. Michael Serpell interviewed him on 23 March 1950. The informant, identified only as 'A', started with an apology: 'I shan't be able to say much. I hope you are not expecting . . .'

Serpell cut in, 'Well, we're very grateful for what you can tell us.'

'There's only one thing actually: I was interned with FUCHS. We were together for roughly five months, in Canada. And very many of those who were interned with him knew he was a communist.'

Serpell established that A's camp was indeed the same as that of Fuchs. They had been together in the Isle of Man, and on the SS *Ettrick* to Canada, but had only met after arrival. After some digressions, Serpell came to the point: what gave rise to the opinion that Fuchs was a communist? He received no direct answer as 'A' admitted that after so long it was 'hard to recapture the atmosphere' revealing whether this person or that was a 'refugee from Nazi oppression' or 'anti-Nazi' or 'communist'.

What struck Serpell was that A's focus on a fine gradation between different degrees of hatred for Hitler did not fit with Roger Hollis' simple description of the camp as a nest of Nazi sympathizers. 'Were there a lot of anti-Nazis in those camps then?' he asked, with surprise. 'Oh yes!' came the reply. 'You see, this camp was predominantly, actually, Jewish.'

In 1946 Serpell had argued that Fuchs' association with Hans Kahle – a communist agent – was potentially significant, only for Roger Hollis to have dismissed this on the grounds that Fuchs and Kahle were two anti-Nazis placed 'by mistake' in a camp of Nazi sympathizers (see chapter 11). Serpell checked that he had the story right:

'Oh, was it?'

'Yes! Predominantly Jewish.'

The conversation continued for a few minutes in mutual misunderstanding, Serpell wanting to establish the Jewish angle, and 'A' responding as if in a debate about racial and religious prejudices, and what defined 'anti-Nazi'.

Serpell brought the interrogation back on track:

'The point I am interested in is: would you have said yourself that in [the camps] there was a large percentage of Nazis?'

His informant cut in: 'Oh no! The camp was predominantly anti-Nazi.'

'Predominantly anti-Nazi was it? There's no doubt of it?'

'Oh yes, exactly. Out of a given 700 I should say 600 were Jewish.'

'I see.'

'And automatically anti-Nazi.'

They continued in this vein, Serpell wanting to establish the facts without leading his informant, and the informant missing the point of Serpell's inquiry: 'Mind you when I say that the Jews were anti-Nazi, I'm not saying that non-Jews were not anti-Nazi.'

'Oh no, no. I'm not suggesting that,' Serpell interjected. 'I'm just trying to get a broad view, you see, because it is quite important in the context to appreciate that if someone who is just left wing is surrounded by a large number of Nazis, naturally it throws his opinions into [the] limelight, doesn't it? It accentuates his opinions. But you tell me it was mainly an anti-Nazi society.'

'Oh yes. Oh yes!'

Serpell now pressed 'A' to determine whether his informant could 'tell [who was] a communist'. His informant painted a picture of the camp – nine huts with some eighty internees crammed in each, each hut having a couple of representatives on a camp committee, which made representations to the Camp commander. That is how 'A' had got to know Fuchs. From the remarks in these meetings, such as attitudes to Russia, 'FUCHS was certainly one of those of whom we knew was [communist.]'

Serpell asked how many of the internees 'A' had identified as communists, and was told, 'About ten'. He asked for some names, and the first one mentioned by his informant was Hans Kahle.

Serpell had established, four years after Hollis had asserted the contrary, that far from being a camp of ardent Nazis, it had contained Jews and predominantly anti-Nazis of various shades of red. Kahle had been singularly visible, Fuchs too, along with others.

This interview was recorded and transcribed in March 1950.[1] Yet in September 1951, when Alan Moorehead asked MI5 for information to aid with his book, he was given the established line that Fuchs and Kahle had been mistakenly placed in a camp of Nazis.[2]

In 1956 Roger Hollis became Director General of MI5 and held that post until his retirement in 1965, as Sir Roger Hollis. Michael Serpell, whose analysis of Fuchs was spot on, was moved away from London to Singapore, where in 1962 he ended his career as head of Security Intelligence Far East.

In 1981 allegations were published claiming that Sir Roger had been a Soviet secret agent. MI5's official website explains: 'These were investigated and found to be groundless.'[3] Hollis' false picture of Fuchs and Kahle, as passed to Moorehead, nevertheless unwittingly polluted its history for nearly half a century.

BACK TO THE FUTURE

It was not until December 1952, nearly three years after Fuchs' arrest, that Harwell appointed his successor as Head of Theoretical Physics. The new leader was Brian Flowers. The media assuaged public concerns that he might be a security risk by emphasizing that Flowers was the son of a clergyman, and therefore beyond reproach. They had clearly forgotten that Fuchs' father too had been a pastor.

Fuchs' former deputy, Oscar Bunemann, missed out on this plum position because he had left Harwell and taken a post at Cambridge University, far from Flowers, in the hope of saving his marriage to Mary. However, he and Mary divorced, and in October 1951 she and Flowers were married. One Oxford colleague wryly commented at the time that Flowers 'first took Bunemann's wife and now he's taken his job'.[4]

Flowers also took the glittering prizes. He died in 2010, shortly before what would have been his and Mary's golden wedding anniversary. Meanwhile he had been enobled as Lord Flowers, having been Rector of Imperial College, Vice-Chancellor of London University, and, according to his obituary in The Guardian, 'the outstanding scientific and academic administrator of his generation'.

Herbert Skinner moved to Liverpool University, as head of the Department of Physics. He died during a visit to CERN in 1960. Erna Skinner was miserable in Liverpool and used alcohol as an escape. She died of a heart attack about fifteen years after Herbert; their daughter Elaine always denied that her mother had an affair with Fuchs and claimed that they were chaperoned when they went overnights to hotels.

In 2009 Mary Flowers, the former Mary Bunemann, whose marriage breakdown had played out alongside Klaus Fuchs' own crisis in 1950, wrote a memoir, which revealed her insider's perspective of Fuchs and Erna Skinner's 'close relationship'.

In it she described Fuchs as what Berliners called a 'Hausfreund' – a man who waits on the lady of the house and is accepted in the family as an auxiliary to the husband. 'Some would simply call such a person a lover, but that is an over-simplification. One man had never been enough for Erna, and she was frequently involved with a supplementary companion.' In Mary's judgement Erna 'obviously had no intention of leaving Herbert', and if the situation kept Erna happy, Herbert accepted it. 'She craved the attention of men and usually got it. Their marriage had already survived a few such adventures.'

In the year of Flowers' succession to Fuchs the Ministry of Supply published a booklet outlining Harwell's history.[5] There was no mention of Fuchs as former head of theoretical physics, nor were his scientific papers included in the list at the end. Fuchs had been airbrushed in a Harwellian rewrite of history, which would have done credit to his new masters in the Soviet Zone of Eastern Germany.*

Settled in the German Democratic Republic, Fuchs was highly regarded, having fulfilled the party's hopes of 1933: 'After the revolution in Germany, people [will] be required with technical knowledge to take part in the building up of the Communist Germany.' He was awarded the Patriotic Order of Merit, and the 'National Prize of East Germany for meritorious achievement in science'. In 1979 he won the GDR's highest honour – the Order of Karl Marx. Ten years earlier, the award had been given to Jürgen Kuzcynski.

Klaus Fuchs did no further work for the KGB. He also refused to cooperate with any potential biographers, which is perhaps no surprise given the complex maze of fluctuating affiliations throughout his life. He spent the rest of his career in Rossendorf (Dresden) as deputy director of the Institute for Nuclear Research, married to Grethe, until his retirement in 1979. He died on 28 January 1988, aged seventy-six; his ashes are buried in the 'Pergolenweg' of the Socialists' Memorial in Berlin's Friedrichsfelde Cemetery. Grete Fuchs-Kielsen died aged ninety-three in 1999.

In 1951 the US Congress had assessed, 'Fuchs alone has influenced the

---

* Sixty years later Fuchs has been restored. A new sculpture outside building B77 at the laboratory includes Fuchs among Harwell luminaries.

safety of more people and accomplished greater damage than any other spy not only in the history of the United States but in the history of nations.'[6] But in both the GDR and the Soviet Union, Fuchs' role in enabling the Russians to develop their atomic bomb remained unacknowledged for decades. In the 1950s his nephew Klaus Kittowski was told to erase the following sentence from his school CV: 'My uncle was sentenced to jail in 1950 for spying for the Soviet Union.' According to Kittowski, the reason for this request was that supposedly the Soviet Union did not engage in espionage.[7] At Fuchs' funeral, friction between the GDR and the Soviet Union was apparent. The eulogy by the Minister for Research of the GDR simply stated that Fuchs was in Los Alamos and then came to the GDR, but did not mention his role in the birth of the Soviet atomic bomb, nor his time in jail.[8]

Any formal appreciation by the Soviet Union of Fuchs' contributions came only after his death, and then only as result of recommendation by the GDR. In June 1989, on the eve of the fortieth anniversary of the founding of the GDR, the East German representative office of the Soviet KGB filed a petition to bestow a Soviet government award posthumously to 'former Central Committee member of the Socialist Unity Party of Germany, Klaus Fuchs, a major scientist in the field of atomic physics'. The Soviet Union awarded Fuchs the 'Order of Friendship of Peoples (posthumous)', which was for strengthening the scientific and cultural development of the USSR.[9]

Even here, however, there was no explicit acknowledgement of his singular contributions to development of the Soviet atomic bomb: the Soviet Union continued to ignore the role of espionage in the creation of their atomic or hydrogen bombs lest it 'lower the image of [Soviet] scientists in the creation of the atomic weapon'.[10] Only after the collapse of the Soviet Union in 1990 did an article by Academician Yulii Khariton give the first public admission that the Soviet atom bomb was developed after the American model with the help of information derived from espionage, especially that received from Klaus Fuchs.[11]

Meanwhile Rudolf Peierls became Professor of Theoretical Physics at Oxford University in 1963, which is where I chanced upon him, four years later, in 12 Parks Road. When I entered his study at that first meeting in 1967, and joined his research team, I never anticipated that this would develop into a lasting friendship and that I would learn so much about his remarkable history.

In addition to attracting leading scientists to Oxford, Peierls brought some of the *esprit de corps* developed during his time at Los Alamos. For many scientists of the 1940s, their time at Los Alamos would be the pinnacle of their career. For the most part they were young then, less than thirty years old, at which age today they would be graduate students or junior academic staff. Yet at Los Alamos they were part of the largest and most exclusive faculty in history, a collection of talent exceeding even that at Cambridge in the 1930s, or at Berkeley, Stanford and Harvard in the post-war decades. Their physics united them, but their social lives there also energized them and released their creativity. This in turn led to life-long friendships among individuals whose geographical origins were widespread but who shared a common, supremely important, purpose.

On that first day in 1967 Rudolf Peierls had told me about the physics that would open before me, and recommended that I attend the research seminars in the department, even though I would understand little at first. But one instruction was mandatory: 'We meet for coffee every morning at eleven o'clock.' It was in such informal gatherings that ideas germinated and that research by what historian Lorna Arnold called 'coffee-housing' took place.

At each year's end there was the Theoretical Physics Department's party, an echo of the festivities that the British delegation at Los Alamos had experienced. It was in helping with these parties that I got to know 'Prof', and then Genia his wife, as well as Jo, their youngest daughter, and began to appreciate how he had been affected by his association with Klaus Fuchs. At one of Peierls' parties I asked his opinion as to whether Bruno Pontecorvo too might also have passed information to the Soviet Union, even though his and Fuchs' personalities could not have been more different.[12] For a moment he appeared far away, in a reverie, and then with deep sadness, in a low voice almost a whisper, said: 'You never can tell.'

This reaction, for me, showed the depth of grief that the Fuchs affair had for Rudolf Peierls. For some people those four words continued also to be addressed to Peierls himself, whose association with Klaus Fuchs left suspicion that he too was indiscreet, or worse.[13] For many years, Genia's Russian origins continued to prejudice MI5's vision of her husband. Not until 1959 were the Security Services' thirty volumes of files on Klaus Fuchs and Rudolf Peierls finally closed. Even then another decade was to elapse before the British establishment recognized Peierls properly. It was during my time in Oxford that Peierls' unique contributions to science and the pursuit of freedom were recognized with the award of a knighthood. Sir Rudolf Peierls published his memoirs in 1985. He died in 1995, Lady Genia Peierls having predeceased him in 1986.

At Peierls' funeral, Lord Flowers gave a fine oration in which he described him as 'one of the greatest figures of the nuclear age. He was the first to show that nuclear weapons were feasible. Later he tried to show us how to live more safely in a world which possesses them.' Flowers concluded with an epitaph for Peierls the human being: 'We shall remember always his honesty and integrity, his quickness of mind, and his gentle but persuasive sense of humour . . . [and] with joy the warmth of the welcome we got in the home he created with Genia, where hospitality and fun were of the highest order.'[14]

Here Flowers, who had been at the eye of the storm when Fuchs was arrested, had isolated the two features of Peierls' character that had most impact on Fuchs' crisis and were key to understanding Fuchs' inner feelings. Fuchs had told the Soviet Union that 'nuclear weapons were feasible', and passed on the work of his colleagues, able to legitimize these acts in his mind. What he was unable to come to terms with was his betrayal of those who had given him 'warmth and welcome' as well as 'hospitality and fun' in their home. The Peierlses had taken in a refugee and given him succour, only for their own 'honesty and integrity' to be questioned when their generosity was exploited. A witness to Genia's reaction at the time of Fuchs' arrest was Freeman Dyson, the brilliant physicist who in 1950 was a lodger in the Peierls' home in Birmingham. 'For Genia with her long experience of living in fear of the Soviet police, the key to survival was to have friends that one could trust, and the unforgivable sin was betrayal of that trust.' Genia Peierls, who years later Dyson's children would lovingly call 'the Loud Lady', was 'for once, speechless with anger'.[15] That Fuchs was unable to respond to Rudolf Peierls' offer of help when he was released from prison in 1959, and never wrote to his closest friend, the man who had in some respects regarded him as a son, ever again, suggests that his nine years of formal imprisonment were accompanied by a lifetime of shame, an inability to face those who had loved him most. Nevertheless he felt he could write to Dyson, who like him had been the Peierlses' lodger. 'I received a letter from Fuchs shortly before his death, seeking to re-establish contact. I replied with an encouraging message, but then he inconsiderately died.'[16]

MI5's papers on Rudolf Peierls remained classified for decades, and those on Klaus Fuchs were released only recently. Even so, there remain many redactions, especially in the records of MI5's eavesdropping on Fuchs at his home and in his office. Also, papers on the hydrogen bomb, and Fuchs' role in the British atomic bomb, remain classified sixty years later, as are Fuchs' notes of Fermi's 1945 lectures on the hydrogen bomb. This is ironic. First, Fuchs had sent these notes to Moscow at the time, and they were openly published there during the Yeltsin era. Second, in 1946 copies of notes on Fermi's lectures went to James Chadwick in Washington, who in turn made copies for a handful of leading British physicists.

One set went to Sir George Thomson, and is freely available in his private papers. Third, a detailed set of notes of the entire lectures, mildly redacted, became available in the United States (see chapter 9). I found all three of these helpful in reconstructing the history.

Fuchs' arrest, followed within months by his colleague Pontecorvo's defection to the Soviet Union, severely strained transatlantic relations. The reputation of the Security Services also suffered. MI5 fought public criticism by sponsoring the publication of a book, called *The Traitors*, in 1953. Its author, Alan Moorehead, was public relations officer at the Ministry of Defence but was expected to have left and 'returned to private life' before the book was published.[17] The resulting encomium to their skills is still advertised on MI5's website as authoritative.

Part of Moorehead's version is that MI5's lead investigator, Jim Skardon, almost single-handedly broke Fuchs' will. As we have seen, the truth is that Skardon benefited from the patient long-term work of Henry Arnold, the Harwell security officer, and at Fuchs' trial the credit for his first confession was attributed to Arnold (though this might also have been to avoid close scrutiny of the circumstances of Fuchs' confession to Skardon, tainted as it was with inducement). Henry Arnold lived to the age of ninety. He remained friends with many of his young charges and, uniquely, maintained contact with Fuchs. In retirement he would take lunchtime walks along the Harwell laboratory byways and sports fields with former colleagues. It was there, when I was a young physicist en route to the Harwell squash club one lunchtime some forty years ago, that a colleague pointed to two ageing men strolling along: 'That's the man who broke Klaus Fuchs.'

Afterword: Who Was Klaus Fuchs?

Seven decades later we can view Klaus Fuchs' life from a different world to the one he knew – except in one respect perhaps: the survival of life on Earth in the atomic age may be due to the mutually assured destruction that Rudolf Peierls and Otto Frisch foresaw, and Fuchs and Ted Hall helped to mature. In 1955 Sir James Chadwick, discoverer of the neutron and head of the British Mission in the Manhattan Project, said to the British Parliamentarian Tam Dalyell,* 'I knew them [the atom spies] very well. I do not approve of what they did, but I understand their motives. You in your generation may come to be grateful to them.'[1]

As to the man Fuchs himself, and the circumstances that determined his life, enigmas remain. Who were the Gunns, who helped establish Fuchs in the United Kingdom? Why, after seven years of espionage, did he confess? And, a parlour game: if VENONA had not revealed the identity of a spy at Los Alamos, how far might Fuchs have risen in the British establishment?

First, the role of the Gunn family, who were his sponsors and landlords during his student days in Bristol, and who maintained contact with him throughout his imprisonment, two decades later. Were they innocent, peace-loving benefactors, out to help a pitiful refugee, or part of some deeper communist agenda, as MI5 seemed to suspect?

The received wisdom in 1950 that Fuchs was involved with left-wing activities during his time in Bristol was in part due to his association with the Gunns. When I read the Ronald Gunn files, with the advantage of seeing them half a century after the myopia of those times had passed, it was apparent that Gunn was a pacifist and that this had made him a focus for antagonism when the nation was in peril. This was, of course, consistent with Fuchs' description of Gunn as a Quaker. Nonetheless, Gunn's file also reveals him operating at the fringes of communism, his visits to

---

* Tam Dalyell was Father of the House of Commons (longest-serving Member of Parliament) from 2001 to 2005.

Leningrad in the 1930s, mail from Moscow, and affiliation with known communists in the Bristol area all providing enough fuel to maintain MI5's interest. There is no evidence, however, that Gunn was intimately involved in a communist cell, let alone that he was a knowing party in a long-term plan to establish Fuchs in the United Kingdom. Fuchs' persistence in describing Gunn as a Quaker was probably an innocent means of protecting a man who had helped him settle in his new homeland, and to avoid dragging Gunn deep into the morass.

Which brings us to the main enigma: who was Klaus Fuchs and why did he confess? Opinions on his character and motives seem to have evolved according to the era in which they first appeared. Thus the earliest, written in the Cold War and influenced by the background of McCarthyism then rife, portrayed him as a scheming communist traitor. The more nuanced works by Norman Moss and by Robert Chadwell Williams were written in the 1980s, which gave them the advantage of a judgement less prejudiced by the McCarthy era but without the benefit of MI5 and Russian files. I was inspired in part to research Fuchs' career by the late Lorna Arnold, the distinguished historian who had known Fuchs during his Harwell period. She insisted that he had not been understood, and that he was an honourable man who stuck by his principles; people might disagree violently with those principles, but there are many who shared them, and to decree what is 'right' or 'wrong' is a profound question of moral philosophy where the line of neutrality itself moves with the era. For Lorna, Fuchs was a man who had yet to receive a fair trial. I hope to have contributed to that.

I was shocked to discover the cavalier manner in which Fuchs was interviewed, and the disturbing feeling that important evidence is still withheld, not for reasons of state security but to keep egregious errors under wraps. The lack of transcripts of Jim Skardon's interview in Fuchs' home, which had been bugged, is one example. The prosecution's attempt to influence Fuchs' defence counsel on the eve of the trial is an astonishing breach of ethical procedure. That said, Fuchs broke the law wilfully and deliberately for several years, so the verdict is hard to fault. The decision process to assess which papers are to remain withheld and which released seems to be a lottery. On the one hand notes on Fermi's H-bomb lectures at Los Alamos remain off limits, yet they are available at other venues in Cambridge, from Los Alamos, and even from the former Soviet Union itself! Meanwhile British connivance to hide Fuchs' communist 'proclivity' from the Americans is now on display, and confirms that J. Edgar Hoover was correct in his criticism.

Fuchs' trial raises as many questions as it answered. Did he receive a fair trial; was he induced to confess? The former is better weighed by legal experts who can assess the significance of his confession, written and signed without the presence of any legal aid, but for which it is doubtful he would have been convicted. The question of inducement was a leitmotif throughout the process and there are several clues to suggest that Skardon, at least, led him on.

We have only Skardon's account of the interrogations, which he wrote several days later; there is no independent corroboration. Fuchs had no legal advice when interviewed, nor did he take any notes for himself. Fuchs later claimed that Skardon lied with an offer to ensure that Fuchs could stay at Harwell – 'I only had to admit one little thing and I could have stayed . . .' Fuchs wrote to Erna – though Fuchs is not necessarily a reliable witness here. Fuchs' claim that he was encouraged not to raise the issue in his trial for reasons of national security, and that he went along with this, beggars belief. It is certainly the case that until Fuchs admitted the whole shebang, MI5 was only pursuing 'one little thing' and that cutting a deal with him remained a real possibility. When the profound nature of his espionage came out, however, the nature of the contest changed.

There are clues nonetheless that Fuchs' claim might have merit and that Skardon offered more than his written account admits. First, the discussions about inducement before the trial are on the record and Guy Liddell's relief when assured that they might 'get away with it' speaks volumes. There is no doubt that Fuchs' prefab was bugged – the decision to do so was taken in October 1949 and the numerous mentions of Fuchs being heard 'stoking his fire', and the record of other movements around the place, all hint that these are the result of microphones. Yet there is no record of Skardon's conversation with Fuchs in that very room, and there are pages withheld in the daily diary accumulated by MI5, all of which point towards a crucial piece of potential evidence being unavailable to us. Finally, the presentation in court of Arnold as the source of Fuchs' first confession was either an attempt to deflect attention from Skardon, or proof that Skardon's account was incorrect, at least in its chronology if not more.

As to the trial itself, Lord Justice Goddard gave short shrift to the claim of 'controlled schizophrenia'. While this has no bearing on Fuchs' guilt, it cannot be easily ignored in an explanation of how he operated now that we know Fuchs' family background. Notwithstanding that he used the term in its colloquial sense of having a split personality rather than a serious mental disease with delusions, three generations of suicides starting with his grandmother, his mother having been a schizophrenic depressive, and his sister Kristel suffering from the condition too, make it very likely that Klaus too had some of these tendencies. He was in denial to a remarkable degree, seemingly unable to recognize that he had committed a major crime. The description of controlled schizophrenia might be truer than even he realized and the means whereby he was able to live two parallel lives so successfully for so long. 'Controlled' schizophrenia is perhaps tolerable, so long as it remains controlled. Fuchs had never been challenged until the end of 1949 when for the first time events were no longer in his control.

Although today it is possible to assess Fuchs' espionage more dispassionately than in the past, and perhaps to sympathize with his reasons, there is also no doubt that Fuchs was first and last a dedicated spy with all the single-minded duplicity that such a role requires.

He told his audience what they wanted to hear, and gave up information only when it suited him. For example, to the KGB he denied having admitted to MI5 or the FBI that he had passed information about the H-bomb, yet in reality Fuchs admitted to the British that he 'told everything he knew', as Michael Perrin and Frederick Lindemann record. When under pressure from Skardon in 1949, Fuchs claimed that he had ceased spying because of dissatisfaction with Soviet ambitions in Europe and because he had grown to love the English way of life; yet to the KGB later he claimed this to have been the result of his exposure to bourgeois propaganda. He withheld evidence, or drip-fed it when the time was ripe. For example, when shown photographs of potential contacts by Skardon and the FBI, at no stage did he recognize the photograph of Ursula Beurton ('Sonya') whereas he picked out Simon Kremer – whom Fuchs knew was out of reach in the Soviet Union. He recognized Harry Gold only after it was obvious that Gold was under arrest; his story of their meetings evolved from one interview to the next, sometimes with trivial matters, such as whether he had a name for his contact, but also in more calculated ways, to protect the safety of Kristel and to hide that they had met at his sister's home.

Once suspicion fell on Fuchs, his singular goal was to ensure that Kristel escaped censure. He tried, and failed, to maintain the spies' charter – of hiding the identity of any contact, including oneself. There was one fact about himself that Fuchs had to withhold, and did so successfully – the date of his entrée into espionage. The continuous reference to 1942, which pollutes the record from his interviews with Skardon, the FBI and the trial, and which became received wisdom in all media reports at the time, became 'late 1941' in the subsequent literature of the twentieth century (and even more recently).[2] Yet we now know that Fuchs passed information to his

Soviet courier, Simon Kremer, as early as August 1941 and that they had met some time before even this, possibly at Kuczynski's celebration. Whatever took place at the Hampstead party in April of 1941, Fuchs was certainly there at Kuczynski's invitation, and it was Kuczynski who introduced Fuchs to Kremer. There was a clear danger that if this came out Fuchs might be accused of having aided the Soviet Union at a time when it was allied with Hitler. Here, at least, Fuchs managed to muddy the waters, aided perhaps by the inability of the British to produce evidence that he had signed the Official Secrets Act before 1942.

In the years of his lonely double life, Fuchs must have spent many hours planning for the day when events threatened his 'control'. It is clear that he knew he was being followed around London, and on the trains, as Erna's concerns about the quality of his driving 'recently' attest. There are unexplained absences when he disappears from MI5's sights at critical moments, such as after two of his interrogations, and the lack of pursuit when he goes off with Erna Skinner – who was still not beyond suspicion – which raise unanswered questions both about Fuchs and the efficiency of the surveillance.

At first sight the available MI5 files appear to suggest gross incompetence, especially in the dark comedy of 'Sonya' – interviewed by Skardon and Michael Serpell in 1947, overlooked by everyone in 1950, and only identified after she had escaped to East Germany. In their defence one could argue that whereas today's electronic data storage would enable immediate correlations between Ursula Beurton and Fuchs to become apparent, the reality in 1950 was very different. When Skardon visited Beurton in 1947, for example, the knowledge that Fuchs had been involved in espionage was still three years in the future. The first they knew that Fuchs had met one of his couriers around Banbury was after his arrest, in February 1950. The remarkable oversight, in my judgement, is Colonel Robertson's in May 1950 when he recommends that Beurton be interviewed because she might be disturbed by the news of Fuchs' arrest, but fails to make a more direct connection between Fuchs – who had already volunteered that he had met a female contact in Middle England – and a woman based in that very area whom MI5 had long and correctly suspected of being active in espionage. In this saga, as in much else, there is no evidence of a mole at work within MI5, let alone that it was Roger Hollis, but equally it is hard to dampen the embers of suspicion that have continued to burn for decades.

Fuchs' core *raisons d'être* were to the communist ideal, his German heritage, and the goal of restoring the lost socialist Germany that his parents had known. Did Fuchs himself feel he had succeeded, that it had been worthwhile? Did he have regrets? He never wrote a memoir; he was the subject of a television programme in East Germany shortly before he died, but his answers gave no more insight into his emotions than those of a sporting hero when asked after a game to explain, 'how do you feel?'

The days immediately following his arrest reveal Fuchs' schizophrenic psyche in action. There was a cost to himself, which he had already discounted, but there was a cost to others, of which he seems to have been unaware until he read Genia Peierls' letter in prison. As William Wordsworth wrote, 'the child is the father of the man', and it is in Fuchs' childhood that the script for his life comes to light. His description of his early years as 'happy', with not a mention of his mother, suggests that this tragic woman was in the background, the intellectual focus of the home being controlled by the driven, austere, pacifist father, Emil. That Emil Jr. chose to be known by his subsidiary name of Klaus shows some level of rebellion, but this was a matter primarily of establishing his personal identity; Klaus and his siblings meanwhile inherited their father's high principles and the mantra to 'do what is right whatever the cost'.

An overriding ethos of liberal ethics became the norm for all the children, and the political climate of Nazi oppression crystallized their beliefs. Many people in Germany at that time felt the same as the Fuchs clan; Klaus, however, chanced upon a role at the heart of the battle against tyranny and in circumstances with such profound potential to alter the nature of warfare and global power where failure to act in accord with his conscience would have been a personal failure. When his political heroes in the Soviet Union joined the war against Hitler in 1941, Fuchs hardly needed the exhortation of Winston Churchill to offer help. Towards the end of his life, now in East Germany, Fuchs' statements show that he never lost that fundamental belief in the communist ideal, whatever he might have claimed during his crisis in 1950. He was doing what his conscience demanded, and his advice to Mary Bunemann as he was about to face his Calvary gives a rare glimpse into Klaus Fuchs' soul.

When confronted by MI5, Fuchs was ready to give up his own freedom in order to save his sister. The family history, however, suggests that this decision was due to the selfish gene – Kristel had been involved in Klaus' espionage as part of the team, and were she to kill herself (like the other members of their family), it would be on Klaus' conscience forever. As for others who regarded him as a friend, but without the ties of family, there was a cost, which he understood too late. He betrayed his colleagues, and even in the case of the Peierlses, friends that were almost an adopted family. His reaction to Genia's letter in prison seems to have been the first time that he faced up to this responsibility. The news a few days later that his actions had put at risk the Skinners' visit to Erna's sick father in America gave empirical proof of Genia's written exhortation, and brought home to Fuchs the broader implications of his actions. I sense that he was ashamed, and for the first time was unable to face himself. I was struck that during his time in jail, and later in East Germany, he maintained contact with his physics colleague Nicholas Kurti and with Henry Arnold, the security officer who had played a role in his exposure and conviction! Yet he was cut off from the Peierlses and the Skinners, who had been his true friends, indeed the only real friends for many years. In the case of the Skinners it is unclear whether this was at their or Fuchs' bidding; in the case of the Peierlses, Fuchs' refusal even to acknowledge the offer of help in 1959 reveals something deep. I sense that Fuchs was ashamed to meet with the two people who knew him so intimately, because he could not face up to the consequences, the loss of trust, the proof that he had cheated those he loved, and who loved him.

VENONA decryption was fragmentary, which is why the contribution of GCHQ at the start of 1950 was so significant. The declassified VENONA messages that are available today are their final forms, the history of their decryptions is not available, so we do not know how much was known at any particular time. There are clues that GCHQ was key to completing the link between GOOSE and thermal diffusion, because this information was available in an MI5 summary by 6 January 1950, and was passed to the FBI via Lish Whitson only on 4 February, after Fuchs' arrest. Released FBI files have no mention of this linkage before that time, and the wording is consistent with the information originating with the British. The format of this report is characteristic of GCHQ (see chapter 22, note 22).

The chronology of decoding the messages that indicated the presence of agent REST, later identified as CHARLES, is also unclear. How well they were understood when decisions were being made about Fuchs' future at Harwell is also obscure. Until the scientist himself confessed, the extent of his espionage was not apparent; if the sole evidence today were the mature versions of VENONA now available, it would be impossible to deduce the profound nature and extent of Fuchs' espionage. Back in September 1949, the fragmentary information made it conceivable that the passing of document MSN-12 to Harry Gold was a minor leak from one scientist to another.

There was another spy at Los Alamos whose importance was in a similar league to that of Fuchs – Ted Hall. When challenged by the FBI, Hall denied everything. As a result his identity was not generally known until the 1990s, and he had a long career as a biophysicist. An American citizen,

Hall emigrated to the United Kingdom and a research post at Cambridge University. The FBI was unable to bring Hall to trial as it was unwilling to make a case based solely on VENONA. It is remarkable that Hoover knew of Hall from the spring of 1950, yet continued to harangue the British for their oversight with Fuchs while keeping the embarrassment of Hall – the agent known as MLAD – quiet. Hall's refusal to confess, and his subsequent career in science, has a significant message for the case of Klaus Fuchs, for had Fuchs remained silent, like Hall, his future career would probably have been stellar and much of the British establishment in the latter half of the twentieth century been changed, perhaps radically.

It is tempting to imagine the alternative universe that might have ensued. Fuchs would have been elected Fellow of the Royal Society in the spring of 1950 and remained head of theoretical physics at Harwell. As a result, the opening for the precocious Brian Flowers would have never happened. Flowers' talent would have taken him far in any event, but the springboard of being leader of Britain's prime team in nuclear physics while still in his twenties, which both honed his skills as an able administrator and enabled him to wield influence as an inspirational scientist, proved a gift that eventually took him to the pinnacle of the British establishment.

There would have been no fallout for Fuchs' colleagues at Harwell, not least Bruno Pontecorvo. While Fuchs was exceedingly able as a mathematical physicist, Pontecorvo was a rare genius, of ability in both experimental and theoretical physics that has been compared to the likes of Ernest Rutherford and Enrico Fermi. Pontecorvo's work touched on at least two Nobel Prizes, and his continued presence in the United Kingdom would have had far-reaching implications for the new field of particle physics.

The national laboratory for research in particle physics – Rutherford Laboratory – was built immediately adjacent to Harwell in the mid-1950s, and its first staff members were Harwell scientists. The founding inspiration for CERN was Eduardo Amaldi, Pontecorvo's former colleague and closest friend, and the role of Pontecorvo in forging Britain's role in that European venture can only be imagined. The intellectual hub of Pontecorvo and Fuchs working at the new heart of British physics, just twelve miles from Oxford University, where Rudolf Peierls became head of theoretical physics in 1963, would have created an international powerhouse of research.

As it was, however, the actions of mathematicians based at GCHQ would prove key in the unravelling of that dream. GCHQ was the United Kingdom's trump card in the transatlantic technical alliance, and its collaboration with Meredith Gardner's team in the VENONA decryptions only became clear years later. In particular it appears that GCHQ played a key role in revealing the link between GOOSE and thermal diffusion, which proved so significant in the FBI's search strategy for Fuchs' contact. Their contribution to the decoding of other messages, in particular those linked to Klaus Fuchs, is unknown. What is certain, however, is that the hero of the affair was VENONA and collaboration between mathematicians and linguists.

But for VENONA, Fuchs' espionage would probably have remained undetected for the rest of his life. His closest friend, Rudolf Peierls, was knighted; his junior colleague Brian Flowers and the leader of the British Atomic Bomb project, William Penney, were both enobled. Would Fuchs, the brains behind the British weapon project, guru at Harwell, have achieved anything less? What irony if the fathers of the H-bomb in the United States and the Soviet Union – Edward Teller and Andrei Sakharov – were remembered in a Trinity with the father of the British bomb – Lord Fuchs of Rüsselsheim, the Red Baron.

Appendix: Fission and Fusion

This appendix should be read in combination with the footnote on p. 15.

Protons are shown as solid circles, neutrons as open circles.

I. FISSION

(a) $\quad$ p $\quad + \quad$ Li$_7$ $\quad \longrightarrow \quad$ He$_4$ $\quad + \quad$ He$_4$

(b) $\quad$ n $\quad + \quad$ Li$_7$ $\quad \quad \quad$ t $\quad + \quad$ He$_4$ $\quad + \quad$ n

Lithium-7 consists of three protons and four neutrons. When struck by a proton (a), lithium fissions into two nuclei of helium-4 (also known as 'alpha particles'). When struck by a neutron (b), the fission produces one helium-4, a triton (nucleus of tritium) and a neutron. This neutron has too little energy to initiate a further fission of lithium-7, so a chain reaction is not possible here (or indeed for any light nuclei). In the case of heavy nuclei, such as uranium-235 (c), the liberated neutron(s) have enough energy to initiate further fissions.

(c)

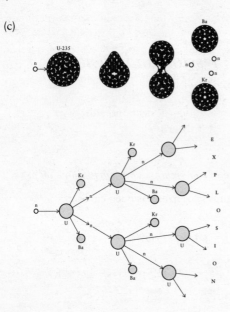

A neutron is absorbed by a uranium-235 nucleus. The nucleus becomes unstable and wobbles like a water drop. The deformed nucleus splits in two. The products are nuclei of lighter elements, such as barium and krypton, and two or three neutrons. Energy is also released. One of these neutrons might hit another fissionable nucleus of uranium so that a chain reaction occurs. Energy is released explosively if more than one neutron induces another fission.

2. DEUTERIUM FUSION

(a) d + d   n He_3

or $\longrightarrow$ + $\wr\wr\wr\wr\wr\wr$ Radiation

(b) d + t $\longrightarrow$ n + He_4

Whether deuterium is fused alone (a) or with tritium (b), a neutron can be produced. If this hits uranium or plutonium, fission is likely. So by having some deuterium and/or tritium along with plutonium or uranium, the power of a conventional atomic bomb can be boosted.

For fusion to happen, two D and/or T nuclei must touch one another. The electrical repulsion of their protons resists this. If by chance the two nuclei are oriented such that their protons are at the rear, the probability that two neutrons will touch is higher. This chance is greater in tritium (c), where there are two neutrons, than in deuterium (d).

(c)

(d)   d   d

3. PRODUCTION OF TRITIUM INSIDE A HYDROGEN BOMB

Lithium-6 consists of three protons and three neutrons. When struck by a neutron (from the fission of uranium or plutonium in an atomic explosion, say), lithium-6 splits into a nucleus of helium-4 and a triton.

Bibliography

Albright, J. and M. Kunstall, *Bombshell: The Secret Story of America's Unknown Atomic Spy Conspiracy*. New York: Times Books, Random House, 1997

Andrew, Christopher, *Defence of the Realm: The Authorized History of MI5*. London: Allen Lane, 2009

Andrew, Christopher and Oleg Gordievsky, *KGB: The Inside Story*. London: Harper Collins, 1990

Andrew, Christopher and Vasili Mitrokhin, *The Mitrokhin Archive*. London: Penguin, 2000

Arnold, Lorna and Kate Pyne, *Britain and the H bomb*. London: Palgrave, 2001

Baggott, Jim, *Atomic: The First War of Physics and the Secret History of the Atomic Bomb, 1939–49*. London: Icon Books, 2009

Badash, Lawrence et al. (eds), *Reminiscences of Los Alamos 1943–1945*. New York: Springer, 1982

Benson, Robert L., *The Venona Story*, Center for Cryptologic History, National Security Agency, Washington DC, 2012

Bernstein, Jeremy, 'A Memorandum that Changed the World', *American Journal of Physics*, vol. 79 (2011), pp. 440–46

Bernstein, Jeremy, *A Bouquet of Dyson, and Other Reflections on Science and Scientists*. London: World Scientific, 2018

Bethe, Hans, *The Road from Los Alamos*. New York: American Institute of Physics, 1991

Born, Max, *My Life: Recollections of a Nobel Laureate*. New York: Charles Scribners Sons, 1975

Bower, Tom, *The Perfect English Spy: Sir Dick White and the Secret War 1939–1945*. London: Heinemann, 1995

Brinson, C. and R. Dove, *A Matter of Intelligence: MI5 and the Surveillance of Anti-Nazi Refugees, 1933–50*. Manchester: Manchester University Press, 2014

Broda, Paul, *Scientist Spies: A Memoir of My Three Parents and the Atom Bomb*. London: Matador, 2011

Burke, David, *The Spy who Came in from the Co-op: Melita Norwood and the Ending of Cold War Espionage*. Martlesham, Suffolk: Boydell Press, 2008

Burke, David, *The Lawn Road Flats: Spies, Writers and Artists*. Martlesham, Suffolk: Boydell Press, 2014

Burt, Leonard, *Commander Burt of Scotland Yard*. London: Heineman, 1959

Cathcart, Brian, *Test of Greatness*. London: John Murray, 1994

Cave Brown, Anthony, *Treason in the Blood*. London: Robert Hale, 1994

Close, Frank, *Half Life: The Divided Life of Bruno Pontecorvo, Scientist or Spy*. New York: Basic Books, 2015; London: OneWorld, 2015

Cohen, Karl, *The Theory of Isotope Separation as Applied to the Large-Scale Production of U-235*. New York: McGraw-Hill, 1951

Dalitz, Richard H. and Sir Rudolf Peierls (eds), *Selected Scientific Papers of Sir Rudolf Peierls with Commentary*. London: World Scientific and Imperial College Press, 1997.

Dombey, Norman, 'The First War of Physics', *Contemporary Physics*, vol. 51 (2010), pp. 85–90, esp. p. 89

Farmelo, Graham, *The Strangest Man: The Hidden Life of Paul Dirac, Quantum Genius*. London: Faber and Faber, 2009

Farmelo, Graham, *Churchill's Bomb: A Hidden History of Science, War and Politics*. London: Faber and Faber, 2013

Feklisov, Alexander, *Overseas and on the Island: On First-Hand Intelligence and Espionage* / За океаном и на острове: О разведке и шпионаже из первых рук. DEM: Moscow, 1994.

Feklisov, Alexander (with the assistance of Sergei Kostin), *The Man Behind the Rosenbergs*. New York: Enigma Books, 2001

Fermi, Laura, *Atoms in the Family*. Chicago, IL: University of Chicago Press, 1954

Flowers (Bunemann), Mary, *Atomic Spice: A Partial Autobiography*, unpublished, 2009. http://homepages.inf.ed.ac.uk/opb/atomicspice/

Ford, Kenneth, *Building the Bomb: A Personal History*. London: World Scientific, 2015

Fort, Adrian, *Prof: The Life of Frederick Lindemann*. London: Jonathan Cape, 2003

Frisch, Otto, *What Little I Remember*. Cambridge: Cambridge University Press, 1979

Fuchs, Emil, *Mein Leben*, vol. 2. Leipzig: Koehler and Amelang, 1959

Fuchs, Klaus, 'Klaus Fuchs – Atomspion', interview with East German television in 1983, transcribed in *Zelluloid*, 31 March 1990, ISSN 07 24-76 56

Fuchs-Kittowski, Klaus, 'Klaus Fuchs and the Humanist Task of Science', *Nature, Society and Thought*, vol. 16, no. 2 (2003), pp. 133–70

Gibbs, Timothy, 'British and American Counter-Intelligence and the Atom Spies, 1941–1950'. Ph.D. thesis, Faculty of History, Cambridge University, 2007

Glees, Anthony, *The Secrets of the Service*. London: Jonathan Cape, 1987

Goncharov, G. A., 'American and Soviet H-Bomb Development Programmes: Historical Background', *Physics–Uspekhi*, vol. 39 (1996), pp. 1,033–44

Goncharov, G. A., 'Beginnings of the Soviet H-Bomb Project', *Physics Today*, vol. 49 (November 1996), pp. 50–55.

Goncharov, G. A., 'On the History of the Creation of the Soviet Hydrogen Bomb', *Physics-Uspekhi*, vol. 40, no. 8 (August 1997), pp. 859–67

Goncharov, G. A. and P. P. Maksimenko (eds), *USSR Atomic Project: Documents and Materials*, vol. 3, *Hydrogen Bomb 1945–1956*. State Corporation for Atomic energy, 2008

Goodman, M. S., 'The Grandfather of the Hydrogen Bomb? Anglo-American Intelligence and Klaus Fuchs', *Historical Studies in the Physical and Biological Sciences*, vol. 34, part 1 (2003), pp. 1–22

Gorelik, Gennady, 'A Russian Perspective on the Father of the American H-Bomb' (April 2002): http://people.bu.edu/gorelik/Minnesota_02_web.htm

Gosling, F. G., *The Manhattan Project: Making the Atomic Bomb. DOE/MA-0001; Washington, DC: History Division, Department of Energy (January 1999)*

Gowing, Margaret, *Britain and Atomic Energy, 1939–1945*. London: Macmillan, 1964

Gowing, Margaret and Lorna Arnold, *Independence and Deterrence, vol. 2: Policy Making*. London: Macmillan, 1974

Gowing, Margaret and Lorna Arnold, *The Atomic Bomb*. London: Butterworths, 1979

Greenspan, Nancy Thorndike, 'The End of the Certain World – The Life and Science of Max Born'. New York: Wiley, 2005

Groves, Leslie, *Now It Can Be Told*. London: Harper, 1962

Hance, Nicholas, *Harwell: The Enigma Revealed*. London: Enhance Publications, 2006, p. 103

Hennessy, Peter, *The Secret State: Whitehall and the Cold War*. London: Penguin, 2002

Hinsley, F. H. (Harry), *British Intelligence in the Second World War*. London: HMSO, 1979

Holloway, David, *Stalin and the Bomb*. New Haven, CT, and London: Yale University Press, 1996

Hughes, R. Gerald, Peter Jackson and Len Scott (eds), *Exploring Intelligence Archives: Enquiries into the Secret State*. London: Routledge, 2008

Hyde, Montgomery, *Atom Bomb Spies*. London: Ballantine Books, 1980

Jeffery, Keith, *MI6: The History of the Secret Intelligence Service 1909–1949*. London: Bloomsbury, 2010

Jeffreys-Jones, Rhodri, *In Spies We Trust: The Story of Western Intelligence*. Oxford: Oxford University Press, 2013

Jones, R. V., *Most Secret War: British Scientific Intelligence 1939–1945*. London: Penguin, 2009

Kimball, Warren F. (ed.), *Churchill and Roosevelt: The Complete Correspondence*, vol. 1. Princeton, NJ: Princeton University Press, 2015, p. 371

Lamphere, R. J. and T. Shachtman, *The FBI–KGB War: A Special Agent's Story*. New York: Random House, 1986

Laucht, Christoph, *Elemental Germans: Klaus Fuchs, Rudolf Peierls and the Making of British Nuclear Culture, 1939–1959*. London: Palgrave Macmillan, 2012

Lee, Sabine, 'The Spy that Never Was', *Joint Intelligence and National Security*, vol. 17 (2002), pp. 77–99

Lee, Sabine, *Sir Rudolf Peierls: Selected Private and Scientific Correspondence*, vol. 1. Singapore: World Scientific, 2007

Lota, Vladimir, *The GRU and the Atomic Bomb*. Moscow: Olma Press, 2002

Louis, William R. and H. Bull (eds), *The Special Relationship: Anglo-American Relations since 1945.* Oxford: Oxford University Press, 1986

Lycett Green, Candida, *The Dangerous Edge of Things: A Village Childhood.* London: Doubleday, 2005.

Mason, Katrina, *Children of Los Alamos.* New York: Twayne Publishers, 1995

McIntyre, Ben, *Double Cross.* London: Picador, 2012

Miller, A. I., *Deciphering the Cosmic Number.* New York: W. W. Norton, 2010

Ministry of Supply and Central Office of Information, *Harwell: The Atomic Energy Research Establishment,* London, 1952

Monk, Ray, *Inside the Centre: The Life of J. Robert Oppenheimer.* London: Jonathan Cape, 2012

Moorehead, Alan, *The Traitors: The Double Life of Fuchs, Pontecorvo and Nunn May.* New York: Dell, 1952

Moss, Norman, *Klaus Fuchs: The Man who Stole the Atom Bomb.* London: Grafton Books, 1987

Pearce, Martin, *Spymaster: The Life of Britain's Most Decorated Cold War Spy and Head of MI6, Sir Maurice Oldfield.* London: Bantam, 2016

Peierls, Rudolf, *Bird of Passage.* Princeton, NJ: Princeton University Press, 1985

Percy, Antony, *Misdefending the Realm.* Buckingham: University of Buckingham, 2018

Perutz, Max, *Is Science Necessary? Essays on Science and Scientists.* Oxford: Oxford University Press, 1992

Philby, Kim, *My Silent War: The Autobiography of a Spy.* London: Arrow, 2018

Pincher, Chapman, *Treachery: Betrayals, Blunders and Cover-Ups: Six Decades of Espionage against America and Great Britain.* London: Random House, 2009

Radosh, R. and J. Milton, *The Rosenberg File: A Search for the Truth,* 2nd edn. New Haven, CT, and London: Yale University Press, 1997

Rhodes, Richard, *The Making of the Atomic Bomb.* London: Penguin, 1988

Rhodes, Richard, *Dark Sun: The Making of the Hydrogen Bomb.* New York: Simon and Schuster, 2005

Rossiter, Mike, *The Spy who Changed the World.* London: Headline, 2014

Shifman, Mikhail, *Love and Physics: The Peierlses.* London: World Scientific, 2019

Smith, Michael, *The Spying Game,* London: Politico's, 2004

Smith, Ralph Carlisle, *Summary of the British Mission at Los Alamos,* 18 July 1949, LAB-ADCS-127, in Ralph Carlisle Smith Collection of papers on Los Alamos, Online archive of New Mexico.

Summers, Anthony, *Official and Confidential: The Secret Life of J. Edgar Hoover.* London: Victor Gollancz, 1993

Szasz, Ferenc, *The Day the Sun Rose Twice: The Story of the Trinity Site Explosion, July 16, 1945.* Albuquerque, NM: University of New Mexico Press, 1984

Szasz, F. M., *British Scientists and the Manhattan Project: The Los Alamos Years.* London: Macmillan, 1992

Teller, Edward (with Judith Shoolery), *Memoirs: A Twentieth-Century Journey in Science and Politics.* New York: Perseus, 2001

Theoharis, Athan and John Stuart Cox, *The Boss: J. Edgar Hoover and the Great American Inquisition*. Temple, AZ: Temple University Press, 1988

Vassiliev, Alexander, *Alexander Vassiliev Papers, 1895–2011*, US Library of Congress. https://www.loc.gov/item/mm2009085460/

Watson, Peter, *Fallout, Conspiracy, Cover-Up and the Making of the Atomic Bomb*. New York: Public Affairs, 2018

Werner, Ruth (Ursula Beurton), *Sonya's Report*. London: Vintage, 1999

Williams, Robert Chadwell, *Klaus Fuchs, Atom Spy*. Cambridge, MA: Harvard University Press, 1987

Notes

TNA refers to files from The National Archives in Kew, followed by the series (e.g. KV, AB, ES), volume and serial number.

1. From Berlin to Birmingham

1. Quoted by Rudolf Peierls, *Bird of Passage* (Princeton University Press, 1985), p. 19.   2. Ibid, p. 26.   3. Quoted by R. Peierls on W. Pauli in *Biographical Memoirs of Fellows of the Royal Society*, vol. 5 (February 1960), pp. 174–92.   4. Quoted by A. I. Miller on p. 108 in *Deciphering the Cosmic Number* (W. W. Norton, 2010). Peierls in *Bird of Passage*, p. 50, however, remarks that this was 'not Pauli's style' and believes that the Russian theorist Lev Landau was the source.   5. R. E. Peierls, 'On the Kinetic Theory of Thermal Conduction in Crystals', *Annalen der Physik*, vol. 3 (1929), pp. 1,055–1,101; 'On the Theory of Electric and Thermal Conductivity of Metals', *Annalen der Physik*, vol. 4 (1930), pp. 121–48.   6. Quotes from Peierls, *Bird of Passage*, p. 63.   7. Peierls papers, Bodleian Library, supplementary collection, File A2.   8. Peierls, *Bird of Passage*, p. 64.   9. Genia Peierls to Frank Close, personal communication following my review of *Bird of Passage* in *New Scientist*, 1986.   10. 'The Englishman of Etretat', in Guy de Maupassant, *The Entire Original Maupassant Short Stories* (Createspace Independent Publishers, 2017).   11. Peierls, *Bird of Passage*, p. 68.   12. Ibid, p. 90ff.   13. H. A. Bethe and R. E. Peierls, 'The Neutrino', *Nature*, vol. 133 (1934), pp. 532–3 and 689–90. The neutrino was discovered experimentally in 1956 and has become a major tool in high-energy particle physics.   14. H. A. Bethe and R. E. Peierls, 'Quantum Theory of the Diplon', *Proceedings of the Royal Society* (1935), A148, pp. 146–56. 'Diplon' is today referred to as the deuteron, the nuclear seed of deuterium as found in heavy water. Their theory of neutron capture explains why ordinary water absorbs low-energy neutrons, and why heavy water – containing deuterium – has been used to slow neutrons in some nuclear reactors.   15. Quote from Peierls, *Bird of Passage*, p. 129.   16. Ibid, p. 130.   17. TNA KV 2/1658, s. 1a.   18. Letter 31 August 1939, entry 294, p. 678 in Sabine Lee, *Sir Rudolf Peierls: Selected Private and Scientific Correspondence*, vol. 1 (World Scientific, 2007); Peierls papers, Bodleian Library, File A38.   19. Letter 13 September 1939, entry 298, ibid, pp. 682–4.   20. 16 February 1940, Peierls papers, Bodleian Library, File A38. British citizenship finally came through on 26 March 1940, and Peierls had taken the Oath of Allegiance on 27 March.   21. Letter to Sir William Bragg, 6 December 1939; entry 302, p. 688, in Lee, *Sir Rudolf Peierls*, vol. 1.   22. Peierls, *Bird of Passage*, p. 148.   23. More energy is used to bind an isotope built from even numbers of both protons and neutrons – 'even–even' – than an isotope where there is an even number of one variety (the protons in the case of uranium) and an odd number of the other (neutron) – 'even–odd'. The result is that 'even–even' nuclei tend to be slightly lighter than their even–odd counterparts. When U235 absorbs a neutron it forms U236, which is 'even–even', and in consequence is lighter than the original combination of U235 and the free neutron. When that neutron is absorbed by U235, there is energy to spare, even if the neutron is barely moving. This excess leads to the instability of

the transient U236, which fissions.   Contrast this with what happens when a neutron hits U238. The addition of this neutron makes U239, which is 'even–odd', and as such slightly more massive than the average. Unless the incident neutron provides some significant amount of energy to produce this extra mass, it will be unable to induce fission. A neutron that originated from the fission of U235 has too little energy to cause the U238 to fission, and it will be captured by the U238, forming an isotope U239.   24. In Gabon at Oklo about 2 billion years ago, there was a natural uranium reactor. The concentration of U235 was larger in prehistoric times. (U235 is less stable than U238, and so more of it has decayed and disappeared in the interim. Specifically, half of a sample of U235 will have decayed at random in about 700,000 years. This 'half-life' is short relative to the 4.5 billion years half-life of U238.) At Oklo ground water seems to have acted as a moderator – the means to slow neutrons to the most efficient conditions for inducing fission – and the rocks were also sufficiently rich in U235 that a natural reactor ensued. It liberated energy for several thousand years until the U235 content had been depleted by natural radioactive decay. See also https://en.wikipedia. org/wiki/Natural_nuclear_fission_reactor   25. N. Bohr and J. A. Wheeler, 'The Mechanism of Nuclear Fission', *Physical Review*, vol. 56 (1939), p. 426ff. This built on Bohr's earlier pedagogic letter of 7 February, 'Resonance in Uranium and Thorium Disintegrations and the Phenomenon of Nuclear Fission', *Physical Review*, vol. 55 (1939), p. 418.   26. Quoted in Richard Rhodes, *The Making of the Atomic Bomb* (Penguin, 1988), p. 314, and Graham Farmelo, *Churchill's Bomb* (Faber and Faber, 2013), p. 129. There was more than one visit to Einstein, involving subgroups of the trio. The full story of the origins of the letter is in Rhodes, *The Making of the Atomic Bomb*, pp. 302–8.   27. Farmelo, *Churchill's Bomb*, p. 129.   28. A. V. Hill, 'Uranium 235', 16 May 1940, TNA AB 1/9.   29. A. O. Nier et al., 'Nuclear Fission of Separated Uranium Isotopes', *Physical Review*, vol. 57 (1940), p. 546, was received by the editor in New York on 3 March 1940 and published on 15 March. The timing is ironic for Frisch and Peierls' memorandum. In those days the journal was shipped by sea and even in peacetime this led to a delay of some weeks. See also Jeremy Bernstein, 'A Memorandum that Changed the World', *American Journal of Physics*, vol. 79 (2011), esp. p. 442.   30. Margaret Gowing, *Britain and Atomic Energy, 1939–1945* (Macmillan, 1964), p. 391.   31. Otto Frisch, *What Little I Remember* (Cambridge University Press, 1979), p. 126.   32. The episode is mentioned in Peierls, *Bird of Passage*, p. 155. The 'digging for victory' refers to the British government's campaign for flowerbeds to be converted into vegetable gardens to provide food during the war.   33. TNA AB 1/210.   34. Graham Farmelo gives more background and the history of MAUD on p. 161 of *Churchill's Bomb*.   35. G. P. Thompson [sic] to Air Marshal Saundby, Assistant Chief of the Air Staff, 3 May 1940. TNA KV 2/1658, s. 3a.   36. TNA AB 1/106.   37. Quoted in Adrian Fort, *Prof: The Life of Frederick Lindemann* (Jonathan Cape, 2003), p. 306. There is no certain date for this meeting but it probably took place in June 1940.   38. For a detailed history of the progress of MAUD research see Gowing, *Britain and Atomic Energy, 1939–1945*, esp. chapter 2. A bibliography of Peierls' papers during the war is listed on pp. 790–94 in *Selected Scientific Papers of Sir Rudolf Peierls with Commentary*, eds R. H. Dalitz and Sir Rudolf Peierls (World Scientific and Imperial College Press, 1997).   39. Gowing, *Britain and Atomic Energy, 1939–1945*, p. 54. For more discussion of the technical reasons for the wrong estimate of the cross section, see Bernstein, 'A Memorandum that Changed the World', pp. 440–46, esp. p. 441, right-hand column.   40. Peierls taped interview about Fuchs, Peierls papers, Bodleian Library, File A176.   41. Peierls, *Bird of Passage*, p. 112; Graham Farmelo, *The Strangest Man: The Hidden Life of Paul Dirac, Quantum Genius* (Faber and Faber, 2009), pp. 248 and 313–15.   42. Peierls, *Bird of Passage*, p. 163.   43. Peierls papers, Bodleian Library, File D53: 13 November 1978 letter to Andrew Boyle.   44. TNA AB 1/572.

2. The Red Fox

1. Klaus Fuchs statement to William Skardon, 27 January 1950; MI5 files, TNA KV 2/1250, s. 439c, p. 1.   2. MI5 files, TNA KV 2/1250 s. 439c, p. 3.   3. Fuchs attributed this remark

to his father in a secret statement to MI5 on 27 January 1950, TNA KV 2/1250 s. 439c, p. 1. Genia Peierls also made this allusion in a letter to Fuchs on 6 February 1950 after his arrest, TNA KV 2/1251, s. 466 – see chapter 18. This hints at the intimate level of discussion between Fuchs and the Peierlses. **4.** Klaus Fuchs to Herbert Skinner, TNA KV 2/1252, s. 518a **5.** Klaus Fuchs to Kristel Heineman, 5 June 1950, TNA KV 2/1255, s. 689. **6.** Genia Peierls, taped interview, Peierls papers, Bodleian Library, File A176. **7.** Robert Chadwell Williams, *Klaus Fuchs, Atom Spy* (Harvard University Press, 1987), p. 10. **8.** Emil Fuchs, *Mein Leben*, vol. 2 (Koehler and Amelang, 1959); cited by Williams, *Klaus Fuchs*, p. 12. **9.** 'I had no friends at school and later it was always a relation based on and dependent on the same political ideas.' Letter to Erna and Herbert Skinner, 27 February 1950, TNA KV 2/1253, s. 563d. **10.** TNA KV 2/1250, 439c and TNA KV 2/1263 contain Fuchs' account of his early life, given in his confession to William Skardon on 27 January 1950. Quotes in this sequence come from these documents. **11.** Klaus Fuchs statement to William Skardon, 27 January 1950, TNA KV 2/1263, p. 1. **12.** Robert Heineman to FBI, 28 February 1950, Fuchs FBI FOIA files 65-58805-408. **13.** Quoted in Norman Moss, *Klaus Fuchs: The Man who Stole the Atom Bomb* (Grafton Books, 1987), p. 6. **14.** TNA KV 2/1250 s. 439c, p. 1. **15.** Williams, *Klaus Fuchs*, p. 15. **16.** Cited in ibid, p. 9. **17.** Klaus Fuchs statement to William Skardon, 27 January 1950; MI5 files, TNA KV 2/1263, p. 3. **18.** Bernard Lovell, as reported in Moss, *Klaus Fuchs*, p. 15. **19.** Klaus Fuchs-Kittowski, 'Klaus Fuchs and the Humanist Task of Science', *Nature, Society and Thought*, vol. 16, no. 2 (2003), pp. 133–70, esp. p. 136. **20.** Medical report, 15 December 1940, TNA KV 2/1253, s. 549. **21.** Klaus Fuchs statement to William Skardon, 27 January 1950; MI5 files, TNA KV 2/1263, p. 3. **22.** 'On 1.3.33 at Fuchs house an inspection was made and books of the Communist Party were found', report of Kiel Police, transmitted to the German Consul in Bristol on 11 October 1934; TNA KV 2/1245 s. 1a. The Gestapo was formed by Hermann Göring on 26 April 1933. **23.** Williams, *Klaus Fuchs*, p. 16. **24.** Photostat of *Ausweiss* (ID) card for the summer found in Fuchs' home, February 1950. TNA KV 2/1253, s. 567a. His communist activities continued to draw attention, and he was excluded from the university on 3 October 1933 (TNA KV 2/1253, s510b, item 73). By this stage, however, he had already fled from Germany. **25.** Klaus Fuchs statement to William Skardon, 27 January 1950; MI5 files, TNA KV 2/1263, p. 4. **26.** Address from copy of registration card, TNA KV 2/1245 s. 18a. **27.** Mike Rossiter, *The Spy who Changed the World* (Headline, 2014), p. 45, and Rossiter interview by author, 7 January 2016. **28.** Mrs J. Gunn to Chapman Pincher, 8 February and 25 April 1983, as reported in Williams, *Klaus Fuchs*, p. 223, n. 3. **29.** Chief Constable Maby of Bristol to Brigadier Harker, Director General of MI5, 15 May 1941, KV 2/3223 s. 7. **30.** Ronald Gunn first came to the attention of the British Security Services in 1932, when he departed on a Russian ship for a three-week visit to Leningrad from Hay's Wharf in London (see TNA KV 2/3223; serial 1 and 2; embark 19.7.32, return 7.8.32). Special Branch recorded that he visited Leningrad again in 1936 (see TNA KV 2/3223; serial 3; embark 2.6.36, no return date recorded). These two pieces of travel documentation appear to have been recovered in May 1940 when MI5 opened a detailed file on Gunn, which focused on his communist links. This classification of Gunn seems to have played no role, however, when Fuchs was vetted for his entry into Peierls' laboratory in 1941, nor in 1943 when he moved to the United States, nor again in 1946 when he returned to work at Harwell. In any event, MI5's evidence about Gunn would have done no more than confirm their perspective on Fuchs: he mixed with socialists. The files on Gunn show that any evidence about him in 1940 was mere gossip driven by national fear of a fifth column at a time when the Battle of Britain raged and the nation's future hung in the balance. By 1941, however, Gunn was being watched for 'his activities in connection with the Communist Party in [Bristol]'. He resigned as an air raid warden following protests by his colleagues, who claimed Gunn was using his position 'to further Communist propaganda'. While there was nothing specific, the accumulation of evidence led to the conclusion: 'Gunn is mixed up with Communism.' **31.** Date and quotes from immigration report, TNA KV 2/1245, s. 3. **32.** Descriptions from MI5 file on Ronald Gunn, TNA KV 2/3223 s. 7. **33.** Registration card, University of Bristol archives, accessed 1 November 2017. **34.** Statement by Rev. L. Folkard, 1934 Chairman of Bristol University

Sociaist Society, to R. Reed of MI5, 13/4/50, in TNA KV 2/1255, s. 648a. 35. Memories of Neville Mott: http://www.bristol.ac.uk/physics/media/histories/11-mott.pdf 'Most of the physics staff': Brian Pollard, email to author, 18 October 2017. Herbert Skinner seems not to have been a member, however, at least in 1941 when MI5 obtained a membership list, which was 'seen to drop from Gunn's car'. This was returned to Gunn after a copy had been made. (TNA KV 2/3223, s. 8). The group was formed in January 1935. 36. Letter from Chief Constable to MI5, 26 May 1940, TNA KV 2/3223, s. 4. 37. Letter of 7 August 1934 in TNA KV 2/1245 s. 1a states 'the validity of the passport for the schoolboy Claus [sic] Fuchs cannot be extended'. 38. Copy dated 6.10.34 found in Fuchs' house, February 1950, TNA KV 2/1252, s510b, item 267. 39. Klaus Fuchs university registration card, University of Bristol archives, accessed 1 November 2017. 'Declared fitted to pursue research for Ph.D. or M.Sc. in Theoretical Physics (Science minutes 4.6.35).' 40. Letter from Peierls to Neville Mott, 20 November 1936, in Fuchs' papers, TNA KV 2/1252, s. 510b, item 184. 41. Mott to Peierls, 4 December 1936, entry 201, p. 496, in Sabine Lee, *Sir Rudolf Peierls: Selected Private and Scientific Correspondence*, vol. 1 (World Scientific, 2007). 42. Peierls to Mott, 9 December 1936, entry 202, p. 499, in ibid. A full year elapsed before Fuchs completed the paper, and correspondence with Peierls continued; letter from Peierls to Fuchs, 25 January 1938, in Fuchs' papers, TNA KV 2/1252, s. 510b, item 183. 43. K. Fuchs, 'The Conductivity of Thin Metallic Films according to the Electron Theory of Metals', *Proceedings of the Cambridge Philosophical Society*, vol. 34 (January 1938), pp. 100–108. 44. Manfred Boniz, as cited by Fuchs-Kittowski, *Klaus Fuchs and the Humanist Task of Science*, p. 134. 45. H. Skinner, TNA KV 2/1259, s. 968, p. 8. 46. 'Notice re registration of German nationals subject to military service', letter from German Consulate, Bristol, to Klaus Fuchs, 6 May 1936, in Fuchs' papers, TNA KV 2/1252, s. 510b, item 269. 47. TNA KV 2/1245, s. 16. 48. TNA KV 2/1245, s. 18A. 49. TNA KV 2/1245, s. 16. 50. TNA KV 2/1259 s. 961b. 51. Letter from Born to Fuchs 7 December 1941, TNA KV 2/1252, s. 510b, item 131. 52. Max Born to Aliens Tribunal, 30 October 1939, TNA KV 2/1259, s. 962a. 53. Entry of 2.11.39 in Alien Registration Form included in 'Papers handed over to [MI5's] representative in Edinburgh by the Edinburgh City Police referring to Emil Julius Klaus FUCHS', TNA KV 2/1259, s. 962a. 54. Statement of Harry Gold to FBI, 10 July 1950, reprinted in Williams, *Klaus Fuchs*, p. 207. 55. Christoph Laucht, *Elemental Germans* (Palgrave Macmillan, 2012); e-version loc 509. 56. Williams, *Klaus Fuchs*, p. 17. This version of Elizabeth's demise also appears in Rossiter, *The Spy who Changed the World*, p. 64. 57. Moss, *Klaus Fuchs*, pp. 17–18. 58. The sinking of the *Arandora Star*: http://www.scotsman.com/lifestyle/seventy-years-after-the-arandora-star-was-sunk-with-loss-of-713-enemy-aliens-the-last-scots-italian-survivor-is-able-to-forgive-but-not-forget-1-814409; accessed 28 October 2017. 59. Max Perutz, *Is Science Necessary? Essays on Science and Scientists* (Oxford University Press, 1992), p. 102. 60. For more about this shipment of enemy aliens, see 'Voyage of SS *Ettrick*: Conditions in Canadian Camps on Arrival', available at TNA HO 215/265 or via http://discovery.nationalarchives.gov.uk/details/r/C2455133. 61. 'In the confusion then existing he was sent to a camp in Canada which was intended for active Nazis only', attachment to letter to author Alan Moorehead, 24 September 1951, 'Summary of Security Action in Fuchs' Case', TNA KV 2/1257, s. 868a. 62. Ibid. 63. Ibid. 64. 'Supplementary notes on Fuchs' background given to Mr Alan Moorehead on 24 September 1951', TNA KV 2/1257, s. 869a. 65. Max Born, letter to Sir Thomas Holland, Principal of Edinburgh University, 29 May 1940, TNA KV 2/1246, s. 136z. Fuchs was not the only physicist to be released at this time. Oskar Bunemann, a mathematical physicist from Hamburg and vehement anti-Nazi, returned to the United Kingdom and the University of Manchester (Bunemann letter to the secretary of the Society for Protection of Science and Learning, 20 January 1941; reference 138 in Christoph Laucht, *Elemental Germans: Klaus Fuchs, Rudolph Peierls and the Making of British Nuclear Culture, 1939–1959* [Palgrave Macmillan, 2012]). He would later (1947) become Fuchs' deputy in Theoretical Physics at Harwell, chapter 11ff. The release of interned scientists came after the Royal Society organized a list of them. Peierls was not elected to the Royal Society until 1943 and so was not directly instrumental in Fuchs' release. (Contrast claims in chapter 9 of Antony Percy,

Misdefending the Realm [University of Buckingham, 2018] that Peierls was involved in a 'conspiracy' for Fuchs' release: '[Peierls] and Max Born conspired, in the summer of 1940, to have Fuchs and other valuable scientists released from internment to join the project'); Chadwick asked Peierls, as a German émigré, for names and Peierls responded on 12 July 1940 with some suggestions and also advised Chadwick to consult the Society for Promotion of Science and Learning. Fuchs' release was authorized on 17 October 1940 following recommendations by Born, Sir Thomas Holland and Chadwick, TNA KV 2/1248, s. 344z, p. 8.   66. 17 October 1940 release: TNA KV 2/1248, s. 344.   67. In TNA KV 2/1879 s. 546A Fuchs told MI5 interrogator Jim Skardon he had 'casually met Jurgen Kuczynski on a couple of occasions and did in fact recognize him as the head of the party here'. Fuchs here referred to an attempted contact with Kuczynski in 1942 (see chapter 6); the 'couple' of previous occasions are then consistent with this visit in April 1941 and their initial meeting prior to internment. Fuchs mentioned the role of Kahle in his interview with Skardon on 21 December 1949, TNA KV 2/1249, s. 388a.   68. Edinburgh Police file A29/107, TNA KV 2/1259 s. 962B.   69. Fuchs to Skardon, 8 February 1950, TNA KV 2/1251, s. 483.   70. Memo on Klaus Fuchs' GRU (Soviet Military Intelligence) history in KGB file 84490, vol. 2, p. 127, as transcribed by Alexander Vassiliev in 'Yellow Notebook #1', *Alexander Vassiliev Papers, 1895–2011* (US Library of Congress), p. 86.   71. Chapman Pincher, *Treachery: Betrayals, Blunders and Cover-Ups: Six Decades of Espionage against America and Great Britain* (Random House, 2009), chapter 15.   72. Metropolitan Police files, TNA KV 2/1259.   73. Rudolf Peierls to Klaus Fuchs, TNA AB 1/572.

3. Defending the Realm

1. TNA CAB 16/8, October 1909; see also chapter 1 in Christopher Andrew, *Defence of the Realm: The Authorized History of MI5* (Allen Lane, 2009).   2. TNA FO 1093/68; Andrew, *Defence of the Realm*, p. 3.   3. Andrew, *Defence of the Realm*, p. 29.   4. Gustav Steinhauer, Head of British Section in the German Admiralty's Intelligence Service, quoted in ibid, p. 51.   5. Chief Constable C. G. Maby to Sir Vernon Kell, 5 November 1934, TNA KV 2/1245, s. 1.   6. Remarks by Sir Dick White, as reported in Tom Bower, *The Perfect English Spy: Sir Dick White and the Secret War 1939–1945* (Heinemann, 1995), p. 20, and Andrew, *Defence of the Realm*, p. 131.   7. Andrew, *Defence of the Realm*, p. 190.   8. Quotes are from Guy Liddell's report, 'The Liquidation of Communism, Left-wing Socialism and Pacifism in Germany (Visit to Berlin 30.3.33–9.4.33)'. TNA KV 4/111.   9. TNA KV 2/1245, s. 3.   10. KV 2/1245; MI5 had 'no later information than that contained in our minute of 21 November 1934'.   11. Andrew, *Defence of the Realm*, p. 117.   12. Ibid, p. 120.   13. Ibid, p. 121.   14. Ibid, p. 127.   15. Ibid, p. 182.   16. Ibid, p. 220.   17. Liddell remark from Liddell diary, 6 December 1940, quoted in Andrew, *Defence of the Realm*, p. 131.   18. Ibid, p. 129.   19. Chapman Pincher, *Treachery: Betrayals, Blunders and Cover-Ups: Six Decades of Espionage against America and Great Britain* (Random House, 2009), chapter 7.   20. Ealing tennis club records reveal that on this date Sissmore signed in White as a visitor. The date also fits with other chronology surrounding Hollis; see Pincher, *Treachery*, chapter 7, loc 1069. The occasion is confirmed also by Dick White; interview with Andrew Boyle, reported in Bower, *The Perfect English Spy*, p. 54.   21. Andrew, *Defence of the Realm*, pp. 207–8.   22. Remark by Kell to French Foreign Intelligence Service, 31 January 1939, quoted in ibid, p. 185.   23. May 1938, File to Miss Sissmore, TNA KV 2/1567 s. 5a.   24. TNA KV 2/1567 s. 1a.   25. 8 June 1938, GPO intercept correspondence, TNA KV 2/1567 s. 5a.   26. David Burke, *The Lawn Road Flats: Spies, Writers and Artists* (Boydell Press, 2014), chapter 4.   27. TNA KV 2/1871, quoted in s. 33a dated 5 October 1939.   28. Mike Rossiter, *The Spy who Changed the World* (Headline, 2014), p. 58.   29. TNA KV 2/1871, minute 37, 22 November 1939.   30. Sissmore (Archer) memorandum, 10 November 1939, TNA KV 2/820 s. 13a. Jane Sissmore's interrogation of Krivitsky is described in detail in Andrew, *Defence of the Realm*, pp. 264–8.   31. Ibid, p. 263.   32. Ibid, p. 264.   33. Ibid, p. 265.   34. Ibid, p. 267.   35. Ibid, pp. 267 and 341.   36. TNA KV 2/1871, s. 73x, 26 March 1940. MI5

cross-referenced Ursula Beurton's application with Jurgen Kuczynski's personal file no. 42628. The status of Beurton's divorce is unclear. Modern biographies (such as https://en.wikipedia.org/wiki/Ursula_Kuczynski#Librarianship_marriage_and_politics) describe her as having divorced in 1939; MI5 files cite her marriage to Len Beurton as a means to obtain a British passport without having legally ended her first marriage. 37. Bower, *The Perfect English Spy*, p. 21. 38. F. H. Hinsley, *British Intelligence in the Second World War* (HMSO, 1979), p. 12, as quoted in Bower, *The Perfect English Spy*, p. 35, 39. 'Good looking but not clever', unnamed former Security Officer quoted in Andrew, *Defence of the Realm*, p. 128; 'Incompetent', Jane Sissmore/Archer, quoted in ibid, p. 220. 40. Quoted in Bower, *The Perfect English Spy*, p. 40. 41. Guy Liddell diary, 18 November 1940; Andrew, *Defence of the Realm*, note 29 on p. 911. 42. Andrew, *Defence of the Realm*, p. 236. 43. Roger Hollis to Col. Vivian, MI6, 9 December 1940. Vivian's reply of 18 December is referred to by Hollis on 16 January 1941. TNA KV 2/1246, s. 118b2. 44. The names of Fuchs' father and mother appear to have been in his Home Office file as early as 1938: extract from Home Office files F.1167 and 1167/3 for FUCHS Emil Julius Klaus, TNA KV 2/1246, s. 136z. 45. Pincher, *Treachery*, loc 1576. 46. TNA KV 2/1872, s. 121k, December 1940, copied to Jurgen Kuczynski's personal file, 29 January 1941. 47. TNA KV 2/1872, s. 128x.

4. Klaus Fuchs in Birmingham

1. For example, Skardon questioned Fuchs about when he first made contact with the Russian Intelligence Service 'in 1942'. Fuchs replied 'at that time . . .' and offered no indication of earlier involvement, TNA KV 2/1879, s. 545a and 546a. Michael Perrin, administrative head of the British Atomic Project, interviewed Fuchs on 30 January 1950, and recorded 'Fuchs gave me full details in chronological order . . . From 1942 to the end of 1943 . . .' (KV 2/1250, s. 443b). Mr Christmas Humphreys at Fuchs' trial gives 1942 as the date – see for example *Daily Telegraph*, 11 February 1950, KV 2/1263, s. 29b, and a record of Mr Humphreys' statements in KV 2/1263. 'Late 1941' – see Norman Moss, *Klaus Fuchs: The Man who Stole the Atom Bomb* (Grafton Books, 1987), p. 38. 2. The possibility that Peierls himself was a spy was claimed by Nicholas Farrell in *The Spectator*, 29 May 1999, and discussed by Nigel West on 23 July 1999. Perhaps most notable in these articles, written four years after Peierls' death, was the lack of any robust evidence for the hypothesis. The identification of Peierls with the Russian spy code named FOGEL was shown to be false when FOGEL was established to be Russell McNutt, based at Oak Ridge, Tennessee. See the final two pages of Dombey: http://www.tandfonline.com/doi/pdf/10.1080/00107510903184422; and the forensic analysis by Richard Dalitz, 'Sir Rudolf Peierls Was Not a Spy', *Physics World*, vol. 12, no. 10 (1999), and Sabine Lee, 'The Spy that Never Was', *Joint Intelligence and National Security*, vol. 17 (2002), pp. 77–99. See also chapter 22 for an account of the demise of an accusation made during Peierls' lifetime. 3. 13 November 1978 letter to Andrew Boyle, Peierls papers, Bodleian Library, File D53. 4. Address to the Court on behalf of the Director of Public Prosecutions, 10 February 1950, KV 2/1263, s. 27b, p. 2. 5. Rudolf Peierls, *Bird of Passage* (Princeton University Press, 1985), p. 163. 6. Born's letter of 29 May is at KV 2/1246, s. 136z. Unless cited otherwise, all subsequent quotes in this section are from the correspondence between Peierls and Born in TNA AB 1/572 or Peierls papers, Bodleian Library, File C140. 7. Ibid. 8. Max Born, *My Life: Recollections of a Nobel Laureate* (Charles Scribners Sons, 1975). 9. Harold Urey, 'Separation of Isotopes', *Reports on Progress in Physics*, vol. 6 (1939), pp. 48–78. For elements as light as oxygen Urey judged electrolysis and chemical reactions to be ideal. For heavier elements he considered differentiating isotopes by use of a centrifuge or by their different rates of diffusion. Urey's paper analyzed these alternatives only for elements no heavier than zinc, however, where two isotopes – $Zn64$ and $Zn68$ – differ in mass by some 6 per cent. For uranium, which is more than three times heavier, the difference between $U235$ and $U238$ is a mere one per cent, hence Peierls' search for an efficient way to separate isotopes of 'heavy' elements. 10. Peierls interviewed by Charles Weiner, American Institute of Physics Oral Histories, 12 August 1969, p. 94.

Available at http://www5.aip.org/history-programs/niels-bohr-library/oral-histories/4816-3   11. Quotes from here on between Peierls and Born are from TNA file AB 1/572.   12. Peierls to Birmingham University, 21 November 1940, Peierls papers, Bodleian Library, File C140.   13. Born, *My Life*, p. 284, and TNA file AB 1/572. Subsequent quotes from the correspondence between Peierls and Born are from this file.   14. Peierls, *Bird of Passage*, p. 163.   15. Born, *My Life*, p. 286.   16. TNA AB 1/572.   17. Permission to reside temporarily in Birmingham issued by Edinburgh Police, 13 May 1941; KV 2/1259 s. 962b.   18. The file AB 1/572 contains one letter from Born, handwritten on 'Monday', but with no date. This is consistent with Monday 12 May, the day when Peierls' letter arrived, as Born thanks Peierls for his 'letter and the offer to Fuchs'.   19. Dates from Fuchs' identity registration certificate, TNA KV 2/1245, s. 18a. His accommodation cost £2 per week out of an annual salary of £400, which was a significant improvement on his Carnegie Fellowship, held at Edinburgh University, of £250 per annum (letter from Birmingham Chief Constable to Home Office, 6 May 1942, TNA KV 2/1245, s. 30a). The children's birthdates, August 1933 and September 1935, are in *Request For Information From Home Office Records (of Rudolf Ernst Peierls)*, KV 2/1658, s. 37a.   20. 'It seemed . . . that you treated him as if he were your son.' Nobel Laureate Max Perutz to Rudolf Peierls, 19 May 1987, Peierls papers, Bodleian Library, File D56.   21. Genia Peierls, taped interview, Peierls papers, Bodleian Library, File A176.   22. Rudolf and Genia Peierls remarks to Frank Close, undated; Jo Hookway (Peierls), interview 11 May 2015.   23. Klaus Fuchs and Rudolf Peierls: 'Effect on separation of isotopes of compound molecules', DTA (Directorate of Tube Alloys) report no. MS. 44, TNA AB 4/838 (1941, no month given) and DTA MS. 12A, TNA AB 4/878 – dated 'early 1942' according to p. 303 in Richard H. Dalitz and Sir Rudolf Peierls (eds), *Selected Scientific Papers of Sir Rudolf Peierls with Commentary* (World Scientific and Imperial College Press, 1997), whereas the bibliography on p. 793 assigns this to 'late 1941'.   24. Peierls personal papers, letter to Hans Halban, TNA AB 1/575.   25. Peierls, quoted in Margaret Gowing, *Britain and Atomic Energy, 1939–1945* (Macmillan, 1964), p. 262.

5. The Amateur Spy

1. 'Mr Winston Churchill's Broadcast on the Soviet–German War', 22 June 1941. Transcript at: https://www.ibiblio.org/pha/timeline/410622dwp.html   2. The decrypt of a message sent from the Soviet Embassy in London to Moscow Centre on 10 August 1941 refers to Fuchs as a 'former acquaintance' of Kremer: https://ia600504.us.archive.org/17/items/1941_10aug_barch_mtg/1941_10aug_barch_mtg.pdf. The decryption project was known as VENONA. This is a made-up word with no special significance.   3. Interview of Fuchs by Skardon, Brixton Prison, 30 November 1950; TNA KV 2/1879 serial 546a. Fuchs told Skardon, 'I informed him [Kuczynski] with the most general expressions about the type of my information, and returned to Birmingham.' As is discussed later, Fuchs may have conflated events of 1941 and 1942 here. His travel records show that the only overnight trips he made were in April 1941 (when he travelled from Scotland to meet Kuczynski and probably Kremer) and in May 1942 (when he re-established contact via Hannah Klopstech by travelling to Scotland). He could have made contact with Kuczynski in London by travelling from Birmingham on a day visit. Fuchs' testimony to Skardon implies that he did not have easy links with Kuczynski – as in 1942 when he was re-introduced by Klopstech – but Fuchs was careful to control the flow of information to Skardon in 1950, so there remain doubts about the reliability of his testimony. The narrative in the text is consistent with his statements but cannot be certain.   4. In 1943, when the control of Fuchs was transferred from the GRU to the KGB, a summary of his activities was prepared for his new masters. KGB file 84490, vol. 1, p. 22, as transcribed in Alexander Vassiliev, 'Yellow Notebook #1', *Alexander Vassiliev Papers, 1895–2011* (US Library of Congress), p. 67, states 'F was recruited for intelligence work in England in August 1941 by Kremer on a lead from Jürgen Kuczynski.' That Kuczynski knew Kremer through 'official connections' originates with the GRU memorandum in Vassiliev's 'Yellow Notebook #1', p. 86.   5. KGB stands for *Komityet*

Gosudarstvennoy Bezopasnosti, the Committee for State Security. The KGB was established in 1954 in succession to the MGB, Soviet Ministry of State Security, which had been formed in 1946. The MGB was immediately preceded by the NKGB, in existence from 1943 to 1946, and before that by the NKVD (People's Ministry of Internal Affairs), which operated from 1934 to 1943. For a guide through this labyrinth see Christopher Andrew and Oleg Gordievsky, *KGB: The Inside Story* (Harper Collins, 1990), p. 9. For ease of comprehension I refer to all these in the main text as the KGB to distinguish them from the second, independent intelligence agency of the Soviet Union, the GRU – *Glavnoye Razvedyvatelnoye Upravleniye* – founded in 1926 as the Chief Intelligence Directorate of the Red Army. 6. Fuchs was initially with the GRU. See GRU archives, edited by Vladimir Lota, *The GRU and the Atomic Bomb* (Olma Press, 2002), as quoted by Chapman Pincher, *Treachery: Betrayals, Blunders and Cover-Ups: Six Decades of Espionage against America and Great Britain* (Random House, 2009), chapter 15, and communications between the author and Michael Goodman. After 1943 Fuchs was a spy for the KGB. KGB Archives reviewed his GRU career, and confirm the 8/8/41 date in file 84490, vol. 2, p. 127, as transcribed in Vassiliev, 'Yellow Notebook #1', p. 86. See also VENONA decrypts, n.2. 7. Documents found in Fuchs' home, February 1950, TNA KV 2/1252, s. 505a. 8. Margaret Gowing, *Britain and Atomic Energy, 1939–1945* (Macmillan, 1964), p. 68. 9. Ibid, p. 55. The listing of his work in Richard H. Dalitz and Sir Rudolf Peierls (eds), *Selected Scientific Papers of Sir Rudolf Peierls with Commentary* (World Scientific and Imperial College Press, 1997), leads to the estimate of 'nine'. 10. The neutrons produced in fission are fast, so the key to a nuclear reactor is to slow them and then reintroduce them into uranium where they can instigate further fission. This is the basis for the arrangement of materials in a nuclear reactor. Typically, uranium is enriched in $U235$ and is then machined into rods of about 1 cm in diameter. These are placed in channels in graphite, which form a grid with each rod about 20 cm apart. When fission occurs in one rod, the secondary neutrons escape into the graphite surrounds. As these neutrons diffuse through the material they slow. Some of these thermalized neutrons by chance enter other uranium rods where they are ideal for inducing fission. The secondary neutrons produced in this subsequent fission escape into the graphite and the process continues. If some of the graphite is removed, the neutrons will retain their energy and be absorbed by the uranium: fission will cease. The ability to remove graphite from the assembly is therefore part of the safety procedures for shutting down a nuclear reactor. 11. 'Rabbit' is described in TNA AB 4/919, 'cascade of cascades' in TNA AB 4/921 and 939, 'cul-de-sac' in TNA AB 4/872, 874 and 876. 12. Their joint paper 'Effect on Separation of Isotopes of Compound Molecules', DTA MS.44, was written in the late summer of 1941 (TNA AB 4/878). Later that year, or early in 1942 (see note 23 in chapter 4), they produced 'Separation of Isotopes', DTA MS 12A (AB 4/838), which is an updated version of Peierls' 1940 manuscript DTA MS12 (AB 4/837), 'Efficiency of Isotope Separation'. 13. VENONA decryption at https://ia600504.us.archive.org/17/items/1941_10aug_barch_mtg/1941_10aug_barch_mtg.pdf 14. A GRU memorandum included in KGB file 84490, vol. 1, p. 25, as transcribed in Vassiliev, 'Yellow Notebook #1', p. 68, records the dates of the first two shipments of Fuchs' information in Moscow to be 22 and 30 September 1941. 15. Notes by Fuchs on Contacts and Meetings, 24 February 1950. TNA KV 2/1252, s. 518d. 16. On p. 8 of his statement of 27 January 1950 to Skardon (exhibit 3 at his trial, TNA KV 2/1263) Fuchs said, 'I concentrated at first mainly on the products of my own work.' Note he says 'mainly', not 'exclusively', contrary to a common misconception. In actuality, it appears that he sent via Kremer almost everything. 17. Lota, *The GRU and the Atomic Bomb*, p. 40. 18. 'Operational letter from the GRU General Staff of the Red Army to the Director of the London *rezidentura* with a task for K Fuchs'; Document 1/10 in Riabev, Atomnyi Proekt SSSR, pp. 447–8, quoted in David Holloway, *Exploring Intelligence Archives – Enquiries into the Secret State*, eds. R. Gerald Hughes, Peter Jackson and Len Scott (Routledge, 2008), p. 138, n. 6. 19. Gowing, *Britain and Atomic Energy, 1939–1945*, p. 46. See also Graham Farmelo, *Churchill's Bomb: A Hidden History of Science, War and Politics* (Faber and Faber, 2013), p. 185. The early drafts of the MAUD report made no mention of radiation; that the final version said that radiation in the vicinity of the blast would be dangerous to human life for long periods was 'at Peierls' suggestion' (Gowing, *Britain and Atomic Energy, 1939–1945*, p. 86). 20. Gowing, *Britain and Atomic Energy, 1939–1945*, p. 53. 21. Reports on German publications, Peierls to Chadwick, 23 September and 20 November 1941, Churchill College Archives, CHAD I/19/6. Reports on Current German Literature, February and August 1942, TNA AB 3/94 and AB 1/356 initialled by 'K.F [and] R.P.' Review of recent German Literature, prepared by Fuchs and transmitted by Peierls to Chadwick, 28 March 1942, TNA AB 1/356. Their work continued into 1943, for on 22 February 1943 Peierls informed Perrin: 'Fuchs and I have gone through the literature and shall shortly report our findings', TNA 1/356. 22. TNA AB 1/356. 23. 'Report by Fuchs on paper by F Houtermans (Energy consumption in separation of isotopes)', 16 March 1942, TNA AB 1/356. 24. Peierls to Perrin, 29 August 1942, TNA AB 1/356. The interest in German work continued after Fuchs and Peierls had moved to North America and was still active in 1945. On 19 May 1944 Peierls sent Chadwick names of German physicists 'likely working in the direction of interest': entry 369, p. 813, in Sabine Lee, *Sir Rudolf Peierls: Selected Private and Scientific Correspondence*, vol. 1 (World Scientific, Singapore, 2007). In a letter about German literature, sent on 19 December 1944 from DSIR to Dr N. Feather, Cavendish Laboratory, the correspondent states 'I hope to prepare other notes at intervals in the future.' There is no indication in these files supporting the claim by Peter Watson in *Fallout* (Public Affairs, 2018) that the British or Americans 'had known since the summer of 1942 that the Germans had no bomb' and were aware by 1944 that German work had reached a 'dead end'. 25. Aliens Control (E.4) to Miss Bagot (F.4. b(2)): 'Request for enquiries about Fuchs' activities in the United Kingdom', 6 August 1941, forwarded to Director General 9 August. TNA KV 2/1245, s. 5. 26. Women Spies: Milicent Bagot: https://girlspy.wordpress.com/2010/06/08/millicent-bagot; accessed 20 November 2017. 27. Anthony Glees, *The Secrets of the Service* (Jonathan Cape, 1987), p. 348; Michael Smith, *The Spying Game* (Politico's, 2004), p. 88, and Christopher Andrew, *Defence of the Realm: The Authorized History of MI5* (Allen Lane, 2009), p. 281, have Hollis in charge of 'F2 [which] was responsible for monitoring Communism and other left wing subversion'. 28. Director General to Chief Constable Moriarty of Birmingham, 9 August 1941. TNA KV 2/1245, s. 6. 29. Chief Constable Moriarty to Sir David Petrie, 11 August 1941, TNA KV 2/1245, s. 8. 30. TNA KV/2 1245, s. 7. From an unidentified member of section F.2.b to Robson-Scott (E.1.a). 31. TNA KV 2/1245, 9 August, s. 7; 29 August, s. 9. 32. TNA KV 2/1245, minute 5, 18 September 1941. 33. It is unclear when Fuchs signed the Official Secrets Act, if indeed he ever did. He received an 'Official circular warning re Official Secrets Act', dated 11 October 1941, which was found in his home in 1950 (TNA KV 2/1252, s. 505a), but it is unclear what action, if any, this led to. M. Perrin in a letter to B. Hill for Fuchs' trial gave the date as 18 June 1942 (*sic*), TNA KV 2/1264, s. 90a. Fuchs' British naturalization was on 30 July 1942; TNA KV 2/1263, serial 19a. However, no evidence of Fuchs' signature was given at his trial (see chapter 20, note 7. 34. D. Griffith (F.2 b) to Mr Cochrane-Wilson (sic) (E.4), 8 October 1941. TNA KV 2/1245, minute 6. KASPAR's identity is revealed to be a Dr Kurt Schreiber, in TNA KV 2/1252, s. 509b. 35. All quotes in this paragraph are taken from J. Robertson, 'Emil Julius Klaus Fuchs', 23 November 1949. TNA KV 2/1248, s. 344z, pp. 2 and 3. 36. Maurice Oldfield (MI6) to Arthur Martin, 8 September 1949, KV 2/1246, s. 118b. 37. This refers to the source mentioned by Roger Hollis, letter to Colonel Vivian (MI6), 9 December 1940 (*sic*). KV 2/1246, s. 118b2. 38. D. Griffith (F.2 b) to Mr Cochrane-Wilson (E.4), 8 October 1941. TNA KV 2/1245, minute 6. 39. KASPAR's information appears in MI5 files eighteen months later, on 29 January 1943 (*sic*) and was 'translated 3 February 1943' (Memo from Alien control E.5 to Daphne Bosanquet, F.2.b., TNA KV 2/1245, s. 21a). This includes the remark that Klaus Fuchs 'like his brother Gerhard . . . belonged to the German Communist Party, in which, however, he never achieved any prominence in Germany'. KASPAR's information is incorrect, however, in its assertion that Klaus 'went to Prague as a refugee'. KASPAR then remarks that although Klaus in Prague 'did not indulge in any political activities', 'Gerhard worked [there] in the Communist Party's Apparat'. This message makes no reference to the '70 Club'; see note 59, which suggests that 'Victoria' forwarded this information to the Czechs and not to KASPAR. 40. J. O. Archer (D 3), 'Application for Employment at Birmingham University'. TNA KV 2/1245, s. 11, 10 October 1941.   41. J. O. Archer, 'no objection', 18 October, minute 13.   42. Stephens to Archer, 15 October 1941, TNA KV 2/1245, minute 12.   43. In 1950 some documents relevant to this chronology were found in Fuchs' house. They are listed in TNA KV 2/1252, s. 505a, items, 240–42. 'Correspondence with M.A.P. re completion of formalities connected with FUCHS' employment at Birmingham', June 1941; Circular letter from M.A.P., 'Official circular warning re Official Secrets Act', 11 October 1941; letter from Box 666, Parliament Street, 'Confirming approval of employment at Birmingham University, 22 October 1941.' The original documents mentioned on this list appear to have been lost.   44. 'Registration Card of Emil Julius Klaus Fuchs', entry of 3 November 1941; TNA TNA KV/2 1245, s. 19a.   45. KGB file 84490, vol. 2, p. 127; Vassiliev, 'Yellow Notebook #1', p. 86: 'To summon Kremer to meetings, F. occasionally called his phone (whether his work phone or home phone is unknown.)'   46. Vladimir Lota in The GRU and the Atomic Bomb, as quoted by Pincher, Treachery, chapter 16, and communications between the author and Michael Goodman. This 'remarkable' occasion is also mentioned by MI5 in TNA KV 2/1256, s. 756, p. 7, and by Fuchs to Skardon in TNA KV 2/1252, s. 519.   47. Genia Peierls, taped interview, Peierls papers, Bodleian Library, File A176.   48. Pincher, Treachery (chapter 16), claims three occasions and Mike Rossiter, The Spy who Changed the World (Headline, 2014), p. 100, four, though there is no source for these. When Fuchs was transferred to the KGB, the GRU report on his activities gave seven dates when information was sent to Moscow, the first two being on 22 and 30 September 1941 (Vassiliev, 'Yellow Notebook #1', p. 68; KGB file 84490, vol. 1, p. 26). No shipments are then mentioned until 26 May 1943, but there were other meetings with Kremer and, later, with 'Sonya' (Ursula Beurton). For example, Fuchs met Kremer in August 1941, and later that year visited the Russian Embassy in London. There is reference to a meeting of April 1943 at which Fuchs recommended Engelbert Broda, then working at Cambridge University, as a GRU contact. Unknown to Fuchs, Broda had already been recruited by the KGB, probably at the end of 1942 or in January 1943; see Paul Broda, Scientist Spies: A Memoir of My Three Parents and the Atom Bomb (Matador, 2011), pp. 150–51.   49. Lota in The GRU and the Atomic Bomb, as quoted by Pincher, Treachery, chapter 16, and communications between the author and Michael Goodman.   50. Gowing, Britain and Atomic Energy, 1939–1945, p. 128.   51. Ibid, p. 71.   52. His application of 30 April 1942 gave his residence as the Peierls' home in Birmingham, his occupation 'Research Worker', and his referees C. G. Barkla and E. G. Whittaker of Edinburgh (Barkla was a Nobel laureate in 1917), Ronald Gunn and Neville Mott. TNA KV 2/1245.   53. Quote from Chief Constable of Birmingham, letter to Miss Bosanquet, F.2.b., 29 July 1943. TNA KV 2/1245, s. 30a.   54. Vetting (Mrs Wyllie C.3.b) to Home Office, 12 May 1942, TNA KV 2/1245, s. 15.   55. D. Griffith (F.2.b) to Mrs Wyllie (Vetting, C.3.b), 11 May 1942. TNA KV 2/1245 s. 15 in response to Ref. No. F.1167/2 (Nat Div), ' "National Interest" case for the favour of your early report', dated 30 April, sent from P.O. Box No. 2, Bournemouth; name of requestor unknown.   56. Quote from Chief Constable of Birmingham, 6 May 1942, TNA KV 2/1245, s. 30a. There is no indication of the nature of the 'discreet enquiries' or when they were made.   57. TNA KV 2/1245, minute 17, 30 May 1942.   58. Extract from Home Office files F.1167 and 1167/3 for 'FUCHS Emil Julius Klaus', TNA KV 2/1246, s. 136z. Fuchs signed the Oath of Allegiance on 31 July and the Certificate of Naturalization was issued on 7 August.   59. 14 February 1950, Unsigned note to Robertson, 'Dr Klaus FUCHS', TNA KV 2/1252, s. 509b.   60. J. Robertson, 9 November 1949, 'Emil Julius Klaus FUCHS', TNA KV 2/1248, s. 344z, p. 9.

6. The Atomic Industry

1. Margaret Gowing, Britain and Atomic Energy, 1939–1945 (Macmillan, 1964), p. 88.   2. Graham Farmelo, Churchill's Bomb: A Hidden History of Science, War and Politics (Faber and Faber, 2013), pp. 164–7.   3. Richard Rhodes, The Making of the Atomic Bomb (Penguin, 1988), pp. 317 and 332.   4. Gowing, Britain and Atomic Energy, 1939–1945, p. 88.   5. James Chadwick interview 20 April 1969; www.aip.org/history/ohilist/3974_4.html

as quoted in Farmelo, *Churchill's Bomb*, p. 179. **6.** Gowing, *Britain and Atomic Energy, 1939–1945*, p. 109. Akers was chair and the scientists were James Chadwick, Franz Simon, Hans Halban, Peierls, together with a Dr Slade from ICI. **7.** Gowing, *Britain and Atomic Energy, 1939–1945*, p. 116. **8.** Quoted in Farmelo, *Churchill's Bomb*, p. 174. **9.** Ibid, p. 182. **10.** Roosevelt to Churchill, 11 October 1941, TNA CAB 126/330. **11.** Sir John Anderson as reported in Farmelo, *Churchill's Bomb*, p. 204. **12.** Quoted in ibid, p. 205. There is no definitive version of the quote, which could be fictitious. For a discussion, see also Richard Langworth: https://richardlangworth.com/churchills-naked-encounter **13.** Farmelo, *Churchill's Bomb*, p. 207. **14.** Gowing, *Britain and Atomic Energy, 1939–1945*, p. 131. 'Teleprinter request for permission to travel to USA'. TNA KV 2/1658, f.5a, and 6a. This request, dated 20 February, states 'leaving UK 21 Feb.' **15.** Ibid, pp. 128 and 141. **16.** Ibid, p. 139. **17.** Rhodes, *The Making of the Atomic Bomb*, p. 10. **18.** Memo from Akers, 11 June 1942, TNA CAB 126/166. See also Farmelo, *Churchill's Bomb*, pp. 214–15. **19.** This is defined in chapter 1, p. 23. Their report, 'Equilibrium time in a separation plant', is DTA rept. MS.47A, May 1942 (TNA AB 4/882), Richard H. Dalitz and Sir Rudolf Peierls (eds), *Selected Scientific Papers of Sir Rudolf Peierls with Commentary* (World Scientific and Imperial College Press, 1997), p. 793. **20.** KGB file 84490, vol. 1, p. 131; Alexander Vassiliev, 'Yellow Notebook #1', *Alexander Vassiliev Papers, 1895–2011* (US Library of Congress), p. 77. **21.** Edinburgh Police File A29/107, TNA KV 2/1259, s. 962B. That the visit was nominally to see Born is clear from a letter dated 24 May 1942, found in Fuchs' house: TNA KV 2/1252, s. 505c, item number 112. **22.** TNA KV 2/1872, serials 79a and 80a. **23.** 'Our illegal station chief in England, "Sonya"': GRU memo to KGB file 84490, vol. 2, p. 127, Vassiliev, 'Yellow Notebook #1', p. 86. Sonya was also the controller at this time for Britain's leading female Soviet agent, Melita Norwood (Christopher Andrew and Vasili Mitrokhin, *The Mitrokhin Archive* [Penguin, 2000], p. 153). Norwood's story is told in David Burke, *The Spy who Came in from the Co-op: Melita Norwood and the Ending of Cold War Espionage* (Boydell Press, 2008). **24.** Robert Chadwell Williams, *Klaus Fuchs, Atom Spy* (Cambridge, MA, 1987), p. 59. **25.** GRU memoir of Klaus Fuchs in KGB file 84490, vol. 2, p. 127, Vassiliev, 'Yellow Notebook #1', p. 86. **26.** Ruth Werner (Ursula Beurton), *Sonya's Report* (Vintage, 1999), chapter 6. Sonya's memories in this chapter come from this source. **27.** Quoted without source in Chapman Pincher, *Treachery: Betrayals, Blunders and Cover-Ups: Six Decades of Espionage against America and Great Britain* (Random House, 2009), chapter 19. Sonya makes no such claim in her memoirs, referring only to a transfer 'more than a hundred pages long' on another occasion. Although the distribution of material among their liaisons is not known, the total was certainly considerable as Fuchs produced a large amount of work for Tube Alloys, and there is no reason for him to have withheld any. **28.** Ursula Beurton interview with Don Chapman, *Oxford Mail*, 1981. Article in *Oxford Mail*, 6 August 2010. **29.** Werner, *Sonya's Report*, chapter 6. **30.** Peierls papers, Bodleian Library, File C152. Letters of 15 July and 2 August found in Fuchs' house, TNA KV 2/1260. Vassiliev, 'Yellow Notebook #1', p. 68, gives the shipment dates for Fuchs' materials in his Birmingham period as 22/9/41; 30/9/41; 26/5/43; 17/6/43; 12/7/43; 16/9/43; and 28/10/43. **31.** K. Fuchs, G. J. Kynch and R. Peierls, 'The Equation of State of Air at High Temperature', DTA rept. MS61 (1942), TNA AB 4/897. The analysis in this paper would later be applied by Fuchs and Peierls to the implosion of plutonium at Los Alamos; chapters 7 and 8. **32.** Werner, *Sonya's Report*, chapter 6. **33.** *The Manhattan Project – Making the Atomic Bomb*, US Department of Energy, 1999, p. 16. The pile's footprint was elliptical, some 1.8 metres wide at the ends and 7.6 metres across its middle. **34.** Akers to Perrin, 21 December 1942, TNA CHAD I 28/2, quoted in Farmelo, *Churchill's Bomb*, p. 215. **35.** R. V. Jones, *Most Secret War: British Scientific Intelligence 1939–1945* (Penguin, 2009), p. 474. **36.** Gowing, *Britain and Atomic Energy, 1939–1945*, p. 217. **37.** Neville Mott proposed and James Chadwick seconded Peierls for the Fellowship. Chadwick offered to propose Peierls on 20 October 1947: Chadwick to Peierls, entry 350, p. 778, in Sabine Lee, *Sir Rudolf Peierls: Selected Private and Scientific Correspondence*, vol. 1 (World Scientific, 2007). Peierls replied on 21 October to say that Mott had already submitted his nomination: entry 351, ibid. **38.** Extract from 'Report of visit to Birmingham University on

11 May by Major G. D. Garrett, R.M.', TNA KV 2/1658, s. 8a.   **39.** Note for Personal File 62251 [Fuchs], 4 July 1943 TNA KV 2/1245, s. 23a.   **40.** TNA KV 2/1245, minute 24, 4 July 1943.   **41.** Memo on Klaus Fuchs by M. D. Bosanquet, 15 March 1943, TNA KV 2/1245, s. 22a.   **42.** Mrs Daphne Bosanquet to Captain Dykes, 7 July 1943, TNA KV 2/1245, s. 25a.   **43.** 'Clever and dangerous': Dykes' reply of 15 July [KV 2/1245,serial 28a] attested that Fuchs 'has been described as being clever and dangerous' – a remark that appears nowhere else in released files. Bosanquet's letter of 19 July (KV 2/1245, serial 29a), in referring to Dykes' (redacted) letter of 11.7.43 (serial 26a), states 'I thought that you had mentioned this to the police as *you then told me their opinion of Fuchs* (my emphasis). This suggests that the redacted letter references this opinion of the police.   **44.** D. Bosanquet to Captain Dykes, 14 July 1943, TNA KV 2/1245, s. 27a.   **45.** Dykes (signed by A. d'Arcy Hughes) to Bosanquet, 15 July 1943, TNA KV 2/1245, s. 28a.   **46.** TNA KV 2/1245, serials 23–30, July 1943.   **47.** TNA KV 2/1245, minutes 31–3.   **48.** H. Shillito [F2C], to Capt. Garrett [D2], after minute 32 in TNA KV 2/1245. Garrett added, 'I agree with your opinion.' Shillito's earlier success is mentioned on p. 82 in Michael Smith, *The Spying Game* (Politico's, 2004).   **49.** Gowing, *Britain and Atomic Energy, 1939–1945*, p. 228.   **50.** As late as 10 November 1950, MI5 still referred to 'the unknown woman', TNA KV 2/1256, m.753. On 30 November Fuchs identified her as Ursula Beurton, TNA KV 1256, s. 759a. See chapter 20 and footnote, p. 358, for more about Beurton's identification.   **51.** R. E. Peierls to Divisional Officer, C Division, National Fire Service, 24 July 1942. Peierls papers, Bodleian Library, File A38   **52.** Farmelo, *Churchill's Bomb*, pp. 240–43.   **53.** 'Indecent haste': Gowing, *Britain and Atomic Energy, 1939–1945*, p. 171. The Quebec Agreement was signed on 19 August and the scientists arrived 'within hours' – Farmelo, *Churchill's Bomb*, pp. 240–44.   **54.** TNA KV 2/1658, s. 9a records that Peierls applied for an exit permit on 10 August for his subsequent visit to the USA. This was 'cleared by Mr Barrs' on 16 August (note at point 10 in TNA KV 2/1658, s. 17a, 17 November 1943).   **55.** Peierls' letter to the AFS in 1942 was now seen to be prescient. He resigned and handed in his equipment. With meticulous accountancy, on 21 October 1943 'FIREMAN PEIERLS 587102' was handed a receipt for having returned one each of 'uniform cap and badge; steel helmet, respirator, pair rubber boots, leggings, belt and pouch, overcoat and overalls. A tunic and a pair of trousers were returned subsequently.' Peierls papers, Bodleian Library, File A38.   **56.** Gowing, *Britain and Atomic Energy, 1939–1945*, p. 239. The terms of collaboration were agreed in mid-November.   **57.** TNA KV 2/1658, s. 15a, 16a, 17a. Their children, aged eight and ten, were already being cared for in Canada, where they had been placed to escape the Blitz. Genia's application explained that the children would join them in the USA.   **58.** Application for Grant of Exit Permit, 10 August 1943, TNA KV 2/1658, s. 9a.   **59.** 'In April 1943, F[uchs] gave a lead for recruiting an Austrian scientist in England named Broda, a physical chemist by specialisation', KGB file 84490, vol. 1: 'Charles'; Vassiliev, 'Yellow Notebook #1', p. 68. For the story of Engelbert Broda and Alan Nunn May, see Paul Broda, *Scientist Spies: A Memoir of My Three Parents and the Atom Bomb* (Matador, 2011).   **60.** Werner, *Sonya's Report*, chapter 6.   **61.** KGB file 84490 v.1, p. 25; Vassiliev, 'Yellow Notebook #1', p. 67.   **62.** Leslie Groves, *Now It Can Be Told* (Harper, 1962), p. 4.   **63.** The Manhattan Project failed to produce a workable centrifuge, suited for industrial separation of uranium isotopes, and in January 1944 Army support for the gas centrifuge method was dropped in favour of gaseous diffusion. An efficient robust centrifuge was developed in the 1950s and is the preferred method of separation today. For the history of isotope separation see pp. 5–6 in the U.S. Department of Energy's official Manhattan Project history: F. G. Gosling, *The Manhattan Project: Making the Atomic Bomb* (DOE/MA-0001; Washington: History Division, Department of Energy, January 1999, available online at https://www.osti.gov/opennet/manhattan-project-history/publications/DE99001330.pdf).   **64.** Groves, *Now It Can Be Told*, p. 20.

7. The New World

1. See David Holloway, *Stalin and the Bomb* (Yale Univerity Press, 1996), p. 77.   **2.** Leslie Groves, *Now It Can Be Told* (Harper, 1962), p. 140 and chapter 10.   **3.** Ibid, p. 145.   **4.** Ibid,

p. 146.   5. Ibid, p. 143.   6. Observation no. 10 on teleprinter application for exit permit, 17 November 1943, TNA KV 2/1245, s. 34a.   7. Milicent Bagot (F.2.b) to Michael Serpell (F.2.a), 22 November 1943, TNA KV 2/1245, minute 35.   8. Serpell to Garrett, 28 November, TNA KV 2/1245, minute 36.   9. Serpell to Garrett, 3 December, TNA KV 2/1245, minute 38.   10. TNA KV 2/1248, s. 349b.   11. Perrin to Garrett, 8 December 1943, TNA KV 2/1248, s. 40a.   12. Groves, *Now It Can Be Told*, p. 143.   13. W. Akers to Chadwick, 10 December 1944, Exhibit 2 in Summary Brief on Klaus Fuchs, 6 February 1950, Fuchs FBI FOIA file 65-58805-1202.   14. W. L. Webster to General Groves, 11 December 1944, Exhibit 2 in Summary Brief on Klaus Fuchs, 6 February 1950, Fuchs FBI FOIA file 65-58805-1202.   15. Groves, *Now It Can Be Told*, p. 143.   16. TNA KV 2/1257, s. 855b.   17. FBI interview with Dr Cohen, Fuchs FBI FOIA file 65-58805-642, p. 104.   18. AEC Oak Ridge records held at FBI Knoxville office, 15 February 1950, Fuchs FBI FOIA file 65-58805-394.   19. FBI interview with Dr Cohen, Fuchs FBI FOIA file 65-58805-642, p. 105.   20. Perrin to Major Garrett, 10 January 1944, TNA KV 2/1245, s. 41b.   21. Groves, *Now It Can Be Told*, p. 144.   22. Note from D.2 to Major Garrett, 16 January 1944, TNA KV 2/1245.   23. Major Garrett, TNA KV 2/1245, s. 42a; 17 January 1944, and serials 39-42, 16 and 17 January 1944   24. Mr Tolson to Hugh Clegg, 'Klaus Fuchs Espionage', 30 December 1953. Fuchs FBI FOIA file, 65-58805-1543.   25. Exhibit in Summary Brief on Klaus Fuchs, FBI FOIA file 65-58805-1202.   26. Rudolf Peierls, *Bird of Passage* (Princeton University Press, 1985), p. 184. The location as number 37 is from FBI file 65-58805-378. Adding to this sense, the ground floor of 37 Wall Street is home to Tiffany's.   27. Fuchs to FBI, 1 June 1950, TNA KV 6/135. 'End' of February – FOIA 65-58805-642 p.19 states that Fuchs 'was said to have taken this apartment from ARMS . . . when ARMS returned to Great Britain on 28 February 1944'. The FBI mistakenly believed Fuchs to have lived at number 128 from 1 February 1944, whereas in fact he lived at 122 from the end of that month. This error explains why in 1950 they were unable to find anyone at 128 who remembered Fuchs, even though several residents had lived there for many years. And it is also the source of Rhodes dating Fuchs' first meeting with Gold – for which Rhodes deduced that Fuchs departed from the Barbizon Plaza hotel and not an apartment in the 77th block – to January rather than February.   The FBI was given the address verbally on 11 February 1950 (TNA KV 6/134, s. 156a). The original source was the physicist Nicholas Kurti, a member of the British Mission, who had recorded Fuchs' address in his diary. This is filed at TNA KV 6/134, s. 156a, which shows clearly 'Address: 122 W 77ᵈ'. Somehow this was misunderstood to be number 128, as on 13 February J. Marriott referred to it as number 128 in KV 2/1252, s. 505a. The arrival of this error can be traced through the Kurti and MI5 papers, and those of the Harwell security officer Henry Arnold in TNA KV 6/134. See also FBI FOIA file 65-58805-642, p. 19.   28. Gold's original reports are available in KGB file 84490, vol. 1 and have been transcribed in Alexander Vassiliev, 'Yellow Notebook #1', *Alexander Vassiliev Papers, 1895–2011* (US Library of Congress), pp. 67–76.   29. The Vassiliev notes record that the original meeting with Fuchs was initially arranged to be the third Saturday in January. The date of Fuchs' entry into espionage in New York is 5 February. This date appears in Gold's report sent to Moscow at the time – Vassiliev, 'Yellow Notebook #1', p. 68 – and with a VENONA decrypted message of 9 February: 'On 5ᵗʰ February a meeting took place between GOOSE and REST.' See: https://www.nsa.gov/news-features/declassified-documents/venona/dated/1944/assets/files/9feb_atomic_energy.pdf   Fuchs' account of the journey to the meeting with his contact, Harry Gold, fits with his starting point being the Barbizon Plaza, which was his residence until at least the end of January. Richard Rhodes, *Dark Sun: The Making of the Hydrogen Bomb* (Simon and Schuster, 2005), p. 104, took Fuchs' move to his apartment to have been 1 February and thereby placed the meeting in January. See note 27 for an alternative interpretation.   30. Description based on Gold's report to Moscow, Vassiliev, 'Yellow Notebook #1', p. 68, and Fuchs' statement to FBI, FOIA file 65-58805-1324, p. 2.   31. This is based on the KGB agreed signals, Vassiliev, 'Yellow Notebook #1', p. 68. Some other versions – e.g. Norman Moss, *Klaus Fuchs: The Man who Stole the Atom Bomb* (Grafton Books, 1987), p. 164, and J. Baggott, *Atomic* (Icon Books, 2009), p. 240 – claim the questioner asked the way to Grand Central Station, but give no original source for this.   32. Harry Gold confession as transmitted to John Cimperman, US Embassy, London, 23 May

1950. Fuchs FBI FOIA file, 65-58805-1196. 'Manny Wolf': Harry Gold statement, 29 May 1950, 65-58805-1355. 33. Fuchs FBI FOIA file 65-58805-1412, p. 12. 34. Report by Harry Gold to Moscow on meeting of 5 February 1944, Vassiliev, 'Yellow Notebook #1', p. 68. In 1950 he gave an account to the FBI in FOIA 65-57449-551, p. 1 et seq. 35. Harry Gold, FBI FOIA file 65-57449-551, p. 2. 36. The meeting point was less than a mile north of the Barbizon Plaza and a similar distance across Central Park from Fuchs' final residence on West 77th Street. 37. Harry Gold, the FBI FOIA file 65-57449-551, p. 2. 38. Vassiliev, 'Yellow Notebook #1', p. 68; KGB file 84490, vol. 1, p. 48. 39. Vassiliev, 'Yellow Notebook #1', p. 69. 40. Harry Gold's statement to FBI, 10 July 1950. FOIA 65-57449-551, p. 1. 41. Fuchs FBI FOIA file 65-58805-1412. 42. Gold FBI FOIA file 65-57449-551, p. 27. See Rhodes, *Dark Sun*, p. 108. 43. Thermal diffusion was later used as a back-up when the gaseous diffusion was delayed, and eventually played a role in isolating U235 for the Hiroshima bomb in August 1945. 44. Fuchs to FBI, 24 February 1950, TNA KV 2/1252, s. 518a. 45. Fuchs interview 1950 by FBI in FOIA file 65-58805-1412, p. 14. 46. Margaret Gowing, *Britain and Atomic Energy, 1939–1945* (Macmillan, 1964), p. 254. 47. The memories of Fuchs and Gold of their meetings do not always agree, which makes construction of an unambiguous history impossible. The meetings of 4 May and 9 June are chronologically inconsistent with other established events, in particular, KGB file 84490 vol. 1, p. 49 (as transcribed in Vassiliev, 'Yellow Notebook #1', p. 70), which reports that Peierls had 'just returned from a three-week trip to Camp Y'. ('Его партнер [и непосредств-й руководитель] Пейерлс только что вернулся из 3-х недельной поездки в лагерь У.' 'Y' would at first sight appear to be Los Alamos but for some reason Fuchs or Gold seems at this stage to have referred to Los Alamos as Camp X – for example, in his report of their meeting of 28 March in the Bronx, Gold refers to 'Camp X in New Mexico'. This, of course, could be simply a slip by Fuchs or Gold. Peierls made a single three-week trip to Los Alamos between 2 and 21 June, yet the reference to his return in Vassiliev appears between the report of a meeting on '4.05.44' and one on '9.06.44' (in the European convention of day, month, year). Given the need to ensure that their theoretical work on diffusion had practical relevance, together with British interest in developing a low-separation plant in England, a visit to Oak Ridge at this juncture would seem appropriate; Gowing, *Britain and Atomic Energy, 1939–1945*, p. 252, says 'The British experts . . . visited the centres where their own type of work was being done', but Peierls is not specifically cited. Peierls makes no mention of a visit in his memoir, but it is rather thinly spread. Gowing mentions that Peierls' colleague Kearton 'was not allowed to visit the full-scale plant [Oak Ridge] itself', which appears to be a comment on the restrictions imposed by the USA and by singling out Kearton implicitly suggests that Peierls might have visited Oak Ridge. Rather than invent a visit for which there is no other evidence, a more likely explanation is that the meeting took place at the end of June or early July. There was no chronological order to the documents, nor were they indexed. Vassiliev remarked (email to author, 6 November 2018): 'One can find a cable in one file and a reply to it in another. A document which should be in an agent's personal file is not there but may be found in an operational correspondence file. The files are not indexed which means it's impossible to tell what kind of information they contain without reading them page by page.' The haphazard nature of the collection appears to have led the month to have been numbered wrongly on at least one occasion, as a reference elsewhere to a meeting on 15.06 (Vassiliev, 'Yellow Notebook #1', p. 70) took place in July according to two other independent reports. Gold later refers to this meeting as taking place in July, which is also consistent with the chronology of Fuchs' meetings with Chadwick – see chapter 8. If the transcription of the meeting on '9.06.44' should also refer to July, a consistent picture emerges where Fuchs is referring to Peierls having returned from Los Alamos (on 21 June) in accord with the established dates for his visit. 48. Harry Gold, FBI FOIA file, 65-57449-551, p. 2. 49. KGB Archives, File 84490, vol. 1, p. 49, in Vassiliev, 'Yellow Notebook #1', p. 67, and VENONA decrypted message of 15 June 1944. 50. Harry Gold, FBI FOIA file, 65-57449-551, p. 3. 51. Harry Gold, FBI FOIA file, 65-57449-551, p. 4. Gold had five minutes to wait for Yatzkov and so 'peeked' at the material; the descriptions of the contents are due to Gold. 52. Quoted in Graham Farmelo, *Churchill's Bomb: A Hidden History of Science, War and Politics* (Faber and Faber, 2013), p. 249, and the Chadwick memorandum on meeting with Groves, 11

February 1944, CHAD IV 3/2. 53. The history of UK–US nuclear relations during the war is in the chapter 'Churchill's Nuclear Deal with FDR', in Farmelo, *Churchill's Bomb*, and it is covered extensively in Gowing, *Britain and Atomic Energy 1939–1945*. 54. Farmelo, *Churchill's Bomb*, p. 241. 55. 'Reference to possible departure of REST' https://www.nsa.gov/news-features/declassified-documents/venona/dated/1944/assets/files/15jun_departure_agent_rest.pdf. See also chapter 13, note 17

8. Trinity

1. MI5 file KV 2/1659 f.113B and 119 gives the dates of Peierls' visit to Los Alamos as 2–20 June 1944. The memo also recorded: 'His posting to Los Alamos was decided at the end of May and would take place in early July.' 2. Gold describes the meeting as 'near an art museum in the 80s and on the west side of 5th Avenue'. FOIA 65-57449-551, p. 6. 3. Fuchs to Peierls, 17 July 1944, 'I saw Chadwick on Friday [14th] and discussed with him the future of Skyrme and myself,' TNA AB 1/575. 4. James Chadwick to Rudolf Peierls, 14 July 1944. TNA AB 1/639. The full letter is quoted on pp. 116–17 of J. Bernstein, *A Bouquet of Dyson* (World Scientific, 2018), and also in 371, pp. 819–22, of Sabine Lee, *Sir Rudolf Peierls: Selected Private and Scientific Correspondence*, vol. 1 (World Scientific, 2007). 5. This question was raised by Brian Cathcart, unpublished, and brought to my attention by Jeremy Bernstein, email, 18 November 2015. 6. Handwritten note by Hoover in *Summary Brief on Dr Emil Julius Klaus Fuchs*, 1949: 'Russia proposed to send F[uchs] back to G[reat] B[ritain]'; FBI files 65-58805-1202, p. 8, quoted in Richard Rhodes, *Dark Sun: The Making of the Hydrogen Bomb* (Simon and Schuster, 2005), pp. 111 and 604. 7. Perrin to Chadwick, 21 July 1944, TNA AB 1/639. 8. Val Fitch, a twenty-year-old soldier, was also assisting with some experiments and became interested in the science. After the war he became an experimental physicist and in 1980 won a Nobel Prize. I am indebted to Jeremy Bernstein for this information. Fitch's Nobel biography is at: https://www.nobelprize.org/nobel_prizes/physics/laureates/1980/fitch-bio.html. 9. Roy Glauber, Remarks in colloquium, Oxford University, 8 May 2015. 10. Quoted in Ferenc Szasz, *The Day the Sun Rose Twice: The Story of the Trinity Site Explosion, July 16, 1945* (University of New Mexico Press, 1984), p. 90. 11. Gaby Gross (Peierls), email to author, 5 January 2019. Katrina Mason, *Children of Los Alamos* (Twayne Publishers, 1995), p. 136. 12. Quoted in Brian Cathcart, *Test of Greatness* (John Murray, 1994), p. 33. 13. This 'Christy gadget' became part of Los Alamos' official history and has been known by Christy's name ever since. However, the patent is in their joint names, and Peierls is credited in authoritative histories as having been its inspiration. Lorna Arnold and Kate Pyne, *Britain and the H Bomb* (Palgrave, 2001), p. 254, note 10, and Ralph Carlisle Smith, summary of British Mission at Los Alamos, 18 July 1949, LAB-ADCS-127. Their joint patent, 'Method and apparatus for explosively releasing nuclear energy', was filed on 27 August 1946. 14. Ralph Carlisle Smith, Summary of British Mission at Los Alamos, 18 July 1949, LAB-ADCS-127, quoted in Szasz, *The Day the Sun Rose Twice*, p. 149. 15. This oft-quoted remark attributed to Feynman appears to originate with Norman Moss, *Klaus Fuchs: The Man who Stole the Atom Bomb* (Grafton Books, 1987), p. 68. Moss, however, gives no source. 16. Harry Gold confession to FBI, FOIA file 65-57449-551, p. 7. 17. The description of the apartment is Gold's to FBI, ibid, p. 9. 18. Ibid, p. 10. 19. KGB file 40159, vol. 3, p. 356, notes, 'If you are unable to establish a connection by 1.04.44 then go through his sister, Heineman, who lives on 144 Lake View Avenue, Cambridge, Massachusetts. Married, she and her husband – fellow countrymen. Password: Our Man: "I bring you greetings from Max"; She: "Oh I heard Max had twins"; Our man: "Yes, seven days ago."' See the 'Black Notebook' in Alexander Vassiliev, *Alexander Vassiliev Papers, 1895–2011*, US Library of Congress: https://www.loc.gov/item/mm2009085460, p. 112. This is strong evidence that Kristel was a willing partner in her brother's affairs. 20. https://www.nsa.gov/news-features/declassified-documents/venona/dated/1944/assets/files/4oct_klaus_fuch_sister.pdf 21. KGB file 84490, vol. 1, pp. 68–71, Vassiliev, 'Yellow Notebook #1', pp. 70–71. 22. The text is based on Gold's

report as transmitted to Moscow by his handler and later transcribed by Vassiliev (see also chapter 13, note 19). Gold's report refers to three visits – 24 October, 2 November and 7 December 1944 – with news of Fuchs having telephoned from Chicago sometime between 24 October and 2 November. Kristel then remembers further information from Fuchs' call when Gold visits on 7 December. MI5 records, on the other hand, list Fuchs as absent from Los Alamos only on two occasions, both in 1945 – his visit to his sister from 13 to 22 February and a visit to Montreal in November followed by a vacation with the Peierlses in Mexico. A possibility is that he made the call from Santa Fe but claimed that he was in Chicago for reasons of security.   23. When questioned by the FBI in 1950, Gold recalled that Kristel didn't know where her brother Klaus was other than he was 'somewhere in the south-west United States'. However, New Mexico is explicitly cited in Gold's 1944 report, which also spelled out that Kristel 'does not know exactly where in New Mexico [Klaus Fuchs] is'.   24. KGB 82702 'Enormos', vol. 1, p. 237, Vassiliev, 'Yellow Notebook #1', p. 16; 'Stayed for lunch': File 84490, vol. 1, p. 69, 2 November 1944, Vassiliev, 'Yellow Notebook #1', p. 71.   25. KGB 84490, vol. 1, p. 71, Vassiliev, 'Yellow Notebook #1', p. 71.   26. Harry Gold to FBI. FBI FOIA file 65-57449-551, p. 12.   27. Klaus Fuchs to agents Clegg and Lamphere. FBI FOIA file 65-58805-1414, p. 15.   28. KGB file 84490, vol. 1, p. 79, Vassiliev, 'Yellow Notebook #1', p. 72.   29. KGB file 84490, vol. 1, p. 80, Vassiliev, 'Yellow Notebook #1', p. 73.   30. KGB file 84490, vol. 1, p. 115. 'The decision to use her as a contact for Ch[arles] was approved by the GRU RA before he was handed over to us.' Vassiliev, Yellow Notebook #1', p. 77.   31. KGB file 40159 v.3, p. 478, Vassiliev 'Black Notebook', p. 133. Undated but in early 1945, prior to 17 February, she is referred to as ANT in the message arranging the meeting between Gold and Fuchs that took place on 21 February; KGB file 40594, vol. 7, p. 77, Vassiliev, 'Black Notebook', p. 135.   32. KGB file 40594 v.7, p. 59; Vassiliev, 'Black Notebook', p. 122.   33. G. A. Goncharev and L. D. Ryabev, 'The Development of the First Soviet Atomic Bomb', Physics-Uspekhi, vol. 44, no. 1 (2001), pp. 71–93. The quote is from M. S. Goodman, 'The Grandfather of the Hydrogen Bomb? Anglo-American Intelligence and Klaus Fuchs', Historical Studies in the Physical and Biological Sciences, vol. 34, part 1 (2003), p. 7   34. KGB file 84490, vol. 1, p. 80, Vassiliev, 'Yellow Notebook #1', p. 73.   35. G. A. Goncharov, 'On the History of the Creation of the Soviet Hydrogen Bomb', Physics-Uspekhi, vol. 40, no. 8 (August 1997), p. 860.   36. Norris Bradbury in Lawrence Badash et al. (eds), Reminiscences of Los Alamos 1943–1945 (Springer, 1982), pp. 161–75, cited in Arnold and Pyne, Britain and the H Bomb.   37. Rhodes, Dark Sun, p. 247. It is ironic that this visionary insight into the use of U235 happened in Japan, and that there seems to have been no analogue there to Peierls and Frisch's observation on the explosive possibility of U235 itself.   38. Arnold and Pyne, Britain and the H Bomb, p. 5.   39. KGB file 40594, vol. 7, p. 75; Vassiliev 'Black Notebook', p. 122. This is also reported in Vassiliev, 'Yellow Notebook #1', p. 73, where Gold's reference to money is also recorded.   40. The description of Fuchs' car is from Harry Gold's confession to FBI, FOIA 65-57449-551, p. 18.   41. Ibid, p. 20, and Fuchs to FBI, FOIA file 65-58805-1324, p. 7.   42. Harry Gold's confession to FBI, FOIA file 65-57449-551, p. 19.   43. Fuchs told Perrin in March 1950 he had 'already written [the report] in Los Alamos with access to the relevant files so that [I] could be sure that all figures mentioned were correct'. Michael Perrin interview with Klaus Fuchs, March 1950, TNA AB 1/695, p. 3.   44. Peierls letter to Brian Cathcart, quoted in Cathcart, Test of Greatness, p. 105.   45. KGB Archives, file 84490, vol. 1, p. 91, Vassiliev, 'Yellow Notebook #1', p. 74.   46. Fuchs to FBI, FOIA file 65-58805-1324, p. 7.   47. Harry Gold's confession to FBI, FOIA 65-57449-551, p. 21.   48. This opinion of Yuri A. Yudin, ed., 'Manuscript on the History of the Soviet Nuclear Weapons and Infrastructure', www.ransac.org/new~web~site/ccc/history-manuscript eng. pdf, pp. 63–5, is quoted by Goodman, 'The Grandfather of the Hydrogen Bomb?', p. 6.

9. The Destroyer of Worlds

1. Ferenc Szasz, The Day the Sun Rose Twice: The Story of the Trinity Site Explosion, July 16, 1945 (Albuquerque, NM, 1984), p. 57.   2. Ibid, p. 77.   3. Ibid, p. 86.   4. Edward Teller,

quoted by Richard Rhodes, *The Making of the Atomic Bomb* (Penguin, 1988), p. 672.   5. Roy Glauber, Remarks at Oxford University Physics Colloquium, 8 May 2015.   6. Philip Morrison, quoted in Rhodes, *The Making of the Atomic Bomb*, p. 673.   7. Rutherford said in a speech at the British Association in 1933, '[Bombarding nuclei with protons is] a very poor and inefficient way of producing energy, and anyone who looked for a source of power in the transformation of the atoms was talking moonshine.' Reported in *The Times*, 12 September 1933.   8. Roy Glauber, Remarks at Oxford University Physics Colloquium, 8 May 2015.   9. I. I. Rabi, quoted by Rhodes, *The Making of the Atomic Bomb*, p. 672.   10. J. Robert Oppenheimer, quoted in ibid, p. 676.   11. Rudolf Peierls, *Bird of Passage* (Princeton University Press, 1985), p. 203.   12. Today, seventy years later, these lectures remain classified in the UK, although the USA has recently released a significant amount of detail (see subsequent references). Furthermore, Klaus Fuchs' own notes made their way to the Soviet Union and have been available there for several years: 'The Super: Lecture Series by Fermi', in G. A. Goncharov and P. P. Maksimenko (eds), *USSR Atomic Project: Documents and Materials, vol. 3, Hydrogen Bomb 1945–1956* (State Corporation for Atomic Energy, 2008), pp. 31–8.   13. Enrico Fermi, 'Super Lecture No. 1: Ideal Ignition Temperature [notes by D. R. Inglis]', LA-344 (1), 2 August 1945, Los Alamos National Laboratory, via Freedom of Information Act Request FOIA 09-00015-H (Alex Wellerstein).   14. Enrico Fermi, 'Super Lecture No. 2: Electron Temperature Lag. Secondary Reactions [notes by D. R. Inglis]', LA-344 (2), 7 August 1945, Los Alamos National Laboratory, via Freedom of Information Act Request FOIA 09-00015-H (Alex Wellerstein).   15. Enrico Fermi, 'Super Lecture No. 3: Addition of Tritium [notes by D. R. Inglis]', LA-344 (3), 18 August 1945, Los Alamos National Laboratory, via Freedom of Information Act Request FOIA 09-00015-H (Alex Wellerstein).   16. Lorna Arnold and Kate Pyne, *Britain and the H Bomb* (Palgrave, 2001), p. 7.   17. Enrico Fermi, 'Super Lecture No. 4: Time Scale. Radiation Cooling [notes by D. R. Inglis]', LA-344 (4), 11 September 1945, Los Alamos National Laboratory, via Freedom of Information Act Request FOIA 09-00015-H (Alex Wellerstein).   18. At which point the text is redacted. Compton scattering (named after its discoverer Arthur Compton) refers to the process where an electrically charged particle – typically an electron – absorbs a high-energy photon, recoils, and in doing so radiates a photon, which usually has lower energy than the original. What Fermi had identified is the 'inverse Compton effect', where absorption of a low-energy photon is followed by the radiation of a higher-energy one. The result is that energy leaks away from the electron: in other words, the gas of electrons cools.   19. Enrico Fermi, 'Super Lecture No. 5: Thermal Conduction as Affected by a Magnetic Field [notes by D. R. Inglis]', LA-344 (5), 17 September 1945, Los Alamos National Laboratory, via Freedom of Information Act Request FOIA 09-00015-H (Alex Wellerstein).   20. Jeremy Bernstein email to author, 30 November 2015. This analogy derives from the physicist George Gamow, who used a ball of cotton wool to represent a fission bomb and a piece of fossilized wood to represent the thermonuclear fuel, to demonstrate the state of the H-bomb at the end of the 1940s. He would light the cotton wool and watch it burn out, the wood remaining unaffected.   21. Enrico Fermi, 'Super Lecture No. 6 (Concluding Lecture): Loss by Particle Ranges [notes by D. R. Inglis]', LA-344 (6), 9 October 1945, Los Alamos National Laboratory, via Freedom of Information Act Request FOIA 09-00015-H (Alex Wellerstein).   22. Chadwick made six copies of Moon's notes. 'Copy No. 2(of 6)' was sent to G. P. Thomson and is in the Catalogue of the papers and correspondence of Sir George Paget Thomson, FRS (1892–1975), Trinity College, Cambridge, CSAC 75.5.80/J84.   23. Fuchs' statement to FBI, 26 May 1950, FBI FOIA 65-58805-1324, p. 8.   24. This was the opinion of Hans Bethe, as transmitted to Jeremy Bernstein (J. Bernstein, communication to the author, 2 May 2018).   25. Remark made by Pike, in a letter to Brian Cathcart, communication to the author by Cathcart, 10 January 2018.   26. Klaus Fuchs confession to FBI, 26 May 1950, FOIA file 65-58805-1324, p. 8.   27. Moon's notes on Fermi's lectures about the hydrogen bomb have remained classified secret, but 'Copy No. 2(of 6)' was sent to G. P. Thomson and was available in the Catalogue of the papers and correspondence of Sir George Paget Thomson, FRS (1892–1975), Trinity College, Cambridge, CSAC 75.5.80/J84. Fuchs' own notes, which made their way to the Soviet Union, were displayed at the International Symposium, 'History of the Soviet Atomic Project', at Dubna in Russia in 1996; see https://blogs.scientificamerican. com/guest-blog/the-riddle-of-the-third-idea-how-did-the-soviets-build-a-thermonuclear-bomb-so-suspiciously-fast/. A printed version is 'The Super: Lecture Series by Fermi', pp. 31–8, in *USSR Atomic Project: Documents and Materials, vol. 3, Hydrogen Bomb 1945–1956* (State Corporation for Atomic Energy), compiled by G. A. Goncharov and P. P. Maksimenko (2008). For an authoritative description of nuclear weapons see also the website of Carey Sublette: The Nuclear Weapon Archive, http://nuclearweaponarchive.org The Los Alamos records of Fermi's lectures are available via a Freedom of Information Act Request by Alex Wellerstein. The first lecture is: Enrico Fermi, 'Super Lecture No. 1: Ideal Ignition Temperature [notes by D. R. Inglis]', LA-344 (1), 2 August 1945, Los Alamos National Laboratory. Subsequent lectures follow this identification scheme. The description in this chapter is based on that. It seems likely that Fuchs also gave a copy of his own notes to Chadwick as closed files in England refer variously to 'Miscellaneous Super Bomb notes by Klaus Fuchs', TNA ES 10/5; 'Fermi lectures on the Super Bomb', ES 10/4; 'Super Bomb: Notes on wartime Los Alamos papers', ES 10/3; and 'Collected notes on Fermi's super bomb lectures', ES 10/21. The Ministry of Defence refused requests for these documents under the following exemptions of the FOI Act: Section 24(1), National Security; 26(1) Defence; 27(1) International Relations. (Defence Nuclear Organisation Secretariat to author, 18 July 2018.) It is therefore impossible to determine the relationship, if any, of these documents to those openly available upon which the text is based.   28. Fuchs' role in stimulating Soviet research into the hydrogen bomb is described in detail in G. A. Goncharov, 'On the History of the Creation of the Soviet Hydrogen Bomb', *Physics-Uspekhi*, vol. 40, no. 8 (August 1997), pp. 859–67, and discussed by M. S. Goodman, 'The Grandfather of the Hydrogen Bomb? Anglo-American Intelligence and Klaus Fuchs', *Historical Studies in the Physical and Biological Sciences*, vol. 34, part 1 (2003), pp. 1–22. As evidence that Fuchs passed this information on 19 September 1945, Goncharov cites 'US Congress Joint Committee on Atomic Energy, Policy and Progress in the H bomb program. A chronology of leading events, US Government Printing Office, Washington DC (1953)', but there is no paper trail to Fuchs or Gold to confirm this. There is no mention in Vassiliev of Fuchs passing such information on this date. Fuchs later denied giving information about the H-bomb while in the USA, though this could have been for self-protection. So it is possible that Fuchs handed over his notes of Fermi's lectures much later, after his return to the UK. On the other hand, Rhodes, *The Making of the Atomic Bomb*, p. 624, suggests that Fuchs may have mentioned the hydrogen bomb to Gold, and cites Moss's transcription (Norman Moss, *Klaus Fuchs: The Man who Stole the Atom Bomb* [Grafton Books, 1987], p. 144) of Perrin and Fuchs' conversation – 'I couldn't explain to [Gold] because he wouldn't understand a thing. All I could give them was something on paper.' Given that Fermi's lectures mesh so neatly with Fuchs meeting Gold on 19 September, on balance it would seem likely that some mention was made; the material was fresh in Fuchs' head and written notes of Fermi's lectures would have been a relatively straightforward exercise at that juncture. It is also notable that Moscow's written version (note 12 above) makes no mention of material from Fermi's final lecture, which took place in October, a month after Fuchs' meeting with Gold. This adds further to the thesis that Fuchs did inform Gold about the hydrogen bomb in September 1945.   29. The decryption project was known as VENONA. This is a made-up word with no special significance.   30. H. Clegg to Mr Tolson, 30 December 1953. Fuchs FBI FOIA file 65-58805-1543, p. 1.   31. Director General Sir Percy Sillitoe sent a message to the MI5 liaison officer at the Washington Embassy in November 1949, which said, 'We have on record a reference to Halperin's notebook but we have never received any further particulars beyond those to be found in the Canadian bluebook pages 633/4' (TNA KV 6/134, s. 25a). Sillitoe's reference to 'on record' may be referring to a telegram received in 1946 after the defection of Gouzenko, which read, 'Large number of documents, papers and books have been siezed [sic] but these have not yet been examined. RCMP corporal who arrested HALPERIN states, however, that latter's notebook contains names of other detainees not previously known to have been associated with this. Examination of this material begins tomorrow' (TNA KV 2/1421, 16 February 1946). Sillitoe further implies that the only further information was in the bluebook, but this lists the names as

'Eric & Jo Adams, Dr. Boyer, Nightingale, Fred Rose, Dave Shugar, et al.' with no explicit mention of Fuchs. FBI records claim that the Canadian police offered the data to Peter Dwyer of MI6, but Dwyer 'did not take it'. (FBI FOIA file 65-58805-1544, see also chapter 21 below). The reasons for this oversight remain obscure. See also the thesis of Timothy Gibbs, 'British and American Counter-Intelligence and the Atom Spies, 1941–1950', Ph.D. thesis, Faculty of History, Cambridge University, 2007. I am indebted to Tony Percy for discussions on this point. 32. KGB file 84490, vol. 1, p. 105; Vassiliev 'Yellow Notebook #1', in Alexander Vassiliev, *Alexander Vassiliev Papers, 1895–2011* (US Library of Congress), p. 76; Klaus Fuchs confession to FBI, 26 May 1950, FOIA file 65-58805-1324, p. 9. 33. KGB file 84490, v.1, p. 105; Vassiliev, 'Yellow Notebook #1', p. 76. 34. KGB file 40594, v.7, p. 318; Vassiliev, 'Black Notebook', p. 125.

10. Harwell, Hydrogen and Plutonium

1. See Richard Rhodes, *Dark Sun: The Making of the Hydrogen Bomb* (Simon and Schuster, 2005), chapter 22. 2. Truman Library online collection, www.trumanlibrary.org/whistlestop/study_collections, cited in Timothy Gibbs, 'British and American Counter-Intelligence and the Atom Spies, 1941–1950', Ph.D. thesis, Faculty of History, Cambridge University, 2007, footnote 291. 3. Margaret Gowing and Lorna Arnold, *Independence and Deterrence, vol. 2: Policy Making* (Macmillan, 1974), p. 23. 4. TNA AB 16/36, p. 13. 5. Graham Farmelo, *Churchill's Bomb: A Hidden History of Science, War and Politics* (Faber and Faber, 2013), p. 324; Peter Hennessy, *The Secret State: Whitehall and the Cold War* (Penguin, 2002). 6. It is possible to deduce some of their patent's features from Russian sources thanks to Fuchs' generosity to the Soviet Union. What follows is the gist of their idea, whose 'paramount importance became evident afterwards'. See G. A. Goncharov, 'American and Soviet H-Bomb Development Programmes: Historical Background', *Physics Uspekhi*, vol. 39 (1996), p. 1,033. 7. Lorna Arnold and Kate Pyne, *Britain and the H Bomb* (Palgrave, 2007), p. 7 etc. The Greenhouse George test in 1951, for example, used a 500-kilotonne atomic bomb to ignite one ounce of DT in an adjoining chamber. This idea of Teller, which was inspired in part by Fuchs and von Neumann, was described by one critic as 'like using a blast furnace to light a match'. Quoted in Rhodes, *Dark Sun*, p. 457. 8. Arnold and Pyne, *Britain and the H bomb*, p. 7; Rhodes, *Dark Sun*, pp. 252–4; G. A. Goncharov, 'Beginnings of the Soviet H-Bomb Project', *Physics Today*, vol. 49 (November 1996). 9. Arnold and Pyne, *Britain and the H Bomb*, p. 7. The radiation is mostly in the form of X-rays. These heat the capsule and its contents so much that they are completely ionized: all the electrons within their atoms are liberated. The vaporized capsule, made of beryllium oxide, produces a total of fourteen charged particles per atom (oxygen has eight electrons; beryllium has four; and there are two nuclei as well). The deuterium and tritium each give up one electron, and when the nuclei are included in the accounts, this gives a total of four charges. The key feature is that atom for atom the fourteen particles of the vaporized capsule numerically exceed the four of the vaporized contents. Why is this important? Because when two gases are in equilibrium, the ratio of their pressures is in proportion to the relative numbers of these particles. So the vaporized capsule exerts a pressure on the gas of deuterium and tritium, and compresses it. The 'one–two punch' of a direct hit by the fission bomb and the radiation-induced implosion of the capsule gives a tenfold compression of the deuterium–tritium mixture, which Fuchs and von Neumann calculated should be enough for ignition. See Kenneth Ford, *Building the Bomb: A Personal History* (World Scientific, 2015), p. 101. 10. Rhodes, *Dark Sun* and Ford, *Building the Bomb* are excellent descriptions of the development of the hydrogen bomb, at least within the USA. 11. Arnold and Pyne, *Britain and the H Bomb*, p. 7. 12. Ford, *Building the Bomb*, pp. 99–102, discusses technical differences between the Ulam–Teller and the Fuchs–von Neumann inventions. Fundamentally, the deuterium cylinder remained uncompressed in the Fuchs–von Neumann device, which was therefore an attempt to improve the ignition of a Classical Super. Ulam–Teller went beyond this and by a sequence of stages also compressed the nuclear fuel. The Fuchs–von

Neumann concept of ignition was tested in the Greenhouse George test of 1951. The fission reaction was separated from the DT capsule, and a long pipe channelled radiation from the fission explosion to the capsule, causing it to ignite. Even so a cylinder of deuterium would have been unable to maintain burning in the Fuchs–von Neumann device. Ulam–Teller extended this and by compression of the main charge enabled a successful thermonuclear explosion. The Ulam–Teller configuration appears to have been common to all early hydrogen bombs. The fact that much information on the hydrogen bomb remains classified makes it hard to assess precisely what relation, if any, there is between the Fuchs–von Neumann idea and the radiation implosion feature of the Ulam–Teller concept of 1951, which led to the United States' hydrogen bomb. G. A. Goncharov in *Physics Today*, November 1996, claims that the Fuchs–von Neumann invention was the first to use radiation implosion and 'was a prototype for the future Ulam–Teller configuration'. A compendium of declassified information, or material that has appeared in the public domain about the Ulam–Teller invention, is at Carey Sublette's website: http://nuclearweaponarchive.org/Library/Teller.html   13. B. Taylor, interview 6 May 2017, and remarks in 'Britain's Nuclear Bomb – the Inside Story', 3 May 2017, BBC4.   Arnold and Pyne, *Britain and the H Bomb*, p. 7 and also note 25, Appendix 1, p. 232. The development of the British bomb seems not to have relied on ideas of Fuchs and von Neumann, however. Fuchs' ideas were locked in the safe of William Penney, and were unfortunately destroyed, leaving a 'gap in the history of the British H bomb which can never be filled' (Lorna Arnold remarks to the author, 30 August 2013).   14. See section 2 in Goncharov, 'American and Soviet H-Bomb Development Programmes', pp. 1,033–44.   15. M. S. Goodman, 'The Grandfather of the Hydrogen Bomb? Anglo-American Intelligence and Klaus Fuchs', *Historical Studies in the Physical and Biological Sciences*, vol. 34, part 1 (2003), pp. 1–22. Goodman's article gives a thorough evaluation of the early development of the H-bomb and analyzes the role of Fuchs. The actual quote originates with Gennady Gorelik, 'A Russian Perspective on the Father of the American H-bomb'; http://people.bu.edu/gorelik/Minnesota_02_web.htm, pp. 8–9.   16. 'No question but that these documents went to the Soviets': US Congress Joint Committee on Atomic Energy, 1951. Letter to Chadwick, 18 June 1946, which enclosed copies of some notes that Fuchs 'wants to speak about': TNA AB 1/444.   17. Letter 24 June from Cockcroft: Fuchs was told of a Harwell steering committee meeting at Harwell on Monday 1 July at 09.30 at which he should be present. This information was sent to him c/o [his sister Kristel] Heineman on 25 June. TNA AB 1/444.   18. Letter about travel reimbursement from K. Fuchs to Geoffrey McMillan, British Supply Office, Washington DC, 27 June 1946, TNA AB 1/444.   19. Source: US departing income-tax statement, TNA AB 1/444.   20. Letter dated 8 March 1946 in Peierls papers, Bodleian Library, File C304, entry 393, p. 34 in Sabine Lee, *Sir Rudolf Peierls: Selected Private and Scientific Correspondence*, vol. 2 (World Scientific, 2007).   21. Peierls to G. P. Thomson, 12 March 1946. Catalogue of the papers and correspondence of Sir George Paget Thomson, FRS (1892–1975), Trinity College, Cambridge, CSAC 75.5.80/J89; and entry 394, p. 35, in Lee, *Sir Rudolf Peierls: Selected Private and Scientific Correspondence*, vol. 2.   22. Peierls to Gardner, 14 March 1946, Peierls papers, Bodleian Library, Box C. Thomson's idea with its implication for plutonium production was classified, but its development would require the solution of many technical problems – such as the physics of magnetic fields – of greater generality. These included unclassified problems, which Gardner was able to investigate for his thesis.   23. Correspondence between Peierls and Thomson, Trinity College, Cambridge, CSAC 75.5.80/J89; entries 393, 394, 397 and 400, in Lee, *Sir Rudolf Peierls: Selected Private and Scientific Correspondence*, vol. 2.   24. Peierls papers, Bodleian Library, File C304.

11. 1947: Harwell Insecurity

1. Henry Arnold memorandum on Klaus Fuchs, October 1951, TNA KV 2/1257, s. 874a, p. 2.   2. Mary Flowers (Bunemann), *Atomic Spice: A Partial Autobiography*, unpublished (2009): http://homepages.inf.ed.ac.uk/opb/atomicspice   3. Ibid, p. 96.   4. Jo Hookway (Peierls), interview, 11 May 2015.   5. Flowers, *Atomic Spice*, p. 125.   6. Lorna Arnold

interview, 4 January 2013. 7. Quotations in this and subsequent paragraphs follow from Henry Arnold's memorandum on Klaus Fuchs, October 1951, TNA KV 2/1257, s. 874a. 8. Fuchs to Arnold, 29 September 1946, TNA KV 2/1245, s. 45x. Minute 45a is Harwell on Fuchs and minute 46 their reply to 45a. 9. Quotes from Henry Arnold's correspondence and phone calls with T. A. Robertson of MI5, October 1946. TNA KV 2/1245, s. 45a and minutes 47–51. 10. Henry Arnold to Lt. Col. Collard, 1 October 1946, TNA KV 2/1245, s. 45a. 11. Collard to Arnold, 8 October 1946, ibid, s. 46a. 12. J. A. Collard, 10 October 1946, TNA KV 2/1245, minute 47. Designation of Section B.1.c – Guy Liddell's diary, 27 September 1947, TNA KV 4/469. 13. T. A. Robertson, [B.4], note about meeting with Arnold sent to [B.1.A and B.1.C], 15 October 1946, TNA KV 2/1245, minute 48. 14. TNA KV 2/3223, s. 8, and note 35 in chapter 2. 15. T. A. Robertson, [B.4], note about meeting with Arnold sent to [B.1.A and B.1.C], 15 October 1946, TNA KV 2/1245, minute 48. 16. Ibid. An unidentified hand has penned 'Oh my sainted aunt' alongside this comment. 17. TNA KV 4/469, 8 December 1947. 18. Ben McIntyre, *Double Cross* (Picador, 2012). 19. Robertson, TNA KV 2/1245, minute 48. 20. TNA KV 2/1245, minutes 32 to 43, as cited by Michael Serpell in minute 49. See also chapter 7, footnote, p. 114. 21. M. F. Serpell (B1c), 13 November 1946, TNA KV 2/1245, minute 49. Serpell is disingenuous here with his allusion to 'difficulty in persuading [*sic*] DSIR'. The exchanges between MI5 and DSIR in chapter 7 show no evidence that MI5 warned DSIR that Fuchs would be a 'danger' in 1943 or 1944, so the need for 'persuasion' never arose. The suggestion that their advice could be overruled comes from within MI5 where T. A. Robertson in minute 48, 15 October 1946, opined, 'It would undoubtedly be said, if FUCHS turns out to be a dangerous character, that his technical ability is such that Atomic Energy Research would suffer very considerably if he were removed from his present employment.' The origins of this angst appear to be the exchanges between Archer and Stephens of the Ministry of Aircraft Production at the time of Fuchs' AWS permit in 1941 (chapter 5). The specific mention of DSIR and 1943 hints at MI5's irritation upon belatedly learning of Fuchs' naturalization only after Fuchs was already en route to the USA on behalf of the DSIR. (Serpell exchanges with Garrett, and Garrett with DSIR, November 1943 to January 1944, TNA KV 2/1245, minutes 34–43.) Serpell's opinion in 1946, minute 49, may be the fallout from that experience. 22. M. F. Serpell, ibid. The assessment makes no mention of Fuchs' name having been found in Halperin's diary or in a list of communists to be apprehended in Germany, both of which were known to the FBI by this time. (Fuchs FBI FOIA file 65-58805-479 and ibid, s. 1543. See also chapter 21 below.) MI5 files only record this information in their possession in 1949 (TNA KV 2/1247, s. 230C). Had these documents been available to Serpell in 1946, it is inconceivable that they could have been ignored in his assessment. 23. M. F. Serpell, 13 November 1946, TNA KV 2/1245, minute 49. 24. M. F. Serpell (B.1.c), note KV 2/1245, minute 49, 13 November 1946; Roger Hollis, minute 55, and Guy Liddell, minute 57, in TNA KV 2/1245, 20 December 1946. 25. Roger H. Hollis (B.1), 19 November 1946, TNA KV 2/1245, minute 50. 26. J. A. Collard to G/C Archer, 24 November 1946, TNA KV 2/1245, minute 51. 27. Arnold's memorandum was written in June 1951 in response to questions from the writer Alan Moorehead. MI5 regarded it as 'too intimate to show to Moorehead' and it was retained in Fuchs' file (Note D. G. White, 16 October 1951, TNA KV 2/1257, s. 874a). 28. Minute 52 in TNA KV 2/1245, 27 November 1946. 29. Kim Philby, *My Silent War: The Autobiography of a Spy* (Arrow, 2018), chapter 7, also quoted in Christopher Andrew, *Defence of the Realm: The Authorized History of MI5* (Allen Lane, 2009), p. 341. 30. Jane Archer is credited erroneously in several places as the author of this memorandum. Pincher seems to have been the first, describing her as having been 'coaxed back to MI5' (chapter 34 loc 4751). Mike Rossiter, *The Spy who Changed the World* (Headline, 2014), chapter 14, Tom Bower, *The Perfect English Spy: Sir Dick White and the Secret War 1939–1945* (Heinemann, 1995), and Wikipedia, https://en.wikipedia.org/wiki/Jane_Sissmore (accessed 21 September 2017) all propagate this myth. There is no source quoted for the Wikipedia entry, other than these books. In existing literature, it appears that only Antony Percy, *Misdefending the Realm* (University of Buckingham, 2018), correctly identifies the author in chapter 8 to be her husband, J. O. Archer, and points out the previous errors.

It remains unexplained how this misattribution arose, but it is possibly a combination of the sharpness of the insight, which has Jane's hallmark, and the fact that she returned to MI5 after the war. As to when this was is a mystery, however. Christopher Andrew confirmed that she returned to MI5 (email to author 13 May 2017), but was unable to give a certain date. When she rejoined MI5, it is notable that this high-flyer was not given charge of any division, yet two Director Generals, Dick White and Roger Hollis, had both been hired, trained and served under her in the past.　I have found two mentions of her, which bear on the question of her later career. There is an ambiguous sentence in Keith Jeffery, *MI6: The History of the Secret Intelligence Service 1909–1949* (Bloomsbury, 2010), p. 657: '[In September 1945 Philby] suggested Jane Archer or Roger Hollis from MI5'; the interpretation of this sentence, however, depends on the absence of a comma before 'or'. She is mentioned in Guy Liddell's diary of 6 September 1947 and again in a heavily redacted entry in November showing that she has some concern meriting attention of the heads of both MI5 and MI6, and Edward Bridges, head of the Home Civil Service. There is the tantalizing possibility that Jane Sissmore-Archer was the Deep Throat who alerted Milicent Bagot to Philby, chapter 5.　Although somewhat peripheral to our primary purpose, I record this in the hope that subsequent investigations might shed light on this episode, and Jane Sissmore's career in general.　**31.** TNA KV 2/1245, minutes 47 to 51.　**32.** 30 November 1950, TNA KV 2/1245, minute 53.　**33.** Formally 'Examination of Credentials', Andrew, *Defence of the Realm*, Appendix 3.　**34.** J. O. Archer (C2), 27 November 1950, TNA KV 2/1245, minute 52.　**35.** Ibid, minute 50.　**36.** Ibid, minute 50; minute 52 (Archer); minute 53.　**37.** Ibid, minute 54.　**38.** Ibid, minute 55, 4 December 1946. This claim was included in the package of information given to author Alan Moorehead in September 1951 (TNA KV 2/1257, s. 868a), even though it had been refuted on 23 March 1950 (TNA KV 2/1270, s. 687a – see the Afterword.　**39.** Chapman Pincher, *Chapman, Treachery: Betrayals, Blunders and Cover-Ups: Six Decades of Espionage against America and Great Britain* (Random House, 2009), chapter 34, has independently highlighted this sequence and added it to his dossier of circumstantial evidence that Hollis was working on behalf of the Soviets.　**40.** J. O. Archer, 5 December 1946, TNA KV 2/1245, minute 56. White wrote on the minute: 'I would like to attend [the meeting] and of course B1 too.'　**41.** TNA KV 2/1245, minute 57 is from Deputy Director General (Liddell) sent on 20 December 1946 to DC and C2 for information and to DB and B1 for action. 'I agree with B1 there is really nothing of a positive nature against either FUCHS or PEIERLS.' The memo is also in KV 2/1658, folio 21a, where someone has penned in '+1934' after the reference to 1937.　**42.** TNA KV 2/1245, minute 57.　**43.** TNA KV 2/1658, s. 22a.　**44.** TNA KV 2/1658, s. 24a.　**45.** Guy Liddell letter to Sir Alexander Maxwell, 23 January 1947, TNA KV 2/1658, s. 25a.　**46.** Guy Liddell, 22 May 1947, TNA KV 2/1245, minute 97. Although Liddell had responded to the concerns raised by Archer, and made direct contact with the Home Office himself, it would seem that he did not regard this as a major issue compared to other affairs that were then on his mind. His diary has no entries between January and May 1947, as he was on a tour of the Middle and Far East; there is no mention of Klaus Fuchs at all until much later.　**47.** KGB file 84490, vol. 1, p. 117, 'Meetings with agents have been suspended [note on 29 September 1946]. In Aug 46 Ch[arles] did not show up for a meeting in London.' Vassiliev, 'Yellow Notebook #1', in Alexander Vassiliev, *Alexander Vassiliev Papers, 1895–2011* (US Library of Congress), p. 77. Formal contacts with agents were renewed from August 1947. Fuchs renewed contact in July 1947. It is not clear whether his exile during this period was imposed by Moscow or was his personal decision.　**48.** For over three decades Harry Chapman Pincher was convinced that Roger Hollis was a Soviet mole within MI5. His final treatise, which subsumes his earlier works, is *Treachery: Betrayals, Blunders and Cover-Ups* (Random House, 2009).　**49.** Guy Liddell to Sir Alexander Maxwell, 23/1/47, Review of all people on highly secret projects, TNA KV 2/1658, s. 25a.　**50.** Peierls' role in the ASA and the Association's fraught relations with government are described extensively in chapters 6 and 7 of Christoph Laucht, *Elemental Germans: Klaus Fuchs, Rudolf Peierls and the Making of British Nuclear Culture, 1939–1959* (Palgrave Macmillan, 2012).　**51.** Peierls to Michael Perrin, 19 February 1948, TNA KV 2/1658, s. 46c.　**52.** The correspondence spans February and March 1948 and is in TNA KV 2/1658, s. 46. This particular quotation is from s. 46d. 53. Rudolf Peierls to Captain Bennett, 17 March 1948, TNA KV 2/1658, s. 46e.

12. 1947–9: Resurrection

1. Brian Cathcart, *Test of Greatness* (John Murray, 1994), p. 40. 2. K. Fuchs, G. J. Kynch and R. E. Peierls, *The Equation of State of the Air at High Temperature*, Tube Alloys Report MS 61, 1942, TNA AB 4/897. 3. Graham Farmelo, *Churchill's Bomb: A Hidden History of Science, War and Politics* (Faber and Faber, 2013), p. 325. The footnote on p. 182 of Margaret Gowing and Lorna Arnold, *Independence and Deterrence, vol. 2: Policy Making* (Macmillan, 1974), lists Attlee, the Foreign Secretary (Ernest Bevin), Lord President (Herbert Morrison), Minister of Defence (A. V. Alexander), Dominions Secretary (Lord Addison) and Minister of Supply (John Wilmot). 4. Gowing and Arnold, *Independence and Deterrence, vol. 2*, pp. 181–2. 5. Lord and Lady Flowers, interview with Michael Goodman, cited in notes 22 and 24 of M. S. Goodman, 'The Grandfather of the Hydrogen Bomb? Anglo-American Intelligence and Klaus Fuchs', *Historical Studies in the Physical and Biological Sciences*, vol. 34, part 1 (2003), pp. 1–22. 6. Peierls to Fuchs, 27 March 1947, TNA KV 2/1658, s. 34a. 7. Gaby Gross (Peierls), email to author, 5 January 2019. Katrina Mason, p. 138, in *Children of Los Alamos* (Twyne Publishers, 1995). 8. KGB Archives, File 84490, vol. 1, p. 235; Alexander Vassiliev, 'Yellow Notebook #1', in Vassiliev, *Alexander Vassiliev Papers, 1895–2011*, US Library of Congress, p. 80, and Fuchs' confession on technical details to Michael Perrin, MI5 files, TNA KV 2/1250 folio 443. 9. TNA KV 6/42, s. 170, shows this to have been on 13 September 1947, not 5 April, contrary to Chapman Pincher, *Treachery: Betrayals, Blunders and Cover-Ups: Six Decades of Espionage against America and Great Britain* (Random House, 2009), chapter 37. 10. Guy Liddell's diary, 23 June 1947, TNA KV 4/469. 11. TNA KV 6/42, s. 149b. 12. Ruth Werner (Ursula Beurton), *Sonya's Report* (Vintage, 1999), p. 278. 13. Ibid, p. 279. 14. Shakespeare, *Henry V*, Act 4, Scene 3, speech before the Battle of Agincourt. 15. White to Tom Bower, p. 95, in Tom Bower, *The Perfect English Spy: Sir Dick White and the Secret War 1939–1945* (Heinemann, 1995). Others would include Kim Philby and Klaus Fuchs. 16. TNA KV 6/42, s. 181. 17. As arranged on 19 September and reported to Moscow, KGB file p. 235, Vassiliev, 'Yellow Notebook #1', p. 80. Fuchs' account given to Skardon on 9 March 1950 is in TNA KV 2/1253, s. 588d. The code phrases differ from what Feklisov remembered decades later, pp. 208–12 in Alexander Feklisov (with the assistance of Sergei Kostin), *The Man Behind the Rosenbergs* (Enigma Books, 2001). 18. KGB Archives, File 84490, vol. 1, p. 264; Vassiliev, 'Yellow Notebook #1', p. 80. 19. I used the form as agreed in KGB files. The quote is in a report of the meeting in KGB file 84490, vol. 1, p. 235; Vassiliev, 'Yellow Notebook #1', p. 80. Some have claimed a different form of words was used but no source has been given. 20. Feklisov, *The Man behind the Rosenbergs*, pp. 211–12. 21. Fuchs to Skardon, 31 January 1950, TNA KV 2/1250, s. 443. 22. G. A. Goncharov, 'American and Soviet H-Bomb Development Programmes: Historical Background', *Physics Uspekhi*, vol. 39 (1996), p. 1,037. 23. Goodman, 'The Grandfather of the Hydrogen Bomb?', p. 8. 24. The reaction is $n + Li6 [3p+3n] \rightarrow t[p+2n] + He4 [2p+2n]$. 25. J. Albright and M. Kunstall, *Bombshell: The Secret Story of America's Unknown Atomic Spy Conspiracy* (Times Books, Random House, 1997), present evidence that the KGB attempted to reactivate Hall into espionage around this time. There is circumstantial evidence to suggest that he agreed; see *Bombshell* especially pp. 189–92, and Joan Hall interviews with author, 25 January 2013 and 1 May 2013. If this is correct, then it is likely that Hall was the source for the information on Teller's idea of lithium deuteride. 26. The 'first idea' in development of the Soviet weapon was to use concentric layers of fission elements, uranium or plutonium, and light isotopes of hydrogen. In this 'layer cake' the explosions in the fission layers compress the thermonuclear fuel. The third idea, which completed the successful Soviet hydrogen bomb, was to use radiation from the atomic explosion to compress the fuel. Historians have argued whether this idea,

which has resemblances to Fuchs–von Neumann, came from Fuchs or was discovered in the USSR independently. See for example https://blogs.scientificamerican.com/guest-blog/the-riddle-of-the-third-idea-how-did-the-soviets-build-a-thermonuclear-bomb-so-suspiciously-fast/ by Gonnady Gorelik. 27. Ferenc Szasz, *The Day the Sun Rose Twice: The Story of the Trinity Site Explosion, July 16, 1945* (University of New Mexico Press, 1984), p. 91. 28. Margaret Farrell interview, 1 May 2015. 29. He was correct. The young physicist Ted Hall provided important technical information on the atomic bomb at Los Alamos and possibly after the war; see note 25 above. 30. KGB file 84490, vol. 1, p. 383, Vassiliev, 'Yellow Notebook #1', p. 82. 31. Guy Liddell's diary, 13 November 1947, TNA KV 4/469. 32. Quotes from Cathcart, *Test of Greatness*, p. 104, based on a private letter from Corner to Cathcart. 33. Ibid, p. 104. 34. K. Fuchs to W. Penney, 2 March 1948; ES 1/493, s. E13. 35. K. Fuchs travel log, March 1948, TNA KV 2/1246. 36. KGB file 84490, vol. 1, p. 384, Vassiliev, 'Yellow Notebook #1', p. 82. In KGB file 84490, vol. 1, p. 267, Vassiliev 'Yellow Notebook #1', p. 81, there is specific mention that Fuchs 'described the working principle of the hydrogen bomb that Fermi and Taylor [*sic*; this is a Russian mistranscription of Teller] were working on at U. Chicago'. 37. Edward Teller (with Judith Shoolery), *Memoirs: A Twentieth-Century Journey in Science and Politics* (Perseus, 2001), p. 237. 38. Fuchs FBI FOIA file, 65-58805-915, p. 36. 39. Harwell to MI5, 19 November 1947, TNA KV 2/1245, s. 101a; MI5 response, J. Collard, 24 November 1947, ibid, minute 102. 40. Ibid, minute 103, M. Furnival Jones, 25 November 1947. 41. Ibid, minute 104, R. H. Hollis, 26 November 1947. 42. Ibid, minute 105, D. White to G. Liddell, 2 December 1947. 43. Roger Hollis report of the 8 December meeting, TNA KV 2/1245, minute 106, 10 December 1947. 44. TNA KV 4/469, 8 December 1947. 45. Report of visit to Harwell by Lt. Col. J. Collard, 18 March 1948, TNA KV 2/1245; minute 110, dated 6 April 1948. 46. Report of visit to AERE Harwell by Lt. Col. J. Collard, 18 March 1948, TNA KV 2/1245, s. 110a. 47. Ibid. 48. Ibid. 49. Ibid. 50. KGB file 84490, vol. 1, pp. 332–7, Vassiliev, 'Yellow Notebook #1', p. 81. 51. KGB report on Fuchs meeting of 10 July 1948. KGB file 84490, vol. 1, p. 343, Vassiliev, 'Yellow Notebook #1', p. 82. 52. G. Peierls communication to the author, undated, and 'Talk about Fuchs', audiotape in Peierls papers, A176. 53. KGB Archives, File 84490, vol. 1, p. 235; Vassiliev, 'Yellow Notebook #1', p. 80, and Fuchs' confession on technical details to Michael Perrin, MI5 files, TNA KV 2/1250, s. 443. 54. R. A. A. Badham to J. McFadden, 1 January 1948, TNA KV 2/1245, s. 109a. 55. J. McFadden (Ministry of Supply) to Major Badham, MI5, 14 August 1948, TNA KV 2/1245, s. 111a. 56. After the minute 111 about Fuchs' employment dated 14 August 1948, file TNA KV 2/1245 closes with minutes 112 (November 1948) concerning a visit by Dr Thirring, and 113a (20 April 1949) noting impending 'Fuchs' family visit to England'. File TNA KV 2/1246 opens with minute 114 dated 7 September 1949, based on information from the USA, which starts the formal investigation into Fuchs' espionage. 57. The first action upon opening the Fuchs inquiry was to collect his travel records. These are filed in TNA KV 2/1246. This records '12 Feb dep. Home or HQ 12 am; Car; From Harwell To Cambridge; Firm, Establishment etc. visited and name of individual contacted: Sir James Chadwick, Prof Feind (?) Prof Hartree. 13 Feb From Cambridge To Harwell; Home or HQ arr. 11pm; Miles by Private Motor Car: 200.' 58. Fuchs' confession on technical details to Michael Perrin, MI5 files TNA KV 2/1250, folio 443. 59. Rudolf Peierls to Klaus Fuchs; 18/3/48, Bodleian Library, C111. 60. Harwell work on thermonuclear reactions. The papers and correspondence of Sir George Paget Thomson, FRS (1892–1975), Trinity College, Cambridge. CSAC 75.5.80/E88. 61. Ibid, Minutes of Technical Committee, 23/1/47, H.881. 62. That Fuchs' group was intimately involved is clear from Cockcroft's letter to Thomson on 29 December 1947, which attests 'the problem [of fusion] is now being considered from the theoretical aspect by Bunemann and Allen here'. On 23 January 1948 Thomson wrote to Klaus Fuchs to say he had seen Cockcroft the previous day and Bunemann would come to work at Imperial College with Thomson for the week of 10 February. The letter is headed in red pen, 'Taken with Sq Ldr Arnold's permission from Bunemann's file at Harwell April 4 1951'. There is evidence of letters exchanged between Bunemann and Thomson in 1948, and of a meeting in Oxford in 1949, which show that this was a continuous programme. 63. J. Gardner, 'Confinement of Slow Charged Particles to a Toroidal Tube', *Proceedings of the Physical Society*, vol. 62 (1949), p. 300. **64.** Peierls to Fuchs, (?) October 1948, Bodleian Library, C111. **65.** Peierls to Fuchs, 20 September 1949, Bodleian Library, C111. **66.** Gardner to Peierls, 11 January 1950, Bodleian Library, C111. **67.** This was never developed. Fusion technology turned out to be a vastly greater engineering challenge than was initially anticipated, and nuclear reactors rapidly became the standard means for breeding plutonium. In Britain, construction of Windscale began in 1947. In Russia, the first working research reactor started on 25 December 1946, and here too reactors became the means for breeding plutonium. So by 1949 the work of Gardner and of his Russian counterparts was already peripheral to any weapons programme, which may explain why Russia too allowed the appearance of this work in the open literature. By the time of Fuchs' arrest the idea that fusion could be used to breed plutonium was already a dead-end, and this item was not mentioned in his oeuvre of espionage. **68.** Henry Arnold, Notes on Dr Klaus Fuchs, KV 2/1257, s. 874, October 1951. **69.** The plan was arranged at a pub in Putney 'about 6 months before his last contact in February 1949' (Fuchs to Skardon, 15 February 1950, TNA KV 2/1252, s. 518d). As Fuchs had missed two assignations, most recently in May, it seems natural that the July meeting was the occasion. **70.** This account follows from TNA KV 2/1256, s. 759a, which appears to be MI5's final assessment following earlier confusing versions in KV 2/1255, s. 700 and KV 2/1256, s. 757a. The specific location of number 14 is given in page 2 of Skardon's report of 14 February 1950, TNA KV 2/1252. **71.** The received wisdom in MI5 was that Fuchs' last meeting with the Russians was in February 1949 (e.g. TNA KV 2/1252, s. 519). KGB records list this as 12 February (KGB file 84490, vol. 1, p. 393, Vassiliev, 'Yellow Notebook #1', p. 83), but KGB file 84490, vol. 1, p. 424 (Vassiliev, 'Yellow Notebook #1', p. 83), records a further rendezvous on 1 April 1949 as their 'last meeting'. **72.** Skardon interview with Skinner, 28 June 1950, TNA KV 2/1255, s. 699b. **73.** Vassiliev, 'Yellow Notebook #1', p. 83, KGB file, p. 393. **74.** Summary of information received from Dr Fuchs regarding his espionage contacts, 2 March 1950, TNA KV 2/1253, s. 564b. Vassiliev, 'Yellow Notebook #1', p. 83, KGB file p. 393. **75.** TNA KV 2/1245, s. 112. **76.** Memo to passport control, 18 March 1949, TNA KV 2/1245, s. 112. This letter also confirms Klaus Fuchs' address as Lacies Court in March. **77.** Hanni Bretscher, note dated 1 April 1987, attached to a letter from Fuchs to Egon Bretscher, 13 May 1948, Egon Bretscher papers, Churchill College, Cambridge, H.29. Christoph Laucht, *Elemental Germans: Klaus Fuchs, Rudolf Peierls and the Making of British Nuclear Culture, 1939–1959* (Palgrave Macmillan, 2012), note 61, claims the visit took place in autumn 1947 and extended to spring 1948. The idea that Emil Fuchs was in Harwell throughout this extended period, when Klaus was active in espionage, is bizarre. The visa application shows that the visit of Emil and Klaus' nephew was for four weeks in July to August 1949. TNA KV 2/1245, s. 112a, April 1949. **78.** MI5's judgement that this was an 'inspired move' is in The Case of Emil Julius Klaus Fuchs, 31 March 1950, TNA KV 2/1256, s. 756, p. 6. **79.** Guy Liddell's diary, TNA KV 4/471, undated. Other entries in the diary place this between 5 and 12 September 1949. **80.** TNA KV 4/471, 13 September 1949. Halperin was Canadian, born of Russian immigrants. **81.** The Soviet bomb test was on 29 August 1949. Nearly a month elapsed before British and American scientists were confident enough to inform their governments. Liddell learned of it with other senior officials on 23 September (MI5 file TNA KV 4/471). It is possible that after missing contacts with the Russians during June and July, the news that the USSR had successfully exploded an atomic bomb gave Fuchs the excuse to quit as, in his mind, his job was now completed. **82.** Guy Liddell's diary, 23 September 1949, TNA KV 4/471. **83.** Ibid. **84.** Ibid. **85.** Ibid. **86.** Ibid.

13. The VENONA Code

1. Quoted in Anthony Summers, *Official and Confidential: The Secret Life of J. Edgar Hoover* (Victor Gollancz, 1993), p. 158. **2.** Quoted in ibid, p. 152. **3.** Ibid. **4.** Ibid, p. 153. **5.** William Sullivan, quoted in ibid, p. 155. **6.** Ibid, p. 156. **7.** The NSA history of

VENONA is given in Robert L. Benson, *The Venona Story*, Center for Cryptologic History, National Security Agency, Washington DC, 2012: https://www.nsa.gov/about/cryptologic-heritage/historical-figures-publications/publications/coldwar/assets/files/venona_story.pdf. The chronology of VENONA decryption remains classified, and material in the public domain 'contains as much as could be released without revealing any of the cryptanalytic techniques which made even partial decryption of the original intercepted messages possible: this is one of the reasons [that only] the final version of each report [has been released].' (Correspondence with GCHQ Departmental Historian, 27 June 2018.)   8. Winston Churchill to President Roosevelt, 25 February 1942, in Warren F. Kimball (ed.), *Churchill and Roosevelt: The Complete Correspondence*, vol. 1 (Princeton University Press, 2015).   9. The London GRU traffic used a variation of the basic VENONA cryptosystems: Benson, *The Venona Story*, p. 49. It is not known what level of decryption was achieved. Certainly the decryption naming 'Doctor Fuchs' (see chapter 5, note 2) was not achieved until 1950 or later.   10. Ibid, pp. 11 and 59.   11. Ibid, p. 51.   12. Ibid, p. 7. For a description of the code, see chapter 9 above.   13. R. J. Lamphere and T. Shachtman, *The FBI–KGB War: A Special Agent's Story* (Random House, 1986), p. 127.   14. Ibid.   15. See Timothy Gibbs, 'British and American Counter-Intelligence and the Atom Spies, 1941–1950', Ph.D. thesis, Faculty of History, Cambridge University, 2007, chapter 2 – 'A SIGINIT partnership', and footnotes 365–7 for analysis of this liaison. He notes a highly redacted FBI memorandum to L. V. Boardman, A. H. Belmont, 1 February 1956. FBI FOIA Electronic Reading Room, http://foia.fbi.gov/foiaindex/venona.htm, which reads 'Both [ ] and [ ] work on this problem and work sheets have been made up and sent to [ ]. Also [ ] has a man in England working with [ ]. In turn, [ ] have a cryptographer working full-time at [ ].' This was written when Gardner was working at GCHQ. Lamphere, *The FBI–KGB War*, gives an FBI perspective on the birth and early period of this collaboration, pp. 127 ff.   16. https://www.nsa.gov/news-features/declassified-documents/venona/dated/1944/assets/files/15jun_departure_agent_rest.pdf. This, the final report issued in 1954, has the hallmarks of originating in GCHQ. Note the appearance of the British spelling of 'speciality' in the text, along with other features discussed in Chapter 22.   17. Decryption was fragmentary, and GCHQ was substantially involved throughout. The first recorded mention of this decryption is in 'Status 16 April 1948: Messages involving cover name ENORMOS and the names of nuclear physicists, p. 1'. Report by Hugh S. Erskine, Lt. Col., Signal Corps, Chief CSGAS-93, TNA HW 15/58.   At this stage the code-breakers had achieved the following:

> 6F report MSN-1* [1 digit or group of letters wanting] EFRENT FLUKTUATSIYA [?efferent fluctuation?] – 1F---2U----37F--...sion method - - work according to (?their?) (?specialities? ?specifications?). (??Radiation?? [very doubtful]) - - 11F - - islanders [British] and urbanites [Americans] final(ly) –14F—The urbanites stated to the representatives of the island [Great Britain] that the construction of the plant on the island inevitably would contradict the spirit of the agreement of ENORMOZ. '(?earnestly?) imputed by the Atlantic Charter'. At the moment –1U—(of) the island [Great Britain] in CARTHAGE [Washington] is looking into the details of the transfer of work to the ISLAND. The work is the cause of the fact that – 2U—left LAT [garble?] via – 1F—

The first mention in files originating in the United Kingdom is on 17 August 1949, and it still refers to MSN-1 (part 3), not to MSN 12 (note 21 below). This reference to MSN-1 is repeated on 30 August ('Unidentified Soviet Agent in the United States' TNA KV 6/134, s. 6a), which suggests that the message was at that date still only partly decrypted. It also raises questions about the accuracy of Lamphere's account, written years after the event. See also chapter 21, note 11.   18. https://www.nsa.gov/news-features/declassified-documents/venona/dated/1944/assets/files/4oct_klaus_fuch_sister.pdf   19. https://www.nsa.gov/news-features/declassified-documents/venona/dated/1944/assets/files/16nov_klaus_fuchs_harry_gold.pdf. These three messages were known to the FBI when they opened the investigation and are mentioned in a summary for Director J. Edgar Hoover on 21 September 1949, Fuchs FOIA file 65-58805-3.   20. https://www.nsa.gov/news-features/declassified-documents/venona/dated/1944/assets/files/2odec_new_lab.pdf.   This decryption, which seems to have originated with GCHQ, was released to the FBI only in February 1950 (see chapter 21, notes 9 and 10, and chapter 22, note 54). The FBI seem to have been unaware of it in September 1949 as it does not appear in FOIA 65-58805-3 or other memoranda at that time. The final report released by the US National Security Agency in 1976 – 'copy number 301' – also has the hallmarks of originating in GCHQ – see note 16 and chapter 22.   21. Dwyer to Oldfield, 16 August 1949; Oldfield to A. Martin of MI5, 17 August; MI5 file TNA KV 6/134, s. 1a. This period of Oldfield's career is described in chapter 6 of Martin Pearce, *Spymaster: The Life of Britain's Most Decorated Cold War Spy and Head of MI6, Sir Maurice Oldfield* (Bantam, 2016).   22. Patterson to Director General, 16 August 1949, TNA KV 6/134, s. 2a.   23. Patterson to Martin, 24 August 1949, TNA KV 6/134, s. 3a.   24. A. Martin note, 30 August 1949, TNA KV 6/134, s. 6a.   25. A. Martin note, 30 August 1949, TNA KV 6/134, s. 7a.   26. Lamphere and Shachtman, *The FBI–KGB War*, p. 134.   Lamphere also recalled that he found the fragment about a week after he learned about the Soviet atomic test, whereby it became: 'immediately obvious that the Russians had stolen crucial evidence from us, and had undoubtedly used it to build their bomb'. The test took place on 29 August 1949 and was not confirmed in the West until mid September (see note 12.5). If Lamphere is correct, this means he would have been unaware of the fragment until well into September (see also p. 226). If so, the FBI source used by Patterson on 1 September could have been Micky Ladd, see later.   27. Patterson to MI5, 1 September 1949, TNA KV 6/134, s. 9a.   28. This appears to originate in Montgomery Hyde, *Atom Bomb Spies* (Ballantine Books, 1980), p. 143, which gives no source. There is no contemporaneous record that Perrin said this, or when, although this is certainly possible, given Patterson's telegram.   29. Report of 6 September meeting, by A. Martin, 7 September 1949, TNA KV 6/134, s. 14a. Perrin's remark that Fuchs wrote this in the UK is presumably an error as this note was written six months after Fuchs' arrival in New York. It is unclear whether Perrin identified the paper as MSN 12 and corrected the MSN-1 error, or whether this had already been established by further decryption.

14. Father or Son? September 1949

1. J. Robertson, Report of meeting of 6 September, written on 7 September 1949. TNA KV 2/1246, s. 114a.   2. Cimperman's ignorance is evident in 'Summary Brief on Klaus Fuchs', Fuchs FBI FOIA file 65-58805-1494. Hoover's anger at his own ignorance of events, and Cimperman's embarrassment, are the theme of a letter from Cimperman to Director Hoover on 21 February 1950, FOIA file 65-58805-705. See also chapter 21.   3. TNA KV 2/1246, s. 118a.   4. TNA KV 2/1246, s. 114a (meeting to discuss investigation) and 123a (letter to Colonel Allen advising discretion).   5. The secreting of a microphone in Fuchs' living room, or his telephone, would have been straightforward, and several reports in files TNA KV 2/1266 to 1269 of Fuchs being overheard in his living room indicate that this had been done. For example, there are sporadic records of his conversation with Arnold after the explosion of the Soviet atomic bomb, 24 September, TNA KV 2/1266, s. 18b, and of 'distant and indistinct' conversation between Fuchs and Erna Skinner on 21 September, KV 2/1266, s. 9e. However, many transcripts on file among the extensive surveillance logs from October 1949 up to his arrest in February 1950 appear to be withheld. In particular, there is no contemporaneous record of his seminal interview with Skardon in that very room in January 1950, at which Fuchs reportedly confessed.   6. J. Robertson, Meeting with Arnold, 9 September 1949. TNA KV 2/1246, s. 121a.   7. TNA KV 2/1246, minute 117.   8. M. Oldfield to A. Martin, 8 September 1949, 'Dr Gerhard FUCHS'. TNA KV 2/1246, s. 118b.   9. SLO Washington, 9 September, to A. Martin, received 10 September 1949. TNA KV 2/1246, s. 122a.   10. Telegram, A. Martin to SLO Washington, 10 September 1949. TNA KV 2/1246, s. 127a.   11. J. Robertson meeting with Arnold, 9 September 1949, TNA KV 2/1246, s. 121a.   12. Dick White, 15 September 1949, TNA KV 2/1246, memo 135.   13. M. B. Hanley, 16 September 1949, TNA KV 2/1246, memo 141.   14. Ibid.   15. TNA KV 2/1658, s. 64b.   16. Robertson to Colonel Allen, G.P.O., 13 September 1949. TNA KV 2/1658,

s. 60a.   **17.** Robertson to SLO Washington, 20 September 1949. TNA KV 2/1658, s. 71a.   **18.** A. Martin to SLO Washington, TNA KV 2/1658, s. 69a, 19 September, and Washington to Martin, s. 91a, 21 September 1949. The origin of this news was a letter, written in 1938. George Newgass of New York had contacted the Home Office on behalf of Peierls' parents, who wanted a visa. Now, eleven years later, MI5 had unearthed this while checking files on Peierls. Newgass said that Heinrich, Rudolf Peierls' father, 'had a son in law and daughter who emigrated to US in 1936 and who intended to become US citizens'. MI5 now noted that Mrs Heinrich Peierls had left the UK for the USA in February or March 1940 and 'may have given daughter's address on landing'. Having identified Peierls' stepmother: 'Can you identify daughter who must be Peierls' sister?' Peierls' sister Annie (Krebs) lived in Montclair, New Jersey, from about 1935 until the 1980s. There appears to be no evidence that MI5 ever identified her.   **19.** R. J. Lamphere and T. Shachtman, *The FBI–KGB War: A Special Agent's Story* (Random House, 1986). Lamphere's erroneous claim that he discovered this information in late September is on p. 134.   **20.** Memorandum for FBI Director, 21(?) September 1949, Fuchs FBI FOIA file, 65-58805-3. The communications section date is clearly 21 September; the date at the head of the memorandum is obscure, but appears to be either 12 or 22 September.   **21.** H. B. Fletcher to D. M. Ladd, 27(?) September 1949, Fuchs FBI FOIA file, 65-58805-7. Other agency stamps suggest this document dates about one week after file 58805-3.   **22.** Fuchs FBI FOIA file, 65-58805-3, 21(?) September 1949.   **23.** H. B. Fletcher to L. Whitson, 26 September 1949, Fuchs FBI FOIA file, 65-58805-9.   **24.** British Embassy, Washington to Arthur Martin, 21 September 1949, TNA KV 2/1658, s. 91a.   **25.** TNA KV 2/1246, s. 144b gives Arnold's address as the Manor House, Marcham.   **26.** Robertson report of visit to Harwell, 20 September 1949, TNA KV 2/1246, s. 167a.   **27.** This observation about Fuchs conveying 'the product of his own brain' originates here with MI5. Later it became attributed to Fuchs as a biopic of his three stages of espionage. However, Fuchs said, 'I concentrated at first mainly (*sic*) on the products of my own work.' See p. 8 of his statement of 27 January 1950 to Skardon (exhibit 3 at his trial, TNA KV 2/1263) and chapter 5, note 16.   **28.** 'Appendix C. Difficulties presented by the investigation into the case of Emil Julius Klaus FUCHS', paragraph 4, undated (September 1949), TNA KV 2/1246.   **29.** Ibid, paragraph 6.   **30.** Report from Fuchs' home by 'R(H)', 21 September 1949, TNA KV 2/1266, s. 9e.   **31.** 'R(H)' to Robertson, 24 September 1949, TNA KV 2/1266, s. 18b.   **32.** 'R(H)' to Robertson, 24 September 1949, TNA KV 2/1266, s. 18b, p. 2.   **33.** Sillitoe to Patterson, 30 September 1949, TNA KV 2/1246, s. 191a.   **34.** SLO Washington to Martin, 21 September 1949, TNA KV 6/134, s. 44a.   **35.** TNA KV 2/1246, s. 92a and 191a.   **36.** Ibid, s. 204a.   **37.** Skardon to Commander Burt, 3 October 1949, TNA KV 2/1658, s. 97a. The information appears linked to Peierls' passport, which is visible on the front cover of his autobiography, *Bird of Passage*. His application of 11 August 1943 for an exit permit refers to 5 feet 7 inches (without a half): TNA KV 2/1658, s. 9a.   **38.** R. Reed [B.2.a] to J. Robertson, 3 October 1949. TNA KV 2/1658, s. 98a.   **39.** MI5 requested Peierls' and Fuchs' passport details on 7 September 1949 (TNA KV 2/1658, s. 55b and TNA KV 2/1246, s. 125b). Peierls' details were received on 12 September, TNA KV 2/1268, s. 56a. The quotes on the surveillance of Peierls are taken from TNA KV 2/1268.   **40.** Robertson priorities for surveillance by section B.4.d, 4 October 1949, TNA KV 2/1247, s. 207a.   **41.** TNA KV 2/1659, s. 119, 19 October 1949. 'Outsiders' refers to Kearton and Skyrme; see chapter 13, note 29.   **42.** Telegram from Washington, 13 October 1949, TNA KV 2/1659, s. 113b.   **43.** Telegram from Washington, 13 October 1949, TNA KV 6/134, s. 57a. This copy is of the same telegram as in note 42 but containing the crucial extra item (3) on MSN 12: 'It was therefore not (repeat) NOT completed before PEIERLS left.'   **44.** Patterson to Director General, 30 September 1949, received 5 October 1949. TNA KV 2/1247, s. 209F.   **45.** TNA KV 2/1247, memo 225; 10 October 1949.   **46.** TNA KV 2/1247, s. 230c; sent 4 October, received 11 October 1949.   **47.** Kim Philby, *My Silent War: The Autobiography of a Spy* (Arrow, 2018), p. 111; Philby reported for duty on 10 October: Anthony Cave Brown, *Treason in the Blood* (Robert Hale, 1994), p. 391.   **48.** Christopher Andrew and Vasili Mitrokhin, *The Mitrokhin Archive* (Penguin, 2000), p. 204; Andrew, *Defence of the Realm*, p. 376, asserts, 'Soon after [arrival in Washington]

Philby reported to Moscow that the atom spy . . . CHARLES . . . had been identified as Klaus Fuchs – thus enabling Moscow to warn those of its American agents who dealt with Fuchs that they might have to flee through Mexico.' Philby admits as much in his memoirs, *My Silent War*, where in chapter 12 he says that Fuchs was arrested 'despite my best efforts'.   49. Robertson's report: 'Visit of W/C Arnold, 17.10.49', TNA KV 2/1247, s. 248a.   50. H. Arnold to J. Robertson, 24 October 1949, TNA KV 2/1247, s. 278a.

15. Private Lives: October 1949

1. J. C. Robertson, Fuchs' possible association with Ronald Hamilton GUNN, 7 November 1949, TNA KV 2/1248, s. 311a.   2. Although Gunn's history could with hindsight have raised enough worries that Fuchs would have been refused security clearance, other obsessions with Gunn appear to have been a waste of time. In 1941 Bristol police reported that Gunn was friendly with a Jacob Cooper, a communist who worked at the Bristol Aeroplane Company. Cooper was regarded as suspicious both for his association with Gunn but also because he owned a 'Cootax camera' and was 'in the habit of developing his own film'. More significant perhaps was that he was stated to have 'taken plans and drawings from the Bristol Aeroplane Company to his lodgings'. In 1946, when Dr Alan Nunn May was arrested for espionage, convicted, and given ten years hard labour, the name and address of Cooper were found in his diary. This seems to have been no more significant than that at that time Cooper was a lecturer at Birkbeck College, and known professionally to May, who was at Kings College London. Nonetheless, the whirlpool of names, with Gunn at its vortex, and Fuchs one of his satellites, tantalized the Security Services, took up resources, and led nowhere.   3. Arnold to Robertson, 29 September 1949, TNA KV 2/1246, s. 185a.   4. TNA KV 2/1246, s. 157A; MI5 officers recorded their surveillance of Fuchs from September 1949 until his arrest in February 1950 in a daily log. This fills files TNA KV 2/1266 to TNA KV 2/1269 in the National Archive. Any unspecified quotes in this chapter and in chapter 16 come from these files.   5. Report from Fuchs' home by 'R(H)', 21 September 1949, TNA KV 2/1266, s. 9e.   6. J. Robertson, 21 September 1949, TNA KV 2/1246, s. 160a.   7. B.4.b to Robertson, TNA KV 2/1266, s. 7a, and Robertson memos TNA KV 2/1246, s. 163a, 167c.   8. Diary, 22 September 1949, TNA KV 2/1266, s. 11b.   9. Arnold to MI5 headquarters, TNA KV 2/1246, s. 171b.   10. D. Storrier to Robertson, Case F.63, TNA KV 2/1246, s. 173a.   11. TNA KV 2/1246, Serials 167c, 171b, 173a.   12. 'R(H)' report on Fuchs' home, 25 September 1949, TNA KV 2/1266, s. 19b.   13. Robertson, 29 September 1949, TNA KV 2/1246, s. 175c.   14. Robertson to D. Storrier, TNA KV 2/1246, s. 151a.   15. 'Preliminary B.4.d report on observation of Fuchs, 27.9.49', TNA KV 2/1246, s. 177b. This is contrary to Mike Rossiter, *The Spy who Changed the World* (Headline, 2014), p. 250, who claimed Fuchs had 'requested two rail warrants for a journey [*sic*] to Paddington'. From this Rossiter drew the conclusion that Fuchs planned to travel with a companion, and so 'would not have made contact with a Soviet agent during the journey'.   16. 'R(H)' report on Fuchs' home, 26 September 1949, TNA KV 2/1266, s. 23b.   17. Erna Skinner to an unknown woman, telephone check on Skinner's home, 29 September 1949, TNA KV 2/1266, s. 31a.   18. D. Storrier report on Fuchs' movements on 27 September 1949, TNA KV 2/1246, s. 181b.   19. TNA KV 2/1246, s. 179a.   20. TNA KV 2/1246, s. 181b.   21. Rudolf Peierls, *Bird of Passage* (Princeton University Press, 1985), p. 205.   22. Edward Teller (with Judith Shoolery), *Memoirs: A Twentieth-Century Journey in Science and Politics* (Perseus, 2001), p. 223.   23. TNA KV 2/1246, Travel records of Fuchs, 1946–49.   24. TNA KV 2/1246, s. 183a.   25. D. Storrier report of Fuchs movements, 7 October 1949, TNA KV 2/1247, s. 223a.   26. Robertson report of meeting with Arnold, 10 October 1949, TNA KV 2/1247, s. 221.   27. Phone log of 29 September 1949, Erna Skinner remarks to an unidentified woman, TNA KV 2/1246.   28. 'R(H)' report on Fuchs' home, 10 October 1949, TNA KV 2/1266, s. 86a.   29. Record of Fuchs' movements, 10 October 1949, TNA KV 2/1247, s. 229a.   30. Robertson, 21 November 1949, TNA KV 2/1248, minute 335. Also, Biographical

Notes on Emil Julius Klaus Fuchs, 23 November 1949, TNA KV 2/1248, s. 344z. **31.** J. Robertson memos, 9 March 1950, TNA KV 2/1253, s. 585, and 30 October 1952, TNA KV 2/1259, minute 975. **32.** Norman Moss, *Klaus Fuchs: The Man who Stole the Atom Bomb* (Grafton Books, 1987), p. 102, and confirmed in Rudolf Peierls' annotated copy (courtesy of Jo Hookway). **33.** Erna Skinner to Genia Peierls, 11 November 1949, MI5 files, TNA KV 2/1659, s. 154a. **34.** Fuchs' last meeting with his KGB contact was on 1 April 1949. He failed to turn up for a meeting due on 25 June and for a back-up meeting on 2 July. KGB file 84490, vol. 1, p. 424, Alexander Vassiliev, 'Yellow Notebook #1', in Vassiliev, *Alexander Vassiliev Papers, 1895–2011*, US Library of Congress, p. 83. **35.** J. Robertson, 'Biographical notes of Emil Julius Klaus Fuchs', 23 November 1949, TNA KV 2/1248, s. 344z, p. 12. **36.** Ibid. **37.** D. Storrier (B.4.d), 'Surveillance report F.63; 4.11.49', TNA KV/2 1248, s. 309a. **38.** Notes by Fuchs on contacts and meetings, TNA KV 2/1252, s. 518a. **39.** J. Robertson, 'Biographical notes of Emil Julius Klaus Fuchs', 23 November 1949, TNA KV 2/1248, s. 344z, p. 13. **40.** Ibid, p. 18. **41.** Report by observer F.63, 14 October 1949, TNA KV 2/1247, s. 244a. **42.** Report summary, 14 October 1949, TNA KV 2/1247, s. 242. **43.** Message from Newbury received 12.00, TNA KV 2/1247, s. 245a. **44.** TNA KV 2/1247, minute 280, 26 October 1949.

16. Guy Liddell's Pursuit: November and December 1949

1. Tom Bower, *The Perfect English Spy: Sir Dick White and the Secret War 1939–1945* (Heinemann, 1995), p. 70. **2.** Christopher Andrew, *The Defence of the Realm: The Authorized History of MI5* (Allen Lane, 2005), p. 320. **3.** Guy Liddell's diary, TNA KV 4/471; 31 October 1949. **4.** Ibid. **5.** Guy Liddell's diary, TNA KV 4/471; 8 November 1949. **6.** Rudolf Peierls, *Bird of Passage* (Princeton University Press, 1985), p. 141. Annie was six years older than Rudolf Peierls. She migrated with her husband Herman Krebs to the USA in about 1935, and lived continuously in the same house in Montclair until the 1980s. **7.** Guy Liddell's diary, TNA KV 4/471; 8 November 1949. **8.** Telegram from Patterson to London, TNA KV 6/134; s. 68a. **9.** Guy Liddell's diary, TNA KV 4/471; 15 November 1949. **10.** TNA KV 2/1247, s. 278d; note to J. Robertson from B4, 24 October 1949. **11.** Guy Liddell's diary, TNA KV 4/471; 15 November 1949. **12.** Ibid. **13.** TNA KV 2/1248, s. 337a; J. Robertson, 22 November 1949. **14.** TNA KV 2/1248, s. 337a; 22 November 1949. **15.** Ibid. **16.** Guy Liddell's diary, TNA KV 4/471; 5 December 1949. **17.** J. Robertson, 'Proposed interrogation of Fuchs', 16 December 1949, TNA KV 2/1249, s. 376c. **18.** Guy Liddell's diary, TNA KV 4/471; 5 December 1949. **19.** Guy Liddell's diary, TNA KV 4/471; 15 December 1949. **20.** Telephone check on Skinner's home, 9 December 1949, TNA KV 2/1268, s. 390b. **21.** Andrew, *Defence of the Realm*, p. 334. **22.** C. Brinson and R. Dove, *A Matter of Intelligence: MI5 and the Surveillance of Anti-Nazi Refugees, 1933–50* (Manchester University Press, 2014), p. 207. **23.** Kim Philby, *My Silent War: The Autobiography of a Spy* (Arrow, 2018), p. 169. **24.** White as quoted by Bower, *The Perfect English Spy*, p. 96. **25.** Paragraph 4 in 'Proposed interrogation of Fuchs', TNA KV 2/1249, s. 376c, J. Robertson, 16 December 1949. **26.** TNA KV 2/1249, s. 382a: 21 December 1949; J. Robertson note on Fuchs interrogation. **27.** TNA KV 2/1249, s. 383a and KV 2/1269, s. 464a; Fuchs movements on 21 December 1949. **28.** Leonard Burt, *Commander Burt of Scotland Yard* (Heineman, 1959), p. 29. **29.** Ibid, p. 32. **30.** Paragraph 5 in J. Skardon report of interview, 22 December 1949, TNA KV 2/1249, s. 388a. **31.** Ibid. **32.** Guy Liddell's diary, TNA KV 4/471, 21 December 1949. **33.** Paragraph 5 in J. Skardon report of interview, 22 December 1949, TNA KV 2/1249, s. 388a. **34.** Burt, *Commander Burt of Scotland Yard*, p. 51. **35.** Paragraph 14, TNA KV 2/1249, s. 388a. **36.** Paragraph 17, TNA KV 2/1249, s. 388a. Other descriptions are based on Skardon's statement of 4 February 1950, TNA KV 2/1263, s. 15b. **37.** 'Two hours' is according to Skardon's report. TNA KV 2/1249, s. 383a, notes Fuchs' movements and confirms the exact time. It seems that he went to his office, where he was heard shutting drawers, between 12.48 and 12.52 and was again in his office between 13.11 and 13.13 as drawers were again heard. This would be when he collected papers to show Skardon, and then returned them. **38.** Fuchs to Skardon, TNA KV 2/1249, s. 388a, paragraph 22. Karl Cohen is famous for his monograph *The Theory of Isotope Separation as Applied to the Large-Scale Production of U-235* (McGraw-Hill, 1951). **39.** TNA KV 2/1249, s. 383a. Phone call from Fuchs to dentist in Fuchs' Movements on 21 December 1949. See also telephone check on Skinner's home, 21 December 1949, TNA KV 2/1269 s. 465a. **40.** Paragraph 25, TNA KV 2/1249, s. 388a. **41.** Paragraph 5 in J. Skardon report of interview, 22 December 1949, TNA KV 2/1249, s. 388a. **42.** Paragraph 25, TNA KV 2/1249, s. 388a. **43.** TNA KV 2/1249 s. 384a, Fuchs movements on 21 December 1949 record '15.46: At that moment Fuchs returned [to his office].' **44.** Paragraph 5 in J. Skardon report of interview, 22 December 1949, TNA KV 2/1249, s. 388a. **45.** Ibid. **46.** Robertson memo, 21 December 1949, TNA KV 2/1249, s. 384a. **47.** Guy Liddell's diary, TNA KV 4/471; 21 December 1949. **48.** Skinner phone log, TNA KV 2/1269, s. 470a. **49.** https://weatherspark.com/history/28729/1949/London-England-United-Kingdom. **50.** Many scientists felt that Portal, a former air vice-marshal, led Atomic Energy with a lack of distinction. One example is the assertion that Portal 'never did anything to help atomic energy'. G. Stafford interview, 20 December 2012. **51.** TNA KV 4/471, 28 December 1949. **52.** Arthur Martin memo, 29 December 1949, TNA KV 6/134, s. 96a. **53.** TNA KV 2/1269, s. 504a. **54.** Fuchs returned to his office from lunch at 2.16. The interview must have lasted about half an hour as eavesdroppers noted: 'quiet in the office. FUCHS out?' from 2.51 to 3.42. There is no mention that anyone heard him leave, and there are records withheld, so it is unclear precisely when or where the interview took place. See TNA KV 2/1269, s. 502a to 506a. Page 505a, however, has been 'retained under section 3(4) of the Public Records Act; this decision dated Nov 2002'. The sole record of Skardon and Fuchs' conversation is therefore, as before, due to Skardon himself. **55.** Skardon's report of his second interview with Fuchs, on 30 December 1949, was written on 2 January 1950. TNA KV 2/1249, s. 397a. **56.** Ibid, paragraph 5. **57.** Dick White interview with Tom Bower, quoted in Bower, *The Perfect English Spy*, p. 95, note 52. **58.** Martin to Patterson, 6 January 1950, TNA KV 6/134, s. 113a. **59.** The guests and their roles are reconstructed from MI5's interceptions of the Skinner residence's phone conversations in TNA KV 2/1268. **60.** Mary Flowers (Bunemann), *Atomic Spice: A Partial Autobiography* (2009), p. 125: http://homepages.inf.ed.ac.uk/opb/atomic-spice. Mary Flowers, whose account was written many years later, writes as if the party was shortly before Christmas and that she then went to her parents in Manchester. The context places this unambiguously as 1949. The MI5 record, however, shows that the Skinners' sole party was at New Year's Eve, and phone conversations between Mary and Erna Skinner place her visit to her parents after her subsequent breakdown in January 1950.

17. Chasing the Fox: January 1950

1. Guy Liddell's diary, 1 January 1950, TNA KV 4/472. **2.** Guy Liddell's diary, 2 January 1950, TNA KV 4/472. **3.** TNA KV 4/472, 4 January 1950. This was reported to White and Robertson on 5 January, TNA KV 2/1249, s. 403a. **4.** TNA KV 4/472, 4 January 1950. **5.** Ibid, 5 January 1950. **6.** Liddell's diary, 5 January 1950, TNA KV 4/472. **7.** TNA KV 2/1269, s. 528a and s. 532a. **8.** Diary of Sir John Cockcroft, Churchill College Archives, Cambridge. **9.** That the crucial meeting was delayed, and that there were two meetings, is evidenced by the MI5 record of a meeting at 3 p.m. on 5 January, TNA KV 2/1269, s. 528a and 532a, and Cockcroft's diary entry of a 10 January meeting. Fuchs' remarks to Erna Skinner at lunch on 10 January show that he had met Cockcroft that morning, TNA KV 2/1269, s. 551a, 554a and 556a. In Skardon's interview on 13 January, Fuchs referred to Cockcroft having already seen him, TNA KV 2/1250, 420a. **10.** J. H. Marriott (B2), 13 January 1950 report of Cockcroft's account of his interview with Fuchs. TNA KV 2/1250, s. 415ab. **11.** Telephone call from Perrin to Robertson, 27 January 1950, TNA KV 2/1250, s. 438a. **12.** TNA KV 2/1250, s. 438a, written on 26 January, records that Skinner learned this 'about a week ago'. If this was from Fuchs at Harwell it ought to have been recorded by MI5's surveillance. Skinner was in Liverpool and London between

16 and 20 January. It is possible that this actually refers to Skinner having learned from Erna Skinner on 19 January, following her tryst with Fuchs in Richmond. 13. Erna Skinner to Eleanor Scott, 29 December 1949, TNA KV 2/1269, s. 498a. 14. TNA KV 2/1269, s. 551a–556a. The verbatim account in the following paragraphs is based on s. 551a. 15. 'Fuchs; Looks; Like an Ascetic; Theoretic.' AERE News, quoted in Norman Moss, *Klaus Fuchs: The Man who Stole the Atom Bomb* (Grafton Books, 1987), p. 98. 16. Fuchs refers to Elaine's age in a letter dated 3 February 1950, TNA KV 2/1252, s. 518a. 17. Dick White to Jim Skardon, as told by White to Tom Bower, cited in Bower, *The Perfect English Spy: Sir Dick White and the Secret War 1939–1945* (Heinemann, 1995), p. 95. 18. Tom Bower interview with Dick White, cited in ibid, p. 96. 19. We have only Skardon's account of the interview. The telephone check on Fuchs' office, which is available on other days, appears to have been withheld. In TNA KV 2/1269, s. 571a, the Fuchs diary records '10.40 Fuchs definitely in his office.' This is followed by 'The office line was then out of order.' Next: '11.30 Fuchs was to be interrogated; 17.05 He was thought to be in his office.' See also s. 569a and 570a. 20. TNA KV 2/1250, s. 420a. 21. Skardon's 18 January 1950 report of his third interview with Fuchs, held on 13 January 1950, TNA KV 2/1250, s. 420a. 22. Emil Fuchs to Klaus Fuchs, letter received 19 October 1949, TNA KV 2/1247, s. 259a; from Kristel in Westboro State Hospital to Klaus, mailed 24 October 1949, intercepted by MI5, 28 October 1949, TNA KV 2/1247, s. 286a. 23. TNA KV 2/1269, s. 572a: '19.31 Fuchs went out. Nothing further was heard of Fuchs's movements. 00.01 Still quiet in the prefab.' This record, titled 'Fuchs Diary', shows that Fuchs' home was bugged. 'Incoming call from Erna SKIN-NER; 11.14 (14 January 1950)', TNA KV 2/1269, s. 573a. 24. MI5 surveillance reports were logged on a daily basis. TNA KV 2/1266 covers the month of October 1949; TNA KV 2/1267 covers November; TNA KV 2/1268 covers December, and TNA KV 2/1269 continues up to Fuchs' arrest on 2 February 1950. Material in this chapter is drawn from these logs and from Liddell's diary for 1950, TNA KV 4/472. 25. TNA KV 2/1269, s. 580a–584a. 26. Det. Sgt. Cyril A. Warren of Berkshire Constabulary, to MI5, 4 March 1950, TNA KV 2/1253, s. 594a. Sgt. Warren's report mistakenly named Fuchs' female companion as Gisela Wagner; Fuchs confirmed to Skardon on 8 March 1950 that it was indeed Erna Skinner: TNA KV 6/135, s. 189a. 27. TNA KV 2/1269, s. 584a. 28. This event is recorded twice in the MI5 files: TNA KV 2/1259, minute 972, and TNA KV 2/1269, s. 589a. Fuchs' liaison in Kew Road is about ten minutes' walk from Richmond railway station. 29. Elaine Wheatley (Skinner), letter to Norman Moss, 17 August 1986; copy in Peierls papers, D57, Bodleian Library. Norman Moss interview, 9 May 2017: Moss said, 'I asked Elaine "Did your mother have an affair with Fuchs" "No!" That was all she said.' Possibly based on this, Moss has Fuchs and Erna in separate rooms at Maidenhead, but the testimony of the manager denies that. 30. Telephone check on Skinner's home, 17 January 1950; TNA KV 2/1269, memo 586a. 31. Telephone check on Skinner's home (extract), 17 January 1950; TNA KV 2/1269, memo 585a. 32. Fuchs' diary, 18 January 1950. 'Fuchs was still on leave in London.' TNA KV 2/1269, s. 593a. 33. Telephone check on Skinner's home, 18 January 1950, TNA KV 2/1269, memo 592a. 34. Telephone check on Skinner's home, 18 January 1950. 'Incoming call from Fuchs from London to Vera.' TNA KV 2/1269, s. 592a. 35. Robertson to the Director General, 'Press comments on Dr Fuchs' espionage methods and contacts', 6 March 1950, TNA KV 2/1254, s. 621. 36. Ibid. 37. 'Letter to W/Cdr Arnold from Prof. Skinner. Received 22.9.52', TNA KV 2/1259, s. 965y. This led to considerable examination in MI5, summarized by E. McBarnet in TNA KV 2/1259, m. 972: 'The probable date of this alleged confession was the 17th January; on that date FUCHS and Erna SKINNER were staying together at the Palm Court Hotel, Richmond.' 38. Ibid. Judgements in this paragraph are based also on MI5's assessments in TNA KV 2/1259, minutes 968, 972 and 975. 39. E. Skinner to H. Arnold, October 1952, TNA KV 2/1259, s. 971a. 40. E. Skinner to H. Skinner, 19 January 1950; H. Skinner letter to H. Arnold, 18 September 1952; 'K. confessed to Erna about the Diff. Plant a day or two prior to Jan 19th' and 'K. denied the bomb to E.' TNA KV 2/1259, s. 965y; also s. 969b 26/9/52. 41. Following Fuchs' arrest, the nomination was withdrawn. Exchange of letters between Peierls and David Brunt of the Royal Society, 22 and 24 April 1950, Peierls papers, Bodleian Library, b.207, C111.

42. 'Klaus Fuchs – Atomspion', Klaus Fuchs interview with East German television in 1983, transcribed in Zelluloid, 31 March 1990, ISSN 07 24-76 56. 43. There is a verbatim transcript of the call at TNA KV 2/1269, s. 599a. 44. Fuchs' diary, 19 January 1950, TNA KV 2/1269, s. 598a, s. 599a and telephone check on Skinner's home, 20 January 1950, s. 600a. 45. TNA KV 2/1250, s. 424b. 46. TNA KV 2/1269, s. 610b. 47. TNA KV 2/1250, s. 429a. 48. Ibid. 49. TNA KV 2/1250, s. 426a. 50. Arnold statement, TNA KV 2/1250, s. 430a; author interview with Norman Moss, 2 March 2017, and p. 138 in Moss, Klaus Fuchs. 51. Moss states that Arnold asked Fuchs directly, 'Have you passed information to a foreign agent?' and that Fuchs admitted he had. There is no contemporaneous mention of this in his report to MI5, however, nor any mention in their files, for example at KV 2/1250, s. 430a. One possibility is that this is a false memory on Arnold's part, recalled more than two decades after the event, as at Fuchs' trial Arnold testified to asking a similar question, but on the morning of 26 January, not 23 January. The conversation between Arnold and Fuchs about the general election is based upon Harwell folklore from the 1970s; I cannot vouch for its accuracy, though it sounds plausible. 52. W. J. Skardon, Report on 'Emil Julius Klaus FUCHS: Fourth Fifth, Sixth, and Seventh Interviews', 31 January 1950, TNA KV 2/1250, s. 443ab. 53. Ibid. 54. 'JIM was with FUCHS in the prefab. 10.59–12.59 [and] 14.22–16.00.' TNA KV 2/1269, s. 619a. Report on activity in Fuchs' home, 24 January 1950. Other than noting the presence of Skardon, there is no verbatim record of what took place. The account in the text is based on Skardon's written account, KV 2/1250, s. 443ab. 55. Robert Chadwell Williams, Klaus Fuchs, Atom Spy (Harvard University Press, 1987), refers solely to the 'grandest' hotel but gives no name. Moss, Klaus Fuchs, p. 139, places this lunch at the Crown and Thistle. While this hotel could lay claim to that title in the 1980s, when Moss' book appeared, back in 1950 the 'grandest hotel' in Abingdon was The Queen's. This was subsumed in a 1960s 'development', which is regarded by long-term Abingdon residents as a symbol of the worst excesses of that era. Part of its frontage remains on the Market Square above a modern shop. Details of its history are at: https://historicengland.org.uk/listing/the-list/list-entry/1283279. Received wisdom in Abingdon is that The Queen's was the location of this historic event. The description of its ambience comes from Margaret Faull (interview 29 June 2015), who remembers going there with her parents when she was a young child. 56. W. J. Skardon, 'Report of fourth interview', 24 January 1950, TNA KV 2/1250, s. 443a, p. 1. 57. Guy Liddell's diary, 25 January 1950, TNA KV 4/472. 58. Skardon's report of Fuchs' confession was written on 31 January 1950, a week after the event. TNA KV 2/1250. The records contain no contemporaneous report. 59. Letter from Klaus Fuchs to Kristel Heineman, (?) February 1950, TNA KV 2/1251. 60. Klaus Fuchs to W. J. Skardon, 'Report of fourth interview', 24 January 1950, TNA KV 2/1250, s. 443a, p. 2. 61. TNA KV 2/1250, s. 434. 62. J. Robertson's note on Mr Skardon's telephone call, 24 January 1950, TNA KV 2/1250, s. 433a.

18. Closing the Net: 1950

1. Guy Liddell's diary, 25 January 1950, TNA KV 4/472. 2. Norman Moss, Klaus Fuchs: The Man who Stole the Atom Bomb (Grafton Books, 1987), p. 141, has Fuchs confessing to Arnold in this talk. 3. 'Diary of events 25.1.50', TNA KV 2/1250, s. 435a. 4. Guy Liddell's diary, 25 January 1950, TNA KV 4/472. 5. Ibid. 6. Ibid. 7. Taken from Arnold's testimony at the Magistrates' Court on 10 February 1950. TNA KV 2/1263, s. 28a. 8. TNA KV 2/1269, s. 632a 26 January 1950: '11.01–13.12 JIM was with FUCHS in the prefab.' As on the first occasion, no verbatim record has been released. 9. GRU memo for KGB, 'Fuchs recruited for intelligence in England in August 1941', KGB file 84490, vol. 2, p. 127, Alexander Vassiliev, 'Yellow Notebook #1', in Vassiliev, Alexander Vassiliev Papers, 1895–2011, US Library of Congress, p. 86. 10. W. J. Skardon, Report on 'Emil Julius Klaus FUCHS: Fourth Fifth, Sixth, and Seventh Interviews', 31 January 1950, TNA KV 2/1250, s. 443, p. 2. 11. Telephone check on Skinner's home, 24 January 1950, TNA KV 2/1269. 12. Telephone check on Skinner's home, 26 January 1950, TNA KV 2/1269, s. 627a. 13. Ibid. 14. Mary Flowers (Bunemann), Atomic Spice: A Partial Autobiography (2009): http://

homepages.inf.ed.ac.uk/opb/atomicspice. 15. W. J. Skardon, Report on 'Emil Julius Klaus FUCHS: Fourth, Fifth, Sixth and Seventh Interviews', 31 January 1950, TNA KV 2/1250, s. 443, p. 3. 16. Fuchs statement to W. J. Skardon, 27 January 1950, TNA KV 2/1263, folio 2, p. 7. 17. Klaus Fuchs to Henry Arnold, 9 February 1950, TNA KV 2/1252, s. 507a. 18. 'Fuchs diary 27.1.50', TNA KV 2/1269, s. 638a, and telephone check on Skinner's home, 27 January 1950, s. 635a. 19. TNA KV 2/1250, s. 438a and 439c. 20. TNA KV 2/1250, s. 439b. 21. Guy Liddell's diary, 27 January 1950, TNA KV 4/472. 22. Ibid. 23. 'FUCHS Exchange of messages. 28.1.50', TNA KV 2/1250, s. 441a. 24. J. C. Robertson memo, 30 January 1950, 'Fuchs interview with Mr Perrin and Mr Skardon at Room 055 on 30.1.50', TNA KV 2/1250, s. 442a. 25. The following paragraphs and quotes follow closely Perrin's report, which was classified for half a century. Information from the report was available to the FBI and has been used by scholars. The popular perception that Fuchs began spying only in 1942 is based in part on this report. Soviet records and other documents, as we have seen, show that in reality he was active by August 1941 and possibly earlier. 26. Today we know this to have been correct: Alan Nunn May had been identified by the Soviets as a potential source of information in November 1942; at that time Nunn May was in Cambridge, and his subsequent move to Canada was known to the USSR. See also Paul Broda, *Scientist Spies: A Memoir of My Three Parents and the Atom Bomb* (Matador, 2011), p .120. 27. There is some debate about this date, what exactly was said, and its implications – see extended note in Richard Rhodes, *Dark Sun: The Making of the Hydrogen Bomb* (Simon and Schuster, 2005), p. 624. Rhodes argues that Perrin incorrectly attributed this to 1947 on the grounds that Fuchs referred to Gold, with whom he only had contact up to 1946. However, it is now clear that Fuchs passed information about the H-bomb from Britain as well. The query referred to was indeed made in 1947 and Perrin's full statement includes the crucial phrase that Fuchs was asked about the hydrogen bomb 'and about a highly secret component material used in connection therewith'. This phrase does not appear in Robert Chadwell Williams, *Klaus Fuchs, Atom Spy* (Harvard University Press, 1987), or Moss, *Klaus Fuchs*, as the report was still classified when they wrote their books. It refers to the problems of maintaining thermonuclear fusion and of sources of tritium, such as the use of lithium deuteride. 28. MI5 was unaware that VENONA had identified other spies, such as MLAD – Ted Hall. The FBI, for their part, did not yet realize the extent of Hall's espionage at Los Alamos. See J. Albright and M. Kunstall, *Bombshell: The Secret Story of America's Unknown Atomic Spy Conspiracy* (Times Books, Random House, 1997), for an account of Hall. 29. Pontecorvo's story is told in my book *Half Life: The Divided Life of Bruno Pontecorvo, Scientist or Spy* (Basic Books, 2015, and OneWorld, 2015). 30. W. J. Skardon, Report on 'Emil Julius Klaus FUCHS: Fourth, Fifth, Sixth and Seventh Interviews', 31 January 1950, TNA KV 2/1250, s. 443, p. 3. 31. Fuchs' diary, 30 January 1950, TNA KV 2/1269, s. 654a. 32. Telephone check on Skinner's home, 31 January 1950, TNA KV 2/1269, s. 654c. 33. TNA KV 2/1251, s. 479B. 'Note on interview with Klaus FUCHS'. 34. Ibid. 'Lists of photographs shown to Fuchs: B.2.b. list'. 35. TNA KV 2/1252, s. 513a. 36. The thesis of Timothy Gibbs, 'British and American Counter-Intelligence and the Atom Spies, 1941–1950', Ph.D. thesis, Faculty of History, Cambridge University, 2007, chapter 3, footnote 562, and TNA KV6/43, Sir Percy Sillitoe to Chief Constable of Oxfordshire, 25 July and 8 August 1950. 37. On 19 December 1950 M. B. Hanley reported, 'On 13 November 1950 Klaus FUCHS identified his second contact (1942/43) as Ursula Maria BEURTON.' TNA KV 2/1256, s. 780b. The '13' appears to be an audio typing error for '30', as on 30 November Skardon visited Fuchs in Stafford Prison and on 1 December reported that Fuchs had identified Beurton's photograph. Skardon's report of visit to Fuchs, 30 November 1950, TNA KV 2/1256, s. 759a. 38. Guy Liddell's diary, 31 January 1950, TNA KV 4/472. 39. J. C. Robertson, 'Meeting with Commander Burt, Special Branch; 1.2.50', TNA KV 2/1250, s. 444a. 40. Guy Liddell's diary, 31 January 1950, TNA KV 4/472. 41. Guy Liddell's diary, 1 February 1950, TNA KV 4/472. 42. Note of conference held at the office of the Director of Public Prosecutions on Wednesday 1 February 1950, TNA KV 2/1263, s. 4a. 43. Fuchs to Under-Secretary of State, Home Office, 28 June 1950, TNA KV 2/1255, s. 710a. 44. Report on Emil Julius Klaus Fuchs, 1 February 1950, paragraph 9 in TNA KV 2/1263, s. 3a. 45. In anticipation of Fuchs' arrest, Robertson contacted the GPO: 'I would be grateful if you would reimpose HOW No. 10801 on Rudolf PEIERLS, at 18 Carpenter Road, Birmingham 15, and at the University, Edgbaston, Birmingham 15.' TNA KV 2/1661, s. 225a. 46. TNA KV 2/1250, s. 448a. 47. TNA KV 2/1250, s. 449a. 48. In response to this, on 26 February the Soviet Council of Ministers adopted a resolution to create a Soviet H-bomb. The direction of Soviet early research built on the intelligence passed by Klaus Fuchs, especially that of 23 March 1948. See G. A. Goncharov, 'On the History of the Creation of the Soviet Hydrogen Bomb', *Physics–Uspekhi*, vol. 40, no. 8 (1997), pp. 859–67, and 'American and Soviet H-Bomb Development Programme: Historical Background', *Physics–Uspekhi*, vol. 39 (1996), p. 1,033. 49. TNA KV 2/1661, s. 227a. 50. Telephone check on Fuchs' office, 1 February 1950, TNA KV 2/1270, s. 655a. 51. TNA KV 2/1270, s. 662a. 52. TNA KV 2/1270, s. 665a, telephone check on Fuchs' office, 2 February 1950. Peierls' call to Fuchs is also logged at TNA KV 2/1661, s. 228a. 53. Nicholas Hance, *Harwell: The Enigma Revealed* (Enhance Publications, 2006), p. 103. 54. TNA KV 4/472, 2 February 1950, p. 1. 55. Ibid. 56. TNA KV 4/472, 2 February 1950, p. 2. 57. Leonard Burt, *Commander Burt of Scotland Yard* (Heineman, 1959), p. 58. Burt claims that Fuchs was twenty minutes late, but this differs from Perrin's account, as described in Moss, *Klaus Fuchs*, p. 147, and with the implications of MI5 and Liddell's record of the delays resulting from the preparatory conference. 58. Fuchs to Erna and Herbert Skinner, 4 February 1950 (dated incorrectly 3 February), TNA KV 2/1251, s. 469c 59. TNA KV 4/472, 2 February 1950, p. 2. 60. TNA KV 2/1250, s. 455a. 61. TNA KV 2/1250, s. 456a. Three scientists were suspected of communist associations: Boris Davison, Morris Rigg and Nathan Shuman. 62. TNA KV 2/1250, s. 454a. 63. TNA KV 2/1250, s. 457a.

19. Arrest

1. Quoted in Anthony Summers, *Official and Confidential: The Secret Life of J. Edgar Hoover* (Victor Gollancz, 1993), p. 172. 2. Athan Theoharis and John Stuart Cox, *The Boss: J. Edgar Hoover and the Great American Inquisition* (Temple University Press, 1988), p. 256. 3. Summers, *Official and Confidential*, p. 172. 4. Lamphere and Shachtman, *The FBI–KGB Wars*, p. 139. 5. Handwritten note, 2 November 1949, on memo by D. M. Ladd, FBI 65-58805-33. Telegram from Patterson to MI5, 10 November 1949, TNA KV 6/134, s. 68a. 6. Timothy Gibbs, 'British and American Counter-Intelligence and the Atom Spies, 1941–1950', Ph.D. thesis, Faculty of History, Cambridge University, 2007, footnote 366 quotes an FBI memorandum to L. V. Boardman and A. H. Belmont of 1 February 1956: 'Both [ ] and [ ] work on this problem and work sheets have been made up and sent to [ ]. Also [ ] has a man in England working with [ ]. In turn, [ ] have a cryptographer working full-time at [ ].' Gibbs concludes: 'Though this portion of the document is highly sanitised, it seems safe to assume that were the words not blacked out, the sentence would describe the cooperation between GCHQ and AFSA on VENONA.' KGB files also lend support to this thesis: KGB file 84490, vol. 3, p. 129; Alexander Vassiliev, 'Yellow Notebook #1', in Vassiliev, *Alexander Vassiliev Papers, 1895–2011*, US Library of Congress, p. 94; see also chapter 22. 7. Sillitoe to Patterson, 1 February 1950, TNA KV 6/134, s. 141a. 8. Hoover to Admiral Souers, 2 February 1950, Fuchs FBI FOIA file 65-58805-586. 9. Ibid. 10. Alden Whitman, obituary of Lewis Strauss, *The New York Times*, 22 January 1974. 11. Lewis Strauss to Hoover, 2 February 1950, Fuchs FBI FOIA file 65-58805-587. 12. The Atomic Energy Commission Chair David Lillienthal as quoted by Ray Monk, *Inside the Centre: The Life of J. Robert Oppenheimer* (Jonathan Cape, 2012), p. 539. 13. Ibid, p. 499. 14. Rudolf Peierls, *Bird of Passage* (Princeton University Press, 1985), p. 223. 15. Telephone conversations involving Rudolf and Genia Peierls, and the Skinners, are logged in MI5 file TNA KV 2/1661, s. 234. 16. TNA KV 2/1251, s. 478d, 7 February 1950, 'Copy of telecheck on PEIERLS dated 3.2.50 mentioning FUCHS'. 17. Ibid. 18. 'It seemed . . . that you treated him as if he were your son.' Nobel Laureate Max Perutz to Rudolf Peierls, 19 May 1987, Peierls papers D56, Bodleian Library. 19. Genia Peierls' remarks to author, undated,

probably at Ettore Majorana Centre, Erice, Sicily, July 1974. 20. TNA KV 2/1251, s. 478d, 7 February 1950, 'Copy of telecheck on PEIERLS dated 3.2.50 mentioning FUCHS'. 21. Telephone conversations involving Rudolf and Genia Peierls, and the Skinners, are logged in MI5 file TNA KV 2/1661, s. 234. 22. TNA KV 2/1661, s. 233A; Athenaeum receipt, s. 242A. 23. TNA KV 2/1661, s. 234b, p. 2. 24. J. Marriott memorandum, 6 February 1950, TNA KV 2/1661, s. 233a. 25. Notes by Special Branch, 6 February 1950, TNA KV 2/1661, s. 234a; Peierls to Burt, 5 February 1950, TNA KV 2/1251, s. 465a. 26. TNA KV 2/1661, s. 233. 27. Peierls' call from London to his wife, 4 February 1950, TNA KV 2/1251, s. 487a. 28. Ibid, p. 2. 29. TNA KV 2/1661, s. 234b. 30. The letter of 4 February is dated 3 February, but mention of Rudolf Peierls' visit indicates that Fuchs put the wrong date. A typed transcript is at 'Copies of Letters sent to SKINNERs by FUCHS from Brixton Prison', TNA KV 2/1252, s. 518a. 31. Telephone check on Skinner's home, 4 February 1950, TNA KV 2/1270, s. 670a. 32. Sir John Cockroft's administrative assistant to Arnold as reported in J. C. Robertson, 'Visit by W/Cdr Arnold on 15.2.50', TNA KV 2/1252, s. 518b. 33. Letter from Max Born to Fuchs, 7 December 1941, TNA KV 2/1252, s. 510b, item 131. 34. As recalled by Max Perutz, *Is Science Necessary? Essays on Science and Scientists* (Oxford University Press, 1992), p. 142. 35. Edward Teller, *Memoirs: A Twentieth-Century Journey in Science and Politics* (Perseus, 2001), p. 275. 36. Quotes from correspondence between Peierls and Pryce are from Peierls' papers, Bodleian Library. 37. Peierls' interview of 6 February 1950 with Commander Burt and his letter to Burt that day are in MI5 file, TNA KV 2/1251, s. 462 and 468. See also TNA KV 2/1661, s. 233. 38. Peierls' letter to Commander Burt, 5 February 1950, TNA KV 2/1251, s. 465a, p. 2. 39. Peierls' letter to Commander Burt, 5 February 1950, TNA KV 2/1251, s. 465a. 40. Telephone check on Skinner's home, 6 February 1950, 9.14 p.m., TNA KV 2/1661, s. 234c. 41. A typed transcript of Genia Peierls' letter to Fuchs is in MI5 file TNA KV 2/1251, s. 466. A photostat of Fuchs' handwritten reply is at s. 478a. The original is in Peierls papers D52, Bodleian Library. 42. Ibid, s. 466a. 43. Ibid, s. 478a. 44. TNA KV 2/1251, s. 474a. Letters to K. Fuchs from H. Skinner (s. 474a) and E. Skinner (s. 475a), 7 February 1950. 45. TNA KV 2/1251, s. 476. The cousin, Gisela Wagner, was a teacher in London. Apart from having sent sporadic letters to Klaus Fuchs, which were opened by MI5, she plays no other significant role in this saga. 46. TNA KV 2/2080, s. 12c. 47. 'Copies of letters sent to SKINNERs by FUCHS from Brixton Prison', TNA KV 2/1252, s. 518a. 48. TNA KV 2/2080, s. 12b. Abstract from Skinner's letter to Fuchs, 10 February 1950. 49. Erna Skinner to Klaus Fuchs, 19 February 1950, TNA KV 2/1252, s. 527a. 50. Klaus Fuchs to Erna and Herbert Skinner, 27 February 1950, TNA KV 2/1253, s. 563d. 51. Erna and Herbert Skinner to Klaus Fuchs, 17 March 1950, TNA KV 2/1254, s. 624a. Subsequent correspondence was sparse. Herbert wrote two letters in the autumn, to which Fuchs replied on 20 December 1950, and Erna wrote to Fuchs on 22 February 1951 having been unable to write previously due to stress. TNA KV 2/2080 s. 19b. There is no record of any further communications between them. 52. Ruth Werner (Ursula Beurton), *Sonya's Report* (Vintage, 1999), p. 288. 53. 'Sonya flew into East Berlin on 28.02.50. It is dangerous to stay in England.' KGB file 84490, vol. 2, p. 205; Vassiliev, 'Yellow Notebook #1', p. 88. 54. Werner, *Sonya's Report*, p. 289.

20. Trials and Tribulations

1. M. Perrin to B. Hill, 7 February 1950, TNA KV 2/1263, s. 23A. 2. 'Note on conference held on 8.2.50 at Mr Christmas Humphreys Chambers', TNA KV 2/1263, s. 26a. 3. B. A. Hill to H. Morgan (for the DPP), 10 February 1950, TNA KV 2/1263, s. 27a. 4. *The Daily Telegraph*, 11 February 1950, TNA KV 2/1263, s. 29a. 5. '*Klaus Fuchs – Atomspion*', Klaus Fuchs interview with East German television in 1983, transcribed in *Zelluloid*, 31 March 1990, ISSN 07 24-76 56. 6. Address to the Court by Mr Christmas Humphreys, 10 February 1950, TNA KV 2/1263, s. 27b. 7. The charges specifically refer to Fuchs violating the Official Secrets Act, but it seems that no copy of any signature before 1944 was available at the Magistrates' Court. Humphreys alludes to Fuchs' career of espionage, which

implicitly is clearly referring to time in or soon after 1942, but at no stage is any date prior to 1944 mentioned explicitly. On 6 February Perrin was asked by Hill to produce a copy of Fuchs' signing of the Official Secrets Act and his naturalization 'at the conference on Wednesday [8 February]' (TNA KV 2/1263, serial 21a). The record of that conference makes no mention of whether Perrin produced the document, nor does a signed copy of the Official Secrets Act appear to have been produced in evidence for the magistrate. The exhibits presented at the trial make no mention of any signed security document by Fuchs prior to 1944. All the evidence suggests that the prosecution were unable to find proof that Fuchs had signed the undertaking in 1941, and so finessed their case accordingly. **8.** Address to the Court by Mr Christmas Humphreys, 10 February 1950, TNA KV 2/1263, s. 27b. **9.** This is an important indication that Fuchs might have confessed to Arnold before he did to Skardon. Arnold would later claim as much to Norman Moss, *Klaus Fuchs: The Man who Stole the Atom Bomb* (Grafton Books, 1987); see above, chapter 17, note 51. Only after the appearance of Alan Moorehead's book *The Traitors: The Double Life of Fuchs, Pontecorvo and Nunn May* (Dell, 1952) does Skardon become the inquisitorial hero, contrary to statements at the court. As we have seen, there was considerable worry that Fuchs might raise a defence based on a claim that Skardon induced him to confess, so by presenting the starting gun as a confession to Arnold on 26 January, the prosecution were able to finesse this delicate matter. It is notable that the interview with Skardon on 24 January was in Fuchs' bugged living room, the bugging of which had been discussed by Robertson and Arnold. Yet among the reports on Fuchs' movements on that day, there is no record of this critical conversation. See chapter 17, note 54. **10.** Notes on Magistrates' Court taken by B. A. Hill, 10 February 1950, TNA KV 2/1263, s. 28a. **11.** Ibid. **12.** For example, 'Atom Scientist's Alleged Confession: I Told Russia', *Daily Telegraph*, 11 February 1950, TNA KV 2/1263, s. 29a. **13.** Notes on Magistrates' Court taken by B. A. Hill, 10 February 1950, TNA KV 2/1263, s. 28a, section 3. **14.** Ibid, section 4. **15.** *Daily Telegraph*, 11 February, TNA KV 2/1263, s. 29a. **16.** Brigadier Taylor to Hon. Elwyn Jones MP, 7 February 1950, TNA KV 2/1263, s. 54a. **17.** Shawcross to the Director of Public Prosecutions, 18 February 1950, TNA KV 2/1263, s. 54a. Shawcross was re-elected, so his alert to a potential future Attorney General was unnecessary. **18.** Hill memorandum, 20 February 1950, TNA KV 2/1263, s. 49a. **19.** B. A. Hill meeting note, 23 February 1950, TNA KV 2/1263, s. 56a. **20.** Ibid. **21.** 'Conference Preceding the Trial of Dr Klaus Fuchs', 28 February 1950, TNA KV 2/1263, s. 62a. **22.** Perrin's report referred to Fuchs having been asked about the tritium weapon. TNA KV 2/1250, s. 442a says Fuchs handed over 'the general picture as far as it was then known to him of how the [so-called Hydrogen bomb] would work'. By 1953 opinion was that Fuchs had passed 'all he knew' about the H-bomb – see Lorna Arnold and Kate Pyne, *Britain and the H bomb* (Palgrave, 2001), pp. 37–8. Later, in 1960, Fuchs would create a different version for the KGB. He told them that while he had admitted to Perrin that he had passed atomic secrets, he did not admit to having passed 'materials on the hydrogen bomb'. See chapter 22. **23.** 'Conference Preceding the Trial of Dr Klaus Fuchs', 28 February 1950, TNA KV 2/1263, s. 62a. **24.** Ibid. **25.** TNA KV 2/1263, s. 62a, 'Note of Conference Preceding the Trial of Dr Klaus Emil Fuchs'. An unidentified person has drawn attention to this with two vertical pencilled lines and an exclamation mark in the margin alongside. **26.** Fuchs to Under-Secretary of State, Home Office, 28 June 1950, TNA KV 2/1255, s. 710a. **27.** This habit of Lord Goddard is recorded in many places, including *Inside Justice – Investigative Unit for Alleged Miscarriage of Justice*: http://www.insidejusticeuk.com/articles/a-principle-of-injustice/113 **28.** The description of the trial follows from the Special Branch report of proceedings, 1 March 1950, TNA KV 2/1264, s. 63b. **29.** Certificate of Naturalization and Oath of Allegiance, 31 July 1942, TNA KV 2/1263, s. 19a. **30.** Mike Rossiter, *The Spy who Changed the World* (Headline, 2014), p. 330, also notes this inconsistency and draws attention to the absence of 1941 and 1942 in the indictment as well as the absence of any evidence that Fuchs actually met 'Sonya' in Birmingham [*sic*] in 1943. **31.** The description of the trial follows from the Special Branch report of proceedings, 1 March 1950, TNA KV 2/1264, s. 63b. **32.** Page 7, line 14 in copy of Fuchs' statement of 27 January 1950, Exhibit number 3 at his trial; page 8 of Fuchs' original handwritten signed statement. Both copies

474 NOTES TO PP. 349–64

are in the 'Prosecution volume', TNA KV 2/1263, the National Archives.   33. The description of the trial follows from the Special Branch report of proceedings, 1 March 1950, TNA KV 2/1264, s. 63b.

21. Going for Gold

1. 21 February 1950. Fuchs FBI FOIA file 65-58805-705; Ladd's accusation of 2 March is in ibid, s. 706.   2. Hoover memo to Ladd, 28 February 1950, Fuchs FBI FOIA file 65-58805-447.   3. FBI Summary brief 65-58805, vol. 38, section C, 12 February 1951.   4. TNA KV 2/1263, s. 17a; telegram from Sir Percy Sillitoe to J. Edgar Hoover, 6 February 1950.   5. According to the FBI report, she was estranged from her husband, whom she claimed to be a sex pest. She also claimed that the father of her three children was one Konstantin Lafazanos, a former fellow student of Robert's at Harvard, a fact which apparently Lafazanos acknowledged. It is unclear whether these were facts or fantasies, and to what extent they were linked to her breakdown.   6. TNA KV 6/135, s. 163a, Patterson to Director General, 24 February 1950, report of FBI interview on 2 February 1950.   7. Ibid, p. 3.   8. Ibid.   9. TNA KV 6/134, s. 145a. Undated summary, 'shown to Mr Whitson on 4 February 1950'. The document refers to 'Top Secret Source', which is undoubtedly VENONA. For analysis that identifies this as a GCHQ breakthrough, see below.   10. There was no mention of Naval research in the decrypted VENONA messages, nor did Gold have any special link with the US Navy. In 1944 the British Mission in New York were aware that the US Navy labs were 'building a pilot plant working with thermal diffusion' – (FBI FOIA file 65-58805-188, 18 January 1950). It appears that when GOOSE's link to diffusion was discovered, the intelligence analysts erroneously assumed that GOOSE was involved with this US Navy venture.   11. Comparison of quotes of VENONA decrypts in FBI files at that time – such as FOIA 65-58805-7 – with the finally released forms, as quoted in chapter 13 here, suggests that GCHQ's analysis from December 1949 put substantial detail into often skeletal structures. See also chapter 13, note 21, and chapter 22, notes 22 and 27, with a specific attribution to the role of GCHQ in the decryption.   12. VENONA 1390, 1 October 1944: https://www.nsa.gov/news-features/declassified-documents/venona/dated/1944/assets/files/1oct_aerosols_ddt.pdf.   This report is in the NSA style (chapter 22, note 22) and also contains two examples of non-British English (at least in 1949) – spelling 'organized' rather than 'organised', and the presence of the Americanism 'chucked'.   13. D. Ladd to H. Fletcher, 'Purpose: Identification of REST and GOOSE', 27 September 1949, Fuchs FBI FOIA file 65-58805-7.   14. Quoted in Richard Rhodes, *Dark Sun: The Making of the Hydrogen Bomb* (Simon and Schuster, 2005), p. 93, and Gold FBI FOIA files 65-57449-591.   15. R. Radosh and J. Milton, *The Rosenberg File: A Search for the Truth*, 2nd edn. (Yale University Press, 1997), pp. 34–7, cited by Timothy Gibbs, 'British and American Counter-Intelligence and the Atom Spies, 1941–1950', Ph.D. thesis, Faculty of History, Cambridge University, 2007, footnote 579.   16. Mr Fletcher to Mr Ladd: 'To obtain authority to interview Kristel Heineman', 1 February 1950. Fuchs FBI FOIA file 65-58805-84.   17. R. J. Lamphere and T. Shachtman, *The FBI–KGB War: A Special Agent's Story* (Random House, 1986), p. 139.   18. TNA KV 6/134, s. 147a.   19. A mole – whether in London or Paris is unknown – alerted Moscow to the inquiry. KGB file 84490, vol. 2, p. 292, Alexander Vassiliev, 'Yellow Notebook #1', in Vassiliev, *Alexander Vassiliev Papers, 1895–2011*, US Library of Congress, p. 89; and 84490, vol. 3, p. 130, Vassiliev, 'Yellow Notebook #1', p. 94.   20. Skardon memo, 8 February 1950, TNA KV 6/134, s. 147a.   21. MI5 files do not give a clear indication of the three names, but Gold's image appears to have been included from the middle of March 1950.   22. TNA KV 2/1252, s. 518b.   23. Ibid.   24. TNA KV 6/134, s. 161b, headed 'Information obtained from Fuchs on 23.2.50'. There is no indication of how or where this was obtained.   25. Lish Whitson to John Marriott, 24 February 1950, TNA KV 6/134, s. 161a.   26. Fuchs to Skardon, 28 February 1950, in MI5 file TNA KV 6/135, s. 187a and TNA KV 2/1879 s. 545a.   27. FBI 65-58805– vol. 14, D. M. Ladd to Director Hoover, 14 March 1950.   28. Lamphere and Shachtman, *The FBI–KGB War*, p. 139.   29. TNA KV 6/135, s. 189a.   30. TNA KV 2/1254, s. 612.   31. KGB file 40159, vol. 3,

p. 478; Alexander Vassiliev, 'Black Notebook', p. 133: 'Charles's sister – Ant'. That Kristel was an integral part of KGB plans is visible in Vassiliev, 'Yellow Notebook #1', p. 67, where on 21 January 1944 the GRU passed to the KGB instructions 'for contacting F[uchs] through his sister, whose last name is Heineman'. 32. 13 March 1950, Fuchs FBI FOIA file 65-58805-713. 33. Letter to Attorney General J. Howard McGrath, 13 March 1950; Gibbs, 'British and American Counter-Intelligence and the Atom Spies, 1941–1950', footnote 488. 34. Letter to Admiral Souers, 22 March 1950, Fuchs FBI FOIA file 65-58805-969. 35. D. M. Ladd to the Director, 13 March, Fuchs FBI FOIA file 65-58805-713. 36. Patterson to the Director General, 9 March 1950, TNA KV 6/135, s. 194a. 37. Director General reply to Patterson, 14 March 1950, TNA KV 6/135, s. 195a. 38. D. de Bardeleben, Chief, Liaison Section, US Embassy, to Sir Percy Sillitoe, TNA KV 2/1254, s. 622z. 39. Guy Liddell response to Cimperman, 26 March 1950, TNA KV 6/135, s. 200a. 40. Fuchs FBI FOIA file 65-58805, vol. 27, FBI memo on conversation with Senator McMahon, 23 March 1950; Gibbs, 'British and American Counter-Intelligence', footnote 496. 41. Fuchs FBI FOIA file 65-58805, vol. 14; Gibbs, 'British and American Counter-Intelligence', footnote 481. 42. Letter to Director D. M. Ladd et al., 5 April 1950. Fuchs FBI FOIA file 65-58805, vol. 22; Gibbs, 'British and American Counter-Intelligence', footnote 495. 43. This inference is due to Gibbs, 'British and American Counter-Intelligence', chapter 3. 44. Minutes of Official Committee on Atomic Energy, 8 May 1950, TNA CAB 134/31. 45. The identification of this event as a bag-job is due to Rhodes, Dark Sun, p. 425, and the note on p. 649. See FBI file 65-58805-1245, p. 5. (Rhodes appears to have made a typo and refers to this incorrectly as 1239, an unrelated document with only a single page.) However, he assumes this took place 'sometime in February or early March'; the only mention of a date in the files is its delivery on 6 May and there is no indication that delivery of the document was delayed. The bag-job – if Rhodes is correct – would seem to have taken place after some delay, however, as Gold did not become the prime suspect for a while. Exactly when remained a source of contention between MI5 and FBI later, when credit for identifying Gold was disputed. See Patterson to Sillitoe, 25 May 1950, TNA KV 6/135, s. 208a, for more about this conflict. 46. TNA KV 2/1255, s. 689a, Skardon report of interviews. 47. TNA KV 2/1255, s. 689a, record by W. J. Skardon written on 9 June 1950. 48. Ladd to Hoover, 'Memorandum on Identification of Harry Gold', 25 May 1950. FBI FOIA file 65-58805-1245, p. 6. 49. TNA KV 6/135, s. 211a. Report of 24 May, 'Mr Clegg opened this interview by reviewing what FUCHS had told them so far, and informed him that Harry GOLD had confessed and been arrested.' 50. Letter from Hoover to Cimperman, 23 May 1950, FBI FOIA file 65-58805-1195, and TNA KV 6/135, s. 205a. Gibbs, 'British and American Counter-Intelligence', p. 221, footnote 601, comments 'The issue of when Gold was identified by Fuchs became a major issue in the Rosenberg case, with certain Rosenberg supporters alleging that Fuchs never identified Gold, or that he only identified him once Gold was in custody', and 'Part of the confusion may have stemmed from the fact that according to the Clegg/Lamphere Report, Fuchs identified Gold on the 24th, but did not confirm the identification by signing the back of the photograph until the 26th.' It is clear from the files that the warrant for Gold was issued in the (Philadelphia) evening of 23 May (65-58805-1245, p. 7). Fuchs had stated on 22 May that the photos were 'very likely' those of his contact; he made a positive identification of Gold only on 24 May. Thus the chronology appears to confirm that Fuchs only identified Gold positively after the latter was in custody. 51. Fuchs to the FBI, 20 May 1950. FBI FOIA file 65-58805-1324, p. 7, and photo of Gold attached to pp. 8–12. 52. TNA KV 1255, s. 689. In detail this was, of course, wrong, as Fuchs met Gold on two occasions, but not both in the same month. Fuchs' signed statement of 29 May admitted that he and Gold met once in June 1945 and again 'a few months later', possibly in September.

22. Aftermath

1. Pontecorvo's life as scientist and possible spy are covered in Frank Close, Half Life: The Divided Life of Bruno Pontecorvo, Scientist or Spy (Basic Books, 2012). 2. Timothy Gibbs,

'British and American Counter-Intelligence and the Atom Spies, 1941–1950'. Ph.D. thesis, Faculty of History, Cambridge University, 2007, 'Introduction: The Politicisation of Espionage'. **3**. Had Groves' desire for compartmentalization been adopted, it would have slowed technical progress while doing nothing to prevent Fuchs' espionage. As Gibbs comments in ibid, chapter 1 – 'Compartmentalization and the Atom Spies' – 'Fuchs was employed in the Theoretical Division where the critical issue of plutonium implosion was first addressed and it was the resolution of this problem that most perplexed the bomb's designers. By Fuchs' own admission, the most important information he handed to the Soviets was the complete design of the plutonium bomb, details which he would have known even if compartmentalization had been rigidly enforced.' **4**. Leslie Groves, *Now It Can Be Told* (Harper, 1962), p. 144. **5**. 16 and 17 January 1944, TNA KV 2/1245, s. 39–42. **6**. Groves, *Now It Can Be Told*, p. 144. **7**. *Sunday Dispatch*, 5 March 1950, in assorted press cuttings, TNA KV 2/1254. **8**. 'The Case of Dr Klaus Fuchs', memo by James Robertson, 2 March 1950, TNA KV 2/1253, s. 568c, Appendix A. **9**. Ibid. **10**. R. J. Lamphere and T. Shachtman, *The FBI–KGB War* (Random House, 1986), p. 134. See also Gibbs, 'British and American Counter-Intelligence', footnote 411 and commentary therein. **11**. 'Preparation of brief on Klaus Fuchs,' 12 February 1950, Fuchs FBI FOIA file 65-58805-479. **12**. 'Klaus Fuchs Espionage'. Letter from D. M. Ladd to A. H. Belmont, 18 December 1953, Fuchs FBI FOIA file 65-58805-1544, p. 3. **13**. Chapman Pincher has long argued that Roger Hollis was that person, and responsible for shielding Klaus Fuchs, among others. It is not possible to draw conclusions from available files. Timothy Gibbs assesses this theory in chapter 3 of 'British and American Counter-Intelligence', p. 162, and also questions whether access to these documents would in practice have made significant difference to the history. For example: 'Had Fuchs been questioned over his connection with Halperin, he would undoubtedly have confirmed that they had never met and that the record of his address in the notebook was not a cause for suspicion. The connection between the pair was explained by Fuchs at his first interrogation and stemmed from the fact that his sister Kristel, whose name also appeared in the address book, was an acquaintance of Halperin.' **14**. MI5 records imply that they first learned of these documents only on 4 October 1949, TNA KV 2/1247, s. 230c. In his critique of MI5, Antony Percy, *Misdefending the Realm* (University of Buckingham, 2018), suggested on p. 255 that early (1946) references to Halperin were removed from Fuchs' file and 'the record edited to make it appear that the FBI had only recently [October 1949] informed MI5 of the discoveries in Halperin's diary.' He offers no direct evidence to support this. **15**. US press reaction, TNA KV 2/1254, s. 614a. **16**. Sir Percy Sillitoe, Memorandum for the Prime Minister, 'Exposure of Dr Klaus Fuchs', TNA PREM 8/1279. **17**. Notice of Parliamentary Questions, 7 March 1950, TNA KV 2/1253, s. 578a. **18**. Confidential notes for Minister, 6 March 1950, TNA PREM 8/1279. The other reviews were listed as June 1942 (naturalization), November 1943 (exit permit to USA), January 1944 (extension of permit to reside in USA), and December 1947 (grant of established status at Harwell). The Prime Minister was unaware of the decision to withhold information about Fuchs' 'proclivities' in January 1944. **19**. Number 2 in Notes for Supplementaries, TNA PREM 8/1279, 6 March 1950. **20**. Extract from Prime Minister's Speech in the Debate on the address: Official Report 6.3.50, cols 71–2, TNA PREM 8/1279. **21**. Gibbs makes this point in 'British and American Counter-Intelligence', based on analysis of the Gold case in R. Radosh and J. Milton, *The Rosenberg File: A Search for the Truth*, 2nd edn (Yale University Press, 1997). **22**. There is no public record of how the initial decryption of these messages was shared between Arlington Hall and GCHQ. All we have are the final VENONA reports released by the US National Security Agency on various occasions between the 1950s and 1970s when decryption of a message was either successfully completed or terminated (3,262 examples are available at https://archive.org/details/thevenonafiles?sort=creatorSo rter). Reports come in two distinct styles, which distinguish their origins. The most immediately noticeable difference is the presence or absence of a prominent redacted circle forming a solid black disc at the top right of the document. The majority of documents have this character. The content of these documents points to this class having originated in GCHQ and their number confirms there was a substantial input from GCHQ to VENONA. An example of this category is the final report of the decrypted Russian message referred to on page 218. In common with others of this style, the report is typewritten, contains a numeric date written in the British style of day/month/year, and has a copy number, which has been added by hand to a typed original. The reports in this format contain some British idioms or spellings (such as the mention of 'postal despatch' in the message that led to Gold's exposure and 'speciality' in the message that first identified the presence of a British spy). Their structure is consistent with a master typed copy having been multiply reproduced, each copy then numbered by hand before being sent to customers. Potential customers for GCHQ reports would have included British security agencies, the Foreign Office and relevant embassies, each with a unique identifier. The United Kingdom's intelligence alliance with Australia, New Zealand, Canada and the United States would also make the corresponding agencies in these countries potential users of this information. In the USA this would have been the NSA, whose copies are now publicly available, but retain their GCHQ copy number. The actual number varies with the period of release (e.g. 205 in the 1950s, 201 in the 1960s and 301 for releases in the late 1970s). The code word for the

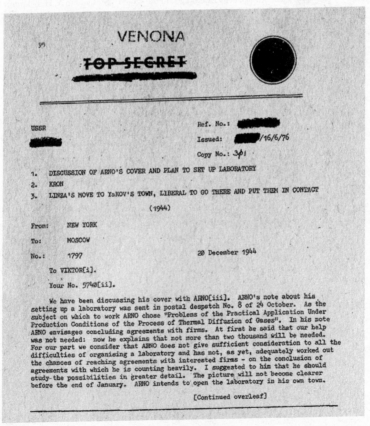

A report in the British style

project was also periodically updated; initially BRIDE, it became DRUG during the early 1960s and then VENONA from 1969 – the name that was in force when the public releases eventually took place and by which the entire project has become known. Above the copy number on all the documents of this class is a release date uniformly in the British numeric style of day/month/year. This alone is not conclusive proof of a British origin, however, as the US military has used the day/month/year format to avoid confusion, but the consistent correlation with the other features is compelling. This class of documents is consistent with being copies delivered to the NSA from an outside source that used British spelling and style. This set contrasts with reports originating in the USA. These have no copy number and are in a different format, although they share the common code names BRIDE, DRUG and VENONA. They are notable by the occasional appearance of American spelling or

---

TOP ~~SECRET DAUNT~~ DRUG

Reissue

1/53

From: NEW YORK

To: MOSCOW

No.: 1390

1 October 1944

To VIKTOR[i].

According to GOOSE's [GUS'][ii] latest advice CONSTRUCTOR[iii] has stopped working at the Cheturgy[a] Design Company where jointly with Henry GOLVINE[b] and Art WEBER he was working on the production of BUNA-5. At the same time CONSTRUCTOR collaborated on the Aerosol problem (the work has partly been sent you) with HENLIG [KhENLIG][iv]. In both cases his partners cheated CONSTRUCTOR. They appropriated his work and chucked him out. Right now C.[K.] at his laboratory at 114 East 32nd Street with the help of the Grover Tank Company and the Bridgeport Brass Company has organized his own company and in the course of two or three weeks proposes to finish work on Aerosol and DDT and consolidate his position with these.

According to GOOSE's advice he had known about the disagreements for three weeks or so but he considered them a temporary quarrel and [B% did not] [1 group unrecoverable] us

[40 groups unrecoverable]

sum of 100 dollars a month. Telegraph your decision. We shall advise in detail by post.

#787

MAY[MAJ][v]
1 October

Notes: [a] Cheturgy: That is: Chemurgy. "Cheturgy" results from misreading a cursive English "m" as a Russian "t".

[b] GOLVINE: ~~This might represent HOLVINE.~~ ... GOLVINNE

Comments:
   [i] VIKTOR: Lt. Gen. P.M. FITIN.

   [ii] GUS': Harry GOLD.

   [iii] CONSTRUCTOR: Abraham BROTHMAN.

   [iv] HENLIG: Theodore HEILIG. KhENLIG instead of KhEJLIG is probably due to misreading.

   [v] MAJ: Stepan APRESYaN.

An American report linking GOOSE and CONSTRUCTOR

idioms and also the lack of a redacted solid circle at the upper right corner. Dates are never in the British (or military) numeric style but have the month spelled out by name. There appears to be a consistent correlation among released reports – namely presence or absence of copy number, redacted black circle with British numeric date style and spelling/idioms – that distinguishes US and UK sources. The final VENONA reports relating to Fuchs all share the same 'British' style and are consistent with the ultimate decryption of these atomic espionage messages having been achieved at GCHQ. While this is not direct evidence for the original decryption of the message that led to Gold's exposure being due to GCHQ, it is nonetheless consistent with the inferences drawn from MI5 and FBI files at the time that GCHQ had a substantial input, and further calls into question Hoover's promotion of the capture of Fuchs and associated agents as being entirely an American FBI triumph.   23. KGB file 84490, vol. 2, p. 60, London to Centre, 3 February 1950; Alexander Vassiliev, 'Yellow Notebook #1', in Vassiliev, *Vassiliev Papers, 1895–2011*, US Library of Congress, p. 8.   24. New York to Moscow Centre, 6 February 1950, KGB file 86194, vol. 2, p. 260; Vassiliev, 'Yellow Notebook #1', p. 109.   25. KGB file 84490, vol. 2, p. 122, A. Raina report on Charles, 6 February 1950; Vassiliev, 'Yellow Notebook #1', pp. 85–6.   26. KGB file 84490, vol. 2, p. 125, A. Raina report on Charles, 6 February 1950; Vassiliev, 'Yellow Notebook #1', p. 86.   27. KGB file 84490, vol. 2, p. 27, V. Zorin note 'To Comrade J. V. Stalin' (V. Zorin 5 February 1950; written by Raina); Vassiliev, 'Yellow Notebook #1', p. 91. Zorin's role is described briefly in Christopher Andrew and Vasili Mitrokhin, *The Mitrokhin Archive* (Penguin, 2000), p. 191.   28. KGB file 84490, vol. 2, p. 129; Vassiliev, 'Yellow Notebook #1', p. 87.   29. KGB file 84490, vol. 2, p. 129; Vassiliev, 'Yellow Notebook #1', p. 87.   30. KGB file 84490, vol. 2, p. 153; Vassiliev, 'Yellow Notebook #1', p. 87.   31. KGB file 84490, vol. 2, p. 168; Vassiliev, 'Yellow Notebook #1', p. 87.   32. KGB file 84490, vol. 2, p. 274; Vassiliev, 'Yellow Notebook #1', p. 88.   33. Telegram from the British Embassy Moscow to the Foreign Office, 8 March 1950, TNA KV 2/1253, s. 600a.   34. KGB file 84490, vol. 2, p. 274; Vassiliev, 'Yellow Notebook #1', p. 88.   35. KGB file 84490, vol. 2, p. 205; Vassiliev, 'Yellow Notebook #1', p. 88.   36. KGB file 84490, vol. 2, p. 279; Vassiliev, 'Yellow Notebook #1', p. 89.   37. KGB file 84490, vol. 2, p. 275; Vassiliev, 'Yellow Notebook #1', p. 88.   38. Vassiliev, 'Yellow Notebook #1', p. 92, refers to p. 167 in an unidentified KGB file, possibly 84490, vol. 3.   39. KGB file 84490, vol. 3, p. 129; Vassiliev, 'Yellow Notebook #1', p. 94.   40. KGB file 84490, vol. 3, p. 130; Vassiliev, 'Yellow Notebook #1', p. 94.   41. KGB file 84490, vol. 3, p. 130; Vassiliev, 'Yellow Notebook #1', p. 94.   42. Gibbs, 'British and American Counter-Intelligence', chapter 2.   43. Groves, *Now It Can Be Told*, p. 408. For more on the position advocated by me, see F. M. Szasz, *British Scientists and the Manhattan Project: The Los Alamos Years* (Macmillan, 1992), p. xviii.   44. M. Gowing, 'Nuclear Weapons and the Special Relationship', in William R. Louis and H. Bull (eds), *The Special Relationship: Anglo-American Relations since 1945* (Oxford University Press, 1986), as discussed in Gibbs, 'British and American Counter-Intelligence', footnote 868.   45. Minutes of the Official Committee on Atomic Energy, 2 January 1950, TNA CAB 134/31. The UK had copious uranium supplies from the Belgian Congo.   46. Congressional Record of the Senate, 81st Congress, 2nd Session, 20 February 1950 (1954–7). The text of the speech is available at http://historymatters.gmu. edu/d/6456.   47. TNA CAB 126/148, Anglo-US-Canadian Security talks, March 1950 to January 1954, Report from Washington to Roger Makins, F. Hoyer Millar, 27 April 1950.   48. Letter from Robert Lamphere to Anthony Murphy, 25 January 1994, Robert Lamphere Collection, Georgetown University, Washington DC.   49. *New York Times*, 5 February 1950.   50. Official Committee on Atomic Energy, Minutes of 8th Meeting, 11 September 1950, TNA CAB 134/31.   51. Autobiographical account, Alec Longair quoted in Gibbs, 'British and American Counter-Intelligence', p. 320.   52. British Foreign Office file FO371/84837, TNA FO 371.   53. MI5 file KV 2/1889, memo 121b.   54. Patterson to Sillitoe, 25 May 1950, TNA KV 6/135, s. 208a.   55. Graham Farmelo, *Churchill's Bomb: A Hidden History of Science, War and Politics* (Faber and Faber, 2013), p. 370.   56. William Penney, quoted in Brian Cathcart, *Test of Greatness* (John Murray, 1994), p 107. One of the university professors would have been Peierls. The identity of the other was probably Frisch or G. Taylor (Cathcart email, 12 December 2017). **57.** The test took place on 3 October off Trimouille Island. Margaret Gowing and Lorna Arnold, *Independence and Deterrence, vol. 2: Policy Making* (Macmillan, 1974), p. 471. **58.** Letter from Sir Freddie Morgan, Controller of Atomic Energy, to Guy Liddell, 28 May 1952, TNA KV 2/1258, s. 918c. **59.** Kate Pyne, cited in M. S. Goodman, 'The Grandfather of the Hydrogen Bomb? Anglo-American Intelligence and Klaus Fuchs', *Historical Studies in the Physical and Biological Sciences*, vol. 34, part 1 (2003), pp. 1–22. **60.** See for example ibid, p. 17. **61.** Lorna Arnold and Kate Pyne, *Britain and the H Bomb* (Palgrave, 2001), pp. 25–6 and 93–4. **62.** Lord Flowers, interview with Mike Goodman, September 2002, cited in Goodman, 'The Grandfather of the Hydrogen Bomb?', note 104; see also paragraph 3. **63.** Letter from Sir Freddie Morgan, Controller for Atomic Energy, to William Penney, 9 February 1953, TNA ES 1/493. See also Goodman, 'The Grandfather of the Hydrogen Bomb?', p. 16, paragraph 3. **64.** Arnold and Pyne, *Britain and the H Bomb*, pp. 37–8. **65.** Author's conversation with Lorna Arnold, 30 August 2013, and with a senior British physicist, name withheld, 2016. **66.** Lorna Arnold interview, 30 August 2013. Her personal opinion also endorses a statement by Gennady Gorelik, 'A Russian Perspective on the Father of the American H-Bomb (April 2002): http://people.bu.edu/gorelik/Minnesota_02_web.htm.

23. Father and Son

1. Telegram, Washington Embassy to Cabinet Office, about difficulties over an American visa for Peierls, 23 August 1951, TNA KV 2/1662, s. 324b. **2.** Extract from *Daily Worker*, 2 February 1950, TNA KV 2/1661, s. 246b. **3.** Telecheck on Atomic Scientists Association, TNA KV 2/1661, s. 246a, 20 February 1950. **4.** Director General of MI5 to Chief Constable of Birmingham, TNA KV 2/1661, s. 252a and 253a, 31 May 1950. **5.** Chief Constable of Birmingham to Director General of MI5, TNA KV 2/1661, s. 253a, 5 June 1950. **6.** Chief Constable of Birmingham to Director General of MI5, 11 September 1950, TNA KV 2/1661, s. 261a. **7.** Chief Constable Dodd to Sir Percy Sillitoe, 11 December 1950, TNA KV 2/1661, s. 267a. **8.** C. Grose-Hodge, 'Rudolf Ernst PEIERLS', December 1950, TNA KV 2/1661, s. 263a. The conclusion in the original draft was dressed with double negatives, 'Such associations cannot be said not to constitute a security risk were PEIERLS to have access to secret information.' **9.** Ibid, s. 269a, Telegram to S.L.O., New Delhi, 11 December 1950. **10.** E. W. Battersby to Ministry of Supply, 28 December 1950, TNA KV 2/1661, s. 273a. **11.** Ibid, s. 275a, 3 January 1951. **12.** E. W. Battersby, note for Peierls' personal file, 5 January 1951, TNA KV 2/1661, s. 277a. **13.** Lord Cherwell as quoted in a letter to Grosse-Hodge of MI5, TNA KV 2/1661, s. 284a. **14.** Sir Charles Darwin, TNA KV 2/1661, s. 285a. **15.** FBI Report, Patterson to Director General, 25 January 1951, TNA KV 2/1661, s. 288a. **16.** Ibid, p. 3. **17.** Ibid, p. 4. **18.** FBI Report, Patterson to Director General, 25 January 1951, TNA KV 2/1661, s. 288a, p. 7. **19.** Top Secret Telegram ANCAM460 from BJSM Washington to Cabinet Office, 23 August 1951, TNA KV 2/1661, s. 324b. **20.** Ibid, s. 330a. **21.** Ibid, s. 332a. **22.** Peierls papers, Bodleian Library, A15. **23.** *Intelligence Digest*, 10 September 1951, vol. 13, chapter 10, p. 17, and vol. 13, no. 155, October 1951, pp. 7 and 8. Peierls Supplementary Papers, Bodleian Library, Box A. **24.** See Kim Philby, *My Silent War: The Autobiography of a Spy* (Arrow, 2018), chapter 12; for his probable role in Pontecorvo's defection, see Frank Close, *Half Life: The Divided Life of Bruno Pontecorvo, Scientist or Spy* (Basic Books and OneWorld, 2015), pp. 201–7. **25.** Peierls supplementary papers, Bodleian Library, Box A. **26.** TNA KV 2/1663, s. 355a, 18 March 1954. **27.** This is the author's summary of TNA KV 2/1663, s. 355a, 18 March 1954, and TNA KV 2/1661, s. 280a, 6 January 1951. **28.** Rudolf Peierls, *Bird of Passage* (Princeton University Press, 1985), p. 325. Deacon's lawyers stated in open court that the book's claims were 'without foundation' and withdrew them 'unreservedly'. Copy of transcript in possession of Peierls family, seen by the author. See also p. 757 in Sabine Lee, *Sir Rudolf Peierls: Selected Private and Scientific Correspondence*, vol. 2 (World Scientific, 2007). **29.** Letter from W. J. Skardon in support of Fuchs' retention of citizenship, TNA KV 2/1255, s. 711a. **30.** Carbon copy in Peierls papers,

Bodleian Library, file D52; transcription at Entry 673, p. 622, in Lee, *Sir Rudolf Peierls*. **31.** KGB File 84490, vol. 5, '"Bras" – Klaus Fuchs', p. 354; Alexander Vassiliev, 'Yellow Notebook #1', in Vassiliev, *Alexander Vassiliev Papers, 1895–2011* (US Library of Congress), p. 57. **32.** KGB File 84490, vol. 5, '"Bras" – Klaus Fuchs', p. 368, Berlin Control to A. M. Korotov, 28 April 1959; Vassiliev, 'Yellow Notebook #1', p. 57. **33.** KGB File 84490, vol. 5, '"Bras"– Klaus Fuchs', p. 369; Vassiliev, 'Yellow Notebook #1', p. 58. **34.** KGB File 84490, vol. 5, '"Bras" – Klaus Fuchs', p. 329, A. Panyushkin to S. N. Kruglov, December 1953; Vassiliev, 'Yellow Notebook #1', p. 56. **35.** KGB File 84490, vol. 5, '"Bras" – Klaus Fuchs', p. 369, A. Panyushkin to S. N. Kruglov, December 1953; Vassiliev, 'Yellow Notebook #1', p. 58. **36.** KGB File 84490, vol. 5, '"Bras" – Klaus Fuchs', p. 381, A. Panyushkin to S. N. Kruglov, December 1953; Vassiliev, 'Yellow Notebook #1', p. 60. **37.** 'Klaus Fuchs – Atomspion', Klaus Fuchs interview with East German television in 1983, transcribed in *Zelluloid*, 31 March 1990, ISSN 07 24–76 56. **38.** Klaus Fuchs-Kittowski, 'Klaus Fuchs and the Humanist Task of Science', *Nature, Society and Thought*, vol. 16, no. 2 (2003), pp. 133–70. **39.** Fuchs' Stasi file contained nothing significant, which suggests that the 'real file' was either transported to the KGB Archives in Moscow or shredded around 1989. Sabine Lee, personal communication. **40.** Klaus Fuchs, as reported on p. 225 in Alexander Feklisov (with the assistance of Sergei Kostin), *The Man behind the Rosenbergs* (Enigma Books, 2001), and quoted on p. 151 of Fuchs-Kittowski, 'Klaus Fuchs and the Humanist Task of Science', pp. 133–70. **41.** KGB file 84490, vol. 6, '"Bras" – Klaus Fuchs', p. 28, Berlin Centre to A. M. Korotov, 14 December 1959; Vassiliev, 'Yellow Notebook #1', p. 60. **42.** KGB file 84490, vol. 6, '"Bras" – Klaus Fuchs', p. 30, Berlin Centre to A. M. Korotov, 15 March 1960; Vassiliev, 'Yellow Notebook #1', p. 61. **43.** KGB file 84490, vol. 6, '"Bras" – Klaus Fuchs', p. 31, Berlin Centre to A. M. Korotov, 15 March 1960. CC CPSU [Central Committee, Communist Party of the Soviet Union] memo, 17 May 1960; Vassiliev, 'Yellow Notebook #1', p. 61. **44.** KGB file 84490, vol. 6, '"Bras" – Klaus Fuchs', p. 38, Berlin Centre to A. M. Korotov, 15 March 1960, 'Report on work with "Charles" during his stay in Moscow'; Vassiliev, 'Yellow Notebook #1', p. 62. **45.** This occasion is described, with further source references, in Close, *Half Life*, p. 281. **46.** KGB file 84490, vol. 6, 'Report on a meeting with "Bras" [Fuchs]', p. 37, 28 May 1960; Vassiliev, 'Yellow Notebook #1', p. 61. **47.** KGB file 84490, vol. 6, 'Report on a meeting with "Bras" [Fuchs]', pp. 43–7, 28 May 1960; Vassiliev, 'Yellow Notebook #1', pp. 63–5. **48.** KGB file 84490, vol. 6, 'Report on a meeting with "Bras" [Fuchs]', p. 44, 28 May 1960; Vassiliev, 'Yellow Notebook #1', p. 63. **49.** KGB file 84490, vol. 6, 'Report on a meeting with "Bras" [Fuchs]', p. 45; Vassiliev, 'Yellow Notebook #1', p. 64. **50.** 'Fuchs interview with Mr Perrin and Mr Skardon at Room 055 on 30.1.50', TNA KV 2/1250, s. 442a, says Fuchs 'gave to the Russian agent the essential nuclear physics data' of the 'so-called Hydrogen bomb and about a highly secret component material used in connection therewith'. This most probably refers to the use of lithium deuteride in the weapon. Fuchs handed over 'the general picture as far as it was then known to him of how the weapon would work'. **51.** KGB file 84490, vol. 6, p. 48: 'Report to Comrade N. S. Krushchev from Committee of State Security Chairman A. Shelepin', 25 June 1960; Vassiliev, 'Yellow Notebook #1', p. 65.

Epilogue

1. Interview by Mr Serpell, 23 March 1950, TNA KV 2/1270, s. 687a. **2.** 'Fuchs . . . was placed in a camp designed to accommodate avowed and unrepentant Nazis', Alan Moorehead, *The Traitors: The Double Life of Fuchs, Pontecorvo and Nunn May* (Dell, 1952), p. 85. **3.** MI5's mini-portrait of Roger Hollis is at https://www.mi5.gov.uk/sir-roger-hollis **4.** This remark probably originated with Denys Wilkinson. **5.** *Harwell: The Atomic Energy Research Establishment*, Ministry of Supply and Central Office of Information, London, 1952. **6.** Report of the 82nd US Congress Joint Committee on Atomic Espionage: Soviet Atomic Espionage April 1951. available at http://archive.org/stream/sovietatomicespi1951unit/ sovietatomicespi1951unit_djvu.txt. **7.** Klaus Fuchs-Kittowski, 'Klaus Fuchs and the Humanist Task of Science', *Nature, Society and Thought*, vol. 16, no. 2 (2003), pp. 133–70, esp. p. 157.   8. Ibid. p. 159.   9. This award was abolished in 1991 and replaced in the Russian Federation by the Order of Friendship.   10. President of the National Academy M. V. Kel'dysh, cited by Alexander Feklisov (with the assistance of Sergei Kostin), *The Man Behind the Rosenbergs* (Enigma Books, 2001), p. 261, and quoted by Klaus Fuchs-Kittowski, 'Klaus Fuchs and the Humanist Task of Science', *Nature, Society and Thought*, vol. 16, no. 2 (2003), note 26.   11. Alexander Feklisov, *Overseas and on the Island: On First-Hand Intelligence and Espionage* (Moscow, 1994), cites Y. Khariton, 'Ядерное оружие СССР: пришло из Америки или создано самостоятельно?' ('Nuclear Weapons of the USSR: Did they Come from America or Were they Created Independently?'), *Izvestiya* (8 December 1992). Note 26 in Fuchs-Kittowski, 'Klaus Fuchs and the Humanist Task of Science', cites this as the 'first public admission of facts that should have come out much sooner: the first Soviet atomic bomb was developed after the American model.' Mikhail Shifman, *Love and Physics: The Peierlses* (World Scientific, 2019), chapter 9, note 2, cites Dmitry Yuryevich Barshchevsky's television film *RISK*, in July 1988, to be the first time Fuchs' name was mentioned in Soviet media. The film stated that Fuchs handed over classified materials, but gave no further details of their nature or implications. I am indebted to Misha Shifman for this information.   12. Bruno Pontecorvo's scientific career, with suspicions of espionage, are described in Frank Close, *Half Life: The Divided Life of Bruno Pontecorvo, Physicist or Spy* (Basic Books, 2015, and OneWorld, 2015).   13. For a forensic refutation of such claims see Norman Dombey, 'The First War of Physics', *Contemporary Physics*, vol. 51 (2010), pp. 85–90, esp. p. 89, available at http://www.tandfonline.com/doi/pdf/10.1080/00107510903184422.   14. Eulogy at funeral of Sir Rudolf Peierls by Lord Flowers, item 941, pp. 1,061–2, in Sabine Lee, *Sir Rudolf Peierls: Selected Private and Scientific Correspondence*, vol. 2 (World Scientific, 2007).   15. Freeman Dyson, in foreword to Lee, *Sir Rudolf Peierls*.   16. Freeman Dyson, email to Frank Close, 3 January 2019.   17. Prison Commissioner to Sir Percy Sillitoe, 7 March 1951, TNA KV 2/1257, s. 817a.

Afterword: Who was Klaus Fuchs?

1. James Chadwick to Tam Dalyell, as quoted in a letter from Dalyell to Frank Close, 30 January 2015.   2. The literature on Fuchs, which asserts that he began his espionage late in 1941, includes the following references to his first contact with either Kuczynski or Kremer: Norman Moss, *Klaus Fuchs: The Man who Stole the Atom Bomb* (Grafton Books, 1987), p. 38; Richard Rhodes, *Dark Sun: The Making of the Hydrogen Bomb* (Simon and Schuster, 2005), p. 57; Christopher Andrew and Vasili Mitrokhin, *The Mitrokhin Archive* (Penguin, 2000), p. 152; Christopher Andrew and Oleg Gordievsky, *KGB: The Inside Story* (Harper Collins, 1990), p. 313; David Holloway, *Stalin and the Bomb* (Yale University Press, 1996), p. 83. Robert Chadwell Williams, *Klaus Fuchs, Atom Spy* (Harvard University Press, 1987), p. 61, has 'autumn 1941' while J. Albright and M. Kunstall, *Bombshell: The Secret Story of America's Unknown Atomic Spy Conspiracy* (Times Books, Random House, 1997), p. 71, have 'summer of 1941' for Fuchs' initial approach to Jürgen Kuczynski. Alan Moorehead, *The Traitors: The Double Life of Fuchs, Pontecorvo and Nunn May* (Dell, 1952), p. 92, is nearest with 'very soon after he arrived in Birmingham in 1941' for this initial approach to Kuczynski, although an impression given is that his actual espionage was not until 'the end of 1941' (p. 94). MI5 documents, the evidence at the trial, and the resulting media reports at the time all asserted 1942. The earliest books known to me that identify Fuchs' first contact to have been before his arrival in Birmingham are Chapman Pincher, *Treachery: Betrayals, Blunders and Cover-Ups: Six Decades of Espionage against America and Great Britain* (Random House, 2009), Mike Rossiter, *The Spy who Changed the World* (Headline, 2014), p. 86.

Index